2

The Films of the Eighties

The Films
of the Eighties

*A Complete, Qualitative Filmography
to Over 3400 Feature-Length English
Language Films, Theatrical and Video-
Only, Released between January 1, 1980,
and December 31, 1989*

ROBERT A. NOWLAN *AND*
GWENDOLYN WRIGHT NOWLAN

Volume 2 : P–Z
(entries 2276–3425; index)

McFarland & Company, Inc., Publishers
Jefferson, North Carolina, and London

The present work is a reprint, in two volumes, of the library bound edition of The Films of the Eighties, *first published in 1991 by McFarland.*

Volume 2

LIBRARY OF CONGRESS CATALOGUING-IN-PUBLICATION DATA

Nowlan, Robert A.
  The films of the eighties : a complete, qualitative filmography
to over 3400 feature-length English language films, theatrical
and video-only, released between January 1, 1980, and
December 31, 1989 / by Robert A. Nowlan and Gwendolyn
Wright Nowlan.
    p.   cm.
  Includes index.

ISBN 0-7864-2737-X (2 volume set : softcover : 50# alkaline paper)
ISBN 0-7864-2738-8 (v. 1 : softcover : 50# alkaline paper)
ISBN 0-7864-2739-6 (v. 2 : softcover : 50# alkaline paper)

  1. Motion pictures—Catalogs. I. Nowlan, Gwendolyn Wright,
  1945– . II. Title.
  PN1998.N78   2006   90-53516
  016.79143'75—dc20

British Library cataloguing data are available

Cover photograph: Kevin Costner as Eliot Ness in *The Untouchables*
(1987) © Paramount Pictures/Photofest

Manufactured in the United States of America

McFarland & Company, Inc., Publishers
  Box 611, Jefferson, North Carolina 28640
  www.mcfarlandpub.com

VOLUME 2 : 0-7864-2739-6
TWO VOLUME SET : 0-7864-2737-X

Table of Contents

• Volume 1 •

....

• Volume 2 •

2276. *Pink Floyd—The Wall* (1982, MGM/United Artists, GB, 99m, c). P Alan Marshall, D Alan Parker, W Roger Waters (based on the album "The Wall" by Pink Floyd), PH Peter Biziou, ED Gerry Hambling, PD Brian Morris.

LP Bob Geldof (Pink), Christine Hargreaves (Pink's Mother), James Laurenson (Pink's Father), Eleanor David (Pink's Wife), Kevin McKeon (Young Pink), Bob Hoskins (Rock & Roll Manager), David Bingham (Little Pink), Jenny Wright (American Groupie), Alex McAvoy (Teacher).

In a surreal, impressionistic movie, Kevin McKeon grows up with the horrors of World War II. As a man he becomes Bob Geldof, a rock star who discovers the power he has to manipulate crowds for his own pleasure. His insensitivity and desensitivity allow him to build a wall around himself to deflect the pain and suffering of life, which he chooses to deny.

2277. *Pink Motel* (1983, New Image, 88m, c, aka *Motel*). P M, James Kouf, Jr. & Ed Elbert, D Mike McFarland, W Kouf, Jr., PH Nicholas J. von Sternberg, M Larry K. Smith, ED Earl Watson.

LP Slim Pickens (Roy), Phyllis Diller (Margaret), John Macchia (Skip), Cathryn Hartt (Charlene), Christopher Nelson (Max), Terri Berland (Marlene), Tony Longo (Mark), Cathy Sawyer-Young (Lola).

In this dreadful sex comedy, Slim Pickens and Phyllis Diller own a pink stucco no-tell motel with rooms for rent by the hour to couples in need of a place to make whoopee.

2278. *Pink Nights* (1985, Koch/Marschall, 84m, c). P Philip Koch & Sally Marschall, D&W Koch, PH Charlie Lieberman, M Jim Tullio & Jeffrey Vanston, ED Koch & Marschall, SD Gail Specht.

LP Kevin Anderson (Danny), Shaun Allen (Terry), Peri Kaczmarek (Esme), Jessica Vitkus (Marcy), Larry King (Jeff), Jonathan Jancovic Michaels (Zero), Mike Bacarella (Bruno), Ron Dean (Pop), Tom Towles (Ralph).

Kevin Anderson doesn't have much luck with the opposite sex. Still he finds a way to live with three pretty girls.

2279. *Pinocchio and the Emperor of the Night* (1987, New World, animated, 88m, c). P Lou Scheimer, D Hal Sutherland, W Robby London, Barry O'Brien & Dennis O'Flaherty (based on a story by O'Flaherty from "The Adventures of Pinochio" by Carlo Collodi), PH Ervin L. Kaplan, M Anthony Marinelli & Brian Banks, ED Jeffrey Patrick Gehr.

VOICES Edward Asner (Scalawag), Tom Bosley (Geppetto), Lana Beeson (Twinkle), James Earl Jones (Emperor of the Night), Rickie Lee Jones (Fairy Godmother), Don Knotts (Gee Willikers), Scott Grimes (Pinocchio), Linda Gary (Bee-atrice), Jonathan Harris (Lt. Grumblebee), William Windom (Puppetino), Frank Welker (Igor).

It's a wholesome but rather too-sweet attempt to rival the great Disney animated story. Pinocchio is lured towards the self-indulgent pleasures of life, but comes down on the side of selflessness in the end.

Piranha II: The Spawning see The Spawning

2280. *The Pirate Movie* (1982, 20th Century-Fox, Australia, 98m, c). P David Joseph, D Ken Annakin, W Trevor Farrant (based on *The Pirates of Penzance* by Sir William Gilbert and Sir Arthur Sullivan), PH Robin Copping, ED Kenneth W. Zemke, PD Tony Woollard.

LP Kristy McNichol (Mabel), Christopher Atkins (Frederic), Ted Hamilton (Pirate King), Bill Kerr (Maj. General), Maggie Kirkpatrick (Ruth), Garry McDonald (Sgt./Inspector), Linda Nagle (Aphrodite), Kate Ferguson (Edith), Rhonda Burchmore (Kate), Catherine Lynch (Isabel).

Savoyards will be aghast at the blending of the work of Gilbert and Sullivan with modern pop music in this amateurish production. A modern girl, Kristy McNichol, daydreams herself into the story of "The Pirates of Penzance." Movie lovers will be equally upset.

2281. *Pirates* (1986, Cannon, France/Tunisian, 124m, c). P Tarak Ben Ammar, D Roman Polanski, W Gerard Brach & Polanski, PH Witold Sobocinski, M Philippe Sarde, ED Herve De Luze & William Reynolds, PD Pierre Guffroy, COS Anthony Powell†.

LP Walter Matthau (Capt. Red), Cris Campion (The Frog), Damien Thomas (Don Alfonso), Olu Jacobs (Boomako),

Ferdy Mayne (Capt. Linares), David Kelly (Surgeon), Anthony Peck, Anthony Dawson (Spanish Officers), Emilio Fernandez (Angelito), Charlotte Lewis (Dolores), Roy Kinnear (Dutch), Michael Elphick (Senery), Bill Fraser (Governor).

Walter Matthau is loads of fun in this robust pirate-comedy. He's the roughest-toughest buccaneer ever to sail the seven seas. With his protégé Cris Campion, he takes on a Spanish galleon filled with Aztec gold. It's a rouser on a grand scale.

2282.   The Pirates of Penzance (1983, Universal, 112m, c). P Joseph Papp, D&W Wilford Leach (based on the operetta by Sir William Gilbert and Sir Arthur Sullivan), PH Douglas Slocombe, M Sullivan, ED Anne V. Coates, PD Elliot Scott.

LP Kevin Kline (Pirate King), Angela Lansbury (Ruth), Linda Ronstadt (Mabel), George Rose (Major-General), Rex Smith (Frederic), Tony Azito (Sergeant), David Hatton (Samuel, sung by Stephen Hanan), Louise Gold (Edith, sung by Alexandra Korey), Teresa Codling (Kate, sung by Marcia Shaw).

This screening of Joseph Papp's successful stage version of the Gilbert and Sullivan classic is lively and fun. Kevin Kline shows some of the glorious goofiness that would win him an Oscar for *A Fish Named Wanda.* George Rose is marvelously cast as the Major-General; Rex Smith makes a quite adequate Frederic and Linda Ronstadt is a brilliant, beautiful, charming Mabel.

2283.   The Pit (1984, New World, 96m, c). P Bennet Fode, D Lew Lehman, W Ian A. Stuart, PH Fred Guthe, M Victor Davies, ED Riko Morden, AD Peter E. Stone.

LP Sammy Snyders (Jamie), Jeannie Elias (Sandra), Laura Hollingsworth (Marg), Sonja Smits (Mrs. Lynde), Laura Press (Mrs. Benjamin), Andrea Swartz (Abergail).

Sammy Snyders, a 12-year-old autistic boy, gets the opportunity to take revenge against all those in his town who humiliated him. He comes across a huge hole in the forest, at the bottom of which are strange and deadly creatures, willing to do his bidding.

2284.   P.K. & The Kid (1987, Sunn Classics/Lorimar, 90m, c). P Joe Roth, D Lou Lombardo, W Neal Barbera, PH Ed Koons, M James Horner, ED Tony Lombardo, PD Chet Allen.

LP Paul LeMat (William "Kid" Kane), Molly Ringwald (Paula Kathleen "P.K." Bayette), Alex Rocco (Les), Charles Hallahan (Bazooka), John Disanti (Benny), Fionnula Flanagan (Flo), Bert Remsen (Al), Leigh Hamilton (Louise).

If Molly Ringwald had not become a star this film would have stayed on the shelves where it was placed after being made in 1982. Molly portrays a likeable 15-year-old who runs away from home because of her sadistic father Alex Rocco. She teams up with Paul LeMat, who dreams of winning a national arm wrestling title. They travel together and meet a series of strange characters along the way. Rocco shows up and must be dealt with by LeMat.

2285.   Places in the Heart† (1984, Tri-Star, 112m, c). P Arlene Donovan, D&W Robert Benton† (for both direction and screenplay), PH Nestor Almendros, M John Kander & Howard Shore, ED Carol Littleton, PD Gene Callahan, AD Sydney Z. Litwack, SD Lee Poll & Derek Hill.

LP Sally Field* (Edna Spalding), Lindsay Crouse† (Margaret Lomax), Ed Harris (Wayne Lomax), Amy Madigan (Viola Kelsey), John Malkovich† (Mr. Will), Danny Glover (Moze), Yankton Hatten (Frank), Gennie James (Possum), Lane Smith (Albert Denby), Terry O'Quinn (Buddy Kelsey).

Sally Field won her second Best Actress Oscar for her portrayal of the widow of a small town Texas sheriff. After his murder in 1935 she struggles to keep and run the family farm, despite tornadoes, falling cotton prices and the Ku Klux Klan. She is aided by itinerant laborer Danny Glover. The film is overly sentimental and makes the dubious point that hard work will overcome adversity every time. Still it's good to look at and John Malkovich, as Field's blind tenant, makes an impressive film debut.

2286.   The Plague Dogs (1984, United International, GB/US, animated, 103m, c). P,D&W Martin Rosen (based on a novel by Richard Adams), PH James

Farrell, Marilyn O'Connor, Ron Jackson, Ted Bemiller, Jr., Bill Bemiller, Robert Velguth & Thane Berti, M Patrick Gleeson & Alan Price, PD Gordon Harrison.

VOICES John Hurt, Christopher Benjamin, James Bolam, Nigel Hawthorne, Warren Mitchell, Bernard Hepton, Brian Stirner, Penelope Lee, Geoffrey Mathews, Barbara Leigh-Hunt.

The film's message gets a bit lost via the animation route. A pair of dogs escape from a scientific research center and race around England scrounging for food. Unfortunately, they are in danger of infecting the nation with a deadly virus with which they have been injected.

2287. *Plain Clothes* (1988, Paramount, 98m, c). P Richard Wechsler & Michael Manheim, D Martha Coolidge, W A. Scott Frank (based on a story by Frank & Dan Vining), PH Daniel Hainey, M Scott Wilk, ED Patrick Kennedy & Edward Abroms, PD Michel Levesque.

LP Arliss Howard (Nick Dunbar/"Nick Springsteen"), Suzy Amis (Robin Torrence), George Wendt (Chet Butler), Diane Ladd (Jane Melway), Seymour Cassel (Ed Malmburg), Larry Pine (Dave Hechtor), Jackie Gayle (Coach Zeffer), Abe Vigoda (Mr. Wiseman), Robert Stack (Mr. Gardner).

Young-looking cop Arliss Howard goes undercover in a high school to find a teacher's killer. His younger brother is the prime suspect. While tracking down the real killer, Howard must fight off the advances of his homeroom teacher and falls in love with the daughter of the gym teacher.

2288. *Planes, Trains & Automobiles* (1987, Paramount, 93m, c). P,D&W John Hughes, PH Don Peterman, M Ira Newborn, ED Paul Hirsch, PD John W. Corso, AD Harold Michelson.

LP Steve Martin (Neal Page), John Candy (Del Griffith), Laila Robins (Susan Page), Michael McKean (State Trooper), Kevin Bacon (Taxi Racer), Dylan Baker (Owen), Carol Bruce (Joy Page), Olivia Burnette (Marti), Diana Douglas (Peg), William Windom (Boss).

For fastidious businessman Steve Martin, trying to get home to Thanksgiving dinner with his family in Chicago after a business trip to New York, is an almost Kafkaesque experience. He spends two days traveling across country, employing various modes of transportation, with loud, obnoxious, overbearing, talkative, shower-curtain salesman John Candy. This may not be exactly hell, but it's certainly purgatory. As is usually the case in road pictures, the two develop an appreciation for each other before reaching their destination—and so does the audience.

Planet of Horrors see Galaxy of Terror

2289. *Platoon** (1986, Orion, 120m, c). P Arnold Kopelson, D&W Oliver Stone* (for directing), PH Robert Richardson†, M Georges Delerue & Budd Carr, ED Claire Simpson*, PD Bruno Rubeo, SOUND John K. Wilkinson, Richard Rogers, Charles "Bud" Grenzbach & Simon Kaye*, AD Rodel Cruz & Doris Sherman Williams.

LP Tom Berenger† (Sgt. Barnes), Willem Dafoe† (Sgt. Elias), Charlie Sheen (Chris), Forest Whitaker (Big Harold), Francesco Quinn (Rhah), John C. McGinley (Sgt. O'Neill), Richard Edson (Sal), Kevin Dillon (Bunny), Reggie Johnson (Junior), Keith David (King), Johnny Depp (Lerner), David Neidorf (Tex), Mark Moses (Lt. Wolfe).

The film is the moving, terrifying account of a group of U.S. infantryman fighting in Vietnam. It is seen mostly through the eyes of young recruit Charlie Sheen, who struggles to retain his humanity in the midst of all the brutality. One sergeant, Tom Berenger, commits an atrocity which another sergeant, Willem Dafoe, intends to report, but Dafoe isn't allowed to live long enough to do so. Many Vietnam vets reported that the film caught the real feeling of the psychological and physical hell of the war.

2290. *Platoon Leader* (1988, Cannon, 100m, c, aka *Nam*). P Harry Alan Towers, D Aaron Norris, W Rick Marx, Andrew Deutsch, David Walker & Peter Welbeck [Towers] (based on the book by James R. McDonough), PH Arthur Wooster, M George S. Clinton, ED Michael J. Duthie.

LP Michael Dudikoff (Lt. Jeff Knight), Robert F. Lyons (Sgt. Michael McNamara), Michael De Lorenzo (Pvt. Raymond Bacera), Rich Fitts (Robert

Hayes), Jesse Dabson (Joshua Parker), Brian Libby (Roach).

Green First Lieutenant Michael Dudikoff must prove his mettle to battle-weary veterans in the jungles of Vietnam.

2291. Play Dead (1981, Troma, 89m, c). P Francine C. Rudine, D Peter Wittman, W Lothrop W. Jordan, PH Robert E. Bethard, AD Robert Burns, M Bob Farrar, ED Eugenie Nicoloff.

LP Yvonne De Carlo (Hester), Stephanie Dunnam (Audrey), David Cullinane (Jeff), Glenn Kezer (Otis), Ron Jackson (Richard).

Strangely twisted Yvonne De Carlo trains her dog to be a vicious killer. Atta boy, be a nice bad doggie.

2292. Play Me Something (1989, BFI, GB, 80m, b&w/c). P Kate Swan, D Timothy Neat, W Neat & John Berger (based on Berger's short story), PH Chris Cox, M Jim Sutherland, ED Russell Fenton, PD Annette Gillies.

LP John Berger (The Stranger), Hamish Henderson (TV repairman), Tilda Swinton (Hairdresser), Stewart Ennis (Motorcyclist), Margaret Bennett (Schoolteacher), Lucia Lanzarini (Marietta), Charlie Barron (Bruno).

As he and other passengers wait for their plane at a small Scottish Outer Hebrides airport, stranger John Berger relates the tale of a short love affair between a musical Italian peasant and a pretty secretary.

2293. Playing Away (1987, Alive Films, GB, 100m, c). P Brian Skilton & Vijay Amarnani, D Horace Ove, W Caryl Phillips, M Junior Giscombe, ED Graham Whitlock.

LP Norman Beaton (Willie-Boy), Robert Urquhart (Godfrey), Helen Lindsay (Marjorie), Nicholas Farrell (Derek), Brian Bovell (Stuart), Gary Beadle (Errol), Suzette Llewellyn (Yvette), Trevor Thomas (Jeff).

In a modest comedy, the lives of the stuffy residents of an English village are disrupted by the arrival of a cricket team from the West Indies.

Playing for Keeps see Lily in the Lake

2294. Plenty (1985, 20th Century-Fox, GB, 125m, c). P Edward R. Pressman & Joseph Papp, D Fred Schepisi, W David Hare (based on his play), PH Ian Baker, M Bruce Smeaton, ED Peter Honess, PD Richard Macdonald, AD Tony Reading & Adrian Smith, SD Peter James.

LP Meryl Streep (Susan Traherne), Charles Dance (Raymond Brock), Tracey Ullman (Alice Park), John Gielgud (Sir Leonard Darwin), Sting (Mick), Ian McKellen (Sir Andrew Charleson), Sam Neill (Lazar), Burt Kwouk (Mr. Aung), Pik Sen Lim (Mme. Aung), Andre Maranne (Villon), Ian Wallace (Medlicott).

As a teenager Meryl Streep fought in the French Resistance. She pines for the emotional charges and purity of purpose that she found in war. When she can't recapture the heroic feelings in herself or others, she drifts into cruelty, irrationality and finally madness.

2295. The Ploughman's Lunch (1984, Goldwyn, GB, 107m, c). P Simon Relph & Ann Scott, D Richard Eyre, W Ian McEwan, PH Clive Tickner, M Dominic Muldowney, ED David Martin, PD Luciana Arrighi.

LP Jonathan Pryce (James Penfield), Tim Curry (Jeremy Hancock), Rosemary Harris (Ann Barrington), Frank Finlay (Matthew Fox), Charlie Dore (Susan Barrington), David De Keyser (Gold), Nat Jackley (Mr. Penfield).

Burnt-out BBC radio journalist Jonathan Pryce plans to write a book on the British role in the 1956 Suez crisis in light of the events of the Falklands War. His research leads to his becoming enamored of TV researcher Charlie Dore, and making love with her mother, Rosemary Harris, an eminent leftwing historian and expert on Suez.

2296. The Plumber (1981, Cinema Ventures, Australia, 76m, c). P Matt Carroll, D&W Peter Weir, PH David Sanderson, M Gerry Tolland, ED G. Tunney-Smith, AD Ken James & Herbert Pinter.

LP Judy Morris (Jill Cowper), Robert Coleby (Brian Cowper), Ivar Kants (Max the Plumber), Candy Raymond (Meg), Henri Szeps (Department Head).

Plumber Ivar Kants invades the home of Judy Morris and Robert Coleby. His few-days' stay almost drives Morris mad. Strangely she gets no sympathy from her husband.

2297. *Police Academy* (1984, Warner, 95m, c). P Paul Maslansky, D Hugh Wilson, W Neal Israel, Pat Proft & Wilson (based on a story by Israel & Proft), PH Michael D. Margulies, M Robert Folk, ED Robert Brown & Zach Staenberg, PD Trevor Williams.

LP Steve Guttenberg (Carey Mahoney), G.W. Bailey (Lt. Harris), George Gaynes (Commandant Lassard), Michael Winslow (Larvell Jones), Kim Cattrall (Karen Thompson), Bubba Smith (Moses Hightower), Andrew Rubin (George Martin), Donovan Scott (Leslie Barbara), Leslie Easterbrook (Sgt. Callahan), David Graff (Eugene Tackleberry), Marion Ramsey (Laverne Hooks).

When the mayor of an American city eliminates all standards for jobs with the police force, an assortment of misfits show up for training at the Police Academy. Steve Guttenberg has been given the choice of attending the academy or having a police record all his own. He tries everything to get out of it, until he falls for fellow recruit Kim Cattrall. The film is basically a series of grade school dirty jokes, stereotypes, and sniggering scenes of ineptitude, until sure enough the recruits put down a riot.

2298. *Police Academy 2: Their First Assignment* (1985, Warner, 87m, c). P Paul Maslansky & Leonard Kroll, D Jerry Paris, W Barry Blaustein & David Sheffield (based on characters created by Neal Israel & Pat Proft), PH James Crabe, M Robert Folk, ED Robert Wyman, PD Trevor Williams.

LP Steve Guttenberg (Carey Mahoney), Bubba Smith (Moses Hightower), David Graff (Eugene Tackleberry), Michael Winslow (Larvell Jones), Bruce Mahler (Doug Fackler), Marion Ramsey (Laverne Hooks), Colleen Camp (Kirkland), Howard Hesseman (Pete Lassard), Art Metrano (Lt. Mauser), George Gaynes (Commandant Lassard), Bob Goldthwait (Zed), Julie Brown (Chloe).

In a moronic, scatological follow-up to the enormously successful *Police Academy,* the nitwits in blue are given their first assignment in the toughest precinct in the city. Art Metrano intends to make hay of their expected failure, but instead, led by Steve Guttenberg, they foil a gang of ruthless street punks headed by Bob Goldthwait.

2299. *Police Academy 3: Back in Training* (1986, Warner, 82m, c). P Paul Maslansky, D Jerry Paris, W Gene Quintano (based on characters created by Neal Israel & Pat Proft), PH Robert Saad, M Robert Folk, ED Bud Molin, PD Trevor Williams.

LP Steve Guttenberg (Sgt. Mahoney), Bubba Smith (Sgt. Hightower), David Graff (Sgt. Tackleberry), Michael Winslow (Sgt. Jones), Marion Ramsey (Sgt. Hooks), Leslie Easterbrook (Lt. Callahan), Art Metrano (Commandant Masur), Tim Kazurinsky (Cadet Sweetchuck), Bobcat Goldthwait (Cadet Zed), George Gaynes (Commandant Lassard), Shawn Weatherly (Cadet Adams).

Having learned very little the first time through, the hapless boys and girls in blue are back at the Police Academy for additional training and hijinks. It's the same old menu, but there were plenty of paying customers, happy to howl at the childish, scatological, sexist jokes.

2300. *Police Academy 4: Citizens on Patrol* (1987, Warner, 87m, c). P Paul Maslansky, D Jim Drake, W Gene Quintano (based on characters created by Neal Israel & Pat Proft), PH Robert Saad, M Robert Folk, ED David Rawlins, PD Trevor Williams.

LP Steve Guttenberg (Carey Mahoney), Bubba Smith (Moses Hightower), Michael Winslow (Larvelle Jones), David Graff (Eugene Tackleberry), Tim Kazurinsky (Sweetchuck), Sharon Stone (Claire Mattson), Leslie Easterbrook (Debbie Callahan), Marion Ramsey (Laverne Hooks), Lance Kinsey (Proctor), G.W. Bailey (Capt. Harris), Bobcat Goldthwait (Zed), George Gaynes (Commandant Lassard).

Near retirement, Commandant Lassard implements a master plan, consisting of supplementing his knucklebrained men and women in blue with John Q. Public. He asks members of the general public to step forward and take training from his cops so they may become active in crime prevention. Naturally Capt. Harris opposes the plan and will stop at nothing to see it fail. The film is filled with tasteless jokes which seem to have audiences both foreign and domestic rolling in the aisles.

2301. *Police Academy 5: Assignment Miami Beach* (1988, Warner, 90m, c). P Paul Maslansky & Donald West, D Alan Myerson, W Stephen J. Curwick (based on the characters created by Neal Israel & Pat Proft), PH James Pergola, M Robert Folk, ED Hubert C. de La Bouillerie, PD Trevor Williams.

LP Matt McCoy (Nick), Janet Jones (Kate Stratton), George Gaynes (Commandant Lassard), G.W. Bailey (Capt. Harris), Rene Auberjonois (Tony Stark), Bubba Smith (Moses Hightower), David Graff (Eugene Tackleberry), Michael Winslow (Larvelle Jones), Leslie Easterbrook (Debbie Callahan), Marion Ramsey (Laverne Hooks).

Commandant Lassard (George Gaynes) is in Miami to accept an award before his retirement. Long time adversary Capt. Harris (G.W. Bailey) is along hoping to gum up the proceedings. The picture that started this series barely had enough laughs to amuse horny boys with subaverage IQs. This fifth film in the series is even less funny than all that have gone before, as impossible as it may seem.

2302. *Police Academy 6: City Under Siege* (1989, Warner, 83m, c). P Paul Maslansky, D Peter Bonerz, W Stephen J. Curwick (based on characters created by Neal Israel & Pat Proft), PH Charles Rosher, Jr., M Robert Folk, ED Hubert de la Bouillerie, PD Tho E. Azzari.

LP Bubba Smith (Moses Hightower), David Graff (Eugene Tackleberry), Michael Winslow (Larvelle Jones), Leslie Easterbrook (Debbie Callahan), Marion Ramsey (Laverne Hooks), Lance Kinsey (Proctor), Matt McCoy (Nick), Bruce Mahler (Fackler), G.W. Bailey (Capt. Harris), George Gaynes (Commandant Lassard), Kenneth Mars (Mayor), Gerrit Graham (Ace), George R. Robertson (Police Commissioner Hurst).

This series of modern day Keystone Kops may continue forever. Explaining what attracts audiences to these films is a service we are unable to provide. It's apparent that a lack of new jokes or a meaningful story line doesn't discourage fans of the series from plopping down their cash for tickets. If the content was as en-joyable as an old Abbott & Costello routine, such as "Who's on First?," we might understand the applauding acceptance of the same old stuff time after time. Commander Lassard and his team of numbskulls are assigned to put an end to a series of robberies and discover the identity of Mr. Big.

2303. *Poltergeist* (1982, MGM/United Artists, 114m, c). P Steven Spielberg & Frank Marshall, D Tobe Hooper, W Spielberg, Michael Grais & Mark Victor, PH Matthew F. Leonetti, M Jerry Goldsmith†, ED Michael Kahn, PD James H. Spencer, VE Richard Edlund, Michael Wood & Bruce Nicholson†.

LP Craig T. Nelson (Steve Freeling), JoBeth Williams (Diane Freeling), Beatrice Straight (Dr. Lesh), Dominique Dunne (Dana), Oliver Robins (Robbie Freeling), Heather O'Rourke (Carol Anne Freeling), Zelda Rubinstein (Tangina), Martin Casella (Marty), Richard Lawson (Ryan).

Menacing spirits terrorize a middle-class family in their perfect new house in the suburbs. The ghosts transport the youngest Freeling, Heather O'Rourke, into a world beyond. Apparently the subdivision was built on a sacred Indian burial ground and the spirits are not pleased.

2304. *Poltergeist II: The Other Side* (1986, MGM, 92m, c). P&W Mark Victor & Michael Grais, D Brian Gibson, PH Andrew Laszlo, M Jerry Goldsmith, ED Thom Noble, PD Ted Haworth, SE Richard Edlund.

LP JoBeth Williams (Diane Freeling), Craig T. Nelson (Steve Freeling), Heather O'Rourke (Carol Ann Freeling), Oliver Robins (Robbie Freeling), Zelda Rubinstein (Tangina Barrons), Will Sampson (Taylor), Julian Beck (Kane), Geraldine Fitzgerald (Grandma Jess), John P. Whitecloud (Old Indian).

Just a few months' screen time after the conclusion of *Poltergeist*, the Freelings are once again at the mercy of ghosts who make their life a living hell.

2305. *Poltergeist III* (1988, MGM/United Artists, 97m, c). P Barry Bernardi, D Gary Sherman, W Sherman & Brian Taggert, PH Alex Nepomniaschy, M Joe Renzetti, ED Ross Albert, PD

Paul Eads, VE Richard Edlund, John Bruno, Garry Waller & William Neilʈ.

LP Tom Skerritt (Bruce Gardner), Nancy Allen (Patricia Gardner), Heather O'Rourke (Carol Anne Freeling), Zelda Rubinstein (Tangina Barrons), Lara Flynn Boyle (Donna Gardner), Kip Wentz (Scott), Richard Fire (Dr. Seaton), Nathan Davis (Rev. Kane), Paul Graham (Martin), Meg Weldon (Sandy).

"They're back . . . " again, or so it would appear. Heather O'Rourke, who has moved to Chicago to live with her aunt Nancy Allen and uncle Tom Skerritt, is not believed by skeptical psychologist Richard Fire, investigating the child's past experiences. He claims the poltergeists that have haunted O'Rourke were caused by mass hypnosis brought about by the child's suggestions. But the evil Rev. Kane has followed her to Chicago, appearing to her in mirrors and reflections, beckoning her "into the light." Twelve-year-old O'Rourke died of a bowel obstruction six months after this film was completed.

2306. *Polyester* (1980, New Line Cinema, 86m, c). P,D&W John Waters, PH David Insley, M Chris Stein & Michael Kamen, ED Charles Roggero, PD Vincent Pernaio.

LP Divine (Francine Fishpaw), Tab Hunter (Todd Tomorrow), Edith Massey (Cuddles), Mink Stole (Sandra), David Samson (Elmer Fishpaw), Joni Ruth White (LaRue, Mother), Mary Garlington (Lulu Fishpaw), Ken King (Dexter Fishpaw), Hans Kramm (Chauffeur), Stiv Bators (Bo-Bo).

In a family of misfits, forlorn housewife Divine pines away for Tab Hunter, the man of her dreams, while the rest of her life is falling apart. Members of the audience were given scratch and sniff cards upon entering the movie with instructions as to when to take a whiff of the unpleasant smells. The picture is probably only for the cult followers of John Waters.

2307. *The Pope of Greenwich Village* (1984, MGM/United Artists, 120m, c). P Gene Kirkwood, D Stuart Rosenberg, W Vincent Patrick (based on his novel), PH John Bailey, M Dave Grusin, ED Robert Brown, PD Paul Sylbert.

LP Eric Roberts (Paulie), Mickey Rourke (Charlie), Daryl Hannah (Diane), Geraldine Pageʈ (Mrs. Ritter), Kenneth McMillan (Barney), Tony Musante (Pete), M. Emmet Walsh (Burns), Burt Young (Bed Bug Eddie), Jack Kehoe (Bunky), Philip Bosco (Paulie's Father), Val Avery (Nunzi).

On the mean streets of New York City, Eric Roberts and his cousin Mickey Rourke commit what seems to be an uncomplicated robbery. But they accidentally kill a corrupt cop and find both the police and the Mafia on their trail.

2308. *Popeye* (1980, Paramount, 114m, c). P Robert Evans, D Robert Altman, W Jules Feiffer (based on the comic strip character created by E.C. Segar), PH Giuseppe Rotunno, M Harry Nilsson, ED Tony Lombardo, PD Wolf Kroeger.

LP Robin Williams (Popeye), Shelley Duvall (Olive Oyl), Ray Walston (Poopdeck Pappy), Paul L. Smith (Bluto), Paul Dooley (Wimpy), Richard Libertini (Geezil), Roberta Maxwell (Nana Oyl), Donald Moffat (Taxman), Wesley Ivan Hurt (Swee' Pea).

Robin Williams is credible as the cartoon sailor who searches for his long-lost father Ray Walston. Along the way he meets Shelley Duvall, adopts little Wesley Ivan Hurt and has plenty of trouble with Paul L. Smith. Director Robert Altman fails to make this dud interesting, amusing or appealing.

2309. *Porky's* (1982, 20th Century-Fox, 94m, c). P Don Carmody & Bob Clark, D&W Clark, PH Reginald H. Morris, M Carl Zittrer & Paul Zaza, ED Stan Cole, PD Reuben Freed.

LP Dan Monahan (Pee Wee), Mark Herrier (Billy), Wyatt Knight (Tommy), Roger Wilson (Mickey), Cyril O'Reilly (Tim), Tony Ganios (Meat), Kaki Hunter (Wendy), Kim Cattrall (Honeywell), Nancy Parsons (Balbricker), Scott Colomby (Brian Schwartz), Boyd Gaines (Coach Brackett), Susan Clark (Cherry Forever), Wayne Maunder (Cavanaugh), Alex Karras (Sheriff Wallace), Chuck Mitchell (Porky).

There's a lot of talking about sex in this teenage sexploitation film, which features a group of unappealing horny Florida high school students of the early 50s.

Dreaming only of how they can get laid, they invade the next county, where Chuck Mitchell runs a raunchy gambling den and whorehouse called Porky's. When they are not treated with the respect they believe they deserve as potential customers, they take revenge by destroying Mitchell's business.

2310.   *Porky's II: The Next Day*   (1983, 20th Century-Fox, 95m, c). P Don Carmody & Bob Clark, D Clark, W Clark, Roger E. Swaybill & Alan Ormsby, PH Reginald H. Morris, M Carl Zittrer, ED Stan Cole.

LP Dan Monahan (Pee Wee), Wyatt Knight (Tommy), Mark Herrier (Billy), Roger Wilson (Mickey), Cyril O'Reilly (Tim), Tony Ganios (Meat), Kaki Hunter (Wendy), Scott Colomby (Brian), Nancy Parsons (Balbricker), Joseph Running Fox (John Henry), Bill Wiley (Rev. Bubba Flavel).

Set the next day after the action of the surprising 1982 hit, this putrid piece doesn't even feature Porky (Chuck Mitchell). Instead it serves up a bigoted fundamentalist minister Bill Wiley and corrupt politicians. There's still plenty of giggling about sex, nudity and to top it all off a vomiting scene in a restaurant. Gross!

2311.   *Porky's Revenge*   (1985, 20th Century-Fox, 92m, c). P Robert L. Rosen, D James Komack, W Ziggy Steinberg (based on characters created by Bob Clark), PH Robert Jessup, M Dave Edmunds, ED John W. Wheeler, PD Peter Wooley.

LP Dan Monahan (Pee Wee), Wyatt Knight (Tommy), Tony Ganios (Meat), Mark Herrier (Billy), Kaki Hunter (Wendy), Scott Colomby (Brian), Nancy Parsons (Ms. Balbricker), Chuck Mitchell (Porky Wallace), Rose McVeigh (Miss Webster), Fred Buch (Mr. Dobbish), Wendy Feign (Blossom), Kimberley Evenson (Inga).

In the second sequel to the surprisingly successful idiotic, tasteless teenage sexploitation film *Porky,* the group of horny high school students (definitely not led by Dan Callahan) once again makes contact with obese title character Chuck Mitchell. He's put together his combination gambling casino–whorehouse on a paddlewheel riverboat and is pressuring the

high school coach to have his boys throw the state championship basketball game. Our heroes snicker all the way as they deal with this threat.

2312.   *Posed for Murder*   (1989, Double Helix, 85m, c). P Carl Fury & Jack Fox, D Brian Thomas Jones, W John A. Gallagher & Chuck Dickenson (based on Fox's story), PH Bob Paone, M Tom Marolda, ED Brian O'Hara, PD Claudia Mohr.

LP Charlotte J. Helmkamp (Laura Shea), Carl Fury (Rick Thompson), Rick Gianasi (Det. Steve Barnes), Michael Merrings (Danny), William Beckwith (Clifford Devereux), Roy MacArthur (Serge LaRue), Terri Brennan (Terri).

Former real-life *Playboy* pinup Charlotte Helmkamp (appearing therein as Charlotte Kemp), here a buxom model for *Thrill* magazine, is trying to break into movies with a role in the horror film *Meat Cleavers from Mars.* Some maniac is stalking our gal, killing off her friends and acquaintances one by one.

2313.   *Positive I.D.*   (1987, Universal, 102m, c). P,D&W Andy Anderson, PH Paul Barton, ED Anderson & Robert J. Castaldo.

LP Stephanie Rascoe (Julie Kenner), John Davies (Don Kenner), Steve Fromholz (Roy/Lt. Mercer), Laura Lane (Dana), Gail Cronauer (Melissa), Audeen Casey (Dr. Sterling), Matthew Sacks (Mr. Tony).

Rape victim Stephanie Rascoe assumes a new identity. She hangs out at a seedy downtown bar playing the role of a seductress. The ending of this low-budget thriller makes the film almost worth watching.

2314.   *The Postman Always Rings Twice*   (1981, Paramount, 125m, c). P Charles Mulvehill & Bob Rafelson, D Rafelson, W David Mamet (based on the novel by James M. Cain), PH Sven Nykvist, M Michael Small, ED Graeme Clifford, PD George Jenkins.

LP Jack Nicholson (Frank Chambers), Jessica Lange (Cora Papadakis), John Colicos (Nick Papadakis), Christopher Lloyd (Salesman), Michael Lerner (Katz), John P. Ryan (Kennedy), Angelica Huston (Madge), William Traylor (Sackett), Tom Hill (Barlow).

This production of James M. Cain's story of infidelity and murder is able to present more explicit love-making scenes, but it doesn't improve on the presentation of the sexual tension shown so effectively in the 1946 movie with John Garfield and Lana Turner. Drifter Jack Nicholson is befriended and given a job by roadhouse owner John Colicos. The latter is repaid when Nicholson and the man's young wife Jessica Lange have an affair and kill him for his insurance money.

2315. ***Pound Puppies and the Legend of Big Paw*** (1988, Tri-Star, animated, 76m, c). P Donald Kushner & Peter Locke, D Pierre DeCelles, W Jim Carlson & Terrence McDonnell, M Richard Kosinski, Sam Winans & Bill Reichenbach, ED John Blizek.

VOICES George Rose (McNasty), B.J. Ward (Whopper), Ruth Buzzi (Nose Marie), Brennan Howard (Cooler), Cathy Cadavini (Collette), Nancy Cartwright (Bright Eyes).

Whether tots will fall for these TV type cartoon characters is debatable. Kids nowadays are more sophisticated. The Pound Puppies try to retrieve the fabled "Bone of Scone," which legend has it enables kids and dogs to communicate.

2316. ***P.O.W. The Escape*** (1986, Cannon, 89m, c). P Menahem Golan & Yoram Globus, D Gideon Amir, W Jeremy Lipp, James Bruner, Malcolm Barbour & John Langley (based on a story by Avi Kleinberger & Amir), PH Yechiel Ne'eman, M Michael Linn, ED Marcus Manton, PD Marcia Hinds.

LP David Carradine (Col. Cooper), Charles R. Floyd (Sparks), Mako (Capt. Vinh), Steve James (Jonston), Phil Brock (Adams), Daniel Demorest (Thomas), Tony Pierce (Waite), Steve Freedman (Scott), James Acheson (McCoy).

In a Rambo-like imitation, American POWs, led by David Carradine, make their escape to freedom as Saigon falls to the Communists.

2317. ***Power*** (1986, 20th Century-Fox, 111m, c). P Reene Schisgal & Mark Tarlov, D Sidney Lumet, W David Himmelstein, PH Andrzej Bartkowiak, M Cy Coleman, ED Andrew Mondshein, PD Peter Larkin.

LP Richard Gere (Pete St. John), Julie Christie (Ellen Freeman), Gene Hackman (Wilfred Buckley), Kate Capshaw (Syd-

ney Betterman), Denzel Washington (Arnold Billings), E.G. Marshall (Senator Sam Hastings), Beatrice Straight (Claire Hastings), Fritz Weaver (Wallace Furman), Michael Learned (Governor Andrea Stannard).

Sidney Lumet, who brought audiences *Network,* once again examines the corruption of a major institution—this time he shows how dehumanized the political process has become. Ruthless hustler Richard Gere helps package candidates, but even he is disappointed when he discovers the only politician he respected, E.G. Marshall, has become a pawn of the political power trade.

2318. ***The Power*** (1984, Film Ventures, 84m, c). P Jeffrey Obrow, D&W Obrow & Stephen Carpenter (based on a story by Obrow, Carpenter, John Penny & John Hopkins), PH Carpenter, M Chris Young, ED Obrow & Carpenter, PD Chris Hopkins.

LP Susan Stokey (Sandy), Warren Lincoln (Jerry), Lisa Erickson (Julie), Chad Christian (Tommy), Ben Gilbert (Matt), Chris Morrill (Ron Prince), Rod Mays (Lee McKennah), J. Dinan Mytretus (Francis Lott), Jay Fisher (Raphael).

As a small Aztec idol is passed down from one generation to the next, it becomes more powerful. Three high school students come into possession of the idol when it is stolen by Warren Lincoln. He becomes possessed by a demon and is transformed into a monster.

2319. ***Powerforce*** (1983, Bedford Entertainment, 98m, c). P George Mason, D Michael King, W Terry Chalmers & Dennis Thompsett, PH Bob Huke & Robert Hope, M Chris Babida.

LP Bruce Baron, Mandy Moore, James Barnett, Jovy Couldry, Frances Fong, Olivia Jeng, Randy Channel, Seon Blake, Sam Sorono, Bruce Li.

In yet another routine martial-arts film, CIA agent Bruce Baron kicks and chops his way through a bunch of baddies.

2320. ***Powwow Highway*** (1989, Handmade Films, GB/US, 91m, c). P Jan Wieringa, D Jonathan Wacks, W Janet Heany & Jean Stawarz (based on the novel by David Seals), PH Toyomichi Kurita, M Barry Goldberg, ED James Austin Stewart, PD Cynthia Sowder.

LP A. Martinez (Buddy Red Bow), Gary Farmer (Philbert Bono), Amanda Wyss (Rabbit Layton), Joanelle Nadine Romero (Bonnie Red Bow), Sam Vlahos (Chief Joseph), Wayne Waterman (Wolf Tooth), Margo Kane (Imogene), Geoff Rivas (Sandy Youngblood), Roscoe Born (Agent Jack Novall).

Based on an underground novel by actor/activist David Seals, this film tells of the comic adventures of two desperate Indians, A. Martinez and Gary Farmer. They rediscover their heritage while on a weekend journey along a scenic interstate, near Lame Deer, Montana, known as the Powwow Highway. Martinez is an angry Vietnam vet and Indian activist, while Farmer is a gentle, generous soul, guided by visions, always looking for links with his people's past.

2321. *Prancer* (1989, Orion, 103m, c). P Raffaella De Laurentiis, D John Hancock, W Greg Taylor (based on his story), PH Misha Suslov, M Maurice Jarre, ED Dennis O'Connor, PD Chester Kaczenski.

LP Sam Elliott (John Riggs), Rebecca Harrell (Jessica Riggs), Cloris Leachman (Mrs. McFarland), Rutanya Alda (Aunt Sarah), John Joseph Duda (Steve Riggs), Abe Vigoda (Dr. Orel Benton), Michael Constantine (Mr. Stewart/Santa), Ariana Richards (Carol Wetherby), Boo (Prancer), Frank Welker (Prancer's Voice).

This one's for the kiddies. A little girl nurses a reindeer back to health, believing the animal to be Santa Claus's Prancer. Writer Greg Taylor admits that he modeled his story on E.T. in that he's taken a child from a troubled household and put her with an alien creature lost in the woods. Nice try. It's sweet, and not too sugary. The reindeer behaves as if he doesn't want to be an actor.

2322. *Pray for Death* (1986, American Distribution Group, 92m, c). P Don Van Atta, D Gordon Hessler, W James Booth, PH Roy Wagner, M Thomas Chase, Steve Rucker, ED Bill Butler, Steve Butler, AD Adrian Gorton.

LP Sho Kosugi (Akira), James Booth (Limehouse), Robert Ito (Koga), Michael Constantine (Newman), Donna Kei Benz (Aiko Saito), Kane Kosugi (Takeshi), Shane Kosugi (Tomoya), Norman Burton (Lt. Anderson), Parley Baer (Sam Green).

A Japanese immigrant and his family are victimized by American mobsters, only to have a Ninja appear to further complicate things.

2323. *A Prayer for the Dying* (1987, Goldwyn, GB, 104m, c). P Peter Snell, D Mike Hodges, W Edmund Ward & Martin Lynch, PH Mike Garfath, M Bill Conti, ED Peter Boyle, PD Evan Hercules.

LP Mickey Rourke (Martin Fallon), Alan Bates (Jack Meehan), Bob Hoskins (Father Da Costa), Sammi Davis (Anna), Christopher Fulford (Billy), Liam Neeson (Liam Docherty), Alison Doody (Siobhan Donovan), Camille Coduri (Jenny).

An IRA detachment to which Mickey Rourke belongs accidentally blows up a school bus in Northern Ireland, instead of the intended troop transport. This causes Rourke to desert the cause and head to London, hoping to make it to America. The IRA doesn't allow desertions or resignations and they are after Rourke, using their London underworld contacts to chase him.

2324. *Predator* (1987, 20th Century–Fox, 107m, c). P Lawrence Gordon, Joel Silver & John Davis, D John McTiernan, W Jim Thomas & John Thomas, PH Donald McAlpine, M Alan Silvestri, ED John F. Link & Mark Helfrich, PD John Vallone, VE Joel Hynek, Robert M. Greenberg, Richard Greenberg & Stan Winston†.

LP Arnold Schwarzenegger (Major Alan "Dutch" Schaefer), Carl Weathers (Dillon), Elpidia Carrillo (Anna), Bill Duke (Mac), Jesse Ventura (Sgt. Blain), Sonny Landham (Billy), Richard Chaves (Pancho), R.G. Armstrong (Gen. Phillips), Shane Black (Hawkins), Kevin Peter Hall (Predator).

Arnold Schwarzennegger leads his troops into a Latin American jungle to rescue some hostages. Arnie must go up against giant, alien, chameleon-like meateater Kevin Peter Hall.

Preppies see Making the Grade

2325. *The President's Women* (1981, Krona, 76m, c). P Cael Gurevich, D&ED John Avildsen, W David Odell, Jack

Richardson & Don Greenberg, PH Ralf D. Bode, M Stan Vincent & Gary William Friedman.

LP Zero Mostel (President/Godfather), Estelle Parsons (First Lady/Barmaid), Pat Paulsen (Norman), Paul Dooley (Salesman), Jerry Orbach (Lorsey), George S. Irving (Roberto/Reverend), Irwin Corey (Professor).

Despite a name cast, this feeble political comedy disappeared before many even knew it had been released.

2326. The Presidio (1988, Paramount, 97m, c). P D. Constantine Conte, D Peter Hyams, W Larry Ferguson, PH Hyams, M Bruce Broughton, ED James Mitchell, PD Albert Brenner.

LP Sean Connery (Lt. Col. Alan Caldwell), Mark Harmon (Jay Austin), Meg Ryan (Donna Caldwell), Jack Warden (Sgt. Maj. Ross "Top" Maclure), Mark Blum (Arthur Peale), Dana Gladstone (Lt. Col. Paul Lawrence), Jenette Goldstein (Patti Jean Lynch).

There's a triangle here, Presidio Military Compound Provost Marshal Sean Connery, San Francisco cop Mark Harmon, and Connery's daughter Meg Ryan. There's a lot of chasing around, but not much of a plot. The two law enforcers reluctantly join forces in a case of murder, corruption and smuggled diamonds. Forget the story, enjoy flinty Connery and sexy Ryan.

2327. Pretty in Pink (1986, Paramount, 96m, c). P Lauren Shuler, D Howard Deutch, W John Hughes, PH Tak Fujimoto, M Michael Gore, ED Richard Marks, PD John W. Corso.

LP Molly Ringwald (Andie), Harry Dean Stanton (Jack), Jon Cryer (Duckie), Annie Potts (Iona), James Spader (Steff), Andrew McCarthy (Blane), Jim Haynie (Donnelly), Alexa Kenin (Jena), Kate Vernon (Benny).

Even though high school girl Molly Ringwald comes from the wrong side of the tracks, wealthy heartthrob Andrew McCarthy asks her to the prom. His friends don't approve and almost ruin the budding romance. It's a bittersweet story, with a none too credible happy ending.

2328. Pretty Smart (1987, New World, 84m, c). P Ken Solomon, Jeff Begun & Melanie J. Alschuler, D Dimitri Logothetis, W Dan Hoskins (based on an original story by Begun & Alschuler), PH Dimitri Papacostantis, M Jay Levy & Eddie Arkin, ED Daniel Gross, PD Beau Peterson.

LP Tricia Leigh Fisher (Daphne "Zigs" Ziegler), Lisa Lorient (Jennifer Ziegler), Dennis Cole (Richard Crawley), Patricia Arquette (Zero), Paris Vaughn (Torch), Kimberly B. Delfin (Yuko), Brad Zutaut (Alexis), Kim Waltrip (Sara Gernhy).

Tricia Leigh Fisher and Lisa Lorient are two extremely different sisters. Sent to the same finishing school, they become enemies, until they discover that the headmaster has been using them in a drug-dealing, pornographic sideline to running the school.

2329. Prettykill (1987, Spectrafilm, 95m, c). P John R. Bowey & Martin Walters, D George Kaczender, W Sandra K. Bailey, PH Joao Fernandes, M Robert O. Ragland, ED Tom Merchant.

LP David Birney (Sgt. Larry Turner), Season Hubley (Heather Todd), Susannah York (Toni), Yaphet Kotto (Lt. Harris), Suzanne Snyder (Francie/Stella/Paul), Germaine Houde (Jacques Mercier), Lenore Zann (Carrie).

Murder and madness menace honest cop David Birney and his callgirl girlfriend Season Hubley. Hubley's seemingly innocent Southern belle protégée Suzanne Snyder is actually a dangerous schizoid.

2330. The Prey (1984, New World, 80m, c). P Summer Brown & Randy Rovins, D Edwin Scott Brown, W Summer Brown & E.S. Brown, PH Teru Hayashi, M Don Peake, ED Michael Barnard.

LP Debbie Thureson (Nancy), Steve Bond (Joel), Lori Lethin (Bobbie), Robert Wald (Skip), Gayle Gannes (Gail), Philip Wenckus (Greg), Carel Struycken (The Giant), Jackson Bostwick (Mark), Jackie Coogan (Lester).

Looking for a mate in the Colorado Rockies, a predator kills five campers in the process.

2331. Prick Up Your Ears (1987, Goldwyn, GB, 111m, c). P Andrew Brown, D Stephen Frears, W Alan Bennett (based on the biography of John Lahr), PH Oliver Stapleton, M Stanley

Myers, ED Mick Audsley, PD Hugo Luczyc-Wyhowski.

LP Gary Oldman (Joe Orton), Alfred Molina (Kenneth Halliwell), Vanessa Redgrave (Peggy Ramsay), Wallace Shawn (John Lahr), Lindsay Duncan (Anthea Lahr), Julie Walters (Elsie Orton), James Grant (William Orton), Janet Dale (Mrs. Sugden), Dave Atkins (Mr. Sugden).

This unflinching look at homosexuality in the British theatre is the story of the relationship between playwright Joe Orton and his longtime lover Kenneth Halliwell. The latter's jealousy of Orton's success leads him to murder the 60s author of black comedies.

2332. *Priest of Love* (1981, Filmways, GB, 125m, c). P Christopher Miles & Andrew Donally, D Miles, W Alan Plater (based on a novel by Harry T. Moore and the writings of D.H. Lawrence), PH Ted Moore, M Joseph James, ED Paul Davies, PD Ted Tester & David Brockhurst.

LP Ian McKellen (D.H. Lawrence), Janet Suzman (Frieda Lawrence), Ava Gardner (Mabel Dodge Luhan), Penelope Keith (The Honorable Dorothy Brett), Jorge Rivero (Tony Luhan), Maurizio Merli (Angelo Ravagli), John Gielgud (Herbert G. Muskett), James Faulkner (Aldous Huxley).

This disappointing, aimless picture explores the last years in the life of D.H. Lawrence. After his books are banned, he seeks a warmer climate to combat his tuberculosis.

2333. *Primal Scream* (1988, Unistar, 92m, c). P Howard Foulkrod, D&W William Murray, PH Dennis Peters, M Mark Knox, ED Keith L. Reamer, SE David Di Pietro.

LP Kenneth J. McGregor (Corby McHale), Sharon Mason (Samantha Keller), Julie Miller (Caitlin Foster), Jon Maurice (Capt. Frank Gitto), Joseph White (Nicky Fingeas), Mickey Shaughnessy (Charlie Waxman), Stephan Caldwell (Olan Robert Foster).

This film combines elements of science fiction and detective thrillers, but not the best parts of either. There's a tenuous relationship between Hellfire, an energy catalyst in the 21st century, and private eye Kenneth J. McGregor's investigation of a series of murders which leave the victims smoldering embers.

2334. *Prime Risk* (1985, Mikas I/Almi, 100m, c). P Herman Grigsby, D&W Michael Farkas, PH Mac Ahlberg, M Phil Marshall, ED Bruce Green, AD Christopher Henry.

LP Toni Hudson (Julie Collins), Lee Montgomery (Michael Fox), Samuel Bottoms (Bill Yeoman), Clu Gulager (Paul Minsky), Keenan Wynn (Dr. Lasser), Lois Hall (Dr. Holt), Rick Rakowski (John), John Lykes (Vance), James O'Connell (Terry Franklin), Randy Pearlman (Ed Harrington).

Not having any luck getting a job, recent college graduate and computer whiz Toni Hudson comes up with a way to electronically break into automatic teller machines. She's doing all right withdrawing all the cash she wants until she comes across a group of secret agents doing the same thing, hoping to destroy the American financial system. Well, it's one thing to be a crook — but at least she's an American crook. Hudson devises a way to foil the foreign competition and wins the gratitude of the FBI, saving the Federal Reserve in the nick of time.

2335. *Prince Jack* (1985, LMF/Castle Hill, 100m, c). P Jim Milio, D&W Bert Lovitt, PH Hiro Narita, M Elmer Bernstein, ED Janice Hampton, PD Michael Corenblith.

LP Robert Hogan (Jack Kennedy), James F. Kelly (Bobby Kennedy), Kenneth Mars (Lyndon B. Johnson), Lloyd Nolan (Joseph Kennedy), Cameron Mitchell (General Walker), Robert Guillaume (Martin Luther King), Theodore Bikel (Russian Ambassador), Dana Andrews (The Cardinal), Jim Backus (Dealy), William Windom (Ferguson).

It's an inconsequential presentation of episodes in the presidential career of John F. Kennedy.

2336. *Prince of Darkness* (1987, Universal, 101m, c). P Larry Franco, D John Carpenter, W Martin Quatermass [Carpenter], PH Gary B. Kibbe, M Carpenter & Alan Howarth, ED Steve Mirkovich, PD Daniel Lomino.

LP Donald Pleasence (Priest), Jameson Parker (Brian), Victor Wong (Professor Birack), Lisa Blount (Catherine), Dennis Dun (Walter), Susan Blanchard (Kelly), Anne Howard (Susan), Ann Yen (Lisa).

Priest Donald Pleasence calls together a group of scientists to stave off the threat from the contents of a 7,000,000-year-old cannister said to contain the very spirit of Satan.

2337. *The Prince of Pennsylvania* (1988, New Line, 87m, c). P Joan Fishman & Kerry Orent, D&W Ron Nyswaner, PH Frank Prinzi, ED Bill Sharf, PD Toby Corbett.

LP Keanu Reeves (Rupert Marshetta), Amy Madigan (Carla Headlee), Bonnie Bedelia (Pam Marshetta), Fred Ward (Gary Marshetta), Joseph De Lisi (Roger Marshetta), Jeff Hayenga (Jack Sike), Tracy Ellis (Lois Sike).

Frustrated and troubled by his right-wing conservative nutcake of a father, Fred Ward, and his mother, Bonnie Bedelia's, affair with her father's best friend, Pennsylvania mining town teen Keanu Reeves comes under the influence of ex-hippie Amy Madigan. The latter convinces the youngster to kidnap his father and hold him for ransom. It's an unusual black comedy, with many of the parts sadly missing.

2338. *Prince of the City* (1981, Warner, 167m, c). P Burtt Harris, D Sidney Lumet, W Jay Presson Allen & Lumet† (based on the book by Robert Daley), PH Andrzej Bartkowiak, W Paul Chihara, ED John J. Fitzstephens, PD Tony Walton.

LP Treat Williams (Daniel Ciello), Jerry Orbach (Gus Levy), Richard Foronjy (Joe Marinaro), Don Billett (Bill Mayo), Kenny Marino (Dom Bando), Carmine Caridi (Gino Mascone), Tony Page (Raf Alvarez), Norman Parker (Rick Cappalino), Paul Roebling (Brooks Paige).

In a long, dragged-out film, Treat Williams, a New York cop on the drug beat, agrees to inform on his corrupt fellow officers as long as he doesn't have to turn in his immediate partners.

2339. *The Princess Academy* (1987, Empire, US/Yugo/France, 90m, c). P Sandra Weintraub, D Bruce Block, W Sandra Weintraub (based on an idea by Fred Weintraub), PH Kent Wakeford, M Roger Bellon, ED Martin Cohen.

LP Eva Gabor (Countess), Lar Park Lincoln (Cindy), Lu Leonard (Fraulein Stickenschmidt), Richard Paul (Drago), Carole Davis (Sonia), Badar Howar (Sarah), Barbara Rovsek (Izzie), Yolande Palfrey (Pamela).

Eva Gabor is the headmistress of a Swiss finishing school where the young ladies are taught how to catch rich husbands, fake an orgasm, shop, and other activities essential to useless females. The acting, story and direction are horrid.

2340. *The Princess Bride* (1987, 20th Century-Fox, 98m, c). P Andrew Scheinman & Rob Reiner, D Reiner, W William Goldman (based on his novel), PH Adrian Biddle, M Mark Knopfler, ED Robert Leighton, PD Norman Garwood, SONG "Storybook Love" by Willy DeVille†, COS Phyllis Dalton.

LP Cary Elwes (Westley), Mandy Patinkin (Inigo Montoya), Chris Sarandon (Prince Humperdinck), Christopher Guest (Count Rugen), Wallace Shawn (Vizzini), Andre the Giant (Fezzik), Fred Savage (The Grandson), Robin Wright (Buttercup), Peter Falk (The Grandfather), Peter Cook (The Impressive Clergyman), Mel Smith (The Albino), Carol Kane (Valerie), Billy Crystal (Miracle Max).

Stuck in bed with the flu, Fred Savage is entertained by his grandfather Peter Falk, who relates the fairy tale story of the true love of the beautiful princess Buttercup, played by Robin Wright, and her one-and-only Westley, bravely portrayed by Cary Elwes. The two are menaced by numerous villains, including Wallace Shawn, Andre the Giant, Mandy Patinkin and, most particularly, Chris Sarandon.

2341. *The Principal* (1987, Tri-Star, 109m, c). P Thomas H. Brodek, D Christopher Cain, W Frank Deese, PH Arthur Albert, M Jay Gruska, ED Jack Hofstra, AD Mark Billerman, SD Rick Brown.

LP James Belushi (Rick Lattimer), Louis Gossett, Jr. (Jake Phillips), Rae Dawn Chong (Hilary Orozco), Michael Wright (Victor Duncan, Jr.), J.J. Cohen ("White Zac"), Esai Morales (Raymi Rojas), Troy Winbush ("Baby" Emile), Jacob

Vargas (Arturo Diego), Thomas Ryan (Robert Darcy).

In his first starring role James Belushi, a messed-up teacher with a failed personal life, is given the ultimatum of becoming principal at the district's most trouble-filled school or being fired. He accepts and finds the high school filled with violent gangs, drug dealers and delinquents of all stripes. Life isn't easy for him, but eventually with the help of Lou Gossett, head of security (a terrible thing to need in a high school), he is able to gain some respect from the students and teachers with his "No More" policy — no more drugs, no more violence, no more arson, no more extortion, etc. He and Gossett have a climactic fight with Michael Wright, the leader of the vicious gang that runs the school.

2342.   *Prison* (1988, Empire, 102m, c). P Irwin Yablans, D Renny Harlin, W C. Courtney Joyner (based on a story by Yablans), PH Mac Ahlberg, M Richard Band & Christopher Stone, ED Andy Horvitch, PD Philip Duffin.

LP Viggo Mortensen (Connie Burke), Chelsea Field (Katherine Walker), Lane Smith (Ethan Sharpe), Lincoln Kilpatrick (Cresus), Tom Everett (Rabbitt), Ivan Kane (Lasagna), Andre De Shields (Sandor), Tom Lister, Jr. (Tiny).

In 1964 an innocent man is executed for the murder of a prison inmate. The deceased was actually killed by brutal prison guard Lane Smith. Shortly thereafter the prison is shut down. Twenty years later, because of overcrowding, the old prison is reopened with Smith as its warden. The vengeful ghost of the unjustly executed man is accidentally released. He begins killing guards and prisoners alike, working his way up to Smith. It's scary!

Prisoner of the Skull see Who?

2343.   *Prisoners of the Lost Universe* (1984, Premier, GB, 91m, c). P Harry Robertson, D Terry Marcel, W Marcel & Robertson, PH Derek Browne, M Robertson, ED Alan Jones.

LP Richard Hatch (Dan Roebuck), Kay Lenz (Carrie Madison), John Saxon (Kleel), Peter O'Farrell (Malachi), Ray Charleson (Greenman), Kenneth Hendel

(Dr. Hartmann), Philip Van Der Byl (Kahar), Larry Taylor (Vosk).

A TV journalist and a martial arts champ are transported to a primitive world via a matter transmitter.

2344.   *Private Benjamin* (1980, Warner, 109m, c). P Nancy Meyers, Charles Shyer & Harvey Miller, D Howard Zieff, W Meyers, Shyer & Miller†, PH David M. Walsh, M Bill Conti, ED Sheldon Kahn, PD Robert Boyle.

LP Goldie Hawn† (Judy Benjamin), Eileen Brennan† (Capt. Doreen Lewis), Armand Assante (Henri Tremont), Robert Webber (Col. Clay Thornbush), Sam Wanamaker (Teddy Benjamin), Barbara Barrie (Harriet Benjamin), Mary Kay Place (Pvt. Mary Lou Glass), Harry Dean Stanton (Sgt. Jim Ballard), Albert Brooks (Yale Goodman), Sally Kirkland (Helga).

When her bridegroom Albert Brooks dies during lovemaking on their wedding day, wealthy Jewish widow Goldie Hawn, at a loss of what to do with her life, joins the army. Her spoiled ways don't sell well with tough officer Eileen Brennan — but Goldie shapes up and does herself proud.

2345.   *The Private Eyes* (1980, Tri-Star/New World, 91m, c). P Lang Elliott & Wanda Dell, D Elliott, W Tim Conway & John Myhers, PH Jacques Haitkin, M Peter Matz, ED Fabien Tordjmann & Patrick M. Crawford.

LP Tim Conway (Dt. Tart), Don Knotts (Inspector Winship), Trisha Noble (Mistress Phyllis Morley), Bernard Fox (Justin), Grace Zabriskie (Nanny), John Fujioka (Mr. Uwatsum), Stan Ross (Tibet), Irwin Keyes (Jock).

Television comedians Tim Conway and Don Knotts once again prove that their humor and popularity cannot be transformed to the big screen. They portray a pair of bungling Scotland Yard detectives investigating murders in a haunted mansion. All the usual stale jokes are brought out in wheelchairs, as it were.

2346.   *A Private Function* (1985, Hand Made/Island Alive, GB, 93m, c). P Mark Shivas, D Malcolm Mowbray, W Alan Bennett (based on a story by Bennett & Mowbray), PH Tony Pierce-Roberts, M John Du Prez, ED Barrie Vince, PD Stuart Walker.

LP Michael Palin (Gilbert Chilvers), Maggie Smith (Joyce Chilvers), Denholm Elliott (Dr. Swaby), Richard Griffiths (Allardyce), Tony Haygarth (Sutcliff), John Normington (Lockwood), Bill Paterson (Wormold).

In a comedy set in 1947 Yorkshire, villagers flaunt food rationing rules and secretly fatten an illicit pig for the Royal Wedding festivities.

Private Investigations see P.I. Private Investigations

2347. *Private Lessons* (1981, Jensen Farley, 87m, c, aka *Philly*). P R. Ben Efraim, D Alan Myerson, W Dan Greenburg (based on the novel *Philly* by Greenburg), PH Jan de Bont, M Various Artists, ED Fred Chulack.

LP Sylvia Kristel (Nicole), Howard Hesseman (Lester), Eric Brown (Philly), Patrick Piccininni (Sherman), Ed Begley, Jr. (Jack Travis), Pamela Bryant (Joyce), Meredith Baer (Miss Phipps), Ron Foster (Philly's Dad).

In another of the many teen sex-fantasy movies, 15-year-old Eric Brown is initiated into the rites by gorgeous maid Sylvia Kristel.

2348. *A Private Life* (1989, Totem, GB, 95m, c). P Francis Gerard & Roland Robinson, D Gerard, W Andrew Davies, PH Nat Crosby, M Trevor Jones, ED Robin Sales, PD Mark Wilby.

LP Bill Flynn (Jack), Jana Cilliers (Stella), Kevin Smith (Older Paul), Embeth Davidtz (Older Karen), Lance Maron (Older Gary), Justin John (Young Paul), Talia Leibman (Young Karen), Warren Hetz (Young Gary).

In the 1950s Cape Town policeman Bill Flynn falls in love with Jana Cilliers. When she applies for a "white" identification card, she is turned down and is classified as colored. When she finds herself pregnant, she and Flynn begin a life of lies. Every attempt to have her reclassified as "white" fails. Over the years the strain of trying to protect their three children from the consequences of colored bias leads to a son's choosing to kill himself when he is unable to marry the white woman he loves.

2349. *Private Property* (1986, Park Lane, 90m, c, aka *Young Lady Chatterley II*). P Alan Roberts & Stanton Korey, D Roberts, W Anthony Williams, PH Bob Brownell & Bryan England, M Misha Segal, ED Gregory Saunders, PD Warren Skip Wildes.

LP Harlee McBride (Cynthia Chatterley), Brett Clark (Thomas), Adam West (Arthur Bohart, Jr.), Sybil Danning (Judith), Alex Sheaf (French Count).

Based on the classic D.H. Lawrence novel, Harlee McBride as Lady Chatterley inherits the family mansion and continues her fooling around.

2350. *Private Resort* (1985, Tri-Star, 82m, c). P R. Ben Efraim & Don Enright, D George Bowers, W Gordon Mitchell (based on a story by Ken Segall, Allen Wenkus & Mitchell), PH Adam Greenberg, ED Sam Pollard, PD Michael Corenblith.

LP Rob Morrow (Ben), Johnny Depp (Jack Marshall), Emily Longstreth (Patti), Karyn O'Bryan (Dana), Hector Elizondo (The Maestro), Dody Goodman (Amanda Rawlings), Leslie Easterbrook (Bobby Sue).

Johnny Depp and Rob Morrow are girl-crazy teens hanging out at a plush Miami resort, hoping to score with the wealthy beauties who stay there. Their hijinks are interrupted by jewel-thief-in-drag Hector Elizondo.

2351. *Private School* (1983, Universal, 97m, c). P R. Ben Efraim & Don Enright, D Noel Black, W Dan Greenburg & Suzanne O'Malley, PH Walter Lassally, ED Fred Chulack, PD Ivo Cristante.

LP Phoebe Cates (Christine), Betsy Russell (Jordan), Kathleen Wilhoite (Betsy), Matthew Modine (Jim), Michael Zorek (Bubba), Fran Ryan (Miss Dutchbok), Ray Walston (Chauncey), Sylvia Kristel (Ms. Copuletta), Jonathan Prince (Roy), Kari Lizer (Rita), Julie Payne (Coach Whelan).

Filmed to appeal to prurient interests, this story of the sexual mingling of students at a boys academy and a neighboring girls school has plenty of T & A, with pouting bad-girl Betsy Russell exposing herself the most frequently.

2352. *Privates on Parade* (1984, Orion Classics, GB, 100m, c). P Simon Relph, D Michael Blakemore, W Peter Nichols (based on his play), PH Ian Wilson, M Dennis King, ED Jim Clark, PD Luciana Arrighi.

LP John Cleese (Maj. Giles Flack), Denis Quilley (Acting Capt. Terri Dennis), Michael Elphick (Sgt. Maj. Reg Drummond), Nicola Pagett (Acting Lt. Sylvia Morgan), Bruce Payne (Flight Sgt. Kevin Artwright), Joe Melia (Sgt. Len Bonny), David Bamber (Sgt. Charles Bishop).

This homosexual farce tells of the none too amusing antics of a British song and dance army unit entertaining the troops in Malaya during the late 1940s.

2353. *Privileged* (1982, Oxford, GB, 94m, c). P Richard Stevenson, D Michael Hoffman, W Hoffman, David Woolcombe & Rupert Walters, PH Fiona Cunningham Reid, M Rachel Portman, ED Derek Goldman, PD Jason Cooper.

LP Robert Woolley (Edward), Diana Katis (Anne), Hughie Grant (Lord Adrian), Victoria Studd (Lucy), James Wilby (Jamie), Simon Shackleton (Justin), Mark Williams (Wilf).

Selfish Oxford undergraduate Robert Woolley gets involved with acting, girls and a suicide.

2354. *Prizzi's Honor†* (1985, 20th Century-Fox, 129m, c). P John Foreman, D John Huston†, W Richard Condon & Janet Roach† (based on the novel by Condon), PH Andrzej Bartkowiak, M Alex North, ED Rudi Fehr & Kaja Fehr†, PD Dennis Washington, AD Michael Helmy & Tracy Bousman, SD Charles Truhan & Bruce Weintraub, COS Donfeld†.

LP Jack Nicholson† (Charley Partanna), Kathleen Turner (Irene Walker), Robert Loggia (Eduardo Prizzi), John Randolph (Angelo "Pop" Partanna), William Hickey† (Don Corrado Prizzi), Lee Richardson (Dominic Prizzi), Michael Lombard (Filargi "Finlay"), Anjelica Huston* (Maerose Prizzi), George Santiopietro (Plumber), Lawrence Tierney (Lt. Hanley), C.C.H. Pounder (Peaches Altamont).

In an entertaining black comedy gem, Jack Nicholson is superb as an aging hit man working for William Hickey, the head of one of New York's powerful Mafia families. Nicholson has been engaged to Hickey's granddaughter, Anjelica Huston, but when he sees Kathleen Turner at a gangster's wedding, he falls in love. Nicholson courts the beautiful Turner, unaware that she also is a hired killer, and her target-to-be is Nicholson. Turner and Nicholson marry, but when it comes to loyalty, marriage means much less than the honor of the Prizzi family to whom Nicholson owes everything.

2355. *The Prodigal* (1984, World Wide, 105m, c). P Ken Wales, D&W James F. Collier, PH Frank Stanley, M Bruce Broughton, ED Bill Brame, PD Bill Creber.

LP John Hammond (Greg Stuart), Hope Lange (Anne Stewart), John Cullum (Elton Stuart), Morgan Brittany (Sheila Holt-Browning), Ian Bannen (Riley Wyndham), Joey Travolta (Tony), Arliss Howard (Scott Stuart), Sarah Rush (Laura).

Pressures of today nearly cause the members of a family to lose their faith.

2356. *Programmed to Kill* (1987, TransWorld, 91m, c, aka *Retaliator*). P Don Stern, D Allan Holzman & Robert Short, W Short, PH Nitcho Lion Nissim & Ernest Holzman, M Jerry Immel & Craig Huxley, ED Michael Kelly, SE Vern Hyde & John Carter.

LP Robert Ginty (Eric Mathews), Sandahl Bergman (Samira), James Booth (Broxk), Alex Courtney (Blake), Paul W. Walker (Jason), Louise Claire Clark (Sharon), Peter Bromilow (Donovan), George Fisher (Mike).

PLO terrorist Sandahl Bergman is fatally wounded in a raid by the CIA. During radical bionic surgery a team of surgeons implant computer chips in her brain-dead body, turning her into a killing machine who obeys orders. When she malfunctions and turns on her creators, only Roberty Ginty can halt her frenzy.

2357. *Project X* (1987, 20th Century-Fox, 108m, c). P Walter F. Parkes & Lawrence Lasker, D Jonathan Kaplan, W Stanley Weiser (based on a story by

Weiser & Lasker), PH Dean Cundey, M James Horner, ED O. Nicholas Brown, PD Lawrence G. Paull.

LP Matthew Broderick (Jimmy Garrett), Helen Hunt (Teresa "Teri" McDonald), Bill Sadler (Dr. Lynnard Carroll), Johnny Ray McGhee (Isaac Robertson), Jonathan Stark (Sgt. "Kreig" Kreiger), Robin Gammell (Col. Niles).

When a young chimpanzee named Virgil is chosen for a deadly military experiment, would-be pilot Matthew Broderick and expert chimp trainer Helen Hunt fight to prevent the certain destruction of the chimps in the program.

2358. *Prom Night* (1980, Avco Embassy, 91m, c). P Peter Simpson, D Paul Lynch, W William Gray (based on a story by Robert Guza, Jr.), PH Robert New, M Carl Zittrer & Paul Zaza, ED Brian Ravok.

LP Leslie Nielsen (Hammond), Jamie Lee Curtis (Kim), Casey Stevens (Nick), Eddie Benton (Wendy), Antoinette Bower (Mrs. Hammond), Michael Tough (Alex), Robert Silverman (Sykes), Pita Oliver (Vicki), David Mucci (Lou).

Some mysterious figure is killing off all the teens involved in the death of Jamie Lee Curtis' little sister some 11 years earlier.

2359. *Promised Land* (1988, Vestron, 92m, c). P Rick Stevenson, D&W Michael Hoffman, PH Ueli Steiger, M James Newton, ED David Spiers, PD Eugenio Zanetti.

LP Jason Gedrick (Davey Hancock), Kiefer Sutherland (Danny Rivers), Meg Ryan (Bev), Tracy Pollan (Mary Daley), Googy Gress (Baines), Deborah Richter (Pammie), Oscar Rowland (Mr. Rivers), Sondra Seacat (Mrs. Rivers).

This crime story takes place in Ashville, Utah. Ex-basketball player Jason Gedrick, now a town cop whose dreams didn't pan out, confronts high school misfit Kiefer Sutherland and his wife, weirdo beauty Meg Ryan, after the latter two rob a local convenience store.

2360. *Prostitute* (1980, Kestrel/Mainline, GB, 98m, c). P,D&W Tony Garnett, PH Charles Stewart, M David Platz, ED Bill Shapter.

LP Eleanor Forsythe (Sandra), Kate Crutchley (Louise), Kim Lockett (Jean), Nancy Samuels (Rose Wilson), Richard Mangan (David Selby), Phyllis Hickson (Mother), Joseph Senior (Joseph), Ann Whitaker (Amanda).

Birmingham prostitute Eleanor Forsythe joins a group to reform the laws regulating her trade and becomes a high-priced London callgirl.

2361. *The Protector* (1985, Golden Harvest, US/Hong Kong, 95m, c). P David Chan, D&W James Glickenhaus, PH Mark Irwin, M Ken Thorne, ED Evan Lottman, AD William F. De Seta & Oliver Wong.

LP Jackie Chan (Billy Wong), Danny Aiello (Danny Garoni), Roy Chiao (Mr. Ko), Victor Arnold (Police Captain), Kim Bass (Stan Jones), Richard Clarke (Supt. Whitehead), Saun Ellis (Laura Shapiro).

In this martial arts film, a Hong Kong to New York heroin ring is broken.

2362. *Protocol* (1984, Warner, 96m, c). P Anthea Sylbert, D Herbert Ross, W Buck Henry (based on a story by Charles Shyer, Nancy Meyers & Harvey Miller), PH William A. Fraker, M Basil Poledouris, ED Paul Hirsch, PD Bill Malley.

LP Goldie Hawn (Sunny), Chris Sarandon (Michael Ransome), Richard Romanus (Emir), Andre Gregory (Nawaf Al Kabeer), Gail Strickland (Mrs. St. John), Cliff De Young (Hilley), Keith Szarabajka (Crowe), Ed Begley, Jr. (Hassler), Kenneth Mars (Lou).

When Washington waitress and dancer Goldie Hawn accidentally prevents the assassination of a visiting Arab dignitary, she is given a job with the State Department as a protocol official. All that glitters is not "Goldie" at her best.

2363. *The Prowler* (1981, Graduation/Sandhurst, 88m, c, aka *Rosemary's Killer*). P Joseph Zito & David Streit, D Zito, W Glenn Leopold & Neal F. Barbera, PH Raoul Lumas, M Richard Einhorn, ED Joel Goodman, PD Lorenzo Mans.

LP Vicki Dawson (Pam McDonald), Christopher Goutman (Mark London), Cindy Weintraub (Lisa), Farley Granger (Sheriff George Fraser), John Seitz (Kingsley).

In this clone of *Halloween,* a returning World War II soldier comes home to find his girl having an affair with another man. He dispatches both with a pitchfork. Thirty-five years later, he returns to his hometown and begins killing all the teens he can get near.

2364. *Psycho from Texas* (1982, New American, 89m, c). P,D&W Jim Feazell, PH Paul Hipp, M Jaime Mendoza-Nava, ED Arjay.

LP John King, III (Wheeler), Herschell Mays (William Phillips), Tommy Lamey (Slick), Candy Dee (Connie Phillips), Janel King (Ellen), Juanne Bruno (Bertha), Reed Johnson (Steve), Jack Collins (Sheriff), Christian Feazell (Young Wheeler).

The message of this poorly-made film is that child-abuse may lead to just about anything, including kidnapping when the kid grows up.

2365. *Psycho II* (1983, Universal, 113m, c). P Hilton A. Green, D Richard Franklin, W Tom Holland (based on characters created by Robert Bloch), PH Dean Cundey, M Jerry Goldsmith, ED Andrew London, PD John W. Corso.

LP Anthony Perkins (Norman Bates), Vera Miles (Lila Loomis), Meg Tilly (Mary), Robert Loggia (Dr. Raymond), Dennis Franz (Toomey), Hugh Gillin (Sheriff Hunt), Claudia Bryar (Mrs. Spool), Robert Alan Browne (Statler), Ben Hartigan (Judge), Lee Garlington (Myrna).

Despite protests from Vera Miles, the sister of his victim 22 years ago, Anthony Perkins is released from a mental institution and returns home to the Bates Hotel . . . and then the murders begin again.

2366. *Psycho III* (1986, Universal, 93m, c). P Hilton A. Green, D Anthony Perkins, W Charles Edward Pogue (based on characters created by Robert Bloch), PH Bruce Surtees, M Carter Burwell, ED David Blewitt, PD Henry Bumstead.

LP Anthony Perkins (Norman Bates), Diana Scarwid (Maureen), Jeff Fahey (Duane), Roberta Maxwell (Tracy), Hugh Gillin (Sheriff Hunt), Lee Garlington (Myrna), Robert Alan Browne (Statler), Gary Bayer (Father Brian), Patience Cleveland (Sister Margaret).

Anthony Perkins directs and stars in this second sequel to the Hitchcock classic. Norman Bates is normal again, but mother still seems to be acting up.

2367. *Psychos in Love* (1987, ICN Bleecker-Infinity, 87m, c). P&D Gorman Bechard, W Carmine Capobianco & Bechard, PH Bechard, M Capobianco & Bechard, ED Bechard.

LP Carmine Capobianco (Joe), Debi Thibeault (Kate), Frank Stewart (Herman), Cecilia Wilde (Nikki), Donna Davidge (Heather), Patti Chambers (Girl in Bed), Carla Bragoli (Girl in Woods), Carrie Gordon (Girl in Toilet), Angela Nicholas (Dianne).

Carmine Capobianco, a lonely psycho killer, kills his dates after having sex with them. Debi Thibeault also eliminates the men in her life when she becomes annoyed by their approaches to get her into bed. It's a match made in hell when they get together.

2368. *The Psychotronic Man* (1980, International Harmony, 90m, c). P Peter Spelson, D Jack M. Sell, W Spelson & Sell (based on a story by Spelson), PH Sell, M Tommy Irons, ED Bill Reese.

LP Peter Spelson (Rocky Foscoe), Christopher Carbis (Lt. Walter O'Brien), Curt Colbert (Sgt. Chuck Jackson), Robin Newton (Kathy), Paul Marvel (Dr. Steinberg), Jeff Caliendo (Officer Maloney), Lindsey Novak (Mrs. Foscoe).

In this cheaply made production from Chicago, Peter Spelson portrays a psychic barber. Unknown forces cause people to die when he blinks at them.

P'Tang, Yang, Kipperbang see Kipperbang

2369. *Puberty Blues* (1983, Limelight/Universal Classics, Australia, 81m, c). P Joan Long & Margaret Kelly, D Bruce Beresford, W Kelly (based on the novel by Kathy Lette & Gabrielle Carey), PH Don McAlpine, M Les Gock, ED Jeanine Chialvo & William Anderson, PD David Copping.

LP Nell Schofield (Debbie), Jad Capelja (Sue), Geoff Rhoe (Garry), Tony Hughes (Danny), Sandy Paul (Tracy), Leander Brett (Cheryl), Jay Hackett (Bruce), Ned Lander (Strach), Joanne Olsen (Vicki), Julie Medana (Kim).

In order to be accepted as part of the in-crowd of their high school, teens Nell Schofield and Jad Capelja join the local surfing scene.

2370. *Pulse* (1988, Columbia, 91m, c). P Patricia A. Stallone, D&W Paul Golding, PH Peter Lyons Collister, M Jay Ferguson, ED Gib Jaffe, PD Holger Gross.

LP Cliff De Young (Bill), Roxanne Hart (Ellen), Joey Lawrence (David), Matthew Lawrence (Stevie), Charles Tyner (Old Man), Dennis Redfield (Pete), Robert Romanus (Paul), Myron D. Healey (Howard).

In a sci-fi version of "the boy who cried wolf," no one will believe Joey Lawrence's explanation for strange behavior in his neighborhood. He claims that an alien force is communicating destructive messages to earth via sudden pulses of electricity through appliances in several homes in the area.

2371. *Pumpkinhead* (1988, MGM/ United Artists, 86m, c, aka *Vengeance: The Devil*). P Richard C. Weinman & Howard Smith, D Stan Winston, W Mark Patrick Carducci & Gary Gerani (based on a story by Carducci, Stan Winston & Weinman), PH Bojan Bazelli, M Richard Stone, ED Marcus Manton, SE Alec Gillis.

LP Lance Henriksen (Ed Harley), Matthew Hurley (Billy Harley), Jeff East (Chris), John DiAquino (Joel), Kimberly Ross (Kim), Joel Hoffman (Steve), Cynthia Bain (Tracy), Kerry Remsen (Maggie), Madeleine Taylor Holmes (Witchwoman), Tom Woodruff, Jr. (Pumpkinhead).

When bikers in a rural area run down the 10-year-old son of kindly widower farmer Lance Henriksen, he seeks help in taking revenge from a vicious demon known as Pumpkinhead. The latter, an eight foot tall alien, hunts down the bikers and dispatches them one by one. With each killing the alien begins to look more and more like Henriksen. Filled with remorse, Henriksen commits suicide, destroying Pumpkinhead in the process.

2372. *Punchline* (1988, Columbia, 128m, c). P Daniel Melnick & Michael Rachmil, D&W David Seltzer, PH Reynaldo Villalobos, M Charles Gross, ED Bruce Green, PD Jackson DeGovia.

LP Sally Field (Lilah Krytsick), Tom Hanks (Steven Gold), John Goodman (John Krytsick), Mark Rydell (Romeo), Kim Greist (Madeline Urie), Paul Mazursky (Arnold), Pam Matteson (Utica Blake), George Michael McGrath (Singing Nun), Taylor Negron (Albert Emperato), Barry Neikrug (Krug), Angel Salazar (Rico), Damon Wayans (Percy), Joycee Katz (Joycee), Mac Robbins (Billy Lane).

In a backstage look at aspiring stand-up comics, Tom Hanks is slightly more successful but no more dedicated than Sally Field to making the mark as a comedian. Her dreams are having a hell of a negative effect on her marriage and family. Hanks, who is supposed to be attending medical school like all the other men in his family, gives Field a boost and some confidence. They think they may have fallen in love, but learn better, as Field realizes that her husband John Goodman is the good and supportive man she needs and wants.

2373. *Puppet Master* (1989, Full Moon, 90m, c). P Hope Perello, D David Schmoeller, W Joseph G. Collodi (based on a story by Charles Band & Kenneth J. Hall), PH Sergio Salvati, M Richard Band, ED Tom Meshelski, PD John Myrhe, PUPPET EFFECTS David Allen Prods.

LP Paul Le Mat (Alex), Irene Miracle (Dana Hadley), Matt Roe (Frank), Kathryn O'Reilly (Clarissa), Robin Frates (Megan Gallagher), Marya Small (Theresa), Jimmie F. Scaggs (Neil), William Hickey (Andre Toulan).

This direct-to-video horror film features cute/scary little puppets, crafted by William Hickey, who committed suicide in 1939 at the Bodega Bay Hotel. Years later, they come to life to terrorize a group of psychics staying at the hotel.

2374. *Purgatory* (1989, New Star, 93m, c). P&D Ami Artzi, W Felix Kroll & Paul Aratow, PH Tom Fraser, M Julian Laxton, ED Ettie Feldman, PD Robert van der Coolwijk.

LP Tanya Roberts (Carly Arnold), Julie Pop (Melanie), Hal Orlandini (Bledsoe), Rufus Swart (Paul Cricks), Adrienne Pearce (Janine), Marie Human (Kirsten), David Sherwood (Stern), Clare Marshall (Ruth Arnold), Hugh Rouse (Rivers), John Newland (Ambassador Whitney).

Sexy Peace Corps worker Tanya Roberts and her pal Julie Pop are arrested in a fictional African country on trumped-up drug charges. They are each sentenced to 11 years in a prison known menacingly as Purgatory. The evil warden turns his prettiest inmates into prostitutes. To this end, Roberts is forced into a discreetly filmed scene of fellatio while Pop is gang-raped by the guards, causing her to commit suicide.

2375. Purple Haze (1983, Triumph, 97m, c). P Thomas Anthony Fucci, D David Burton Morris, W Vittoria Wozniak (based on the story by Wozniak, Morris & Tom Kelsey), PH Richard Gibb, ED Dusty Dennisson.

LP Peter Nelson (Matt Caulfield), Chuck McQuary (Jeff Maley), Bernard Baldan (Derek Savage), Susanna Lack (Kitty Armstrong), Bob Breuler (Walter Caulfield), Joanne Bauman (Margaret Caulfield), Kay Horsch (Phoebe Caulfield), Heidi Helmer (Angela).

Two friends Peter Nelson and Chuck McQuary experience the 60s — drugs, avoiding the draft, dealing with insensitive parents, and fighting the "Establishment." Anyone seeing this film who was unfamiliar with the period would surely think the decade was rather dull.

2376. Purple Hearts (1984, Warner, 115m, c). P&D Sidney J. Furie, W Rick Natkin & Furie, PH Jan Kiesser, M Robert Folk, ED George Grenville, AD Francisco Balangue.

LP Ken Wahl (Don Jardian), Cheryl Ladd (Deborah Solomon), Stephen Lee (Wizard), Annie McEnroe (Hallaway), Paul McCrane (Brenner), Cyril O'Reilly (Zuma), David Harris (Hanes), Hillary Bailey (Jill), Lee Ermey (Gunny).

This film is about the nothing romance of Navy doctor Ken Wahl who falls in love with nurse Cheryl Ladd in Vietnam during the war.

2377. The Purple People Eater (1988, Concorde, 92m, c). P Brad Krevoy &

Steve Stabler, D&W Linda Shayne (based on the song by Sheb Wooley), PH Peter Deming, M Various Artists, ED Cari Ellen Coughlin, PD Stephen Greenberg.

LP Ned Beatty (Grandpa), Neil Patrick Harris (Billy Johnson), Shelley Winters (Rita), Peggy Lipton (Mom), James Houghton (Dad), Thora Birch (Molly Johnson), John Brumfeld (Mr. Noodle), Little Richard (Mayor), Chubby Checker (Singer).

Most viewers of this film probably weren't around when Sheb Wooley had a 1958 hit song with a silly novelty number called "Purple People Eater." In the film a one-eyed, purple, people-eater alien drops in on earth when 12-year-old daydreaming Neil Patrick Harris plays a record from his parents' 50s collection. Fear not, the visitor is not hungry for human flesh — just music.

2378. Purple Rain (1984, Warner, 111m, c). P Robert Cavallo, Joseph Ruffalo & Steven Fargnoli, D Albert Magnoli, W Magnoli & William Blinn, PH Donald Thorin, M Michel Colombier, ED Magnoli & Ken Robinson, PD Ward Preston, M/L "When Doves Cry," "The Beautiful Ones," "Darling Nikki" & "Purple Rain" by Prince*.

LP Prince (The Kid), Apollonia Kotero (Apollonia), Morris Day (Morris), Olga Karlatos (Mother), Clarence Williams, III (Father), Jerome Benton (Jerome), Billy Sparks (Billy), Jill Jones (Jill), Charles Huntsberry (Chick), Dez Dickerson (Dez).

In this quasiautobiographical showcase for pop star Prince, audiences learn of his struggle for love, attention, admiration and recognition. What he comes away with is more money than most people could ever imagine.

2379. The Purple Rose of Cairo (1985, Orion, 84m, c/b&w). P Robert Greenhut, D&W Woody Allen† (for writing), PH Gordon Willis, M Dick Hyman, ED Susan E. Morse, PD Stuart Wurtzel, AD Edward Pisoni, SD Carol Joffe.

LP Mia Farrow (Cecilia), Jeff Daniels (Tom Baxter/Gil Shepherd), Danny Aiello (Monk), Dianne Wiest (Emma), Van Johnson (Larry), Zoe Caldwell (The Countess), John Wood (Jason), Milo

O'Shea (Father Donnelly), Deborah Rush (Rita).

During the Depression, mousy housewife Mia Farrow escapes the harshness of her existence and marriage to loutish womanizer Danny Aiello by attending movies. She sees *The Purple Rose of Cairo* over and over again. On one occasion, Jeff Daniels, a character on the screen, turns and begins talking directly to Farrow in the audience. Finally he leaves the screen to be with her and learn what real life is about.

2380. *The Purple Taxi* (1980, Quartet, Fr./Ital./Ireland, 107m, c). P Peter Rawley & Hugo Lodrini, D Yves Boisset, W Michel Deon & Boisset (based on the book by Deon), PH Tonino Delli Colli, M Philippe Sarde, ED Albert Jurgensen.

LP Charlotte Rampling (Sharon), Philippe Noiret (Philippe), Agostina Belli (Anne Taubelman), Peter Ustinov (Taubelman), Fred Astaire (Dr. Scully), Edward Albert (Jerry), Mairin O'Sullivan (Colleen), Jack Watson (Sean).

Despite its origins, this multinational effort is an English language film. A collection of expatriates come together for a brief period to share angst, love and friendship and then go their separate ways.

2381. *The Pursuit of D.B. Cooper* (1981, Universal, 100m, c). P Daniel Wigutow & Michael Taylor, D Roger Spottiswoode, W Jeffrey Alan Fiskin (based on the book *Free Fall* by J.D. Reed), PH Harry Stradling, M James Horner, ED Robbe Roberts & Allan Jacobs, PD Preston Ames.

LP Robert Duvall (Gruen), Treat Williams (Meade), Kathryn Harrold (Hannah), Ed Flanders (Brigadier), Paul Gleason (Remson), R.G. Armstrong (Dempsey), Dorothy Fielding (Denise), Nicolas Coster (Avery).

Skyjacker Treat Williams bails out of a plane with the $200,000 ransom he was paid not to blow it up. He's chased by various people after the reward for his capture.

2382. *Puss in Boots* (1989, Cannon, 96m, c). P Menahem Golan & Yoram Globus, D Eugene Marner, W Carole Lucia Satrina (based on the fairy tale by Charles Perrault), PH Avi Karpick, M Rafi Kadishson, ED Satrina & Marner, PD Marek Dobrowolski.

LP Christopher Walken (Puss), Jason Connery (Corin), Carmela Marner (Vera), Yossi Graber (King), Elki Jacobs (Lady Clara), Amnon Meskin (Ogre).

Christopher Walken portrays a song and dance cat who helps young Jason Connery make his fortune by fooling a king into awarding his daughter, Carmela Marner, to Connery. He also appropriates the vast wealth of ogre Amnon Meskin.

2383. *Q: Quetzalcoatl* (1982, UFD, 100m, c, aka *Winged Serpent*). P,D&W Larry Cohen, PH Fred Murphy, M Robert O. Ragland, ED Armond Lebowitz, SE David Allen, Randy Cook & Peter Kuran.

LP Michael Moriarty (Jimmy), Candy Clark (Joan), David Carradine (Shepard), Richard Roundtree (Powell), James Dixon (Lt. Murray), Malachy McCourt (Commissioner), Fred J. Scollay (Capt. Fletcher).

A prehistoric Aztec deity flies from its nest atop a Manhattan skyscraper to tear off the heads of sunbathers and other unwary victims.

2384. *Quarantine* (1989, Atlantis, Canada, 97m, c). P,D&W Charles Wilkinson, PH Tobias Schliessler, ED Allan Lee, AD Robert Logevall.

LP Beatrice Boepple (Ivan Joad), Garwin Sanford (Spencer Crown), Jerry Wasserman (Sen. Edgar Ford), Tom McBeath (Lt. Beck), Michele Goodger (Berlin Ford), Kaj-Erik Eriksen (The Kid), Susan Chappelle (Councilwoman Campbell), Lee Taylor (Dr. Jim).

In a confusing mishmash, dictatorial Senator Jerry Wasserman arranges to move those caring for people dying of some unnamed disease to camps where they are kept as prisoners. A super computer is working on the eradication of the disease, but few viewers will care.

2385. *Quartet* (1981, New World, GB/Fr., 101m, c). P Ismail Merchant & Jean Pierre Mahot de la Querantonnais, D James Ivory, W Ruth Prawer Jhabvala & Ivory (based on the novel by Jean Rhys), PH Pierre Lhomme, M Richard

Robbins, ED Humphrey Dixon, AD Jean Jacques Caziot.

LP Alan Bates (H.J. Heidler), Maggie Smith (Lois), Isabelle Adjani (Marya), Anthony Higgins (Stephen), Armelia McQueen (Nell), Daniel Chatto (Guy), Pierre Clementi (Theo), Suzanne Flon (Mme. Hautchamp).

When her husband Anthony Higgins is sent to prison, Isabelle Adjani is taken in by Alan Bates and his indulgent painter wife Maggie Smith. Bates seduces Adjani, who becomes his lover. It's a story by Jean Rhys, loosely based on her life with Ford Madox Ford in Paris in the 1920s. Adjani loses out all around by the end of the film.

2386. *Quatermass Conclusion* (1980, Euston, GB, 105m, c). P Ted Childs, D Piers Haggard, W Nigel Kneale, PH Ian Wilson, M Marc Wilkinson & Nick Rowley, ED Keith Palmer.

LP John Mills (Prof. Bernard Quatermass), Simon MacCorkindale, Barbara Kellerman, Margaret Tyzack, Brewster Mason.

John Mills gives an outstanding interpretation of the sometimes eccentric scientist in this Armageddon epic. The old gent saves mankind from a killer broadcast beam, but sacrifices his life in the effort.

2387. *Queen of Hearts* (1989, Cinecom, GB, 112m, c). P John Hardy, D Jon Amiel, W Tony Grisoni, PH Mike Southon, M Michael Convertino, ED Peter Boyle, PD Jim Clay.

LP Vittorio Duse (Nonno), Joseph Long (Danilo), Anita Zagaria (Rosa), Eileen Way (Mama Sibilla), Vittorio Amandola (Barbariccia), Ian Hawkes (Eddie), Tat Whalley (Beetle).

The story is seen through the eyes of Ian Hawkes, a young boy living in the Italian community in London. He loves his mischievous grandfather Vittorio Duse, but learns of the harshness of life when Vittorio Amandola, once a contender for his mother's hand, arrives to take his revenge, causing the family to lose their modest cafe.

2388. *Quest for Fire* (1982, 20th Century-Fox, Fr./Canada, 97m, c). P John Kemeny, Denis Heroux, Jacques Dorf-

mann & Vera Belmont, D Jean-Jacques Annaud, W Gerard Brach (based on the novel *La Guerre de Feu* by J.H. Rosny, Sr.), PH Claude Agostini, M Philippe Sarde, ED Yves Langlois, PD Brian Morris & Guy Comtois, MK Sarah Monzani & Michele Burke*.

LP Everett McGill (Naoh), Ron Perlman (Amoukar), Nameer El-Kadi (Gaw), Rae Dawn Chong (Ika), Gary Schwartz, Frank Oliver Bonnet, Jean-Michel Kindt, Kurt Schiegl, Brian Gill.

The film is an imaginative and usually exciting story of prehistoric man's (and woman's) attempt to survive the Ice Age. Three members of the Ulam tribe are sent to find fire after their only source is accidentally extinguished. They encounter the barbarous Ivakas tribe that has knowledge of creating fire, using sticks and flints.

2389. *Quest for Love* (1989, Distant Horizon, South Africa, 93m, c). P Shan Moodley, D&W Helena Noguiera (based on the novel *Q.E.D.* by Gertrude Stein and the writings of Antonio A. Goncalves), PH Roy Macgregor, M Tony Rudner, ED Noguiera, PD Beverly Lanyon.

LP Jana Cilliers (Alex), Sandra Prinsloo (Dorothy), Andrew Buckland (Michael), Joanna Weinberg (Mabel), Wayne Bowman (Zaccharia), Lynn Gaines (Isabella), S. Prince Mokhini (Cokwana), Frances Ndlazilwana (Mapule).

Tormented Jana Cilliers, recently released from prison in South Africa, must sort out her political and sexual feelings. She ultimately commits herself to building a school destroyed by the South Africans and becoming Sandra Prinsloo's full-time lover.

2390. *Quicker Than the Eye* (1989, Condor, Switzerland, 92m, c). P Peter-Christian Fueter, D Nicolas Gessner, W Joseph Morhaim & Gessner (based on the novel by Claude Cueni), PH Wolfgang Treu, M George Garvarentz, ED Daniela Roderer, PD Max Stubenrauch.

LP Ben Gazzara (Ben Norell), Mary Crosby (Mary Preston), Jean Yanne (Inspector Sutter), Catherine Jarrett (Catherine Lombard), Wolfgang Berger (Kurt), Dinah Hinz (Gertrude), Ivan

Desny (Schneider), Sophie Carle (Silke), Robert Liensol (Pres. Makabutu).

Made especially for the U.S. video market, this Swiss production stars Ben Gazzara as a magician touring Europe with his assistant Mary Crosby. Ivan Desny plans to use Gazzara in a plot to kill an African leader attending a summit conference being held in Lucerne.

2391. *Quicksilver* (1986, Columbia, 106m, c). P Michael Rachmil & Daniel Melnick, D&W Tom Donnelly, PH Thomas Del Ruth, M Tony Banks, ED Tom Rolf, PD Charles Rosen.

LP Kevin Bacon (Jack Casey), Jami Gertz (Terri), Paul Rodriguez (Hector), Rudy Ramos (Gypsy), Andrew Smith (Gabe), Gerald S. O'Loughlin (Mr. Casey), Larry Fishburne (Voodoo), Louis Anderson (Tiny).

After blowing his and his parents' savings, Wall Street wizard Kevin Bacon is reduced to being a bicycle messenger. In this guise he becomes involved with drug dealers and an independent girl Jami Gertz who gets in over her head with the villains.

2392. *Quiet Cool* (1986, New Line Cinema, 86m, c). P Robert Shaye & Gerald T. Olson, D Clay Borris, W Borris & Susan Vercellino, PH Jacques Haitkin, M Jay Ferguson, ED Bob Brady.

LP James Remar (Joe Dillon), Adam Coleman Howard (Joshua Greer), Daphne Ashbrook (Katy Greer), Jared Martin (Mike Prior), Nick Cassavetes (Valence), Fran Ryan (Ma).

In a ludicrous action film, New York cop James Remar goes to the Pacific Northwest with Adam Coleman Howard to confront the maniacal marijuana growers who have killed Howard's parents.

2393. *The Quiet Earth* (1985, Skouras, New Zealand, 91m, c). P Sam Pillsbury & Don Reynolds, D Geoffrey Murphy, W Bill Baer, Bruno Lawrence & Pillsbury (based on the novel by Craig Harrison), PH James Bartle, M John Charles, ED Michael Horton, PD Josephine Ford.

LP Bruno Lawrence (Zac Hobson), Alison Routledge (Joanne), Peter Smith (Api), Anzac Wallace (Api's Mate), Norman Fletcher (Perrin), Tom Hyde (Scientist).

In what is probably New Zealand's first science fiction movie, scientist Bruno Lawrence wakes up one morning to find himself the only person left on earth. All others having mysteriously vanished. Eventually a few other survivors show up.

2394. *Rabid Grannies* (1989, Troma, 83m, c). P James Desert & Jonathan Rambert, D&W Emmanuel Kervyn, PH Hugh Labye, M Peter Castelain & J.B. Castelain, ED Philippe Ravoet, PD Luke Bertrand, SE Steven Fernandez.

LP Catherine Aymerie (Helen), Caroline Braekman (Suzie), Danielle Daven (Elisabeth), Raymond Lescot (Rev. Father), Elliot Lison (John), Michel Lombet (Roger), Anne Marie Fox (Victoria), Paule Herreman (Miss Barnstable), Bobette Jouret (Erika).

How about that for a great title? Various members of a family gather to celebrate the birthdays of wealthy grannies Danielle Daven and Anne Marie Fox, whose money they hope to soon inherit. A gift arrives from the black sheep of the family, one into satanic activities. When the present is opened it turns the old gals into cannibalistic monsters. Special effects expert Steven Fernandez has created some effects which should gross out just about everyone.

2395. *Race for Glory* (1989, New Century/Vista, 96m, c). P Jon Gordon & Daniel A. Sherkow, D Rocky Lang, W Scott Swanton (based on a story by Lang), PH Jack N. Green, M Jay Ferguson, ED Maryann Brandon, PD Cynthia Charette.

LP Alex McArthur (Cody), Peter Berg (Chris), Pamela Ludwig (Jenny), Ray Wise (Jack), Oliver Stritzel (Klaus), Burt Kwouk (Yoshiro Tanaka), Jerome Dempsey (Ray Crowley), Lane Smith (Joe Gifford).

Alex McArthur, a daredevil motorcycle racer, is trying for the big-time in International racing. He abandons his best friend and mechanic Peter Berg and his hometown girlfriend, Pamela Ludwig, when a Japanese company offers to sponsor him. Only later does he learn that they have given him an inferior bike so he won't threaten their big star Oliver Stritzel. Will McArthur come to his senses in time for the big race? Will his former friend and girlfriend rally around when his father dies? Are there any clichés this picture doesn't use?

Race for the Yankee Zephyr see Treasure of the Yankee Zephyr

2396.   The Rachel Papers (1989, United Artists/Virgin, GB, 95m, c). P Andrew S. Karsch, D&W Damian Harris (based on the novel by Martin Amis), PH Alex Thomson, M Chaz Jankel, ED David Martin, PD Andrew McAlpine.

LP Dexter Fletcher (Charles Highway), Ione Skye (Rachel Seth-Smith), Jonathan Pryce (Norman), James Spader (DeForrest), Bill Paterson (Charles' father), Lesley Sharp (Jenny), Michael Gambon (Oxford Don).

Nineteen-year-old Dexter Fletcher has plenty of money and all the sexual conquests he can handle. He meets and falls in love with beautiful 19-year-old American Ione Skye. She resists his charms for a short time, but comes around. They have a steamy passionate affair, but the fires burn out and it's over. Finis.

2397.   Rachel River (1989, Taurus, 90m, c). P Timothy Marx, D Sandy Smolan, W Judith Guest (based on the stories of Carol Bly), PH Paul Elliott, M Arvo Part, ED Susan Crutcher, PD David Wasco.

LP Pamela Reed (Mary Graving), Viveca Lindfors (Harriet White), Craig T. Nelson (Marlyn), Zeljko Ivanek (Momo), James Olson (Jack Canon), Ailene Cole (Svea).

This slice-of-life film stays on the sentimental and depressing side of Rachel River, a fictional town in Northern Minnesota. It appears to have died long ago and its residents are only awaiting their time to join it in the grave.

Racing Fury see Hell High

2398.   Racing with the Moon (1984, Paramount, 108m, c). P Alain Bernheim & John Kohn, D Richard Benjamin, W Steven Kloves, PH John Bailey, M Dave Grusin, ED Jacqueline Cambas, PD David L. Snyder.

LP Sean Penn (Henry "Hopper" Nash), Elizabeth McGovern (Caddie Winger), Nicolas Cage (Nicky), John Karlen (Mr. Nash), Rutanya Alda (Mrs. Nash), Max Showalter (Mr. Arthur),

Crispin Glover (Gatsby Boy), Barbara Howard (Gatsby Girl), Bob Maroff (Al).

In 1942 two young California men, Sean Penn and Nicolas Cage, have six months to say goodbye to their girlfriends before entering the Marine Corps. The main failure of this movie is that no one connected with the film seems to have any feeling for the period.

2399.   Rad (1986, Tri-Star, 93m, c). P Robert L. Levy, D Hal Needham, W Sam Bernard & Geoffrey Edwards, PH Richard Leiterman, M James Di Pasquale, ED Carl Kress, AD Shirley Inget.

LP Bill Allen (Cru), Lori Laughlin (Christian), Talia Shire (Mrs. Jones), Ray Walston (Burton Timmer), Alfie Wise (Elliott Dole), Jack Weston (Duke Best), Bart Connor (Bart Taylor), Marta Kober (Becky).

In this almost unwatchable sports drama, teen Bill Allen moves from his paper route to competition in BMX bike competition against arrogant champ Bart Connor. The latter, an ex–Olympic gold-medalist gymnast, should have stuck to the rings and parallel bars.

2400.   Radio Days (1987, Orion, 85m, c). P Robert Greenhut, D&W Woody Allen† (for screenplay), PH Carlo Di Palma, MD Dick Hyman, ED Susan E. Morse, PD Santo Loquasto†, AD/SD Santo Loquasto, Carol Joffe, Les Bloom & George DeTitta, Jr.†

LP Woody Allen (Narrator), Seth Green (Little Joe), Julie Kavner (Mother), Michael Tucker (Father), Dianne Wiest (Aunt Bea), Josh Mostel (Uncle Abe), Renee Lippin (Aunt Ceil), William Magerman (Grandpa), Leah Carrey (Grandma), Joy Newman (Ruthie), Mia Farrow (Sally White), Julie Kurnitz (Irene), Wallace Shawn (Masked Avenger), Jeff Daniels (Biff Baxter), Danny Aiello (Rocco), Gina DeAngelis (Rocco's Mother), Kenneth Mars (Rabbi Baumel), Tony Roberts ("Silver Dollar" Emcee), Diane Keaton (New Year's Singer).

Woody Allen provides a warmly nostalgic and comical look at his extended Jewish family. Living in a Brooklyn neighborhood in the 40s, the radio was everyone's contact with the big outside world. Allen presents not so much a story as a series of incidents and vignettes which take place in the family and to the various radio personalities brought into their home through the ever-playing instrument.

2401. *Radio On* (1980, Unifilm, GB/Ger., 101m, c). P Keith Griffiths, D Christopher Petit, W Petit & Heidi Adolph, PH Martin Schafer, M David Bowie, Sting, Kraftwerk, Eddie Cochran & Wreckless Eric, ED Anthony Sloman, AD Susannah Buxton.

LP David Beames (Robert), Lisa Kreuzer (Ingrid), Sandy Ratcliff (Kathy), Andrew Byatt (Deserter), Sue Jones-Davies (Girl), Sting (Just Like Eddie), Sabina Michael (Aunt), Katja Kersten (German Woman), Paul Hollywood (Kid).

Emotionally dead disc jockey David Beames returns to his Bristol home to investigate the mysterious circumstances of his brother's death.

2402. *Radioactive Dreams* (1986, De Laurentiis, 94m, c). P Thomas Karnowski & Moctesuma Esparza, D&W Albert F. Pyun, PH Charles Minsky, M Pete Robinson, ED Dennis O'Connor, PD Chester Kaczenski.

LP John Stockwell (Phillip), Michael Dudikoff (Marlowe), George Kennedy (Spade), Don Murray (Dash), Michele Little (Rusty), Norbert Weisser (Sternwood), Lisa Blount (Miles).

It's as funny as you might expect a post-apocalypse story to be. Two jerks, John Stockwell and Michael Dudikoff, raised on 1940s pulp detective novels, emerge from their hiding after the danger of radiation has worn off. They travel through a world filled with mutants, bikers and punks. Everyone including beautiful Michele Little and Lisa Blount are searching for the world's last atomic bomb.

2403. *Rage of Honor* (1987, Trans-World, 91m, c). P Don Van Atta, D Gordon Hessler, W Robert Short & Wallace Bennett (based on a story by Short), PH Julio Bragado, M Stelvio Cipriani, ED Robert Gordon, PD Adrian Gorton.

LP Sho Kosugi (Shiro Tanaka), Lewis Van Bergen (Drug Lord), Robin Evans (Jennifer), Richard Wiley (Ray Jones), Armando Caro (Juan), Marlee Jepson (Girl in Convertible).

Martial arts expert Sho Kosugi is a narcotics agent working out of Phoenix. His partner Richard Wiley is set up and murdered by a drug kingpin. Kosugi gets angry. It's routine stuff.

2404. *Rage to Kill* (1989, Action International, 92m, c). P&D David Winters, W Winters & Ian Yule, PH Vincent Cox, M Tim James, Steven McClintock & Mark Mancina, ED Bill Asher.

LP James Ryan (Blaine Striker), Oliver Reed (Gen. Turner), Cameron Mitchell (Miller), Maxine John (Trishia Baker), Henry Cele (Wally Arn), Ian Yule (Slade).

US racing driver James Ryan heads to the Caribbean island of St. Heron to check on his medical student brother now that control of the island nation has been taken over by Oliver Reed. Ryan is taken hostage, but organizes the students and with the aid of CIA man Cameron Mitchell teams up with the rebels headed by Henry Cele to kick out Reed.

2405. *Raggedy Man* (1981, Universal, 94m, c). P Burt Weissbourd & William D. Wittliff, D Jack Fisk, W Wittliff, PH Ralf Bode, M Jerry Goldsmith, ED Edward Warschilka, AD John Lloyd.

LP Sissy Spacek (Nita), Eric Roberts (Teddy), Sam Shepard (Bailey), William Sanderson (Calvin), Tracey Walter (Arnold), R.G. Armstrong (Rigby), Henry Thomas (Harry), Carey Hollis, Jr. (Henry), Ed Geldart (Mr. Calloway), Bill Thurman (Sheriff), Suzi McLaughlin (Jean Lester).

It's World War II in a small Texas town. Lonely divorcée Sissy Spacek, raising two sons alone, risks the anger of several determined suitors, who believe all divorcées are "hot-to-trot," when she allows sailor Eric Roberts to move in with her. The period atmosphere and naturalistic dialogue almost make up for the understated plot.

2406. *The Raggedy Rawney* (1988, Handmade Films, GB, 104m, c). P Bob Weis, D Bob Hoskins, W Hoskins & Nicole de Wilde, PH Frank Tidy, M Michael Kamen, ED Alan Jones, PD Jiri Matolin.

LP Bob Hoskins (Darky), Dexter Fletcher (Tom), Zoe Nathenson (Jessie), Dave Hill (Lamb), Ian Drury (Weasel), Zoe Wanamaker (Elle), J.G. Devlin (Jake).

A Rawney is a half-made creature with magical powers. So says actor Bob Hoskins who invented the creature for his debut as both screenwriter and director. The Rawney in Hoskins story is Dexter Fletcher, a young soldier, so traumatized by the horrors of war that he flees into the forests of the night and finally finds some comfort with a band of gypsies.

2407.   *Raging Bull*† (1980, United Artists, 129m, b&w). P Irwin Winkler & Robert Chartoff, D Martin Scorsese†, W Paul Schrader & Mardik Martin (based on the book by Jake LaMotta with Joseph Carter & Peter Savage), PH Michael Chapman†, ED Thelma Schoonmaker†, PD Gene Rudolf, SOUND Donald O. Mitchell, Bill Nicholson, David J. Kimball & Les Lazarowitz†.

LP Robert De Niro* (Jack LaMotta), Cathy Moriarty† (Vickie LaMotta), Joe Pesci† (Joey), Frank Vincent (Salvy), Nicholas Colasanto (Tommy Como), Theresa Saldana (Lenore), Frank Adonis (Patsy), Mario Gallo (Mario), Frank Topham (Toppy/Handler), Lori Anne Flax (Irma), Joseph Bono (Guido).

Boxing films make the best sports movies, because the film concentrates on individual struggles, achievements and problems, rather than contributions to a team. Robert DeNiro, an actor who really gets into his parts, went so far as to gain 50 pounds so that he would be more credible as the washed up middleweight boxer Jake LaMotta. This marvelous cinematic achievement details the life and career of a talented but basically unlikeable champion. Many critics have designated the film as the best picture of the eighties. We find it hard to believe that anyone could seriously rank movies by any criteria so as to isolate one as the "best." This one would certainly make our unranked list of outstanding films of the decade.

2408.   *Ragtime* (1981, Paramount, GB, 156m, c). P Dino De Laurentiis, D Milos Forman, W Michael Weller† (based on the novel by E.L. Doctorow), PH Miroslav Ondricek†, M Randy Newman†, ED Anne V. Coates, Antony Gibbs & Stanley Warnow, PD John Graysmark, AD/SD Graysmark, Patrizia Von Brandenstein, Anthony Reading, George de Titta, Sr., George de Titta, Jr. & Peter Howitt†, M/L "One More Hour" by Newman† (sung by Jennifer Warnes), COS Anna Hill Johnstone†.

LP James Cagney (Police Commissioner Rhinelander Waldo), Brad Dourif (Younger Brother), Moses Gunn (Booker T. Washington), Elizabeth McGovern† (Evelyn Nesbit), Kenneth McMillan (Willie Conklin), Pat O'Brien (Delmas), Donald O'Connor (Evelyn's Dance Instructor), James Olson (Father), Mandy Patinkin (Tateh), Howard E. Rollins† (Coalhouse Walker, Jr.), Mary Steenburgen (Mother), Debbie Allen (Sarah), Jeff DeMunn (Harry Houdini), Robert Joy (Harry K. Thaw), Norman Mailer (Stanford White).

Based on a patchwork novel which examined how world events just prior to World War I affected various Americans; the movie is confused and confusing. The film concentrates on a minor event in the book which the moviemakers must have felt was more relevant to modern times. The performances by Elizabeth McGovern as "The Girl in the Red Velvet Swing" and Howard Rollins as an early black activist are splendid. Of considerable interest to many fans is the final teaming (if it can be said to be a teaming, they don't appear together in any scene) of James Cagney and Pat O'Brien. This isn't the way to remember the two grand, spunky, Irish actors.

2409.   *Raiders of the Living Dead* (1989, Cineronde-Canada, 83m, c). P Dan Q. Kennis, D Samuel M. Sherman, W Sherman & Brett Piper, PH Douglas Meltzer, M Tim Ferrante, ED John Donaldson, PD Ruth Seidman.

LP Robert Deveau (Morgan Randall), Donna Asali (Shelly), Scott Schwartz (Jonathan), Bob Allen (Dr. Carstairs), Bob Sacchetti (Man in Black), Zita Johann (Librarian), Corri Burt (Michelle).

Begun in 1983 as *Graveyard* this minor zombie picture is the tale of newspaper reporter Robert Deveau who tracks down a mad scientist at an abandoned island prison. The bad doctor is up to no good, reanimating corpses. Zita Johann appeared with Boris Karloff in Universal's classic 1932 horror film, *The Mummy*. Welcome back, Zita. Where have you been for so long?

2410.   *Raiders of the Lost Ark*† (1981, Paramount, 115m, c). P Frank Marshall, D Steven Spielberg†, W Lawrence

Kasdan (based on a story by George Lucas & Philip Kaufman), PH Douglas Slocombe†, M John Williams†, ED Michael Kahn*, PD Norman Reynolds, AD/SD Reynolds, Leslie Dilley & Michael Ford*, SE Richard Edlund, Kit West, Bruce Nicholson & Joe Johnston*, SOUND Bill Varney, Stew Maslow, Gregg Landaker & Roy Charman*.

LP Harrison Ford (Indiana Jones), Karen Allen (Marion Ravenswood), Paul Freeman (Belloq), Ronald Lacey (Toht), John Rhys-Davies (Sallah), Denholm Elliott (Brody), Wolf Kahler (Dietrich), Anthony Higgins (Gobler), Alfred Molina (Satipo), Vic Tablian (Barranca), Don Fellows (Col. Musgrove), William Hootkins (Maj. Eaton).

Some critics dismiss this action-adventure film as merely a piece of exciting fluff, meant to entertain children of all ages. But perhaps they forget that one of the several functions of movies is to entertain and provide harmless escape from the everyday cares of the world. And that's precisely what this enjoyable spoof of every adventure film ever made does with great vigor and fun. American archaeologist Harrison Ford struggles with 30s Nazis for possession of the priceless treasure and holy relic, the Ark of the Covenant. The film is a never ending series of visual shocks, like a roller coaster, constantly diving from a very high drop. The acting is adequate for what it needs to be and the story, incredible but absorbing.

2411. *Rain Man** (1988, MGM/United Artists, 140m, c). P Mark Johnson, D Barry Levinson*, W Ronald Bass & Barry Morrow* (based on a story by Morrow), PH John Seale†, M Hans Zimmer†, ED Stu Linder†, PD Ida Random, AD/SD Random & Linda DeScenna†.

LP Dustin Hoffman* (Raymond Babbitt), Tom Cruise (Charlie Babbitt), Valeria Golino (Susanna), Jerry Molen (Dr. Bruner), Jack Murdock (John Mooney), Michael D. Roberts (Vern), Ralph Seymour (Lenny).

In one of the finest movies to come down the pike in many a year, Tom Cruise portrays a selfish young hustler who returns home for the reading of his estranged father's will. He learns that he has an older brother who has been left the bulk of the $3 million estate. The brother, brilliantly interpreted by Dustin Hoffman, is an autistic savant, a person extremely limited in most mental areas but supremely gifted in others. Cruise effectively kidnaps Hoffman from the safety of the institution where he has lived for many years. He hopes to be named Hoffman's guardian and get his hands on the money. Driving cross country gives the two a chance to know each other, not that Hoffman changes much. But Cruise, so lacking in kindness and understanding, undergoes a slow and believable transformation, as he learns to care for the brother he called "Rainman" as a child, being unable to pronounce "Raymond." Director Barry Levinson took risks with the movie. If he had played it for more humor, it might have seemed that he was having a laugh at Hoffman's plight; any less humor and the film would be unbearably depressing; any more spirit-raising and it would be pure sentimentality; any offered hope that Hoffman's condition would change and it wouldn't be credible. Hoffman, who almost acted himself out of movies with *Ishtar,* is back at the top of his form. Cruise, oddly cast in the part of Hoffman's younger, almost cruelly uncaring brother, nevertheless does a credible job. Italian actress Valeria Golino is most effective as Cruise's sensitive, long-suffering girlfriend who is touched by and touches Hoffman.

2412. *The Rainbow* (1989, Vestron, GB, 112m, c). P&D Ken Russell, W Ken Russell & Vivian Russell (based on the novel by D.H. Lawrence), PH Billy Williams, M Carl Davis, ED Peter Davies, PD Luciana Arrighi, AD Ian Whittaker.

LP Sammi Davis (Ursula Brangwen), Paul McGann (Anton Skrebensky), Amanda Donohoe (Winifred), Christopher Gable (Will Brangwen), David Hemmings (Uncle Henry), Glenda Jackson (Anna Brangwen), Dudley Sutton (MacAllister), Jim Carter (Mr. Harby), Judith Paris (Miss Harby), Ken Colley (Mr. Brunt), Glenda McKay (Gudrun).

Director Ken Russell returns to the works of D.H. Lawrence, filming a sort of prequel to *Women in Love,* which Russell brought brilliantly to the screen in

1970. It's the story of the sexual awakening of Ursula Brangwen, played this time by Sammi Davis, and by Jennie Linden in the earlier film. Glenda Jackson who portrayed Ursula's sister Gudrun in the 1970 picture, appears here as the girls' mother. Davis' initiation to sex comes from her swimming instructor, beautiful Amanda Donohoe. Davis later finds herself attracted to a man, career soldier Paul McGann, whose lovemaking is not as gentle as that of Donohoe. The film is a fine companion piece to *Women in Love*.

2413. Rainbow Brite and the Star Stealer (1985, Warner, 97m, animated, c). P John Chalopin, Andy Heyward & Tetsuo Katayama, D Bernard Deyries & Kimio Tabuki, W Howard R. Cohen (based on characters developed by Hallmark Properties), M Haim Saban & Shuki Levy, ED Yutaka Chikura.

VOICES Bettina (Rainbow Brite), Patrick Fraley (Lurky, On-X, Buddy Blue, Dog, Spectran, Slurthie, Glitterbot), Peter Cullen (Murky, Castle Monster, Glitterbot, Guard, Skydancer, Slurthie), Robbie Lee (Twink, Shy Violet, Indigo, La La Orange, Spectran, Sprites), Andre Stojka (Starlite, Wizard, Spectran), David Mendenhall (Krys), Rhonda Aldrich (The Princess, The Creature).

Rainbow Brite (Bettina) saves the world's color from an evil princess who has stolen the planet Spectra, the universe's source of all light.

2414. Raise the Titanic (1980, Associated Film Distribution, GB, 112m, c). P William Frye, D Jerry Jameson, W Adam Kennedy & Eric Hughes (based on the novel by Clive Cussler), PH Matthew F. Leonetti, M John Barry, ED J. Terry Williams & Robert F. Shugrue, PD John F. De Cuir.

LP Jason Robards (Adm. James Sandecker), Richard Jordan (Dirk Pitt), David Selby (Dr. Gene Seagram), Anne Archer (Dana Archibald), Alec Guinness (John Bigalow), J.D. Cannon (Capt. Joe Burke), Bo Brundin (Capt. Andre Prelov), M. Emmet Walsh (MCPO Vinnie Giordino), Robert Broyles (Willis).

In a film with surprisingly little action, suspense or plot, a group of Americans led by Jason Robards and Richard Jordan attempt to recover rare minerals from the wreck of the *Titanic* that sunk on its maiden voyage in 1912 when it hit an iceberg in the North Atlantic. The Russians are also interested.

2415. Raising Arizona (1987, 20th Century-Fox, 94m, c). P Ethan Coen & Mark Silverman, D Joel Coen, W Ethan Coen & Joel Coen, PH Barry Sonnenfeld, M Carter Burwell, ED Michael R. Miller, PD Jane Musky.

LP Nicolas Cage (H.I. McDonnough), Holly Hunter (Edwina), Trey Wilson (Nathan Arizona, Sr.), John Goodman (Gale), William Forsythe (Evelle), Sam McMurray (Glen), Frances McDormand (Dot), Randall "Tex" Cobb (Leonard Smalls), T.J. Kuhn (Nathan Arizona, Jr.).

Nicolas Cage makes a living robbing convenience stores. Each time he's arrested, his mug shot is taken by pretty officer Holly Hunter. As a result the two fall in love and marry. Their happiness is almost ruined when they discover they can't have children. Because of his record, they are unable to adopt a child. When a local wealthy family is blessed with quints, Cage and Hunter decide that one won't be missed. They kidnap Nathan Arizona, Jr., whom they hope to raise as their own. Their problems are far from over in this quirky comedy.

2416. Rambo: First Blood Part II (1985, Tri-Star, 92m, c). P Buzz Feitshans, D George P. Cosmatos, W Sylvester Stallone & James Cameron (based on a story by Kevin Jarre & characters by David Morrell), PH Jack Cardiff, M Jerry Goldsmith, ED Mark Goldblatt & Mark Helfrich, PD Bill Kenney, SE ED Frederick J. Brown†.

LP Sylvester Stallone (John Rambo), Richard Crenna (Trautman), Charles Napier (Murdock), Steven Berkoff (Podovsky), Julia Nickson (Co Bao), George Kee Cheung (Tay), Andy Wood (Banks), Martin Kove (Ericson), William Ghent (Vinh), Vojo Goric (Yushin).

The message of this violent film is that neither the United States' former enemies in Southeast Asia nor the U.S. government can be trusted to deal with the problem of the MIAs. Direct action by killing moron Sylvester Stallone is the answer.

2417. *Rambo III* (1988, Tri-Star, 101m, c). P Buzz Feitshans, D Peter Mac-Donald, W Sylvester Stallone & Sheldon Lettich (based on characters created by David Morrell), PH John Stanier, M Jerry Goldsmith, ED James Symons, Andrew London, O. Nicholas Brown & Edward Warschilka, PD Bill Kenney.

LP Sylvester Stallone (John Rambo), Richard Crenna (Colonel Trautman), Marc de Jonge (Colonel Zaysen), Kurtwood Smith (Griggs), Spiros Focas (Masoud), Sasson Gabai (Mousa), Doudi Shoua (Hamid), Randy Raney (Gen. Kourov), Marcus Gilbert (Tomask).

Having "cleaned-up" Southeast Asia, Sylvester Stallone turns his attention to other commies; this time those in Afghanistan. He's there to rescue his buddy Richard Crenna. For those who enjoy jingoistic films, this one ought to prove a treat.

2418. *Rampage* (1987, DEG, 97m, c). P David Salven, D&W William Friedkin (based on the novel by William P. Wood), PH Robert D. Yeoman, M Ennio Morricone, ED Jere Higgins, PD Buddy Cone.

LP Michael Biehn (Anthony Fraser), Alex McArthur (Charles Reece), Nicholas Campbell (Albert Morse), Deborah Van Valkenburgh (Kate Fraser), John Harkins (Dr. Keddie), Art Lafleur (Mel Sanderson), Billy Green Bush (Judge McKinsey), Royce D. Applegate (Gene Tippetts), Grace Zabriskie (Namoi Reece).

Although personally opposed to capital punishment, prosecutor Michael Biehn is forced to ask for the death penalty for serial killer Alex McArthur. The latter's lawyer is trying to get his client off on an insanity plea.

Rap Attack see Krush Grove

2419. *Rappin'* (1985, Cannon, 92m, c). P Menahem Golan & Yoram Globus, D Joel Silberg, W Robert Litz & Adam Friedman, PH David Gurfinkel, M Michael Linn, ED Andy Horvitch & Bert Glatstein, PD Steve Miller.

LP Mario Van Peebles (John Hood), Tasia Valenza (Dixie), Charles Flohe (Duane), Leo O'Brien (Allan), Eriq La Salle (Ice), Richie Albanes (Richie), Kadeem Hardison (Moon), Melvin Plowden (Fats), Harry Goz (Thorndike), Rony Clanton (Cedric).

Ex-con Mario Van Peebles wants to go straight but finds that his girlfriend Tasia Valenza has taken up with the leader of a street gang. The latter works for an evil contractor who is trying to evict his tenants so he can tear down the whole neighborhood. Van Peebles rallies the tenants and legally defeats the contractor. He also wins a record contract for his rap songs.

2420. *A Rare Breed* (1981, New World, 94m, c). P Jack Cox, D David Nelson, W Gardner Simmons, PH Darryl Cathcart.

LP George Kennedy (Nathan Hill), Forrest Tucker (Jess Cutler), Tom Hallick (Lou Nelson), Don Defore (Frank Nelson), Tracy Vaccaro (Anne Cutler).

While en route to Europe for training, young Tracy Vaccaro and her filly Carnauba are kidnapped, setting off a race against time to rescue them before the big race.

2421. *Ratboy* (1986, Warner, 104m, c). P Fritz Manes, D Sondra Locke, W Rob Thompson, PH Bruce Surtees, M Lennie Niehaus, ED Joel Cox, PD Edward Carfagno.

LP Sondra Locke (Nikki Morrison), Robert Townsend (Manny), Christopher Hewett (Acting Coach), Larry Hankin (Jewell), Gerrit Graham (Billy Morrison), Louie Anderson (Omer Morrison), S.L. Baird (Ratboy).

Sondra Locke's directorial debut sees actress Locke as a journalist who discovers and exploits S.L. Baird, part boy, part rodent. We don't like rats, even partial rats. Very few people, except for some French critics, bothered to watch it.

The Rats see Deadly Eyes

2422. *Raw Courage* (1984, New World, 90m, c, aka *Courage*). P Ronny Cox & Robert L. Rosen, D Rosen, W Ronny & Mary Cox, PH F. Pershing Flynn, M Johnny Harris, ED Steven Polivka, PD Don Nunley.

LP Ronny Cox (Pete Canfield), Lois Chiles (Ruth), Art Hindle (Roger Bower), M. Emmet Walsh (Colonel Crouse), Tim Maier (Craig Jensen), William Russ (Sonny), Lisa Sutton (Stephanie), Noel Conlon (Clay Matthews).

While participating in a 72-mile supermarathon race, three runners pass through a New Mexico desert, where they get more than they bargained for from a group of survivalists, training for war.

2423.   *Raw Deal* (1986, De Laurentiis, 97m, c). P Martha Schumacher, D John Irvin, W Gary M. DeVore & Norman Wexler (based on a story by Luciano Vincenzoni & Sergio Donati), PH Lucio Trentini, M Clifford Capone, ED Anne V. Coates, PD Giorgio Postiglione.

LP Arnold Schwarzenegger (Kaminski), Kathryn Harrold (Monique), Sam Wanamaker (Patrovita), Paul Shenar (Rocca), Robert Davi (Max), Ed Lauter (Baker), Darren McGavin (Shannon), Joe Regalbuto (Baxter), Mordecai Lawner (Marcellino), Steven Hill (Lamanski), Blanche Baker (Amy Kaminski).

Kicked out of the FBI because of his unconventional means of conducting investigations, Arnold Schwarzenegger gets another chance when the bureau needs someone to infiltrate the Chicago mob machine and tear it apart. The mass-destruction finale is awesome, but we're forced to inform the makers of this movie that Arnie must have let some of the baddies get away, because the mob is alive and well in the Windy City.

2424.   *Raw Force* (1982, American Panorama, 86m, c, aka *Shogun Island*). P Frank Johnson, D&W Edward Murphy, PH Johnson, M Walter Murphy, ED Eric Lindemann.

LP Cameron Mitchell (Captain), Geoff Binney (Mike), Jillian Kesner (Cookie), John Dresden (John), Jennifer Holmes (Ann), Hope Holiday (Hazel), Rey King (Chin), Vic Diaz (Monk).

Three karate experts travel to an island inhabited by a tribe of cannibalistic monks with the power to raise the dead.

2425.   *Rawheard Rex* (1987, Empire, GB, 89m, c). P Kevin Attew & Don Hawkins, D George Pavlou, W Clive Barker (based on his short story), PH John Metcalfe, M Colin Towns, ED Andy Horvitch, AD Len Huntingford.

LP David Dukes (Howard Hallenbeck), Kelly Piper (Elaine Hallenbeck), Ronan Wilmot (Declan O'Brien), Niall Toibin (Rev. Coot), Niall O'Brien (Det. Insp. Isaac Gissing), Heinrich Von Schellendorf (Rawhead Rex).

A satanic demon terrorizes a small Ireland village when it is accidentally unearthed.

2426.   *Razorback* (1984, UAA/Warner, Australia, 95m, c). P Hal McElroy, D Russell Mulcahy, W Everett DeRoche (based on the novel by Peter Brennan), PH Dean Semler, M Ira Davies, ED William Anderson, PD Bryce Walmsley.

LP Gregory Harrison (Carl Winters), Arkie Whiteley (Sarah Cameron), Bill Kerr (Jake Cullen), Chris Haywood (Benny Baker), Judy Morris (Beth Winters), John Howard (Danny), John Ewart (Turner), Don Smith (Wallace).

In a small Australian outback community, a man is tried for the murder of his grandson. The child actually has been carried off by a giant wild boar. Shades of *A Cry in the Dark.*

2427.   *The Razor's Edge* (1984, Columbia, 128m, c). P Robert P. Marcucci, Harry Benn, D John Byrum, W Byrum & Bill Murray (based on the novel by W. Somerset Maugham), PH Peter Hannan, M Jack Nitzsche, ED Peter Boyle, PD Philip Harrison.

LP Bill Murray (Larry Darrell), Theresa Russell (Sophie), Catherine Hicks (Isabel), Denholm Elliott (Elliott Templeton), James Keach (Gray Maturin), Peter Vaughan (MacKenzie), Brian Doyle-Murray (Piedmont), Stephen Davies (Malcolm), Saeed Jaffrey (Raaz), Faith Brook (Louisa Bradley).

Audiences found it difficult to take Bill Murray seriously in a dramatic role. But its not all their fault. Murray failed to deliver a dramatic performance in the Somerset Maugham story of a well-to-do young man who spends the years between the world wars looking for essential truth. Murray is a charming performer but he doesn't convey the necessary spirituality of the part. But for that matter Tyrone Power also had difficulty with that chore in 1946. Denholm Elliott as Murray's uncle is his usual fine form.

2428.   *Reaching Out* (1983, Par Films, 87m, c). P,D&W Pat Russell, PH David Sperling, M Elizabeth Mazel, ED Russell, Sperling & Jim McCreading.

LP Pat Russell (Pat Stuart), Tony Craig (John Stevens), Frank McCarthy

(Frank Mesina), Betty Andrews (Mrs. Stuart), Douglas Stark (Mr. Stuart), Tyre Alls (Florence), Ralph Carlson (Agent), Marketa Kimbrel (Acting Teacher).

Originally shot in 1973, this film's initial release was ten years later. Considering the thinness of the story about actress Pat Russell trying to make it on Broadway, one is surprised it was ever released.

Reactor see Deadly Reactor

2429. *Real Genius* (1985, Tri-Star, 105m, c). P Brian Grazer, D Martha Coolidge, W Neal Israel, Pat Proft & Peter Torokvei (based on a story by Israel & Proft), PH Vilmos Zsigmond, M Thomas Newman, ED Richard Chew, PD Josan F. Russo.

LP Val Kilmer (Chris Knight), Gabe Jarret (Mitch Taylor), Michelle Meyrink (Jordan), William Atherton (Prof. Hathaway), Patti D'Arbanville (Sherry Nugil), Robert Prescott (Kent), Louis Giambalvo (Maj. Carnagle), Ed Lauter (Decker).

When the brilliant students at a California technical institute discover that their class projects are being used for offensive military purposes, they come up with a strategic defensive initiative of their own. It's a disappointing comedy from director Martha Coolidge.

2430. *Real Life* (1984, Bedford, GB, 92m, c). P Mike Dineen, D Francis Megahy, W Megahy & Bernie Cooper, PH Peter Jessop, M David Mindel, ED Peter Delfgou, PD John White.

LP Rupert Everett (Tim), Cristina Raines (Laurel), Catherine Rabett (Kate), James Faulkner (Robin), Isla Blair (Anna), Norman Beaton (Leon), Warren Clarke (Gerry), Lynsey Baxter (Jackie), Annabel Leventon (Carla), Michael Cochrane (Lipton).

Mischievous lad Rupert Everett spices up his life by telling tall tales. He creates a story about the theft of a Rembrandt painting, taken by a gang working for a big-shot boss, who in turn is operating in behalf of South African guerrillas. Everett's in trouble when his story comes true.

2431. *Real Men* (1987, MGM/United Artists, 96m, c). P Martin Bregman, D&W Dennis Feldman, PH John A. Alonzo, AD William J. Cassidy & James Allen.

LP James Belushi (Nick Pirandello), John Ritter (Bob Wilson), Barbara Barrie (Mom), Bill Morey (Cunard), Iva Andersen (Dolly), Gail Berle (Sherry), Mark Herrier (Bradshaw), Matthew Brooks (Bob, Jr.).

Bond-like CIA agent James Belushi attempts to build up the confidence of a wimpy partner who is reluctantly posing as a dead spy. It's a candidate for a short shelf life in a video store.

2432. *Re-Animator* (1985, Empire, 86m, c). P Brian Yuzna, D Stuart Gordon, W Dennis Paoli, William J. Norris & Gordon (based on the story "Herbert West: The Re-Animator" by H.P. Lovecraft), PH Mac Ahlberg, M Richard Band, ED Lee Percy, AD Robert A. Burns, SE Anthony Doublin & John Naulin.

LP Jeffrey Combs (Herbert West), Bruce Abbott (Dan Cain), Barbara Crampton (Megan Halsey), David Gale (Dr. Carl Hill), Robert Sampson (Dean Halsey), Gerry Black (Mace), Peter Kent (Melvin the Re-animated).

This black-humor horror film, based on the work of H.P. Lovecraft, in which medical student Jeffrey Combs is able to reanimate the dead, has become a cult favorite.

2433. *Rebel* (1985, Vestron, Australia, 91m, c). P Phillip Emanuel, D Michael Jenkins, W Jenkins & Bob Herbert (based on the play *No Names...No Packdrill* by Herbert), PH Peter James, M Chris Neal, ED Michael Honey, PD Brian Thompson.

LP Matt Dillon (Rebel), Debbie Byrne (Kathy McLeod), Bryan Brown (Tiger Kelly), Bill Hunter (Browning), Ray Barrett (Bubbles), Julie Nihill (Joycie), John O'May (Bernie), Kim Deacon (Hazel).

In Sydney during World War II, young U.S. Marine Matt Dillon goes AWOL and falls in love with a married nightclub singer, Debbie Byrne. He's torn between wanting to escape the war and staying with her in Australia. There are too many suds in this soap opera.

2434. *Rebel Love* (1985, Troma, 90m, c). P John Quenelle, D&W Milton

Bagby, Jr., PH Joseph A. Whigham, M Bobby Horton, ED Melinda Bridges, PD Bill Teague.

LP Jamie Rose (Columbine Cromwell), Terence Knox (McHugh/Hightower), Fran Ryan (Granny Plug), Carl Spurlock (Sergeant), Rick Wain (Corporal), Larry Larson (Aaron Cromwell), Charles Hill (The Captain).

In a cheaply-made Civil War drama, Yankee widow Jamie Rose finds escape from her loneliness on a solitary Indiana farm in the arms of rebel spy Terence Knox.

Rebel Waves see Rising Storm

2435. *Reckless* (1984, MGM/United Artists, 90m, c). P Edgar J. Scherick & Scott Rudin, D James Foley, W Chris Columbus, PH Michael Ballhaus, M Thomas Newman, ED Albert Magnoli, PD Jeffrey Townsend.

LP Aidan Quinn (Johnny Rourke), Daryl Hannah (Tracey Prescott), Kenneth McMillan (John Rourke, Sr.), Cliff De Young (Phil Barton), Lois Smith (Mrs. Prescott), Adam Baldwin (Randy Daniels), Dan Hedaya (Peter Daniels).

Aidan Quinn, the son of the town drunk, has a bad reputation. He falls in love with straitlaced cheerleader Daryl Hannah, a girl from a good family. Their passion and rebellion upset their little West Virginia town.

2436. *Recruits* (1986, Concorde, 82m, c). P Maurice Smith, D Rafal Zielinski, W Charles Wiener, B.K. Roderick, PH Peter Czerski, M Steve Parsons, ED Stephan Fanfara & Christie Wilson, AD Craig Richards.

LP Steve Osmond (Steve), Doug Annear (Mike), Alan Deveau (Howie), John Terrell (Winston), Lolita Davidoff (Susan), Tracey Tanner (Brazil), Annie McAuley (Tanya), Tony Travis (Stonewall), Mike McDonald (Magruder).

In a cheap rip-off of *Police Academy* (how is that possible, you ask?), a sheriff hires hookers, thieves, winos and bums as deputies.

2437. *Red Dawn* (1984, MGM/United Artists, 100m, c). P Buzz Feitshans & Barry Beckerman, D John Milius, W Kevin Reynolds & Milius (based on the novel by Reynolds), PH Ric Waite, M Basil Poledouris, ED Thom Noble, PD Jackson de Govia.

LP Patrick Swayze (Jed), C. Thomas Howell (Robert), Lea Thompson (Erica), Charlie Sheen (Matt), Darren Dalton (Daryl), Jennifer Grey (Toni), Brad Savage (Danny), Doug Toby (Aardvark), Ben Johnson (Mason), Harry Dean Stanton (Mr. Eckert), Ron O'Neal (Bella), William Smith (Strelnikov), Vladek Sheybal (Bratchenko), Powers Boothe (Andy).

In this commie-bashing movie which makes the NRA's point about the need for keeping guns, Russian invaders overrun the United States heartland, taking over the country. Eight small-town teenagers hide out in the rugged countryside and harrass the Russkies with guerrilla warfare. It's not a very believable story, but the youngsters work hard to make it exciting.

2438. *Red-Headed Stranger* (1986, Alive Films, 105m, c). P Willie Nelson & William Wittliff, D&W Wittliff, PH Neil Roach, M Willie Nelson, ED Eric Austin Williams & Stephen H. Purvis, PD Cary White.

LP Willie Nelson (Julian), Morgan Fairchild (Raysha), Katharine Ross (Laurie), R.G. Armstrong (Scoby), Royal Dano (Larn Claver), Sonny Carl Davis (Odie Claver), Marinell Madden (Cindy), Ted J. Crum (Cauley Felps).

Montana preacher Willie Nelson is troubled by his wayward wife Morgan Fairchild, good woman Katharine Ross and some bad guys headed by Royal Dano who rule the roost in his town. He'll just have to do something about all of this other than sing.

2439. *Red Heat* (1988, Tri-Star, 106m, c). P Walter Hill & Gordon Carroll, D Hill, W Harry Kleiner, Hill & Troy Kennedy Martin (based on a story by Hill), PH Matthew F. Leonetti, M James Horner, ED Freeman Davies, Carmel Davies & Donn Aron, PD John Vallone.

LP Arnold Schwarzenegger (Capt. Ivan Danko), James Belushi (Det. Sgt. Art Ridzik), Peter Boyle (Police Comdr. Lou Donnelly), Ed O'Ross (Viktor Rostavili), Larry Fishburne (Lt. Stobbs), Gina Gershon (Cat Manzetti), Richard Bright (Sgt. Gallagher), J.W. Smith (Salim).

No nonsense Soviet police officer Arnold Schwarzenegger follows Georgian drug dealer Ed O'Ross to Chicago. He's forced to team up with slovenly wise-cracking cop James Belushi to catch his man. It's close enough to director Walter Hill's *48 Hours* to be considered a reworking of the plot, but it's fast moving and fun.

2440. *Red Heat* (1988, Vestron, US/Ger., 104m, c). P Ernst R. Theumer, D Robert Collector, W Collector & Gary Drucker, PH Wolfgang Dickmann, M Tangerine Dream, ED Anthony Redman.

LP Linda Blair (Chris Carlson), Sylvia Kristel (Sofia), Sue Kiel (Hedda), William Ostrander (Michael), Elisabeth Volkmann (Einbeck), Albert Fortell (Ernst), Herb Andress (Werner), Barbara Spitz (Meg), Kati Marothy (Barbara), Dagmar Michal-Schwarz (Lillian).

Although completed 1984 this dumb women-in-prison film wasn't released in the US until 1988. In Berlin to be with her soldier fiancé, American Linda Blair witnesses the abduction of an East German woman who has just defected. The kidnappers throw Blair into the van as well. Blair is convicted of espionage and sent to an East German prison. Pens for women are the same the world over, ruthless guards, rampant lesbianism, nudity, violence, etc.

2441. *Red Nights* (1988, TransWorld, 89m, c). P Ron Wolotzky, D Izhak Hanooka, W Hanooka, PH Jacob Eleasari, M Tangerine Dream, ED David Lloyd, PD Rina Binyamini.

LP Christopher Parker (Randy), Brian Matthews (David), Tom Badal (Bruce), Patti Bauer (Betty), Jack Carter (Uncle Solly), James Mayberry (Jeff), William Smith (Phillip), Ivan E. Roth (Peter), Tawny Capriccio (Helen), Anna Louise (Stripper).

New Hampshire lad Christopher Parker goes to Hollywood to pursue a career as an actor. He puts his career plans on hold long enough to go after the killers of a friend. Not too surprisingly the film went direct to video.

Red on Red see **Scarred**

2442. *Red Riding Hood* (1987, Cannon, 80m, c). P Menahem Golan & Yoram Globus, D Adam Brooks, W Carole Lucia Satrina (based on the fairytale by the Brothers Grimm), PH Danny Shnegur & Ye'ehi Neyman, M Stephen Lawrence, ED David Tour.

LP Craig T. Nelson (Godfrey/Percival), Isabella Rossellini (Lady Jeanne), Amelia Shankley (Red Riding Hood), Rocco Sisto (Dagger/The Wolf), Linda Kaye (Badger Kate), Helen Glazary (Nancy Bess), Julian Joy-Chagrin (Allen Owen).

Here's another of Cannon's fairytale films having a brief theater release before heading for home video. The familiar tale has been replaced with a new storyline and several songs. Craig T. Nelson plays twin princes, one good, one evil. Amelia Shankley as Red Riding Hood possesses a magic coat which protects her from Rocco Sisto, the evil prince's lackey. He has been changed into a wolf by a magic spell.

2443. *Red Scorpion* (1989, Shapiro Glickenhaus, 102m, c). P Jack Abramoff, D Joseph Zito, W Arne Olsen (based on a story by Robert and Jack Abramoff & Olsen, PH Joao Fernandes, M Jay Chattaway, ED Daniel Loewenthal, PD Ladislav Wilhelm.

LP Dolph Lundgren (Lt. Nikolai), M. Emmet Walsh (Dewey Ferguson), Al White (Kallunda), T.P. McKenna (Gen. Vortek), Carmen Argenziano (Zayas), Alex Colon (Mendez), Brion James (Krasnov), Regopstaan (Gao, bushman).

Dull! Dull! Dull! Unless you are taken by musclebound men with nothing between their ears, this grade Z story has stone-faced Dolph Lundgren playing a Russian special services officer. It would seem that he carries a can of Crisco with him so he can get that all-over glistening look. Besides flexing his muscles, the Soviet killing machine is assigned to assassinate a rebel leader fighting the Communist regime in some faraway country.

2444. *Red Sonja* (1985, MGM/United Artists, 89m, c). P Christian Ferry, D Richard Fleischer, W Clive Exton & George MacDonald Fraser (based on characters created Robert E. Howard), PH Giuseppe Rotunno, M Ennio Morricone, ED Frank J. Urioste, PD Danilo Donati.

LP Arnold Schwarzenegger (Kalidor), Brigitte Nielsen (Red Sonja), Sandahl Bergman (Queen Gedren), Paul Smith (Falkon), Ernie Reyes, Jr. (Tarn), Ronald Lacey (Ikol), Pat Roach (Brytag), Terry Richards (Djart), Janet Agren (Varna), Donna Osterbuhr (Kendra, the High Priestess).

It says here that Arnold Schwarzenegger is not portraying Conan in this sword-and-sorcery fantasy, but it's hard to tell the difference. At least he has a costar, Brigitte Nielsen, whose lack of talent makes him look like quite a thespian. The statuesque Nielsen joins forces with Arnie to fight an evil queen who has killed her family.

The Red Tide see ***Blood Tide***

2445. Reds† (1981, Paramount, 200m, c). P&D Warren Beatty* (for direction), W Beatty & Trevor Griffiths†, PH Vittorio Storaro*, M Stephen Sondheim & Dave Grusin, ED Dede Allen & Craig McKay†, PD Richard Sylbert, AD/SD Sylbert & Michael Seirton†, COS Shirley Russell†, SOUND Dick Vorisek, Tom Fleischman & Simon Kaye†.

LP Warren Beatty† (John Reed), Diane Keaton† (Louise Bryant), Edward Herrmann (Max Eastman), Jerzy Kosinski (Grigory Zinoviev), Jack Nicholson† (Eugene O'Neill), Paul Sorvino (Louis Fraina), Maureen Stapleton* (Emma Goldman), Nicolas Coster (Paul Trullinger), M. Emmet Walsh (Speaker at the Liberal Club), Ian Wolfe (Mr. Partlow), Bessie Love (Mrs. Partlow), MacIntyre Dixon (Carl Walters), Pat Starr (Helen Walters), Eleanor D. Wilson (Mrs. Reed), Max Wright (Floyd Dell), George Plimpton (Horace Whigham), Henry Miller, Adela Rogers St. John, Hamilton Fish, Rebecca West, Will Durant, Adele Nathan, George Jessel, Harry Carlisle (Witnesses).

The film is long but well worth the time. It is the story of the last years of American writer John Reed, inspiringly played by Warren Beatty. After a stormy romance with free-lover feminist Louise Bryant, impersonated by Diane Keaton, he helped found the American Communist Party. Reed travels to Russia in time for the Bolshevik Revolution, which he documented in his book *Ten Days That Shook the World*. Reed became the only American to be buried within the walls of the Kremlin. It's rather amazing that this project succeeded in 1981, but it was widely praised and even broke even at the box-office.

2446. Reflections (1984, Film Four, GB, 103m, c). P David Deutsch & Kevin Billington, D Billington, W John Banville, PH Mike Malloy, M Rachel Portman, ED Chris Risdale, AD Martin Johnson.

LP Gabriel Byrne (William Masters), Donal McCann (Edward Lawless), Harriet Walter (Ottilie Granger), Fionnula Flanagan (Charlotte Lawless), Gerard Cummins (Michael Lawless), Niall Toibin (Prunty), Paedar Lamb (Doctor), Des Nealon (Tom Mittler), Margaret Wade (Bunny Mittler).

Made for British TV, this film was shown theatrically. Researcher Gabriel Byrne, preparing a study of the life of Sir Isaac Newton, rents a cottage in Ireland in which to do his writing. Instead he falls in love with Harriet Walter and her married aunt Fionnula Flanagan.

2447. Reform School Girls (1986, New World, 94m, c). P Jack Cummings, D&W Tom DeSimone, PH Howard Wexler, M Various Artists, ED Michael Spence, PD Becky Block.

LP Linda Carol (Jenny), Wendy O. Williams (Charlie), Pat Ast (Edna), Sybil Danning (Sutter), Charlotte McGinnis (Dr. Norton), Sherri Stoner (Lisa), Denise Gordy (Claudia), Laurie Schwartz (Nicky), Tiffany Helm (Fish).

Knowledgeable drive-in movie fans will hear the title of this film and know they are in for some female nudity, stereotyped prisoners, cruel guards, one understanding authority figure, suggested lesbianism, etc. — and this spoof of the subgenre won't disappoint them.

2448. The Rejuvenator (1988, SVS, 86m, c). P Steven Mackler, D Brian Thomas Jones, W Simon Nuchtern & Jones, PH James McCalmont, M Larry Juris, ED Brian O'Hara, PD Susan Bolles.

LP Vivian Lanko (Elizabeth Warren/ Monster), John MacKay (Dr. Gregory Ashton), James Hogue (Wilhelm), Katell

Pleven (Dr. Stella Stone), Marcus Powell (Dr. Germaine), Jessica Dublin (Ruth Warren), Roy MacArthur (Hunter), Louis F. Homyak (Tony).

Wealthy old Jessica Dublin funds mad scientist John MacKay's experiment with a serum, made from human gray matter, which reverses the aging process. When Dublin tries the formula, it works and she becomes young, beautiful Vivian Lanko. The catch is the serum periodically turns Lanko into a monster, and greater amounts of the serum is needed to bring her back to normal.

2449. *Relentless* (1989, New Line Cinema, 92m, c). P Howard Smith, D William Lustig, W "Jack T.D. Robinson" (Phil Alden Robinson), PH James Lemmo, M Jay Chattaway, ED David Kern, PD Gene Abel.

LP Judd Nelson (Buck Taylor), Robert Loggia (Bill Malloy), Leo Rossi (Sam Dietz), Meg Foster (Carol Dietz), Patrick O'Bryan (Todd Arthur), Mindy Seger (Francine), Ron Taylor (Capt. Blakely), Beau Starr (Ike Taylor).

Judd Nelson appears as a maniacal serial murderer, known as the "Sunset Killer." The character is kept under control by the actor, making him all the more frightening in this taunt suspense thriller. Through flashbacks audiences learn the reason for Nelson's psychotic behavior. He is pursued by Leo Rossi and Robert Loggia, both giving excellent performances.

2450. *Religion, Inc.* (1989, Chronicle, 87m, c). P Michael Mailer, D Daniel Adams, W Adams & Mailer (based on a story by Adams), PH John Drake, M Kip Martin, ED Thomas R. Rondinella, PD Paola Ridolfi.

LP Jonathan Penner (Morris Codman), Gerald Orange (Dr. Ian Clarity), Sandra Bullock (Debby), George Plimpton (God), Wendy Adams (Peggy).

God, in the person of preppie-like George Plimpton, appears on the TV screen of failing and executive Jonathan Penner. The Almighty suggests that Penner start a new religion—and so he does. Its tenets are selfishness, greed, cruelty and adultery, because this is what market research says religious consumers want. A bit cynical, would you say?

2451. *Rembrandt Laughing* (1989, Jost, 100m, c). P Jon Jost & Henry Rosenthal, D Jost, W Jost & Den Darstellern, PH Jost, M Jon A. English.

LP Jon A. English, Barbara Hammes, Jennifer Johanson, Ed Green, Nathaniel Dorsky, Jerry Barrish.

In cinéma verité fashion independent producer-director Jon Jost follows the daily encounters of ex-lovers Jon A. English and Barbara Hammes five years after their break-up. As a cameraman Jost is too artsy for the good of the movie.

2452. *Remo Williams: The Adventure Begins* (1985, Orion, 121m, c). P Larry Spiegel, D Guy Hamilton, W Christopher Wood (based on characters created by Warren Murphy & Richard Sapir in "The Destroyer" series), PH Andrew Laszlo, M Craig Safan, ED Mark Melnick, PD Jackson de Govia, MK Carl Fullerton†.

LP Fred Ward (Remo Williams), Joel Gray (Chiun), Wilford Brimley (Harold Smith), J.A. Preston (Conn MacCleary), George Coe (Gen. Scott Watson), Charles Cioffi (George Grove), Kate Mulgrew (Maj. Rayner Fleming).

Remo Williams, the hero of "The Destroyer" adventure novel series, a James Bond–like good guy, can walk on water and dodge bullets after being instructed by a Korean martial arts master.

2453. *Remote Control* (1988, Vista, 88m, c). P Scott Rosenfelt & Mark Levinson, D&W Jeff Lieberman, PH Timothy Suhrstedt, M Peter Bernstein, ED Scott Wallace, PD Curtis Schnell.

LP Kevin Dillon (Cosmo), Deborah Goodrich (Belinda), Christopher Wynne (Georgie), Frank Beddor (Victor), Jennifer Tilly (Allegra), Kaaren Lee (Patricia), Bert Remsen (Bill Denver).

When the manager of a video store discovers that several of his customers have been brutally murdered after viewing a particular cassette, he figures he'd better investigate.

2454. *Renegades* (1989, Universal, 107m, c). P David Madden, D Jack Sholder, W David Rich, PH Phil Meheux, M Michael Kamen, ED Caroline Biggerstaff, PD Carol Spier.

LP Kiefer Sutherland (Buster), Lou

Diamond Phillips (Hank), Jami Gertz (Barbara), Rob Knepper (Marino), Bill Smitrovich (Finch), Floyd Westerman (Red Crow), Joe Griffin (Matt), Clark Johnson (J.J.).

In a fast-moving, violent, implausible film, Philadelphia cop Kiefer Sutherland infiltrates a gang in order to expose a rogue cop. As the gang escapes they kill Lou Diamond Phillips' brother and steal a lance sacred to the Lakota Sioux Indian tribe. Phillips teams with Sutherland, going after the killer and retrieving the lance.

2455. *Reno and the Doc* (1984, New World, Canada, 88m, c). P David Mitchell & Sean Ryerson, D&W Charles Dennis (based on a story by Damien Lee), PH Ludek Bogner, M Betty Lazebnik & Brian Bell, ED Jim Lahti & Mairin Wilkison, PD Stephen Surjik.

LP Ken Walsh (Reginald "Reno" Coltchinsky), Henry Ramer (Hugo "Doc" Billings), Linda Griffiths (Savannah Gates), Gene Mack (Stan Kukamunga), Cliff Welsh (Cliff), Laura Dickson (Agnes), Sean Ryerson (Long Jack).

Middleaged Ken Walsh and Henry Ramer, both battling mid-life crises, team up to test themselves in the world of professional skiing.

2456. *Rent-a-Cop* (1988, Kings Road, 96m, c). P Raymond Wagner, D Jerry London, W Dennis Shryack & Michael Blodgett, PH Giuseppe Rotunno, M Jerry Goldsmith, ED Robert Lawrence, PD Tony Masters.

LP Burt Reynolds (Church), Liza Minnelli (Della), James Remar (Dancer), Richard Masur (Roger), Dionne Warwick (Beth), Bernie Casey (Lemar), Robby Benson (Pitts), John Stanton (Alexander), John P. Ryan (Wieser).

Busted cop Burt Reynolds is reduced to taking a job as a security guard after a blown drug arrest. Liza Minnelli is a kooky but affectionate lady-of-the-evening. Their performances makes one nostalgic for earlier films of these two talented performers when they seemed to try harder to please. Reynolds does his usual number, but with not much enthusiasm. Liza shows spunk, but it's a shame the day of the musicals, where her singing and dancing could turn on an audience, is past.

2457. *Rent Control* (1981, Group S, 95m, c). P Benni Korzen, D Gian L. Polidoro, W John Menegold & Sherill Tippins, PH Benito Frattari, M Oscar De Mejo & Ian North, ED Ed Orshan & Jim Cookman.

LP Brent Spiner (Leonard), Elizabeth Stack (Anne), Leonard Melfi (Milton), Jeanne Ruskin (Margaret), Annie Korzen (Nancy), Leslie Cifarelli (Barbara), Charles Laiken (Jim), Roy Brocksmith (Stan).

Aspiring writer Brent Spiner makes the near-impossible quest to find a rent-controlled apartment in Manhattan. He believes that's what it will take to get his wife, who has run away with a cosmetician, to return to him.

2458. *Rented Lips* (1988, Vista, 80m, c). P Mort Engelberg, D Robert Downey, W Martin Mull, PH Robert D. Yeoman, M Van Dyke Parks, ED Christopher Greenbury, Brian Berdan & Jay Ignaszewski, PD George Costello.

LP Martin Mull (Archie Powell), Dick Shawn (Charlie Slater), Jennifer Tilly (Mona Lisa), Edy Williams (Heather Darling), Robert Downey, Jr. (Wolf Dangler), Kenneth Mars (Rev. Farrell), Shelley Berman (Bill Slotnik).

Documentary filmmakers Martin Mull and Dick Shawn (in his last screen appearance), are induced by public TV station manager Shelley Berman to complete a porno movie, left unfinished when the director died. This silly movie dies long before that.

2459. *Repo Man* (1984, Universal, 92m, c). P Jonathan Wacks & Peter McCarthy, D&W Alex Cox, PH Robby Muller, M Tito Larriva & Steven Hufsteter, ED Dennis Dolan.

LP Harry Dean Stanton (Bud), Emilio Estevez (Otto), Tracey Walter (Miller), Olivia Barash (Leila), Sy Richardson (Lite), Susan Barnes (Agent Rogers), Fox Harris (J. Frank Parnell), Tom Finnegan (Oly).

Spaced out L.A. teen Emilio Estevez is recruited by Harry Dean Stanton to become a repossession man for an auto loan company. The youngster finds himself in a nightmarish world, constantly on the run from all kinds of dangers.

2460. *The Rescue* (1988, Buena Vista, 98m, c). P Laura Ziskin, D Ferdinand Fairfax, W Jim Thomas & John Thomas, PH Russell Boyd, M Bruce Broughton, ED David Holden & Carroll Timothy O'Meara, PD Maurice Cain.

LP Kevin Dillon (J.J. Merrill), Christina Harnos (Adrian Phillips), Marc Price (Max Rothman), Ned Vaughn (Shawn Howard), Ian Giatti (Bobby Howard), Charles Haid (Cmdr. Howard), Edward Albert (Cmdr. Merrill), Timothy Carhart (Lt. Phillips), Michael Gates Phenicie (Wicks).

A team of Americans are captured by North Koreans as they attempt to locate and destroy a United States nuclear submarine sunk in North Korean waters. Their children, Kevin Dillon, Christina Harnos, Ned Vaughn and Ian Giatti, are outraged that the government is doing nothing to rescue their fathers from the godless commies. The kids take things in their own hands and make the rescue.

2461. *The Rescuers [Re-issue]* (1989, Disney, animated, 76m, c). P Wolfgang Reitherman, D Reitherman, John Lounsbery & Art Stevens, W Ken Anderson, Vance Gerry, Larry Clemmons, David Michener, Burny Mattinson, Frank Thomas, Fred Lucky, Ted Berman & Dick Sebast (based on the stories "The Rescurers" and "Miss Bianca" by Margery Sharp), M Artie Butler, ED James Melton & Jim Koford, ANIM D Ollie Johnston, Milt Kahl & Don Bluth, AD Don Griffith.

VOICES Bob Newhart (Bernard), Eva Gabor (Miss Bianca), Geraldine Page (Mme. Medusa), Joe Flynn (Mr. Snoops), Jeanette Nolan (Ellie Mae), Pat Buttram (Luke), Jim Jordan (Orville), John McIntire (Rufus), Michelle Stacy (Penny).

Initially released in 1977, the film demonstrated that the Disney studio still had it when it came to producing a first-rate animated feature. In the story two mice (voices of Bob Newhart and Eva Gabor) set out to rescue a girl (Michelle Stacy) from the evil Mme. Medusa (Geraldine Page). It gets a bit scary in parts and may be too much for real little tykes.

2462. *Restless Natives* (1985, EMI, GB, 89m, c). P Rick Stevenson, D Michael Hoffman, W Ninian Dunet, PH Oliver Stapleton, M Stuart Adamson, ED Sean Barton, PD Adrienne Atkinson.

LP Vincent Friell (Will Bryce), Joe Mullaney (Ronnie Wotherspoon), Teri Lally (Margot), Ned Beatty (Fritz Bender), Robert Urquhart (Detective Inspector Baird), Anne Scott-James (Mother).

In Edinburgh, two bored lads, Vincent Friell and Joe Mullaney, decide to become latter-day highwaymen. They don disguises and comical masks to rob tourists.

2463. *Resurrected* (1989, St. Pancras/Hobo, GB, 94m, c). P Tara Prem & Adrian Hughes, D Paul Greengrass, W Martin Allen, PH Ivan Strasburg, ED Dan Rae, PD Christopher Burke.

LP David Thewlis (Kevin Deakin), Tom Bell (Mr. Deakin), Rita Tushingham (Mrs. Deakin), Michael Pollitt (Gregory Deakin), Rudi Davies (Julie), William Hoyland (Capt. Sinclair).

Eighteen-year-old David Thewlis is reported missing, presumed dead, during fighting in the Falklands. Several weeks later he appears at a nearby farmhouse. When he returns to England, the press alleges that he was a deserter.

2464. *Resurrection* (1980, Universal, 103m, c). P Renee Missel & Howard Rosenman, D Daniel Petrie, W Lewis John Carlino, PH Mario Tosi, M Maurice Jarre, ED Rita Roland, PD Paul Sylbert.

LP Ellen Burstyn† (Edna McCauley), Sam Shepard (Cal Carpenter), Richard Farnsworth (Esco), Roberts Blossom (John Harper), Clifford David (George), Pamela Payton-Wright (Margaret), Jeffrey DeMunn (Joe McCauley), Eva LeGallienne† (Grandma Pearl), Lois Smith (Kathy).

Ellen Burstyn has an out-of-body experience and "comes back from the dead" following an automobile accident in L.A. that killed her husband. She returns to her rural Kansas home where she discovers she has the power of healing. She also attracts Sam Shepard, the troubled young son of a preacher, with whom she has an affair. He comes to believe that Burstyn is the second coming of Jesus and to prove her godness he shoots her.

Retaliator   see   Programmed to Kill

2465.   Retribution (1988, Renegade/United, 107m, c). P&D Guy Magar, W Guy Magar & Lee Wasserman, PH Gary Thieltges, M Alan Howarth, ED Magar & Alan Shefland, PD Robb Wilson King.

LP Dennis Lipscomb (George Miller), Leslie Wing (Dr. Jennifer Curtis), Suzanne Snyder (Angel), Jeff Pomerantz (Dr. Alan Falconer), George Murdock (Dr. John Talbot), Pamela Dunlap (Sally Benson), Susan Peretz (Mrs. Stoller), Clare Peck (Carla Minelli).

On Halloween night, destitute, wimpy artist Dennis Lipscomb attempts to take his life by jumping from the roof of the seedy hotel where he lives. When he hits the pavement he has an out-of-body-experience and survives. Three months later upon being released from a sanitarium he returns home. He has horrible dreams of visiting places he's never been before and killing people he's never seen before. When he wakes the papers are filled with stories of his dream murders.

The Retrievers   see   Hot and Deadly

2466.   Return (1986, A Silver Prod., 82m, c). P Philip Spinelli, D&W Andrew Silver, PH Janos Zsombolyai, M Ragnar Grippe & Michael Shrieve, ED Gabrielle Gilbert.

LP Karlene Crockett (Diane Stoving), John Walcutt (Day Whittaker), Lisa Richards (Ann Stoving), Frederic Forrest (Brian Stoving), Anne Lloyd Francis (Eileen Sedgely), Lenore Zann (Susan), Thomas Rolopp (Lucky).

Her investigation of the mysterious death of her grandfather leads Karlene Crockett to make several bizarre discoveries at her birthplace.

2467.   The Return of Captain Invincible (1983, Keys, Australia/US, 90m, c, aka *Legend in Leotards*). P Andrew Gaty, D Philippe Mora, W Steve de Souza & Gaty, PH Mike Molloy, M William Motzing, ED John Scott, PD David Copping.

LP Alan Arkin (Capt. Invincible), Christopher Lee (Mr. Midnight), Kate Fitzpatrick (Patty), Bill Hunter (Tupper), Graham Kennedy (Prime Minister), Michael Pate (President), Hayes Gordon (Kirby), Max Phipps (Admiral), Noel Ferrier (General).

In an unsuccessful parody, retired superhero Alan Arkin is called back to deal with super-villain Christopher Lee.

2468.   The Return of Josey Wales (1987, Reel Movies Intl., 90m, c). P Mickey Grant, D Michael Parks & R.O. Taylor, W Forrest Carter & Taylor (based on the novel *Vengeance Trail of Josey Wales* by Carter), PH Brant A. Hughes, M Rusty Thornhill, ED Ivan L. Bigley, AD Larry Melton.

LP Michael Parks (Josey Wales), Rafael Campos (Chato), Charlie McCoy (Charlie), Everett Sifuentes (Capt. Jesus Escobedo), Suzie Humphreys (Rose), John Galt (Kelly), Joe Kurtzo (Nacole), Paco Vela (Paco).

While reminiscing about gunman Josey Wales, two friends are gunned down by marauding Rurales. When the Rurales take Wales' last remaining ex-comrade as a hostage, Wales (Michael Parks) comes out of hiding and sets off on a trail of bloody vengeance.

The Return of Maxwell Smart   see   The Nude Bomb

2469.   Return of the Jedi (1983, 20th Century-Fox, 133m, c). P Howard Kazanjian, Robert Watts & Jim Bloom, D Richard Marquand, W Lawrence Kasdan & George Lucas (based on a story by Lucas), PH Alan Hume, Jack Lowin & Jim Glennon, M John Williams†, ED Sean Barton, Marcia Lucas, Duwayne Dunham & Arthur Repola, PD Norman Reynolds, AD/SD Reynolds, Fred Hole, James Schoppe & Michael Ford, SE Roy Arbogast, Kit West, Richard Edlund, Dennis Muren & Ken Ralston, SOUND Ben Burtt, Gary Summers, Randy Thom & Tony Dawe†, SE ED Burtt†.

LP Mark Hamill (Luke Skywalker), Harrison Ford (Han Solo), Carrie Fisher (Princess Leia), Billy Dee Williams (Lando Calrissian), Anthony Daniels (See Threepio [C-3PO]), Peter Mayhew (Chewbacca), Sebastian Shaw (Anakin Skywalker), Ian McDiarmid (Emperor Palpatine), Frank Oz (Yoda), David Prowse (Darth Vader), James Earl Jones (voice of Darth Vader), Alec Guinness (Ben Obi-Wan Kenobi), Kenny Baker (Artoo-Detoo [R2-D2]), Michael Pennington (Moff Jerjerrod), Ken Colley (Adm. Piett).

George Lucas presents "Episode Six" on the *Star Wars* serial in which Luke Skywalker (Mark Hamill) and his friends combat Darth Vader and Jabba the Hutt. Luke learns how to become a Jedi warrior from Yoda (Frank Oz) and that Vader is actually his father. In the end Vader sacrifices his own life for Luke. These entertaining movies with all of their spectacular special effects and impressive sets are, after all, only huge video games, but they manage to capture the attention of millions of fans.

2470. Return of the Killer Tomatoes (1988, New World, 98m, c). P J. Stephen Peace & Lowell D. Blank, D John De-Bello, W DeBello, Stephen F. Andrich & Constantine Dillon, M Rick Patterson & Neal Fox, ED DeBello & Andrich, PD Dillon.

LP Anthony Starke (Chad), George Clooney (Matt), Karen Mistal (Tara), Steve Lundquist (Igor), John Astin (Prof. Gangrene), Charlie Jones, Rock Peace, Frank Davis, C.J. Dillon, Teri Weigel.

This sequel to *Attack of the Killer Tomatoes* (1977), picks up where the latter left off. Earth has made ketchup of the killer tomatoes, but are they all really gone? Surround them with pasta!

2471. The Return of the Living Dead (1985, Orion, 91m, c). P Tom Fox & Graham Henderson, D&W Dan O'Bannon (based on a story by Rudy Ricci, John Russo & Russell Streiner), M Matt Clifford, ED Robert Gordon, PD William Stout, SE MK Bill Munns.

LP Clu Gulager (Burt), James Karen (Frank), Don Calfa (Ernie), Thom Mathews (Freddy), Beverly Randolph (Tina), John Philbin (Chuck), Jewal Shepard (Casey), Miguel A. Nunez, Jr. (Spider), Brian Peck (Scuz).

In a fast-moving spoof of the living dead subgenre, the army is called in to repel an attack of zombies.

2472. Return of the Living Dead Part II (1988, Lorimar, 89m, c). P Tom Fox, D&W Ken Wiederhorn, PH Robert Elswit, M J. Peter Robinson, ED Charles Bornstein.

LP Michael Kenworthy (Jesse Wilson), Thor Van Lingen (Billy), Jason Hogan (Johnny), James Karen (Ed), Marsha Dietlein (Lucy Wilson), Thom Mathews (Joey), Suzanne Snyder (Brenda), Dana Ashbrook (Tom Essex), Philip Bruns (Doc Mandel).

This sequel to *The Return of the Living Dead* has nothing to do with the 1968 cult favorite *Night of the Living Dead*. It does have sloppy creatures oozing out of their graves at night to terrorize the local townsfolks. Seems for the dead, live human brains are a delicacy.

2473. The Return of the Musketeers (1989, Universal, GB/Fr./Span., 94m, c). P Pierre Spengler, D Richard Lester, W George MacDonald Fraser (based on *Twenty Years After* by Alexander Dumas), PH Bernard Lutic, M Jean-Claude Petit, ED John Victor Smith, PD Gil Arrondo.

LP Michael York (D'Artagnan), Oliver Reed (Athos), Frank Finlay (Porthos), C. Thomas Howell (Raoul), Kim Cattrall (Justine De Winter), Richard Chamberlain (Aramis), Philippe Noiret (Cardinal Mazarin), Roy Kinnear (Planchet), Geraldine Chaplin (The Queen), Christopher Lee (Rochefort), Eusebio Lazaro (Beaufort), Jean-Pierre Cassel (Cyrano De Bergerac), David Birkin (King Louis), Alan Howard (Oliver Cromwell).

Set 20 years after director Richard Lester's hits *The Three Musketeers* and *The Four Musketeers,* this film finds everyone older and looking very tired. Its a convoluted story of the reunited musketeers serving the widowed Queen (Geraldine Chaplin), her 10-year-old son (David Birkin), now king, and the Queen's lover and prime minister (Philippe Noiret). Somehow they must foil the plot to execute England's king by Madame de Winter's daughter (Kim Cattrall), working in league with Oliver Cromwell (Alan Howard).

2474. The Return of the Secaucus Seven (1980, Salsipuedes/Libra, 110m, c). P William Aydelott & Jeffrey Nelson, D&W John Sayles, PH Austin de Besche, M K. Mason Daring, ED Sayles.

LP Matt Arnold (Jeff), Gordon Clapp (Chip), Maggie Cousineau (Frances), Brian Johnston (Norman Gaddis), Adam

LeFevre (J.T.), Bruce MacDonald (Mike), Jean Passanante (Irene), Maggie Renzi (Kate), John Sayles (Howie).

In sort of a precursor to the more polished *The Big Chill*, seven friends who were activists during the 60s gather years later for a weekend reunion. It's earnest and intelligent.

2475.   The Return of the Soldier (1983, 20th Century–Fox, GB, 102m, c). P Ann Skinner & Simon Relph, D Alan Bridges, W Hugh Whitemore (based on the novel by Rebecca West), PH Stephen Goldblatt, M Richard Rodney Bennett, ED Laurence Clark, PD Luciana Arrighi.

LP Alan Bates (Capt. Chris Baldry), Ann-Margret (Jenny), Glenda Jackson (Margaret Gray), Julie Christie (Kitty Baldry), Jeremy Kemp (Frank), Edward D. De Souza (Edward), Frank Finlay (William Grey), Jack May (Brigadier), Ian Holm (Dr. Gilbert Anderson), Emily Irvin (Jenny as a child), William Booker (Chris as a child).

In 1919, shell-shocked World War I officer Alan Bates forgets his wife Julie Christie but remembers his love for his childhood sweetheart Ann-Margret.

2476.   The Return of Swamp Thing (1989, Millimeter Films, 86m, c). P Ben Melniker & Michael Uslan, D Jim Wynorski, W Derek Spencer & Grant Morris (based on the characters appearing in magazines published by DC Comics, Inc.), PH Zoran Hochstatter, M Chuck Cirino, ED Leslie Rosenthal, PD Robb Wilson King.

LP Louis Jourdan (Dr. Anton Arcane), Heather Locklear (Abby Arcane), Sarah Douglas (Dr. Lana Zurrell), Dick Durock (Swamp Thing), Joey Sagal (Gunn), Ace Mask (Dr. Rochelle), Chris Doyle (Leechman).

This horror is meant to be comical and on occasion succeeds. Louis Jourdan, a mad doctor who lives in a mansion on the edge of the bayou, performs unspeakable experiments in his quest to maintain his youth. Swamp Thing is all that remains of one of his former colleagues. This more-vegetable-than-man does his best to save the beautiful women fleeing Jourdan's unholy experiments. If the film sounds much like the 1982 original *Swamp Thing*, that's only because it is.

2477.   Return to Horror High (1987, New World, 95m, c). P Mark Lisson, D Bill Froehlich, W Froehlich, Lisson, Dana Escalante & Greg H. Sims, PH Roy Wagner, M Stacy Widelitz, ED Nancy Forner, PD Greta Grigorian.

LP Lori Lethin (Callie Cassidy/Sarah/Susan), Brendan Hughes (Steven Blake), Alex Rocco (Harry Sleerik), Scott Jacoby (Josh Forbes), Andy Romano (Principal Kastleman), Richard Brestoff (Arthur Lyman [Kastleman]), Vince Edwards (Richard Birnbaum).

The murderer of several students at Crippen High was never found and now he's back. The finale is a disappointing cop-out.

2478.   Return to Oz (1985, Buena Vista, 110m, c). P Paul Maslansky, D Walter Murch, W Murch & Gill Dennis (based on the novels *The Land of Oz* and *Ozma of Oz* by L. Frank Baum), PH David Watkin, M David Shire, ED Leslie Hodgson, PD Norman Reynolds, VE Will Vinton, Ian Wingrove, Zoran Perisic & Michael Lloyd†.

LP Fairuza Balk (Dorothy), Nicol Williamson (Dr. Worley/Nome King), Jean Marsh (Nurse Wilson/Princess Mombi), Piper Laurie (Aunt Em), Matt Clark (Uncle Henry), Michael Sundin & Tim Rose (Tik Tok), Sean Barrett (Tik Tok's voice), Mak Wilson (Billina), Denise Bryer (Billina's voice), Brian Henson (Jack Pumpkinhead's voice), Stewart Larange (Jack Pumpkinhead), Emma Ridley (Ozma), Justin Case (Scarecrow), Deep Roy (Tin Man), John Alexander (Cowardly Lion).

After returning from Oz, Dorothy is placed by Auntie Em and Uncle Henry in the care of an electroshock therapist who promises to cure her delusions about the land over the rainbow. But another natural disaster transports Dorothy back to Oz where she must confront the evil Nome King and Princess Mombi. Kids of all ages will hate it.

2479.   A Return to Salem's Lot (1988, Warner, 95m, c). P Paul Kurta, D Larry Cohen, W Cohen & James Dixon, PH Daniel Pearl, M Michael Minard, ED Armond Lebowitz, SE Steve Neill.

LP Michael Moriarty (Joe Weber), Ricky Addison Reed (Jeremy), Samuel

Fuller (Van Meer), Andrew Duggan (Judge Axel), Evelyn Keyes (Mrs. Axel), Jill Gatsby (Sherry), June Havoc (Aunt Clara), Ronee Blakley (Sally).

Anthropologist Michael Moriarty and his estranged teenage son Ricky Addison Reed travel to Salem's Lot, Maine, to refurbish a house left to him by his aunt. To their surprise the community is the home to 300-year-old vampires who crossed the Atlantic at the same time as did the Pilgrims. Having grown rich through shrewd real estate investments they have become conservative Republicans. They drink cattle blood for substance, because human blood has become contaminated with things like AIDS. They want Moriarty to write their history and clear up all the myths about how horrible they are.

2480. *Return to Snowy River, Part II* (1988, Buena Vista, Australia, 100m, c). P&D Geoff Burrowes, W John Dixon & Burrowes, PH Keith Wagstaff, M Bruce Rowland, ED Gary Woodyard, PD Leslie Binns.

LP Tom Burlinson (Jim Craig), Sigrid Thornton (Jessica Harrison), Brian Dennehy (Harrison), Nicholas Eadie (Alistair Patton), Mark Hembrow (Seb), Bryan Marshall (Hawker), Rhys McConnochie (Patton, Sr.), Peter Cummins (Jake), Cornelia Frances (Mrs. Darcy).

While still quite a treat for the eyes, this sequel to *The Man from Snowy River* (1982) is not as good. Tom Burlinson is back, taking on villain Nicholas Eadie who has his sights set on Burlinson's beloved Sigrid Thornton.

2481. *Return to the River Kwai* (1989, Rank, GB, 98m, c). P Kurt Unger, D Andrew V. McLaglen, W Sargon Tamimi & Paul Mayersberg (based on the book by Joan and Clay Blair, Jr.), PH Arthur Wooster, M Lalo Schifrin, ED Alan Strachan, PD Michael Stringer.

LP Nick Tate (Hunt), Timothy Bottoms (Miller), George Takei (Tanaka), Edward Fox (Benford), Christopher Penn (Crawford), Richard Graham (Perry), Tatsuya Nakadai (Harada), Denholm Elliott (Grayson), Masato Nagamori (Yamashita), Etsushi Takahashi (Ozawa), Michael Dante (Davidson).

This artless action film, filled with war movie stereotypes, picks up where the classic 1957 *Bridge on the River Kwai* left off, that is with the blowing up of the bridge in enemy-occupied Thailand. The remaining prisoners, now mostly Australian, are herded by rail and sea to Japan to serve as slave labor. In the climax the POWs have taken over the Japanese ship, but it is sunk by a U.S. submarine in the South China Sea.

2482. *Reuben, Reuben* (1983, 20th Century-Fox, 101m, c). P Walter Shenson, D Robert Ellis Miller, W Julius J. Epstein† (based on the novel by Peter DeVries and the play *Spofford* by Herman Shumlin), PH Peter Stein, M Billy Goldenberg, ED Skip Lusk, PD Peter Larkin.

LP Tom Conti† (Gowan McGland), Kelly McGillis (Geneva Spofford), Roberts Blossom (Frank Spofford), Cynthia Harris (Bobby Springer), E. Katherine Kerr (Lucille Haxby), Joel Fabiani (Dr. Haxby), Kara Wilson (Edith McGland), Lois Smith (Mare Spofford), Ed Grady (Dr. Ormsby).

Tom Conti is charming as a drunken Irish poet who sponges off women. He's on a speaking tour in New England when he meets Kelly McGillis in a small community. She decides that Conti is worth saving. Her love makes him wish to turn his life around, but her dog Reuben is his undoing.

2483. *Reunion* (1989, Les Films Ariane-Fr3/Nef/CLG, Fr./West Ger./GB, 110m, c). P Anne Francois, D Jerry Schatzberg, W Harold Pinter (based on the novel by Fred Uhlman), PH Bruno de Keyzer, M Philippe Sarde, ED Martine Barraque, PD Alexandre Trauner.

LP Jason Robards (Henry Strauss), Christian Anholt (Hans Strauss), Samuel West (Konrad von Lohenburg), Francoise Fabian (Countess von Lohenburg), Maureen Kerwin (Lisa), Barbara Jefford (Mme. Strauss), Bert Parnaby (Dr. Jakob Strauss), Dorothea Alexander (Old Countess Gertrud).

This interesting English-language film is the story of two German boys, Jewish Christian Anholt and his aristocratic friend Samuel West. In 1933 Stuttgart, they witness the rise of the Nazis and the increase in anti-Semitism. The long central part of the film is framed by a contemporary narrative in which Anholt, grown to become Jason Robards, returns to Stuttgart, which he hasn't visited since 1933, to find out what has happened to his boyhood friend.

Revenge of the Innocents see *South Bronx Heroes*

2484. *Revenge of the Living Zombies* (1989, H&G Films, 84m, c). P&D Bill Hinzman, W Bill Randolph & Hinzman (based on a story by Hinzman), PH Simon Manses, M Erica Portnoy, ED Paul McCullough & Hinzman, SE Gerald Gergely.

LP Bill Hinzman (Flesh Eater), John Morwood (Bob), Leslie Ann Wick (Sally), Kevin Kindlin (Ralph), James J. Rutan (Eddie), Denise Morrone, Charles Kirkpatrick Acuff, Lisa Smith, Mark Strycula.

In a tribute to George Romero's *Night of the Living Dead* (1968), Bill Hinzman rises from the ground to reprise his role as "Flesh Eater." He attacks teens on Halloween, turning them into cannibalistic ghouls.

2485. *Revenge of the Nerds* (1984, 20th Century–Fox, 90m, c). P Ted Field & Peter Samuelson, D Jeff Kanew, W Steve Zacharias & Jeff Buhai (based on a story by Tim Metcalfe, Miguel Tejada-Flores, Zacharias & Buhai, PH King Baggot, M Thomas Newman, ED Alan Balsam, PD James Schoppe.

LP Robert Carradine (Lewis), Anthony Edwards (Gilbert), Tim Busfield (Poindexter), Andrew Cassese (Wormser), Curtis Armstrong (Booger), Larry B. Scott (Lamar), Brian Tochi (Takashi), Julie Montgomery (Betty), Michelle Meyrink (Judy), Ted McGinley (Stan), Donald Gibb (Ogre), Bernie Casey (U.N. Jefferson).

A group of nerdish college freshmen led by Robert Carradine get even with a fraternity of jocks which had them evicted from their dorm. For the sub-genre to which this belongs, teenage college capers, it's quite a funny movie. That is if you can get around the notion that bright people are weird looking, talk funny, have poor eyesight and coordination, and lack common sense; while the college in-crowd consists of good-looking, athletic clods, who get all the great-looking women.

2486. *Revenge of the Nerds II: Nerds in Paradise* (1987, 20th Century–Fox, 92m, c). P Ted Field, Robert Cort & Peter Bart, D Joe Roth, W Dan Guntzelman & Steve Marshall (Based on characters created by Tim Metcalfe, Miguel Tejada-Flores, Steve Zacharias & Jeff Buhai), PH Charles Correll, M Mark Mothersbaugh & Gerald V. Casale, ED Richard Chew, PD Trevor Williams.

LP Robert Carradine (Lewis Skolnick), Curtis Armstrong (Dudley "Booger" Dawson), Larry B. Scott (Lamar Latrelle), Timothy Busfield (Arnold Poindexter), Courtney Thorne-Smith (Sunny Carstairs), Andrew Cassese (Harold Wormser), Donald Gibb (Ogre), Bradley Whitford (Roger), Ed Lauter (Buzz), Anthony Edwards (Gilbert).

The nerds, geeky as ever, attend the National United Fraternity Conference at Fort Lauderdale. The manager of the hotel at which they are registered tries just about any dirty trick to get them out of his hotel.

2487. *Revenge of the Ninja* (1983, MGM/United Artists/Cannon, 88m, c). P Menahem Golan & Yoram Globus, D Sam Firstenberg, W James R. Silke, PH David Gurfinkel, M Rob Walsh, W. Michael Lewis & Laurin Rinder, ED Mark Helfrich & Michael J. Duthie, SE Joe Quinlivan.

LP Sho Kosugi (Cho), Keith Vitali (Dave), Virgil Frye (Lt. Dime), Arthur Roberts (Braden), Mario Gallo (Caifano), Grace Oshita (Grandmother), Ashley Ferrare (Cathy), Kane Kosugi (Kane), John LaMotta (Joe).

Ninja Sho Kosugi is in Los Angeles, hoping to put his bloody past behind him. Unfortunately, he gets mixed up with drug trafficker Arthur Roberts, an American Ninja, who is his archenemy.

2488. *Revenge Squad* (1983, Comworld, 94m, c, aka *Hit and Run*). P&D Charles Braverman, W Don Enright (based on the novel *80 Dollars to Stamford* by Lucille Fletcher), PH Tony Mitchell, M Brad Fiedel, ED Dale Beldin, PD Paul Eads.

LP Paul Perri (David Marks), Claudia Cron (Diana Douglas), Will Lee (Joseph Kahn), Bart Braverman (Jerry Ramundi).

Manhattan cab driver Paul Perri is haunted by recurring flashbacks of the freakish hit-and-run accident that took his wife's life.

2489. *Revolution* (1985, Warner, 125m, c). P Irwin Winkler, D Hugh Hudson, W Robert Dillon, PH Bernard Lutic, M John Corigliano, ED Stuart Baird, PD Assheton Gorton.

LP Al Pacino (Tom Dobb), Donald Sutherland (Sgt. Maj. Peasy), Nastassja Kinski (Daisy McConnahay), Joan Plowright (Mrs. McConnahay), Dave King (Mr. McConnahay), Steven Berkoff (Sgt. Jones), John Wells (Corty), Annie Lennox (Liberty Woman), Dexter Fletcher (Ned Dobb), Sid Owen (Young Ned).

Living in the colonies, Scottish trapper Al Pacino is caught up in the American Revolution. This would-be epic film fails on just about every level. Somehow, films about the American Revolution don't seem to attract audiences. Maybe it's not the subject, but as in this case, the poor quality of the stories and performances.

2490. *Rhinestone* (1984, 20th Century-Fox, 111m, c). P Howard Smith, Marvin Worth, Bill Blake & Richard M. Spitalny, D Bob Clark, W Phil Alden Robinson & Sylvester Stallone (based on the song "Rhinestone Cowboy" by Larry Weiss, story by Robinson), PH Timothy Galfas, M Mike Post, ED Stan Cole & John Wheeler, PD Robert Boyle.

LP Sylvester Stallone (Nick), Dolly Parton (Jake), Richard Farnsworth (Noah), Ron Leibman (Freddie), Tim Thomerson (Barnett), Steven Apostle Pec (Father), Penny Santon (Mother), Russell Buchanan (Elgart).

Dolly Parton brags that she can turn anyone into a country and western singer. Her bluff is called and she must put up or shut up when faced with turning sow's ear cabbie Sylvester Stallone into a silk purse Conway Twitty.

2491. *Rich and Famous* (1981, MGM/ United Artists, 117m, c). P William Allyn, D George Cukor, W Gerald Ayres (based on the play *Old Acquaintance* by John Van Druten), PH Don Peterman, M Georges Delerue, ED John F. Burnett, PD Jan Scott.

LP Jacqueline Bisset (Liz Hamilton), Candice Bergen (Merry Noel Blake), David Selby (Doug Blake), Hart Bochner (Chris Adams), Steven Hill (Jules Levi), Meg Ryan (Debby at 18), Matt Lattanzi (Jim as a boy), Daniel Faraldo (Ginger Trinidad), Nicole Eggert (Debby at 8).

This film is a contemporary sexed-up remake of the bitchy production *Old Acquaintance* (1943), which starred wild cats Bette Davis and Miriam Hopkins as two novelists who interfere in each other's lives over a period of many years. In the modern version, Jacqueline Bisset and Candice Bergen meet at Smith in 1959. A decade later their paths cross once again. Bisset is an acclaimed but unsold novelist. She gives Bergen some advice which helps the latter become a Jackie Collins–like success writing trashy novels. It's talky and not very good talk.

2492. *Richard's Things* (1981, New World, GB, 104m, c). P Mark Shivas, D Anthony Harvey, W Frederic Raphael (based on his novel), PH Freddie Young, M Georges Delerue, ED Lesley Walker, AD Ian Whittaker.

LP Liv Ullmann (Kate), Amanda Redman (Josie), Tim Pigott-Smith (Peter), Elizabeth Spriggs (Mrs. Sells), David Markham (Morris), Mark Eden (Richard), Gwen Taylor (Margaret), John Vine (Dr. Mace).

After a man's death, his wife Liv Ullmann and mistress Amanda Redman (with whom he was making love when he suffered a fatal heart attack) find love and comfort in each other's arms.

2493. *Ricky* (1988, Tapeworm, 90m, c). P,D&W Bill Naud, PH David Golia, M Joel Goldsmith, ED Naud.

LP Michael Michaud (Ricky Wanero), Maggie Hughes (Angela), James Herbert, Lane Montano, Peter Zellers, Jon Chaney, Brent Beckett.

Filmed in 1983, this spoof of *Rocky* features Michael Michaud as a boxer who's given up the sport to please his girl, but still would like a shot at the champ.

2494. *Riddle of the Sands* (1984, Rank, GB, 102m, c). P Drummond

Challis, D Tony Maylam, W Maylam & John Bailey (based on the novel by Erskine Childers), PH Christopher Challis, M Howard Blake, ED Peter Hollywood, AD Terry Pritchard.

LP Michael York (Charles Carruthers), Jenny Agutter (Clara Dollman), Simon MacCorkindale (Arthur Davies), Alan Badel (Dollmann), Jurgen Andersen (Von Bruning), Olga Lowe (Frau Dollman), Hans Meyer (Grimm).

Made in 1979, the film was released in the U.S. in 1984. It's based on the novel considered the forerunner of the modern espionage novel. In 1901 yachtsman Simon MacCorkindale learns of a plot by the Kaiser to invade England. He enlists his college chum Michael York to foil the plan.

Riders of the Storm   see   The American Way

2495.   *Riding High* (1981, Enterprise, GB, 96m, c). P Michael & Tony Klinger, D Derek Ford, W Ross Cramer (based on a story by Ford), PH Brian Tufano, M Paul Fishman, ED John Jympson.

LP Eddie Kidd (Dave Munday), Irene Handl (Gran), Marella Oppenheim (Zoro), Murray Salem (Marvin Ravensdorf), Bill Mitchell (Judas S. Charriot), Zoot Money (Dorking), Paul Humpoletz (Gelt), Lynda Bellingham (Miss Mott).

Motorcyclist Eddie Kidd becomes a stunt rider.

2496.   *Riding the Edge* (1989, Trans-World, 95m, c). P Wolf Schmidt, D James Fargo, W Ronald A. Suppa, PH Bernard Salzmann, M Michael Gibbs, ED James Ruxin, PD James Shanahan.

LP Raphael Sbarge (Matt Harman), Catherine Mary Stewart (Maggie Kemp), Peter Haskell (Dean Stradling), Lyman Ward (Dr. Harman), Asher Sarfati (Moussa), Benny Bruchim (Boy), Michael Sarne (Kroll), Nili Zomer (Karima).

When terrorists in North Africa kidnap Lyman Ward, they demand that his son Raphael Sbarge act as a courier. The youth is to deliver a secret microprocessor in exchange for his father. Sbarge teams up with secret agent Catherine Mary Stewart and an Arab princeling to rescue dear old dad without giving up the hardware.

2497.   *Rigged* (1985, CineStar, 94m, c). P K.A. Roberson, Jr., D C.M. Cutry, W John Goff (based on the novel *Hit and Run* by James Hadley Chase), PH Eddy Van Der Enden, M Brian Banks & Anthony Marinelli, ED John R. Bowen.

LP Ken Roberson (Mason Morgan), Pamela Bryant (Monique), George Kennedy (Benjamin Wheeler), Dene Hofteizer Anton (Cheryl), John Goff (West), Ramon Gonzales Cuevas (Lopez).

Rigger Ken Roberson learns of oil baron George Kennedy's plot to import not only petroleum from Venezuela but cocaine as well. This information and his overly friendly ways with Kennedy's girlfriend Pamela Bryant, mark Roberson for extermination.

2498.   *The Right Hand Man* (1987, New World, Australia, 101m, c). P Steven Grives, Tom Oliver & Basil Appleby, D Di Drew, W Helen Hodgman (based on the novel by Kathleen Peyton), PH Peter James, M Alan Zavod, ED Don Saunders, PD Neil Angwin.

LP Rupert Everett (Harry Ironminster), Hugo Weaving (Ned Devine), Arthur Dignam (Dr. Redbridge), Jennifer Claire (Lady Ironminster), Catherine McClements (Sarah Redbridge), Ralph Cotterill (Sam), Adam Cockburn (Violet Head), Tim Eliott (Lord Ironminster).

Rupert Everett, the wealthy diabetic heir to a 1860 Australian fortune, goes into a coma while driving the family buggy. As a result his father is killed and Everett loses an arm. His domineering mother blames Everett for the death of her husband, causing the young man to become deeply depressed. Everett hires Hugo Weaving to be his righthand man, to run his estate and even to be the surrogate father of his children, as he is unwilling to risk bringing diabetic children into the world.

2499.   *The Right Stuff†* (1983, Warner, 192m, c). P Irwin Winkler & Robert Chartoff, D&W Philip Kaufman (based on the book by Tom Wolfe), PH Caleb Deschanel†, M Bill Conti*, ED Glenn Farr, Lisa Fruchtman, Stephen A. Rotter, Tom Rolf & Douglas Stewart*, PD Geoffrey Kirkland, AD/SD Kirkland, Richard J. Lawrence, W. Stewart Campbell, Peter Romero, Pat Pending &

George R. Nelson†, SOUND Mark Berger, Tom Scott, Randy Thom & David MacMillan*, SE ED Jay Boekelheide*.

LP Sam Shepard† (Chuck Yeager), Scott Glenn (Alan Shepard), Ed Harris (John Glenn), Dennis Quaid (Gordon Cooper), Fred Ward (Gus Grissom), Barbara Hershey (Glennis Yeager), Kim Stanley (Bancho Barnes), Veronica Cartwright (Betty Grissom), Pamela Reed (Trudy Cooper), Scott Paulin (Deke Slayton), Charles Frank (Scott Carpenter), Lance Henriksen (Wally Schirra), Donald Moffat (Lyndon B. Johnson), Levon Helm (Jack Ridley), Mary Jo Deschanel (Annie Glenn).

The film is a reasonably gripping examination of the Mercury Space program, which consisted of the first men recruited and trained to become astronauts. It also is the story of test pilot Chuck Yeager (Sam Shepard), who took aviation to new heights within the earth's atmosphere.

2500. *Rikky and Pete* (1988, MGM/United Artists, Australia, 101m, c). P Nadia Tass & David Parker, D Tass, W Parker (based on a story by Parker), PH Parker, M Phil Judd & Eddie Raynor, ED Ken Sallows, PD Josephine Ford.

LP Stephen Kearney (Pete), Nina Landis (Rikky), Tetchie Agbayani (Flossie), Bill Hunter (Whitstead), Bruno Lawrence (Sonny), Bruce Spence (Ben), Dorothy Alison (Mrs. Menzies), Don Reid (Mr. Menzies), Lewis Fitz-gerald (Adam), Peter Cummins (Delahunty).

This quirky comedy-drama features Stephen Kearney as a Melbourne genius of Rube Goldberg–like inventions. His sister Nina Landis is trying to find herself. Together they flee in their mother's Bentley to a remote mining village. Before long, his inventions and her resourcefulness set them up in business for themselves, each finding romance in the bargain.

2501. *The Rise and Fall of Idi Amin* (1981, Intermedia, GB/Kenya, 105m, c, aka *Amin — The Rise and Fall*). P Sharad Patel & Christopher Sutton, D Patel, W Wade Huie, PH Harvey Harrison, M Christopher Gunning, ED Keith Palmer.

LP Joseph Olita (Idi Amin), Geoffrey Keen (High Commissioner), Denis Hills (Himself), Leonard Trolley (Bob Astles), Andre Maranne (Ambassador), Diane Mercier (Wife), Tony Sibbald (Commissioner Davis), Thomas Baptiste (Dr. Michael Oloya), Louis Mahoney (Ofumbi).

This purports to be the true story of the 1971–78 reign of a soldier who proclaimed himself president of Uganda. He ruled by genocide, using most cruel and horrible ways of torturing and killing any who opposed him.

2502. *Rising Damp* (1980, Black Lion/ITC, GB, 98m, c). P Roy Skeggs, D John McGrath, W Eric Chappell (based on the TV series by Chappell), PH Frank Watts, M David Lindup, ED Peter Weatherley.

LP Leonard Rossiter (Rigsby), Frances de la Tour (Miss Jones), Denholm Elliott (Seymour), Don Warrington (Philip), Christopher Strauli (John), Carrie Jones (Sandra), Glynn Edwards (Cooper), John Cater (Bert).

In this comedy, landlord Leonard Rossiter attempts to woo stand-offish spinster Frances de la Tour.

2503. *Rising Storm* (1989, Gibraltar, 96m, c, aka *Rebel Waves*). P Jay Davidson & James Buchfuehrer, D Francis Schaeffer, W Gary Rosen & William Fay, PH Robb D. Hinds, M Julian Laxton, ED Alan Baumgarten.

LP Zach Galligan (Artie Gage), Wayne Crawford (Joe Gage), June Chadwick (Mila Hart), John Rhys-Davies (Don Waldo), Elizabeth Keifer (Blaise Hart), Graham Clark (Lt. Ulmer).

In the year 2009, what's left of the U.S. is ruled by a totalitarian theocracy headed by an oily television evangelist. Just out of jail, brothers Zach Galligan and Wayne Crawford team with blond sisters June Chadwick and Elizabeth Keifer. They are being chased by villain John Rhys-Davies who enjoys sadistically torturing his victims.

2504. *Risky Business* (1983, Warner, 98m, c). P Jon Avnet & Steve Tisch, D&W Paul Brickman, PH Reynaldo Villalobos & Bruce Surtees, M Tangerine Dream, ED Richard Chew, PD William J. Cassidy.

LP Tom Cruise (Joel), Rebecca De

Morney (Lana), Joe Pantoliano (Guido), Richard Masur (Rutherford), Bronson Pinchot (Barry), Curtis Armstrong (Miles), Nicholas Pryor (Joel's Father), Janet Carroll (Joel's Mother), Shera Danese (Vicki), Raphael Sbarge (Glenn), Bruce A. Young (Jackie).

Tom Cruise became a star after this appearance as a 17-year-old Chicago youngster left in charge of his parents' luxurious house while they are off on a vacation. As soon as they are out of sight, honor student Cruise is no longer honor-bright. Before long his home is filled with prostitutes, pimps and customers—providing our young man with a lucrative business. His dancing in his BVD's didn't hurt his career as far as female members of the audience were concerned.

2505. *Rita, Sue and Bob Too!* (1987, Orion Classics, GB, 95m, c). P Sandy Lieberson & Patsy Pollock, D Alan Clarke, W Andrea Dunbar (based on her plays *The Arbor* and *Rita, Sue and Bob Too!*), PH Ivan Strasburg, M Michael Kamen, ED Stephen Singleton, AD Len Huntingford.

LP Michelle Holmes (Sue), Siobhan Finneran (Rita), George Costigan (Bob), Lesley Sharp (Michelle), Willie Ross (Sue's Father), Patti Nicholls (Sue's Mother), Kulvinder Ghir (Aslam), Paul Oldham (Lee), Bryan Heeley (Michael).

Hefty teenagers Michelle Holmes and Siobhan Finneran babysit for George Costigan and his frigid wife Lesley Sharp. Rather than take them home at the end of the evening, Costigan drives the girls to the Moors where he rather easily convinces them to have sex with him. This cozy arrangement is continued, until Sharp grows wise, and takes the children and leaves Costigan. He's not too broken up, inviting Holmes and Finneran to move in with him, which they do.

Rituals see The Creeper

2506. *The River* (1984, Universal, 122m, c). P Edward Lewis & Robert Cortes, D Mark Rydell, W Robert Dillon & Julian Barry (based on a story by Dillon), PH Vilmos Zsigmond†, M John Williams†, ED Sidney Levin, PD Charles Rosen, SOUND Nick Alphin, Robert Thirlwell, Richard Portman & David Ronnet†.

LP Mel Gibson (Tom Garvey), Sissy Spacek† (Mae Garvey), Shane Bailey (Lewis Garvey), Becky Jo Lynch (Beth Garvey), Scott Glenn (Joe Wade), Don Hood (Sen. Neiswinder), Billy Green Bush (Harve Stanley), James Tolkan (Howard Simpson), Bob W. Douglas (Hal Richardson), Andy Stahl (Dave Birkin), Lisa Sloan (Judy Birkin).

Husband and wife team Mel Gibson and Sissy Spacek struggle to save the family farm from the bank, developers, the elements and a wide assortment of other trials and challenges. It was a banner year for films featuring hard working farmers, their families and assorted tribulations.

2507. *River of Death* (1989, Cannon, 100m, c). P Harry Alan Towers & Avi Lerner, D Steve Carver, W Andrew Deutsch & Edward Simpson (based on a novel by Alistair MacLean), PH Avi Karpick, M Sasha Matson, ED Ken Bornstein.

LP Michael Dudikoff (John Hamilton), Robert Vaughn (Dr. Mantueffel), Donald Pleasence (Heinrich Spaatz), Herbert Lom (Col. Diaz), L.Q. Jones (Hiller), Cynthia Erland (Maria), Sarah Maur Thorp (Anna), Foziah Davidson (Dahlia), Ian Yule (Long John).

When his pretty client Sarah Maur Thorp is captured in the Amazon jungle by cannibals, guide Michael Dudikoff puts together a motley crew to fetch her back. For most, the interest in the missing girl is secondary to reaching a lost city.

2508. *The River Rat* (1984, Paramount, 93m, c). P Bob Larson, D&W Tom Rickman, PH Jan Keisser, M Mike Post, ED Dennis Virkler, PD John J. Lloyd.

LP Tommy Lee Jones (Billy), Martha Plimpton (Jonsy), Brian Dennehy (Doc), Shawn Smith (Wexel), Nancy Lea Owen (Vadie), Norman Bennett (Sheriff Cal), Tony Frank (Poley), Angie Bolling (Joyce), Roger Copeland (Young Billy).

Ex-convict Tommy Lee Jones is reunited with his young daughter Martha Plimpton along the Mississippi River after wrongly spending 13 years in prison. She teaches him the value of love.

2509. *Riverbend* (1989, Intercontinental/Vandale, 100m, c). P Sam Vance,

D Sam Firstenberg, W Vance, PH Ken Lamkin, M Paul Loomis, ED Marcus Manton.

LP Steve James (Major Quinton), Margaret Avery (Bell), Tony Frank (Sheriff Jake), Julius Tennon (Tony), Alex Morris (Butch), Vanessa Tate (Pauline), T.J. Kennedy (Capt. Monroe).

The time is 1966, the place is Riverbend, Georgia. Three black soldiers, headed by Steve James, have escaped from MPs taking them to a court martial for failing to follow orders in Vietnam. The escapees help the local blacks train themselves to face the cruel white folk, led by evil sheriff Tony Frank. The new allies take over the town and focus media attention on the hotspot. Both the injustices visited on the black people of the town and the unfairness to James and his buddies are placed in the spotlight.

2510. *River's Edge* (1987, Hemdale/Island, 99m, c). P Sarah Pillsbury, Midge Sanford & David Streit, D Tim Hunter, W Neal Jimenez, PH Frederick Elmes, M Jurgen Knieper, ED Howard Smith & Sonya Sones, PD John Muto.

LP Crispin Glover (Layne), Keanu Reeves (Matt), Ione Skye Leitch (Clarissa), Daniel Roebuck (Samson "John" Tollette), Dennis Hopper (Feck), Joshua Miller (Tim), Roxana Zal (Maggie), Josh Richman (Tony), Phil Brock (Mike), Tom Bower (Bennett), Constance Forslund (Madeleine), Leo Rossi (Jim).

Based on an actual incident, this is the frightening story of a closely-knit group of teenagers who do not divulge that one of their numbers has killed a girlfriend. They visit her body which lies near the river's edge, but are able to find a way to blame the poor dead girl, rather than their friend.

2511. *Roadgames* (1981, Avco Embassy, Australia, 101m, c). P Barbi Taylor & Richard Franklin, D Franklin, W Everett DeRoche, PH Vincent Monton, M Brian May, ED Edward McQueen-Mason, PD/AD Jon Dowding.

LP Stacy Keach (Pat Quid), Jamie Lee Curtis (Hitch/Pamela), Marion Edward (Frita Frugal), Grant Page (Smith or Jones), Thaddeus Smith (Abbott), Bill Stacey (Capt. Careful), Stephen Millichamp (Costello).

Long-distance truck driver Stacy Keach unwittingly picks up a murderer on the run. The killer targets truck drivers.

Road Gangs see Spacehunter: Adventures in the Forbidden Zone

2512. *Road House* (1989, MGM/United Artists, 114m, c). P Joel Silver, D Rowdy Herrington, W David Lee Henry & Hilary Henkin (based on a story by Henry), PH Dean Cundey, M Michael Kamen, ED Frank Urioste & John Link.

LP Patrick Swayze (Dalton), Kelly Lynch (Doc), Sam Elliott (Wade Garrett), Ben Gazzara (Brad Wesley), Marshall Teague (Jimmy), Julie Michaels (Denise), Red West (Red Webster), Sunshine Parker (Emmet).

Patrick Swayze, the heartthrob from *Dirty Dancing,* is stuck in a turkey. He plays a loner hired to clean up a bar, frequented by lowlifes and bikers. The film degenerates into an endless round of fistfights and a little gratuitous nudity with leggy local doctor Kelly Lynch.

Road Trip see Jacks

2513. *The Road Warrior* (1982, Warner, Australia, 94m, c, aka *Mad Max II*). P Byron Kennedy, D George Miller, W Terry Hayes, Miller & Brian Hannat, PH Dean Semler, M Brian May, ED David Stiven, Tim Wellburn & Michael Chirgwin, AD Graham Walker.

LP Mel Gibson (Max), Bruce Spence (Gyro Captain), Vernon Wells (Wez), Emil Minty (Feral Kid), Mike Preston (Pappagallo), Kjell Nilsson (Humungus), Virginia Hey (Warrior Woman), Syd Heylen (Curmudgeon), Moira Claux (Big Rebecca), David Slingsby (Quiet Man).

In this action-filled sequel to *Mad Max,* Mel Gibson is the only one who can save terrorized pilgrims, barricaded in a desert commune. They are beseiged by punk villains after their primitive oil refinery.

2514. *Roadhouse 66* (1984, Atlantic, 90m, c). P Scott M. Rosenfelt & Mark Levinson, D John Mark Robinson, W Galen Lee & George Simpson (based on a story by Lee), PH Tom Ackerman, M Gary Scott, ED Jay Lash Cassidy, PD Chester Kaczenski.

LP Willem Dafoe (Johnny Harte), Judge Reinhold (Beckman Hallsgood,

Jr.), Kaaren Lee (Jesse Duran), Kate Vernon (Melissa Duran), Stephen Elliott (Sam), Alan Autry (Hoot), Kevyn Major Howard (Dink), Peter Van Norden (Moss), Erica Yohn (Thelma).

Hitchhiker Willem Dafoe and Ivy Leaguer Judge Reinhold are stuck overnight in an Arizona town while their car is being repaired. They enter their 1955 T-bird in a drag race and fall in love with a couple of local girls. It's not as exciting as it sounds.

2515. Roadie (1980, United Artists, 105m, c). P Carolyn Pfeiffer, D Alan Rudolph, W Big Boy Medlin & Michael Ventura (based on a story by Medlin, Ventura, Rudolph & Zalman King), PH David Myers, M Craig Hundley, ED Carol Littleton & Tom Walls, PD Paul Peters.

LP Meatloaf (Travis W. Redfish), Kaki Hunter (Lola Bouilliabase), Art Carney (Corpus C. Redfish), Gailard Sartain (B.B. Muldoon), Don Cornelius (Mohammed Johnson), Rhonda Bates (Alice Poo), Richard Marion (George).

Roadie Meatloaf and Kaki Hunter (you remember her, she was the goodtime had by all in the *Porky's* series) waste nearly two hours of audiences' time trying to meet Alice Cooper.

2516. Roadkill (1989, Cinephile, Canada, 80m, b&w). P Bruce McDonald & Colin Brunton, D McDonald, W Don McKellar, PH Miroslaw Baszak, M Nash the Slash, ED Mike Munn.

LP Valerie Buhagiar (Ramona), Gerry Quigley (Roy Seth), Larry Hudson (Buddie), Bruce McDonald (Bruce Shack), Shaun Bowring (Matthew), Don McKellar (Russel), Mark Tarantino (Luke).

Compliant Valerie Buhagiar, an employee of a big time rock promoter, is sent from Toronto to northern Ontario to track down a missing touring band. Unable to drive, she takes a cab. Her driver promptly strands her. Her on-the-road experiences include meeting an intinerant documentary film director, a would-be serial killer and a 15-year-old country boy who seduces her.

2517. Robbers of the Sacred Mountain (1982, Heller Prods., Canada, 97m, c, aka *Falcon's Gold*). P Keith Rothman, D Bob Schulz, W Olaf Pooley & Walter Bell, PH Laszlo George, M Lalo Schifrin, ED Ralph Brunjes, PD Dave Davis.

LP John Marley (Dr. Falcon), Simon MacCorkindale (Hank Richards), Louise Vallance (Tracey Falcon), Blanca Guerra (B.G. Alvarez), George Touliatos (Murdoch), Jorge Reynoso (Marques).

The late John Marley stars as an archaeologist called from an Arabian dig to Mexico. His expertise is needed to identify a fertility goddess statuette, part of a fabulous treasure lost in a 1645 earthquake. The film resembles *Raiders of the Lost Ark* in numerous ways, unfortunately not in the quality of the acting.

2518. Robbery Under Arms (1985, ITC, Australia, 141m, c). P Jock Blair, D Ken Hannam & Donald Crombie, W Graeme Koestveld & Tony Morphett (based on the novel by Rolf Boldrewood), PH Ernest Clark, M Garry McDonald & Laurie Stone, ED Andrew Prowse, PD George Liddle.

LP Sam Neill (Capt. Starlight), Steven Vidler (Dick Marston), Christopher Cummins (Jim Marston), Liz Newman (Gracey), Deborah Coulls (Kate), Susie Lindeman (Jeannie), Tommy Lewis (Warrigal), Ed Devereux (Ben Marston).

The story of Australian highwayman Capt. Starlight and two farming brothers who join his gang has been filmed four times before. It still isn't much to see.

2519. Robocop (1987, Orion, 103m, c). P Arne Schmidt, D Paul Verhoeven, W Edward Neumeier & Michael Miner, PH Jost Vacano, M Basil Poledouris, ED Frank J. Urioste†, PD William Sandell, SOUND Michael J. Kohut, Carlos de Larios, Aaron Rochin & Robert Wald†.

LP Peter Weller (Alex J. Murphy/Robocop), Nancy Allen (Anne Lewis), Ronny Cox (Richard "Dick" Jones), Kurtwood Smith (Clarence J. Boddicker), Miguel Ferrer (Robert Morton), Robert DoQui (Sgt. Reed), Daniel O'Herlihy (The Old Man), Ray Wise (Leon Nash).

In a crime-ridden, corrupt Detroit of the future, a large corporation has assumed responsibility for policing the city. Peter Weller, a brave cop killed in the line of duty, is transformed into a cyborg (half-man, half-robot), designed to be a superinforcer of the law. In reality, Robocop is merely a pawn of the internecine struggles of executives in the corporation. The latter hadn't counted on the human part of Robocop assuming control.

2520. *Robot Holocaust* (1987, Wizard Video-Infinity, 79m, c). P Cynthia DePaula, D&W Tim Kincaid, PH Arthur D. Marks, ED Barry Zetlin, PD Medusa, SE Jeremie Frank, Ralph Cordero & Valarie McNeill.

LP Norris Culf (Neo), Nadine Hart (Deeja), Joel Von Ornsteiner (Klyton), Jennifer Delora (Myta), Andrew Howarth (Kai), Angelika Jager (Valaria), Rick Gianasi (Torque), Michael Dowend (Jorn), George Gray (Bray).

Millions of servant robots have revolted, with the result that humans are nearly extinct. Those remaining are slaves of the "Dark One" who control them by poisoning the atmosphere. But if you could keep good men and women down forever, there wouldn't be an excuse for this movie, would there? Now there's a thought.

2521. *Rock & Rule* (1983, Canada Trust Co., Canada, animated, 85m, c). D Clive A. Smith, M Lou Reed, Iggy Pop, Debbie Harry, Cheap Trick.

VOICES Don Francks, Paul Le Mat, Susan Roman, Sam Langevin, Catherine O'Hara.

This animated rock and roll fantasy is from Canada's Nelvana animation studio. The music is good, the humor is adult, and there is no story to speak of.

2522. *Rock 'n' Roll Nightmare* (1987, Shapiro, Canada, 83m, c, aka *The Edge of Hell*). P Jon-Miki Thor, D John Fasano, W Thor, PH Mark MacKay, ED Robert Williams, AD Wolfgang Siebert, M/L Various Artists.

LP Jon-Miki Thor (John Triton), Jillian Peri (Lou Anne), Frank Dietz (Roger Eburt), Dave Lane (Max), Teresa Simpson (Randy), Clara Pater (Mother), Jesse D'Angelo (Little Boy), Chris Finkel (Father), Liane Abel (Mary).

When a hot new rock 'n' roll group takes their sexy young girlfriends to an out of the way farm for a fun weekend, they didn't count on terror.

2523. *Rocket Gibralter* (1988, Columbia, 100m, c). P Jeff Weiss & Marcus Viscidi, D Daniel Petrie, W Amos Poe, PH Jost Vacano, M Andrew Powell, ED Melody London, PD Bill Groom.

LP Burt Lancaster (Levi Rockwell), Suzy Amis (Aggie Rockwell), Patricia Clarkson (Rose Black), Frances Conroy (Ruby Hanson), Sinead Cusack (Amanda "Billi" Rockwell), John Glover (Rolo Rockwell), Bill Pullman (Crow Black), Kevin Spacey (Dwayne Hanson), John Bell (Orson Rockwell).

The family of Burt Lancaster gathers for his 77th birthday at his Coastal Long Island estate. His children love but don't understand the dying old man. His grandchildren resolve to give him what they think he wants, a Viking funeral. When he dies without his children noting his passing, the youngest generation haul his corpse down to the water, and lovingly place it in an old boat, the Rocket Gibralter, which they had prepared for the event. They set the vessel adrift and shoot burning arrows into it. You may find a tear or two in your eyes at this point.

2524. *Rocky III* (1982, MGM/United Artists, 99m, c). P Irwin Winkler & Robert Chartoff, D&W Sylvester Stallone, PH Bill Butler, M Bill Conti, ED Don Zimmerman & Mark Warner, PD William J. Cassidy, M/L "Eye of the Tiger" by Jim Peterik & Frankie Sullivan, III†.

LP Sylvester Stallone (Rocky Balboa), Carl Weathers (Apollo Creed), Mr. T (Clubber Lang), Talia Shire (Adrian Balboa), Burt Young (Paulie), Burgess Meredith (Mickey), Ian Fried (Rocky, Jr.), Hulk Hogan (Thunderlips), Al Silvani (Al).

Would you believe that someone could be found to make Rocky Balboa look bright? Well just take a look at brutal loud-mouthed slugger Clubber Lang played by that fine thespian Mr. T. He beats our hero in the ring the first time, but we know that Sylvester Stallone's character has to take several shots to the head before one has his attention. Watch out for that rematch, Mr. T.

2525. *Rocky IV* (1985, MGM/United Artists, 91m, c). P Irwin Winkler &

Robert Chartoff, D&W Sylvester Stallone, PH Bill Butler, M Vince DiCola & Bill Conti, ED Don Zimmerman & John W. Wheeler, PD Bill Kenney.

LP Sylvester Stallone (Rocky Balboa), Talia Shire (Adrian Balboa), Burt Young (Paulie), Carl Weathers (Apollo Creed), Brigitte Nielsen (Ludmilla), Tony Burton (Duke), Michael Pataki (Nicoli Koloff), Dolph Lundgren (Drago).

The Russian champion, blond coldblooded giant Dolph Lundgren, who looks like a perfect Aryan Nazi, kills Carl Weathers in an exhibition match. Sylvester Stallone wraps the flag around himself and goes through intense training so he can climb into the ring and wipe up the floor with the dirty commie killer. Statuesque Brigitte Nielsen, briefly Stallone's wife, appears as Lundgren's wife and keeper.

2526. *Roller Blade* (1986, New World, 97m, c). P,D&PH Donald G. Jackson, W Jackson & Randall Frakes (based on a story by Jackson), M Robert Garrett, ED Ron Amick.

LP Suzanne Solari (Sister Sharon Cross), Jeff Hutchinson (Marshall Goodman), Shaun Michelle (Hunter/Sister Fortune), Katina Garner (Mother Speed), Sam Mann (Waco), Robby Taylor (Deputy/Dr. Saticoy).

In a postholocaust world, a group of Amazons use martial arts and mysticism to battle the forces of evil.

2527. *Rolling Vengeance* (1988, Apollo, 90m, c). P&D Steven H. Stern, W Michael Montgomery, PH Laszlo George, M Phil Marshall, ED Ron Wisman, AD Harold Thrasher.

LP Don Michael Paul (Joey Rosso), Lawrence Dane (Big Joe), Ned Beatty (Tiny Doyle), Susan Hogan (Big Joe's Wife), Lisa Howard (Misty), Barclay Hope (Steve), Todd Duckworth (Vic Doyle), Michael J. Reynolds (Lt. Sly).

When his family is killed and his girlfriend raped, trucker Don Michael Paul builds an 8-ton killing machine with 73-inch tires and a 600 horsepower engine. Then he sets out to take revenge against nasty redneck Ned Beatty, the latter's rotten family, and all their vehicles.

2528. *Rollover* (1981, Warner, 118m, c). P Bruce Gilbert, D Alan J. Pakula, W

David Shaber (based on a story by Shaber, Howard Kohn & David Weir), PH Giuseppe Rotunno & William Garroni, M Michael Small, ED Evan Lottman, PD George Jenkins & John Jay Moore.

LP Jane Fonda (Lee Winters), Kris Kristofferson (Hub Smith), Hume Cronyn (Maxwell Emery), Josef Sommer (Roy Lefcourt), Bob Gunton (Sal Naftari), Macon McCalman (Mr. Fewster), Ron Frazier (Gil Hovey), Jodi Long (Betsy Okamoto), Crocker Nevin (Warner Ackerman).

Jane Fonda, the widow of a murdered bank president, becomes involved with banker Kris Kristofferson. The two are caught up in a high-powered Arab investment plot. The plot is so complex, it's difficult to know what's going on.

2529. *Romancing the Stone* (1984, 20th Century–Fox, 105m, c). P Michael Douglas, D Robert Zemeckis, W Diane Thomas, PH Dean Cundey, M Alan Silvestri, ED Donn Cambern & Frank Morriss†, PD Lawrence G. Paull.

LP Michael Douglas (Jack Colton), Kathleen Turner (Joan Wilder), Danny DeVito (Ralph), Zack Norman (Ira), Alfonso Arau (Juan), Manuel Ojeda (Zolo), Holland Taylor (Gloria), Mary Ellen Trainor (Elaine), Eve Smith (Mrs. Irwin), Kym Herrin (Angelina), Bill Burton (Jessie), Ted White (Grogan).

When she is forced to go to Colombia to rescue her kidnapped sister, bestselling romance novelist Kathleen Turner finds herself living the exciting, dangerous and romantic life of one of her heroines. She teams up with handsome hunter Michael Douglas. Together they encounter various villains, including the hilarious Danny De Vito, who wish to get hold of a treasure map she unwittingly possesses. It's all good boisterous fun.

2530. *Romantic Comedy* (1983, MGM/United Artists, 103m, c). P Walter Mirisch & Morton Gottlieb, D Arthur Hiller, W Bernard Slade (based on his play), PH David M. Walsh, M Marvin Hamlisch, ED John C. Howard, PD Alfred Sweeney.

LP Dudley Moore (Jason), Mary Steenburgen (Phoebe), Frances Sternhagen (Blanche), Janet Eilber (Allison), Robyn Douglass (Kate), Ron Leibman

(Leo), Roziska Halmos (Maid), Alexander Lockwood (Minister).

Broadway playwright Dudley Moore takes on New England schoolteacher Mary Steenburgen as a collaborator and then falls in love with her. It's a tedious comedy that isn't very romantic.

2531. *Romero* (1989, Four Seasons, 105m, c). P Rev. Ellwood E. Keiser, D John Duigan, W John Sacret Young, PH Geoff Burton, M Gabriel Yared, ED Frans Vandenburg, PD Roger Ford.

LP Raul Julia (Archbishop Oscar Arnulfo Romero), Richard Jordan (The Rev. Rutilio Grande), Ana Alicia (Arista Zelada), Eddie Velez (Lt. Columa), Alejandro Bracho (The Rev. Alfonzo Osuna), Tony Plana (The Rev. Manuel Morantes), Harold Gould (Francisco Galedo), Lucy Reina (Lucia).

Raul Julia is convincing if not inspiring as the heroic liberal archbishop of San Salvador. The prelate was assassinated by right wingers while saying mass in 1980, because he refused to be a tool of the rich, speaking out against the injustices and the misery of the poor in his country.

2532. *Rooftops* (1989, New Visions, 95m, c). P Howard W. Koch, Jr., D Robert Wise, W Terence Brennan (based on a story by Allan Goldstein & Tony Mark), PH Theo Van de Sande, M David A. Stewart & Michael Kamen, ED William Reynolds, PD Jeannine C. Oppewall.

LP Jason Gedrick (T), Troy Beyer (Elana), Eddie Velez (Lobo), Tisha Campbell (Amber), Alexis Cruz (Squeak), Allen Payne (Kadim), Steve Love (Jackie-Sky), Rafael Baez (Raphael).

Squatter Jason Gedrick lives in an abandoned water tower atop a tenement. He's a martial arts enthusiast who decides to take a stand against Eddie Velez when the latter turns the tenement into a crack house.

2533. *A Room with a View*† (1986, Cinecom, GB, 115m, c). P Ismail Merchant, D James Ivory†, W Ruth Prawer Jhabvala* (based on the novel by E.M. Forster), PH Tony Pierce-Roberts†, M Richard Robbins, ED Humphrey Dixon, AD Gianni Quaranta & Brian Ackland-Snow*, SD Brian Savegar & Elio Altra-

mura*, COS Jenny Beaven & John Bright*.

LP Maggie Smith† (Charlotte Bartlett), Helena Bonham Carter (Lucy Honeychurch), Denholm Elliott† (Mr. Emerson), Julian Sands (George Emerson), Daniel Day-Lewis (Cecil Vyse), Simon Callow (Rev. Beebe), Judi Dench (Miss Lavish), Rosemary Leach (Mrs. Honeychurch), Rupert Graves (Freddy Honeychurch), Patrick Godfrey (Mr. Eager), Fabia Drake (Catherine Alan), Joan Henley (Teresa Alan).

Films seldom look or sound better than this one. The photography is magnificent, the settings are a delight, and throughout the film some of the most beautiful music ever written perfectly sets the mood. Innocent Edwardian girl Helena Bonham Carter, travelling in Italy with her aunt, Maggie Smith, has her eyes opened to real life and the excitement of romance. It's a precious, simple movie, with no great story line – but with most enjoyable performances by all of the principals.

2534. *The Rosary Murders* (1987, New Line, 105m, c). P Robert G. Laurel, D Fred Walton, W Elmore Leonard & Walton (based on the novel by William X. Kienzle), PH David Golia, M Bobby Laurel & Don Sebesky, ED Sam Vitale.

LP Donald Sutherland (Father Bob Koesler), Charles Durning (Father Ted Nabors), Josef Sommer (Lt. Walt Koznicki), Belinda Bauer (Pat Lennon), James Murtaugh (Javison), John Danelle (Detective Harris), Addison Powell (Father Killeen), Kathleen Tolan (Sister Ann Vania).

What is unorthodox priest Donald Sutherland to do when the serial murderer of Detroit priests and nuns confesses his crimes in the confessional? Why team with beautiful reporter Belinda Bauer and crack the case without cracking the seal of the confessional. Just remember to avoid occasions of sin, Father!

2535. *The Rose Garden* (1989, Pathe Intl., West Ger./US, 112m, c). P Artur Brauner, D Fons Rademakers, W Paul Hengge, PH Gernot Roll, M Egisto Macchi, ED Kees Lindhorst, PD Jan Schlubach.

LP Liv Ullmann (Gabriele Schlueter-

Freund), Maximilian Schell (Aaron Reichenbacher), Peter Fonda (Herbert Schlueter), Jan Niklas (Paessler), Katarina Lena Muller (Tina), Kurt Hubner (Arnold Krenn), Hanns Zischler (Prof. Eckert), Gila Almagor (Ruth Levi).

The title refers to a plot of flowered land next to a Hamburg street. As the British army approached the city in 1945, the Nazis hanged 20 Jewish children being used for medical experiments. Years later, Maximilian Schell, the only child to escape this fate, is determined to bring the SS officer responsible for the order to trial. Beware! The film shows the hangings in a documentary-like style.

2536.   The Rosebud Beach Hotel (1984, Almi, 105m, c). P Irving Schwartz & Harry Hurwitz, D Hurwitz, W Harry Narunsky, Schwartz & Thomas Rudolph, PH Joao Fernandes, M Jay Chattaway, ED Daniel Lowenthal.

LP Colleen Camp (Tracy), Peter Scolari (Elliott), Christopher Lee (King), Fran Drescher (Linda), Eddie Deezen (Sydney), Chuck McCann (Dorfman), Hank Garrett (Kramer), Hamilton Camp (Matches), Jonathan Schmock (Dennis).

In a mediocre adult comedy, Peter Scolari tries his hand at managing a run down hotel in order to please his girlfriend Colleen Camp. Bellhop Fran Drescher doubles as a call girl and Camp's father Christopher Lee plots to blow the place up for the insurance money.

Rosemary's Killer see The Prowler

2537.   R.O.T.O.R. (1988, Imperical, 90m, c). P Cullen Blaine, Budd Lewis & Richard Gesswein, D Blaine, W Lewis, PH Glenn Roland, M David Adam Newman, ED Douglas Bryan.

LP Richard Gesswein, Margaret Trigg, Jayne Smith, James Cole, Clark Moore, Carroll Brandon Baker.

The acronym R.O.T.O.R. stands for Robot Officer Tactical Operation Research, so you know you're in for a rip-off of *Terminator* and *Robocop,* and not a very good one at that.

2538.   Rotweiler: Dogs of Hell (1984, Owensby, 3-D, 90m, c, aka *Dogs of Hell*). P Earl Owensby, D Worth Keeter, III, W Tom McIntyre.

LP Earl Owensby, Bill Gribble, Jerry Rushing.

This boring horror film, produced to be shown in Southern drive-ins, features a pack of dogs attacking the inhabitants of a small North Carolina mountain retreat.

2539.   Rough Cut (1980, Paramount, GB, 112m, c). P David Merrick, D Don Siegel, W Francis Burns [Larry Gelbart] (based on the novel *Touch the Lion's Paw* by Derek Lambert), PH Freddie Young, M Nelson Riddle (adapted from the music of Duke Ellington and collaborators), ED Doug Stewart, PD Ted Haworth.

LP Burt Reynolds (Jack Rhodes), Lesley-Anne Down (Gillian Bromley), David Niven (Chief Inspector Cyril Willis), Timothy West (Nigel Lawton), Patrick Magee (Ernst Mueller), Al Matthews (Ferguson), Susan Littler (Sheila), Joss Ackland (Insp. Vanderveld), Isabel Dean (Mrs. Willis).

Retiring Scotland Yard inspector David Niven has never been able to apprehend notorious jewel thief Burt Reynolds. Desperate to remove this blotch from his record he sets up a trap, employing kleptomaniac society woman Lesley-Anne Down as bait. Instead she falls in love with Reynolds and becomes his partner in a plan to steal $30,000,000 in jewels during a flight from Antwerp to Amsterdam. Neither Niven nor Reynolds are up for this tepid comedy.

2540.   Round Midnight (1986, Warner, US/Fr., 133m, c). P Irwin Winkler, D Bertrand Tavernier, W David Rayfiel & Tavenier (based on incidents in the lives of Francis Paudras and Bud Powell), PH Bruno de Keyzer, M Herbie Hancock*, ED Armand Psenny, PD Alexandre Trauner.

LP Dexter Gordon† (Dale Turner), Francois Cluzet (Francis Borier), Gabrielle Haker (Berangere), Sandra Reaves-Phillips (Buttercup), Lonette McKee (Darcey Leigh), Christine Pascal (Sylvie), Herbie Hancock (Eddie Wayne), Bobby Hutcherson (Ace).

This jazz buff's tribute to Bud Powell and Lester Young features the late real-life musician Dexter Gordon in a sparkling performance as a talented but self-destructive saxophonist whose career is rescued by French fan Francois Cluzet. The Herbie Hancock score won a much deserved Oscar.

2541. *Roxanne* (1987, Columbia, 107m, c). P Michael Rachmil & Daniel Melnick, D Fred Schepisi, W Steve Martin (based on the play *Cyrano de Bergerac* by Edmond Rostand), PH Ian Baker, M Bruce Smeaton, ED John Scott, PD Jack DeGovia.

LP Steve Martin (Charlie "C.D." Bales), Daryl Hannah (Roxanne Kowalski), Rick Rossovich (Chris McDonell), Shelley Duvall (Dixie), John Kapelos (Chuck), Fred Willard (Mayor Deebs), Max Alexander (Dean), Michael J. Pollard (Andy), Shandra Beri (Sandy), Brian George (Dr. David Schepisi).

In a very appealing, romantic update of Cyrano de Bergerac, Steve Martin is the fire chief in a sleepy ski town in Washington state. Because of a rather long and distinctive nose, he's afraid of expressing his true feelings for recently arrived Daryl Hannah. Instead he fronts for dumb hunk Rick Rossovich. However since Martin is the screenwriter, he makes certain he gets the girl by the final reel.

2542. *R.S.V.P.* (1984, Platinum, 86m, c). P John Amero, D Lem Amero, W LaRue Watts, PH Larry Revene, M Ian Shaw, ED L. Amero, AD Watts & Fabian Stuart.

LP Adam Mills (Toby), Lynda Wiesmeier (Jennifer), Veronica Hart (Ellen), Ray Colbert (Bill), Harry Reems (Grant), Katt Shea (Rhonda), Lola Mason (Polly), Allene Simmons (Patty), Dustin Stevens (Jonathan).

For some of these performers, making a soft core picture must be a nice change. Several, including Veronica Hart and Harry Reems, have usually starred in executive producer Chuck Vincent's XXX films. In this one, things go wrong at a Hollywood party being held to honor a writer when a body (dead, that is) is found in the guest of honor's pool.

2543. *Ruckus* (1981, New World, 91m, c, aka *The Loner*). P Paul Maslansky, D&W Max Kleven, M/L Willie Nelson & Hank Cochran.

LP Dirk Benedict, Linda Blair, Richard Farnsworth, Matt Clark, Jon Van Ness, Ben Johnson, Taylor Lacher.

No one gets killed in this Rambo-like story. Vietnam vet Dirk Benedict escapes from a military psychiatric ward and ends up in a little Southern town where the locals hassle him. But they are made to feel sorry for it.

2544. *Rude Awakening* (1989, Orion, 100m, c). P Aaron Russo, D David Greenwalt, Russo, W Neil Levy & Richard LaGravenese, PH Tim Sigel, M Jonathan Elias, ED Paul Fried, PD Mel Bourne.

LP Cheech Marin (Hesus), Eric Roberts (Fred), Julie Hagerty (Petra), Robert Carradine (Sammy), Buck Henry (Lloyd), Louise Lasser (Ronnie), Cindy Williams (June), Andrea Martin (April), Cliff De Young (Brubaker).

Flower children Cheech Marin and Eric Roberts emerge after 20 years of living in a jungle commune in a fictitious Latin American country. On their return to the U.S., they encounter several old friends, who have changed in attitude and outlook. It's moderately amusing; but preachy. Gurus of the 60s Timothy Leary, Jerry Rubin and Bobby Seale make cameo appearances.

2545. *Rude Boy* (1980, Atlantic, GB, 120m, c). P&D Jack Hazan & David Mingay, W Hazan, Mingay & Ray Gange, PH Hazan, M Joe Strummer & Mick Jones, ED Mingay & Peter Goddard.

LP Ray Gange (Ray), The Clash (Themselves), John Green (Road Manager), Barry Baker (Roadie), Terry McQuade (Terry), Caroline Coon (Clash Girl Friend), Elizabeth Young & Sarah Hall (Ray's Girl Friends).

Ray Gange, a London young man with no prospects, takes a job as a roadie with the rock group The Clash, but ends up back where he started from. If you're into the alienated punk generation this picture ought to pleasingly bum you out.

2546. *Rumble Fish* (1983, Universal, 105m, c). P Fred Roos & Doug Claybourne, D Francis Ford Coppola, W S.E. Hinton & Coppola (based on a novel by Hinton), PH Stephen H. Burum, M Stewart Copeland, ED Barry Malkin, PD Dean Tavoularis.

LP Matt Dillon (Rusty-James), Mickey Rourke (Motorcycle Boy), Diane Lane

(Patty), Dennis Hopper (Father), Diana Scarwid (Cassandra), Vincent Spano (Steve), Nicolas Cage (Smokey), Christopher Penn (B.J.), Larry Fishburne (Midget), William Smith (Patterson).

Tulsa teen Matt Dillon, living with his drunken father Dennis Hopper, strives to be like his biker brother Mickey Rourke. He works in a petshop and likens himself to the rumble fish, which fights even its own image in the glass. Rourke knows that his way leads nowhere and he tries to redirect his brother's hero-worship.

2547. *Rumpelstiltskin* (1987, Cannon, 92m, c). P Menahem Golan & Yoram Globus, D&W David Irving, PH David Gurfinkel, M Max Robert, ED Tova Neeman, PD Marek Dobrowolski, COS Debbie Leon.

LP Amy Irving (Katie), Clive Revill (King Mezzer), Billy Barty (Rumpelstiltskin), Priscilla Pointer (Queen Grizelda), Robert Symonds (Victor), John Moulder-Brown (The Prince).

Menahem Golan and Yoram Globus please audiences with a charming version of the familiar story of the foolish miller who claims his daughter can spin straw into gold. She does so with the help of dwarf Billy Barty who demands her baby as payment, unless she can guess his name.

2548. *Runaway* (1984, Tri-Star, 100m, c). P Michael Rachmil, D&W Michael Crichton, PH John A. Alonzo, M Jerry Goldsmith, ED Glenn Farr, PD Douglas Higgins.

LP Tom Selleck (Sgt. Jack Ramsey), Cynthia Rhodes (Sgt. Karen Thompson), Gene Simmons (Luther), Kirstie Alley (Jackie), Stan Shaw (Marvin), G.W. Bailey (Chief), Joey Cramer (Bobby), Chris Mulkey (Johnson).

Robotics expert Tom Selleck and his pretty blond policewoman partner Cynthia Rhodes are given the assignment of tracking down killer robots. The latter, termed runaways (they were household help until they were deliberately short-circuited), are wreaking havoc in a metropolitan city.

2549. *Runaway Train* (1985, Cannon, 111m, c). P Menahem Golan & Yoram Globus, D Andrei Konchalovsky, W

Djordje Milicevic, Paul Zindel & Edward Bunker (based on the screenplay by Akira Kurosawa, Ryuzo Kikushima & Hideo Oguni), PH Alan Hume, M Trevor Jones, ED Henry Richardson†, PD Stephen Marsh.

LP Jon Voight† (Manny), Eric Roberts† (Buck), Rebecca DeMornay (Sara), Kyle T. Heffner (Frank Barstow), John P. Ryan (Ranken), T.K. Carter (Dave Prince), Kenneth McMillan (Eddie MacDonald), Stacey Pickren (Ruby).

One can never accuse Jon Voight of repeating a role. Here he plays an almost samurai-like convict in an Alaskan prison. He's a hero to all the other prisoners because he stands up to sadistic warden John P. Ryan, no matter what the consequences. Voight escapes from the pen for the third time; this time taking along young Eric Roberts, by crawling through a smelly, filthy sewer. They board a passing train consisting of four engines coupled together. Unbeknownst to them the engineer suffers a fatal heart attack, his dead body moving the throttle to full speed ahead. The cons and Rebecca DeMornay, a railroad employee and the only other person on the train, are on a runaway train. In the end Voight saves Roberts and DeMornay but takes his hated enemy Ryan, who has boarded the speeding train via a helicopter, with him to their doom.

The Runaways* see *South Bronx Heroes

2550. *Runners* (1983, Cinegate, GB, 106m, c). P Barry Hanson, D Charles Sturridge, W Stephen Poliakoff, PH Howard Atherton, M George Fenton, ED Peter Coulson.

LP Kate Hardie (Rachel Lindsay), James Fox (Tom Lindsay), Jane Asher (Helen), Eileen O'Brien (Gillian Lindsay), Ruti Simon (Lucy Lindsay), Bridget Turner (Teacher), Robert Lang (Wilkins).

A Nottingham father and a Reading mother search all over London for their runaway children.

2551. *Running Brave* (1983, Buena Vista, Canada, 105m, c). P Ira Englander, D D.S. Everett [Donald Shebib], W Henry Bean & Shirl Hendryx, PH

Francois Protat, M Mike Post, ED Tony Lower & Earl Herdan, PD Carol Spier.

LP Robby Benson (Billy Mills), Pat Hingle (Coach Easton), Claudia Cron (Pat Mills), Jeff McCracken (Dennis), August Schellenberg (Billy's Father), Denis Lacroix (Frank), Graham Greene (Eddie), Margo Kane (Catherine).

This film wouldn't make a good made-for-TV movie. It purports to tell the true story of a young Sioux from the reservation who faces extreme pressures from the world of the white man as he becomes an Olympic runner. Looks like the movies are still in the mood to massacre the redman.

2552. *Running Hot* (1984, New Line, 95m, c, aka *Lucky 13*). P David Calloway & Zachary Feuer, D&W Mark Griffiths, PH Tom Richmond, M Al Capps, ED Andy Blumenthal, PD Katherine Vallin.

LP Monica Carrico (Charlene Andrews), Eric Stoltz (Danny Hicks), Stuart Margolin (Officer Trent), Virgil Frye (Ross the Pimp), Richard Bradford (Tom Bond), Louise Baker (Shane), Joe George (Officer Berman), Laurel Patrick (Angie).

Seventeen-year-old Eric Stoltz has been convicted of murdering his father and is sentenced to be executed. Instead he escapes and hides out with prostitute Monica Carrico, who has written to him while he was in prison. Stoltz may really be innocent, but nevertheless he's killed in the end.

2553. *The Running Man* (1987, Tri-Star, 100m, c). P Tim Zinnemann & George Linder, D Paul Michael Glaser, W Steven E. de Souza (based on the novel by Richard Bachman [Stephen King]), PH Thomas Del Ruth & Reynaldo Villalobos, M Harold Faltermeyer, ED Mark Roy Warner, Edward A. Warschilka & John Wright, PD Jack T. Collis.

LP Arnold Schwarzenegger (Ben "Butcher of Bakersfield" Richards), Maria Conchita Alonso (Amber Mendez), Yaphet Kotto (Laughlin), Jim Brown (Fireball), Richard Dawson (Damon Killian), Dweezil Zappa (Stevie), Mick Fleetwood (Mic), Jesse Ventura (Captain Freedom), Erland Van Lidth (Dynamo).

In the year 2019 A.D., the U.S. is a totalitarian state. Framed as a mass murderer Arnold Schwarzenegger has a Hobson's choice of appearing on "A Most Dangerous Game"-inspired TV program. Convicted felons are given the chance to run for their lives, but with the stalkers on their tails, none have ever escaped or survived—until now. You just know Arnie means it when he tells unctuous game show host Richard Dawson, "I'll be back!"

2554. *Running on Empty* (1988, Warner, 116m, c). P Amy Robinson & Griffin Dunne, D Sidney Lumet, W Naomi Foner†, PH Gerry Fisher, M Tony Mottola, ED Andrew Mondshein, PD Philip Rosenberg.

LP Christine Lahti (Annie Pope), River Phoenix† (Danny Pope), Judd Hirsch (Arthur Pope), Martha Plimpton (Lorna Phillips), Jonas Arby (Harry Pope), Ed Crowley (Mr. Phillips), L.M. Kit Carson (Gus Winant), Steven Hill (Mr. Patterson), Augusta Dabney (Mrs. Patterson).

Former 60s radicals Judd Hirsch and Christine Lahti are still sought by the FBI twenty years later. They are also parents of two children, River Phoenix and Jonas Arby, the former desperately wanting to emerge from the underground and make a life for himself. His biggest fear is that his parents may be exposed if he enters college.

2555. *Running Scared* (1986, MGM/UA, 107m, c). P David Foster & Lawrence Turman, D&PH Peter Hyams, W Gary DeVore & Jimmy Huston (based on a story by DeVore), M Rod Temperton, ED James Mitchell, PD Albert Brenner.

LP Gregory Hines (Ray Hughes), Billy Crystal (Danny Costanzo), Steven Bauer (Frank), Darlanne Fluegel (Anna Costanzo), Joe Pantoliano (Snake), Dan Hedaya (Captain Logan), Jonathan Gries (Tony), Tracy Reed (Maryann), Jimmy Smits (Julio Gonzales), John DiSanti (Vinnie).

Before retiring to the sunny south, two long-time Chicago cops, Gregory Hines and Billy Crystal, have one last murdering drug dealer to put away. It's an exciting, likeable comedy-action film, with a great car chase on the El (elevated train) tracks. The nonstop banter in this male-bonding film is often very funny.

2556. *Russkies* (1987, New Century/ Vista, 98m, c). P Mark Levinson & Scott Rosenfelt, D Rick Rosenthal, W Allan Jay Glueckman, Sheldon Lettich & Michael Nankin, PH Reed Smoot, M James Newton Howard, ED Antony Gibbs, PD Linda Pearl, SE Tom Anderson & Karl Herrmann.

LP Whip Hubley (Mischa), Leaf Phoenix (Danny), Peter Billingsley (Adam), Stefan DeSalle (Jason), Susan Walters (Diane), Patrick Kilpatrick (Raimy), Vic Polizos (Sulock), Charles Frank (Mr. Vandermeer).

In this formula teen comedy, three Florida youngsters pick up Russian sailor Whip Hubley. He has become stranded when his raft capsizes, forcing him to abort his mission to pick up a stolen American defense weapon. This reworking of *The Russians Are Coming!, The Russians Are Coming!* is well meaning, but rather corny.

2557. *Rustler's Rhapsody* (1985, Paramount, 88m, c). P David Giler, D&W Hugh Wilson, PH Jose Luis Alcaine, M Steve Doriff, ED John Victor Smith, PD Gil Parrondo.

LP Tom Berenger (Rex O'Herlihan), G.W. Bailey (Peter), Marilu Henner (Miss Tracy), Fernando Rey (Railroad Colonel), Andy Griffith (Col. Ticonderoga), Sela Ward (Colonel Ticonderoga's Daughter), Brant Van Hoffman (Jim), Christopher Malcolm (Jud), Patrick Wayne (Bob Barber).

In a satire of the 30s and 40s B Westerns, singing cowboy Tom Berenger rides into town. He picks town drunk G.W. Bailey to be his sidekick, deals with a whore with a heart of gold, a corrupt sheriff, a shy young schoolteacher, terrified sheepherders, and an evil cattle baron. Finally he faces a hired gunman dressed all in white, in the person of Patrick Wayne. All the clichés are here — even if they are a bit skewed.

2558. *Ruthless People* (1986, Buena Vista, 93m, c). P Michael Peyser, D Jim Abrahams, David Zucker & Jerry Zucker, W Dale Launer, PH Jan De Bont, M Michel Colombier, ED Arthur Schmidt & Gib Jaffe, AD Donald Woodruff.

LP Danny DeVito (Sam Stone), Bette Midler (Barbara Stone), Judge Reinhold (Ken Kessler), Helen Slater (Sandy Kessler), Anita Morris (Carol), Bill Pullman (Earl), William G. Schilling (Police Commissioner), Art Evans (Lt. Bender), Clarence Felder (Lt. Walters).

Having been cheated out of a design process that made a millionaire of rascally Danny De Vito, Judge Reinhold and his wife Helen Slater kidnap the Spandex king's wife Bette Midler, demanding a large ransom. Wishing to be free of Midler so he can be with Anita Morris (who is two-timing him with dumb Bill Pullman), DeVito refuses to pay the money. He hopes the kidnappers will go through with their threat to kill Midler. Instead, Reinhold and Slater, two of the most spiritless people you'd ever encounter, team up with Midler to give DeVito his comeuppance.

2559. *Ryder P.I.* (1986, YGB Distribution, 92m, c). P Karl Hosch, D Hosch, W Hosch, Chuck Walker, Dave Hawthorne, Bob Nelson, PH Phil Arfman, M Kevin Kelly, ED Keith Brooke, AD Kenneth Hosch.

LP Dave Hawthorne (Sky Ryder), Bob Nelson (Eppie), Frances Raines (Valerie), John Mulrooney (Gang Leader), Bob Woods (Prof. Throckmorton), Howard Stern (Ben Wah), Kim Lurie (Maria), Chuck Rader (Det. Hoolihan).

This routine private eye film made on a shoestring has little to recommend it.

2560. *Sacred Ground* (1984, Pacific International, 100m, c). P Arthur R. Dubs, D,W&PH Charles B. Pierce, M Gene Kauer & Don Bagley, ED David E. Jackson, Steven L. Johnson & Lynne Sutherland.

LP Tim McIntire (Matt), Jack Elam (Witcher), L.Q. Jones (Tolbert), Mindi Miller (Wannetta), Eloy Phil Casados (Prairie Fox), Serene Hedin (Little Doe), Vernon Foster (Wounded Leg), Lefty Wild Eagle (Medicine Man), Larry Kenoras (Brave Beaver).

Trapper Tim McIntire and his pregnant wife unwittingly build their shelter on sacred Indian burying grounds. When the wife dies in childbirth, McIntire kidnaps an Indian woman, who has just buried her deceased infant, to care for his child.

2561. *Sacred Hearts* (1984, Reality/ Film Four, GB, 89m, c). P Dee Dee Glass, D&W Barbara Rennie, PH Diane Tammes, M Dirk Higgins, ED Martin Walsh, AD Hildegard Echtler.

LP Anna Massey (Sister Thomas), Katrin Cartlidge (Doris), Oona Kirsh (Maggie), Fiona Shaw (Sister Felicity), Anne Dyson (Sister Perpetua), Annette Badland (Sister Mercy), Sadie Wearing (Mary), Ann-Marie Gwatkin (Lizzie).

Even though she's not Catholic, at the start of World War II, Katrin Cartlidge enters an English convent school run by tyrannical Anna Massey. Cartlidge, a German Jew, is attempting to avoid persecution by the Nazis in case they successfully invade Britain.

2562. *Safari 3000* (1982, MGM/United Artists, 92m, c). P Arthur Gardner & Jules V. Levy, D Harry Hurwitz, W Michael Harreschou (based on a story by Levy, Gardner & Harreschou), PH Adam Greenberg, M Ernest Gold, ED Samuel E. Beetley, AD Peter Williams.

LP David Carradine (Eddie), Stockard Channing (J.J. Dalton), Christopher Lee (Count Borgia), Hamilton Camp (Feodor), Ian Yule (Freddie), Hugh Rouse (Hawthorne), Mary Ann Berold (Victoria), Peter J. Elliott (Stewart).

Top race-car driver David Carradine is forced to take *Playboy* photograper Stockard Channing along for the ride in a trans-African auto race. Amid much adversity and antagonism, love blossoms.

2563. *Sahara* (1984, MGM/United Artists, GB, 104m, c). P Menahem Golan & Yoram Globus, D Andrew V. McLaglen, W James R. Silke (based on a story by Golan), PH David Gurfinkel & Armando Nannuzzi, M Ennio Morricone, ED Alan Strachan & Michael J. Duthie, PD Luciano Spadoni.

LP Brooke Shields (Gordon Dale), Lambert Wilson (Jaffar), John Rhys-Davies (Rasoul), Horst Buchholz (Von Glessing), Perry Lang (Andy), Cliff Potts (String), John Mills (Cambridge), Steve Forrest (R.J. Gordon).

Brooke Shields, the daughter of a deceased Detroit car designer, disguises herself as a boy in order to enter and win a 1927 Sahara car race. Her sheik Lambert Wilson is a bit of a sissy, but she carries off the masquerade because the people she's around aren't too swift.

2564. *Saigon Commandos* (1988, Concorde, 83m, c). P John Schouweiler & Isabel Sumayao, D Clark Henderson, W Thomas McKelvey Cleaver (based on the novel *Saigon Commandos—Mad Minute* by Jonathan Cain), PH Juanito Pereira & Conrado Baltazar, M Samuel Asuncion & Noli Aurillo, ED Pacifico Sanchez.

LP Richard Young (Sgt. Mark Stryker), P.J. Soles (Jean Lassiter), John Allen Nelson (Tim Bryant), Jimi B., Jr. (Will Thomas), Spanky Manikan (Jon Toi), Joonee Gamboa (Nguyen Huu Tri), Fred Bailey (Capt. Daniels).

A.P. reporter P.J. Soles finds a link between drug-related murders in South Vietnam and corrupt politicians.

2565. *St. Elmo's Fire* (1985, Columbia, 110m, c). P Lauren Shuler, D Joel Schumacher, W Schumcher & Carl Kurlander, PH Stephen H. Burum & Jim Hovey, M David Foster, ED Richard Marks, AD William Sandell.

LP Emilio Estevez (Kirbo), Rob Lowe (Billy), Andrew McCarthy (Kevin), Demi Moore (Jules), Judd Nelson (Alex), Ally Sheedy (Leslie), Mare Winningham (Wendy), Martin Balsam (Mr. Beamish), Andie MacDowell (Dale Biberman), Joyce Van Patten (Mrs. Beamish), Jenny Wright (Felicia).

Seven recent graduates from Georgetown University must confront adult problems for the first time. It's tough to have midlife crises when you're only 22. The cast almost makes their plight believable.

2566. *St. Helens* (1981, Parnell, 90m, c). P Michael Murphy, D Ernest Pintoff, W Peter Bellwood & Larry Ferguson, PH Jacques Haitkin, M Goblin and Buckboard, ED George Berndt, SE Magic Lantern.

LP Art Carney (Harry Truman), David Huffman (Geologist), Cassie Yates (His Girlfriend), Ron O'Neal (Helicopter Pilot), Bill McKinney, Albert Salmi, Tim Thomerson, Henry Darrow, Nehemiah Persoff.

On May 18, 1980, after plenty of warning, active volcano Mount St. Helen's erupted. This cheap production is Hollywood's memorial to an old man with the improbable name of Harry Truman (Art Carney) who refused to leave his home on the slope of the mountain and naturally was killed.

2567.   The Salamander (1982, ITC, US/Ital./GB, 101m, c). P Paul Maslansky, D Peter Zinner, W Robert Katz (based on a novel by Morris West), PH Marcello Gatti, M Jerry Goldsmith, ED Claudio Cutry, AD Giantito Burchiellaro.

LP Franco Nero (Dante Matucci), Anthony Quinn (Bruno Manzini), Martin Balsam (Stefanelli), Sybil Danning (Lili Anders), Christopher Lee (Director Baldassare), Cleavon Little (Maj. Malinowsky), Eli Wallach (Leporello), Claudia Cardinale (Elena).

Despite an international cast of talented performers, this intriguing thriller about a possible coup d'état by fascists in modern-day Italy suffers from a hokey script.

2568.   Salome's Last Dance (1988, Vestron, 89m, c). P Penny Corke & Robert Littman, D Ken Russell, W Russell (based on the play *Salome* by Oscar Wilde), PH Harvey Harrison, MD Richard Cooke & Ray Beckett, ED Timothy Gee, AD Michael Buchanan, SD Christopher Hobbs, COS Michael Arrals.

LP Glenda Jackson (Herodias/Lady Alice), Stratford Johns (Herod/Alfred Taylor), Nickolas Grace (Oscar Wilde), Douglas Hodge (John the Baptist/Lord Alfred "Bosie" Douglas), Imogen Millais-Scott (Salome/Rose), Denis Ull (Tigellenus/Chilvers), Russell Lee Nash (Pageboy), Alfred Russell (Cappadodem), Ken Russell (Kenneth).

In this play within a film, Oscar Wilde (Nickolas Grace) and his lover "Bosie" Douglas (Douglas Hodge) attend a bordello in London on a rainy November 5, 1892. As a surprise for the author a performance of his banned play *The Tragedy of Salome* is to be performed, with Douglas portraying John the Baptist and various bordello employees appearing in other roles. It's director Ken Russell's most interesting work in years.

2569.   Salsa (1988, Cannon, 97m, c). P Menahem Golan & Yoram Globus, D Boaz Davidson, W Davidson, Tomas Benitez & Shepard Goldman (based on a story by Davidson & Eli Tabor), PH David Gurfinkel, M/L Various Artists, ED Alain Jakubowicz, PD Mark Haskins.

LP Robby Rosa (Rico), Rodney Harvey (Ken), Magali Alvarado (Rita), Miranda Garrison (Luna), Moon Orona (Lola), Angela Alvarado (Vicki), Loyda Ramos (Mother), Valente Rodriguez (Chuey), Daniel Rojo (Orlando).

In a scriptless clone of *Dirty Dancing*, automobile mechanic Robby Rosa would rather be swaying to a salsa beat.

2570.   The Salute of the Jugger (1989, Filmpac, Australia, 102m, c). P Charles Roven, D&W David Webb Peoples, PH David Eggby, M Todd Boekelheide, ED Richard Francis-Bruce, PD John Stoddart.

LP Rutger Hauer (Sallow), Joan Chen (Kidda), Vincent Phillip D'Onofrio (Young Gar), Delroy Lindo (Mbulu), Anna Katarina (Big Cimber), Gandhi Macintyre (Gandhi), Justin Monju (Dog Boy), Max Fairchild (Gonzo), Hugh Keays-Byrne (Lord Vile).

Juggers are a band of futuristic wandering gladiators, led by Rutger Hauer, once a member of the ruling elite, called the League, but since banished over a misdemeanor. He has plans for a comeback and challenges the League's juggers to do battle.

2571.   Salvador (1986, Hemdale, 123m, c). P Gerald Green & Oliver Stone, D Stone, W Stone & Richard Boyle†, PH Robert Richardson, M Georges Delerue, ED Claire Simpson, PD Bruno Rubeo.

LP James Woods† (Richard Boyle), James Belushi (Dr. Rock), Michael Murphy (Ambassador Thomas Kelly), John Savage (John Cassidy), Elpedia Carrillo (Maria), Tony Plana (Major Max), Colby Chester (Jack Morgan), Cindy Gibb (Cathy Moore), Will MacMillan (Col. Hyde), Valerie Wildman (Pauline Axelrod).

Based on the 1980–81 experiences of journalist Richard Boyle in strife-ridden El Salvador, this compelling drama has James Woods and James Belushi as a pair of not-completely likeable newsmen. Slowly their indifference to the people of El Salvador changes as the brutality of the regime and the right-wing death squads radicalize them.

2572. *Salvation* (1987, B Movies/Circle, 80m, c, aka *Salvation! Have You Said Your Prayers Today?*). P Beth B. & Michael H. Shamberg, D Beth B., W Beth B. & Tom Robinson, PH Francis Kenny, ED Elizabeth Kling, PD Lester Cohen.

LP Stephen McHattie (Rev. Edward Randall), Dominique Davalos (Lenore Finley), Exene Cervenka (Rhonda Stample), Viggo Mortensen (Jerome Stample), Rockets Redglare (Oliver), Billy Bastiani (Stanley).

This black comedy takes on TV evangelism. Stephen McHattie makes the fire-and-brimstone sermons, appealing for money from the unwashed and uneducated out in TV-land. He's a fake with feet of clay, set up by some of his followers for a bit of blackmail.

Salvation: Have You Said Your Prayers Today? see *Salvation*

Sam Marlow: Private Eye see *The Man with Bogart's Face*

2573. *Sammy and Rosie Get Laid* (1987, Cinecom, GB, 97m, c). P Tim Bevan & Sarah Radclyffe, D Stephen Frears, W Hanif Kureishi, PH Oliver Stapleton, M Stanley Myers, ED Mick Audsley, PD Hugo Luczyc Wyhowski.

LP Shashi Kapoor (Rafi), Frances Barber (Rosie), Claire Bloom (Alice), Ayub Khan Din (Sammy), Roland Gift (Danny), Wendy Gazelle (Anna), Suzette Llewellyn (Vivia), Meera Syal (Rani), Badi Uzzaman (Ghost).

Pakistani politician Shashi Kapoor takes up exile in England, which he remembers fondly from times spent there years before. He finds his English mistress Claire Bloom has grown tired of waiting for him. His accountant son Khan Din and the latter's social worker wife Frances Barber sleep only with others, and their neighborhood has erupted into a race riot. Nothing stays the same anymore.

2574. *Sam's Son* (1984, Worldvision/Invictus, 104m, c). P Kent McCray, D&W Michael Landon, PH Ted Voigtlander, M David Rose, ED John Loeffler, AD George Renne.

LP Eli Wallach (Sam Orowitz), Anne Jackson (Harriet Orowitz), Timothy Patrick Murphy (Gene Orowitz), Hallie Todd (Cathy Stanton), Alan Hayes (Robert Woods), Jonna Lee (Bonnie Barnes), Michael Landon (Gene Orman).

Timothy Patrick Murphy's athletic prowess at throwing the javelin opens the door for a Hollywood acting career. Orowitz is the real name of "Bonanza's" and "Little House on the Prairie's" Michael Landon.

2575. *Santa Claus: The Movie* (1985, Tri-Star, 112m, c). P Ilya Salkind & Pierre Spengler, D Jeannot Szwarc, W David Newman (based on a story by David Newman & Leslie Newman), PH Arthur Ibbetson, M Henry Mancini, ED Peter Hollywood, PD Anthony Pratt.

LP Dudley Moore (Patch), John Lithgow (B.Z.), David Huddleston (Claus), Burgess Meredith (Ancient Elf), Judy Cornwell (Anya), Jeffrey Kramer (Towzer), Christian Fitzpatrick (Joe), Carrie Kei Heim (Cornelia).

We suppose this movie featuring Dudley Moore as an elf won't harm anybody but we wouldn't want our granddaughter to see it. Moore leaves the North Pole, gets mixed up with crooked toy manufacturer John Lithgow and needs Santa to straighten things out.

2576. *Satan's Mistress* (1982, Motion Picture Marketing, 91m, c, aka *Fury of the Succubus; Demon Rage; Dark Eyes*). P James Polakof & Beverly Johnson, D Polakof, W Polakof & Johnson, PH James L. Carter, M Roger Kellaway, ED George Trirogoff, AD Fred Cutter & John Flaherty, SE Karen Kubeck, Dennis Dion & Tom Shouse.

LP Britt Ekland (Anne-Marie), Lana Wood (Lisa), Kabir Bedi (The Spirit), Don Galloway (Carl), John Carradine (Father Stratton), Sherry Scott (Michelle), Elise-Anne (Belline), Chris Polakof (Cissy), Howard Murphy (The Beast).

Neglected housewife Britt Ekland comes under the power of a demented lover.

2577. *Satisfaction* (1988, 20th Century-Fox, 92m, c). P Aaron Spelling & Alan Greisman, D Joan Freeman, W

Charles Purpura, PH Thomas Del Ruth, M Michel Colombier, ED Joel Goodman, PD Lynda Paradise.

LP Justine Bateman (Jennie Lee), Liam Neeson (Martin Falcon), Trini Alvarado (May "Mooch" Stark), Scott Coffey (Nickie Longo), Britta Phillips (Billy Swan), Julia Roberts (Daryle Shane), Debbie Harry (Tina), Chris Nash (Frankie Malloy).

In this bomb, four girls and a guy form a garage rock 'n' roll band. They get their first professional gig at a seaside resort owned by Liam Neeson, once a Grammy-winning songwriter. The five musicians crash in one small room and the film makes as much of the sleeping arrangements as it can before going on to pairing everyone in more equitable proportions.

2578. *Saturday the 14th* (1981, New World, 75m, c). P Julie Corman & Jeff Begun, D&W Howard R. Cohen (based on a story by Begun), PH Daniel Lacambre, ED Joanne D'Antonio & Kent Beyda, AD Arlene Alen.

LP Richard Benjamin (John), Paula Prentiss (Mary), Severn Darden (Van Helsing), Jeffrey Tambor (Waldemar), Kari Michaelsen (Debbie), Kevin Brando (Billy), Nancy Lee Andrews (Yolanda), Craig Coulter (Duane).

If the intent of this spoof of holiday slasher movies was to put them to rest, it failed miserably. As a comedy, it wasn't very funny either.

2579. *Saturday the 14th Strikes Back* (1988, Concorde, 78m, c). P Julie Corman, D&W Howard R. Cohen, PH Levie Isaacks, M Parmer Fuller, ED Bernard Caputo.

LP Ray Walston (Gramps), Jason Presson (Eddie Baxter), Avery Schreiber (Frank), Patty McCormack (Kate), Julianne McNamara (Linda), Rhonda Aldrich (Alice), Daniel Will-Harris (Bert), Pamela Stonebrook (Charlene).

More is less in this sequel to the 1981 turkey. This dimwitted spoof of horror movies has an assortment of monsters attacking Presson on his birthday.

2580. *Saturn 3* (1980, Associated Film Distributors, 88m, c). P&D Stanley Donen, W Martin Amis (based on the story by John Barry), PH Billy Williams, M Elmer Bernstein, ED Richard Marden, PD Stuart Craig.

LP Farrah Fawcett (Alex), Kirk Douglas (Adam), Harvey Keitel (Benson), Douglas Lambert (Capt. James), Ed Bishop (Harding), Christopher Muncke (2nd Crewman).

Research scientists Farrah Fawcett and Kirk Douglas create a futuristic Garden of Eden in an isolated part of the solar system. Their tranquility is interrupted with the arrival of crazed scientist Harvey Keitel and his eight-foot robot who lusts after Fawcett.

2581. *Savage Beach* (1989, Malibu Bay, 95m, c). P Arlene Sidaris, D&W Andy Sidaris, PH Howard Wexler, M Gary Stockdale, ED Michael Haight, PD Jimmy Hadder.

LP Dona Speir (Donna), Hope Marie Carlton (Taryn), John Aprea (Capt. Andreas), Bruce Penhall (Bruce Christian), Rodrigo Obregon (Martinez), Michael Mikasa (Japanese Warrior), Michael Shaner (Shane Abilene).

Government drug enforcement officers Dona Spier and Hope Marie Carlton's plane crashlands on a remote island where numerous opposing forces are searching for a cache of gold stolen from the Philippines by the Japanese in 1943.

2582. *Savage Dawn* (1984, Media Home Ent., 102m, c). D Simon Nuchtern, W William P. Milling, PH Gerald Feil, ED Gerald B. Greenberg.

LP George Kennedy (Tick Rand), Lance Henriksen (Ben Stryker), Karen Black, Richard Lynch, Claudia Udy.

A group of motorcycle creeps terrorize a small Southern town, until a macho hero stomps their asses.

2583. *Savage Harvest* (1981, 20th Century-Fox, 87m, c). P Ralph Helfer, Sandy Howard & Lamar Card, D Robert Collins, W Collins & Robert Blees (based on a story by Helfer & Ken Noyle), PH Ronnie Taylor, M Robert Folk, ED Patrick Kennedy & Scott Wallace, PD Brian Eatwell.

LP Tom Skerritt (Casey), Michelle Phillips (Maggie), Shawn Stevens (Jon), Anne-Marie Martin (Wendy), Derek Partridge (Derek), Arthur Malet (Dr. MacGruder), Tana Helfer (Kristie), Vincent Isaac (Jurogi).

In this scary but senseless film, lions prey on Tom Skerritt, Michelle Phillips and some children in Africa.

2584. *Savage Island* (1985, Empire, US/Ital./Span., 74m, c). P Robert Amante & Mark Alabiso, D Edward Muller & Nicholas Beardsley, W Michelle Tomski & Beardsley, M Mark Ryder, ED Tomski.

LP Linda Blair (Daly), Anthony Steffen (Laredo), Ajita Wilson (Marie), Christina Lai (Muriel), Leon Askin (Luker).

Linda Blair, a former inmate of a brutal South American labor camp, escapes and takes revenge.

Savage Islands see Nate and Hayes

2585. *Savage Streets* (1984, Motion Picture Marketing, 93m, c). P John C. Strong III, D Danny Steinmann, W Norman Yonemoto & Steinmann, PH Stephen Posey, M Michael Lloyd & John D'Andrea, ED Bruce Stubblefield & John O'Connor, AD Ninkey Dalton.

LP Linda Blair (Brenda), John Vernon (Principal Underwood), Robert Dryer (Jake), Johnny Venocur (Vince), Sal Landi (Fargo), Scott Mayer (Red), Debra Blee (Rachel), Lisa Freeman (Francine), Linnea Quigley (Heather).

Linda Blair, wearing a revealing commando outfit and a crossbow, leads a no-nonsense girl gang called the "Satins." They teach a lesson to the "Scars," a male gang, led by Robert Dryer, which gang-raped Blair's deafmute sister.

Savage Sunday see Low Blow

2586. *Savage Weekend* (1983, Cannon, 83m, c, aka *The Killer Behind the Mask; The Upstate Murders*). P John Mason Kirby & David Paulsen, D&W Paulsen, PH Zoli Vidor, M Dov Seltzer, ED Zion Avrahamian & Jonathan Day.

LP Christopher Allport (Nicky), James Doerr (Robert), Marilyn Hamlin (Marie), Kathleen Heaney (Shirley), David Gale (Mac), Devin Goldenberg (Jay), Jeffrey David Pomerantz (Greg), William Sanderson (Otis).

Originally filmed in 1976, this soft-core porno horror film was briefly released in 1981 and re-released in 1983. Two families visit upstate New York for a weekend and are picked off one-by-one.

2587. *Savannah Smiles* (1983, Gold Coast, 104m, c). P Clark L. Paylow, D Pierre DeMoro, W Mark Miller (based on his story), PH Stephen W. Gray, M Ken Sutherland, ED Eva Ruggiero, PD Charles Stewart.

LP Mark Miller (Alvie), Donovan Scott (Boots), Bridgette Andersen (Savannah Driscoll), Peter Graves (Harland Dobbs), Chris Robinson (Richard Driscoll), Michael Parks (Lt. Savage), Barbara Stanger (Joan Driscoll), Pat Morita (Father O'Hara), Philip Abbott (Chief Pruitt).

Six-year-old runaway Bridgette Andersen befriends two escaped convicts, Mark Miller and Donovan Scott. Their plans to hold her for ransom go out the window when this cute little tyke smiles at them.

2588. *Saving Grace* (1986, Embassy, 112m, c). P Herbert Solow, D Robert M. Young, W David S. Ward & Richard Kramer (based on the novel by Celia Gittelson), PH Reynaldo Villalobos, ED Peter Zinner, PD Giovanni Natalucci.

LP Tom Conti (Pope Leo XIV), Giancarlo Giannini (Abalardi), Erland Josephson (Monsignor Francesco Ghezzi), Fernando Rey (Cardinal Stefano Biondi), Patricia Mauceri (Lucia Fedelia), Edward James Olmos (Ciolino).

This man-of-the-people pope (Tom Conti) leaves the Vatican one day and ends up in a remote village which has no priest. Everyone pretends to be quarantined in order to receive relief money. The Pope's absence is kept from the world until he's able to redeem the townspeople.

2589. *Say Anything* (1989, 20th Century-Fox, 100m, c). P Polly Platt, D&W Cameron Crowe, PH Laszlo Kovacs, M Richard Gibbs & Anne Dudley, ED Richard Marks, PD Mark Mansbridge.

LP John Cusack (Lloyd Dobler), Ione Skye (Diane Court), John Mahoney (James Court), Lili Taylor (Corey Flood), Amy Brooks (D.C.), Pamela Segall (Rebecca), Jason Gould (Mike Cameron), Loren Dean (Joe), Glenn Walker Harris, Jr. (Jason).

John Cusack, an appealing young actor, usually plays appealing young men. This film is no exception. He's an aimless high school jock with no plans until he falls for beautiful Ione Skye, a cool princess type and class valedictorian. Can this relationship work? What a silly question. It's good escapism.

2590. *Say Yes* (1986, CineTel, 90m, c). P Rosemary Le Roy Layng & Larry Yust, D&W Yust, PH Isidore Mankofsky, ED Margaret Morrison.

LP Jonathan Winters (W.D. Westmoreland), Art Hindle (Luke), Lissa Layng (Annie), Logan Ramsey (George), Maryedith Burrell (Gladys), Jensen Collier (Belinda), Jacque Lynn Colton (Message Taker), Devon Ericson (Cynthia), Art La Fleur (Ernest), John Milford (Sailor), Laurie Prange (First Bride), Anne Ramsey (Major).

When multimillionaire Jonathan Winters dies, he leaves his fortune to his son Art Hindle on the condition that he marry before his 35th birthday, just one day away. He finds a bride and love with Lissa Layng just in the nick of time.

2591. *Scalps* (1983, 21st Century, 82m, c). P The Eel (T.L. Lankford), D&W Fred Olen Ray, PH Brett Webster & Larry van Loon, M Drew Neumann & Eric Rasmussen, ED John Barr.

LP Kirk Alyn (Dr. Howard Machen), Carroll Borland (Dr. Reynolds), Jo Ann Robinson (D.J.), Richard Hench (Randy), Roger Maycock (Kershaw), Barbara Magnusson (Ellen), Frank McDonald (Ben), Carol Sue Flockhart (Louise).

In this horribly amateurish film, a group of teens stir up the spirit of an Indian warrior when they mess around in a sacred burial ground.

2592. *Scandal* (1989, Miramax, GB, 106m, c). P Stephen Woolley, D Michael Caton-Jones, W Michael Thomas, PH Michael Molloy, M Carl Davis, ED Angus Newton, PD Simon Holland.

LP John Hurt (Stephen Ward), Joanne Whalley-Kilmer (Christine Keeler), Bridget Fonda (Mandy Rice-Davies), Ian McKellen (John Profumo), Leslie Phillips (Lord Astor), Britt Ekland (Mariella Novotny), Daniel Massey (Mervyn Griffith-Jones), Jeroen Krabbe (Eugene Ivanov), Deborah Grant (Valerie Hobson Profumo).

Ambitious London osteopath Dr. Stephen Ward (John Hurt) finds ways to ingratiate himself with the high born and powerful of British society. One method is to introduce the powerful and rich to the young and beautiful, such as Christine Keeler (Joanne Whalley-Kilmer). This compelling examination of the affair with Keeler of John Profumo (Ian McKellen), the Secretary of State for War under Harold Macmillan, makes Hurt out to be a victim rather than the villain of the scandal as he was painted by the real-life press in 1963. Whatever the truth, Ward took his own life. Hurt is an extraordinary actor, particularly adept at portraying flawed men such as Ward.

2593. *Scandalous* (1984, GB, Orion, 92m, c). P Arlene Sellers & Alex Winitsky, D Rob Cohen, W Cohen & John Byrum (based on a story by Byrum, Rob Cohen & Larry Cohen), PH Jack Cardiff, M Dave Grusin, ED Michael Bradsell, PD Peter Mullins.

LP Robert Hays (Frank Swedlin), Pamela Stephenson (Fiona Maxwell Sayle), Ron Travis (Porno Director), M. Emmet Walsh (Simon Reynolds), John Gielgud (Uncle Willie), Ed Dolan (Purser), Paul Reeve (Flight Coordinator).

Bungling American TV reporter Robert Hays becomes involved with a gang of British con artists led by Pamela Stephenson and John Gielgud. They see to it that he is framed for the murder of his wife.

2594. *Scanners* (1981, Avco Embassy, Canada, 102m, c). P Claude Heroux, D&W David Cronenberg, PH Mark Irwin, M Howard Shore, ED Ron Sanders, AD Carol Spier, SE Dick Smith, Gary Zeller, Henry Pierrig & Chris Walas.

LP Stephen Lack (Cameron Vale), Jennifer O'Neill (Kim), Patrick McGoohan (Dr. Paul Ruth), Lawrence Dane (Keller), Charles Shamata (Gaudi), Adam Ludwig (Crostic), Michael Ironside (Darryl Revok), Victor Desy (Dr. Gatineau).

"Scanners" are mutants born to pregnant women who had been given a thalidomide-like drug. The Scanners are able to will other people to literally explode. Some plan to use this power for evil purposes. Well, who would've have thought it?

2595. *Scarecrows* (1988, Effigy/Forum, 88m, c). P Cami Winikoff &

William Wesley, D Wesley, W Richard Jefferies & Wesley (based on a story by Wesley), PH Peter Deming, M Terry Plumeri, ED Wesley, SE J.B. Jones & Norman Cabrera.

LP Ted Vernon (Corbin), Michael Simms (Curry), Richard Vidan (Jack), Kristina Sanborn (Roxanne), Victoria Christian (Kellie), David Campbell (Al), B.J. Turner (Bert), Dax Vernon (Dax the Dog).

The film starts with a group of paramilitary types pulling off a heist at a Marine base, hijacking a plane, kidnapping the pilot and his daughter, and then being double-crossed by one of their numbers. The real meat is about mysterious scarecrows who kill their victims with scythes. When the jolly little band of mercenaries land their plane in a remote area with only one abandoned house around, the battle is joined.

2596. Scared to Death (1981, Lone Star, 95m, c, aka *The Terror Factor*). P Rand Marlis & Gil Shelton, D&W William Malone, PH Patrick Prince, M Tom Chase & Ardell Hake, ED Warren Chadwick, SE Malone & Robert Short.

LP John Stinson (Ted Lonergan), Diana Davidson (Jennifer Stanton), Jonathan David Moses (Lou Capell), Toni Jannotta (Sherry Carpenter), Kermit Eller (Syngenor), Walker Edmiston, Pamela Bowman.

Police inspector David Moses and ex-cop John Stinson had never seen murder victims like this before. Their bodies have been mutilated. Well, what do you expect, their killer isn't human. . . .

The Scaremaker* see *Girls Night Out

2597. Scarface (1983, Universal, 170m, c). P Martin Bregman & Peter Saphier, D Brian De Palma, W Oliver Stone (based on the 1932 script by Ben Hecht), PH John A. Alonzo, M Giorgio Moroder, ED Jerry Greenberg & David Ray, AD Ed Richardson.

LP Al Pacino (Tony Montana), Steven Bauer (Manny Ray), Michelle Pfeiffer (Elvira), Mary Elizabeth Mastrantonio (Gina), Robert Loggia (Frank Lopez), Miriam Colon (Mama Montana), F. Murray Abraham (Omar), Paul Shenar (Alejandro Sosa), Harris Yulin (Bernstein), Angel Salazar (Chi Chi).

Optimists tend to have high expectations for updated reworkings of film classics, especially when the production has the cast and crew of this film. This said, we must report that this remake of the 1932 film *Scarface* starring Paul Muni is a ghastly bomb. The extra 71 minutes is not used to advantage. It only gives Cuban refugee Al Pacino, who works his way up to becoming a major Miami drug lord, a greater opportunity to exhibit his foul-mouthed vocabulary. The film's grisly scenes put the various splatter exploitation films to shame. It seems that the spilling of blood and guts in various nauseatingly cruel ways takes the place of story and acting. We don't so much object to director Brian De Palma's making a movie for sickies, but it's so poorly done.

2598. Scarred (1984, Seymour Borde, 85m, c, aka *Red on Red; Street Love*). P Marie Turko, Mark Borde & Dan Halperine, D&W Turko, PH Michael Miner, ED Turko, AD Cecilia Rodarte.

LP Jennifer Mayo (Ruby Star), Jackie Berryman (Carla), David Dean (Easy), Rico L. Richardson (Jojo), Debbie Dion (Sandy), Lili (Rita), Randolph Pitts & Walter Klenhard (Tricks).

In order to support her baby, unwed mother Jennifer Mayo turns to street prostitution. It's an honest look at a seedy life but budget restrictions hurt it.

2599. Scavengers (1988, Anglo Pacific/Triax, 94m, c). P Chris Davies & David Barrett, D&W Duncan McLachlan, PH Johan Van Der Veer, M Nick Picard & Ferdi Brendgen, ED C.J. Appel, PD Roy Rudolphe.

LP Kenneth David Gilman (Tom Reed), Brenda Bakke (Kimberly Blake), Crispin De Nys (Col. Chenko), Cocky "Two-Bull" Tihothalemaj (February), Norman Anstey (Boris), Somizi Mhlongo (Jeffrey), Patrick Mynhart (Pavloski).

Ornithologist Kenneth David Gilman, known as the "Vulture Man," is mistaken for a government agent. He soon finds himself in Africa with his former girlfriend Brenda Bakke being chased by both Russian agents and drug-runners.

2600. Scenes from the Class Struggle in Beverly Hills (1989, Cinecom, 102m, c).

P James C. Katz. D Paul Bartel, W Bruce Wagner (based on a story by Bartel & Wagner), PH Steven Fierberg, M Stanley Myers, ED Alan Toomayan, PD Alex Tavoularis.

LP Jacqueline Bisset (Clare), Ray Sharkey (Frank), Robert Beltran (Juan), Mary Woronov (Lisabeth), Ed Begley, Jr. (Peter), Wallace Shawn (Howard), Arnetia Walker (To-bel), Paul Mazursky (Sidney), Rebecca Schaeffer (Zandra), Edith Diaz (Rosa), Paul Bartel (Dr. Mo Van de Kamp).

This farce from the maker of *Eating Raoul,* like that black comedy, is a series of comical set pieces with a great number of funny lines, but no cohesive plot. It's really more the presentation of a group of unusual characters interacting in strange but amusing ways. It definitely isn't for every one, but if camp is your ticket, it might please.

2601. *Scenes from the Goldmine* (1988, Hemdale, 105m, c). P Danny Eisenberg, Marc Rocco & Pierre David, D Rocco, W Rocco, John Norvet & Danny Eisenberg, PH Cliff Ralke, M Steve Delacy, Rocco & Eisenberg, ED Russell Livingstone, PD Matthew Jacobs.

LP Catherine Mary Stewart (Debi Di-Angelo), Cameron Dye (Niles Dresden), Steve Railsback (Harry), Joe Pantoliano (Manny), John Ford Coley (Kenny Bond), Timothy B. Schmit (Dennis), Alex Rocco (Nathan DiAngelo).

Things are not all peaches and cream in the rock 'n' roll world. Promising female keyboardist/songwriter Catherine Mary Stewart has a hellish time when her unscrupulous manager convinces band leader Cameron Dye and Stewart's current lover to take credit for the songs she's written.

2602. *Schizoid* (1980, Cannon, 91m, c, aka *Murder by Mail*). P Menahem Golan & Yoram Globus, D&W David Paulsen, PH Norman Leigh, M Craig Hundley, ED Robert Fitzgerald & Dick Brummer, AD Kathy Curtis Cahill.

LP Klaus Kinski (Dr. Peter Fales), Marianna Hill (Julie), Craig Wasson (Doug), Donna Wilkes (Alison Fales), Richard Herd (Donahue), Joe Regalbuto (Jake), Christopher Lloyd (Gilbert), Flo Gerrish (Pat).

One-by-one, the nubile young women who make up psychiatrist Klaus Kinski's group-therapy patients are being slashed by someone wielding a pair of scissors. These same cutting instruments are being used to cut out letters for a correspondence between the killer and advice columnist Marianna Hill, who just happens to be a member of the therapy group.

2603. *School Daze* (1988, Columbia, 120m, c). P,D&W Spike Lee, PH Ernest Dickerson, M Bill Lee, ED Barry Alexander Brown, PD Wynn Thomas.

LP Larry Fishburne (Dap Dunlap), Giancarlo Esposito (Julian "Big Brother Almighty" Eaves), Tisha Campbell (Jane Toussaint), Kyme (Rachel Meadows), Joe Seneca (President McPherson), Art Evans (Cedar Cloud), Ellen Holly (Odrie McPherson), Ossie Davis (Coach Odom), Spike Lee (Half-Pint), Gregg Burge (Virgil Cloyd).

Spike Lee shows a split in the attitudes of blacks by examining the social and political divisions of two fraternities in a fictional Southern black school. The dark-skinned "Jigaboos" want total and immediate divestment of the school's South African investments, and the light-skinned "Wannabees" (wanna be white) favor a more gradual approach.

2604. *School Spirit* (1985, Concorde, 90m, c). P Ashok Amritraj & Jeff Begun, D Alan Holleb, PH Robert Ebinger, M Tom Bruner, ED Sonya Sones, PD Peter Knowlton.

LP Tom Nolan (Billy Batson), Elizabeth Foxx (Judith Hightower), Larry Linville (President Grimshaw), Daniele Arnaud (Madeleine), Nick Segal (Gregg), Marta Kober (Ursula), Robert Collins (Helen Grimshaw).

Racing his car to get back to campus for an assignation with sorority cutey Elizabeth Foxx, Tom Nolan runs into a truck and is killed. Game fellow, he gets up and portrays his ghost for the rest of the movie. He especially enjoys his ability to be seen or not at will as he roams the sorority shower room. Try and imagine a ghostly *Porky's* and you have the idea.

2605. *Scorpion* (1986, Crown Intl., 98m, c, aka *The Summons*). P,D&W William Riead, PH Bill Philbin, M Sean Murray, ED Gigi Coello.

LP Tommy Tulleners (Steve), Don Murray (Gifford), Robert Logan (Gordon), Allen Williams (Keller), Kathryn Daley (Jackie), Ross Elliott (Sam), John Anderson (Neal), Bart Braverman (Mehdi), Thom McFadden (Lt. Woodman).

Tommy Tulleners, a martial arts expert who takes on a bunch of terrorists, makes other martial arts actors look like Lord Olivier.

2606. *Scream* (1985, Vestron, 81m, c, aka *The Outing*). P Clara Huff, Hal Buchanan & Larry Quisenberry, D&W Byron Quisenberry, PH Rick Pepin, M Joseph Conlan, ED B.W. Kestenberg.

LP Pepper Martin (Bob), Hank Worden (John), Alvy Moore (Al), John Ethan Wayne (Stan), Julie Marine (Laura), Gregg Palmer (Ross), Woody Strode (Charlie).

Vacationers in a western ghost town are bumped off one-by-one. It's a slow-moving, lifeless squandering of film.

2607. *Scream for Help* (1984, Lorimar, 88m, c). P&D Michael Winner, W Tom Holland, PH Robert Paynter, M John Paul Jones, ED Arnold Ross, AD Tony Reading.

LP Rachel Kelly (Christie Cromwell), Marie Masters (Karen Cromwell Fox), David Brooks (Paul Fox), Lolita Lorre (Brenda Bohle), Rocco Sisto (Lacey Bohle), Corey Parker (John Dealey), Sandra Clark (Janey).

Rachel Kelly can't get the police to take seriously her fears that her stepfather David Brooks is plotting to kill her mother Marie Masters, even when a couple of murder traps kill two innocent parties by mistake.

2608. *Screamplay* (1985, Boston Movie Co., 90m, b&w). P Dennis M. Piana, D Rufus Butler Seder, W Seder & Ed Greenberg, PH Piana, M George Cordeiro & Basil J. Bova, ED Seder, AD Cheryl Hirschman.

LP Rufus Butler Seder (Edgar Allen), George Kuchar (Holly), George Cordeiro (Sgt. Joe Blatz), Basil J. Bova (Tony Cassano), M. Lynder Robinson (Mina Ray), Eugene Seder (Al Weiner).

It's just one more low-budget horror film featuring a crazy killer.

2609. *Screamtime* (1986, Rugged Films, GB, 89m, c). P&D Al Beresford, W Michael Armstrong, PH Don Lord, Alain Pudney & Mike Spera, M KPM, ED Uncredited.

LP Robin Bailey (Jack Grimshaw), Ann Lynn (Lena), Ian Saynor (Tony), Yvonne Nicholson (Susan), David Van Day (Gavin), Dora Bryan (Emma).

When two fiendish friends swipe some horror videos, strange things happen after they watch them.

2610. *Screen Test* (1986, CinTel Films, 88m, c). P&W Sam Auster & Laura Auster, D Sam Auster, PH Jeff Jur, M Don Harrow, ED Carol Eastman.

LP Michael Allan Bloom (Terry), Monique Gabrielle (Roxanne), David Simpatico (Stevie), Paul Leuken (Dan), William Dick (Dr. DeSade), Robert Bundy (Clayton).

Four horny teen boys arrange for phony porno video screen tests to attract girls. The casting call is a mixed bag — the Mafia princess causes the most trouble for our heroes.

2611. *Screwball Hotel* (1989, Universal, US/GB, 101m, c). P Maurice Smith, D Rafal Zielinski, W B.K. Roderick, Phil Kueber, Charles Wiener & Nick Holeris, PH Thomas F. De Nove, M Nathan Wang, ED Joseph Tornatore, PD Naomi Shohan.

LP Michael C. Bendetti (Mike), Jeff Greenman (Norman), Andrew Zeller (Herbie), Kelly Monteith (Mr. Ebbel), Corinne Alphen (Cherry Amour), Charles Ballinger (Stoner), Laurah Guillen (Miss Walsh).

Michael C. Bendetti, Jeff Greenman and Andrew Zeller are loose in a resort setting, surrounded by beautiful girls. They work for the Rochester Hotel, which they try to save from being taken over by corrupt schemer Charles Ballinger. They come up with some bizarre fundraising techniques, not all legal.

2612. *Screwballs* (1983, New World, 80m, c). P Maurice Smith, D Rafal Zielinski, W Linda Shayne & Jim Wynorski, PH Miklos Lente, M Tim McCauley, ED Brian Ravok, AD Sandra Kybartas.

LP Peter Keleghan (Rick McKay), Linda Speciale (Purity Busch), Alan

Daveau (Howie Bates), Kent Deuters (Brent Van Dusen, III), Jason Warren (Melvin Jerkovski), Linda Shayne (Bootsie Goodhead), Jim Coburn (Tim Stevenson).

A group of teenage boys at T&A High go *Porky's* one better. Their sport is strip bowling. They also cause a lot of trouble for the school's snooty and virginal homecoming queen, Linda Speciale.

2613. *Scrooged* (1988, Paramount, 101m, c). P Richard Donner, Art Linson & Ray Hartwick, D Donner, W Mitch Glazer & Michael O'Donoghue, PH Michael Chapman, M Danny Elfman, ED Fredric Steinkamp & William Steinkamp, PD J. Michael Riva, MK Tom Burman & Bari Dreiband-Burman†.

LP Bill Murray (Frank Cross), Karen Allen (Claire Phillips), John Forsythe (Lew Hayward), John Glover (Brice Cummings), Bobcat Goldthwait (Eliot Loudermilk), David Johansen (Ghost of Christmas Past), Carol Kane (Ghost of Christmas Present), Robert Mitchum (Preston Rhinelander), Nicholas Phillips (Calvin Cooley), Michael J. Pollard (Herman).

Bill Murray, a cynical TV network executive, has lost the meaning of Christmas. While overseeing a production of Dickens' *A Christmas Carol,* three ghostly figures from the past, present and future arrive to rekindle the spirit within him. Give us Alastair Sim if you don't mind.

2614. *Scrubbers* (1984, Orion, GB, 90m, c). P Don Boyd, D Mai Zetterling, W Zetterling, Roy Minton & Jeremy Watt, PH Ernest Vincze, M Michael Hurd & Ray Cooper, ED Rodney Holland, AD Celia Barnett.

LP Amanda York (Carol), Chrissie Cotterill (Annetta), Elizabeth Edmonds (Kathleen), Kate Ingram (Eddie), Debbie Bishop (Doreen), Dana Gillespie (Budd), Camille Davis (Sharon), Amanda Symonds (Mac), Kathy Burke (Glennis).

This is an unflinching look at British girls' reform schools. Amanda York is the naive youngster who is the target of the obligatory lesbian.

2615. *Scum* (1980, World Northal, GB, 96m, c). P Davina Belling & Clive Parsons, D Alan Clarke, W Roy Minton, PH Phil Meheux, ED Mike Bradsell, AD Mike Porter.

LP Ray Winstone (Carlin), Mick Ford (Archer), John Judd (Sands), Phil Daniels (Richards), John Blundell (Banks), Ray Burdis (Eckersley), Julian Firth (Davis), Alrick Riley (Angel), John Fowler (Woods).

Transferred to a rough and tough prison for his rebellious behavior, Ray Winstone runs afoul of John Blundell who violently attacks the newcomer. Winstone befriends Mick Ford, an older con, and eventually leads the prisoners in a riot to protest conditions.

2616. *Sea of Love* (1989, Universal, 110m, c). P Martin Bregman & Louis A. Stroller, D Harold Becker, W Richard Price, PH Ronnie Taylor, M Trevor Jones, ED David Bretherton, PD John Jay Moore.

LP Al Pacino (Frank Keller), Ellen Barkin (Helen), John Goodman (Sherman), Michael Rooker (Terry), William Hickey (Frank, Sr.), Richard Jenkins (Gruber), Paul Calderon (Serafino), Gene Canfield (Struk), Barbara Baxley (Miss Allen), Jacqueline Brookes (Helen's Mother).

Lonely cop Al Pacino drinks too much and is essentially an emotional and physical wreck. He and his partner John Goodman are working on a case of murders committed by someone who is ridding the world of womanizers who meet females by answering ads in personal columns. Each man has been found face down on a bed, nude, with fatal wounds in his back. Pacino and Goodman put their own ads in the personal columns to see what they can come up with. The chief suspect among the respondents is Ellen Barkin who also seems the most likely solution to Pacino's loneliness. Unfortunately Pacino makes very few movies and when he does, fans hope they will be better than this sluggish, long-winded puffball.

2617. *The Sea Wolves* (1981, Paramount, GB, 120m, c). P Euan Lloyd, D Andrew V. McLaglen, W Reginald Rose (based on the novel *The Boarding Party* by James Leasor), PH Tony Imi, M Roy Budd, ED John Glen, PD Syd Cain.

LP Gregory Peck (Col. Lewis Pugh), Roger Moore (Capt. Gavin Stewart), David Niven (Col. Bill Grice), Trevor Howard (Jack Cartwright), Barbara Kellerman (Mrs. Cromwell), Patrick MacNee (Maj. Yogi Crossley), Patrick Allen (Colin MacKenzie), Bernard Archard (Underhill).

Gregory Peck leads a fine cast in this wartime true-story thriller about a commando style operation undertaken in 1943 India by a group of middle-aged boozing British businessmen.

2618. *Search and Destroy* (1981, Film Ventures, 93m, c). P James Margellos, D William Fruet, W Don Enright, PH Rene Verzier, M FM, ED Donald Ginsberg.

LP Perry King (Kip Moore), Don Stroud (Buddy Grant), Tisa Farrow (Kate), Park Jong Soo (Assassin), George Kennedy (Anthony Fusqua), Tony Sheer (Frank Malone).

After the Vietnam war, a Vietnamese official left behind by the U.S. troops during the evacuation travels to the U.S. to get revenge for his abandonment.

Search for the Mother Lode see Mother Lode

Searchers of the Voodoo Mountain see Warriors of the Apocalypse

2619. *Season of Fear* (1989, MGM/ United Artists, 89m, c). P Scott J. Mulvaney, D Doug Campbell, W Campbell (based on a story by Campbell & Mulvaney), PH Chuy Elizondo, M David Wolinski, ED Dan Selakovich, PD Phillip Michael Brandes.

LP Michael Bowen (Mick Drummond), Ray Wise (Fred Drummond), Clancy Brown (Ward), Clara Wren (Sarah Drummond), Michael J. Pollard (Bob).

Even though Michael Bowen's father Ray Wise left him and his mother 20 years earlier, the bitter and resentful son responds positively when his father invites him for a visit. When Bowen arrives for the weekend, there's no sign of his father, but beautiful blond Clara Wren makes him feel right at home in her bed. She's his stepmother and has some plans for him and his father, à la *Body Heat*.

2620. *Second-Hand Hearts* (1981, Paramount, 102m, c). P James William Guercio, D Hal Ashby, W Charles Eastman, PH Haskell Wexler, M Willis Alan Ramsey, ED Amy Holden Jones, PD Peter Wooley.

LP Robert Blake (Loyal Muke), Barbara Harris (Dinette Dusty), Collin Boone (Human), Amber Rose Gold (Iota), Jessica Stansbury & Erica Stansbury (Sandra Dee), Bert Remsen (Voyd), Sondra Blake (Ermy), Shirley Stoler (Maxy).

Robert Blake and Barbara Harris are two dumb Texans, who meet, marry and decide that they can find more happiness in California, so they travel there. Along the way they see a bit of the country and a few characters. Something's missing here.

2621. *Second Sight* (1989, Warner, 83m, c). P Mark Tarlov, D Joel Zwick, W Tom Schulman & Patricia Resnick, PH Dana Christiaansen, M John Morris, ED David Ray, PD James L. Schoppe.

LP John Larroquette (Wills), Bronson Pinchot (Bobby McGee), Stuart Pankin (Dr. Preston Pickett), Bess Armstrong (Sister Elizabeth), John Schuck (Lt. Manoogian), James Tolkan (Captain Coolidge), Christine Estabrook (Priscilla).

TV comedians John Larroquette ("Night Court") and Bronson Pinchot ("Perfect Strangers") haven't altered their characters much for their roles in this not-so-funny story. Upon being hit by lightning simple-minded Pinchot becomes a psychic who is exploited by his misanthropic business partner Larroquette.

2622. *Second Thoughts* (1983, Universal, 98m, c). P Lawrence Turman & David Foster, D Turman, W Steve Brown (based on a story by Brown & Terry Louise Fisher), PH King Baggot, M Henry Mancini, ED Neil Travis, PD Paul Peters.

LP Lucie Arnaz (Amy), Craig Wasson (Will), Ken Howard (John Michael), Anne Schedeen (Janis), Arthur Rosenberg (Dr. Eastman), Peggy McCay (Dr. Martha Carpenter), Tammy Taylor (Sharon), Alan Stock (Hondo).

Frustrated attorney Lucie Arnaz divorces her husband Ken Howard to move in with one of her hippie clients Craig Wasson. She soon finds the new relationship isn't working out and leaves him. When she finds she's pregnant and opts for an abortion, Wasson kidnaps her to prevent it.

2623. *Second Time Lucky* (1984, United International, Australia/New Zealand, 98m, c). P Anthony I. Ginnane, D Michael Anderson, W Ross Dimsey, David Sigmund & Howard Grigsby (based on a story by Dimsey & Sigmund), PH John McLean, M Garry McDonald & Laurie Stone, ED Terry Paterson, PD David Copping.

LP Diane Franklin (Eve), Roger Wilson (Adam), Robert Helpmann (The Devil), Jon Gadsby (Gabriel), John-Michael Howson (The Devil's Assistant), Bill Ewens (Chuck), Robert Morley (God).

The devil makes a bet with God that if the world were to start over again, Adam and Eve would make the same mistake. Sounds like a sucker bet to us.

2624. *Secret Admirer* (1985, Orion, 98m, c). P Stephen J. Roth & Jim Kouf, D David Greenwalt, W Kouf & Greenwalt, PH Victor J. Kemper, M Jan Hammer, ED Dennis Virkler, PD William J. Cassidy.

LP C. Thomas Howell (Michael Ryan), Lori Loughlin (Toni), Kelly Preston (Debora Anne Fimple), Dee Walker Stone (Connie Ryan), Cliff De Young (George Ryan), Fred Ward (Lou Fimple), Leigh Taylor-Young (Elizabeth Fimple), Casey Siemaszko (Roger Despard).

Teen Lori Loughlin leaves love notes for C. Thomas Howell but they are misdirected. Loughlin and Howell's respective parents believe that the notes are indications of unfaithlessness of their mates. The story insults the intelligence of even the most hardened teen exploitation fans.

2625. *The Secret Diary of Sigmund Freud* (1984, 20th Century-Fox, 99m, c). P Wendy Hyland & Peer Oppenheimer, D Danford B. Greene, W Roberto Mitrotti & Linda Howard, PH George Nikolic, M V. Boris, AD Miodrag Miric.

LP Bud Cort (Sigmund Freud), Carol Kane (Martha Bernays), Klaus Kinski (Dr. Max Bauer), Marisa Berenson (Emma Herrmann), Carroll Baker (Mama Freud), Dick Shawn (The Ultimate Patient), Ferdinand Mayne (Herr Herrmann), Nikola Simic (Papa Freud), Rade Markovic (Dr. Schtupmann).

In this strange comedy, Bud Cort as Sigmund Freud learns about sex from his mother Carroll Baker, experiments with drugs, and hypnotizes his assistant Carol Kane into falling madly in love with him. The latter becomes extremely jealous of Cort's first patient Marisa Berenson.

2626. *Secret Honor* (1984, Cinecom, 90m, c, aka *Secret Honor: The Last Testament of Richard M. Nixon; Secret Honor: A Political Myth*). P&D Robert Altman, W Donald Freed & Arnold M. Stone (based on their stage play), PH Pierre Mignot, M George Burt, ED Juliet Weber, AD Stephen Altman.

LP Philip Baker Hall (President Richard M. Nixon).

In this scathing portrait of Richard M. Nixon, actor Philip Baker Hall portrays the ex-president pacing around his study, reminiscing and bitterly attacking the memories of politicians with whom he interacted over the years. Even Nixon-haters will find it difficult to enjoy this mean-spirited and malicious film.

Secret Honor: The Last Temptation of Richard M. Nixon see Secret Honor

Secret Honor: A Political Myth see Secret Honor

2627. *The Secret of My Success* (1987, Universal, 110m, c). P&D Herbert Ross, W Jim Cash & Jack Epps, Jr., A.J. Carothers (based on a story by Carothers), PH Carlo Di Palma, M David Foster, ED Paul Hirsch, PD Edward Pisoni, Peter Larkin.

LP Michael J. Fox (Brantley Foster), Helen Slater (Christy Wills), Richard Jordan (Howard Prescott), Margaret Whitton (Vera Prescott), John Pankow (Fred Melrose), Christopher Murney (Barney Rattigan), Gerry Banman (Art Thomas), Fred Gwynne (Donald Davenport).

Michael J. Fox tries to prove that one can succeed in the business world on the basis of talent, not through sleeping your way to the top. He seems defeated by the notion that advancement is made in the sack. He's bedded by Margaret Whitton, his boss' wife, while Helen Slater, the girl of his dreams, is sleeping with his boss, Richard Jordan.

2628. *The Secret of N.I.M.H.* (1982, MGM/United Artists, animated, 82m, c). P Don Bluth, Gary Goldman & John Pomeroy, D Bluth, W Bluth, Goldman, Pomeroy & Will Finn (based on the novel *Mrs. Frisby and the Rats of N.I.M.H.* by Robert C. O'Brien), PH Joe Jiuliano, Charles Warren & Jeff Mellquist, M Jerry Goldsmith, ED Jeffrey Patch.

VOICES Derek Jacobi (Nicodcmus), Elizabeth Hartman (Mrs. Brisby), Arthur Malet (Ages), Dom DeLuise (Jeremy), Hermione Baddeley (Auntie Shrew), John Carradine (Great Owl), Peter Strauss (Justin), Paul Shenar (Jennar).

Disney-trained animators bring to the screen Robert C. O'Brien's charming tale about a newly-widowed mouse and her four little ones that need to be protected from danger. They get some help from escaped laboratory rats with superior intelligence.

2629. *The Secret of the Sword* (1985, Atlantic, animated, 100m, c). P Arthur H. Nadel, D Ed Friedman, Lou Kachivas, Marsh Lamore, Bill Reed & Gwen Wetzler, W Larry Ditillo & Robert Forward, M Shuki Levy, Haim Saban & Erika Lane, ED Joe Gall, Rich Gehr & Robert Crawford.

VOICES John Erwin (He-Man), Melendy Britt (She-Ra), George DiCenzo (Hordak), Linda Gary, Erika Scheimer, Erick Gunden, Alan Oppenheimer.

He-Man must rescue his sister She-Ra from the evil clutches of evil ruler Hordak. Not for anyone over 10 — or under.

2630. *Secret Places* (1984, 20th Century-Fox, GB, 98m, c). P Simon Relph & Ann Skinner, D Zelda Barron, W Barron (based on the novel by Janice Elliott), PH Peter MacDonald, M Michel Legrand, ED Laurence Mery-Clark, PD Eileen Diss.

LP Marie-Theres Relin (Laura Meister), Tara MacGowran (Patience), Claudine Auger (Sophy Meister), Ann-Marie Gwatkin (Rose), Pippa Hinchley (Barbara), Klaus Barner (Wolfgang Meister), Jenny Agutter (Miss Lowrie), Cassie Stuart (Nina), Sylvia Coleridge (Miss Trott), Rosemary Martin (Mrs. MacKenzie).

This drama is the story of the friendship of shy ugly-duckling Tara MacGowran and sophisticated refugee Marie-Theres Relin at a 1942 British girls school. Relin is the daughter of a German gentile couple, forced to flee Nazi Germany when they were denounced by their Hitler Youth son.

2631. *Secrets* (1984, Samuel Goldwyn, GB, 78m, c). P Chris Griffin, D Gavin Millar, W Noella Smith, PH Christopher Challis, M Guy Woolfenden, ED Eric Boyd-Perkins, AD Jeffrey Woolbridge.

LP Helen Lindsay (Mother), John Horsley (Dr. Jefferies), Anna Campbell-Jones (Louise), Daisy Cockburn (Sydney), Rebecca Johnson (Trottie), Lucy Goode (Jane), Richard Tolan (Paul), Carol Gillies (Miss Quick), Jane Briers (Miss Strickland).

Thirteen-year-old Anna Campbell-Jones, an innocent British school girl, is the victim of a mess of misunderstanding when a box of condoms is found in her room.

2632. *The Seduction* (1982, Avco Embassy, 104m, c). P Irwin Yablans & Bruce Cohn Curtis, D&W David Schmoeller, PH Mac Ahlberg, M Lalo Schifrin, ED Tony DiMarco.

LP Morgan Fairchild (Jamie), Michael Sarrazin (Brandon), Vince Edwards (Maxwell), Andrew Stevens (Derek), Colleen Camp (Robin), Kevin Brophy (Bobby), Wendy Smith Howard (Julie), Woodrow Parfrey (Salesman).

Newscaster Morgan Fairchild is stalked and tormented by psychotic photographer Andrew Stevens, obsessed with her beauty.

2633. *Seduction: The Cruel Woman* (1989, First Run Features, Ger., 90m, c). P,D&W Elfi Mikesch & Monika Treut, PH Mikesch, ED Renate Merck.

LP Mechthild Grossmann (Wanda), Carola Regnier (Caren), Udo Kier (Gregor), Sheila McLaughlin (Justine), Georgette Dee (Friederike), Peter Weibel (Herr Marsch).

Mechthild Grossmann runs a sex gallery where her friends and lovers perform S&M scenes for the entertainment of her audiences.

2634. See No Evil, Hear No Evil (1989, Tri-Star, 103m, c). P Marvin Worth, D Arthur Hiller, W Earl Barret, Arne Sultan, Eliot Wald, Andrew Kurtzman & Gene Wilder (based on a story by Barret, Sultan & Worth), PH Victor J. Kemper, M Stewart Copeland, ED Robert C. Jones, PD Robert Gundlach.

LP Richard Pryor (Wally), Gene Wilder (Dave), Joan Severance (Eve), Kevin Spacey (Kirgo), Alan North (Braddock), Anthony Zerbe (Sutherland), Louis Giambalvo (Gatlin), Kirsten Childs (Adele).

Once upon a time Gene Wilder and Richard Pryor appeared together in a movie and were moderately funny together. Ever since they have been trying to recapture that minor glory. Once again they have only partially succeeded. Their movie about deaf Wilder and blind Pryor who somehow complement each other is not this year's *Rain Man*. Somehow the two must solve a murder involving a beautiful woman, whose perfume Pryor remembers and whose legs have made a deep impression on Wilder. Most of the jokes are predictable and fall flat, just short of being offensive and insensitive to the physically challenged.

2635. See You in the Morning (1989, Warner, 116m, c). P,D&W Alan J. Pakula, PH Donald McAlpine, M Michael Small, ED Evan Lottman, PD George Jenkins.

LP Jeff Bridges (Larry Livingston), Alice Krige (Beth Goodwin), Farrah Fawcett (Jo), Drew Barrymore (Cathy), Lukas Haas (Petey), David Dukes (Peter), Frances Sternhagen (Neenie), Linda Lavin (Sidney).

Director Alan J. Pakula's film deals with adjustments which must be made in second marriages while everyone still feels guilty for messing up their first less-than-blissful union. Talented photographer Alice Krige can't forgive herself for her concert pianist husband's taking his own life when he became despondent due to a paralyzed left hand. Psychiatrist Jeff Bridges was married to Farrah Fawcett, America's most famous TV model, and couldn't deal with it. Almost reluctantly Krige and Bridges marry, hoping they and their respective children can suc-

cessfully make the needed adjustments. This romantic comedy is advertised as "a personal family drama."

Seed of Innocence see Teen Mothers

2636. Seems Like Old Times (1980, Columbia, 102m, c). P Ray Stark, D Jay Sandrich, W Neil Simon, PH David M. Walsh, M Marvin Hamlisch, ED Michael A. Stevenson, PD Gene Callahan.

LP Goldie Hawn (Glenda), Chevy Chase (Nick), Charles Grodin (Ira), Robert Guillaume (Fred), Harold Gould (Judge), George Grizzard (Governor), Yvonne Wilder (Aurora), T.K. Carter (Chester), Judd Omen (Dex), Marc Alaimo (Bee Gee).

When Chevy Chase innocently gets involved in a bank robbery, he seeks help from his ex-wife Goldie Hawn, a very liberal lawyer. She's now married to the local district attorney, Charles Grodin. By the end of the film, the latter is out of the picture as far as Chase and Hawn are concerned.

Self Defense see Siege

2637. The Sender (1982, Paramount, GB, 91m, c). P Edward S. Feldman, D Roger Christian, W Thomas Baum, PH Roger Pratt, M Trevor Jones, ED Alan Strachan, PD Malcolm Middleton.

LP Kathryn Harrold (Gail Farmer), Zeljko Ivanek (The Sender), Shirley Knight (Jerolyn), Paul Freeman (Dr. Denman), Sean Hewitt (The Messiah), Harry Ditson (Dr. Hirsch), Olivier Pierre (Dr. Erskine).

Psychiatrist Kathryn Harrold discovers her amnesiac patient Zeljko Ivanek is a "sender" who can transmit his nightmares to others. Ivanek's mother Shirley Knight is raising him to be another Messiah.

2638. Senior Week (1988, Skouras, 98m, c). P Ken Schwenker & Matt Ferro, D Stuart Goldman, W Jan Kubicki, Goldman & Stacey Lynn Fravel, PH John A. Corso, M Ken Mazur & Russ Landau, ED Richard Dama, PD John Lawless.

LP Michael St. Gerard (Everett), Gary Kerr (Jody), George Klek (Jamie), Jennifer Gorey (Tracy), Leesa Bryte (Stacy), Alan Naggar (Kevin), Barbara Gruen (Miss Bagley).

A group of New Jersey teens hit the road for Daytona Beach and a final fling before graduation. It's the usual teenage sexploitation nonsense. Films like this and hardcore pornography both suffer from a lack of any real sexiness.

2639. *A Sense of Freedom* (1985, Island, GB, 85m, c). P Jeremy Isaacs, D John Mackenzie, W Peter McDougall (based on the book by Jimmy Boyle), PH Chris Menges, M Frankie Miller & Rory Gallagher, PD Geoff Nixon.

LP David Hayman (Jimmy Boyle), Alex Norton (Malkie), Jake D'Arcy (Robbie), Sean Scanlon (Jackie), Fulton Mackay (Inspector Davidson), John Murtagh (Piper), Roy Hanlon (Chief Officer), Martin Black (Bobbie).

The film is based on the real-life career of a Glaswegian gangster who was quick with his fists. He was seemingly unintimidated by anyone as he was transferred from one prison to another. Ultimately, he reformed and married a psychiatrist, with whom he established a series of halfway houses for the rehabilitation of convicts.

2640. *Separate Vacations* (1986, RSL Entertainment, Canada, 82m, c). P Robert Lantos & Stephen J. Roth, D Michael Anderson, W Robert Kaufman, PH Francois Protat, ED Ron Wisman, PD Csaba Kertesz.

LP David Naughton (Richard Moore), Jennifer Dale (Sarah Moore), Mark Keyloun (Jeff Ferguson), Laurie Holden (Karen), Blanca Guerra (Alicia), Suzie Almgren (Helen Gilbert), Lally Cadeau (Shelle).

David Naughton and Jennifer Dale decide to take separate vacations. He travels to Mexico where he constantly strikes out with beautiful women. She takes the kids skiing and is pursued by a ski instructor. They each have flashbacks of their courting days, trying to figure why the romance went out of their relationship.

2641. *Separate Ways* (1983, Crown Intl., 92m, c). P&D Howard Avedis, W Leah Appet (based on the story by Appet, Avedis & Marlene Schmidt), PH Dean Cundey, M John Cacavas, ED John Wright, AD Chuck Seaton.

LP Karen Black (Valentine Colby), Tony LoBianco (Ken Colby), Arlene Golonka (Annie), David Naughton (Jerry), Jack Carter (Barney), Sharon Farrell (Karen), William Windom (Huey), Robert Fuller (Woody).

Unhappy housewife Karen Black begins an affair with art student David Naughton. When she discovers that her bored husband Tony LoBianco is also having an affair, she moves out and takes a job as a waitress. The rest of the movie is about how the couple get back together and form a new perspective of themselves and their marriage.

2642. *September* (1987, Orion, 82m, c). P Robert Greenhut, D&W Woody Allen, PH Carlo di Palma, ED Susan E. Morse, PD Santo Loquasto.

LP Mia Farrow (Lane), Elaine Stritch (Diane), Dianne Wiest (Stephanie), Sam Waterston (Peter), Denholm Elliott (Howard), Jack Warden (Lloyd), Rosemary Murphy (Mrs. Mason), Ira Wheeler (Mr. Raines), Jane Cecil (Mrs. Raines).

A funny thing happened during the production of this Woody Allen film. When the principal photography was first completed, Maureen O'Sullivan was Diane, Sam Shepard was Peter and Charles Durning was Howard. Allen wanted to re-shoot part of the movie, but these three actors were no longer available so Allen started over. The film is not a comedy. It features Mia Farrow as the emotionally crippled daughter of celebrity Elaine Stritch. Mia confronts Elaine with their disturbing past (something akin to that of Lana Turner and daughter Cheryl Crane). The action or shall we say lack of action all takes place in a Vermont country house.

2643. *Serial* (1980, Paramount, 91m, c). P Sidney Beckerman, D Bill Persky, W Rich Eustis & Michael Elias (based on the novel by Cyra McFadden), PH Rexford Metz, M Lalo Schifrin, ED John W. Wheeler, AD Bill Sandell.

LP Martin Mull (Harvey), Tuesday Weld (Kate), Jennifer McAlister (Joan), Sam Chew, Jr. (Bill), Sally Kellerman (Martha), Anthony Battaglia (Stokeley), Bill Macy (Sam), Nita Talbot (Angela), Pamela Bellwood (Carol).

Nothing is sacred in this film, which

spoofs open marriage, health foods, exercise, psychiatry, cult religions and anything else which makes life worthwhile in California's Marin county.

2644.   The Serpent and the Rainbow (1988, Universal, 98m, c). P David Ladd & Doug Claybourne, D Wes Craven, W Richard Maxwell & A.R. Simoun, PH John Lindley, M Brad Fiedel, ED Glenn Farr, PD David Nichols.

LP Bill Pullman (Dennis Alan), Cathy Tyson (Marielle Celine), Zakes Mokae (Dargent Peytraud), Paul Winfield (Lucien Celine), Michael Gough (Schoonbacher), Paul Guilfoyle (Andrew Cassedy), Dey Young (Mrs. Cassedy), Theresa Merritt (Simone), Brent Jennings (Mozart).

Harvard anthropologist Bill Pullman journeys to Haiti to investigate voodoo ceremonies. He wishes to determine if the poison they use is responsible for turning participants into zombies. Pullman was the extremely stupid, but funny Earl in *Ruthless People,* and Cathy Tyson was the extremely beautiful call girl chauffeured by Bob Hoskins in *Mona Lisa.*

2645.   Sesame Street Presents: Follow That Bird (1985, Warner, 88m, c). P Tony Garnett, D Ken Kwapis, W Tony Geiss & Judy Freudberg, PH Curtis Clark, M Van Dyke Parks & Lennie Niehaus, ED Evan Landis, AD Carol Spier.

LP Carroll Spinney (Big Bird/Oscar), Jim Henson (Kermit the Frog/Ernie), Frank Oz (Cookie Monster/Bert/Grover), Paul Bartel (Grouch Cook), Sandra Bernhard (Grouch Waitress), John Candy (State Trooper), Chevy Chase (Newscaster), Waylon Jennings (Truck Driver), Sally Kellerman (Miss Finch).

Suffering an identity crisis, Big Bird leaves Sesame Street to live with real birds, but soon misses his home. His return journey is filled with danger.

Set-Up   see   Tango and Cash

2646.   Seven Doors of Death (1983, Aquarius, 89m, c). P Terry Levene, D Louis Fuller, W Ray Corchoran, PH Glenn Kimbell, M Mitchell Yuspeh & Ira Yuspeh.

LP Katherine MacColl, David Warbeck, Sarah Keller, Tony Saint John, Veronica Lazar.

Katherine MacColl inherits a hotel inhabited by evil zombies who came from the netherworld to invade Earth. It's pretty gruesome.

2647.   Seven Hours to Judgement (1988, TransWorld, 88m, c). P Mort Abrahams, D Beau Bridges, W Walter Davis & Elliot Stephens, PH Hanania Baer, M John Debney, ED Bill Butler, PD Phedon Papamichael.

LP Beau Bridges (Judge John Eden), Ron Leibman (David Reardon), Julianne Phillips (Lisa Eden), Tiny Ron (Ira), Al Freeman, Jr. (Danny Larwin), Reggie Johnson (Chino), Glen-Michael Jones (Doctor), Chris Garcia (Victor).

Judge Beau Bridges is forced to release a gang of punks charged with the brutal mugging death of Ron Leibman's wife. The latter gives Bridges seven hours to produce the evidence that will convict the street gang, or have his own wife Julianne Phillips killed.

2648.   The Seven Magnificent Gladiators (1984, MGM/United Artists, 86m, c). P Menahem Golan & Yoran Globus, D Bruno Mattei, W Claudio Fragasso, PH Silvano Ippoliti, M Ennio Morricone, AD Amedeo Mellone.

LP Lou Ferrigno (Gan), Sybil Danning (Julia), Brad Harris (Scipio), Dan Vadis (Nicerote), Carla Ferrigno (Pandora), Mandy Rice-Davies (Lucello), Yehuda Erfoni (Emperor).

This is sort of a *Magnificent Seven* set in mythical times. Seven gladiators do battle with a tyrant forcing a village to pay him tribute.

2649.   Seven Minutes in Heaven (1986, Warner, 90m, c). P Fred Roos, D Linda Feferman, W Jane Bernstein & Feferman, PH Steven Fierberg, M Robert Kraft, ED Marc Laub, PD Vaughan Edwards.

LP Jennifer Connelly (Natalie), Maddie Corman (Polly), Byron Thames (Jeff), Alan Boyce (Casey), Polly Draper (Aileen), Marshall Bell (Gerry), Michael Zaslow (Bob), Denny Dillon (Aunt Gail).

In this endearing coming-of-age story, Jennifer Connelly is an earnest student competing both in an essay contest and, with her best friend Maddie Corman, for a handsome classmate.

Seven Sisters see *The House on Sorority Road*

2650. *The Seventh Sign* (1988, Tri-Star, 97m, c). P Ted Field & Robert W. Cort, D Carl Schultz, W W.W. Wicket [Ellen Green] & George Kaplan [Clifford Green], PH Juan Ruiz Anchia, M Jack Nitzsche, ED Caroline Biggerstaff, PD Stephen Marsh.

LP Demi Moore (Abby Quinn), Michael Biehn (Russell Quinn), Jurgen Prochnow (David, the Boarder), Peter Friedman (Father Lucci), Manny Jacobs (Avi), John Taylor (Jimmy Zaragoza), Lee Garlington (Dr. Inness), Akosua Busia (Penny).

Demi Moore is convinced that the Apocalypse is now and that Jurgen Prochow is an avenging angel, perhaps even Christ come again. She believes he wants her baby for some end-of-the-world machinations. It's a finely crafted suspense film.

2651. *Severance* (1988, 20th Century-Fox/Lorber, 95m, c). P Ann Bohrer & David Max Steinberg, D Steinberg, W Steinberg & Cynthia Hochman, PH Steinberg, M Daniel May, ED Steinberg, Thomas R. Rodinella & Cecilia Zanuso.

LP Lou Liotta (Ray Ponti), Lisa Nicole Wolpe (Cly Ponti), Linda Christian-Jones (P.J.), Carl Pistilli (Marty), Sandra Soehngen (Sonia), Martin Haber (Lyle), Lou Bonaki (Georgie).

When Air Force officer Lou Liotta loses his wife in an automobile accident, he hits the bottle hard. Having no place else to go, he moves in with Lisa Nicole Wolpe, his go-go dancer daughter who has just purchased the house where she lived as a child.

2652. *Sex Appeal* (1986, Platinum Pictures, 84m, c). P&D Chuck Vincent, W Vincent & Craig Horrall (based on film by Jimmy James and Vincent), PH Larry Revene, M Ian Shaw & Kai Joffe, ED Marc Ubell [Vincent].

LP Louie Bonnano (Tony), Tally Brittany (Corinne), Marcia Karr (Christina), Jerome Brenner (Joseph), Marie Sawyer (Louise), Philip Campanaro (Ralph), Jeff Eagle (Donald Cromronic).

Trying to make it in the straight film world, porno-maker Chuck Vincent here shoots a softcore version of one of his XXX films. Many in his cast and production team worked with him in his more explicit features.

2653. *Sex, Lies and Videotape* (1989, Miramax, 100m, c). P Robert Newmyer & John Hardy, D&W Steven Soderbergh† (for original screenplay), PH Walt Lloyd, M Cliff Martinez, ED Soderbergh, AD Joanne Schmidt.

LP James Spader (Graham), Andie MacDowell (Ann Millaney), Peter Gallagher (John Millaney), Laura San Giacomo (Cynthia Bishop), Ron Vawter (Therapist), Steven Brill (Barfly).

Twenty-six-year-old director and writer Steven Soderbergh presents a unique look at a group of young people for whom sex is everything and nothing. Andie MacDowell can no longer stand to have her yuppie husband Peter Gallagher touch her, but she's hiding a sexuality which she doesn't understand. Meanwhile Gallagher is having an affair with Laura San Giacomo, MacDowell's sister. San Giacomo's interest in Gallagher seems more as competition with her "perfect" sister than any passion for him. Into all this walks James Spader, a one-time buddy of Gallagher, and just what MacDowell seems to be missing. But he announces he's impotent and his sexual kicks comes from making videotapes of women he interviews about their sex lives. It's an intelligent, beautifully controlled film and one of the most appealing independently made movies to come along in years.

2654. *Sexbomb* (1989, Phillips & Mora Ent., 89m, c). P Rick Eye, D Jeff Broadstreet, W Robert Benson, PH Dale Larson, M Leonard Marcel, ED Todd Felker, AD Liz Simakis.

LP Robert Quarry (King Faraday), Linnea Quigley (Phoebe Love), Stuart Benton (Lou Lurrod), Delia Sheppard (Candy), Stephan Liska (Gersch/Steve), Kathryn Stanleigh (Lola), Spice Williams (Rake).

This is an ultra-low-budget dark comedy parody of ultra-low-budget filmmaking. Some will check it out of a video store for its modest humor. Others will do so to get a look at B-movie queen Linnea Quigley bare-breasted and in a black garter belt. To each his own.

2655. *Sexpot* (1988, Platinum, 93m, c). P&D Chuck Vincent, W Craig Horrall (based on the film *Mrs. Barrington* by James Vidos & Vincent), PH Larry Revene, M Joey Mennonna, ED James Davalos, AD Edmond Ramage.

LP Ruth Collins (Ivy Barrington), Joyce Lyons (Boopsie), Frank Stewart (Jackson), Gregory Patrick (Damon), Jane Hamilton (Beth), Jennifer Delora (Barbara), Christina Veronica (Betty), Troy Donahue (Phillip), Jack Carter (Cal Farnsworth), Scott Bergold (Gorilla).

This remake of Chuck Vincent's 1974 movie *Mrs. Barrington* is about a woman who marries wealthy old men and then murders them. The deaths all seem accidental, but three disinherited daughters compare notes and smell something rotten. *Black Widow* it isn't.

2656. *Shadey* (1987, Skouras, GB, 90m, c). P Otto Plaschkes, D Philip Saville, W Snoo Wilson, PH Roger Deakins, M Colin Towns, ED Chris Kelly, PD Norman Garwood.

LP Antony Sher (Oliver Shadey), Billie Whitelaw (Dr. Cloud), Patrick Macnee (Sir Cyril Landau), Leslie Ash (Carol Landau), Bernard Hepton (Capt. Amies), Larry Lamb (Dick Darnley), Katherine Helmond (Lady Constance Landau), Jon Cartwright (Shulman).

Auto mechanic Antony Sher has the ability to transmit visions of his mind to film. Secret agent Billie Whitelaw wants him to use his power to uncover strategic Russian submarine plans. But peace-loving Sher only wants to earn enough money to pay for a sex-change operation.

2657. *Shadow Play* (1986, New World, 101m, c). P Dan Biggs, Susan Shadburne & Will Vinton, D&W Susan Shadburne, PH Ron Orieux, M John Newton, ED Kenji Yamamoto.

LP Dee Wallace Stone (Morgan Hanna), Cloris Leachman (Millie Crown), Ron Kuhlman (John Crown), Barry Laws (Jeremy Crown), Delia Salvi (Bette Mertz), Susan Dixon (Zelda), Al Strobel (Byron Byron), Glen Baggerly (Archie).

After her lover takes his own life, New York playwright Dee Wallace Stone goes to his hometown where she has visions of him. Whether this is her imagination or something more sinister is the subject of the remainder of the movie. Whatever the explanation, Stone goes mad very nicely.

2658. *Shadows in the Storm* (1988, Mediacom/Vidmark, 81m, c). P Strath Hamilton & J. Daniel Dusek, D&W Terrell Tannen, PH John Connor, M Sasha Matson, ED Marcy Hamilton, AD Elizabeth Moore.

LP Ned Beatty (Thelo), Mia Sara (Melanie), Michael Madsen (Earl), Donna Mitchell, James Widdoes, Joe Dorsey, William Bumiller.

In an unusual casting decision, Ned Beatty is a John Dunne–quoting librarian and poet, fired for drunkenness. He takes to the woods to live a quiet existence, but is soon joined by exotic Mia Sara and her companion Michael Madsen. Beatty and Sara becomes lovers. He commits murder because of her and is blackmailed.

2659. *Shag* (1989, Hemdale, 98m, c). P Julia Chasman & Stephen Woolley, D Zelda Barron, W Robin Swicord, Lanier Laney & Terry Sweeney (based on a story by Laney & Sweeney), PH Peter MacDonald, ED Laurence Mery-Clark, PD Buddy Cone.

LP Phoebe Cates (Carson), Scott Coffey (Chip), Bridget Fonda (Melaina), Annabeth Gish (Pudge), Page Hannah (Luanne), Robert Rusler (Buzz), Tyrone Power, III (Harley), Jeff Yagher (Jimmy Valentine).

In the summer of 1963, three of Phoebe Cates' friends, Bridget Fonda, Annabeth Gish and Page Hannah, have mixed feeling about her imminent marriage to unliberated Tyrone Power, III. They whisk her off to Myrtle Beach for a few fun-filled days. Nothing much happens — but catch young Fonda.

2660. *Shakedown* (1988, Universal, 105m, c). P J. Boyce Harman, Jr., D&W James Glickenhaus, PH John Lindley, M Jonathan Elias, ED Paul Fried, PD Charles Bennett.

LP Peter Weller (Roland Dalton), Blanche Baker (Gail Feinberger), Patricia Charbonneau (Susan Cantrell), Sam Elliott (Richie Marks), Antonio Fargas

(Nicky Carr), Tom Waites (Officer Kelly), Kathryn Rossetter (Mrs. O'Leary).

Public defender Peter Weller teams with undercover cop Sam Elliott to fight corruption in the NYC police force. This sleazy thriller is packed with action, but the story is farfetched.

2661. *Shaker Run* (1985, Mirage/Aviscom/Laurelwood, New Zealand, 90m, c). P Larry Parr & Igo Kantor, D Bruce Morrison, W James Kouf, Jr., Henry Fownes & Morrison, PH Kevin Hayward, M Stephen McCurdy, ED Ken Zamke & Bob Richardson, PD Ron Highfield.

LP Cliff Robertson (Judd Pierson), Leif Garrett (Casey Lee), Lisa Harrow (Dr. Christine Rubin), Shane Briant (Paul Thoreau), Peter Hayden (Michael Connolly), Ian Mune (Barry Gordon).

Out-of-work stunt drivers Cliff Robertson and Leif Garrett help research scientist Harrow transport a vial of viral culture from New Zealand to America. Their assignment is menaced by terrorists intent on getting the culture from them.

2662. *Shallow Grave* (1988, E.L.F./Intl. Film, 89m, c). P Barry H. Waldman, D Richard Styles, W George E. Fernandez (based on a story by Fernandez & Carolyn J. Horton), PH Orson Ochoa, M Mason Daring, ED Horton.

LP Tony March (Sheriff Dean), Lisa Stahl (Sue Ellen), Tom Law (Deputy Scott), Carol Cadby (Patty), Donna Baltron (Rose), Just Kelly (Cindy), Vince Tumeo (Chad), Gregory Todd Davis (Owen).

On their way to Florida, four college girls stop in Medley, Georgia. Two are killed after witnessing a man murder his girlfriend. All three females are buried together in a shallow grave. The local authorities, good ol' boys, rednecks and ignoramuses, don't believe the survivors.

2663. *Shame* (1988, Skouras, Australia, 92m, c). P Damien Parer & Paul D. Barron, D Steve Jodrell, W Beverly Blankenship & Michael Brindley, PH Joseph Pickering, M Mario Millo, ED Kerry Regan, PD Phil Peters.

LP Deborra-Lee Furness (Asta Cadell), Tony Barry (Tim Curtis), Simone Buchanan (Lizzie Curtis), Gillian Jones (Tina Farrel), Peter Aanensen (Sgt. Wal Cuddy), Marjorie Ford (Norma Curtis), David Franklin (Danny Fiske), Bill McClusky (Ross).

In this stirring feminist film, tough, independent lawyer Deborra-Lee Furness is on a motorbiking holiday in rural Australia. She is forced to stay over in a small town when her bike needs repairs. She is put up by the owner of the service station. She discovers that the owner's daughter, Simone Buchanan, and several other young women of the town have been gang-raped. The rapists have gone unpunished because no one will bring charges. It takes the death of Buchanan to get the women and responsible men of the town to finally deal with the rapists.

2664. *Shanghai Surprise* (1986, MGM, 97m, c). P John Kohn, D Jim Goddard, W Kohn & Robert Bentley (based on the novel *Faraday's Flowers* by Tony Kenrick), PH Ernie Vincze, M George Harrison & Michael Kamen, ED Ralph Sheldon, PD Peter Mullins.

LP Sean Penn (Glendon Wasey), Madonna (Gloria Tatlock), Paul Freeman (Walter Faraday), Richard Griffiths (Willis Tuttle), Philip Sayer (Justin Kronk), Clyde Kusatsu (Joe Go), Kay Tong Lim (Mei Gan), Sonserai Lee (China Doll), Victor Wong (Ho Chong).

The break-up of Madonna and Sean Penn's marriage is not too high a prize to pay to guarantee that the two won't be teamed again in a stinker like this picture. The time is 1937 and the material girl is a missionary who hires roguish Penn to track down an opium shipment.

2665. *Sharkey's Machine* (1981, Warner, 122m, c). P Hank Moonjean, D Burt Reynolds, W Gerald Di Pego (based on the novel by William Diehl), PH William A. Fraker, M Snuff Garrett & Al Capps, ED William Gordean, PD Walter Scott Herndon.

LP Burt Reynolds (Tom Sharky), Vittorio Gassman (Victor), Brian Keith (Papa), Charles Durning (Friscoe), Earl Holliman (Hotchkins), Bernie Casey (Arch), Henry Silva (Billy Score), Richard Libertini (Nosh), Darryl Hickman (Smiley), Rachel Ward (Dominoe).

Undercover cop Burt Reynolds is on the trail of underworld Atlanta drug kingpin Vittorio Gassman. He turns a crew of vice cops into his personal avenging army, falling for Rachel Ward, a high-priced call girl whom he has under surveillance.

2666. *Sharma and Beyond* (1986, Cinecom, GB, 82m, c). P Chris Griffin, D&W Brian Gilbert, PH Ernest Vincze, ED Max Lemon, AD Maurice Cain.

LP Suzanne Burden (Natasha Gorley-Peters), Robert Urquhart (Evan Gorley-Peters), Michael Maloney (Stephen Archer), Antonia Pemberton (Myrna), Benjamin Whitrow (Anton Heron), Tom Wilkinson (Vivian).

Would-be science fiction writer Michael Maloney falls in love with Suzanne Burden whose father Robert Urquhart is a famous science fiction author.

2667. *She Dances Alone* (1982, D.H.D./CD, Austria/US, 87m, c). P Frederico DeLaurentiis & Earle Mack, D Robert Dornhelm, W Paul Davis & Jon Bradshaw (based on an idea by Dornhelm), PH Karl Kofler, M Gustavo Santolalla, ED Tina Frese.

LP Kyra Nijinsky (Herself), Bud Cort (Director), Patrick Dupond (Dancer), Sauncey LeSueur (Kyra as a child), Walter Kent (Doctor), Rosine Bena (Ballerina), Jeanette Etheridge (Girlfriend), Max von Sydow (Voice of Nijinsky).

This film within a film shows the attempt to make a documentary about famous Russian dancer Nijinsky's daughter. She tried to pursue her own career as a dancer. Sixty-year-old Kyra Nijinsky adds authority to the production.

2668. *She-Devil* (1989, Orion, 99m, c). P Jonathan Brett & Susan Seidelman, D Susan Seidelman, W Mark R. Burns & Barry Strugatz (based on the novel *The Life and Loves of a She-Devil* by Fay Weldon), PH Oliver Stapleton, M Howard Shore, ED Craig McKay, PD Santo Loquasto.

LP Meryl Streep (Mary Fisher), Roseanne Barr (Ruth Patchett), Ed Begley, Jr. (Bob Patchett), Linda Hunt (Hooper), Sylvia Miles (Mrs. Fisher), Elizabeth Peters (Nicolette), Bryan Larkin (Andy), A. Martinez (Garcia).

TV's Roseanne Barr makes her film debut as a dowdy wife who loses her husband Ed Begley, Jr., to glamorous romance novelist Meryl Streep. Having been accused of being a she-devil, Barr decides to become one for real, taking delicious revenge. That's the plot—but the execution works only in the case of Streep, who is a delight every time she is before the camera. Barr is given seedy material she can't do a thing with. Begley is a zero.

She Drives Me Crazy see ***Crazy Horse***

2669. *She Must Be Seeing Things* (1987, McLaughlin, 90m, c). P,D&W Sheila McLaughlin, PH Mark Daniels & Heinz Emigholz, M John Zorn, ED Ila Von Hasperg, AD Leigh Kyle.

LP Sheila Dabney (Agatha), Lois Weaver (Jo), Kyle DeCamp (Catalina), John Erdman (Eric).

Lesbian filmmaker Lois Weaver is working on a new project. Jealous lover Sheila Dabney must learn to deal with Weaver's innocent flirtations.

2670. *She'll Be Wearing Pink Pajamas* (1985, Film Four Intl., GB, 90m, c). P Tara Prem & Adrian Hughes, D John Goldschmidt, W Eva Hardy, PH Clive Tickner, M John du Prez, ED Richard Key, PD Colin Pocock.

LP Julie Walters (Fran), Anthony Higgins (Tom), Jane Evers (Catherine), Janet Henfrey (Lucy), Paula Jacobs (Doreen), Penelope Nice (Ann), Maureen O'Brien (Joan), Alyson Spiro (Anita), Jane Wood (Judith).

Eight women volunteer to take part in an outdoor survival course in the hills of Britain's Lake District and learn more than they bargained for.

2671. *She's Back* (1989, Vestron, 90m, c, aka *Dead and Married*). P Cynthia DePaula, D Tim Kincaid, W Buddy Giovinazzo, PH Arthur D. Marks, M Jimmie Haskell, ED Mary Hickey.

LP Carrie Fisher (Beatrice), Robert Joy (Paul), Matthew Cowles (Sherman Bloom), Joel Sweto (Razorface), Sam Coppola (Det. Brophy), Donna Drake (Sally), Bobby DiCicco (Bob).

Robert Joy and his wife Carrie Fisher move to Queens. When their home is robbed by a neighborhood gang, Fisher is killed, but she's soon back as a ghost only Joy can see. She was a nag when alive, but now she's really on Joy's case to go out each night and kill another member of the gang that did her in. With a little bit of help from gung-ho Korean vet Matthew Cowles, the body count grows higher and higher.

2672. *She's Been Away* (1989, BBC Films, GB, 106m, c). P Kenith Trodd, D Peter Hall, W Stephen Poliakoff, PH Philip Bonham-Carter, M Richard Hartley, ED Ardan Fisher, PD Gary Wilkinson.

LP Peggy Ashcroft (Lillian Huckle), Geraldine James (Harriet Ambrose), James Fox (Hugh Ambrose), Jackson Kyle (Dominic Ambrose), Rebecca Pidgeon (Young Lillian), Rosalie Crutchley (Gladys), Rachel Kempson (Matilda), Hugh Lloyd (George).

Peggy Ashcroft's performance as an old woman who emerges from a mental institution after 60 years is glorious. She can't cope with the modern world and would rather be back in the now closed hospital. Her return to the home she lived in when she was first institutionalized brings back too many painful memories. She lives with her great-nephew James Fox and his wife Geraldine James. The latter's behavior is every bit as strange as was that of Ashcroft when she was put away.

2673. *She's Gotta Have It* (1986, Island Pictures, 100m, c/b&w). P Sheldon J. Lee, D,W&ED Spike Lee, PH Ernest Dickerson, M Bill Lee, PD Wynn Thomas.

LP Tracy Camila Johns (Nola Darling), Tommy Redmond Hicks (Jamie Overstreet), John Canada Terrell (Greer Childs), Spike Lee (Mars Blackmon), Raye Dowell (Opal Gilstrap), Joie Lee (Clorinda Bradford), Epatha Merkinson (Dr. Jamison), Bill Lee (Sonny Darling).

In this sexually frank film from auteur Spike Lee, beautiful black Brooklynite Tracy Camila Johns juggles three lovers, vain actor John Canada Terrell, sensitive romantic Tommy Redmond Hicks, and class clown Spike Lee. Among the many amusing scenes is a montage of male come-ons.

2674. *She's Having a Baby* (1988, Paramount, 106m, c). P,D&W John Hughes, PH Don Peterman, M Stewart Copeland, ED Alan Heim, PD John Corso.

LP Kevin Bacon (Jefferson "Jake" Briggs), Elizabeth McGovern (Kristy Briggs), Alec Baldwin (Davis McDonald), Isabel Lorca (Fantasy Girl), William Windom (Russ Bainbridge), James Ray (Jim Briggs), Holland Taylor (Sarah Briggs), James Ray (Jim Briggs).

As if his Ferris Bueller wasn't enough of a selfish drop-out, writer-director John Hughes presents audiences with Kevin Bacon. He marries a women he doesn't care for, takes a job in which he has no interest and moves to a home in a suburb that's enough to make anyone blue. Poor Elizabeth McGovern gets stuck with being an unintentional ball and chain in this dreadful look at blissless marriage.

2675. *She's Out of Control* (1989, Columbia, 97m, c, aka *Daddy's Little Girl*). P Stephen Deutsch, D Stan Dragoti, W Seth Winston & Michael J. Nathanson, PH Donald Peterman, M Alan Silvestri, ED Dov Hoenig, PD David L. Snyder.

LP Tony Danza (Doug Simpson), Catherine Hicks (Janet Pearson), Wallace Shawn (Dr. Fishbinder), Dick O'Neill (Mr. Pearson), Ami Dolenz (Katie Simpson), Laura Mooney (Bonnie Simpson), Derek McGrath (Jeff), Dana Ashbrook (Joey), Matthew L. Perry (Timothy).

Tony Danza is a single father trying to cope with teenage daughter Ami Dolenz, who goes from an ugly-duckling wallflower to an in-demand beautiful swan almost over night. Danza merely plays his TV role on "Who's the Boss." If you can get it for free, why pay to see it in the theater?

2676. *Sheena* (1984, Columbia, 117m, c). P Paul Aratow, D John Guillermin, W David Newman & Lorenzo Semple, Jr. (based on a story by Newman & Leslie Stevens from the comic strip "Sheena, Queen of the Jungle" by W. Morgan Thomas "S.M. Eiger & Will Eisner"), PH Pasqualino De Santis, M Richard Hartley, ED Ray Lovejoy, PD Peter Murton.

LP Tanya Roberts (Sheena), Ted Wass (Vic Casey), Donovan Scott (Fletcher), Elizabeth of Toro (Shaman), France Zobda (Countess Zanda), Trevor Thomas (Prince Otwani), Clifton Jones (King Jabalani), John Forgeham (Jorgenson).

Tanya Roberts, once one of TV's Charlie's Angels, is a gorgeous woman, and her undress in this film is remarkable for a PG film. But the picture is a miserable failure, filled with inconsistencies and laughable lapses. It's the story of a white child, lost in an African jungle, raised by the Zambouli tribe, who grows up to be Roberts. She champions her adopted tribe when bad guys threaten them. Strangely, Roberts speaks in a halting English, while the natives sound like they were educated at Oxford.

2677. *The Shining* (1980, Warner, 146m, c). P&D Stanley Kubrick, W Kubrick & Diane Johnson (based on the novel by Stephen King), PH John Alcott, M Bela Bartok, Wendy Carlos, Rachel Elkind, Gyorgy Ligeti & Krzysztof Penderecki, ED Ray Lovejoy, PD Roy Walker.

LP Jack Nicholson (Jack Torrance), Shelley Duvall (Wendy Torrance), Danny Lloyd (Danny Torrance), Scatman Crothers (Halloran), Barry Nelson (Ullman), Philip Stone (Grady), Joe Turkel (Lloyd), Anne Jackson (Doctor).

Terror overwhelms a family isolated and snowbound in a huge closed resort hotel with a macabre history of violence. Jack Nicholson is excellent as the father who threatens his wife and son when he cracks. Who will forget his maniacal "Heeeeeere's Johnny" as he smashes through a door with a fire axe.

2678. *Shirley Valentine* (1989, Paramount, 108m, c). P&D Lewis Gilbert, W Willy Russell (based on his play), PH Alan Hume, M George Hatzinassios, ED Lesley Walker, PD John Stoll, SONG "The Girl Who Used to Be Me" by Willy Russell†.

LP Pauline Collins† (Shirley Valentine Bradshaw), Tom Conti (Costas Caldes), Alison Steadman (Jane), Julia McKenzie (Gillian), Joanna Lumley (Marjorie), Bernard Hill (Joe Bradshaw), Sylvia Syms (Headmistress), Gillian Kearney (Young Shirley), Catherine Duncan (Young Marjorie).

Pauline Collins recreates her acclaimed stage role in this romantic comedy. She's a 42-year-old mother and housewife from Liverpool, who dreams of getting away from it all. She does when she accompanies her best friend on a two-week vacation in Greece. She encounters Tom Conti, falling in love with him and life.

2679. *Shock Treatment* (1981, 20th Century–Fox, 94m, c). P John Goldstone, D Jim Sharman, W Sharman, Richard O'Brien & Brian Thomson (based on a book by O'Brien), PH Mike Molloy, M Richard Hartley, ED Richard Bedford, PD Thomson.

LP Jessica Harper (Janet Majors), Cliff DeYoung (Brad Majors/Farley Flavors), Richard O'Brien (Cosmo McKinley), Patricia Quinn (Nation McKinley), Charles Gray (Judge Oliver Wright), Ruby Wax (Betty Hapschatt).

This turkey is meant to be a followup to the midnight cult film *The Rocky Horror Picture Show*. Jessica Harper and Cliff DeYoung, in the roles played earlier by Susan Sarandon and Barry Bostwick, are married contestants on the TV game show "Marriage Maze." Their problem is to get off the show. Audiences have the problem of finding theater exits.

2680. *Shocker* (1989, Universal, 110m, c). P Marianne Maddalena & Barin Kumar, D&W Wes Craven, PH Jacques Haitkin, M William Goldstein, ED Andy Blumenthal, PD Cynthia Kay Charette.

LP Michael Murphy (Lt. Don Parker), Peter Berg (Jonathan Parker), Mitch Pileggi (Horace Pinker), Cami Cooper (Alison), Richard Brooks (Rhino), Theodore Raimi (Pac Man), John Tesh (TV newscaster), Dr. Timothy Leary (TV evangelist), Heather Langenkamp (Victim), Bingham Ray (Bartender).

The ads read "On October 2nd, at 6:45 a.m. mass murderer Horace Pinker was put to death. Now, he's really mad." Director-writer Wes Craven provides audiences craving sick humor all they can stomach in this mayhem-filled action thriller.

Shogun Island see Raw Force

2681. *Shoot the Moon* (1982, MGM, 124m, c). P Alan Marshall, D Alan Parker, W Bo Goldman, PH Michael Seresin, ED Gerry Hambling, PD Geoffrey Kirkland.

LP Albert Finney (George Dunlap), Diane Keaton (Faith Dunlap), Karen Allen (Sandy), Peter Weller (Frank

Henderson), Dana Hill (Sherry), Viveka Davis (Jill), Tracey Gold (Marianne), Tina Yothers (Molly), George Murdock (French DeVoe), Leora Dana (Charlotte DeVoe).

The film is the less than compelling story of the disintegration of the marriage of Albert Finney and Diane Keaton, and the effect this has on the affluent Marin county couple and their four daughters.

2682. *Shoot to Kill* (1988, Buena Vista, 106m, c). P Daniel Petrie, Jr. & Ron Silverman, D Roger Spottiswoode, W Petrie, Harv Zimmel & Michael Burton, PH Michael Chapman, M John Scott, ED Garth Craven & George Bowers, PD Richard Sylbert.

LP Sidney Poitier (Warren Stantin), Tom Berenger (Jonathan Knox), Kirstie Alley (Sarah), Clancy Brown (Steve), Richard Masur (Norman), Andrew Robinson (Harvey), Kevin Scannell (Ben), Frederick Coffin (Ralph), Michael MacRae (Fournier).

Shot in Vancouver and the mountainous regions of British Columbia, the film teams Sidney Poitier, a streetwise FBI agent, with skilled wilderness trail guide Tom Berenger. They go after Berenger's girlfriend Kirstie Alley who has been taken hostage by a savage killer who has fled with her across the border into the mountains.

2683. *The Shooting Party* (1985, European Classics, GB, 97m, c). P Geoffrey Reeve, D Alan Bridges, W Julian Bond (based on the novel by Isabel Colegate), PH Fred Tammes, M John Scott, ED Peter Davies, PD Morley Smith, COS Tom Rand.

LP James Mason (Sir Randolph Nettleby), Dorothy Tutin (Lady Minnie Nettleby), Edward Fox (Lord Gilbert Hartlip), Cheryl Campbell (Lady Aline Hartlip), John Gielgud (Cornelius Cardew Gordon Jackson (Tom Harker), Aharon Ipale (Sir Reuben Hergesheimer), Rupert Frazer (Lionel Stephens), Robert Hardy (Lord Bob Lilburn), Judi Bowker (Lady Olivia Liburn), Sarah Badel (Ida Nettleby), Rebecca Saire (Cicely Nettleby), Joris Stuyck (Count Tibor Rakassyi), Frank Windsor (Glass).

To describe this film as a nostalgic look at the English aristocracy in the period just before World War I would do it a great disservice. It is a perfectly splendid period piece, beautifully capturing a time when the classes were separate and apparently content to be so. English nobleman James Mason has a variety of guests staying at his country estate for a weekend of shooting pheasants and other game. Mason senses that the times are changing and his order is about over. He will not fight the change but is sad to see the life he knew and loved come to an end. Mason could not have wanted for a better curtain call to his long and distinguished career. He is sheer brilliance. Everyone involved in the production can forever be proud of their contribution. The acting, right down to the smallest part is thoroughly convincing and touching. The photography is superb, and the director has put his performers through their paces as if they were willing them. To one and all, bravo!

2684. *Short Circuit* (1986, Tri-Star, 99m, c). P David Foster & Lawrence Turman, D John Badham, W S.S. Wilson & Brent Maddock, PH Nick McLean, M David Shire, ED Frank Morriss, AD Dianne Wager.

LP Ally Sheedy (Stephanie Speck), Steve Guttenberg (Newton Crosby), Fisher Stevens (Ben Jabituya), Austin Pendleton (Howard Marner), G.W. Bailey (Skroeder), Brian McNamara (Frank), Tim Blaney (Voice of Number Five), Marvin McIntyre (Duke).

When lightning hits a robot made for military purposes, it acquires human qualities. Number Five, as it is called, escapes, taking refuge with animal-lover Ally Sheedy, who thinks it's some adorable alien. Its creators, Steve Guttenberg and Fisher Stevens, search for the missing robot, while insensitive military man G.W. Bailey orders its mission aborted and the charming robot destroyed.

2685. *Short Circuit 2* (1988, Tri-Star, 110m, c). P David Foster, Lawrence Turman & Gary Foster, D Kenneth Johnson, W S.S. Wilson & Brent Maddock, PH John McPherson, M Charles Fox, ED Conrad Buff, PD Bill Brodie.

LP Fisher Stevens (Ben Jahrvi), Michael McKean (Fred Ritter), Cynthia

Gibb (Sandy Banatoni), Jack Weston (Oscar Baldwin), Dee McCafferty (Saunders), David Hemblen (Jones), Tim Blaney (Voice of Johnny Five), Don Lake (Manic Mike), Damon D'Oliveira (Bones).

Inventor Fisher Stevens, whose shtik is mangling the English language, goes into the toy business with street hustler Michael McKean. Their greatest asset is Johnny Five, a most appealing, intelligent and trusting robot. Bad guys working for Jack Weston take advantage of this trio of unlikely heroes and almost kill Johnny Five, who is really alive.

2686. Shy People (1988, Cannon, 119m, c). P Menahem Golan & Yoram Globus, D Andrei Konchalovsky, W Gerard Brach, Konchalovsky & Marjorie David (based on a story by Konchalovsky), PH Chris Menges, M Various Artists, ED Alain Jakubowicz, PD Stephen Marsh.

LP Jill Clayburgh (Diana Sullivan), Barbara Hershey (Ruth Sullivan), Martha Plimpton (Grace Sullivan), Merritt Butrick (Mike Sullivan), John Philbin (Tommy Sullivan), Don Swayze (Mark Sullivan), Pruitt Taylor Vince (Paul Sullivan), Mare Winningham (Candy), Michael Audley (Louie).

New York writer Jill Clayburgh and her troubled, troublesome daughter Martha Plimpton travel to Louisiana to visit their Cajun cousins, headed by strong-willed matriarch Barbara Hershey. It's a half-baked drama of a strange and violent family, with beliefs and behavior bordering on the maniacal. Hershey's acting almost makes up for the film's excesses.

2687. The Sicilian (1987, 20th Century-Fox, 115m, c). P Michael Cimino & Joann Carelli, D Cimino, W Steve Shagan (based on the novel by Mario Puzo), PH Alex Thomson, M David Mansfield, ED Francoise Bonnot, PD Wolf Kroeger.

LP Christopher Lambert (Salvatore Giuliano), Terence Stamp (Prince Borsa), Joss Ackland (Don Masino Croce), John Turturro (Aspanu Pisciotta), Richard Bauer (Prof. Hector Adonis), Barbara Sukowa (Camilla), Giulia Boschi (Giovanna Ferra).

Based on a second-rate Mario Puzo novel, directed by Michael Cimino, and starring over-eager actor Christopher Lambert, this dull but violent movie is the story of a sort-of Sicilian Robin Hood who stands up to the Mafia chiefs before being betrayed by his best friend.

2688. Sid & Nancy (1986, Samuel Goldwyn, GB, 111m, c). P Eric Fellner, D Alex Cox, W Cox & Abbe Wool, PH Roger Deakins, M The Pogues, Joe Strummer, Pray for Rain, ED David Martin, PD Andrew McAlpine.

LP Gary Oldman (Sid Vicious), Chloe Webb (Nancy Spungen), Drew Schofield (Johnny Rotten), David Hayman (Malcolm McLaren), Debby Bishop (Phoebe), Tony London (Steve), Perry Benson (Paul), Ann Lambton (Linda).

This is the true story of the sordid relationship between Sex Pistol's bassist Sid Vicious and American junkie-groupie Nancy Spungen. Gary Oldman and Chloe Webb are excellent in this depressing examination of a downward spiral into tragedy in the drug and music world of London in the 70s.

2689. Sidewalk Stories (1989, Island, silent, 97m, b&w). P,D&W Charles Lane, PH Bill Dill, M Marc Marder, ED Anne Stein & Lane, PD Lyn Pinezich.

LP Charles Lane (Artist), Nicole Alysia (Child), Sandye Wilson (Young Woman), Darnell Williams (Father), Trula Hoosier (Mother), George Riddick (Street Partner), Tom Hoover (Portrait Artist).

In this Chaplin-inspired silent comedy, Charles Lane portrays a street artist who draws charcoal caricatures in Greenwich Village. When he witnesses the murder of a man, Lane adopts the deceased's baby daughter, providing her shelter in the abandoned building which is his "home." He hopes to reunite the child with her mother, but first there is a chase sequence, involving the murderers, Lane and the baby in a horse-drawn carriage.

2690. Siege (1983, Summa Vista, Canada, 83m, c, aka *Self Defense*). P Michael Donovan, John Walsch, Maura O'Connell & Paul Donovan, D P. Donovan & O'Connell, W P. Donovan (based on an idea by Marc Vautour), PH Les Krizsan, M Peter Jermyn & Drew King, ED Ian McBride, PD Malachi Salter.

LP Doug Lennox (Cube), Tom Nardini (Horatio), Brenda Bazinet (Barbara), Darel Haney (Chester), Terry-David (Daniel), Jeff Pustil (Goose), Jack Blum (Patrick), Keith Knight (Steve), Brad Wadden (Ian).

The film is the story of the clash between a vigilante right-wing group and the patrons of a gay bar called the Crypt. Things get pretty violent.

2691. *The Siege of Firebase Gloria* (1988, Fries Entertainment, Australia, 100m, c). P Howard Grigsby & Rudolfos S.M. Confesor, D Brian Trenchard-Smith, W William Nagle & Tony Johnston, PH Kevan Lind, M Paul Shutze, ED Andrew Prowse, PD Toto Castillo.

LP Wings Hauser (DiNardo), R. Lee Ermey (Hafner), Albert Popwell (Sgt. Jones), Robert Arevalo (Cao Van), Mark Neely (Murphy), Gary Hershberger, Clyde R. Jones, Margi Gerard, Richard Kuhlman.

Wings Hauser portrays a sadistic marine who, with a few others, holds on at the forward outpost Gloria during the 1968 Tet Offensive in Vietnam.

2692. *Siesta* (1987, Lorimar, 97m, c). P Gary Kurfirst & Chris Brown, D Mary Lambert, W Patricia Louisiana Knop (based on the novel by Patrice Chaplin), PH Bryan Loftus & Michael Lund, M Marcus Miller, ED Glenn A. Morgan, PD John Beard.

LP Ellen Barkin (Claire), Gabriel Byrne (Augustine), Julian Sands (Kit), Isabella Rossellini (Marie), Martin Sheen (Del), Alexi Sayle (Cabbie), Grace Jones (Conchita), Jodie Foster (Nancy), Anastassia Stakis (Desdra).

This experimental, shaggy-dog film follows the romantic exploits of daredevil skydiver Ellen Barkin with various lovers and an insistent rapist.

2693. *Signal 7* (1984, Taylor-Myron, 92m, c). D&W Rob Nilsson, PH Geoff Schaaf & Tomas Tucker, M Andy Narrell, ED Richard Harkness, AD Hildy Burns & Steve Burns.

LP Bill Ackridge (Speed), Dan Leegant (Marty), John Tidwell (Johnny), Herb Mills (Steve), Don Bajema (Roger), Phil Polakoff (Phil), Don Defina (Setts), Frank Triest (Tommy), Jack Tucker (Hank).

This is a touching but muddled stream-of-consciousness story of two aging San Francisco cabdriver friends, Bill Ackridge and Dan Leegant. Some may find it one of the better films of the decade.

2694. *Signs of Life* (1989, Avenue, 91m, c). P Marcus Viscidi & Andrew Reichsman, D John David Coles, W Mark Malone, PH Elliot Davis, M Howard Shore, ED William A. Anderson & Angelo Corrao, PD Howard Cummings.

LP Beau Bridges (John Alder), Vincent Philip D'Onofrio (Daryl Monahan), Arthur Kennedy (Owen Coughlin), Kevin J. O'Connor (Eddie Johnson), Will Patton (Mr. Coughlin, Sr.), Kate Reid (Mrs. Wrangway), Michael Lewis (Joey Monahan), Kathy Bates (Mary Beth Alder), Georgia Engel (Betty).

This film is about the salt-of-the-earth folks in the small town of Easthasset, Maine. It explores the effect on the residents of the closing of the 200-year-old family boat business owned by Kennedy. It's a dreary business with enough subplots to delight any soap opera fan.

2695. *The Silence at Bethany* (1988, American Playhouse, 90m, c). P Tom Cherones & Fred Gerber, D Joel Oliansky, W Joyce Keener, PH Charles Minsky, M Lalo Schifrin, ED Pasquale Buba, PD Cletus Anderson.

LP Tom Dahlgren (Phares Mitgang), Richard Fancy (Elam Swope), Dakin Matthews (Sam Mitgang), Mark Moses (Ira Martin), Susan Wilder (Pauline Mitgang Martin), Megan Bellwoar (Phyllis Mitgang), Robert Billbrough (Junior Mitgang).

Set in a Mennonite Pennsylvania farm community, the film is the story of the doctrinal conflicts between two good men of faith: liberal, newly ordained minister Mark Moses, and his wife's uncle, older, orthodox bishop Tom Dahlgren.

2696. *Silence of the North* (1981, Universal, Canada, 94m, c). P Murray Shostak, D Allan Winton King, W Patricia Louisiana Knop (based on the book by Olive Fredrickson & Ben East), PH Richard Leiterman, M Allan MacMillan, ED Arla Saare, PD Bill Brodie.

LP Ellen Burstyn (Olive Fredrickson), Tom Skerritt (Walter Reamer), Gordon

Pinsent (John Fredrickson), Jennifer McKinney (Little Olive Reamer), Donna Dobrijevic (Vala Reamer), Jeff Banks (Lewis Reamer).

This is the true story of a widow with three children who survived rugged pioneer conditions in 1919 on the Canadian frontier.

2697. Silent Assassins (1988, Action/Panache-Forum, 92m, c). P Jun Chong & Phillip Rhee, D Lee Doo-yong & Scott Thomas, W Will Gates & Ada Lin (based on a story by John Bruner), PH Son Hyun-Chae, M Paul Gilman, ED William Hoy, AD John Nakayama.

LP Sam J. Jones (Sam Kettle), Linda Blair (Sara), Jun Chong (Jun Kim), Phillip Rhee (Bernard), Bill Erwin (Dr. London), Gustav Vintas (Kendrick), Mako (Oyama), Rebecca Ferratti (Miss Amy), Peter Looney (Dr. Thomas).

LA cop Sam Jones comes out of retirement to go up against a former CIA agent gone bad. The villain, earlier responsible for the death of Jones' partners during a stakeout, now has kidnapped a research scientist to get his hands on a formula for a new biological weapon.

2698. Silent Madness (1984, Almi, 3-D, 97m, c). P Simon Nuchtern & William P. Milling, D Nuchtern, W Milling, Robert Zimmerman & Nelson de Mille, PH Gerald Feil, M Barry Salmon, ED Philip Stockton, AD Brian Martin.

LP Belinda Montgomery (Dr. Joan Gilmore), Viveca Lindfors (Mrs. Collins), Solly Marx (Howard Johns), David Greenan (Mark McGowan), Sidney Lassick (Sheriff Liggett), Roderick Cook (Dr. Kruger), Stanja Lowe (Dr. Anderson).

Brilliant psychiatrist Belinda Montgomery is shocked to learn that maniacal killer Solly Marx has mistakenly been released from a mental institution. She flies to a small college where Marx committed his original murders to pose as a sorority girl in a hope to catch him before he kills again.

2699. Silent Night, Deadly Night (1984, Tri-Star, 79m, c). P Ira Richard Barmak, D Charles E. Sellier, Jr., W Michael Hickey (based on a story by Paul Caimi), PH Henning Schellerup, M Perry Botkin, ED Michael Spence, PD Dian Perryman.

LP Lilyan Chauvin (Mother Superior), Gilmer McCormick (Sister Margaret), Toni Nero (Pamela), Robert Brian Wilson (Billy at 18), Britt Leach (Mr. Sims), Nancy Borgenicht (Mrs. Randall), H.E.D. Redford (Capt. Richards), Danny Wagner (Billy at 8), Linnea Quigley (Denise).

The combination of witnessing the killing of his parents killed by someone wearing a Santa Claus suit when he was only 8 and cruel treatment in an orphanage has unhinged Robert Brian Wilson. He takes a job as a department-store Santa, but is definitely not a jolly old elf. He goes off on a murder spree, wearing his red suit.

2700. Silent Night, Deadly Night Part II (1987, Ascot, 88m, c). P Lawrence Applebaum, D Lee Harry, W Harry & Joseph H. Earle (based on a story by Harry, Earle, Dennis Paterson, Applebaum and a character created by Michael Hickey & Paul Caimi), PH Harvey Genkins, M Michael Armstrong.

LP Eric Freeman, James L. Newman, Elizabeth Clayton, Jean Miller, Lilyan Chauvin.

In this unnecessary follow-up to the story of a Santa Claus–dressed killer, the latter's younger brother has taken up his psychotic sibling's slaughtering ways.

2701. Silent Night, Deadly Night III: Better Watch Out! (1989, Quiet Films, 91m, c). P Arthur H. Gorson, D Monte Hellman, W Carlos Laszlo (based on a story by Laszlo, Hellman & Richard N. Gladstein), PH Josep M. Civit, M Steven Soles, ED Ed Rothkowitz, PD Philip Thomas.

LP Richard Beymer (Dr. Newbury), Bill Moseley (Ricky), Samantha Scully (Laura), Eric Da Re (Chris), Laura Herring (Jerri), Elizabeth Hoffman (Granny), Robert Culp (Lt. Connelly), Isabel Cooley (Receptionist).

This third entry in the series of notorious "Santa Claus" horror series went directly to video. It's fairly standard stuff and won't disappoint the audience for whom it has been made—others will eagerly avoid it.

2702. The Silent One (1984, Gibson, New Zealand, 95m, c). P Dave Gibson, D Yvonne Mackay, W Ian Mune (based on the novel by Jan Crowley), PH Ian Paul, Ron Taylor & Valerie Taylor, M Jenny McLeod, ED Jamie Selkirk, PD Tony Rabbitt.

LP Telo Malese (Jonasi), George Henare (Paul Tel Po), Pat Evison (Luisa), Anzac Wallace (Tasiri), Rongo Tupatea Kahu (Taruga), Jo Pahu (Etika), Reg Ruka (Bulai), Anthony Gilbert (Aesake).

Having arrived from the sea as an infant, strange mysterious Telo Malese, tagged the "silent one" because he neither speaks nor hears, maintains a nautical relationship with a sea turtle.

2703. *Silent Rage* (1982, Columbia, 100m, c). P Anthony B. Unger, D Michael Miller, W Joseph Fraley, PH Robert Jessup & Neil Roach, M Peter Bernstein & Mark Goldenberg, ED Richard C. Meyer, AD Jack Marty.

LP Chuck Norris (Dan Stevens), Ron Silver (Dr. Tom Halman), Steven Keats (Dr. Philip Spires), Toni Kalem (Alison Halman), William Finley (Dr. Paul Vaughn), Brian Libby (John Kirby), Stephen Furst (Charlie), Stephanie Dunnam (Nancy Halman).

Martial arts star Chuck Norris portrays a small town Texas sheriff. He must contend with a mysterious killer made almost indestructible by genetic breeding.

2704. *Silkwood* (1983, 20th Century–Fox, 131m, c). P Mike Nichols & Michael Hausman, D Nichols†, W Nora Ephron & Alice Arlen†, PH Miroslav Ondricek, M Georges Delerue, ED Sam O'Steen†, PD Patrizia Von Brandenstein.

LP Meryl Streep† (Karen Silkwood), Kurt Russell (Drew Stephens), Cher† (Dolly Pelliker), Craig T. Nelson (Winston), Diana Scarwid (Angela), Fred Ward (Morgan), Ron Silver (Paul Stone), Charles Hallahan (Earl Lapin), Josef Sommer (Max Richter), Sudie Bond (Thelma Rice).

The film is a dramatization of the life of nuclear plant worker and activist Karen Silkwood, who died in 1974 under suspicious circumstances while investigating unsafe practices at the plant where she worked. The film raises many intriguing questions, but offers few answers. The work of Meryl Streep, Kurt Russell and Cher makes the film worth seeing.

2705. *Silver City* (1985, Samuel Goldwyn, Australia, 110m, c). P Joan Long, D Sophia Turkiewicz, W Turkiewicz & Thomas Keneally, PH John Seale, M William Motzing, ED Don Saunders, AD Igor Nay.

LP Gosia Dobrowoska (Nina), Ivar Kants (Julian), Anna Jemison (Anna), Steve Bisley (Viktor), Debra Lawrance (Helena), Ewa Brok (Mrs. Bronowska), Joel Cohen (Young Daniel), Tim McKenzie (Mr. Roy), Dennis Miller (Max).

The film details the plight of Polish immigrants and their conflicts with native Australians in 1949.

2706. *Silver Dream Racer* (1983, Rank/Almi, GB, 111m, c). P Rene Dupont, D&W David Wickes, PH Paul Beeson, M David Essex, ED Peter Hollywood, AD Malcolm Middleton.

LP David Essex (Nick Freeman), Beau Bridges (Bruce McBride), Cristina Raines (Julie Prince), Clarke Peters (Cider Jones), Harry H. Corbett (Wiggins), Diane Keen (Tina), Lee Montague (Jack Freeman), Sheila White (Carol).

Garage mechanic David Essex inherits his late brother's super motorcycle which he enters in a race in which his main competition is American punk racer Beau Bridges.

2707. *Silverado* (1985, Columbia, 132m, c). P&D Lawrence Kasdan, W L. Kasdan & Mark Kasdan, PH John Bailey, M Bruce Broughton†, ED Carol Littleton & Mia Goldman, PD Ida Random, SOUND Donald O. Mitchell, Rick Kline, Kevin O'Connell & David Ronne†.

LP Kevin Kline (Paden), Scott Glenn (Emmett), Rosanna Arquette (Hannah), John Cleese (Sheriff Langston), Kevin Costner (Jake), Brian Dennehy (Cobb), Danny Glover (Mal), Jeff Goldblum (Slick), Linda Hunt (Stella), Ray Baker (McKendrick), Joe Seneca (Ezra), Lynn Whitfield (Ray), Jeff Fahey (Tyree), Patricia Gaul (Kate), Amanda Wyss (Phoebe).

This attempt to revise the Western genre had a lot going for it; a talented and enthusiastic young cast, lots of action and gunfighting, traditional western subplots, and the excitement of a lawless time. Unfortunately, the public didn't take to the movie in sufficient numbers to offer hope that the western genre, frequently described as moribund, was on its way to a healthy recovery. Maybe it was the lack of Indians.

2708. *Simon* (1980, Orion, 97m, c). P Martin Bregman, D&W Marshall Brickman, PH Adam Holender, M Stanley Silverman, ED Nina Feinberg, PD Stuart Wurtzel.

LP Alan Arkin (Simon), Austin Pendleton (Becker), Judy Graubart (Lisa), William Finley (Fichandler), Jayant (Barundi), Wallace Shawn (Von Dongen), Max Wright (Hundertwasser), Fred Gwynne (Korey), Madeline Kahn (Cynthia), Adolph Green (Commune Leader).

A group of demented think tank geniuses convince inept college professor Alan Arkin that he's an alien from outerspace. Things get out of hand when Arkin becomes a TV messiah.

2709. *Simply Irresistible* (1983, Essex, 100m, c). P Summer Brown, D Edwin Brown, W Sandra Winters & E. Brown, PH Teru Hyashi, M Geoffrey Petrofsky, ED Terrance O'Reilly.

LP Richard Pacheco (Walter), Samantha Fox (Arlene), Gayle Sterling (Juliet), Star Wood (Cleopatra), Gina Gianetti (Sunshine), Nicole Black (Mata Hari), Dorothy Lemay (Hitchhiker), Misha Garr (Miracle).

For reasons not totally apparent Richard Pacheco is "simply irresistible" to a variety of women in this soft porno piece.

2710. *A Sinful Life* (1989, New Line, 90m, c). P Daniel Raskov, D William Schreiner, W Melanie Graham, PH Jonathan West, M Todd Hayen, ED Jeffrey Reiner, PD Robert Zentis.

LP Anita Morris (Claire Vin Blanc), Rick Overton (Janitor Joe), Dennis Christopher (Nathan Flowers), Blair Tefkin (Baby), Mark Rolston (Teresa Tremaine), Cynthia Szigeti (Mrs. Crow), Kirsten Price (Sweetie).

Anita Morris, a former dancer with the Sonny and Cher show, is raising a mentally handicapped daughter named Baby. Unless Morris can find a husband who will take them away from their squalid living conditions, she may have Baby taken from her. It's meant to be a black comedy, in case you care.

2711. *Sing* (1989, Tri-Star, 97m, c). P Craig Zadan, D Richard Baskin, W Dean Pitchford, PH Peter Sova, M Jay Gruska, ED Bud Smith, Jere Huggins & Scott Smith, PD Carol Spier.

LP Lorraine Bracco (Miss Lombardo), Peter Dobson (Dominic), Jessica Steen (Hannah), Louise Lasser (Rosie), George DiCenzo (Mr. Marowitz), Patti LaBelle (Mrs. DeVere), Susan Peretz (Mrs. Tucci), Laurnea Wilkerson (Zena), Rachel Sweet (Cecelia).

Probably hoping to have another *Fame, Flashdance* or *Footloose,* instead, the genius behind this teen musical disappoints with stale music and stereotyped characters.

Singleton's Pluck   see   Laughter House

2712. *Sir Henry at Rawlinson End* (1980, Charisma, GB, 72m, b&w). P Tony Stratton Smith, D Steve Roberts, W Roberts & Vivian Stanshall, PH Martin Bell, M Stanshall, ED Chris Rose, AD Jim Acheson.

LP Trevor Howard (Sir Henry Rawlinson), Patrick Magee (Rev. Slodden), Denise Coffey (Mrs. E), J.G. Devlin (Old Scrotum), Harry Fowler (Buller Bullethead), Sheila Reed (Florrie), Vivian Stanshall (Hubert).

Eccentric gentleman Trevor Howard seeks to exorcise the ghost of his brother Vivian Stanshall during an annual dinner.

2713. *Sister, Sister* (1988, New World, 91m, c). P Walter Coblenz, D Bill Condon, W Condon, Joel Cohen & Ginny Cerrella, PH Stephen M. Katz, M Richard Einhorn, ED Marion Rothman, SE Wayne Beauchamp & Paul Hickerson.

LP Eric Stoltz (Matt Rutledge), Jennifer Jason Leigh (Lucy Bonnard), Judith Ivey (Charlotte Bonnard), Dennis Lipscomb (Sheriff Cleve Doucet), Anne Pitoniak (Mrs. Bettleheim), Benjamin Mouton (Etienne LeViolette), Natalia Nogulich (Fran Steuben).

In an unappealing Southern gothic horror story, Jennifer Jason Leigh and Judith Ivey, the siblings of the title, have transformed their parents' Louisiana bayou mansion into a dreary guest house. Released repressed sexual tensions and murder arrive at about the same time as does Congressional aide Eric Stolz.

2714. *Sisterhood* (1988, Concorde, 76m, c). P&D Cirio H. Santiago, W Thomas McKelvey Cleaver, PH Ricardo Remias, MD Jun Latonio, ED Edgar Viner, PD Joe Mari Avellana.

LP Rebecca Holden (Alee), Chuck Wagner (Mikal), Lynn-Holly Johnson (Marya), Barbara Hooper (Vera), Henry Strzalkowski (Jon), Robert Dryer (Lord Barah).

After the apocalypse, female warriors led by Rebecca Holden and Barbara Hooper have no intention of allowing surviving males ever to become dominant again. The Sisterhood makes a dangerous trek across the deadly Forbidden Zone to find a place of peace.

2715. *Sitting Ducks* (1980, International Rainbow, 90m, c). P Meira Attia Dor, D&W Henry Jaglom, PH Paul Glickman, M Richard Romanus.

LP Michael Emil (Simon), Zack Norman (Sidney), Patrice Townsend (Jenny), Irene Forrest (Leona), Richard Romanus (Moose), Henry Jaglom (Jenny's Friend).

In this rollicking comedy, friends Michael Emil and Zack Norman steal money from gangsters so they can go to Central America and live the good life.

2716. *Six Pack* (1982, 20th Century-Fox, 110m, c). P Michael Trikilis, D Daniel Petrie, W Mike Marvin & Alex Matter, PH Mario Tosi, M Charles Fox, ED Rita Roland, PD William J. Creber.

LP Kenny Rogers (Brewster Baker), Diane Lane (Breezy), Erin Gray (Lilah), Barry Corbin (Sheriff), Terry Kiser (Terk), Bob Hannah (Diddler), Tom Abernathy (Louis), Robbie Fleming (Little Harry), Anthony Michael Hall (Doc), Robby Still (Swifty), Benji Wilhoite (Steven).

Racing car driver Kenny Rogers returns to the circuit with the help of six larcenous orphans adept at mechanics.

2717. *Six Weeks* (1982, Universal, 107m, c). P Peter Guber & Jon Peters, D Tony Bill, W David Seltzer (based on a novel by Fred Mustard Stewart), PH Michael D. Margulies, M Dudley Moore, ED Stu Linder, PD Sandy Veneziano.

LP Dudley Moore (Patrick Dalton), Mary Tyler Moore (Charlotte Dreyfus), Katherine Healy (Nicole Dreyfus), Shannon Wilcox (Peg Dalton), Bill Calvert (Jeff Dalton), Joe Regalbuto (Bob Crowther), John Harkins (Arnold Stillman).

In a hollow, pretentious and unconvincing tearjerker, politician Dudley Moore meets precocious little Katherine Healy, who is dying of leukemia. Despite being married, he enters into a romance with the child's mother Mary Tyler Moore.

2718. *Sixteen Candles* (1984, Universal, 93m, c). P Hilton Green, D&W John Hughes, PH Bobby Byrne, M Ira Newborn, ED Edward Warschilka, PD John W. Corso.

LP Molly Ringwald (Samantha Baker), Justin Henry (Mike Baker), Michael Schoeffling (Jake), Haviland Morris (Caroline), Gedde Watanabe (Long Duk Dong), Anthony Michael Hall (Ted the Geek), Paul Dooley (Jim Baker), Carlin Glynn (Brenda Baker), Blanche Baker (Ginny), Edward Andrews (Howard), Billie Bird (Dorothy), John Cusack (Bryce).

It's difficult to remember a teen performer arriving on the scene in a more appealing role than Molly Ringwald. She's a sweet, normal, redheaded teen whose 16th birthday is completely forgotten by her family because of excitement over her older sister's marriage. She admires senior hunk Michael Schoeffling from afar and is in turn idolized by nerdish but marvelous Anthony Michael Hall. He promises Molly he will use his good offices to set her up with Schoeffling if she will give him a pair of her panties. She does. Hall makes a tidy sum, charging his freshmen classmates to view the undergarments. Somehow Schoeffling, who has grown tired of trampy Blanche Baker, takes notice of Ringwald on his own.

2719. *'68* (1988, New World, 98m, c). P Dale Djerassi, Isabel Maxwell & Steven Kovacs, D&W Kovacs, PH Daniel Lacambre, M Various Artists, ED Cari Coughlin.

LP Eric Larson (Peter Szabo), Robert Locke (Sandy Szabo), Sandor Tecsi (Zoltan Szabo), Anna Dukasz (Zsuzsa Szabo), Miran Kwun (Alana Chan), Terra Vandergaw (Vera Kardos), Shony

Alex Braun (Tibor Kardos), Donna Pecora (Piroska Kardos).

Hungarian immigrant Sandor Tecsi and his wife Anna Dukasz fled the old country during the 1956 revolution. They settle in San Francisco where they start a small restaurant. Years later, Tecsi is constantly at odds with his two sons, Eric Larson, a political activist of the protest era, and Robert Locke, who is gay.

2720. *Sizzle Beach U.S.A.* (1987, Troma Team, 93m, c). P Eric Louzil, D Richard Brander, W Craig Kusaba, PH John Sprung.

LP Terry Congie (Janice Johnston), Leslie Brander (Dit McCoy), Roselyn Royce (Cheryl Percy), Robert Acey (Steve), Kevin Costner (John Logan), Larry DeGraw (Brent Richardson), James Pascucci (Von Titale).

Made in 1974 and never seen in a darkened theater, this extremely low-budget bikini-beach-bimbos film was released because one of its young players, Kevin Costner, became a star.

2721. *Skeleton Coast* (1989, Sivertree Pictures, 98m, c). P Harry Alan Towers, D John (Bud) Cardos, W Nadia Calliou (based on a story by Peter Welbeck [Towers]), PH Hanro Mohr, M Colin Shapiro & Barry Bekker, ED Allan Morrison & Mac Errington.

LP Ernest Borgnine (Col. Smith), Robert Vaughn (Col. Schneider), Oliver Reed (Capt. Simpson), Herbert Lom (Elia), Daniel Greene (Rick Weston), Leon Isaac Kennedy (Chuck), Simon Sabela (Gen. Sekatri), Nancy Mulford (Sam).

Ernest Borgnine organizes a seven member rescue team to move into Angola to bring out his son. The latter is a CIA agent captured and being tortured by evil East German commandant Robert Vaughn.

2722. *Ski Country* (1984, Warren Miller, 93m, c). P,D,W Warren Miller, PH Don Brolin, Fletcher Manley, Gary Nate, Gary Capo, Lex Fletcher, Gary Bigham, Fletcher Anderson, Brian Sissleman, Karl Herrimann, Miller, ED Michael Usher, Ray Laurent, Kim Schneider, Robert Knop, Hamilton Camp.

LP Greg Smith, Hans Fahlen, Lhasa Fahlen, Gunner Moberg, Pierre Vuarnet, John Low, Fred Noble, Otto Lang, Scott Brookshank, Mike Chew.

In this adventure film, expert skiers risk their limbs on slopes all over the world. For skiers, it's the peaks; for winter-haters, it's the pits.

2723. *Skin Deep* (1989, 20th Century-Fox, 102m, c). P Tony Adams, D&W Blake Edwards, PH Isidore Mankofsky, M Various Artists, ED Robert Pergament, PD Rodger Maus.

LP John Ritter (Zach), Vincent Gardenia (Barney), Alyson Reed (Alex), Joel Brooks (Jake), Julianne Phillips (Molly), Chelsea Field (Amy), Peter Donat (Sparky), Nina Foch (Alex's Mother).

John Ritter is a Hollywood screenwriter whose preoccupation with sex and beautiful women wreaks havoc with both his marriage and his mistresses. When one mistress finds him in bed with a new one, Ritter says, "What can I say?" The offended woman responds as she pulls out a pistol, "Try 'the Lord is my shepherd.'"

2724. *Skull: A Night of Terror* (1989, Geonib/Lightshow, Canada, 77m, c, aka *Don't Turn Out the Light*). P&D Robert Bergman, W Bergman & Gerard Ciccoritti (based on his story), PH Bergman, M Philip Strong, ED Bergman.

LP Robert Bideman (David King), Nadia Capone (Jennifer King), Robbie Rox (Skull), Erica Lancaster (Lisa King), Paul Saunders (Kiel Adams), Nial Lancaster (Gideon King), Bonnie Beck (Sarah Adams), Isabelle Merchant (Ash).

Cop Robert Bideman is haunted by the memory of killing an innocent woman being used by young toughs as a human shield. When some cons take a woman as a hostage to make their escape, they take refuge in his farmhouse home. They torment his wife Nadia Capone and kill Bonnie Beck, his secret mistress and wife of his partner Paul Saunders. Well, a man's gotta do what a man's gotta do.

2725. *Skullduggery* (1989, BBC-TV, GB, 90m, c). P Ann Scott, D&W Philip Davis (based on his play), PH Barry McCann, M Carl Davis, ED Peter Harris, PD Gerry Scott.

LP David Thewlis (Tony), Steve Sweeney (Sweeney), Paul McKenzie (Terry), Chris Pitt (Gombo), Robin Weaver (Kak), Gillian Raine (Tony's mum).

This production starts out as an amusing study of four young friends in a British public housing project. By the end it's a weird black comedy.

2726. *Sky Bandits* (1986, Galaxy Intl., GB, 93m, c). P Richard Herland, D Zoran Perisic, W Thom Keyes, PH David Watkin, M Alfie Kabiljo & Roland Shaw, ED Peter Tanner, PD Tony Woollard.

LP Scott McGinnis (Barney), Jeff Osterhage (Luke), Ronald Lacey (Fritz), Miles Anderson (Bannock), Valerie Steffen (Yvette), Ingrid Held (Mitsou), Keith Buckley (Commander von Schlussel), Terrence Harvey (Col. Canning).

Scott McGinnis and Jeff Osterhage are miscast as two Western buddies who become pilots during World War I. These latter-day Butch Cassidy and Sundance Kid characters stink up the screen. The film is reportedly the most expensive independent British production ever made.

2727. *Slamdance* (1987, Island/Zenith, US/GB, 99m, c). P Rupert Harvey & Barry Opper, D Wayne Wang, W Don Opper, PH Amir Mokri, M Mitchell Froom, ED Lee Percy, PD Eugenio Zanetti.

LP Tom Hulce (C.C. Drood), Mary Elizabeth Mastrantonio (Helen Drood), Adam Ant (Jim), Judith Barsi (Bean Drood), Rosalind Chao (Mrs. Bell), Sasha Delgado (Girl at Nursery), Joshua Caceras (Boy at Nursery), Don Opper (Buddy).

Down-on-his luck cartoonist Tom Hulce becomes the main suspect in the murders of high-priced L.A. call girls. It's a decent thriller.

2728. *Slammer Girls* (1987, Vestron, 80m, c). P&D Chuck Vincent, W Craig Horrall, Vincent, Rick Marx & Larue Watts, PH Larry Revene, M Ian Shaw & Kai Joffe, ED Marc Ubell.

LP Devon Jenkin (Melody), Jeff Eagle (Harry Wiener), Jane Hamilton [Veronica Hart] (Miss Crabapples), Ron Sullivan (Gov. Caldwell), Tally Brittany, Darcy Nychols, Stasia Micula [Samantha Fox], Sharon Cain.

Chuck Vincent and some of his hardcore porno stars present a softcore story about busty females in the Loch Ness Penitentiary for Women. It has all the predictable bawdy goings-on.

2729. *Slapstick of Another Kind* (1984, Intl. Film Marketing, 87m, c). P,D&W Steven Paul (based on the novel *Slapstick* by Kurt Vonnegut), PH Anthony Richmond, M Morty Stevens, ED Doug Jackson, PD Joel Schiller.

LP Jerry Lewis (Wilbur Swain/Caleb Swain), Madeline Kahn (Eliza Swain/Letitia Swain), Marty Feldman (Sylvester), John Abbott (Dr. Frankenstein), Jim Backus (U.S. President), Samuel Fuller (Col. Sharp), Merv Griffin (Anchorman), Virginia Graham (Gossip Specialist), "Noriyuki" Pat Morita (Ambassador Ah Fong), Orson Welles (Voice of Alien Father).

Jerry Lewis and Madeline Kahn give birth to enormous twins (also Lewis and Kahn), aliens sent to earth to solve its woes. Once their mission is discovered, a group of midget Chinese try to kidnap the pair. You'll have to be a devoted and uncritical fan of Jerry Lewis to like this dismal production of Kurt Vonnegut's intriguing novel.

2730. *Slash Dance* (1989, Glencoe, 83m, c). P Andrew Maisner, D&W James Shyman, PH Geza Sinkovics, M Emilio Kauderer, ED Lawrence Rosen.

LP Cindy Maranne (Tori Raines), James Carroll Jordan (Logan), Jay Richardson (Edison), Joel Von Ornsteiner (Amos), John Bluto (Rupert), Jackson Daniel (Jeff).

After several women auditioning for a musical show are killed by a maniac, beautiful cop Cindy Maranne goes undercover as a dancer to smoke out the murderer.

2731. *Slate, Wyn & Me* (1987, Hemdale, Australia, 90m, c). P Tom Burstall, D&W Don McLennan (based on the novel *Slate and Wyn and Blanche McBride* by Georgia Savage), PH David Connell, M Peter Sullivan, ED Peter Friedrich, PD Paddy Reardon.

LP Sigrid Thornton (Blanche McBride), Simon Burke (Wyn Jackson), Martin Sacks (Slate Jackson), Tommy Lewis (Morgan), Lesley Baker (Molly), Harold Baigent (Sammy), Michelle Torres (Daphne), Murray Fahey (Martin).

Brothers Simon Burke and Martin Sacks rob a bank, kill a cop and kidnap

Sigrid Thornton who witnessed the crime. All the good stuff happens in the first 20 minutes. From then on, it's boring!

2732. *Slaughter High* (1987, Vestron, 88m, c). P Steve Minasian & Dick Randall, D&W George Dugdale, Mark Ezra & Peter Litten, PH Alain Pudney, M Harry Manfredini, ED Jim Connock, PD Geoff Sharpe.

LP Caroline Munro (Carol), Simon Scuddamore (Marty), Carmine Iannaccone (Skip), Donna Yaeger (Stella), Gary Hartman (Joe), Billy Martin (Frank), Michael Saffran (Ted), John Segal (Carl), Kelly Baker (Nancy).

Everyone makes fun of nerd Simon Scuddamore. The jocks' and pretty girls' teasing continues until one of their jokes at his expense backfires, disfiguring him for life. Five years later, he throws a reunion party for all those he considers responsible. He's still mad, but he's going to get even....

2733. *Slaughter in San Francisco* (1981, World Northal, 87m, c). P Leonard K.C. Ho, D&W William Lowe, PH David Bailes, M Joe Curtis, ED Fred Cumings.

LP Don Wong, Chuck Norris, Sylvia Channing, Robert Jones, Dan Ivan, Bob Talbert, Robert J. Herguth, James Economides, Chuck Boyde.

In this routine martial arts entry, Chinese-American cop Don Wong leads a one-man fight against corruption in the San Francisco Police Department.

2734. *Slaughterday* (1981, Intercontinental, 86m, c). D Peter Patzak, W Patzak, Walter Kindler & Ossi Bronner, PH Kindler.

LP Rita Tushingham, Michael Hausserman, Frederick Jaeger, William Berger, Gordon Mitchell, Vicki Wolf, Klaus Dahlen.

Once prominent British actress Rita Tushingham's star must have fallen quite far, for her to appear in this cheap horror film.

2735. *Slaughterhouse* (1988, American Artists, 85m, c). P Ron Matonak, D&W Rick Roessler, PH Richard Benda, M Joseph Garrison, ED Sergio Uribe, PD Michael Scaglione, SE Barney Burman & Mark Lane.

LP Sherry Bendorf (Liz Borden), Don Barrett (Lester Bacon), William Houck (Sheriff), Joe Barton (Buddy), Jane Higginson (Annie), Eric Schwartz (Skip), Jeff Grossi (Buzz).

A slasher film without dumb teens wouldn't have a chance. Don't worry, the boys and girls in this gory movie are really obtuse. The star maniac is a nut who slaughters people as if they were farm animals.

2736. *Slaughterhouse Rock* (1988, First American/Arista, 90m, c). P Louis George, D Dimitri Logothetis, W Ted Landon, PH Nicholas Von Sternberg, M/L Mark Mothersbaugh & Gerald V. Castle, ED Daniel Gross, PD Peter Paul Raubertas.

LP Nicholas Celozzi (Alex Gardner), Tom Reilly (Richard Gardner), Donna Denton (Carolyn Harding), Toni Basil (Sammy Mitchell), Hope Marie Carlton (Krista Halpern), Steven Brian Smith (Jack), Ty Miller (Marty), Al Fleming (The Commandant).

Nicholas Celozzi dreams about a prison of the dead where he's an inmate. When these nightmares begin interfering with his everyday life, Celozzi goes to an expert on the occult who identifies the prison as Alcatraz, and advises Celozzi to visit "the Rock" to confront his fears head-on. Turns out this isn't sound advice.

2737. *Slave Girls from Beyond Infinity* (1987, Titan/Urban Classics, 72m, c). P Ken Dixon, John Eng & Mark Wolf, D&W Dixon, PH Ken Wiatrak & Thomas Callaway, M Carlo Dante, ED Bruce Stubblefield & James A. Stewart.

LP Elizabeth Cayton (Daria), Cindy Beal (Tisa), Brinke Stevens (Shela), Don Scribner (Zed), Carl Horner (Rik), Kirk Graves (Vak), Randolph Roehbling (Krel).

Years and years from now, two beautiful girls are serving life on a prison galley ship. With no hope of a future, they escape, believing anything has to be an improvement. They are incorrect.

2738. *Slaves of New York* (1989, Tri-Star, 125m, c). P Ismail Merchant & Gary Hendler, D James Ivory, W Tama Janowitz (based on her stories), PH Tony

Pierce-Roberts, M Richard Robbins, ED Katherine Wenning, PD David Gropman.

LP Bernadette Peters (Eleanor), Chris Sarandon (Victor Okrent), Marybeth Hurt (Ginger Booth), Madeleine Potter (Daria), Adam Coleman Howard (Stash), Nick Corri (Marley), Mercedes Ruehl (Samantha), Betty Comden (Mrs. Wheeler), Steve Buscemi (Wilfredo), Tama Janowitz (Abby), Bruce Peter Young (Mikell), Tammy Grimes (Georgette).

The film drifts rather aimlessly from situation to situation. Scads of talented young people try to make it in New York, but find the Big Apple almost unbearable to live in.

2739. *The Slayer* (1982, 21st Century, 80m, c, aka *Nightmare Island*). P William R. Ewing, D J.S. Cardone, W Cardone & Ewing, PH Karen Grossman, M Robert Folk, ED Edward Salier, SE Robert Babb.

LP Sarah Kendall (Kay), Frederick Flynn (Eric), Carol Kottenbrook (Brooke), Alan McRae (David), Michael Holmes (Marsh), Carl Kraines (The Slayer).

While vacationing on a small island off the coast of Georgia four friends become dinner for an unseen monster.

2740. *Slayground* (1984, Universal, GB, 89m, c). P John Dark & Gower Frost, D Terry Bedford, W Trevor Preston (based on the novel by Richard Stark), PH Stephen Smith & Herb Wagreitch, M Colin Towns, ED Nicolas Gaster, PD Keith Wilson.

LP Peter Coyote (Stone), Mel Smith (Terry Abbott), Billie Whitelaw (Madge), Philip Sayer (Costello), Bill Luhrs (Joe Sheer), Marie Masters (Joni), Clarence Felder (Orxel), Ned Eisenberg (Lonzini).

During a botched armored car robbery, Peter Coyote's little girl is killed. He sets out to revenge his daughter's death.

2741. *Sleepaway Camp* (1983, United Film, 85m, c). P Michele Tatosian & Jerry Silva, D&W Robert Hiltzik, PH Benjamin Davis, M Edward Bilous, ED Ron Kalish & Sharyn L. Rose, PD William Billowit, SE Ed Fountain.

LP Mike Kellin (Mel), Felissa Rose

(Angela), Jonathan Tierston (Ricky), Karen Fields (Judy), Christopher Collet (Paul), Paul De Angelo (Ron), Robert Earl Jones (Ben), Katherine Kamhi (Meg), John E. Dunn (Kenny).

A crazed killer hacks to death unhappy campers at a once peaceful summer camp.

2742. *Sleepaway Camp 2: Unhappy Campers* (1988, Double Helix, 80m, c). P Jerry Silva & Michael A. Simpson, D Simpson, W Fritz Gordon (based on a story idea by Robert Hiltzik), PH Bill Mills, M James Oliverio, ED John David Allen, SE Bill Johnson.

LP Pamela Springsteen (Angela Baker), Brian Patrick Clarke (T.C.), Renee Estevez (Molly), Walter Gotell (Uncle John), Susan Maria Snyder (Mare), Heather Binion (Phoebe).

Bruce Springsteen's younger sister Pamela teaches a harsh lesson to the "bad kids" of Camp Rolling Hills, who smoke, drink, swear and fornicate at every opportunity. She murders them in an assortment of grisly ways, including slashing, drilling, choking, drowning and beating.

2743. *Sleepaway Camp 3: Teenage Wasteland* (1989, Double Helix, 79m, c). P Jerry Silva & Michael A. Simpson, D Simpson, W Fritz Gordon (based on an idea by Robert Hiltzik), PH Bill Mills, M James Oliverio, ED Amy Carey & John David Allen.

LP Pamela Springsteen (Angela), Tracy Griffith (Marcia), Michael J. Pollard (Herman), Mark Oliver (Tony), Kim Wall (Cindy), Kyle Holman, Daryl Wilcher, Haynes Brooke, Stacie Lambert, Kashina Kessler.

Pamela Springsteen is back killing kids attending a summer camp (catering to both rich kids and underprivileged kids). Not content with merely dispatching those whose behavior offends her in some grisly fashion, Springsteen likes to crack jokes about her victims while she's offing them.

2744. *Sleeping Beauty* (1987, Cannon, 90m, c). P Menahem Golan & Yoram Globus, D David Irving, W Michael Berz (based on a story by Charles Perrault), PH David Gurfinkel, ED Tova Neeman, PD Marek Dobrowlski.

LP Morgan Fairchild (Queen), David Holliday (King), Tahnee Welch (Rosebud), Nicholas Clay (Prince), Sylvia Miles (Red Fairy), Kenny Baker (Elf), Jane Weidlin (White Fairy), Julian Chagrin (Court Advisor).

It's the familiar story of the beautiful princess put under an evil magic spell, dooming her to sleep for 100 years unless Prince Charming comes along and awakens her with a kiss.

2745. *Sleeping Dogs* (1982, Aardvark/Satori, New Zealand, 107m, c). P&D Roger Donaldson, W Ian Mune & Arthur Baysting (based on the novel *Smith's Dream* by Karl Stead), PH Michael Seresin, M Murray Grindlay, David Calder & Mathew Brown, ED Ian John.

LP Sam Neill (Smith), Bernard Kearns (Prime Minister), Nevan Rowe (Gloria), Ian Mune (Bullen), Ian Watkin (Dudley), Don Selwyn (Taupiri), Tommy Tinirau (Old Maori Man), Bill Johnson (Cousins).

Set in the near future, New Zealand has come under the control of extreme right-wing forces, following the assassination of democratic leaders. Sam Neill joins a violent resistance movement.

2746. *Slime City* (1988, Slime City, 85m, c). P Gregory Lamberson, Peter Clark & Marc Makowski, D&W Lamberson, PH Peter Clark, M Robert Tomaro, ED Lamberson & Britton Petrucelly, PD Bonnie Brinkley.

LP Robert C. Sabin (Alex), Mary Huner (Lori/Nicole), T.J. Merrick (Jerry), Dick Biel (Irish), Jane Reibel (Lizzy), Bunny Levine (Ruby), Dennis Embry (Roman), Marilyn Oran (Selina).

A crazed cultist turns the inhabitants of an apartment building into slime monsters that ooze into humans, possessing them. Well what do you expect for a measly $50,000?

2747. *Slipping into Darkness* (1989, MCEG, 87m, c). P Jonathan D. Krane, D&W Eleanor Gaver, PH Loren Bivens, M Joey Rand, ED Barbara Pokras, PD Patricia Woodbridge.

LP Michelle Johnson (Carlyle), John DiAquino (Fritz), Neill Barry (Ebin), Anastasia Fielding (Genevieve), Cristen Kaufman (Alex), Vyto Ruginis (Otis).

River's Edge was the inspiration for this film featuring Michelle Johnson, Anastasia Fielding and Cristen Kauffman as three college coeds looking for and finding trouble in a small town filled with bikers.

2748. *Slow Burn* (1989, North American Releasing, Canada, 100m, c, aka *Brothers in Arms*). P Geoff Griffiths, D John E. Eyres, W Steven Lister, PH Nathaniel Massey, M Alan Grey.

LP Anthony James, William Smith, Ivan Rogers, Scott Andersen, Mellisa Conroy.

In the beginning of the film, a Mafia hood murders a family, sparing the youngest son. He will regret this good deed.

2749. *Slow Moves* (1984, Jon Jost, 93m, c). P,D,W,PH,M&ED Jon Jost.

LP Roxanne Rogers, Marshall Gaddis, Debbie Krant, Barbara Hammes, Geoffrey Rotwein, Bebe Bright, Roger Ruffin.

Roxanne Rogers and Marshall Gaddis meet on the Golden Gate Bridge and become lovers. They wander across the country in a beat-up car, robbing stores to finance the trip. It finally comes to an end when Gaddis is killed by a store owner unwilling to be robbed.

2750. *The Slugger's Wife* (1985, Columbia, 105m, c). P Ray Stark, D Hal Ashby, W Neil Simon, PH Caleb Deschanel, M Patrick Williams, ED George Villasenor & Don Brochu, PD J. Michael Riva.

LP Michael O'Keefe (Darryl Palmer), Rebecca De Mornay (Debby Palmer), Martin Ritt (Burley De Vito), Randy Quaid (Goose Granger), Cleavant Derricks (Manny Alvarado), Lisa Langlois (Aline Cooper), Loudon Wainwright, III (Gary), Georgann Johnson (Marie De Vito).

Michael O'Keefe is an outfielder for the Atlantic Braves. His wife Rebecca De Morney is a rock singer. The conflicts of their careers take the glue out of their marriage.

2751. *The Slumber Party Massacre* (1982, Santa Fe/PFC, 78m, c). P Amy Jones, D Jones & Aaron Lipstadt, W Rita Mae Brown, PH Steve Posey, M Ralph

Jones, ED Wendy Green, AD Francesca Bartoccini.

LP Michele Michaels (Trish), Robin Stille (Valerie), Michael Villela (Russ), Andre Honore (Jackie), Debra Deliso (Kim), Gina Mari (Diane), David Milbern (Jeff), Joe Johnson (Neil), Pamela Roylance (Coach Joan).

Mad killer Michael Villela invades a girl's slumber party wielding a power drill. The film, meant to be a spoof of the subgenre of slasher films, misses the mark.

2752. *Slumber Party Massacre II* (1987, Concorde/Embassy, 75m, c). P Deborah Brock & Don Daniel, D&W Brock, PH Thomas Callaway, ED William Flicker, AD Frank Novak, M Various Artists.

LP Crystal Bernard (Courtney), Jennifer Rhodes (Mrs. Bates), Kimberly McArthur (Amy), Patrick Lowe (Matt), Juliette Cummins (Sheila), Heidi Kozak (Sally), Cynthia Eilbacher (Valerie), Atanas Ilitch (The Driller Killer), Joel Hoffman (T.J.).

Crystal Bernard dreams of the return of the killer with a power drill. Ultimately her nightmare becomes reality.

2753. *A Small Circle of Friends* (1980, United Artists, 113m, c). P Tim Zinnemann, D Rob Cohen, W Ezra Sacks, PH Michael Butler, M Jim Steinman, ED Randy Roberts, PD Joel Schiller.

LP Brad Davis (Leo DaVinci), Karen Allen (Jessica), Jameson Parker (Nick Baxter), Shelley Long (Alice), John Friedrich (Haddox), Gary Springer (Greenblatt), Craig Richard Nelson (Harry), Harry Caesar (Jimmy the Cook).

This attempt to depict the conditions on college campuses during the turbulent 60s winds up being just an examination of the questionable mores of three inseparable friends, Brad Davis, Karen Allen and Jameson Parker, as they live and love at Harvard during the demonstrations and riots.

2754. *Smash Palace* (1982, Atlantic, New Zealand, 100m, c). P&D Roger Donaldson, W Peter Hanson, Donaldson & Bruno Lawrence, PH Graeme Cowley, M Sharon O'Neill, ED Mike Horton, AD Reston Griffiths.

LP Bruno Lawrence (Al Shaw), Anna Jemison (Jacqui Shaw), Greer Robson (Georgie Shaw), Keith Aberdein (Ray Foley), Desmond Kelly (Tiny).

Former race car champion Bruno Lawrence is torn between his love for his sport and his wife Anna Jemison.

2755. *Smithereens* (1982, New Line, 90m, c). P&D Susan Seidelman, W Ron Nyswaner & Peter Askin (based on a story by Nyswaner & Seidelman), PH Chririne El Khadem, M Glenn Mercer & Bill Million, ED Seidelman, AD Franz Harland.

LP Susan Berman (Wren), Brad Rinn (Paul), Richard Hell (Eric), Nada Despotovitch (Cecile), Roger Jett (Billy), Kitty Summerall (Blondie), Robynne White (Landlady), D.J. O'Neill (Ed), Joel Rooks (Xerox Boss).

In her directorial debut, Susan Seidelman *(Desperately Seeking Susan),* uses a tried-and-true formula to present the tribulations of Susan Berman, who comes to the Big Apple to become a star.

Smokey and the Bandit Ride Again see Smokey and the Bandit II

2756. *Smokey and the Bandit II* (1980, Universal, 95m, c, aka *Smokey and the Bandit Ride Again*). P Hank Moonjean, D Hal Needham, W Jerry Belson & Brock Yates (based on a story by Michael Kane and characters created by Needham & Robert L. Levy), PH Michael Butler, M Snuff Garrett, ED Donn Cambern & William Gordean, PD Henry Bumstead.

LP Burt Reynolds (Bandit), Jackie Gleason (Sheriff Buford T. Justice/Reginald Van Justice/Gaylord Van Justice), Jerry Reed (Cledus), Dom DeLuise (Doc), Sally Field (Carrie), Paul Williams (Little Enos), David Huddleston (John Conn), Mike Henry (Junior), Pat McCormick (Big Enos).

Working on the principle that nothing succeeds like excess, Burt Reynolds and Hal Needham go back to the wall for a sequel to their 1977 hit *Smokey and the Bandit.* They add little to the almost nonexistent plotline, except to make Reynolds a crushed alcoholic who has lost his cult status, his girlfriend Sally Field and just about everything else. He gets rolling again by monotonous repeats of the mindless chases of the first film.

2757. Smokey and the Bandit—Part 3 (1983, Universal, 88m, c). P Mort Engelberg, D Dick Lowry, W Stuart Birnbaum & David Dashev (based on characters created by Hal Needham & Robert L. Levy), PH James Pergola, M Larry Cansler, ED Byron "Buzz" Brandt, David Blewitt & Christopher Greenbury, AD Ron Hobbs.

LP Jackie Gleason (Buford T. Justice), Jerry Reed (Cledus/Bandit), Paul Williams (Little Enos), Pat McCormick (Big Enos), Mike Henry (Junior), Colleen Camp (Dusty Trails), Faith Minton (Tina), Burt Reynolds (The Real Bandit).

Burt Reynolds had the good grace to take only a cameo role in this third in the series of infantile and moronic chase films. Jerry Reed moves up to the "bandit" chased by Jackie Gleason's rednecked sheriff.

2758. Smokey and the Hotwire Gang (1980, NMD, 85m, c). P,D&ED Anthony Cardoza, W T. Gary Cardoza (based on his story), PH Gregory Sandor, M Valerie Jeanne & Danny Bravin.

LP James Keach (Joshua), Stanley Livingston (Russ), Tony Lorea (Filbert), Alvy Moore (Sheriff), Skip Young (Junior), Carla Ziegfeld (Elena/Hotwire), George Barris (Billy), Ray Cantrell (Ron), Tanya George (Nancy).

This "comedy" features CB'ers, "hot babes," fast cars and an armored car robbery.

2759. Smokey Bites the Dust (1981, New World, 85m, c). P Roger Corman & Gale Hurd, D Charles B. Griffith, W Max Apple (based on a story by Brian Williams), PH Gary Graver, M Bent Myggen, ED Larry Bock.

LP Jimmy McNichol (Roscoe Wilton), Janet Julian (Peggy Sue Turner), Walter Barnes (Sheriff Turner), Patrick Campbell (Lester), Kari Lizer (Cindy), John Blythe Barrymore (Harold), Kedric Wolfe (Deputy Bentley), Bill Forsythe (Kenny).

Small town delinquent Jimmy McNichol smashes stolen car after stolen car with the town's homecoming queen Janet Julian as his passenger.

2760. Smooth Talk (1985, Spectrafilm, 92m, c). P Martin Rosen, D Joyce Chopra, W Tom Cole (based on the story "Where Are You Going, Where Have You Been?" by Joyce Carol Oates), PH James M. Glennon, M Bill Payne, Russell Kunkel & George Massenburg, ED Patrick Dodd, PD David Wasco.

LP Treat Williams (Arnold Friend), Laura Dern (Connie), Mary Kay Place (Katherine), Elizabeth Berridge (June), Levon Helm (Harry), Sarah Inglis (Jill), Margaret Welch (Laura), Geoff Hoyle (Ellie), William Ragsdale (Jeff), David Berridge (Eddie).

In this adaptation of Joyce Carol Oates' short story, small town teenage beauty Laura Dern plays with fire when she innocently attracts potentially dangerous stranger Treat Williams.

2761. Smorgasbord (1983, Warner, 83m, c, aka *Cracking Up*). P Peter Nelson & Arnold Orgolini, D Jerry Lewis, W Lewis & Bill Richmond, PH Gerald Perry Finnerman, M Morton Stevens, ED Gene Fowler, Jr., AD Terry Bousman.

LP Jerry Lewis (Warren Nefron/Dr. Perks), Herb Edelman (Dr. Jonas Pletchick), Zane Busby (Waitress), Foster Brooks (Pilot), Buddy Lester (Passenger), Milton Berle (Female Patient).

It's long past the time that Jerry Lewis should be put out to pasture. His slapstick routines had their day, but can now only be viewed as an embarrassment to the comedian. In this film he's a goofy nut who visits his psychiatrist and relates through flashbacks his failed attempts at keeping a job.

Snapshot see **The Day After Halloween**

2762. Sno-Line (1986, Vandom Intl., 89m, c). P Robert Burge, D Douglas F. O'Neons, W Robert Hilliard, PH Guy Thieltges, M Richard Bellis, ED Beth Conwell, PD Chuck Stewart.

LP Vince Edwards (Steve King), Paul Smith (Duval), June Wilkinson (Audrey), Phil Foster (Ralph Salerno), Louis Guss (Gus), Carey Clark (Michael), Charity Ann Zachary (Tina).

New York gangster Vince Edwards moves to Texas where he wipes out all competition in his way to becoming a drug and gambling king.

2763. *Snow White* (1987, Cannon, 83m, c). P Menahem Golan & Yoram Globus, D&W Michael Berz, AD Etan Levy.

LP Diana Rigg (Mean Queen), Billy Barty (Iddy), Sarah Patterson (Snow White at 16), Nicola Stapleton (Snow White at 7), Mike Edmunds (Biddy), Ricardo Gil (Kiddy), Malcolm Dixon (Diddy), Gary Friedkin (Fiddy), Tony Cooper (Liddy), Douglas Sheldon (King).

Diana Rigg hams it up as the nasty queen not taken with the beauty of Snow White in this version of the fairy tale, which won't steal admirers from the Disney version.

2764. *Snow White and the Seven Dwarfs* (1987, Walt Disney, animated, 82m, c). P Walt Disney, SUPERVISING DIRECTOR David Hand, SEQUENCE DIRECTORS Perce Pearce, Larry Morey, William Cottrell, Wilfred Jackson & Ben Sharpsteen, SUPERVISING ANIM Hamilton Luske, Vladimir Tytla, Fred Moore & Norman Ferguson, M Frank Churchill, Leigh Harline & Paul Smith†.

VOICES Adriana Caselotti (Snow White), Harry Stockwell (Prince Charming), Lucille LaVerne (The Queen), Moroni Olsen (Magic Mirror), Billy Gilbert (Sneezy), Pinto Colvig (Sleepy/Grumpy), Otis Harlan (Happy), Scotty Mattraw (Bashful), Roy Atwell (Doc), Stuart Buchanan (Humbert, the Queen's Huntsman).

Originally released December 21, 1937, this Disney classic was his first feature animation, a mammoth undertaking which many called Disney's Folly. Once upon a time, there lived a princess named Snow White whose beauty enraged her vain stepmother, the Queen. The latter ordered her huntsman to take Snow White into the woods, kill her and bring back her heart as proof the deed was done. The huntsman could not bring himself to kill one so good, kind, beautiful and young, so he abandoned her in the woods and brought back the heart of an animal. Snow White was discovered by seven Dwarfs: Doc, Happy, Grumpy, Sleepy, Sneezy, Bashful and Dopey, who lived and worked in the forest. They took her in and she cared for their house. The Queen discovered she had been tricked when she asked her magic mirror the now famous line, "Who's the fairest one of all?" and the mirror once again replied, "Snow White!" Disguising herself as an old hag, the Queen tempted Snow White with a poisoned apple which put the fair one into a death-like sleep, from which she could only be awakened by the kiss of her Prince Charming. He showed up and everyone lived happily ever after. The marvelous songs of the film included "Whistle While You Work," "Heigh-Ho," "Some Day My Prince Will Come" and "One Song."

Snowman see *The Land of No Return*

2765. *S.O.B.* (1981, Paramount, 121m, c). P Blake Edwards & Tony Adams, D&W Edwards, PH Harry Stradling, Jr., M Henry Mancini, ED Ralph E. Winters, PD Rodger Maus.

LP Julie Andrews (Sally Miles), William Holden (Tim Culley), Marisa Berenson (Mavis), Larry Hagman (Dick Benson), Robert Loggia (Herb Maskowitz), Stuart Margolin (Gary Murdock), Richard Mulligan (Felix Farmer), Robert Preston (Dr. Irving Finegarten), Craig Stevens (Willard), Loretta Swit (Polly Reed), Robert Vaughn (David Blackman), Robert Webber (Ben Coogan), Shelley Winters (Eva Brown), Jennifer Edwards (Lila).

In Blake Edward's bitter farce about Hollywood and the movie business, Julie Andrews portrays an actress whose sweetness and purity in films have seen their day. Her latest multimillion-dollar film is a flop. Her husband, Richard Mulligan, gets the idea of rescripting and shooting the film as an X-rated feature. For her art Andrews exposes her breasts. No big deal, everyone knew she had 'em. There just was no clamor to see them.

2766. *Society* (1989, Wild Street Pictures, 99m, c). P Keith Walley, D Brian Yuzna, W Woody Keith & Rick Fry, PH Rick Fichter, M Mark Ryder & Phil Davies, ED Peter Teschner, PD Mathew C. Jacobs.

LP Billy Warlock (Bill Whitney), Devin Devasquez (Clarissa), Evan Richards, Ben Meyerson, Charles Lucia, Connie Danese, Patrice Jennings.

In this obnoxious horror film, everyone believes that teen Billy Warlock is paranoid when he suspects that not only is he adopted but that his "parents" are having incestuous orgies with his sister.

2767. *Soggy Bottom U.S.A.* (1982, Gaylord, 90m, c). P Elmo Williams, D Ted Flicker, W Eric Edson & Stephen C. Burnham & Joy N. Houck, Jr. (based on a story by Hal L. Harrison, Jr.).

LP Ben Johnson, Ann Wedgeworth, Lois Nettleton, Dub Taylor, Anthony Zerbe, Jack Elam, P.J. Soles, Lane Smith, Don Johnson.

The cast tries diligently in this story of a sheriff having difficulty keeping the peace in a small Southern community. But they don't have much to work with.

2768. *Solarbabies* (1986, MGM/United Artists, 94m, c). P Irene Walzer & Jack Frost Sanders, D Alan Johnson, W Walon Green & Douglas Anthony Metrov, PH Peter MacDonald, M Maurice Jarre, ED Conrad Buff, PD Anthony Pratt, VE Richard Edlund.

LP Richard Jordan (Grock), Jami Gertz (Terra), Jason Patric (Jason), Lukas Haas (Daniel), James Le Gros (Metron), Claude Brooks (Rabbit), Peter DeLuise (Tug), Pete Kowanko (Gavial), Adrian Pasdar (Darstar), Sarah Douglas (Shandray), Charles Durning (Warden), Frank Converse (Greentree).

In the distant future, a group of teens who play a version of hockey on roller skates join forces with a mystical force to wrestle the control of the world's water supply from an evil empire.

2769. *The Soldier* (1982, Embassy, 96m, c, aka *Codename: The Soldier*). P,D&W James Glickenhaus, PH Robert M. Baldwin, Jr., M Tangerine Dream, ED Paul Fried, PD William DeSeta.

LP Ken Wahl (The Solider), Klaus Kinski (Dracha), William Prince (U.S. President), Alberta Watson (Susan Goodman), Jeremiah Sullivan, Joaquim DeAlmeida, Peter Hooten, Steve James, Alexander Spencer.

The Russians hold the world ransom to their demands because of a pile of stolen plutonium. A single soldier, Ken Wahl, is in the position of carrying out a dangerous unauthorized plan which may preserve the world's balance of power.

2770. *A Soldier's Story*† (1984, Columbia, 101m, c). P Norman Jewison, Ronald L. Schwary & Patrick Palmer, D Jewison, W Charles Fuller† (based on his stage play *A Soldier's Play*), PH Russell Boyd, M Herbie Hancock, ED Mark Warner & Caroline Biggerstaff, PD Walter Scott Herndon.

LP Howard E. Rollins, Jr. (Capt. Davenport), Adolph Caesar† (Sgt. Waters), Art Evans (Pvt. Wilkie), David Alan Grier (Cpl. Cobb), David Harris (Pvt. Smalls), Dennis Lipscomb (Capt. Taylor), Larry Riley (C.J. Memphis), Robert Townsend (Cpl. Ellis), Denzel Washington (Pfc. Peterson), William Allen Young (Pvt. Henson), Patti LaBelle (Big Mary), Wings Hauser (Lt. Byrd).

Black army attorney Howard E. Rollins, Jr., is sent to a Southern military base to investigate the murder of unpopular black sergeant Adolph Caesar. A series of flashbacks reveal much about the character of the deceased and his relationship with his men. Caesar, a fine character actor, gives the performance of his career.

2771. *Sole Survivor* (1984, Grand National, 90m, c). P Don Barkemeyer, D&W Thom Eberhardt, PH Russ Carpenter, M David F. Anthony, ED Eberhardt.

LP Anita Skinner (Denise Watson), Caren Larae Larkey (Karla Davis), Robin Davidson (Kristy Cutler), Kurt Johnson (Brian Richardson).

A group of zombies search for beautiful advertising executive Anita Skinner, the only survivor of an airplane crash in a remote area.

2772. *Some Girls* (1988, MGM/United Artists, Canada, 94m, c). P Rick Stevenson, D Michael Hoffman, W Rupert Walters, PH Ueli Steiger, M James Newton Howard, ED David Spiers.

LP Patrick Dempsey (Michael), Jennifer Connelly (Gabby), Sheila Kelly (Irenka), Andre Gregory (Father), Ashley Greenfield (Simone), Florinda Bolkan (Mrs. D'Arc), Lila Kedrova (Granny).

In this mildly amusing comedy, American college student Patrick Dempsey has accepted the offer of his sleep-in girlfriend Jennifer Connelly to spend Christmas with her family in Quebec City. When Dempsey arrives, she informs him that she no longer loves him and he will be sleeping alone. That doesn't fit with Dempsey's needs and the randy youngster makes every effort to win back his bedtime privileges. Connelly's two nubile sisters seem more than willing to accommodate Dempsey's needs for sleeping companions.

2773. *Some Kind of Hero* (1982, Paramount, 97m, c). P Howard W. Koch, D Michael Pressman, W James Kirkwood & Robert Boris (based on the novel by Kirkwood), PH King Baggot, M Patrick Williams, ED Christopher Greenbury, AD James L. Schoppe.

LP Richard Pryor (Eddie Keller), Margot Kidder (Toni), Ray Sharkey (Vinnie), Ronny Cox (Col. Powers), Lynne Moody (Lisa), Olivia Cole (Jesse), Paul Benjamin (Leon), David Adams (The Kid), Martin Azarow (Tank).

When Vietnam prisoner-of-war Richard Pryor comes home, he finds his world a much changed place. His wife has left him for another man. The government is suspicious of the statements he signed while a prisoner to prevent his buddies from being tortured and he's low on cash. He meets high-priced call girl Margot Kidder with the proverbial heart-of-gold. Together, they briefly use some mob money to arrange for their future.

2774. *Some Kind of Wonderful* (1987, Paramount, 93m, c). P John Hughes, D Howard Deutch, W Hughes, PH Jan Kiesser, M Stephen Rague & John Musser, ED Bud Smith & Scott Smith, PD Josan Russo.

LP Eric Stoltz (Keith Nelson), Mary Stuart Masterson (Watts "Drummer Girl"), Lea Thompson (Amanda Jones), Craig Sheffer (Hardy Jenns), John Ashton (Cliff Nelson), Elias Koteas (Skinhead), Molly Hagan (Shayne), Maddie Corman (Laura Nelson), Jane Elliot (Carol Nelson).

Eric Stoltz is a high school student who has this thing for Lea Thompson. Not being able to get to first base with her, he turns to tomboy Mary Stuart Masterson for help. He's too dense to see that she's mad for him and it takes the whole film to realize that she's better for him than the more glamorous but shallow Thompson.

2775. *Someone to Love* (1988, Rainbow-Castle Hill, 110m, c). P M.H. Simonsons, D&W Henry Jaglom, PH Hanania Baer, M Various Artists, ED Ruth Wald.

LP Orson Welles (Danny's Friend), Henry Jaglom (Danny Sapir), Andrea Marcovicci (Helen Eugene), Michael Emil (Mickey Sapir), Sally Kellerman (Edith Helm), Oja Kodar (Yelena), Stephen Bishop (Blue), Dave Frishberg (Harry).

While filmmaker Henry Jaglom has people at a St. Valentine's Day party speak to the camera, explaining why they are lonely, Orson Welles, in his last screen appearance, sits near by and makes profound comments.

2776. *Someone to Watch Over Me* (1987, Columbia, 106m, c). P Thierry de Ganay & Harold Schneider, D Ridley Scott, W Howard Franklin, PH Stephen Poster, M Michael Kamen, ED Claire Simpson, PD Jim Bissell.

LP Tom Berenger (Mike Keegan), Mimi Rogers (Claire Gregory), Lorraine Bracco (Ellie Keegan), Jerry Orbach (Lt. Garber), John Rubinstein (Neil Steinhart), Andreas Katsulas (Joey Venza), Tony DiBenedetto (T.J.).

Detective Tom Berenger is assigned to protect Mimi Rogers, the prime witness in a murder case. He finds he doesn't quite fit into her glamorous life style, but he falls for her nevertheless and that's dangerous for both of them.

2777. *Something Special* (1987, Concorde, 90m, c, aka *Willy Milly*). P M. David Chilewich & Fred Berner, D Paul Schneider, W Walter Carbone & Carla Reuben (based on the story "Willy Milly" by Alan Friedman), PH Dominique Chapuis, M David McHugh, ED Michael R. Miller, PD Nora Chavooshian.

LP Pamela Segall (Milly/Willy Niceman), Eric Gurry (Alfie Bensdorf), Mary Tanner (Stephanie), Patty Duke (Mrs. Doris Niceman), John Glover (Mr. Fred Niceman), Seth Green (Malcolm), John David Cullum (Tom).

Teenage girl Pamela Segall wants to become a teenage boy. She succeeds with the help of some magical powder and a solar eclipse. Then "he" discovers that it's not just girls who have problems.

2778. *Something Wicked This Way Comes* (1983, Buena Vista, 94m, c). P Peter Vincent Douglas, D Jack Clayton, W Ray Bradbury (based on his novel), PH Stephen H. Burum, M James Horner, ED Argyle Nelson & Barry Mark Gordon, PD Richard MacDonald.

LP Jason Robards, Jr. (Charles Halloway), Jonathan Pryce (Mr. Dark), Diane Ladd (Mrs. Nightshade), Pam Grier (Dust Witch), Royal Dano (Tom Fury), Vidal Peterson (Will Halloway), Shawn Carson (Jim Nightshade), Angelo Rossitto (Little Person No. 1), Peter D. Risch (Little Person No. 2).

Ray Bradbury's classic fantasy novel is the basis for an excellent moody piece featuring Jonathan Pryce and his mysterious traveling carnival. When it arrives in a small Illinois town in the early part of the century, it proves to be much more than it seems. The film lost lots of money, but is well worth viewing if one gets the Disney Channel.

2779. *Something Wild* (1986, Orion, 113m, c). P Jonathan Demme & Kenneth Utt, D Demme, W E. Max Frye, PH Tak Fujimoto, M John Cale & Laurie Anderson, ED Craig McKay, PD Norma Moriceau.

LP Jeff Daniels (Charles Driggs), Melanie Griffith (Audrey Hankel), Ray Liotta (Ray Sinclair), Margaret Colin (Irene), Tracey Walter (The Country Squire), Dana Preu ("Peaches"), Jack Gilpin (Larry Dillman).

In a kooky comedy, straight-shooting businessman Jeff Daniels takes off for a few days with wild, flaky, sexy Melanie Griffith, who turns his life inside out.

2780. *Somewhere in Time* (1980, Universal, 103m, c). P Stephen Deutsch, D Jeannot Szwarc, W Richard Matheson (based on his novel *Bid Time Return*), PH Isidore Mankofsky, M John Barry (Sergei Rachmaninov), ED Jeff Gourson, PD Seymour Klate, COS Jean-Pierre Dorleac.

LP Christopher Reeve (Richard Collier), Jane Seymour (Elise McKenna), Christopher Plummer (W.F. Robinson), Teresa Wright (Laura Roberts), Bill Erwin (Arthur), George Voskovec (Dr. Gerald Finney), Susan French (Older Elise), John Alvin (Arthur's Father).

Playwright Christopher Reeve falls in love with an old portrait of Jane Seymour and through self-hypnosis transforms himself back in time to discover what their relationship might have been.

Son see Bad Blood

2781. *Songwriter* (1984, Tri-Star, 94m, c). P Sydney Pollack, D Alan Rudolph, W Bud Shrake, PH Matthew F. Leonetti, M Kris Kristofferson†, ED Stephen Lovejoy & George A. Martin, PD Joel Schiller.

LP Willie Nelson (Doc Jenkins), Kris Kristofferson (Blackie Buck), Melinda Dillon (Honey Carder), Rip Torn (Dino McLeish), Lesley Ann Warren (Gilda), Mickey Raphael (Arly and Harmonica), Rhonda Dotson (Corkie).

In yet another attempt to show the way it really is in the country and western music world, Willie Nelson and Kris Kristofferson portray one time performing partners who break away to work solo. Nelson becomes the dean of C&W, wracked with personal and tax problems, while Kristofferson maintains his stance as a rebel.

2782. *Sons* (1989, Pacific Pictures, 88m, c). P Marc Toberoff, D Alexandre Rockwell, W Rockwell & Brandon Cole, PH Stefan Czapsky, M Mader, ED Jay Freund.

LP William Forsythe (Mikey), D.B. Sweeney (Ritchie), Robert Miranda (Fred), Samuel Fuller (Father), Stephane Audran (Florence), Judith Godreche (Florence, Jr.), William Hickey (Roger), Bernard Fresson (Baker), Jennifer Beals (Transvestite), Shirley Stoler (German Housewife).

Three sons take their incapacitated father Samuel Fuller on a trip to Normandy to find his long lost love Stephane Audran.

2783. *Sophie's Choice* (1982, Universal, 157m, c). P Alan J. Pakula & Keith Barish, D Pakula, W Pakula† (based on the novel by William Styron), PH Nestor Almendros†, M Marvin Hamlisch†, ED Evan Lottman, PD George Jenkins, COS Albert Wolsky†.

LP Meryl Streep* (Sophie Zawistowska), Kevin Kline (Nathan Landau), Peter MacNicol (Stingo), Josef Sommer

(Narrator), Rita Karin (Yetta Zimmerman), Stephen D. Newman (Larry), Greta Turken (Leslie Lapidus), Josh Mostel (Morris Fink), Marcell Rosenblatt (Astrid Weinstein), Moishe Rosenfeld (Moishe Rosenblum), Gunther Maria Halmer (Rudolf Hoess), Karlheinz Hackl (SS Doctor), Ulli Fessl (Frau Hoess).

Polish Auschwitz survivor Meryl Streep settles in Brooklyn after the war and tries to forget her past. But the recollection that she was forced to choose which of her children was to be sent to the gas chamber immediately on arriving at the death camp and which would be allowed to live a bit longer, proves to be too much for her. Her stormy relationship with unstable Kevin Kline doesn't help.

2784. *Sorceress* (1983, New World, 75m, c). P Jack Hill, D Brian Stuart, W Jim Wynorski, PH Alex Phillips, Jr., ED Larry Bock & Barry Zetlin, PD Charles Grodin.

LP Leigh Harris (Mira), Lynette Harris (Mara), Bob Nelson (Erlick), David Milbern (Pando), Bruno Rey (Baldar), Ana De Sade (Dellisia), Robert Ballesteros (Traigon), Douglas Sanders (Hunnu), Tony Stevens (Khrakannon).

Despotic ruler and master of the Black Arts Robert Ballesteros plans to become master of the world. The film is just an excuse to exploit the beautiful bodies of the Harris twins, who have been disguised as males to prevent their father Ballesteros from sacrificing them to gain more power. They experience each other's feeling — you know, like, orgasms.

2785. *Sorority Babes in the Slimeball Bowl-O-Rama* (1988, Urban Classics, 78m, c, aka *The Imp*). P David DeCoteau & John Schouweiler, D David DeCoteau, W Sergei Hasenecz, PH Stephen Ashley Blake, M Guy Moon, ED Barry Zetlin & Tom Meshelski, PD Royce Mathew.

LP Linnea Quigley (Spider), Michelle Bauer (Lisa), Andras Jones (Calvin), Robin Rochelle (Babs), Brinke Stevens (Taffy), Kathi Obrecht (Rhonda), Carla Baron (Frankie), Hal Havins (Jimmie), John Stuart Wildman (Keith), George [Buck] Flower (Janitor), Michael D. Sonye (The Imp's Voice).

Sorority pledges Michelle Bauer and Linnea Quigley, along with some college nerds caught spying on the kinky initiation rites, are forced to steal a bowling trophy. They succeed, but drop it, and out pops a surly genie, who gives each of the college students a wish. When he tricks the girls, turning them into monsters, the movie gets down to business.

2786. *Sorority House Massacre* (1987, Concorde, 73m, c). P Ron Diamond, D&W Carol Frank, PH Marc Reshovsky, M Michael Wetherwax, ED Eve Gage.

LP Angela Maegan O'Neill (Laura/Beth), Wendy Martel (Linda), Pamela Ross (Sara), Nicole Rio (Tracy), John C. Russell (Killer/Bobby), Marcus Vaughter (Andy), Vinnie Bilancio (John), Joe Nassi (Craig).

While most of her snippy sisters are away on holiday, shy sorority pledge Angela Maegan O'Neill becomes the prey of a psychopath who used to live in the sorority house.

Sorority Sisters   see   Nightmare Sisters

2787. *Soul Man* (1986, New World, 101m, c). P Steve Tisch, D Steve Miner, W Carol Black, PH Jeffrey Jur, M Tom Scott, ED David Finfer, PD Gregg Fonseca, AD Don Diers & John Rienhart.

LP C. Thomas Howell (Mark Watson), Arye Gross (Gordon Bloomfeld), Rae Dawn Chong (Sarah Walker), James Earl Jones (Professor Banks), Melora Hardin (Whitney Dunbar), Leslie Nielsen (Mr. Dunbar), James B. Sikking (Bill Watson).

In order to earn a scholarship to Harvard, C. Thomas Howell dons an Afro wig, uses tanning pills and passes for black. Howell discovers much about racial stereotyping and falls in love with Rae Dawn Chong.

2788. *Soup for One* (1982, Warner, 87m, c). P Marvin Worth, D&W Jonathan Kaufer, PH Fred Schuler, M Nile Rodgers, Bernard Edwards & Johnny Mandel, ED David Rawlins, PD Philip Rosenberg.

LP Saul Rubinek (Allan), Marcia Strassman (Maria), Gerrit Graham (Brian), Teddy Pendergrass (Nightclub Singer), Richard Libertini (Angelo), Andrea Martin (Concord Seductress), Mordecai Lawner (Furniture Salesman).

Young conservative Jewish New

Yorker Saul Rubinek searches for his "dream girl" in this bittersweet comedy. When various dates fizzle, womanizer friend Graham takes Rubinek to the Catskills for a singles weekend.

Soup to Nuts see Waitress

2789. *South Bronx Heroes* (1985, Zebra/Continental, 85m, c, aka *The Runaways; Revenge of the Innocents*). P&D William Szarka, W Szarka & Don Schiffrin, PH Eric Schmitz, M Al Zima & Mitch Herzog, ED Jim Rivera, Eli Haviv & Szarka.

LP Brendan Ward (Paul), Mario van Peebles (Tony), Megan van Peebles (Chrissie), Melissa Esposito (Michelle), Martin Zurla (Bennett), Jordan Abeles (Scott), Barry Lynch, Dan Lauria, Bo Rucker, Sean Ward.

Mario Van Peebles stars in this obscure independent film which poignantly tells the story of victims of child abuse and pornography.

2790. *South of Reno* (1988, Open Road/Castle-Hill, 94m, c). P Robert Tinnell, D Mark Rezyka, W Rezyka & T.L. Lankford, PH Bernard Auroux, M Nigel Holton & Clive Wright, ED Marc Grossman, PD Philip Duffin.

LP Jeffrey Osterhage (Martin Clark), Lisa Blount (Anette Clark), Joe Phelan (Hector), Lewis Van Bergen (Willard), Julie Montgomery (Susan), Brandis Kemp (Brenda), Danitza Kingsley (Louise).

None-too-bright Jeffrey Osterhage and his wife Lisa Blount live in a remote desert shack in Nevada, spending most of their time watching their one channel TV. He dreams of visiting Reno, but must be content with the make-believe Reno which he creates with thousands of Christmas lights. She has a rather apparent affair with auto mechanic Joe Phelan. Ultimately Osterhage fights the latter for Blount's affection.

2791. *Southern Comfort* (1981, 20th Century-Fox, 100m, c). P David Giler, D Walter Hill, W Michael Kane, Hill & Giler, PH Andrew Laszlo, M Ry Cooder, ED Freeman Davies, PD John Vallone.

LP Keith Carradine (Spencer), Powers Boothe (Hardin), Fred Ward (Reece), Franklyn Seales (Simms), T.K. Carter (Cribbs), Lewis Smith (Stuckey), Les Lannom (Casper), Peter Coyote (Poole), Carlos Brown (Bowden).

In a frightening story, nine members of a National Guard patrol, on routine weekend maneuvers in Louisiana, are marked for death by Cajuns who have mistaken the purpose of the soldiers.

2792. *Space Avenger* (1989, Manley Prods., 88m, c). P Ray Sundlin, Robert A. Harris & Richard W. Haines, D Haines, W Haines & Lynwood Sawyer, PH Mustupha Barat, M Richard Fiocca, ED Haines.

LP Robert Prichard, Mike McClerie, Charity Staley, Gina Mastrogiacomo, Kirk Fairbanks Fogg, Angela Nicholas.

Four alien convicts escape from an outer galaxy prison, ending up in an American woods circa 1930. They possess the bodies of two couples driving by, hoping to put the agents on their trail off their scent. To repair their spaceship they realize that they'll have to wait until earth technology has advanced sufficiently. When this takes place 50 years later, the aliens are just as ornery as ever.

2793. *Space Mutiny* (1989, Action Intl., 91m, c). P&D David Winters, W Maria Dante, PH Vincent Cox, M Tim James, Steve McClintock & Mark Mancina, ED Bill Asher, Charlotte Konrad & Catherine Meyburgh.

LP Reb Brown (Dave Ryder), John Phillip Law (Kaglan), James Ryan (MacPhearson), Cameron Mitchell (Alex Jansen), Cissie Cameron (Lea Jansen), Graham Clark (Scott Dyers).

Reb Brown helps Cameron Mitchell and his daughter Cissy Cameron fight off a spaceship mutiny led by John Phillip Law and James Ryan.

2794. *Space Rage* (1987, Vestron, 77m, c). P Morton Reed & Eric Barrett, D Conrad E. Palmisano & Peter McCarthy, W Jim Lenahan (based on a story by Reed), PH Timothy Suhrstedt & Tom Richmond, M Billy Ferrick & Zander Schloss, ED W. Peter Miller & Arthur Bressan, Jr.

LP Richard Farnsworth (The Colonel), Michael Pare (Grange), John Laughlin (Walker), Lee Purcell (Maggie), William Windom (Gov. Tovah), Lewis Van Bergen (Drago), Dennis Redfield (Quinn), Hank Worden (Old Codger).

Set on a prison planet, Richard Farnsworth must strap on a six-laser and teach the baddies a lesson. The film is a disgrace to several genres.

2795. *Space Raiders* (1983, New World, 82m, c, aka *Star Child*). P Roger Corman, D&W Howard R. Cohen, PH Alec Hirschfeld, M James Horner, ED Anthony Randel & Robert J. Kizer, AD Wayne Springfield, SE Tom Campbell.

LP Vince Edwards (Hawk), David Mendenhall (Peter), Patsy Pease (Amanda), Thom Christopher (Flightplan), Luca Bercovici (Ace), Drew Snyder (Alderbarian), Ray Stewart (Zariatin), George Dickerson (Tracton).

Lucky ten-year-old David Mendenhall blasts off to a fantastic world filled with intergalactic desperadoes, alien mercenaries and star ship battles. Producer Roger Corman has put together this dud from leftovers of earlier pictures including *Battle Beyond the Stars, Sorceress* and *Screwballs*.

2796. *Spaceballs* (1987, MGM/United Artists, 96m, c). P&D Mel Brooks, W Brooks, Thomas Meehan & Ronny Graham, PH Nick McLean, M John Morris, ED Conrad Buff IV, PD Terence Marsh.

LP Mel Brooks (President Skroob/Yogurt), John Candy (Barf the Mawg), Rick Moranis (Lord Dark Helmet), Bill Pullman (Lone Starr), Daphne Zuniga (Princess Vespa), Dick Van Patten (King Roland), George Wyner (Col. Sandurz), Michael Winslow (Radar Technician), Joan Rivers (Voice of Dot Matrix), Lorene Yarnell (Dot Matrix).

Mel Brooks' spoof of *Star Wars* misses the target by light-years. The story is just about the same as Steven Spielberg's, except where Brooks takes a few liberties to show more of his childish attempts at humor. The performances of the cast match the ineptitude of producer-director-writer Brooks.

2797. *Spacecamp* (1986, 20th Century–Fox, 112m, c). P Patrick Bailey & Walter Coblenz, D Harry Winer, W W.W. Wicket & Casey T. Mitchell (based on a story by Bailey & Larry B. Williams,

PH William Fraker, M John Williams, ED John W. Wheeler & Timothy Board, PD Richard MacDonald.

LP Kate Capshaw (Andie), Lea Thompson (Kathryn), Kelly Preston (Tish), Larry B. Scott (Rudy), Leaf Phoenix (Max), Tate Donovan (Kevin), Tom Skerritt (Zach), Barry Primus (Brennan), Terry O'Quinn (Launch Director).

Astronaut Kate Capshaw, a reluctant instructor at the U.S. Space Camp in Alabama, and five of her teenage and younger charges board a real space ship and are accidentally launched on a space journey.

2798. *Spaced Out* (1981, Miramax, GB, 90m, c, aka *Outer Touch*). P David Speechley, D Norman J. Warren, W Andrew Payne, Bob Saget & Jeff de Hart, PH John Metcalfe & Peter Sinclair, M Alan Brawer & Anna Pepper, ED Edward Glass.

LP Barry Stokes (Oliver), Tony Maiden (Willy), Glory Annen (Cosia), Michael Rowlatt (Cliff), Ava Cadell (Partha), Kate Ferguson (Skipper), Lynne Ross (Prudence).

This British sex comedy is a parody of films such as *Star Wars* and *2001: A Space Odyssey*.

2799. *Spacehunter: Adventures in the Forbidden Zone* (1983, Columbia, 3-D, 90m, c, aka *Adventures in the Creep Zone; Road Gangs*). P Don Carmody, Andre Link & John Dunning, D Lamont Johnson, W David Preston, Edith Rey, Dan Goldberg & Len Blum (based on a story by Stewart Harding & Jean LaFleur), PF Frank Tidy, M Elmer Bernstein, ED Scott Conrad, PD Jackson DeGovia.

LP Peter Strauss (Wolff), Molly Ringwald (Niki), Ernie Hudson (Washington), Andrea Marcovicci (Chalmers), Michael Ironside (Overdog McNabb), Beeson Carroll (Grandma Patterson), Hrant Alianak (Chemist).

Molly Ringwald's career has withstood this stupid science fiction film featuring galactic bounty hunter Peter Strauss, who agrees to rescue three stranded girls whose space ship has crashed on the planet Terra Eleven. But in years to come she may well wish to leave it out of her filmography.

2800. *Spaceship* (1983, Creature Features, 88m, c, aka *The Creature Wasn't Nice*). P Mark Haggard, D&W Bruce Kimmel, PH Denny Lavil, M David Spear, ED David Blangsted, PD Lee Cole.

LP Cindy Williams (McHugh), Bruce Kimmel (John), Leslie Nielsen (Jameson), Gerrit Graham (Rodzinski), Patrick Macnee (Stark), Ron Kurowski (Creature).

Stopping at a small planet, the crew of a lone spaceship picks up a clump of matter which turns into a monster. When hooked up with a communication computer it does a song and dance routine called "I Want to Eat Your Face."

2801. *Spasms* (1983, Famous Players/PDC, Canada, 89m, c, aka *Death Bite*). P John G. Pozhke & Maurice Smith, D William Fruet, W Don Enright (based on the novel *Death Bite* by Mitchell Maryk & Brent Monahan), PH Mark Irwin, M Eric N. Robertson & Tangerine Dream, ED Ralph Brunjes.

LP Peter Fonda (Dr. Brasilian), Oliver Reed (Jason), Kerrie Keane (Susanne), Al Waxman (Crowley), Miguel Fernandes (Mendes), Marilyn Lightstone (Dr. Rothman), Angus MacInnes (Duncan), Laurie Brown (Allison).

In this forgettable sf/horror film a killer devil-snake resurfaces every seven years to claim the souls of the dead.

2802. *The Spawning* (1983, Saturn Intl., Italy/US, 95m, c, aka *Piranha II: The Spawning*). P Chako van Leuwen & Jeff Schechtman, D James Cameron, W H.A. Milton, PH Roberto D'Ettore Piazzoli, M Steve Powder, ED Roberto Silvi.

LP Tricia O'Neil (Anne), Steve Marachuk (Tyler), Lance Henriksen (Steve), Ricky G. Paul (Chris), Ted Richert (Raoul), Leslie Graves (Allison).

Those who are turned-off by flesh-eating fish shouldn't see this movie. That's just one of many groups of people who shouldn't see this dreadful sequel to *Piranha* (1978).

2803. *Speaking Parts* (1989, Cinephile, Canada, 92m, c). D Atom Egoyan, W Egoyan, PH Paul Sarossy, M Mychael Danna, ED Bruce McDonald.

LP Michael McManus (Lance), Arsinee Khanjian (Lisa), Gabrielle Rose (Clara), David Hemblen (Producer), Patricia Collins (Housekeeper), Gerard Parkes (The Father), Jackie Samuda (The Bride), Peter Krantz (The Groom).

Michael McManus works for a hotel, cleaning rooms and servicing female guests on orders of the housekeeper. After getting some parts as an extra, he wants to break into movies.

2804. *Special Effects* (1984, New Line, 93m, c). P Paul Kurta, D&W Larry Cohen, PH Paul Glickman, M Michael Minard, ED Armond Lebowitz.

LP Zoe Tamerlis (Andrea/Elaine), Eric Bogosian (Neville), Brad Rijn (Keefe), Kevin O'Connor (Delroy), Bill Oland, Richard Greene.

Having just finished a major special effects movie failure, film director Eric Bogosian meets aspiring actress Zoe Tamerlis. He kills her while a hidden camera records the murder, then sets about to find another actress who looks just like the deceased (again Tamerlis), and makes a movie about the killing.

2805. *Speed Zone!* (1989, Orion, US/Canada, 95m, c). P Murray Shostak, D Jim Drake, W Michael Short, PH Francois Protat & Robert Saad, M David Wheatley, ED Mike Economou, PD Richard Hudolin.

LP John Candy (Charlie), Donna Dixon (Tiffany), Matt Frewer (Alec), Joe Flaherty (Vic), Tim Matheson (Jack), Mimi Kuzyk (Heather), Melody Anderson (Lee), Shari Belafonte (Margaret), Peter Boyle (Chief Edsel).

This film about a *Cannonball Run*-like cross-country car chase stars John Candy. Guest stars in cameo roles, such as Tom & Dick Smothers, John Schneider, Jamie Farr, Lee Van Cleef, Eugene Levy, Michael Spinks, Brooke Shields and Carl Lewis, don't take it out of the boring zone.

2806. *Spellbinder* (1988, MGM/United Artists, 98m, c). P Joe Wizan & Brian Russell, D Janet Greek, W Tracey Torme, PH Adam Greenberg, M Basil Poledouris, ED Steve Mirkovich, PD Rodger Maus.

LP Timothy Daly (Jeff Mills), Kelly Preston (Miranda Reed), Rick Rossovich

(Derek Clayton), Audra Lindley (Mrs. White), Anthony Crivello (Aldys), Diana Bellamy (Grace Woods), Cary-Hiroyuki Tagawa (Lt. Lee).

In a *Fatal Attraction*–inspired film, yuppie lawyer Timothy Daly goes after woman-in-distress Kelly Preston, only to discover that she's a witch trying to escape her coven, which wants her back.

2807.   *Sphinx* (1981, Warner, 117m, c). P Stanley O'Toole, D Franklin J. Schaffner, W John Byrum (based on the novel by Robin Cook), PH Ernest Day, M Michael J. Lewis, ED Robert E. Swink & Michael F. Anderson, PD Terence Marsh.

LP Lesley-Anne Down (Erica Baron), Frank Langella (Ahmed Khazzan), Maurice Ronet (Yvon), John Gielgud (Abdu Hamdi), Vic Tablian (Khalifa), Martin Benson (Muhammed), John Rhys-Davies (Stephanos Markoulis).

Tough archaeologist Lesley-Anne Down stumbles across a secret hidden for centuries in the tomb of an Egyptian king. The experience nearly costs her life as well as worse things.

2808.   *Spies Like Us* (1985, Warner, 109m, c). P Brian Grazer & George Folsey, Jr., D John Landis, W Dan Aykroyd, Lowell Ganz & Babaloo Mandel (based on a story by Aykroyd & Dave Thomas), PH Robert Paynter, M Elmer Bernstein, ED Malcolm Campbell, PD Peter Murton.

LP Chevy Chase (Emmett Fitz-Hume), Dan Aykroyd (Austin Millbarge), Steve Forrest (Gen. Sline), Donna Dixon (Karen Boyer), Bruce Davison (Mr. Ruby), Bernie Casey (Col. Rhombus), William Prince (Mr. Keyes), Tom Hatten (Gen. Miegs), Frank Oz (Test Monitor).

Other than make fools of themselves, we don't know what Chevy Chase and Dan Aykroyd accomplish in this sad tale of a pair of the dumbest CIA agents ever recruited. Even dumber than Chase and Aykroyd are those they encounter as they bungle through their mission. Aykroyd deserves a double-dose of shame-shame, to be shared with director Landis, because he had a hand in writing the trash. It's Chase and Aykroyd's *Ishtar*.

2809.   *Spike of Bensonhurst* (1988, Film Dallas, 101m, c). P David Weisman,

Nelson Lyon & Mark Silverman, D Paul Morrissey, W Alan Bowne & Morrissey, PH Steven Fierberg, M Coati Mundi, ED Stan Salfas, PD Stephen McCabe.

LP Sasha Mitchell (Spike Fumo), Ernest Borgnine (Baldo Cacetti), Anne DeSalvo (Sylvia Cacetti), Sylvia Miles (Congresswoman), Geraldine Smith (Helen Fumo), Antonio Rey (Bandana's Mother), Rick Aviles (Bandana), Maria Pitillo (Angel), Talisa Soto (India).

Big dumb Sasha Mitchell is under the protection of Mafia boss Ernest Borgnine, because his father is doing a term in Sing Sing for Borgnine. Mitchell sees himself as a boxer. Most of the fights he wins are fixed by Borgnine. Mitchell falls in love with Borgnine's daughter, Maria Pitillo, who the mob boss has plans to marry to the son of congresswoman Sylvia Miles. Pitillo comes up for a plan to win her father's acceptance of Mitchell as a son-in-law by becoming pregnant. Unfortunately, Mitchell has also impregnated Talisa Soto. Everything is sorted out in a boxing ring.

2810.   *Spiker* (1986, Seymour Borde & Associates, 104m, c). P&D Roger Tilton, W Marlene Matthews (based on a story by Tilton & Matthews), PH Robert A. Sherry, M Jeff Barry, ED Richard S. Brummer.

LP Patrick Houser, Kristi Ferrell, Jo McDonnel, Natasha Shneider, Stephan Burns, Christopher Allport, Michael Parks, Ken Michelman, Eric Matthew.

In what is probably the first film with a volleyball theme, Patrick Houser and the Olympic gold medal–winning U.S. Men's National Team star in the drama of a young man who sacrifices everything for a chance at Olympic gold in 1984.

Spinal Tap   see   This Is Spinal Tap

2811.   *Spirits of the Air: Gremlins of the Clouds* (1989, Meaningful Eye Contact Prod., Australia, 93m, c). P Andrew McPhail & Alex Proyas, D&W Proyas, PH David Knaus, M Peter Miller, ED Craig Wood, PD Sean Callinan.

LP Michael Lake (Felix Crabtree), Melissa Davis (Betty Crabtree), Norman Boyd (Smith).

Manic Michael Lake and his sister Melissa Davis live in a wooden house in the middle of a desert. The two have a religious fixation, and their house is filled with crucifixes and other icons. Trapped in this primitive setting, the two are struggling to build a flying machine to escape. Along comes Norman Boyd, lost in the wilderness. He helps them build their primitive plane, but by this time Davis is completely off her rocker. Lake decides to stay with his sister and Boyd flies off alone. What does it all mean? We have no idea. We wonder if director-writer Alex Proyas has any clue.

2812. *Splash* (1984, Buena Vista, 111m, c). P Brian Grazer, D Ron Howard, W Lowell Ganz, Babaloo Mandel & Bruce Jay Friedman† (based on the story by Grazer & Friedman), PH Don Peterman, M Lee Holdridge, ED Daniel P. Hanley & Michael Hill, PD Jack T. Collis.

LP Tom Hanks (Allen Bauer), Daryl Hannah (Madison), Eugene Levy (Walter Kornbluth), John Candy (Freddie Bauer), Dody Goodman (Mrs. Stimler), Shecky Greene (Mr. Buyrite), Richard B. Shull (Dr. Ross), Bobby Di Cicco (Jerry), Howard Morris (Dr. Zidell).

Mermaid Daryl Hannah arrives buck naked in New York City looking for Tom Hanks, the man she has fallen for. She needs to avoid water or her legs turn to a tail. She's very affectionate and a quick study in everything from making love to learning English and charging things at Bloomingdale's. This surprise hit from Ron Howard is fun if it's not examined too closely.

2813. *Splatter University* (1984, Troma, 77m, c). P Richard W. Haines & John Michaels, D Haines, W Haines, Michaels & Michael Cunningham, PD Fred Cohen & Jim Grib, M Chris Burke, ED Haines.

LP Francine Forbes (Julie Parker), Dick Biel (Father Janson/Daniel Grayham), Cathy Lacommare (Cathy), Ric Randig (Mark), Joanna Mihalakis, George Seminara, Don Eaton, Sal Lumetta, Denise Texeira.

After escaping from an asylum, a deranged killer begins a reign of terror at a local college where he slaughters and mutilates pretty coeds.

2814. *Split* (1989, Starker Film, 85m, c). P Barbara Horscraft, D,W,PH&ED Chris Shaw, M Chris Shaw, Robert Shaw & Ugi Tojo.

LP Chris Shaw, Tim Dwight, Joan Bechtel, John Flynn.

In this futuristic chase-thriller, a prophet of peace, who wishes to liberate humankind from the mass media and junk ideas, is menaced by an evil genius. It doesn't seem to be a completed film and the plot is vague.

2815. *Split Decisions* (1988, New Century/Vista, 95m, c). P Joe Wizan, D David Drury, W David Fallon, PH Timothy Suhrstedt, M Basil Poledouris, ED John W. Wheeler, Jeff Freeman & Thomas Stanford.

LP Craig Sheffer (Eddie McGuinn), Jeff Fahey (Ray McGuinn), Gene Hackman (Dan McGuinn), John McLiam (Pop McGuinn), Jennifer Beals (Barbara Uribe), Eddie Velez (Julian "Snake" Pedroza), Carmine Caridi (Lou Rubia), James Tolkan (Benny Platone).

Things look up for the youngest son (Craig Sheffer) of the Fighting McGuinn family when he is offered a boxing scholarship to a major university. His hopes for the Olympics are dashed when he feels he must become a professional to enter the ring against the man responsible for his brother's (Jeff Fahey) killing by mobsters when the latter refuses to throw a fight.

2816. *Split Image* (1982, Orion, 111m, c). P&D Ted Kotcheff, W Scott Spencer, Robert Kaufman & Robert Mark Kamen (based on the story by Spencer), PH Robert Jessup, M Bill Conti, ED Jay Kamen, PD Wolf Kroeger.

LP Michael O'Keefe (Danny), Karen Allen (Rebecca), Peter Fonda (Kirklander), James Woods (Pratt), Elizabeth Ashley (Diana), Brian Dennehy (Kevin), Ronnie Scribner (Sean), Pamela Ludwig (Jane).

Possible Olympian gymnast Michael O'Keefe falls in with a religious cult, headed by Peter Fonda. His parents Brian Dennehy and Elizabeth Ashley hire James Woods, an expert in deprogramming, to get him back.

2817. *Splitz* (1984, Film Ventures, 83m, c). P Kelly Van Horn & Stephen

Low, D Domonic Paris, W Paris, Bianca Littlebaum, Harry Azorin & Van Horn, PH Ronnie Taylor, M George Small, AD Tom Allen.

LP Robin Johnson (Gina), Patti Lee (Joan), Chuck McQuary (Chuck), Barbara M. Bingham (Susie), Shirley Stoler (Dean Hunta), Raymond Serra (Vito), Martin Rosenblatt (Louie), Sal Carollo (Tony).

When a female rock band helps a sorority at Hoofer College win a strip basketball game and a lingerie wrestling conquest, it doesn't sit well with dictatorial dean Shirley Stoler. (Those deans are such party-poopers.) Don't movie colleges ever have anything higher than a dean?

2818. *Spookies* (1988, Safir, 84m, c). P Eugenie Joseph, Thomas Doran, Brendan Faulkner & Frank M. Farel, D Joseph, Doran & Faulkner, W Farel, Doran, Faulkner & Joseph Burgund, PH Robert Chappell & Ken Kelsch, M Kenneth Higgins & James Calabrese, ED Joseph.

LP Felix Ward (Kreon), Dan Scott (Kreon's Servant), Alec Nemser (Billy), Maria Pechukas (Isabelle).

Trying to resurrect his wife, dead for 70 years, ancient sorcerer Felix Ward is in need of some human sacrifices. A group of youngsters show up at his mansion and they'll do just fine, thank you.

2819. *Spring Break* (1983, Columbia, 101m, c). P&D Sean S. Cunningham, W David Smilow, PH Stephen Poster, M Harry Manfredi, ED Susan Cunningham & Angie Ross, PD Virginia Field.

LP David Knell (Nelson), Steve Bassett (O.T.), Perry Lang (Adam), Paul Land (Stu), Richard B. Shull (Eddie), Corinne Alphen (Joan), Jayne Modean (Susie), Donald Symington (Ernest Dalby), Mimi Cozzens (May Dalby).

Four college students are thrown together in a small motel room in Fort Lauderdale during Spring Break, looking for fun and to get laid. That's about the extent of the minuscule plot.

2820. *Spring Fever* (1983, Amulet/Comworld, Canada, 100m, c). P John F. Bassett, D Joseph L. Scanlan, W Fred Stefan & Stuart Gillard, PH Donald

Wilder, M Fred Mollin, ED Kirk Jones & Tony Lower, AD Bruno Rubeo & Carmi Gallo.

LP Susan Anton (Stevie Castle), Frank Converse (Louis Corman), Jessica Walter (Celia Berryman), Stephen Young (Neil Berryman), Carling Bassett (Karen Castle), David Mall (Beechman), Lisa Brady (Rhoda), Barbara Cook (Chris).

Young tennis star Carling Bassett finds it difficult to establish friendships at a junior tennis championship because her mother Susan Anton is just too good looking.

2821. *Square Dance* (1987, Island, 112m, c). P&D Daniel Petrie, W Alan Hines (based on his novel), PH Jacek Laskus, M Bruce Broughton, ED Bruce Green, PD Jan Scott.

LP Jason Robards, Jr. (Dillard), Jane Alexander (Juanelle), Winona Ryder (Gemma Dillard), Rob Lowe (Rory), Deborah Richter (Gwen), Guich Koock (Frank), Elbert Lewis (Beecham), Charlotte Stanton (Aggie), J. David Moeller (Dub Mosley), Dixie Taylor (Dolores).

Thirteen-year-old, Godfearing Winona Ryder becomes disenchanted with life on her crotchety grandfather Jason Robards' farm and runs away to live with her mother, Jane Alexander, who left her years before. Ryder falls in love with Rob Lowe, an emotionally disturbed young man. It's a poignant coming of age drama with Ryder quite good.

2822. *The Squeeze* (1987, Tri-Star, 101m, c). P Rupert Hitzig & Michael Tannen, D Roger Young, W Daniel Taplitz, PH Arthur Albert, M Miles Goodman, ED Harry Keramidas, PD Simon Waters.

LP Michael Keaton (Harry Berg), Rae Dawn Chong (Rachel Dobs), John Davidson (Honest Tom T. Murray), Ric Abernathy (Bouncer), Danny Aiello, III (Ralph Vigo), Bobby Bass (Poker Player), Leslie Bevis (Gem Vigo).

Down-and-out new wave artist Michael Keaton tries every scam to make it big with little success. He teams up with Rae Dawn Chong, a would-be detective, to uncover an outrageous lottery-fixing scheme worth $56 million.

2823. *Squizzy Taylor* (1984, Satori, Australia, 98m, c). P Roger LeMesurier,

D Kevin Dobson, W Roger Simpson, PH Dan Burstall, M Bruce Smeaton, ED David Pulbrook, PD Logan Brewer.

LP David Atkins (Squizzy Taylor), Jacki Weaver (Dolly), Kim Lewis (Ida), Michael Long (Inspector Piggot), Fred Cullen (Henry), Alan Cassell (Detective Brophy), Steve Bisley (Snowy), Peter Paulsen (Harry).

The film is the true story of the rise and fall of an Australian mob boss, Squizzy Taylor.

2824. *Stacking* (1987, Spectrafilm, 97m, c). P&D Martin Rosen, W Victoria Jenkins, PH Richard Bowen, M Patrick Gleeson, ED Patrick Dodd, PD David Wasco.

LP Christine Lahti (Kathleen Morgan), Frederic Forrest (Buster McGuire), Megan Follows (Anna Mae Morgan), Jason Gedrick (Gary Connaloe), Ray Baker (Dan Morgan), Peter Coyote (Photographer), James Gammon (Clate Connaloe).

Some of the performances in this dull account of the growing up of young Megan Follows in the rural West of the 50s, are laudable, but they are not enough to prevent audiences from becoming bored. "Stacking" refers to the operation of stacking bales of hay with the help of a large tractor-like piece of farm machinery.

2825. *Stacy's Knights* (1983, Crown, 100m, c, aka *Double Down*). P JoAnn Locktov & Freddy Sweet, D Jim Wilson, W Michael Blake, PH Raoul Lomas, M Norton Buffalo, ED Bonnie Koehler, AD Florence Fellman.

LP Andra Millian (Stacy), Kevin Costner (Will), Eve Lilith (Jean), Mike Reynolds (Shecky), Ed Semenza (Kid), Don Hackstaff (Lawyer), Gary Tilles (Rudy), Garth Howard (Mr. C.), Cheryl Ferris (Marion).

Andra Millian is an innocent young girl with amazing skills at blackjack. She teams up with a group of backers, her "knights," to set up an incredible sting operation.

2826. *Stakeout* (1987, Buena Vista, 115m, c). P Jim Kouf & Cathleen Summers, D John Badham, W Kouf, PH John Seale, M Arthur B. Rubinstein, ED

Tom Rolf & Michael Ripps, PD Philip Harrison.

LP Richard Dreyfuss (Chris Lecce), Emilio Estevez (Bill Reimers), Madeleine Stowe (Maria McGuire), Aidan Quinn (Richard "Stick" Montgomery), Dan Lauria (Phil Coldshank), Forest Whitaker (Jack Pismo), Earl Billings (Capt. Gilles).

When nasty killer Aidan Quinn escapes from prison, Seattle police figure he will come for his former girlfriend Madeleine Stowe. Richard Dreyfuss and Emilio Estevez make up one of the teams staking out her apartment. Dreyfuss makes things more complex than usual by becoming romantically involved with Stowe. The film has some nice humor and decent excitement when Quinn finally shows up.

2827. *Stand Alone* (1985, New World, 94m, c). P Leon Williams, D Alan Beattie, W Roy Carlson, PH Tom Richmond & Tim Suhrstedt, M David Richard Campbell, ED Fabien Dahlen Tordjmann, AD Pam Warner.

LP Charles Durning (Louis), Pam Grier (Catherine), James Keach (Isgro), Bert Remsen (Paddie), Barbara Sammeth (Meg), Lu Leonard (Mrs. Whitehead), Luis Contreras (Look-Out), Willard Pugh (Macombers), Bob Tzudiker (Farley), Mary Ann Smith (Nurse Warren).

Decorated World War II veteran Charles Durning witnesses a street-gang killing. Despite warnings from his lawyer Pam Grier not to get involved, Durning refuses to be intimidated, even when the low-lifes responsible for the killing beat up his buddy Bert Remsen. Durning arms himself to the teeth and waits in his home for them to come for him. He doesn't have long to wait.

2828. *Stand and Deliver* (1988, Warner, 105m, c). P Tom Musca, D Ramon Menendez, W Menendez & Musca, PH Tom Richmond, M Craig Safan, ED Nancy Richardson, AD Milo.

LP Edward James Olmos† (Jamie Escalante), Lou Diamond Phillips (Angel), Rosanna De Soto (Fabiola Escalante), Andy Garcia (Ramirez), Ingrid Oliu (Lupe), Karla Montana (Claudia), Vanessa Marquez (Ana), Mark Eliot (Tito), Patrick Baca (Javier), Will Gotay

(Pancho), Daniel Villarreal (Chuco), Carmen Argenziano (Molina), Virginia Paris (Raquel Ortega), Lydia Nicole (Rafaela).

This is the inspiring, hopeful true story of someone who has made a difference. Edward James Olmos superbly portrays the electronics employee Escalante who gives up a good job so he can teach in East L.A.'s Garfield High to barrio kids. Although initially very few of his students see any advantage in learning mathematics, their dedicated and demanding teacher gets a bunch of them to study advanced placement calculus. They all pass the exam, which means they get college credit for their study, but at first there is some suspicion, probably racially motivated, that they cheated. This is cleared up in this stand-up-and-cheer film, and as we learn at the closing credits, each year more and more Garfield students take and pass AP calculus, because of the efforts of Escalante. The only complaint that we can make about this marvelous movie is that more isn't shown as to how Escalante was able to get indifferent students to overcome their suspicion that education wouldn't do much for them and become diligent pupils who would come to school early, stay late and skip vacations so they might learn. Now that's a lesson our schools and teachers need to learn.

2829. *Stand by Me* (1986, Columbia, 87m, c). P Andrew Scheinman, Bruce A. Evans & Raynold Gideon, D Rob Reiner, W Gideon & Evans† (based on the novella *The Body* by Stephen King), PH Thomas Del Ruth, M Jack Nitzsche, ED Robert Leighton, PD Dennis Washington.

LP Wil Wheaton (Gordie Lachance), River Phoenix (Chris Chambers), Corey Feldman (Teddy Duchamp), Jerry O'Connell (Vern Tessio), Richard Dreyfuss (The Writer), Kiefer Sutherland (Ace Merrill), Casey Siemaszko (Billy Tessio), Gary Riley (Charlie Hogan), Bradley Gregg (Eyeball Chambers).

In a spectacular film, four young boys spend the last weekend of summer searching for the body of a boy believed hit by a train. Sometimes funny, sometimes sad, this coming of age film is perfectly

enhanced by the old title song, sung by Ben E. King.

2830. *The Stand-In* (1985, Stand-In, 87m, c). P&D Robert N. Zagone, W Zagone & Edward Azlant, PH Rick Butler, M Don Lewis, ED Kenji Yamamoto & Norm Levy, AD Don De Fina.

LP Danny Glover, Christa Victoria, Joe Bellan, Jane Dornacker, Marc Hayashi, Bob Sarlatte.

Made in San Francisco before becoming a star, Danny Glover is featured as the independent filmmaker who accidentally kills a crude biker. To cover up the crime, he assumes the identity of his victim.

2831. *The Star Chamber* (1983, 20th Century-Fox, 109m, c). P Frank Yablans, D Peter Hyams, W Roderick Taylor & Hyams (based on a story by Taylor), PH Richard Hannah, M Michael Small, ED Jim Mitchell & Charles Tetoni, PD Bill Malley.

LP Michael Douglas (Steven Hardin), Hal Holbrook (Benjamin Caulfield), Yaphet Kotto (Detective Harry Lowes), Sharon Gless (Emily Hardin), James B. Sikking (Dr. Harold Lewin), Joe Regalbuto (Arthur Cooms), Don Calfa (Lawrence Monk), John DiSanti (Detective James Wickman).

A team of judges gets together to retry defendents who have escaped justice because of legal technicalities. If found guilty, the jurists have them executed by hired assassins.

2832. *Star 80* (1983, Warner, 102m, c). P Wolfgang Glattes & Kenneth Utt, D&W Bob Fosse (based on *Death of a Playmate* by Teresa Carpenter), PH Sven Nykvist, M Ralph Burns, ED Alan Heim, AD Jack G. Taylor, Jr.

LP Mariel Hemingway (Dorothy Stratten), Eric Roberts (Paul Snider), Cliff Robertson (Hugh Hefner), Carroll Baker (Dorothy's Mother), Roger Rees (Aram Nicholas), David Clennon (Geb), Josh Mostel (Private Detective).

This is the unappetizing account of the short life and career of Playmate of the Year Dorothy Stratten, who was murdered by her husband, after which he took his own life. Mariel Hemingway had her breasts enlarged by surgery for the role.

2833. *Star Slammer: The Escape* (1988, Vidmark, 86m, c, aka *Prison Ship*). P Jack H. Harris & Fred Olen Ray, D Ray, W Michael D. Sonye (based on a story by Sonye, Miriam Preissel & Ray), PH Paul Elliott, M Anthony Harris, ED Preissel, PD Michael Novotny.

LP Sandy Brooke (Taura), Susan Stokey (Mike), Ross Hagen (Bantor), Marya Gant (Warden Exene), Aldo Ray (The Inquisitor), Dawn Wildsmith (Muffin), Richard Alan Hench (Garth), Michael D. Sonye (Krago), Lindy Skyles (The Sovereign), Bobbie Bresee (Marai), John Carradine (The Judge).

Fred Olen Ray has made a women's prison film with a science-fiction setting and for good measure throws in some decent laughs. It went directly to the shelves of your local video store.

2834. *Star Trek II: The Wrath of Khan* (1982, Paramount, 113m, c). P Robert Sallin, D Nicholas Meyer, W Jack B. Sowards (based on a story by Harve Bennett, Sowards and the TV program "Star Trek" created by Gene Roddenberry), PH Gayne Rescher, M James Horner, ED William P. Dornisch, PD Joseph R. Jennings.

LP William Shatner (Adm. James T. Kirk), Leonard Nimoy (Mr. Spock), DeForest Kelley (Dr. Leonard "Bones" McCoy), James Doohan (Chief Engineer Montgomery "Scotty" Scott), Walter Koenig (Chekov), George Takei (Sulu), Nichelle Nichols (Cmdr. Uhura), Bibi Besch (Dr. Carol Marcus), Merritt Butrick (David), Paul Winfield (Starship Reliant Captain Terrell), Kirstie Alley (Saavik), Ricardo Montalban (Khan).

The crew of the starship *Enterprise* must counter the evil genius Ricardo Montalban, an old foe who blames William Shatner for the death of his wife.

2835. *Star Trek III: The Search for Spock* (1984, Paramount, 105m, c). P Harve Bennett, D Leonard Nimoy, W Bennett (based on the TV production "Star Trek" by Gene Roddenberry), PH Charles Correll, M James Horner, ED Robert F. Shugrue, AD John E. Chilberg, II, SD Tom Pedigo, SE Rocky Gehr.

LP William Shatner (Kirk), Leonard Nimoy (Spock), DeForest Kelley (Mc-

Coy), James Doohan (Scotty), Walter Koenig (Chekov), George Takei (Sulu), Nichelle Nichols (Uhura), Robin Curtis (Saavik), Merritt Butrick (David), Phil Morris (Trainee Foster), Scott McGinnis ("Mr. Adventure"), Robert Hooks (Adm. Morrow), Christopher Lloyd (Kurge, Klingon), John Larroquette (Maltz, Klingon), James B. Sikking (Capt. Styles), Judith Anderson (High Priestess of Vulcans).

Captain Kirk (William Shatner) and the remaining crew of the starship *Enterprise* journey to the Genesis planet to discover if Spock (Leonard Nimoy) still lives.

2836. *Star Trek IV: The Voyage Home* (1986, Paramount, 119m, c). P Harve Bennett, D Leonard Nimoy, W Steve Meerson & Peter Krikes (based on a story by Nimoy & Bennett and the TV series "Star Trek" created by Gene Roddenberry), PH Don Peterman†, M Leonard Rosenman†, ED Peter E. Berger, PD Jack T. Collis, SOUND Terry Porter, Dave Hudson, Mel Metcalfe & Gene Cantamessa†, SOUND EFFECTS ED Mark Mangini†.

LP William Shatner (Kirk), Leonard Nimoy (Spock), DeForest Kelley (McCoy), James Doohan (Scotty), Walter Koenig (Chekov), Nichelle Nichols (Uhura), George Takei (Sulu), Jane Wyatt (Amanda), Catherine Hicks (Gillian), Mark Lenard (Sarek), Robin Curtis (Lt. Saavik), John Schuck (Klingon Ambassador), Brock Peters (Admiral Cartwright).

In an uncharacteristic but welcomed switch, the crew of the *Enterprise* try their hands at comedy. They exit the 23rd century universe, which is on the verge of destruction by an alien probe, to seek humanity's salvation in the 20th century United States.

2837. *Star Trek V: The Final Frontier* (1989, Paramount, 106m, c). P Harve Bennett, D William Shatner, W David Loughery (based on a story by Shatner, Bennett & Loughery and the TV series "Star Trek" created by Gene Roddenberry), PH Andrew Laszlo, M Jerry Goldsmith, ED Peter Berger.

LP William Shatner (Kirk), Leonard Nimoy (Spock), DeForest Kelley

(McCoy), James Doohan (Scotty), Walter Koenig (Chekov), Nichelle Nichols (Uhura), George Takei (Sulu), David Warner (St. John Talbot), Laurence Luckinbill (Sybok), Charles Cooper (Korrd), Cynthia Gouw (Caithlin Dar), Todd Bryant (Captain Klaa), Spice Williams (Vixis).

In this disappointing entry in the Star Trek series, unimaginatively directed by William Shatner, Laurence Luckinbill, in Kabuki-like makeup, is a renegade Vulcan who kidnaps the crew of the *Enterprise* and makes them fly to a never-before explored galaxy to seek the meaning of life. They don't find it.

2838. *Starchaser: The Legend of Orin* (1985, Atlantic, animated, 3-D, 101m, c). P Steven Hahn, D Hahn & John Sparey, W Jeffrey Scott, M Andrew Belling, ED Donald W. Ernst, PD Louis Zingarelli.

VOICES Joe Colligan (Orin), Carmen Argenziano (Dagg), Noelle North (Elan/Aviana), Anthony Delongis (Zygon), Les Tremayne (Arthur), Tyke Caravelli (Silica), Ken Sansom (Magreb), John Moschitta, Jr. (Auctioneer/Z. Gork), Mickey Morton (Minemaster).

In this animated fantasy, Orin, using a magic sword, saves the world of the future from malevolent hordes.

Starchild see ***Space Raiders***

2839. *Stardust Memories* (1980, United Artists, 90m, b&w). P Robert Greenhut, D&W Woody Allen, PH Gordon Willis, ED Susan E. Morse, PD Santo Loquasto.

LP Woody Allen (Sandy Bates), Charlotte Rampling (Dorrie), Jessica Harper (Daisy), Marie-Christine Barrault (Isobel), Tony Roberts (Tony), Daniel Stern (Actor), Amy Wright (Shelley), Helen Hanft (Vivian Orkin), John Rothman (Jack Abel).

In a painfully autobiographical film, Woody Allen as an increasingly melancholy comedian attends a retrospective of his career and is plagued by feelings of failure and inadequacy. Allen pokes fun at those who admire his films to the point of making them cult pieces.

2840. *Stark Raving Mad* (1983, Independent Artists, 88m, c). P Tiger Warren & Don Gronquist, D George F. Hood, W Uncredited, PH J. Wilder, ED Hood, AD W.S. Warren.

LP Russell Fast (Richard), Marcie Severson (Laura), B. Joe Medley (Francis), Mike Walter (David), Janet Galen (Barbara), Don Beekman (Norman), Mildred Card (Dorothy), Marjorie Hall (Maid).

The title tells it all in this cheaply produced independent horror film.

2841. *Starlight Hotel* (1988, Republic Pictures, New Zealand, 93m, c). P Finola Dwyer & Larry Parr, D Sam Pillsbury, W Grant Hinden Miller (based on his novel *The Dream Monger*), PH Warrick Attewell, ED Mike Horton, PD Mike Becroft.

LP Peter Phelps (Patrick), Greer Robson (Kate), Marshall Napier (Detective Wallace), The Wizard (Spooner), Alice Fraser (Aunt), Patrick Smyth (Uncle), Bruce Phillips (Dave Marshall), Donogh Rees (Helen).

In 1929, 12-year-old runaway Peter Phelps, bound for Australia, travels across the New Zealand countryside. It's violent.

2842. *Starman* (1984, Columbia, 115m, c). P Larry J. Franco, D John Carpenter, W Bruce A. Evans & Raynold Gideon, PH Donald M. Morgan, M Jack Nitzsche, ED Marion Rothman, PD Daniel Lomino.

LP Jeff Bridges† (Starman), Karen Allen (Jenny Hayden), Charles Martin Smith (Mark Shermin), Richard Jaeckel (George Fox), Robert Phalen (Maj. Bell), Tony Edwards (Sgt. Lemon), John Walter Davis (Brad Heinmuller).

When an alien from an advanced civilization lands in Wisconsin, he finds a less than warm welcome from the military. To disguise himself, he clones himself into the form of Jeff Bridges, the recently deceased husband of grieving Karen Allen. With hostile authorities in hot pursuit, the alien and the widow race to his rendezvous spot in Arizona, falling in love along the way.

2843. *Stars and Bars* (1988, Columbia, 94m, c). P Sandy Lieberson, D Pat O'Connor, W William Boyd (based on his novel), PH Jerzy Zielinski, M Stanley Myers, ED Michael Bradsell, PD Leslie Dilley & Stuart Craig.

LP Daniel Day-Lewis (Henderson

Dores), Harry Dean Stanton (Loomis Gage), Kent Broadhurst (Sereno), Maury Chaykin (Freeborn Gage), Matthew Cowles (Beckman Gage), Joan Cusack (Irene Stein), Keith David (Teagarden), Spalding Gray (Rev. Cardew), Glenne Headly (Cora Gage).

In this overbaked, misfiring comedy, very proper British Daniel Day-Lewis is sent to Georgia to negotiate the purchase of a Renoir and runs afoul of boorish, combative Southerners.

2844.   *Starstruck* (1982, Cinecom, Australia, 102m, c). P David Elfick & Richard Brennan, D Gillian Armstrong, W Stephen Maclean, PH Russell Boyd, ED Nicholas Beauman, PD Brian Thomson.

LP Jo Kennedy (Jackie Mullens), Ross O'Donovan (Angus Mullens), Pat Evison (Nana), Margo Lee (Pearl), Max Cullen (Reg), Melissa Jaffer (Mrs. Booth), Ned Lander (Robbie), John O'May (Terry Lambert).

In a pleasant musical 14-year-old Ross O'Donovan decides to make his new wave, punk-rock cousin Jo Kennedy into a major star, no matter what it takes.

2845.   *The State of Things* (1983, Gray City/Artificial Eye, 121m, b&w). P Chris Sievernich, D Wim Wenders, W Wenders & Robert Kramer, PH Henri Alekan & Fred Murphy, M Jurgen Knieper, ED Barbara von Weitershausen.

LP Isabelle Weingarten (Anna), Rebecca Pauly (Joan), Jeffrey Kime (Mark), Geoffrey Carey (Robert), Camilla Mora (Julia), Alexandra Auder (Jane), Patrick Bauchau (Friedrich, Director), Paul Getty, III (Dennis, Writer).

The film is the saga of filmmaker Patrick Bauchau and his crew shooting a remake of a Hollywood B movie, *The Most Dangerous Man on Earth,* in the boondocks of Spain.

2846.   *Static* (1985, Film Forum, 93m, c). P Amy Ness, D Mark Romanek, W Romanek & Keith Gordon, PH Jeff Jur, ED Emily Paine, SD Cynthia Sowder.

LP Keith Gordon (Ernie), Amanda Plummer (Julia), Bob Gunton (Frank), Barton Heyman (Sheriff William Orling), Lily Knight (Patty), Jane Hoffman (Emitly), Reathel Bean (Fred Savins), Kitty Mei Mei Chen (Li).

In a film which is sometimes fascinating, sometimes deadly dull, Keith Gordon has invented an unusual TV. Sometimes it picks up heaven.

2847.   *Staying Alive* (1983, Paramount, 96m, c). P Robert Stigwood & Sylvester Stallone, D Stallone, W Stallone & Norman Wexler (based on characters created by Nik Cohn), PH Nick McLean, M The Bee Gees, Frank Stallone & Johnny Mandel, ED Don Zimmerman & Mark Warner, PD Robert F. Boyle.

LP John Travolta (Tony Manero), Cynthia Rhodes (Jackie), Finola Hughes (Laura), Steve Inwood (Jesse), Julie Bovasso (Mrs. Manero), Charles Ward (Butler), Steve Bickford (Sound Technician), Patrick Brady (Derelict).

Sylvester Stallone almost ended John Travolta's career with this horrible sequel to *Saturday Night Live.* Sly has John sweating à la Rocky as a supposed star dancer in a hit musical. Fred Astaire always insisted that full body shots of his dancing be shown so that audiences could see what he was doing. Travolta is not so much dancing as moving from one pose to another with the camera doing the dancing. It's one of the all-time turkeys.

2848.   *Staying Together* (1989, Hemdale, 91m, c). P Joseph Feury, D Lee Grant, W Monte Merrick, PH Dick Bush, ED Katherine Wenning, PD Stuart Wurtzel, AD W. Steven Graham.

LP Sean Astin (Duncan McDermott), Stockard Channing (Nancy Trainer), Melinda Dillon (Eileen McDermott), Jim Haynie (Jake McDermott), Levon Helm (Denny Stockton), Dinah Manoff (Lois Cook), Dermot Mulroney (Kit McDermott), Tim Quill (Brian McDermott).

The McDermott clan, Mom, Dad and three strapping boys run a home-cooked chicken restaurant in a small South Carolina town. Everything is just ducky until yuppies move into the area with their condos and unlimited supply of money. Dad sells the restaurant when he is offered an almost obscene profit. The three lads are now forced to re-evaluate their lives, learning that there is more to life than good times.

2849.   *Stealing Heaven* (1989, Scotti Bros., GB/Yugo., 116m, c). P Simon

MacCorkindale, D Clive Donner, W Chris Bryant (based on the novel by Marion Meade), PH Mikael Salomon, M Nick Bicat, ED Michael Ellis, PD Voytek Roman.

LP Derek de Lint (Pierre Abelard), Kim Thompson (Heloise), Denholm Elliott (Fulbert), Mark Jax (Jourdain), Rachel Kempson (Prioress), Angela Pleasence (Sister Cecilia), Bernard Hepton (Bishop Martin), Kenneth Cranham (Vice Chancellor Suger).

This modest production is surprisingly well done. It is the true story of 12th-century philosopher Pierre Abelard and his beautiful gifted student Heloise. They become lovers, have a child and are secretly married. This does not set well with Heloise's powerful uncle, who had other plans for her. He has Abelard castrated. The latter becomes a monk, while Heloise reluctantly retires to a convent.

2850. *Stealing Home* (1988, Warner, 98m, c). P Thom Mount & Hank Moonjean, D&W Steven Kampmann & Will Aldis, PH Bobby Byrne, M David Foster, ED Antony Gibbs, AD Vaughan Edwards, SD Robert Franco.

LP Mark Harmon (Billy Wyatt as an adult), Blair Brown (Ginny Wyatt), Jodie Foster (Katie Chandler), Jonathan Silverman (Alan Appleby as a teen), Harold Ramis (Alan Appleby as an adult), John Shea (Sam Wyatt), William McNamara (Billy Wyatt as a teen), Thatcher Goodwin (Billy Wyatt as a child), Judith Kahan (Laura Appleby).

Flashbacks tell the story of minor league baseball player Mark Harmon's bittersweet relationship with Jodie Foster, an older woman who was both his lover and mentor.

2851. *Steaming* (1985, Columbia, GB, 95m, c). P Paul Mills, D Joseph Losey, W Patricia Losey (based on the play by Nell Dunn), PH Christopher Challis, M Richard Harvey, ED Reginald Beck, PD Maurice Fowler.

LP Vanessa Redgrave (Nancy), Sarah Miles (Sarah), Diana Dors (Violet), Patti Love (Josie), Brenda Bruce (Mrs. Meadows), Felicity Dean (Dawn Meadows), Sally Sagoe (Celia).

The performances are better than average in this story of the interactions of a group of women in a run-down London steam bath. The film could use a bit more humor to make it palatable.

2852. *Steel* (1980, World/Northal, 99m, c, aka *Look Down and Die; Men of Steel*). P Peter S. Davis & William N. Panzer, D Steven Carver, W Leigh Chapman (based on a story by Rob Ewing, Davis & Panzer), PH Roger Shearman, M Michel Colombier, ED David Blewitt, PD Ward Preston.

LP Lee Majors (Mike Catton), Jennifer O'Neill (Cass Cassidy), Art Carney (Pignose Moran), George Kennedy (Lew Cassidy), Harris Yulin (Eddie Cassidy), Redmond Cleason (Harry), Terry Kiser (Valentino).

When construction boss George Kennedy is killed, his daughter Jennifer O'Neill vows to complete his last project. It's harmless hokum.

2853. *Steel Dawn* (1987, Vestron/Silver Lion, 100m, c). P Lance Hool & Conrad Hool, D L. Hool, W Doug Lefler, PH George Tirl, M Brian May, ED Mark Conte, PD Alex Tavoularis.

LP Patrick Swayze (Nomad), Lisa Niemi (Kasha), Christopher Neame (Sho), Brion James (Tark), John Fujioka (Cord), Brett Hool (Jux), Anthony Zerbe (Damnil), Marcel Van Heerden (Lann), Arnold Vosloo (Makker).

In a modern version of *Shane*, Patrick Swayze is a sword-wielding martial arts expert who wanders the desert wasteland, becoming Lisa Niemi and her son's champion against the evil Anthony Zerbe and his men.

2854. *Steel Magnolias* (1989, Tri-Star, 118m, c). P Ray Stark, D Herbert Ross, W Robert Harling (based on his play), PH John A. Alonzo, M Georges Delerue, ED Paul Hirsch, PD Gene Callahan & Edward Pisoni.

LP Sally Field (M'Lynn Eatenton), Dolly Parton (Truvy Jones), Shirley MacLaine (Ouiser Boudreaux), Daryl Hannah (Annelle Dupuy Desoto), Olympia Dukakis (Clairee Belcher), Julia Roberts† (Shelby Eatenton Latcherie), Tom Skerritt (Drum Eatenton), Sam Shepard (Spud Jones), Dylan McDermott (Jackson Latcherie), Kevin J. O'Connor (Sammy Desoto), Bill McCutcheon (Owen Jenkins).

Here's the one to see at the end of the 1980s. It's a superb cast which makes audiences laugh and cry and cheer a bit. The movie differs from the still-running play, in that it opens up and introduces the men (only talked about on stage) of the wild, lively group of Southern women who meet in a beauty parlor to gossip, crack jokes and help each other. Each of the six women stars check their egos at the door of the beauty parlor and work surprisingly well together. It's tough to say which one gives the best performance, but if forced to vote, we'd say Olympia Dukakis squeaks by Shirley MacLaine by an eyelash. Others may choose Sally Field, who handles the chores of the mother of doomed Julia Roberts with a sure sense.

2855.   Steele Justice (1987, Atlantic, 95m, c). P John Strong, D&W Robert Boris, PH John M. Stephens, M Misha Segal, ED John O'Connor & Steve Rosenblum, PD Richard N. McGuire.

LP Martin Kove (John Steele), Sela Ward (Tracy), Ronny Cox (Bennett), Bernie Casey (Reese), Joseph Campanella (Harry), Soon-Teck Oh (Gen. Bon Soong Kwan), Jan Gan Boyd (Cami Van Minh), David Froman (Kelso), Sarah Douglas (Kay).

Vietnam vet Martin Kove's investigation of the murders of the family of a Vietnamese friend in L.A. puts him on the trail of former Vietnam general Soon-Teck Oh, who's now a druglord in the U.S.

2856.   The Stepfather (1987, New Century/Vista, 90m, c). P Jay Benson, D Joseph Ruben, W Donald E. Westlake (based on a story by Carolyn Lefcourt, Brian Garfield & Westlake), PH John W. Lindley, M Patrick Moraz, ED George Bowers, PD James William Newport.

LP Terry O'Quinn (Jerry Blake, the Stepfather/Henry Morrison/Bill Hodgkins), Jill Schoelen (Stephanie Maine), Shelley Hack (Susan Blake), Charles Lanyer (Dr. Bondurant), Stephen Shellen (Jim Ogilvie), Stephen E. Miller (Al Brennan), Robyn Stevan (Karen), Jeff Schultz (Paul Baker).

Terry O'Quinn's stepdaughter Jill Schoelen has good instincts in not liking him. He's been married before, with a

family. When he grew tired of them, he killed them and assumed a new identity. Will Schoelen and her mother Shelley Hack be next?

2857.   Stepfather II: Make Room for Daddy (1989, Millimeter Films, 88m, c). P William Burr & Darin Scott, D Jeff Burr, W John Auerbach, PH Jacek Kaskus, M Jim Manzie, ED Pasquale A. Buba.

LP Terry O'Quinn (The Stepfather), Meg Foster (Carol Grayland), Jonathan Brandis (Todd Grayland), Caroline Williams (Matty Crimmins), Henry Brown (Dr. Joseph Danvers), Mitchell Laurance (Phil Grayland).

Terry O'Quinn reprises his role of what appears to be an average middleclass male. However, his tight little smile suggests a menace which doesn't stay hidden. The film appears to miss the hand of director Joseph Ruben, who has gone on to better things.

2858.   Stephen King's Silver Bullet (1985, Paramount, 95m, c). P Martha Schumacher, D Daniel Attias, W Stephen King (based on his novelette *Cycle of the Werewolf*), PH Armando Nannuzzi, M Jay Chattaway, ED Daniel Loewenthal, PD Giorgio Postiglione.

LP Gary Busey (Uncle Red), Everett McGill (Rev. Lowe/Werewolf), Corey Haim (Marty Coslaw), Megan Follows (Jane Coslaw), Robin Groves (Nan Coslaw), Leon Russom (Bob Coslaw), Terry O'Quinn (Sheriff Joe Haller).

Once again, our contention is that if moviemakers use the name of a popular writer *in the title,* they are advertising that the film is a stinker and needs the boost of a well-known name. Plucky, handicapped, young Corey Haim, with the help of his drunken uncle Gary Busey, his disbelieving sister Megan Follows, and a silver bullet put an end to the rampage of a nasty werewolf ravaging their small town.

2859.   Stewardess School (1987, Columbia, 87m, c). P Phil Feldman, D&W Ken Blancato, PH Fred J. Koenekamp, M Robert Folk, ED Lou Lombardo & Kenneth C. Paonessa, PD Daniel A. Lomino.

LP Brett Cullen (Philo Henderson), Mary Cadorette (Kelly Johnson), Donald

Most (George Bunkle), Sandahl Bergman (Wanda Polanski), Wendie Jo Sperber (Jolean Winters), Judy Landers (Sugar Dubois).

The curriculum of this school features a lot of foolin' around. The interiors of airplanes apparently are aphrodisiacs.

2860. *Stick* (1985, Universal, 109m, c). P Jennings Lang, D Burt Reynolds, W Elmore Leonard & Joseph C. Stinson (based on the novel by Leonard), PH Nick McLean, M Barry De Vorzon & Joseph Conlan, ED William Gordean, PD James Shanahan.

LP Burt Reynolds (Stick), Candice Bergen (Kyle), George Segal (Barry), Charles Durning (Chucky), Jose Perez (Rainy), Richard Lawson (Cornell), Castulo Guerra (Nestor), Dar Robinson (Moke), Alex Rocco (Firestone).

Director Burt Reynolds should have canned actor Burt Reynolds, who seems to be just going through the motions. He's an ex-con who wants to start a new life in Miami, but keeps running into various bad guys who make him mad enough to seek revenge. Actor Reynolds should have insisted on a new director, one who knew something about pacing and actors working together.

2861. *Sticky Fingers* (1988, Spectrafilm, 97m, c). P Catlin Adams & Melanie Mayron, D Adams, W Adams & Mayron, PH Gary Thieltges, M Gary Chang, ED Bob Reitano, PD Jessica Scott-Justice.

LP Helen Slater (Hattie), Melanie Mayron (Lolly), Danitra Vance (Evanston), Eileen Brennan (Stella), Carol Kane (Kitty), Loretta Devine (Diane), Stephen McHattie (Eddie), Christopher Guest (Sam), Gwen Welles (Marcie), Shirley Stoller (Reeba).

Helen Slater and Melanie Mayron are charmless as two struggling musicians who discover a suitcase containing $900,000 left in their care by a friendly dope dealer. They spend, spend, spend.

2862. *Stitches* (1985, Intl. Film Marketing, 89m, c). P William B. Kerr & Robert P. Marcucci, D Alan Smithee [Rod Holcomb], W Michel Choquette & Michael Paseornek, PH Hector R. Figueroa, M Bob Floke, ED John Duffy, AD Diane Campbell.

LP Parker Stevenson (Bobby Stevens), Geoffrey Lewis (Ralph Rizzo), Brian Tochi (Sam Boon Tong), Robin Dearden (Nancy McNaughton), Bob Dubac (Al Rosenberg), Tommy Koenig ("Barfer" Bogan), Sidney Lassick (Sheldon Mendelbaum), Eddie Albert (Dean Bradley), Susanne Wasson (Judith Bradley).

Didn't the British have a string of hits on their hands a decade or so ago about the hijinks of medical students and their amorous times with sexy nurses? Why can't nice American boys like Parker Stevenson, Bob Dubac and Brian Tochi make a successful American version? Because they are untalented clods who smirk and giggle like horny 13 year olds while carrying off unfunny sexist and scatological practical jokes, most at the expense of poor old Eddie Albert.

2863. *Still of the Night* (1982, MGM/United Artists, 91m, c). P Arlene Donovan, D&W Robert Benton (based on a story by David Newman & Benton), PH Nestor Almendros, M John Kander, ED Jerry Greenberg, PD Mel Bourne.

LP Roy Scheider (Sam Rice), Meryl Streep (Brooke Reynolds), Jessica Tandy (Grace Rice), Joe Grifasi (Joseph Vitucci), Sara Botsford (Gail Phillips), Josef Sommer (George Bynum), Rikke Borge (Heather Wilson).

Manhattan psychiatrist Roy Scheider is suspected of having killed one of his patients or at least knowing more about the death than he's telling. He claims doctor-patient confidentiality. The deceased's mistress Meryl Streep is also a likely candidate as the murderer. Director Robert Benton is trying to play like Alfred Hitchcock, but he's out of his league.

2864. *Still Smokin'* (1983, Paramount, 91m, c, aka *Cheech and Chong's Still Smokin'*). P Peter MacGregor-Scott, D Thomas Chong, W Chong & Cheech Marin, PH Harvey Harrison, M George S. Clinton, ED David Ramirez & James Coblentz, AD Ruud Van Dijk.

LP Cheech Marin, Tommy Chong (Themselves), Hans Van In't Veld (Promoter), Carol Van Herwijen (Hotel Manager), Shireen Strooker (Assn't Manager), Susan Hahn (Maid), Arjan Ederveen & Kees Prins (Bellboys), Mariette

Bout (Waitress), Fabiola (Barge Lady), Carla Van Amstel (Queen Beatrix).

Cheech and Chong travel to Amsterdam to raise money for a film festival by holding a dope-a-thon. They're dopes for sure and even their staunchest fans will be hard pressed to follow their hallucinations in this one.

2865.   A Sting in the Tale   (1989, Rosa Colosimo Films, Australia, 96m, c). P Rosa Colosimo & Reg McLean, D Eugene Schlusser, W Patrick Edgeworth, PH Nicholas Sherman, M Allan Zavod, ED Zbigniew Friedrich, PD Lisa Blitz Brennan.

LP Diane Craig (Diane Lane), Gary Day (Barry Robbins), Lynne Williams (Louise Parker), Edwin Hodgeman (Roger Monroe), Don Barker (Prime Minister Falcon), Jon Noble (P.M.'s minder), Tony Mack (Michael Meadows).

In a corny Australian soap opera, Diane Craig becomes Australia's first female prime minister and ruins a powerful media baron at the same time.

2866.   The Sting II   (1983, Universal, 102m, c). P Jennings Lang, D Jeremy Paul Kagan, W David S. Ward, PH Bill Butler, M Lalo Schifrin†, ED David Garfield, PD Edward C. Carfagno.

LP Jackie Gleason (Henry Gondorff), Mac Davis (Johnny Hooker), Teri Garr (Veronica), Karl Malden (Macalinski), Oliver Reed (Doyle Lonnegan), Bert Remsen (Kid Colors), Jose Perez (Carlos), Larry Bishop (Gallecher).

The competition is stiff, but this film definitely is in the running for worst sequel to a good movie. Jackie Gleason and Mac Davis play the Paul Newman and Robert Redford roles, respectively. They come up with a boxing scam involving nightclub owner Karl Malden, but also must deal with Oliver Reed who as Doyle Lonnegan is still steamed at the pair for the sting they pulled on him in the original. Only Teri Garr is worth seeing in this dull film.

2867.   Stir Crazy   (1980, Columbia, 111m, c). P Hannah Weinstein, D Sidney Poitier, W Bruce Jay Friedman, PH Fred Schuler, M Tom Scott, ED Harry Keller, PD Alfred Sweeney.

LP Gene Wilder (Skip Donahue), Richard Pryor (Harry Monroe), Georg Stanford Brown (Rory Schultebrand), JoBeth Williams (Meredith), Miguelangel Suarez (Jesus Ramirez), Craig T. Nelson (Deputy Ward Wilson).

New Yorkers Gene Wilder and Richard Pryor, heading for California to change their luck, are wrongly convicted of a bank robbery. Once in prison they plan their escape. There are a number of amusing moments in the film, but overall it's disappointing.

2868.   The Stone Boy   (1984, 20th Century–Fox, 93m, c). P Joe Roth & Ivan Bloch, D Chris Cain, W Gina Berriault (based on her short story), PH Juan Ruiz Anchia, M James Horner, ED Paul Rubell, PD Joseph G. Pacelli.

LP Robert Duvall (Joe Hillerman), Frederic Forrest (Andy Jansen), Glenn Close (Ruth Hillerman), Wilford Brimley (George Jansen), Jason Presson (Arnold Hillerman), Gail Youngs (Lu Jansen), Dean Cain (Eugene Hillerman).

In a film which easily could have been called "Ordinary People," the lives of poor farmer Robert Duvall, his wife Glenn Close, and their family is torn asunder when their two sons, Jason Presson and Dean Cain (the director's son) go out early one morning duck hunting, with the result that the former accidentally kills the latter. Immediately Presson retreats into a shell, which Duvall misreads as either being uncaring or not realizing the enormity of his deed. Left out of his parents' grief, Presson withdraws even more, becoming completely silent, a "stone boy." It isn't easy for these simple folks, without the means to hire any professional help to sort out their problems and unite as a family once more.

2869.   Stone Cold Dead   (1980, Ko-Zak/Dimension, Canada, 97m, c). P George Mendeluk & John Ryan, D&W Mendeluk (based on the novel *The Sin Sniper* by Hugh Garner), PH Dennis Miller, ED Martin Pepler, AD Ted Watkins.

LP Richard Crenna (Sgt. Boyd), Paul Williams (Julius Kurtz), Linda Sorenson (Monica Page), Belinda J. Montgomery (Sandy MacAuley), Charles Shamata

(Sgt. Tony Colabre), Alberta Watson (Olivia Page).

Police sergeant Richard Crenna hunts a sniper who only shoots prostitutes. He taunts the police with photographs of the girls at their moments of death.

2870. *Stoogemania* (1986, Atlantic, 83m, c/b&w). P Chuck Workman & James Ruxin, D Workman, W Jim Geoghan & Workman, PH Christopher Tufty, M Hummie Mann & Gary Tigerman, ED Ruxin.

LP Josh Mostel (Howard F. Howard), Melanie Chartoff (Beverly), Mark Holton (Son of Curly), Sid Caesar (Dr. Fixyer Minder), Patrick DeSantis (Moe, Jr.), Armin Shimermann (Larry II), Thom Sharp (Bob), Josh Miller (Young Howard), Victoria Jackson (Nurse Grabatit), Ron House (Stooge Hills Director).

Nerdish Josh Mostel becomes so obsessed with the Three Stooges that they begin to take over and ruin his life.

2871. *Storm* (1987, Cannon, Canada, 81m, c). P,D&W David Winning, PH Tim Hollings, M Amin Bhatia, ED Bill Campbell.

LP David Palfy (Lowell), Stan Kane (Jim), Tom Schioler (Booker), Harry Freedman (Burt), Lawrence Elion (Stanley), Stacy Christensen (Corbi), Tibi (Lisa), Sean O'Byrne (Danny), James Hutchison (Hostage).

This dull rip-off of *Gotcha* has two college students playing assassination tag with paint-pellet guns.

2872. *Stormy Monday* (1988, Atlantic, GB, 93m, c). P Nigel Stafford-Clark, D&W Mike Figgis, PH Roger Deakins, M Figgis, ED David Martin, PD Andrew McAlpine.

LP Melanie Griffith (Kate), Tommy Lee Jones (Cosmo), Sting (Finney), Sean Bean (Brendan), James Cosmo (Tony), Mark Long (Patrick), Brian Lewis (Jim), Heathcote Williams (Peter Reed), Prunella Gee (Mrs. Finney), Alison Steadman (Mayor), Al Matthews (Radio DJ), Guy Manning.

In this interesting thriller, unlikely lovers Melanie Griffith and Sean Bean work to prevent self-serving American business magnate/gangster Tommy Lee Jones from taking over a Newcastle jazz club owned by Sting.

2873. *Straight to Hell* (1987, Island, GB, 86m, c). P Eric Fellner, D Alex Cox, W Dick Rude & Cox, PH Tom Richmond, M The Pogues & Pray for Rain, ED Dave Martin, PD Andrew McAlpine, SE Juan Ramon Molina.

LP Sy Richardson (Norwood), Joe Strummer (Simms), Dick Rude (Willy), Courtney Love (Velma), Zander Schloss (Karl), Del Zamora (Poncho), Luis Contreras (Sal), Jim Jarmusch (Mr. Amos Dade), Miguel Sandoval (George).

This spoof of spaghetti westerns is about as digestible as two-week old pasta with clam sauce.

2874. *Stranded* (1987, New Line, 80m, c). P Scott Rosenfelt & Mark Levinson, D Tex Fuller, W Alan Castle, PH Jeff Jur, M Stacy Widelitz, ED Stephen E. Rivkin, SE Allen Hall.

LP Ione Skye (Deirdre Clark), Joe Morton (Sheriff McMahon), Maureen O'Sullivan (Grace Clark), Susan Barnes (Helen Anderson), Cameron Dye (Lt. Scott), Michael Greene (Vernon Burdett), Brendan Hughes (Prince).

Aliens land on earth and take Ione Skye and her grandmother Maureen O'Sullivan hostage. It's science fiction all right, but it owes more to *The Desperate Hours* than fantasy writers.

Strange Behavior see Dead Kids

2875. *Strange Brew* (1983, MGM/ United Artists, 90m, c). P Louis M. Silverstein, D Dave Thomas & Rick Moranis, W Thomas, Moranis & Steven DeJarnatt, PH Steven Poster, M Charles Fox, ED Patrick McMahon, PD David L. Snyder.

LP Dave Thomas (Doug McKenzie), Rick Moranis (Bob McKenzie), Max von Sydow (Brewmeister Smith), Paul Dooley (Claude Elsinore), Lynne Griffin (Pam Elsinore), Agnus MacInnes (Jean LaRose), Tom Harvey (Inspector).

Dave Thomas and Rick Moranis bring their "SCTV" comedy skit of the beer-swilling, plaid-shirted Canadian brothers to the big screen. The hoseheads must stop mad brewmaster Max von Sydow from taking control of the world.

2876. *Strange Invaders* (1983, Orion, 94m, c). P Walter Coblenz, D Michael Laughlin, W William Condon & Laughlin, PH Louis Horvath, M John Addison, ED John W. Wheeler, PD Susanna Moore.

LP Paul LeMat (Charles Bigelow), Nancy Allen (Betty Walker), Diana Scarwid (Margaret), Michael Lerner (Willie Collins), Louise Fletcher (Mrs. Benjamin), Wallace Shawn (Earl), Fiona Lewis (Waitress/Avon Lady), Kenneth Tobey (Arthur Newman), June Lockhart (Mrs. Bigelow).

During the 1950s a small Illinois town is invaded by aliens that replace the townspeople whom they beam by small blue spheres to their spaceship. After three decades the aliens decide to go home, but must take all of their race with them including the half-alien, half-human daughter of earthling Paul LeMat and alien Diana Scarwid. Mixed marriages can be a problem.

2877. *The Stranger* (1987, Columbia, US/Arg., 88m, c). P Hugo Lamonica, D Adolfo Aristarain, W Dan Gurskis, PH Horacio Maira, M Craig Safan, ED Eduardo Lopez.

LP Bonnie Bedelia (Alice Kildee), Peter Riegert (Dr. Harris Kite), Barry Primus (Sgt. Drake), David Spielberg (Hobby), Marcos Woinski (Macaw), Julio de Grazia (Jay), Cecilia Roth (Anita).

Bonnie Bedelia witnesses some killings and then develops amnesia with the murderers on her trail.

2878. *A Stranger Is Watching* (1982, MGM/United Artists, 92m, c). P Sidney Beckerman, D Sean S. Cunningham, W Earl MacRauch & Victor Miller (based on the novel by Mary Higgins Clark), PH Barry Abrams, M Lalo Schifrin, ED Cunningham, AD Virginia Field.

LP Kate Mulgrew (Sharon Martin), Rip Torn (Artie Taggart), James Naughton (Steve Peterson), Shawn von Schreiber (Julie Peterson), Barbara Baxley (Lally), Stephen Joyce (Detective), James Russo (Ronald Thompson).

In this unpleasant, sadistic thriller, Rip Torn is a psychopathic killer who kidnaps and terrorizes Shawn von Schreiber and her mother Kate Mulgrew, whom he rapes and kills.

2879. *Stranger Than Paradise* (1984, Goldwyn/ZDF, US/Ger., 95m, b&w). P Sara Driver, D&W Jim Jarmusch, PH Tom Di Cillo, M John Lurie & Aaron Picht, ED Jarmusch & Melody London.

LP John Lurie (Willie), Eszter Balint (Eva), Richard Edson (Eddie), Cecilla Stark (Aunt Lottie), Danny Rosen (Billy), Rammellzee (Man with Money), Tom Di Cillo (Airline Agent), Richard Boes (Factory Worker).

Three lost souls, John Lurie, who came to New York from Hungary 10 years ago, expecting but not finding paradise, his visiting adorable cousin Eszter Balint and his friend Richard Edson, survive a comically empty life. It's a semi-avant garde film.

2880. *Strangers Kiss* (1984, Orion Classics, 93m, c). P Douglas Dilge, D Matthew Chapman, W Blaine Novak & Chapman (based on a story by Novak), PH Mikhail Suslov, M Gato Barbieri, ED William Carruth, AD Ginny Randolph.

LP Peter Coyote (Stanley the Director), Victoria Tennant (Carol Redding/Betty). Blaine Novak (Stevie Blake), Dan Shor (Farris the Producer), Richard Romanus (Frank Silva), Linda Kerridge (Shirley), Carlos Palomino (Estoban), Vincent Palmieri (Scandelli).

Peter Coyote, the director of a 1955 film, encourages his leading lady Victoria Tennant and his leading man Blaine Novak to have an off-screen affair to bring more realism to their on-screen romance. Things are OK until Tennant's boyfriend Richard Romanus, the producer of the film, gets wind of the method acting techniques being employed.

2881. *Strapless* (1989, Granada, GB, 97m, c). P Rick McCallum, D&W David Hare, PH Andrew Dunn, M Nick Bicat, ED Edward Marnier, PD Roger Hall.

LP Blair Brown (Dr. Lillian Hempel), Bruno Ganz (Raymond Forbes), Bridget Fonda (Amy Hempel), Alan Howard (Mr. Cooper), Michael Gough (Douglas Brodie), Hugh Laurie (Colin), Suzanne Burden (Romaine Salmon).

After living in Britain for 12 years, American physician Blair Brown has come to care for British values even more so than the native born. She secretly marries apparently wealthy stranger Bruno Ganz. He has no money, but he does have a wife and son, whom he has abandoned. He also has no intention of staying with Brown. Contrasted with Brown is her flighty sister Bridget Fonda, who has many affairs but changes her attitude and behavior when she discovers she is pregnant.

2882. *Streamers* (1983, United Artists Classics, 118m, c). P Robert Altman & Nick J. Mileti, D Altman, W David Rabe (based on his play), PH Pierre Mignot, ED Norman Smith, PD Wolf Kroeger.

LP Matthew Modine (Billy), Michael Wright (Carlyle), Mitchell Lichtenstein (Richie), David Alan Grier (Roger), Guy Boyd (Rooney), George Dzundza (Cokes), Albert Macklin (Martin), B.J. Cleveland (Pfc. Bush).

This version of David Rabe's claustrophobic play about tensions at a training camp for the 83rd Airborne Division features young macho recruits baring their souls.

Street Gang *see* ***Vigilante***

2883. *Street Justice* (1989, Lorimar, 94m, c). P David Witz & Michael Masciarelli, D Richard C. Sarafian, W James J. Docherty, PH Roland (Ozzie) Smith, M James Szmadzinski & Paul Hertzog, ED Mark Goldberg, AD Jo-Ann Chorney.

LP Michael Ontkean (Curt Flynn), Joanna Kerns (Katharine Watson), Catherine Bach (Tamarra), J.D. Cannon (Arthur Dante), Jeanette Nolan (Edith Chandler), Richard Cox (Sam Chandler), William Windom (Father Burke), Sondra Currie (Mandy), Richard C. Sarafian (Taxi Driver).

This drama, which went direct to video, is the story of former government agent Michael Ontkean who returns home after spending 12 years in a Soviet prison after his mission was terminated by the CIA out of expediency. He not only has a hit on him ordered by the "Company," but finds his wife remarried, and his daughter seriously injured by the powerful Chandler clan which runs his home town. He goes on the warpath.

Street Love *see* ***Scarred***

2884. *Street Music* (1982, Pacificon, 92m, c). P Richard Bowen, D Jenny Bowen, PH R. Bowen, M Ed Bogas & Judy Munson, ED Lisa Fruchtman & Diana Pelligrini, AD Don De Fina.

LP Elizabeth Daily (Sadie), Larry Breeding (Eddie), Ned Glass (Sam), Mar-jorie Eaton (Mildred), W.F. Walker (Jasper), Miriam Phillips (Hattie), D'Alan Moss (Monroe), Sam Morford (Slim), John Romano (Potts).

Singer Elizabeth Daily and her boyfriend Larry Breeding organize senior citizens in danger of losing their housing in fighting for their rights.

2885. *Street Smart* (1987, Cannon, 95m, c). P Menahem Golan & Yoram Globus, D Jerry Schatzberg, W David Freeman, PH Adam Holender, M Robert Irving, III & Miles Davis, ED Priscilla Nedd, PD Dan Leigh.

LP Christopher Reeve (Jonathan Fisher), Morgan Freeman† (Fast Black), Kathy Baker (Punchy), Mimi Rogers (Alison Parker), Jay Patterson (Leonard Pike), Andre Gregory (Ted Avery), Anna Maria Horsford (Harriet).

Christopher Reeve, an out-of-favor reporter for a Manhattan magazine, is given the assignment of writing the story of a pimp. Unable to get a cooperative subject, he fakes the story. Things boomerang when the D.A. believes Reeve knows something about a murder suspect. Morgan Freeman gives an outstanding Oscar-nominated performance in a movie that has little else to recommend it.

2886. *Street Story* (1988, Films Around the World, 90m, c). P,D,W, PH&ED Joseph B. Vasquez, M Edward W. Burrows.

LP Angelo Lopez (Junior), Cookie (Joey), Lydia Ramirez (Cecilia), Melvin Muza (T.C.), Soraya Andrade (Rosa), Zerocks (Willie), Rena Zentner (Nadia), Edward W. Burrows (Father).

Two South Bronx brothers fight the local drug-pusher gangs who demand protection money from their barber father.

2887. *A Street to Die* (1985, Mermaid Beach, Australia, 91m, c). P,D&W Bill Bennett, PH Geoff Burton, M Michael Atkinson & Michael Spicer, ED Denise Hunter, PD Igor Nay.

LP Chris Haywood (Col Turner), Jennifer Cluff (Lorraine Turner), Peter Hehir (Peter Townley), Arianthe Galani (Dr. Walsea), Peter Kowitz (Craig), Sussanah Fowle (Julie), Pat Evison (Sister Sweet).

Chris Haywood struggles to get financial compensation from the government for Australian Vietnam veterans dying of leukemia and other cancers brought on by American use of Agent Orange defoliant. When he dies of his disease, his wife continues his crusade.

2888. *Street Trash* (1987, Chaos/Lightning, 91m, c). P Roy Frumkes, D Jim Muro, W Frumkes, PH David Sperling, M Rick Ulfik, ED Dennis Werner, PD Robert Marcucci.

LP Mike Lackey (Fred), Vic Noto (Bronson), Bill Chepil (Bill the Cop), Mark Sferrazza (Kevin), Jane Arakawa (Wendy), Nicole Potter (Winette), R.L. Ryan (Frank Schnizer), Clarenze Jarmon (Burt).

Bums and winos are being killed in a Brooklyn junkyard ruled by a Vietnam vet. The cause is a fatal brand of alcohol called Tenafly Viper.

Streetfighters see Ninja Turf

2889. *Streets of Fire* (1984, Universal/RKO, 94m, c). P Lawrence Gordon & Joel Silver, D Walter Hill, W Hill & Larry Gross, PH Andrew Laszlo, M Ry Cooder, ED Freeman Davies, Michael Ripps, James Coblentz & Michael Tronick, PD John Vallone.

LP Michael Pare (Tom Cody), Diane Lane (Ellen Aim), Rick Moranis (Billy Fish), Amy Madigan (McCoy), Willem Dafoe (Raven), Deborah Van Valkenburgh (Reva), Richard Lawson (Ed Price), Rick Rossovich (Officer Cooley), Bill Paxton (Clyde).

Soldier-of-fortune Michael Pare rescues his former girlfriend, rock sensation Diane Lane, when she is kidnapped by a dangerous motorcycle gang called the "Bombers."

2890. *Streets of Gold* (1986, 20th Century–Fox, 95m, c). P Joe Roth & Harry Ufland, D Roth, W Heywood Gould, Richard Price & Tom Cole (based on a story by Dezso Magyar, PH Arthur Albert, M Jack Nitzsche, Brian Banks & Anthony Marinelli, ED Richard Chew, PD Marcos Flaksman.

LP Klaus Maria Brandauer (Alek Neuman), Adrian Pasdar (Timmy Boyle), Wesley Snipes (Roland Jenkins), Angela Molina (Elena Gitman), Elya Baskin (Klebanov), Rainbow Harvest (Brenda), Adam Nathan (Grisha), John Mahoney (Lineman).

Former Russian boxing champion Klaus Maria Brandauer, now a Brooklyn dishwasher, helps train two street kids for the U.S. boxing team, hoping to defeat his former Russian coach.

2891. *Streetwalkin'* (1985, Concorde, 86m, c). P Robert Alden, D Joan Freeman, W Freeman & Alden, PH Steven Fierberg, M Matthew Ender & Doug Timm, ED John K. Adams & Patrick Rand, PD Jeffrey Robbins.

LP Melissa Leo (Cookie), Dale Midkiff (Duke), Leon Robinson (Jason), Julie Newmar (Queen Bee), Randall Batinkoff (Tim), Annie Golden (Phoebe), Antonio Fargas (Finesse), Deborah Offner (Heather).

Melissa Leo is an innocent, seductive teenager, forced onto the streets by the advances of her lecherous stepfather. She falls for the come-on of pimp Dale Midkiff.

2892. *Strikebound* (1984, TRM/Mainline, Australia, 100m, c). P Miranda Bain & Timothy White, D&W Richard Lowenstein (based on the novel *Dead Men Don't Dig Coal* by Wendy Lowenstein), PH Andrew De Groot, M Declan Affley, ED Jill Bilcock, PD Tracy Watt.

LP Chris Haywood, Carol Burns, Hugh Keays-Byrne, Rob Steele, Nik Forster, David Kendall, Anthony Hawkins, Marion Edward, Lazar Rodic.

This familiar coal mine story is set in Australia. It features the troubles of the miners with scabs who take their jobs when the union strikes.

2893. *Striking Back* (1981, Film Ventures, 91m, c). P James Margellos, D William Fruet, W Don Enright, M FM.

LP Perry King (Kip), Tisa Farrow (Kate), Don Stroud (Buddy), George Kennedy (Capt. Fusqua), Park Jong Soo (Assassin).

Having paid George Kennedy's price to appear in this action/adventure turkey, there apparently wasn't any money left to hire a good director or screenwriter.

2894. *Stripes* (1981, Columbia, 106m, c). P Ivan Reitman & Dan Goldberg, D Reitman, W Len Blum, Goldberg & Harold Ramis, PH Bill Butler, M Elmer Bernstein, ED Eva Ruggiero, Michael Luciano & Harry Keller, PD James H. Spencer.

LP Bill Murray (John), Harold Ramis (Russell), Warren Oates (Sgt. Hulka), P.J. Soles (Stella), Sean Young (Louise), John Candy (Ox), John Larroquette (Capt. Stillman), John Voldstad (Aide), John Diehl (Cruiser), Lance LeGault (Col. Glass), Roberta Leighton (Anita).

In a sort of "Saturday Night Live meets Abbott and Costello in *Buck Privates*," Bill Murray and Harold Ramis go through some of the usual army recruit hijinks, adding a bit of sex and hip comedy to generally dull proceedings.

2895. *Stripped to Kill* (1987, Concorde, 84m, c). P Andy Ruben, Mark Byers & Matt Leipzig, D Katt Shea Ruben, W K.S. Ruben & A. Ruben, PH John Leblanc, M John O'Kennedy, ED Zach Staenberg, AD Paul Raubertas.

LP Kay Lenz (Cody/Sunny), Greg Evigan (Sgt. Heineman), Norman Fell (Ray), Tracy Crowder (Fanny), Athena Worthey (Zeena), Carlye Byron (Cinnamon), Debbie Nassar (Dazzle), Lucia Nagy Lexington (Brandy).

A serial killer is killing dancers at a L.A. topless bar. Undercover cop Kay Lenz is the tasty bait used to catch the killer. Before this happens she has to show more than her dancing talents.

2896. *Stripped to Kill II: Live Girls* (1989, Concorde, 82m, c). P Andy Ruben, D&W Katt Shea Ruben, PH Phedon Papamichael, M Gary Stockdale, ED Stephen Mark, PD Virginia Lee.

LP Maria Ford (Shady), Eb Lottimer (Decker), Karen Mayo Chandler (Cassandra), Birke Tan (Dazzle), Marjean Holden (Something Else), Debra Lamb (Montra), Lisa Glaser (Victoria), Tommy Ruben (Ike).

Stripper Maria Ford is tormented by dreams in which she kills other strippers, slashing their throats with a razor blade held in her teeth. When strippers are found with their throat slashed and Ford awakens with blood dribbling from her lips, things look pretty grim for our girl in a G-string. There's a plethora of barely clad bodies and imaginative strip routines

for those who like their sadism with a little sex.

2897. *Stroker Ace* (1983, Universal/Warner, 96m, c). P Hank Moonjean, D Hal Needham, W Needham & Hugh Wilson (based on the novel *Stand On It* by William Neely & Robert K. Ottum), PH Nick McLean, M Al Capps, ED Carl Kress & William Gordean, AD Paul Peters.

LP Burt Reynolds (Stroker Ace), Ned Beatty (Clyde Torkle), Jim Nabors (Lugs), Parker Stevenson (Aubrey James), Loni Anderson (Pembroke Feeney), John Byner (Doc Seegle), Frank O. Hill (Dad Seegle), Bubba Smith (Arnold).

Flamboyant race car driver Burt Reynolds tries to get out of his long term contract with chicken franchise magnate Ned Beatty. It's a clucky movie with not enough yolks.

2898. *Stryker* (1983, New World, Phil./US, 84m, c). P&D Cirio H. Santiago, W Howard R. Cohen (based on a story by Leonard Hermes), PH Ricardo Remias, M Ed Gatchalian & Susan Justin, ED Bas Santos & Ruby Cabrales, PD Pol Dimalanta.

LP Steve Sandor (Stryker), Andria Savio (Delha), William Ostrander (Bandit), Michael Lane (Kardis), Julie Gray (Laurenz), Monique St. Pierre (Cerce), Ken Metcalfe (Trun), Jon Harris, III (Oiric).

In another of Philippine helmer Cirio H. Santiago's postholocaust films, bands of marauders fight each other for the scarcest resource—water.

2899. *Stuck on You* (1984, Troma, 90m, c). P Lloyd Kaufman & Michael Herz, D Herz, Samuel Weil, W Weil, ED Darren Kloomok & Richard Haines.

LP Prof. Irwin Corey (Judge), Virginia Penta (Carol), Mark Mikulski (Bill), Albert Pia (Artie), Norma Pratt (Bill's Mother), Daniel Harris (Napoleon), Denise Silbert (Cavewoman), Eddie Brill (Caveman).

Having all of the intelligence of a cancelled check, this film features looney judge Irwin Corey, presiding over a palimony case.

2900. ***Stuckey's Last Stand*** (1980, Royal Oak, 92m, c). P,D&W Lawrence G. Goldfarb, PH Anthony J. Fitzsimmons, M Carson Whitsett, ED Fitzsimmons & Ethan Edwards, AD Julia Norris.

LP Whit Reichert (Whit), Ray Anzalone (Russ), Will Shaw (Will), Tom Murray (Pete), Richard Cosentino (Duke), Marilyn Terschluse (Billie), Jeanne L. Austin (Marianne), John Zimmerman (Gordon), Dan Dierdorf (Angry Father).

In this Hamburger-Helper version of *Meatballs,* unhappy campers and inept counselors are played by talentless actors, stuck with an impossible script.

2901. ***Student Affairs*** (1988, Platinum, 94m, c). P&D Chuck Vincent, W Craig Horrall & Vincent (based on a story idea by John Weidner), PH Larry Revene, ED Vincent, James Davalos & Chip Lambert, AD D. Gary Phelps.

LP Louie Bonanno (Louie Balducci), Jim Abele (Andy Armstrong), Deborah Blaisdell [Veronica Hart] (Kelly), Beth Broderick (Alexis), Alan Fisler (Devon Wheler), Jane Hamilton (Veronica Harper), Richard Parnes (Rudy).

Former porno-movie maker Chuck Vincent is back with another effort to crack the mainstream market with several of his triple-X performers appearing in a film within a film as characters in a 50s teen movie.

2902. ***Student Bodies*** (1981, Paramount, 86m, c). P Allen Smithee (Michael Ritchie), D&W Mickey Rose, PH Robert Ebinger, M Gene Hobson, ED Kathryn Ruth Hope, PD Donald Nunley.

LP Kristin Ritter (Toby), Matthew Goldsby (Hardy), Richard Brando (The Breather), Joe Flood (Mr. Dumpkin), Joe Talarowski (Principal Peters), Mimi Weddell (Miss Mumsley), Carl Jacobs (Dr. Sigmund).

Here's another spoof of high school *Halloween*-like horror films. Young couples are murdered by person or persons unknown just as they are about to have sex. Funny, it's not.

2903. ***Student Confidential*** (1987, Troma, 94m, c). P,D&W Richard Horian, PH James Dickson, M&ED Horian, PD David Wasco.

LP Eric Douglas (Johnny Warshetsky), Marlon Jackson (Joseph Williams), Susan Scott (Susan Bishop), Elizabeth Singer (Elaine Duvat), Ronee Blakley (Jenny Selden), Richard Horian (Michael Drake), Paula Sorenson (Carla).

In a ludicrous story, millionaire Richard Horian's help to a group of troubled teens is repaid when he considers suicide.

2904. ***The Stuff*** (1985, New World, 93m, c). P Paul Kurta, D&W Larry Cohen, PH Paul Glickman, M Anthony Guefen, ED Armond Lebowitz, PD Larry Lurin, SE David Allen.

LP Michael Moriarty (David "Moe" Rutherford), Andrea Marcovicci (Nicole Kendall), Garrett Morris (Chocolate Chip Charlie), Paul Sorvino (Col. Spears), Scott Bloom (Jason), Danny Aiello (Vickers), Alexander Scourby (Evans).

Ice cream executive Alexander Scourby hires industrial spy Michael Moriarty to discover the secret ingredients in a new yogurt-like desert sensation, known only as "The Stuff." He finds that its popularity is because it's addictive, altering consumers' minds.

2905. ***The Stunt Man*** (1980, 20th Century-Fox, 129m, c). P&D Richard Rush† (as director), W Lawrence B. Marcus & Rush† (based on the novel by Paul Brodeur), PH Mario Tosi, M Dominic Frontiere, ED Jack Hofstra & Caroline Ferriol, AD James Schoppe.

LP Peter O'Toole† (Eli Cross), Steve Railsback (Cameron), Barbara Hershey (Nina Franklin), Allen Goorwitz (Sam), Alex Rocco (Jake), Sharon Farrell (Denise), Adam Roarke (Raymond Bailey), Philip Bruns (Ace), Chuck Bail (Chuck Barton).

Vietnam veteran Steve Railsback, on the run from the police, takes refuge with a movie company on location, headed up by megalomaniac director Peter O'Toole, who blackmails Railsback into assuming the role of a stuntman who is killed. It's an enjoyable behind-the-scenes look at making movies.

2906. ***Suburbia*** (1984, New World, 99m, c, aka *The Wild Side*). P Bert Dragin, D&W Penelope Spheeris, PH

Tim Suhrstedt, M Alex Gibson, ED Ross Albert, AD Randy Moore.

LP Timothy Eric O'Brien (Tom), Grant Miner (Keef), Michael Bayer (Razzle), Bill Coyne (Evan), Andrew Pece (Ethan), Chris Pederson (Jack), Wade Walston (Joe Schmo), De Waldron (De Generate), Jennifer Clay (Sheila).

When a group of punk teens becomes squatters in a condemned suburban development, the locals form a vigilante group to evict them.

2907. *Subway Riders* (1981, Hep/Mainline, 118m, c). P Johanna Heer & Amos Poe, D&W Poe, PH Heer, M Various Artists, ED Orlando Gallini, Heer & Poe.

LP Robbie Coltrane (Detective Fritz Langley), Charlene Kaleina (Claire Smith), Cookie Mueller (Penelope Trasher), John Lurie (The Saxaphonist), Amos Poe (Writer Ant), Susan Tyrrell (Eleanor Langley), Bill Rice (Mr. Gollstone), Leigh Taylor (Susannah).

Psychopath saxophonist John Lurie draws an audience on the streets of Manhattan, first plays, then slays a listener before fleeing into the subway. The musical score by a group of avant garde artists is probably the best thing about this underground 16mm film.

2908. *Success Is the Best Revenge* (1984, Gaumont, GB, 90m, c). P&D Jerzy Skolimowski, W Michael Lyndon & Skolimowski, PH Mike Fash, M Stanley Myers & Hans Zimmer, ED Barrie Vince, PD Voytek.

LP Michael York (Alex Rodak), Janna Szerzerbic (Wife), Michael Lyndon (Adam), George Skolimowski (David), Michel Piccoli (French Official), Anouk Aimee (Monique de Fontaine), John Hurt (Dino Montecurva).

In this unusual comedy, complications abound when an expatriate Pole, George Skolimowski, attempts to direct a play.

2909. *Sudden Death* (1985, Lodestar/Marvin, 95m, c). P Steven Shore & David Greene, D&W Sig Shore, PH Benjamin Davis, M Arthur Baker, ED John Tintori, AD Charles Weaver.

LP Denise Coward (Valarie Wells), Frank Runyeon (Det. Marty Lowery), Jamie Tirelli (Willie), Robert Trumbull

(Herbert), Rebecca Hollen (Peggy), J. Kenneth Campbell (Kosakowski), Joe Maruzzo (Raphael).

In this hyper-feminist, man-hating movie, New York businesswoman Denise Coward vows to kill every rapist she can, after she is raped and beaten.

2910. *Sudden Impact* (1983, Warner, 117m, c). P&D Clint Eastwood, W Joseph C. Stinson (based on a story by Earl E. Smith & Charles B. Pierce, based on characters by Harry Julian Fink & R.M. Fink), PH Bruce Surtees, M Lalo Schifrin, ED Joel Cox, PD Edward Carfagno.

LP Clint Eastwood (Harry Callahan), Sondra Locke (Jennifer Spencer), Pat Hingle (Chief Jannings), Bradford Dillman (Capt. Briggs), Paul Drake (Mick), Audrie J. Neenan (Ray Parkins), Jack Thibeau (Kruger), Michael Currie (Lt. Donnelly), Albert Popwell (Horace King).

Clint Eastwood in his role as "Dirty Harry" tracks down revenged-obsessed murderer Sondra Locke, who is one-by-one brutally killing the guys who gang-raped her and her sister, leaving the latter in a catatonic state. Eastwood catches up with her, but as she finishes her vengeful chore, he lets her go. This is the film in which Clint delivers his classic line: "Go ahead, make my day."

2911. *The Suicide Club* (1988, Angelika, 90m, c). P&D James Bruce, W Matthew Gaddis, Susan Kouguell & Carl Caportoto (based on a story by Robert Louis Stevenson), PH Frank Prinzi, M Joel Diamond, ED Bruce & Keith Rouse, PD Stephen McCabe.

LP Mariel Hemingway (Sasha Michaels), Robert Joy (Michael Collins), Lenny Henry (Cam), Madeleine Potter (Nancy), Michael O'Donaghue (Mervin), Anne Carlisle (Catherine), Sullivan Brown (Brian), Leta McCarthy (Cowgirl).

Feeling guilty over her brother's suicide, Mariel Hemingway and other bored rich kids participate in a lethal card game in which the "winner" must swallow a fatally poisonous drink.

2912. *Sullivan's Pavilion* (1987, Adirondack Alliance, 83m, c). P,D&W Fred G. Sullivan, PH Hal Landen, M Kenneth

Higgins & James Calabrese, ED Fred G. Sullivan, AD Susan Neal.

LP Polly Sullivan, Tate Sullivan, Katie Sullivan, Kirk Sullivan, Ricky Sullivan, Fred G. Sullivan (Themselves), Jon Granik (Bear/Narrator), James R. Hogue (Conrad P. Drizzle), Jan Jalenak (The Temptress), Judith Mayes (Sister Mary Anthony).

Independent filmmaker Fred G. Sullivan makes an autobiographical film about the trials of his family and himself as he tries to make it as an independent filmmaker.

2913. Summer Camp Nightmare (1987, Concorde, 87m, c, aka *The Butterfly Revolution*). P Robert T. Crow, Emilia Lesniak-Crow & Andy Howard, D Bert L. Dragin, W Dragin & Penelope Spheeris (based on the novel *The Butterfly Revolution* by William Butler), PH Don Burgess, M Ted Neeley & Gary Chase, ED Michael Spence, PD Richard McGuire.

LP Chuck Connors (Mr. Warren), Charles Stratton (Franklin Reilly), Harold B. Pruett (Chris Wade), Adam Carl (Donald Poultry), Tom Fridley (John Mason), Melissa Brennan (Heather), Stuart Rogers (Stanley Runk).

In a muddled story, idealistic counselor Charles Stratton organizes a revolt of the kids at a summer camp run by despotic Chuck Connors. For good measure they also liberate a nearby girl's camp.

2914. Summer Heat (1987, Atlantic, 90m, c). P William Tennant, D&W Michie Gleason (based on the novel *Here to Get My Baby Out of Jail* by Louise Shivers), PH Elliot Davis, M Steve Tyrell, ED Mary Bauer, PD Marcia Hinds.

LP Lori Singer (Roxanna "Roxy" Walston), Anthony Edwards (Aaron Walston), Bruce Abbott (Jack Ruffin), Clu Gulager (Will Stanton), Kathy Bates (Ruth Stanton), Jessie Kent (Baby Walston), Noble Willingham (Strother).

This torpid romantic triangle drama involving tobacco farmer Anthony Edwards, his young wife Lori Singer and hired hand Bruce Abbott takes place in North Carolina in 1937. Things get a bit out of hand, but hardly enough to stir the audience from its nap.

2915. Summer Job (1989, SVS Films, 90m, c). P Josi W. Konski, D Paul Madden, W Ralph Wilson, PH Orson Ochoa, M Ike Stubblefield, ED Christopher Cibelli.

LP Amy Baxter (Susan), Sherrie Rose (Kathy), Cari Mayor (Donna), George O. (Herman), Renee Shugart (Karen), James Summer, Chantal, Dave Clouse.

Here's a loser that very few people will see or miss, even in video stores. It's filled with stupid dialogue, dumb gags, poor performances and no plot. Sherrie Rose is the supervisor of college kids working at a Florida resort one summer. The college kids do what college kids do. It doesn't look like much fun.

2916. Summer Lovers (1982, Filmways/Orion, 98m, c). P Mike Modor, D&W Randal Kleiser, PH Peter Collister, Timothy Galfas & Dimitri Papacostandis, M Basil Poledouris, ED Robert Gordon, PD Bruce Weintraub.

LP Peter Gallagher (Michael Papas), Daryl Hannah (Cathy Feathererst), Valerie Quennessen (Lina), Barbara Rush (Jean Feathererst), Carole Cook (Barbara Foster), Hans Van Tongeren (Jan Tolin), Lydia Lenosi (Aspa).

Rich-kid lovers Peter Gallagher and Daryl Hannah spend their summer vacation at a Greek island villa, adding archaeologist Valerie Quennessen to their exploitations of life and love. Give it an X for content, language, nudity, sex and an F for dramatic values.

2917. Summer of the Colt (1989, Cinema Plus, Canada, 100m, c). P Rock Demers & Lita Stantic, D Andre Melancon, W Genevieve Lefebvre & Rodolfo Otero (based on Otero's story), PH Thomas Vamos, M Osvaldo Montes, ED Andre Corriveau.

LP Hector Alterio (Federico), China Zorrilla (Ana), Alexandra London-Thompson (Laura), Juan de Benedictis (Daniel), Santiago Gonzalez (Martin), Mariano Bertolini (Felipe), Gabriela Felperin (Manuela), Manuel Callau (Luis), Emilia Farah (Damasia).

Filmed in Argentina, four children come to visit their grandfather and his sister on the former's beautiful horse ranch for the summer. Unfortunately for Alexandra London-Thompson, she reminds her grandfather of his young wife who long ago deserted him and his children. He turns against the poor 13-year-old, but everything is satisfactorily resolved before the children return to their Buenos Aires home at the end of the summer.

2918. *Summer Rental* (1985, Paramount, 88m, c). P George Shapiro, D Carl Reiner, W Jeremy Stevens & Mark Reisman, PH Ric Waite, M Alan Silvestri, ED Bud Molin & Lee Burch, PD Peter Wooley.

LP John Candy (Jack Chester), Richard Crenna (Al Pellet), Rip Torn (Scully), Karen Austin (Sandy Chester), Kerri Green (Jennifer Chester), John Larroquette (Don Moore), Joey Lawrence (Bobby Chester), Aubrey Jene (Laurie Chester), Dick Anthony Williams (Dan Gardner).

Suffering from burnout, Chicago air traffic controller John Candy takes his family to Florida for a vacation in a beach house and runs afoul of wealthy snob Richard Crenna. Candy challenges Crenna to a sailing race, with Candy's ship being a floating restaurant owned by Rip Torn. Doesn't sound very funny, does it?

2919. *Summer School* (1987, Paramount, 98m, c). P George Shapiro & Howard West, D Carl Reiner, W Jeff Franklin (based on a story by Stuart Birnbaum, Dave Dashev & Jeff Franklin), PH David M. Walsh, M Danny Elfman, ED Bud Molin, PD David L. Snyder.

LP Mark Harmon (Freddy Shoop), Kirstie Alley (Robin Bishop), Robin Thomas (Phil Gills), Patrick Laborteaux (Kevin Winchester), Courtney Thorne-Smith (Pam House), Dean Cameron (Francis "Chainsaw" Gremp), Gary Riley (Dave Frazier).

Mark Harmon is given a chance to earn a regular teaching job by working in summer school with a group of remedial students who must pass a big test. Kirstie Alley also keeps Harmon guessing.

2920. *A Summer Story* (1988, Atlantic, US/GB, 96m, c). P Danton Rissner, D Piers Haggard, W Penelope Mortimer (based on a story "The Apple Tree" by John Galsworthy), PH Kenneth Mac-Millan, M Georges Delerue, ED Ralph Sheldon, PD Leo Austin.

LP Imogen Stubbs (Megan David), James Wilby (Frank Ashton), Kenneth Colley (Jim), Sophie Ward (Stella Halliday), Susannah York (Mrs. Narracombe), Jerome Flynn (Joe Narracombe), Lee Billett (Nick Narracombe), Oliver Perry (Rick Narracombe).

Set in rural 1902 southwest England, this beautiful film is the story of the love of farm girl Imogen Stubbs and young London lawyer James Wilby, each faced with decisions which will change their lives forever.

The Summons see Scorpion

2921. *Sunburn* (1980, Paramount, 99m, c). P John Daly & Gerald Green, D Richard C. Sarafian, W Daly, Stephen Oliver & James Booth (based on the novel *The Bind* by Stanley Ellin), PH Alex Phillips, Jr., M John Cameron, ED Geoff Foot, PD Ted Tester.

LP Farah Fawcett [Majors] (Ellie), Charles Grodin (Jake), Art Carney (Marcus), Joan Collins (Nera), William Daniels (Crawford), John Hillerman (Webb), Eleanor Parker (Mrs. Thoren), Keenan Wynn (Mark Elmes).

In this comedy-mystery, private eye Charles Grodin hires model Farrah Fawcett to pose as his wife as he travels to Acapulco while he investigates the violent death of an aging industrialist. Farrah looks great, but has little to do related to acting.

2922. *Sunset* (1988, Tri-Star, 107m, c). P Tony Adams, D&W Blake Edwards (based on a story by Rod Amateau), PH Anthony B. Richmond, M Henry Mancini & Duke Ellington, ED Robert Pergament, PD Rodger Maus, COS Patricia Norris.

LP Bruce Willis (Tom Mix), James Garner (Wyatt Earp), Malcolm McDowell (Alfie Alperin), Mariel Hemingway (Cheryl King), Kathleen Quinlan (Nancy Shoemaker), Jennifer Edwards (Victoria Alperin), Patricia Hodge (Christina Alperin), Richard Bradford (Capt. Blackworth), M. Emmet Walsh (Chief Marvin Dibner), Joe Dallesandro (Dutch Kieffer).

In this fictional story, legendary lawman Wyatt Earp (James Garner) and cowboy movie star Tom Mix (Bruce Willis) become fast friends. They team up to try to solve a William Desmond Taylor-like murder case.

2923. *Super Fuzz* (1981, Avco Embassy, 97m, c, aka *Supersnooper*). P Maximilian Wolkoff, D Sergio Corbucci, W Corbucci & Sabatino Ciuffini, PH Silvano Ippoliti, M La Bionda, ED Eugene Alabiso, PD Marco Dentici.

LP Terence Hill (Dave Speed), Ernest Borgnine (Willy Dunlop), Joanne Dru (Rosy Labouche), Marc Lawrence (Torpedo), Julie Gordon (Evelyn), Lee Sandman (Chief McEnroy), Herb Goldstein (Silvius).

After being exposed to radiation, rookie cop Terence Hill develops super powers which he uses to fight crime.

2924. *The Super Jocks* (1980, Brenner, 100m, c). P&W Emil Nofal, D Nofal & Ray Sargeant.

LP Joe Stewardson (Will), Ken Leach (Tony), John Higgins (Barry), Richard Loring (Paul), Jenny Meyer (Sandra), Madeleine Usher, Diane Ridler, Tony Jay.

Look if you want, but you're not likely to find this dumb film in any of your friendly video stores. A group of athletes flex their muscles for the usual assortment of adoring girls.

2925. *Supergirl* (1984, Tri-Star, GB, 114m, c). P Timothy Burrill, D Jeannot Szwarc, W David Odell (based on the comic book character), PH Alan Hume, M Jerry Goldsmith, ED Malcolm Cooke, PD Richard MacDonald.

LP Faye Dunaway (Selena), Helen Slater (Kara, Supergirl/Linda Lee), Peter O'Toole (Zaltar), Mia Farrow (Alura), Brenda Vaccaro (Bianca), Peter Cook (Nigel), Simon Ward (Zor-El), Marc McClure (Jimmy Olsen), Hart Bochner (Ethan), Maureen Teefy (Lucy Lane).

Several fine performers might like to forget this film when putting together their résumés. None is more poorly used than Faye Dunaway, whose career seems to be in one long downward spin. Cute young Helen Slater probably will survive portraying Superman's cousin, who leaves Krypton (yeah, we thought it had been destroyed, too) to recover the Omegahedron Stone.

2926. *The Supergrass* (1985, Comic Strip, GB, 105m, c). P Elaine Taylor, D Peter Richardson, W Pete Richens & Richardson, PH John Metcalfe, M Keith Tippet & Working Week Big Band, ED Geoff Hogg, AD Niki Wateridge.

LP Adrian Edmondson (Dennis), Jennifer Saunders (Lesley), Peter Richardson (Harvey Duncan), Dawn French (Andrea), Keith Allen (Wong), Nigel Planer (Gunter), Robbie Coltrane (Troy), Daniel Peacock (Jim Jarvis).

In this comedy set in England's West Country, the police are convinced that boastful young Adrian Edmondson is a drug smuggler.

2927. *Superman II* (1981, Warner, 127m, c). P Pierre Spengler, D Richard Lester, W Mario Puzo, David Newman & Leslie Newman (based on a story by Puzio, from characters created by Jerry Siegel & Joe Shuster), PH Geoffrey Unsworth & Robert Paynter, M Ken Thorne (based on original music composed by John Williams), ED John Victor Smith, PD John Barry & Peter Murton, AD Maurice Fowler, SE Colin Chilvers, Roy Field & Zoran Perisic.

LP Gene Hackman (Lex Luthor), Christopher Reeve (Clark Kent/Superman), Ned Beatty (Otis), Jackie Cooper (Perry White), Sarah Douglas (Ursa), Margot Kidder (Lois Lane), Jack O'Halloran (Non), Valerie Perrine (Eve Teschmacher), Susannah York (Lara), Clifton James (Sheriff), Marc McClure (Jimmy Olsen), Terence Stamp (General Zod).

Three renegade Kryptonians, Terence Stamp, Sarah Douglas and Jack O'Halloran threaten earth with a space bomb, while Superman is away at his North Pole retreat, becoming a mere mortal so he can become Kidder's lover. Even when he regains his powers, the trio of villains are his match in super powers. What will he do? What will he do?

2928. *Superman III* (1983, Warner, 123m, c). P Pierre Spengler, D Richard Lester, W David Newman & Leslie Newman (based on characters created by Jerry Siegel & Joe Shuster), PH Robert Paynter, M Ken Thorne & John Williams, ED John Victor Smith, PD Peter Murton, SE Roy Field, Colin Chilvers, Martin Gutteridge & Brian Warner.

LP Christopher Reeve (Clark Kent/ Superman), Richard Pryor (Gus Gorman), Jackie Cooper (Perry White), Margot Kidder (Lois Lane), Annette O'Toole (Lana Lang), Annie Ross (Vera Webster), Pamela Stephenson (Lorelei Ambrosia), Robert Vaughn (Ross Webster), Marc McClure (Jimmy Olsen).

Computer whiz Richard Pryor is employed by villainous Robert Vaughn and his nasty sister Annie Ross to manufacture some synthetic Kryptonite. The phony material warps Superman's character, but he snaps out of it just in time.

2929. *Superman IV: The Quest for Peace* (1987, Warner, 89m, c). P Menahem Golan & Yoram Globus, D Sidney J. Furie, W Lawrence Konner & Mark Rosenthal (based on a story by Konner, Rosenthal & Christopher Reeve), PH Ernest Day, M John Williams & Alexander Courage, ED John Shirley, PD John Graysmark.

LP Christopher Reeve (Superman/ Clark Kent), Gene Hackman (Lex Luthor), Jackie Cooper (Perry White), Marc McClure (Jimmy Olsen), Jon Cryer (Lenny), Sam Wanamaker (David Warfield), Mark Pillow (Nuclear Man), Mariel Hemingway (Lacy Warfield), Margot Kidder (Lois Lane).

It may be time to close the book on the Superman series. With this film, the man of steel becomes rather preachy as he rids the world of all nuclear weapons when asked to do so in a letter from a child. Villain Gene Hackman takes advantage of the situation to create a worthy opponent for Superman, solar energized Mark Pillow. Mariel Hemingway gives Margot Kidder some competition for Christopher Reeve, with Mariel after Clark Kent and Kidder still hot for Superduperman.

2930. *The Supernaturals* (1987, Republic Ent. Intl., 80m, c). P Michael S. Murphey & Joel Soisson, D Armand Mastroianni, W Michael S. Murphey & Soisson, PH Peter Collister, M Robert O. Ragland, AD Jo Ann Chorney.

LP Maxwell Caulfield (Lt. Ray Ellis), Nichelle Nichols (Sgt. Leona Hawkins), Talia Balsam (Pvt. Angela Lejune), Bradford Bancroft (Pvt. Tom Weir), LeVar Burton (Pvt. Michael Osgood), Bobby Di Cicco (Pvt. Tim Cort).

Sgt. Nichelle Nichols' present-day soldiers are troubled by a group of zombies, former Confederate soldiers forced by Union forces to cross a mine field at the time of the Civil War.

Supersnooper see Super Fuzz

2931. *Superstition* (1985, Almi, 84m, c, aka *The Witch*). P Ed Carlin, John D. Schwartz & Robert L.J. Lewis, D James W. Roberson, W Michael Sajbel, Bret Plate, Brad White & Donald G. Thompson (based on the story "The Witch" by Sajbel), PH Lee Madden, M David Gibney, ED Al Rabinowitz, AD Penny Hadfield.

LP James Carl Houghton (Rev. David Thompson), Albert Salmi (Inspector Sturgess), Larry Pennell (George Leahy), Lynn Carlin (Melinda Leahy), Maylo McCaslin (Sheryl Leahy), Heidi Bohay (Ann Leahy), Billy Jacoby (Justin Leahy).

Despite warnings from the locals, a reverend and his family move into a vacant house near Black Pond, where the remains of a 200-year-old witch burned at the stake refuses to rest.

2932. *The Sure Thing* (1985, Embassy, 94m, c). P Roger Birnbaum & Andrew Scheinman, D Rob Reiner, W Steven L. Bloom & Jonathan Roberts, PH Robert Elswit, M Tom Scott, ED Robert Leighton, PD Lily Kilvert.

LP John Cusack (Walter "Gib" Gibson), Daphne Zuniga (Alison Bradbury), Anthony Edwards (Lance), Boyd Gaines (Jason), Lisa Jane Persky (Mary Ann Webster), Viveca Lindfors (Prof. Taub), Nicollette Sheridan (The Sure Thing), Tim Robbins (Gary Cooper), Fran Ryan (Louise).

In a charming film in the same way *It Happened One Night* was charming five decades earlier, horny Yale college student John Cusack is induced to spend Christmas vacation with friend Anthony Edwards on the West Coast by the promise of a "sure thing." Somehow Cusack and Daphne Zuniga, a classmate with whom he doesn't get along, are teamed in a cross country trip and as would be expected they fall in love—demonstrating that mere casual sex isn't the prescription for happiness.

2933. *Surf Nazis Must Die* (1987, Troma, 95m, c). P Robert Tinnell, D Peter George, W Jon Ayre, PH Rolf Kesterman, M Jon McCallum, ED Craig Colton, AD Byrnadette diSanto.

LP Gail Neely (Mama Washington), Robert Harden (LeRoy Washington), Barry Brenner (Adolf), Dawn Wildsmith (Eva), Michael Sonye (Mengele), Joel Hile (Hook), Gene Mitchell (Brutus), Tom Shell (Smeg), Bobbie Bresee (Smeg's Mom).

The favorite activities of the Nazis in this movie are surfing and killing on California beaches. Gail Neely, the mother of one of their victims, uses guns, grenades and motorcycles to take revenge.

2934. *Surf II* (1984, Intl. Film Marketing, 91m, c). P George G. Braunstein & Ron Hamady, D&W Randall Badat, PH Alex Phillips, M Peter Bernstein, ED Jacqueline Cambas, PD Jeff Staggs.

LP Morgan Paull (Dad), Ruth Buzzi (Chuck's Mother), Lyle Waggoner (Chief Boyardie), Cleavon Little (Daddy-O), Linda Kerridge (Sparkle), Carol Wayne (Mrs. O'Finlay), Eddie Deezen (Menlo Schwartzer), Peter Isacksen (Beaker), Eric Stoltz (Chuck).

Bet you wonder why you can't find *Surf I*. Well, none was ever made. Bet you often wondered what had happened to the likes of Ruth Buzzi, Lyle Waggoner and Cleavon Little. Bet you don't care enough to rent this film from your local video store to watch surfers getting sick from drinking tainted soda pop.

2935. *Surrender* (1987, Warner, 96m, c). P Aaron Spelling & Alan Greisman, D&W Jerry Belson, PH Juan Ruiz Anchia, M Michel Colombier, ED Wendy Greene Briemont, PD Lilly Kilvert.

LP Sally Field (Daisy Morgan), Michael Caine (Sean Stein), Steve Guttenberg (Marty Caesar), Peter Boyle (Jay Bass), Julie Kavner (Ronnie), Jackie Cooper (Ace Morgan), Louise Lasser (Joyce), Iman (Hedy).

Wealthy writer Michael Caine, tired of being taken to the cleaners by women, pretends he's poor. Struggling artist Sally Field falls for him, but their courtship is not exactly what either hopes for.

2936. *The Surrogate* (1984, Cinepix, Canada, 99m, c). P John Dunning & Don Carmody, D Carmody, W Carmody & Robert Geoffrian, PH Francois Protat, M Daniel Lanois, ED Rit Wallace, AD Charles Dunlop.

LP Art Hindle (Frank Waite), Carole Laure (Anouk Van Derlin), Shannon Tweed (Lee Waite), Michael Ironside (George Kyber), Marilyn Lightstone (Dr. Harriet Forman), Jim Bailey (Eric), Jackie Burroughs (Fantasy Woman).

Sexually dissatisfied with their marriage, Art Hindle and Shannon Tweed seek help from sex therapist Carol Laure, who helps couples release their most hidden sexual fantasies. When a series of sexually related murders result in the couple's friends being killed one by one, the question is who has gone too far.

2937. *Survival Game* (1987, TransWorld, 91m, c). P Gideon Amir, D Herb Freed, W Freed, Susannah de Nimes & P.W. Swann (based on a story by Freed), PH Avraham Karpick, M Tom Simonec & Michael Linn, ED Charles Simmons & Karen Gebura, PD Diana Morris.

LP Mike Norris (Mike Falcon), Deborah Goodrich (C.J. Forrest), Seymour Cassel (Dave Forrest), Ed Bernard (Sugar Bear), John Sharp (Charles), Rick Grassi (Ice), Arlene Golonka (Mike's Mom), Michael Halton (Harlan).

Chuck Norris' son Mike, a survival-camp trainee, falls for Deborah Goodrich, whom he meets after a car crash. When she and her 60s drug guru are kidnapped, the martial arts chip-off-the-block takes on their abductors.

2938. *Survival Quest* (1989, MGM/United Artists, 96m, c). P Roberto Quezada, D&W Don Coscarelli, PH Daryn Okada, M Fred Myrow, ED Coscarelli, PD Andrew Siegel.

LP Lance Henriksen (Hank), Mark Rolston (Jake), Steve Antin (Raider), Michael Allen Ryder (Harper), Paul Provenza (Joey), Ben Hammer (Hal), Dominic Hoffman (Jeff), Traci Lin (Olivia), Dermot Mulroney (Gray).

This almost direct-to-video film isn't worth a rental. It deals with two separate survival course runs over the same rugged northern Rockies terrain. The two groups get into it and blood is spilled, but the good guys win.

2939. *Survival Run* (1980, Film Ventures, 90m, c). P Lance Hool, D Larry Spiegel, W Spiegel, G.M. Cahill & Fredric Shore (based on a story by Cahill & Shore), PH Alex Phillips, Jr., M Gary William Friedman, ED Chris Greenbury.

LP Peter Graves, Ray Milland, Vincent Van Patten, Pedro Armendariz, Jr., Alan Conrad, Anthony Charnota, Gonzalo Vega, Cosie Costa, Randi Meryl.

Six teenagers stranded in the desert are harrassed by Peter Graves and Ray Milland when the kids see the pair making a shady deal.

2940. *Survivor* (1988, Vestron, GB, 91m, c). P Martin Wragge, D Michael Shackleton, W Bima Stagg, PH Fred Tammes, M Andraan Strydom, ED Max Lemon.

LP Chip Mayer (Survivor), Richard Moll (Kragg), Sue Kiel, Richard Haines, John Carson, Rex Garner, Sandra Duncan, Sven Forsell, Bima Stagg.

NASA astronaut Chip Mayer returns to earth after World War III has made the world one vast desert wasteland. He comes across a subterranean society headed by crazy Richard Moll (Bull, of TV's "Night Court"). The latter, not so dumb as he looks, has gathered together all the surviving beautiful women with whom he plans to repopulate the world.

2941. *The Survivors* (1983, Columbia, 102m, c). P William Sackheim, D Michael Ritchie, W Michael Leeson, PH Billy Williams, M Paul Chihara, ED Richard A. Harris, PD Gene Callahan.

LP Walter Matthau (Sonny Paluso), Robin Williams (Donald Quinelle), Jerry Reed (Jack Locke), James Wainwright (Wes Huntley), Kristen Vigard (Candice Paluso), Annie McEnroe (Doreen), Anne Pitoniak (Betty).

Young executive Robin Williams and former gas station owner Walter Matthau find themselves the target of Jerry Reed, an out-of-work hit man, whom they disarm in a robbery attempt. Williams takes off for a survivalist camp, followed by Matthau and shortly thereafter by Reed.

2942. *Suspect* (1987, Tri-Star, 121m, c). P Daniel A. Sherkow, D Peter Yates, W Eric Roth, PH Billy Williams, M Michael Kamen, ED Ray Lovejoy, PD Stuart Wurtzel.

LP Cher (Kathleen Riley), Dennis Quaid (Eddie Sanger), Liam Neeson (Carl Wayne Anderson), John Mahoney (Judge Matthew Helms), Joe Mantegna (Charlie Stella), Philip Bosco (Paul Gray), E. Katherine Kerr (Grace Comisky), Fred Melamed (Morty Rosenthal).

Washington, D.C., public defender Cher is given the assignment of defending homeless, mentally unstable, deaf-mute Vietnam vet Liam Neeson against a charge of murdering a woman. Things look bad for her client but with the unwelcome help of juror Dennis Quaid, who becomes romantically obsessed with Cher during the trial, justice prevails.

2943. *Swamp Thing* (1982, Embassy, 90m, c). P Benjamin Melniker & Michael E. Uslan, D&W Wes Craven (based on DC comic characters), PH Robin Goodwin, M Harry Manfredini, ED Richard Bracken, PD Robb Wilson King.

LP Louis Jourdan (Arcane), Adrienne Barbeau (Alice Cable), Ray Wise (Dr. Alec Holland), David Hess (Ferret), Nicholas Worth (Bruno), Don Knight (Ritter), Al Ruban (Charlie), Dick Durock (Swamp Thing), Ben Bates (Arcane Monster).

Filmed in comic book format, the movie is the story of a group of scientists performing a top secret experiment in a swamp and their troubles with their lunatic archenemy, Louis Jourdan.

2944. *Sweet Country* (1987, Cinema Group, 147m, c). P Michael Cacoyannis & Costas Alexakis, D&W Cacoyannis (based on a novel by Caroline Richards), PH Andreas Bellis, M Starvos Xarhakos, ED Dinos Katsourides & Cacoyannis.

LP Jane Alexander (Anna Willing), John Cullum (Ben Willing), Carole Laure (Eva Araya), Franco Nero (Paul), Joanna Pettet (Monica Araya), Randy Quaid (Juan), Irene Papas (Mrs. Araya), Jean-Pierre Aumont (Mr. Araya).

In 1973, American activist Jane Alexander, her teacher husband John Cullum, and their friends, divorced sisters Carole Laure and Joanna Pettet, become involved in political intrigue in Chile when Marxist leader Salvador Allende is overthrown.

2945. *Sweet Dirty Tony* (1980, Key West, 90m, c, aka *Cuba Crossing; Kill*

Castro; Assignment: Kill Castro). P Peter J. Barton, D&W Chuck Workman.

LP Stuart Whitman (Capt. Tony Terracino), Robert Vaughn (Hudd), Raymond St. Jacques (Bell), Caren Kaye (Tracy), Woody Strode (Titi), Sybil Danning (Veronica), Mary Lou Gassen (Maria), Albert Salmi (Delgato), Michael Gazzo (Rosselini).

In a dreadful film, soldier-of-fortune Stuart Whitman gets mixed up in a plot to assassinate Castro.

2946. *Sweet Dreams* (1985, Tri-Star, 115m, c). P Bernard Schwartz, D Karel Reisz, W Robert Getchell, PH Robbie Greenberg, M Charles Gross, ED Malcolm Cooke, PD Albert Brenner.

LP Jessica Lange† (Patsy Cline), Ed Harris (Charlie Dick), Ann Wedgeworth (Hilda Hensley), David Clennon (Randy Hughes), James Staley (Gerald Cline), Gary Basaraba (Woodhouse), John Goodman (Otis), P.J. Soles (Wanda).

In a well-acted biopic, Jessica Lange shines in the story of the short turbulent life of country singer Patsy Cline. The hits of the latter lip-synched by Lange include "San Antonio Rose," "Lovesick Blues," "Foolin' Around," "Your Cheatin' Heart," "Seven Lonely Days," "Walking After Midnight," "I Fall to Pieces" and the title song.

2947. *Sweet Heart's Dance* (1988, Tri-Star, 101m, c). P Jeffrey Lurie, D Robert Greenwald, W Ernest Thompson, PH Tak Fujimoto, M Richard Gibbs, ED Robert Florio, PD James Allen.

LP Don Johnson (Wiley Boon), Susan Sarandon (Sandra Boon), Jeff Daniels (Sam Manners), Elizabeth Perkins (Adie Nims), Kate Reid (Pearne Manners), Justin Henry (Kyle Boon), Holly Marie Combs (Debs Boon), Heather Coleman (BJ Boon), Matthew Wohl (Dick Merezini), Laurie Corbin (Claire Norton).

Conflicts arise between two Vermont friends, as one, Jeff Daniels, falls in love for the first time with Elizabeth Perkins, while the other, Don Johnson, is ending a 15-year marriage to Susan Sarandon. The film isn't much but the four main performers are charming.

2948. *Sweet Liberty* (1986, Universal, 107m, c). P Martin Bregman, D&W Alan Alda, PH Frank Tidy, M Bruce Brough-

ton, ED Michael Economou, PD Ben Edwards.

LP Alan Alda (Michael Burgess), Michael Caine (Elliott James), Michelle Pfeiffer (Faith Healy), Bob Hoskins (Stanley Gould), Lise Hilboldt (Gretchen Carlsen), Lillian Gish (Cecelia Burgess), Lois Chiles (Leslie), Saul Rubinek (Bo Hodges), Linda Thorson (Grace).

Small town historian Alan Alda finds his prize-winning saga of the Revolutionary War and his hometown being ruined by the film crew making a movie based on his work. Besides everything else, the star of the movie, Michael Caine, tries to bed every female around, including Alda's love, Lise Hilboldt. Young director Saul Rubinek believes that all ages are filled with alienation and the desire to remove everyone's clothes.

2949. *Sweet Lies* (1989, Island, 96m, c). P Serge Touboul & Chris Blackwell, D Nathalie Delon, W Rob Dunn (based on Delon's story), PH Dominique Chapuis, M Trevor Jones, ED Marie-Sophie Dubus, AD Bruno Held.

LP Treat Williams (Peter Nicholl), Joanna Pacula (Joelle), Julianne Phillips (Dixie), Laura Manszky (Lisa), Marilyn Dodds Frank (Maggie), Norbert Weisser (Bill), Aina Walle (Isabelle), Gisele Casadesus (Nemo).

Joanna Pacula and Julianne Phillips make a wager as to who will be the first to bed American detective Treat Williams, in Paris to investigate insurance fraud.

2950. *Sweet Lorraine* (1987, Angelika, 91m, c). P&D Steve Gomer, W Michael Zettler & Shelly Altman (based on a story by Zettler, Altman & George Malko), PH Rene Ohashi, M Richard Robbins, ED Laurence Solomon, PD David Gropman.

LP Maureen Stapleton (Lillian Garber), Trini Alvarado (Molly), Lee Richardson (Sam), John Bedford Lloyd (Jack), Freddie Roman (Phil Allen), Giancarlo Esposito (Howie), Edith Falco (Karen), Todd Graff (Leonard).

Young Trini Alvarado pitches in to help her grandmother Maureen Stapleton keep her run-down Catskills resort, which is facing bankruptcy.

2951. *Sweet Revenge* (1987, Concorde, 78m, c). P Brad Krevoy & Steven

Stabler, D Mark Sobel, W Steven Krauzer & Tim McCoy (based on an original story by Michael Jones & Randy Kornfield), PH Shane Kelly, M Ernest Troost, ED Michael S. Murphy, PD Vic Dabao.

LP Nancy Allen (Jillian Grey), Ted Shackelford (Boone), Martin Landau (Cicero), Sal Landi (Gil), Michele Little (Lee), Gina Gershon (K.C.), Lotis Key (Sonya), Stacey Adams (Tina), Leo Martinez (Buddha).

Investigating a white slavery ring run by Martin Landau in the Far East, reporter Nancy Allen is kidnapped and finds herself the ring's latest recruit.

2952. *Sweet 16* (1983, Century Intl., 90m, c). P&D Jim Sotos, W Erwin Goldman, PH James L. Carter, M Tommy Vig, ED Drake Silliman.

LP Bo Hopkins (Dan), Susan Strasberg (Joanne), Don Stroud (Billy), Dana Kimmell (Marci), Aleisa Shirley (Melissa), Don Shanks (Jason), Steve Antin (Hank), Logan Clarke (Jimmy).

Beautiful, mysterious, promiscuous 16-year-old Aleisa Shirley finds her boyfriends always turning up dead. What a bother!

2953. *Sweet William* (1982, World Northal, GB, 92m, c). P Jeremy Watt, D Claude Whatham, W Beryl Bainbridge (based on her novel), PH Les Young, ED Peter Coulson, PD Eileen Diss.

LP Sam Waterston (William), Jenny Agutter (Ann), Anna Massey (Edna), Geraldine James (Pamela), Daphne Oxenford (Mrs. Walton), Rachel Bell (Mrs. Kershaw), David Wood (Vicar).

Londoner Jenny Agutter finds her Scottish lover Sam Waterston constantly unfaithful.

2954. *Sweetie* (1989, Filmpac, Australia, 97m, c). P John Maynard, D Jane Campion, W Campion & Gerard Lee, PH Sally Bongers, M Martin Armiger, ED Veronika Heussler, PD Peter Harris.

LP Genevieve Lemon (Dawn [Sweetie]), Karen Colston (Kay), Tom Lycos (Louis), Jon Darling (Gordon), Dorothy Barry (Flo), Michael Lake (Bob).

In this tragicomedy, Karen Colston is afraid of trees and a believer in fortune-tellers. She initially figures that Tom Lycos, who has just become engaged to a coworker, is the one foretold to be the man in her life. She goes about seducing him, but after awhile she's no longer so sure he's the one. Her sister Genevieve Lemon, plump and plain, and eager for a show biz career, may be more to Lycos' liking.

2955. *Swing Shift* (1984, Warner, 113m, c). P Jerry Bick, D Jonathan Demme, W Rob Morton, PH Tak Fujimoto, M Patrick Williams, ED Craig McKay, PD Peter Jamison.

LP Goldie Hawn (Kay Walsh), Kurt Russell (Lucky Lockhart), Christine Lahti† (Hazel Zanussi), Fred Ward (Biscuits Toohey), Ed Harris (Jack Walsh), Sudie Bond (Annie), Holly Hunter (Jeannie Sherman), Patty Maloney (Laverne), Lisa Pelikan (Violet Mulligan).

In this nostalgic look at the times of World War II's "Rosie the Riveter," Goldie Hawn takes a job in an aircraft factory to make ends meet while her sailor husband Ed Harris is away at war. She has a fling with a fellow worker, 4-F Kurt Russell. This complicates things for her when her man comes home at the end of the war.

2956. *Switching Channels* (1988, Tri-Star, 105m, c). P Martin Ransohoff, D Ted Kotcheff, W Jonathan Reynolds (based on *The Front Page,* a play by Ben Hecht & Charles MacArthur), PH Francois Protat, M Michel Legrand, ED Thom Noble, PD Anne Pritchard.

LP Kathleen Turner (Christy Colleran), Burt Reynolds (John L. Sullivan, IV), Christopher Reeve (Blaine Bingham), Ned Beatty (Roy Ridnitz), Henry Gibson (Ike Roscoe), George Newbern (Siegenthaler), Al Waxman (Berger), Joe Silver (Morosini), Monica Parker (Jessica), Laura Robinson (Karen Ludlow).

While male viewers may never grow tired of seeing Kathleen Turner in another wholesomely sexy role, few will feel the same about Burt Reynolds and Christopher Reeve, who are charmless in this atrocious remake of *The Front Page* and *His Girl Friday.* The newspaper people are changed to TV news gatherers (make that inventors). For the record, ace TV reporter Turner is quitting the business to marry boring Reeve. Her ex-husband Reynolds tries anything to prevent her leaving. All is resolved as TV covers the planned execution of innocent Henry Gibson. It's hard to describe just how bad this film really is.

2957.   The Sword and the Sorcerer (1982, Group 1, 100m, c). P Brandon & Marion Chase, D Albert Pyun, W Pyun, Thomas Karnowski & John Stuckmeyer, PH Joseph Mangine, M David Whittaker, ED Marshall Harvey, AD George Costello.

LP Lee Horsley (Talon), Kathleen Beller (Alana), Simon MacCorkindale (Mikah), George Maharis (Machelli), Richard Lynch (Cromwell), Richard Moll (Xusia), Anthony DeLongis (Rodrigo), Nina Van Pallandt (Malia).

Lee Horsley regains control of a kingdom seized by an evil tyrant with the help of a powerful magician.

2958.   Sword of Heaven (1985, Trans-World, 85m, c). P Joseph J. Randazzo & Britt Lomond, D Byron Meyers, W James Bruno, Lomond, William P. O'Hagan & Randazzo, PH Gil Hubbs, M Christopher L. Stone, ED Warren Chadwick.

LP Tadashi Yamashita (Tadashi), Mel Novak (Dirk), Gerry Gibson (Patrick), Joe Randazzo (Cain), Mika (Satoko), Wynston A. Jones (Cal), Bill "Superfoot" Wallace, Karen Lee Shepherd, Venus Jones.

Crooked L.A. cop Wynston A. Jones and his martial arts buddy Mel Novak scheme to strip rich men of their money in order to equip a paramilitary crime-fighting unit, but they are stopped by visiting Japanese police officer Tadashi Yamashita.

2959.   The Sword of the Barbarians (1983, Cannon, US/Ital., 88m, c). P Pino Burricchi, D Michael E. Lemick, W Pietro Regnoli, PH Giancarlo Ferrando, M Franco Campanino, ED Alessandro Lucidi.

LP Peter MacCoy (Sangral), Margareta Rance, Yvonne Fraschetti, Anthony Freeman, Sabrina Siani, Ziomaria Rodriguez, Al Huang.

In this routine sword-and-fantasy film, Peter MacCoy seeks the "Golden Goddess."

2960.   Sword of the Valiant (1984, Cannon, GB, 101m, c). P Menahem Golan & Yoram Globus, D Stephen Weeks, W Weeks, Philip M. Breen & Howard C. Pen, PH Freddie A. Young & Peter Hurst, M Ron Geesin, ED Richard Marden & Barry Peters, PD Maurice Fowler & Derek Nice.

LP Miles O'Keeffe (Gawain), Cyrielle Claire (Linet), Leigh Lawson (Humphrey), Sean Connery (Green Knight), Trevor Howard (King Arthur), Peter Cushing (Seneschal), Ronald Lacey (Oswald), Lila Kedrova (Lady of Lyonesse), John Rhys-Davies (Baron Fortinbras), Wilfred Brambell (Porter).

Sean Connery as the Green Knight arrives in Camelot to challenge anyone to take a blow at him with a sword as long as he can return the blow. After awhile Miles O'Keeffe as Sir Gawain accepts the challenge and with a broadsword severs Connery's head from his body. At this the decapitated knight picks up his head and walks out, informing Gawain that he'll take his turn later. Readers will be relieved to learn that O'Keeffe, who was so miserable in Bo Derek's *Tarzan, the Ape Man,* is just as bad this time and required his lines to be dubbed. Unfortunately he's allowed to keep his head.

Swordkill   see   Ghost Warrior

2961.   Sylvester (1985, Columbia, 103m, c). P Martin Jurow, D Tim Hunter, W Carol Sobieski, PH Hiro Narita, M Lee Holdridge, ED Howard Smith, Suzanne Pettit & David Garfield, PD James W. Newport.

LP Richard Farnsworth (Foster), Melissa Gilbert (Charlie), Michael Schoeffling (Matt), Constance Towers (Muffy), Pete Kowanko (Harris), Yankton Hatten (Grant), Shane Serwin (Seth), Chris Pedersen (Red).

Sixteen-year-old Melissa Gilbert and cranky stockyard boss Richard Farnsworth team up to train a battered horse named Sylvester for the National Equestrian trials. It's not *National Velvet,* but it's enjoyable.

2962.   Sylvia (1985, MGM/United Artists, New Zealand, 98m, c). P Don Reynolds & Michael Firth, D Firth, W Michael Quill, F. Fairfax & Firth (based on the books *Teacher and I Passed This Way* by Sylvia Ashton-Warner), PH Ian Paul, M Leonard Rosenman, ED Michael Horton.

LP Eleanor David (Sylvia Henderson), Nigel Terry (Aden Morris), Tom Wilkinson (Keith Henderson), Mary Regan (Opal Saunders), Joseph George (Seven), Eileen Glover (Lilac), Graham Glover (Ashton), Tessa Wells (Jasmine).

Eleanor David gives an excellent portrayal of Sylvia Ashton-Warner, who in the early 40s bucked the New Zealand educational structure to offer innovative reading instructions to the Maori children.

2963. *Table for Five* (1983, Warner, 122m, c). P Robert Schaffel, D Robert Lieberman, W David Seltzer, PH Vilmos Zsigmond, M Miles Goodman & John Morris, ED Michael Kahn, PD Robert R. Boyle.

LP Jon Voight (J.P. Tannen), Richard Crenna (Mitchell), Marie-Christine Barrault (Marie), Millie Perkins (Kathleen), Roxana Zal (Tilde), Robby Kiger (Truman-Paul), Son Hoang Bui (Trung), Maria O'Brien (Mandy).

Trying to show that daddies make just as good parents as mommies and sometimes even better ones, this sickeningly sentimental soap opera stars Jon Voight as a divorced father. He tries to re-establish a relationship with the children he has let get away, while they all take an ocean cruise.

2964. *Taffin* (1988, MGM/United Artists, US/GB, 96m, c). P Peter Shaw, D Francis Megahy, W David Ambrose (based on the book by Lyndon Mallett), PH Paul Beeson, M Stanley Myers & Hans Zimmer, ED Rodney Holland, PD William Alexander.

LP Pierce Brosnan (Mark Taffin), Ray McAnally (O'Rourke), Alison Doody (Charlotte), Jeremy Child (Martin), Patrick Bergan (Mo Taffin), Ronan Wilmot (The Deacon), Alan Stanford (Sprawley), Gerald McSorley (Ed).

An ex-seminarian and now a debt-collector, Pierce Brosnan learns that the athletic field in his small Irish home town is the planned site of a dangerous chemical plant. He mounts a vigorous campaign against the plant's owners.

Things turn violent when hired thugs are turned loose on the conservationists.

2965. *Tail of the Tiger* (1984, Roadshow, Australia, 82m, c). P James M. Vernon, D&W Rolf de Heer, PH Richard Michalak, M Steve Arnold & Graham Tardif, ED Surresh Ayyar, PD Judi Russell.

LP Grant Navin (Orville Ryan), Gordon Poole (Harry), Caz Lederman (Lydia Ryan), Gayle Kennedy (Beryl), Peter Feeley (Spike), Dylan Lyle (Rabbit), Walter Sullivan (Stan), Basil Clarke (Jack).

The neighborhood boys won't allow airplane enthusiast Grant Navin to join them in flying model planes. He takes to hanging around old Gordon Poole who is trying to restore an ancient deHaviland Tiger in an abandoned warehouse. The efforts of the two are frequently aided by the ghosts of deceased pilots.

2966. *Tainted* (1989, Cardinal, 93m, c). P Orestes Matacena & Phyllis Redden, D&W Matacena, PH Ramon Suarez, M Hayden Wayne, ED Stephen Sheppard, AD Randy Barcelo.

LP Shari Shattuck (Cathy Lowell), Park Overall (Marian), Gene Tootle (Frank), Magilla Schaus (Tom), Blaque Fowler (Rapist), Ross Taylor (Principal), Ruben Rabasa (Guard).

Filmed in 1984, it was planned to release this film theatrically as *Body Passion,* but instead it went directly to video shelves. Shari Shattuck, a small-town school teacher, is raped by a prowler who in turn is killed by her mortician husband Gene Tootle. The latter promptly expires from a heart attack. Rather than call in the police, Shattuck decides to cover up the incident.

Tai-Pan see James Clavell's Tai-Pan

2967. *Take This Job and Shove It* (1981, Avco Embassy, 100m, c). P Greg Blackwell, D Gus Trikonis, W Barry Schneider (based on a story by Jeffrey Bernini & Schneider from a song by David Allen Coe), PH James Devis, M Billy Sherrill, ED Richard Belding, AD Jim Dultz.

LP Robert Hays (Frank Maclin), Art Carney (Charlie Pickett), Barbara Hershey (J.M. Halstead), David Keith (Harry Meade), Tim Thomerson (Ray

Binkowski), Martin Mull (Dick Ebersol), Eddie Albert (Samuel Ellison).

Robert Hays, a junior executive for a megaconglomerate, is sent to his home town to modernize a brewery. By this film's end, his disgust for his company makes him shout the title which was named after a song. That's the kiss of death for any movie.

2968. Take Two (1988, Hadar/TBJ, 100m, c). P Ronnie Hadar, D Peter Rowe, W Moshe Hadar, PH James Mathers, M Donald Hulette, ED Terry Chiappe.

LP Grant Goodeve (Barry/Frank), Robin Mattson (Susan Bentley), Frank Stallone (Ted Marvin), Nita Talbot (Betty Griffith), Warren Berlinger (Apartment Manager), Mickey Morton (Det. Stratton).

A wealthy man arranges for Nita Talbot to serve as a surrogate mother. She gives birth to twins but only presents her client with one of the boys, keeping the other to raise herself. Later when the lad has grown to be Grant Goodeve, Talbot tells him of his parentage and encourages him to collect his share of his deceased father's estate. When he presents this notion to his twin (also Goodeve), Bro wants nothing to do with it. The disinherited lad seduces his brother's abused wife Robin Mattson and the two plot to do away with the unwanted twin.

2969. Tales from the Gimli Hospital (1989, Extra Large/Winnipeg Film Group, Canada, 72m, b&w). D,W, PH&ED Guy Maddin, AD Jeff Solylo.

LP Kyle McCulloch (Einar), Michael Gottli (Gunnar), Angela Heck (Snjofridur), Margaret-Anne MacLeod (Amma), Heather Neale (Fjola), Caroline Bonner (Elfa Egilsdottir).

This midnight movie creation of 31-year-old Guy Maddin seems headed for cult status. It is the story of the rivalry of two men, Kyle McCulloch and Michael Gottli, who share the same dirty hospital room in turn-of-the-century Icelandic village of Gimli. They are in quarantine because of an epidemic. They pass the time regaling each other with stories of their miserable lives which involved wife-killing and grave robbing. Their surreal relationship supposedly draws upon strange ancient Icelandic customs.

2970. Tales of the Third Dimension (1985, Owensby/Shapiro, 90m, c). P Earl Owensby, D Thom McIntyre ("Young Blood"), Worth Keeter ("The Guardians"), Todd Durham (Visions of Sugar-Plum"), W McIntyre, Keeter & Durham, M Dee Barton.

LP "Young Blood"—Robert Bloodworth, Kate Hunter, Fran Taylor, Kevin Campbell. "The Guardians"—William Hicks, Terry Laughlin, Leon Rippy. "Visions of Sugar-Plum"—Helene Tryon, Kathy O'Toole, Neal Powell.

Earl Owensby, the king of the Southern drive-ins, presents three comedy-horror stories. In "Young Blood" a vampire couple have a problem child who is actually a werewolf. In "The Guardians," greedy grave robbers dig up more than they bargained for. In "Visions of Sugar-Plum," visiting grandmother takes on a murderous twist.

2971. Tale of Two Sisters (1989, Vista Street, 89m, b&w/c). P Lawrence Bender & Randolf Turrow, D Adam Rifkin, W Improvised by the cast, PH John F.K. Parenteau, M Marc David Decker, ED King Wilder.

LP Valerie Breiman (Phil), Claudia Christian (Liz), Sidney Lassick (Dad), Dee Coppola (Mom), Tom Hodges (Butler/Auntie Sparkle), Jeff Conaway (Taxi driver), Pete Berg (Gardener).

Surreal images are used to illustrate the feelings of two adult sisters Valerie Breiman and Claudia Christian. They have a reunion after five years and recall their childhood and their mutual resentments.

2972. Talk Radio (1988, Universal, 110m, c). P Edward R. Pressman, D Oliver Stone, W Eric Bogosian & Stone (based on the play created by Bogosian & Tad Savinar, and the book *Talked to Death: The Life and Murder of Alan Berg* by Stephen Singular), PH Robert Richardson, M Stewart Copeland, ED David Brenner, PD Bruno Rubeo.

LP Eric Bogosian (Barry Champlain), Alec Baldwin (Dan), Ellen Greene (Ellen), Leslie Hope (Laura), John C.

McGinley (Stu), John Pankow (Chuck Dietz), Michael Wincott (Kent), Zach Grenier (Sid Greenberg).

Recreating his stage role, Eric Bogosian is in the mold of a Morton Downey, Jr., talk show host. His abrasive and abusive style with callers provokes the crazies in his audience, leading to a violent conclusion.

2973. *Talking to Strangers* (1988, Baltimore Film Factory, 92m, c). P J.K. Eareckson, D&W Rob Tregenza, PH Tregenza.

LP Ken Gruz (Jesse), Dennis Jordan (Red Coat), Marvin Hunter (General), Caron Tate (Ms. Taylor), Brian Constantini (Angry Man), Bill Sanders (Manager), Henry Strozier (Priest), Richard Foster (Slick).

This independent film is about a pompous artist trying to find material for a movie by "talking to strangers." Nine continuous takes are arranged in random order, so the audience never really knows the director's intentions—assuming he had any.

2974. *Talking Walls* (1987, New World, 83m, c, aka *Motel Vacancy*). P Philip A. Waxman, D&W Stephen Verona (based on the novel *The Motel Tapes* by Mike McGrady), PH Scott Miller, M Richard Glasser, ED Jonathan Lawton, AD Rick Carter.

LP Stephen Shellen (Paul Barton), Marie Laurin (Jeanne), Barry Primus (Prof. Hirsh), Karen Lee Hopkins (Luna), Sybil Danning (Bathing Beauty), Don Davis (Don), Rae Davis (Rae), Hector Elias (Roberto).

Seeking the secret of romance, intimacy and lasting relationships, sociology student Stephen Shellen videotapes trysts held at the Total Media Hotel via one-way mirrors. His incessant use of a camera just about ruins his chance to have a meaningful relationship with beautiful French art student Marie Laurin.

2975. *The Tall Guy* (1989, Vestron, GB, 92m, c). P Paul Webster, D Mel Smith, W Richard Curtis, PH Adrian Biddle, M Peter Brewis, ED Dan Rae, PD Grant Hicks.

LP Jeff Goldblum (Dexter King), Emma Thompson (Kate Lemon), Rowan Atkinson (Ron Anderson), Emil Wolk (Cyprus Charlie), Geraldine James (Carmen), Kim Thomson (Cheryl), Susan Field (Dr. Freud), Hugh Thomas (Karabekian).

American actor Jeff Goldblum has been performing as straight man for comedian Rowan Atkinson for several years in London's West End. He falls for nurse Emma Thompson and about the time the two sexually connect, Atkinson fires Goldblum. The latter turns this defeat into triumph when he is cast in the title role in a musical version of *The Elephant Man*. Is any further comment called for?

2976. *Tango and Cash* (1989, Warner, 98m, c). P Jon Peters & Peter Guber, D Andrei Konchalovsky, W Randy Feldman, PH Donald E. Thorin, M Harold Faltermeyer, ED Stuart Baird, Hubert de la Bouillerie & Robert Ferretti, PD J. Michael Riva.

LP Sylvester Stallone (Tango), Kurt Russell (Cash), Teri Hatcher (Kiki), Jack Palance (Yves Perret), Brion James (Courier/Requin), James Hong (Quan), Marc Alaimo (Lopez).

Appearing as a macho Laurel and Hardy, Sylvester Stallone and Kurt Russell are Los Angeles narcotics officers. They are framed by drugpin Jack Palance and sent to prison. This buddy picture is merely a poor excuse to show off the muscles of the two stars, but it is their ignorance that is shown to greatest advantage. There's abundant mindless violence and gore, but little that can pass for plot or acting.

2977. *Tango Bar* (1989, Zaga-Beco/Manley, 90m, b&w). P Roberto Gandara and Juan Carlos Codazzi, D Marcos Zurinaga, W Jose Pablo Feinman, Codazzi & Zurinaga, PH Zurinaga, M Atilio Stampone, ED Pablo Mari, PD Maria Julia Bertotto.

LP Raul Julia (Ricardo), Valerie Lynch (Elena), Ruben Juarez (Antonio).

In this musical, Raul Julia is the foremost tango singer in the world. Reunited in Buenos Aires with Valerie Lynch and Ruben Juarez, the three stars of the nightspot called the Tango Bar form a romantic triangle in a bones-bare plot.

2978. *Tank* (1984, Universal, 113m, c). P Irwin Yablans, D Marvin J. Chomsky, W Dan Gordon, PH Don Birnkrant, M Lalo Schifrin, ED Donald R. Rode, PD Bill Kenney.

LP James Garner (Zack), Shirley Jones (LaDonna), C. Thomas Howell (Billy), Mark Herrier (Elliott), Sandy Ward (Gen. Hubik), Jenilee Harrison (Sarah), James Cromwell (Deputy Euclid), Dorian Harewood (Sgt. Tippet), G.D. Spradlin (Sheriff Buelton).

G.D. Spradlin is a delightful villain, worthy of resounding hisses and boos. He's the tyrannical sheriff of a small Southern town outside a military base where James Garner is the top sergeant. Garner's hobby is restoring tanks. He owns a working Sherman tank. He uses it to break his son C. Thomas Howell out of a harsh prison farm. Spradlin used Howell to punish Garner for coming to the assistance of prostitute Jenilee Harrison when Deputy James Cromwell began slapping her around. Garner, Howell and Harrison try to escape by tank to the next state where they hope to get a fair shake from the authorities. Spradlin and his rednecks are intent on preventing this from happening.

2979. *Tank Malling* (1989, Pointlane Films, GB, 108m, c). P Glen Murphy & Jamie Foreman, D James Marcus, W Marcus & Mick Southworth, PH Jason Lehel, M Rick Fenn & Nick Mason, ED Brian Peachey, PD Geoffrey Sharpe.

LP Ray Winstone (Tank Malling), Amanda Donohoe (Helen Searle), Peter Wyngarde (Robert Knights), Glen Murphy (Cashman), Jason Connery (Dunboyne), Marsha Hunt (Salena), Jamie Foreman (Danny), John Bett (Campbell Sinclaire).

In this clichéd and caricature-filled crime thriller, investigative reporter Ray Winstone has just been released from prison. He had been framed for perjury. He's approached by high-priced callgirl Amanda Donohoe who has some dirt on powerful national figure Peter Wyngarde. While he's busy gathering facts on the corruption in high places, he and Donohoe are being tracked by killer Glen Murphy, not too particular whom he kills.

2980. *Tanya's Island* (1980, Intl. Film Exchange, Canada, 82m, c). P Pierre Brousseau, D Alfred Sole, W Brousseau, PH Mark Irwin, M Jean Musy, ED Michael MacLaverty, AD Angelo Stea, SE Rick Baker & Rob Bottin.

LP D.D. Winters (Tanya), Richard Sargent (Lobo), Mariette Levesque (Kelly), Don McCleod (Blue).

In a Beauty and the Beast story, beautiful D.D. Winters, abused by her artist husband Richard Sargent, dreams about living on an island where she makes friends with an ape.

2981. *Tap* (1989, Tri-Star, 110m, c). P Gary Adelson & Richard Vane, D&W Nick Castle, Jr., PH David Gribble, M James Newton Howard, ED Patrick Kennedy, PD Patricia Norris.

LP Gregory Hines (Max), Suzanne Douglas (Amy), Sammy Davis, Jr. (Little Mo), Savion Glover (Louis), Joe Morton (Nicky), Dick Anthony Williams (Francis), Sandman Sims (Sandman), Bunny Briggs (Bunny), Steve Condos (Steve), Jimmy Slyde (Slim), Pat Rico (Spats), Arthur Duncan (Arthur), Harold Nicholas (Harold).

Talented tap dancer Gregory Hines is just out of jail after serving a robbery stretch. The plot is merely an excuse to feature his superb dancing talent. In one memorable sequence he works with seven great old-time tap dancers, each showing what made them great. Fortunately for the audience the camera is drawn back and their routines are shown in full figures.

2982. *Tapeheads* (1988, Avenue, 97m, c). P Peter McCarthy, D Bill Fishman, W Fishman & McCarthy (based on a story by Fishman, McCarthy, Jim Herzfeld & Ryan Rowe), PH Bojan Bazelli, M Fishbone, ED Mondo Jenkins, PD Catherine Hardwicke.

LP John Cusack (Ivan Alexeev), Tim Robbins (Josh Tager), Mary Crosby (Samantha Gregory), Connie Stevens (June Tager), Clu Gulager (Norman Mart), Katy Boyer (Belinda Mart), Jessica Walter (Kay Mart), Sam Moore (Billy Diamond), Junior Walker (Lester Diamond), King Cotton (Roscoe).

In this spoof of the music business, John Cusack and Tim Robbins are fired from their jobs as security guards. They move into the video production business and get their hands on a video damaging to the career of politician Clu Gulager. Thugs are sent to recover the incriminating video.

2983. *Taps* (1981, 20th Century–Fox, 119m, c). P Stanley R. Jaffe & Howard B. Jaffe, D Harold Becker, W Darryl Ponicsan, Robert Mark Kamen & James Lineberger (based on the novel *Father Sky* by Devery Freeman), PH Owen Roizman, M Maurice Jarre, ED Maury Winetrobe, AD Stan Jolley & Alfred Sweeney.

LP George C. Scott (Gen. Harlan Bache), Timothy Hutton (Brian Moreland), Ronny Cox (Col. Kerby), Sean Penn (Alex Dwyer), Tom Cruise (David Shawn), Brendan Ward (Charlie Auden), Evan Handler (Edward West), John P. Navin, Jr. (Derek Mellott), Billy Van Zandt (Bug).

When the students of an elite military school learn that the trustees plan to close the school and sell the grounds to the developer of condominiums, they arm themselves and defend their turf. The result is a bloodbath.

2984. *Target* (1985, Warner, 117m, c). P Richard D. Zanuck & David Brown, D Arthur Penn, W Howard Berk & Don Petersen (based on a story by Leonard Stern), PH Jean Tournier & Robert Jessup, M Michael Small, ED Stephen A. Rotter & Richard P. Cirincione, AD Willy Holt & Richard James.

LP Gene Hackman (Walter Lloyd), Matt Dillon (Chris Lloyd), Gayle Hunnicutt (Donna Lloyd), Victoria Fyodorova (Lise), Ilona Grubel (Carla), Herbert Berghof (Schroeder), Josef Sommer (Taber), Guy Boyd (Clay), Richard Munch (The Colonel).

When his wife Gayle Hunnicutt is kidnapped in Paris, Dallas lumberyard owner Gene Hackman and son Matt Dillon fly to France to find her. When assassins try to kill Hackman, he must reveal to Dillon his past as a CIA agent. Hackman and Dillon team up to get mom back safely.

2985. *Tarzan, The Ape Man* (1981, MGM/United Artists, 112m, c). P Bo Derek, D John Derek, W Tom Rowe & Gary Goddard (based on the characters created by Edgar Rice Burroughs), PH John Derek, M Perry Botkin, ED James B. Ling, AD Alan Roderick-Jones.

LP Bo Derek (Jane), Richard Harris (Parker), John Phillip Law (Holt), Miles O'Keeffe (Tarzan), Akushula Selayah (Africa), Steven Strong (Ivory King), Maxime Philoe (Riano), Leonard Bailey (Feathers).

Anyone who believes that a movie which features a naked Bo Derek frolicking with the animals on a beach and in the jungle can't be all bad, hasn't seen this film. Everything about the movie is amateurish, and the acting is atrocious. But Miles O'Keeffe as the Ape Man is an embarrassment to the simian parents who raised him.

2986. *The Taste of Hemlock* (1989, Intl. Artists, GB, 90m, c). P Eric Tynan Young, D Geoffrey Darwin, W Young (based on the play *The Astrakhan Coat* by Pauline Macaulay), PH Roger Tonry, M Young, ED Henry Te.

LP Randy Harrington (Claud Thatch), Eric Tynan Young (James Hattan), Anne Elizabeth Ramsey (Barbara), Reed Armstrong (Barry), David McKnight (Lt. Jordan), Barbara Pilavin (Mrs. Dobrowski), Shea Young (Sgt. Narducci).

The plot seems to be one large shaggy dog story made at the expense of both Randy Harrington, who buys an expensive coat from manipulative Eric Tynan Young, even though he can't afford it, and the audience.

2987. *A Taste of Sin* (1983, New West/Ambassador, 84m, c). P&D Ulli Lommel, W Lommel, John P. Marsh & Ron Norman, PH Lommel, Jochen Breitenstein, Jon Kranhouse, Dave Sperling & Jurg Walthers, M Joel Goldsmith, ED Terrell Tannen.

LP Suzanna Love (Olivia), Robert Walker (Michael Grant), Jeff Winchester (Richard), Bibbe Hansen (Mother), Amy Robinson (Olivia at age 6), Nicholas Love (G.I.), Ulli Lommel (Detective).

As a child Suzanna Love witnessed the

murder of her prostitute mother by a G.I. As an adult, she hears her mother's voice from the grave and becomes a killer, dressed as a hooker, hitting the pavement on London Bridge.

2988.   *Tattoo* (1981, 20th Century-Fox, 103m, c). P Joseph E. Levine & Richard P. Levine, D Bob Brooks, W Joyce Bunuel (based on a story by Brooks), PH Arthur Ornitz & Michael Seresin, M Barry DeVorzon, ED Thom Noble, PD Stuart Wurtzel.

LP Bruce Dern (Karl Kinski), Maud Adams (Maddy), Leonard Frey (Halsey), Rikke Borge (Sandra), John Getz (Buddy), Peter Iacangelo (Dubin), Alan Leach (Customer), Cynthia Nixon (Cindy), Trish Doolin (Cheryl).

Maniacal tattoo artist Bruce Dern almost jumps out of his skin with his obsession of making Adams his ultimate canvas.

2989.   *Teachers* (1984, MGM/United Artists, 106m, c). P Aaron Russo, D Arthur Hiller, W W.R. McKinney (based on a story by A. Russo & Irwin Russo), PH David M. Walsh, ED Don Zimmerman, MD Sandy Gibson, PD Richard MacDonald.

LP Nick Nolte (Alex), JoBeth Williams (Lisa), Judd Hirsch (Roger), Ralph Macchio (Eddie), Allen Garfield (Rosenberg), Lee Grant (Dr. Burke), Richard Mulligan (Herbert), Royal Dano (Ditto), William Schallert (Horn), Art Metrano (Troy), Laura Dern (Diane), Crispin Glover (Danny), Morgan Freeman (Lewis).

For anyone who has ever taught at the high school level, this film is a chilling reminder of all the things that are wrong with American public schools. The students aren't much interested in learning, the administration cares more for appearances than education and many of the teachers are an incompetent, frightened lot. The best teacher shown in the film is Richard Mulligan, an escapee from a looney bin who is mistaken for a substitute teacher and really turns students on to American history before he is taken away with a net. Royal Dano has developed a technique of conducting his classes which does not require any interaction with his students. It's so effective that one day he dies at his desk during the first period and no one notices all day. Nick Nolte is the obligatory caring pedagogue and Ralph Macchio is the student he wishes to salvage when he's not otherwise occupied bedding reporter JoBeth Williams.

2990.   *Teen Mothers* (1980, Cannon, 90m, c, aka *Seed of Innocence*). P Yoram Globus, D Boaz Davidson, W Stuart Krieger, PH Adam Greenberg, M Shalom Chanach, ED Jon Koslowsky, PD Brent Swift.

LP Timothy Wead (Danny), Mary Cannon (Alice), Vincent Schiavelli (Leo), T.K. Carter (Captain), Azizi Johari (Denise), Julianna McCarthy (Nadine), Sonja O. Menor (Teacher), Mary Ellen O'Neill (Sister Mary).

Teenage couple Timothy Wead and Mary Cannon (she's pregnant) run away to New York City and find it an unfriendly place.

2991.   *Teen Vamp* (1989, New World, 89m, c). P Jim McCullough, D&W Samuel Bradford, PH Richard Mann, M Robert Sprayberry, ED Uncredited.

LP Clu Gulager (Reverend), Karen Carlson (Mom), Angie Brown (Connie), Beau Bishop (Murphy), Mike Lane, Evans Dietz, Edd Anderson, Jude Gerard.

Nerdish Beau Bishop is turned into a hip, leather-jacketed, 50s cool-cat after he's bitten in the neck by a whore at a road house.

2992.   *Teen Witch* (1989, TransWorld Ent., 105m, c). P Alana Lambros, Rafael Eisenman, D Dorian Walker, W Robin Menkin & Vernon Zimmerman, PH Marc Reshovsky, M Richard Elliot, ED Natan Zahavi, PD Stephen Rice.

LP Robyn Lively (Louise Miller), Zelda Rubinstein (Madame Serena), Dan Gauthier (Brad), Joshua Miller (Richie), Caren Kaye (Margaret), Dick Sargent (Frank), Lisa Fuller (Randa), Shelley Berman (Mr. Weaver).

In this comedy-fantasy, music and dance are incorporated into a contemporary fable about designated loser Robyn Lively, a member of the "out-crowd" at her school. She runs into fortuneteller Zelda Rubinstein, who predicts Lively will turn into a witch before her

16th birthday. She does and her attempts at "turn-about-is-fair-play" are moderately funny.

2993. *Teen Wolf* (1985, Atlantic, 91m, c). P Mark Levinson, Scott Rosenfelt & George Perkins, D Rod Daniel, W Joseph Loeb III & Matthew Weisman, PH Tim Suhrstedt, M Miles Goodman, ED Lois Freeman-Fox, AD Chester Kaczenski.

LP Michael J. Fox (Scott Howard), James Hampton (Harold Howard), Susan Ursitti (Lisa "Boof" Marconi), Jerry Levine (Rupert "Stiles" Stilinsky), James MacKrell (Russell Thorne), Lorie Griffin (Pamela Wells), Mark Arnold (Mick McAllister).

Life as a teenager is the pits for Michael J. Fox. The high school basketball team for which the short little actor plays is putrid. He can't get to first base with beauty Lorie Griffin and he can't shake persistent Susan Ursitti. Things improve when he discovers that he's a werewolf. His howl is worse than his bite, however.

2994. *Teen Wolf Too* (1987, Atlantic, 95m, c). P Kent Bateman, D Christopher Leitch, W R. Timothy Kring (based on a story by Joseph Loeb, III & Matthew Weisman), PH Jules Brenner, M Mark Goldenberg, ED Steven Polivka, Kim Secrist, Harvey Rosenstock & Raja Gosnell.

LP Jason Bateman (Todd Howard), Kim Darby (Prof. Brooks), John Astin (Dean Dunn), Paul Sand (Coach Finstock), James Hampton (Uncle Howard), Mark Holton (Chubby), Estee Chandler (Nicki), Robert Neary (Gustavson).

Jason Bateman, the heartthrob star of television's "Valerie," plays the cousin of Michael J. Fox, who had the title role in the original film about a teenage werewolf. Bateman also has lycanthrophy ability, but this film didn't pull in the big bucks at the box office as did the Fox number.

2995. *The Telephone* (1988, New World, 82m, c). P Robert Katz & Moctesuma Esparza, D Rip Torn, W Harry Nilsson & Terry Southern, PH David Claessen, M Christopher Young, ED Sandra Adair, AD Jim Pohl.

LP Whoopi Goldberg (Vashti Blue),

Severn Darden (Max), Amy Wright (Honey Boxe/Irate Neighbor), Elliott Gould (Rodney), John Heard (Telephone Man), Ronald J. Stallings (Saxaphone Player).

The movie serves as a vehicle for Whoopi Goldberg to do a variety of her monologs. She appears as an out-of-work actress with no money to pay her bills. She vents her anger on her telephone, employing various accents and personas.

2996. *Tell Me a Riddle* (1980, Filmways, 90m, c). P Mindy Affrime, Rachel Lyon & Susan O'Connell, D Lee Grant, W Joyce Eliason & Alev Lytle (based on the novella by Tillie Olsen), PH Fred Murphy, M Sheldon Shkolnik, ED Suzanne Pettit, PD Patrizia von Brandenstein.

LP Melvyn Douglas (David), Lila Kedrova (Eva), Brooke Adams (Jeannie), Lili Valenty (Mrs. Mays), Dolores Dorn (Vivi), Bob Elross (Sammy), Jon Harris (Mathew), Zalman King (Paul), Winifred Mann (Hannah).

After years of quarreling, elderly Melvyn Douglas and his dying wife of 40 years Lila Kedrova rediscover the love they once had.

2997. *Tempest* (1982, Columbia, 140m, c). P&D Paul Mazursky, W Mazursky & Leon Capetanos (based on the play by William Shakespeare), PH Donald McAlpine, M Stomu Yamashta, ED Donn Cambern, PD Pato Guzman.

LP John Cassavetes (Phillip), Gena Rowlands (Antonia), Susan Sarandon (Aretha), Vittorio Gassman (Alonzo), Raul Julia (Kalibanos), Molly Ringwald (Miranda), Sam Robards (Freddy), Paul Stewart (Phillip's Father), Jackie Gayle (Trinc), Anthony Holland (Sebastian).

In this contemporary version of Shakespeare's *The Tempest,* John Cassavetes is an architect in the mold of Gary Cooper in *The Fountainhead.* He leaves his wife Gena Rowlands, for a Greek island, taking along Susan Sarandon and his teenage daughter Molly Ringwald. Cassavetes and Sarandon have not consummated their affair. Raul Julia is the Caliban-like character. The film makes a grand effort and Cassavetes gives a peak performance, but the result is a valiant failure.

Temptation Blues see Nowhere to Run (1989)

2998. Ten Little Indians (1989, Cannon, 98m, c). P Harry Alan Towers, D Alan Birkinshaw, W Jackson Hunsicker & Gerry O'Hara (based on Agatha Christie's play), PH Arthur Lavia, M George C. Clinton, ED Penelope Shaw, PD Roger Orpen.

LP Donald Pleasence (Justice Wargrave), Frank Stallone (Capt. Lombard), Sarah Maur Thorp (Vera Claythorne), Herbert Lom (Gen. Romensky), Brenda Vaccaro (Marion Marshall), Warren Berlinger (Blore), Yehuda Efroni (Dr. Hans Werner), Paul L. Smith (Elmo Rodgers), Moira Lister (Ethel Rodgers), Neil McCarthy (Anthony Mardsen).

This new version of Agatha Christie's masterful mystery story is even worse than the 1965 and the 1975 versions and should not even be mentioned in the same breath with the 1945 classic directed by Rene Clair. Set in the 30s, ten disparate individuals are summoned to an African safari party where they are dispatched one-by-one by their unseen host using means corresponding to the way the little Indians died in the nursery rhyme "Ten Little Indians."

2999. 10 to Midnight (1983, Cannon, 101m, c). P Pancho Kohner & Lance Hool, D J. Lee Thompson, W William Roberts, PH Adam Greenberg, M Robert O. Ragland, ED Peter Lee Thompson, AD Jim Freiburger.

LP Charles Bronson (Leo Kessler), Lisa Eilbacher (Laurie Kessler), Andrew Stevens (Paul McAnn), Gene Davis (Warren Stacy), Geoffrey Lewis (Dave Dante), Wilford Brimley (Capt. Malone), Robert Lyons (Nathan Zager).

In this thoroughly unpleasant movie, Charles Bronson is a cop who makes his own rules in dealing with psychopathic killer Gene Davis. The latter wearing only his birthday suit preys on young women, including Bronson's daughter Lisa Eilbacher. The film finds many ways to offend all but bloody-thirsty voyeurs.

3000. 10 Violent Women (1982, New American/Aquarius, 95m, c). P&D Ted V. Mikels, W Mikels & James Gordon White, PH Yuval Shousterman, M Nicholas Carras, ED Mikels, PD Mike McClusky.

LP Sherri Vernon (Samantha), Dixie Lauren (Maggie), Georgia Morgan (Bri Terry), Jane Farnsworth (Madge), Ted V. Mikels (Leo), Anne Gaybis (Vickie), Melodie Bell, Christina de Cattani.

Bored with their jobs, ten lovely ladies embark on a million dollar jewel heist. They end up in a women's prison where the guards subject them to cruel indignities.

3001. Tender Mercies† (1983, Universal, 89m, c). P Philip S. Hobel, Mary-Ann Hobel, Horton Foote & Robert Duvall, D Bruce Beresford†, W Horton Foote*, PH Russell Boyd, M George Dreyfus, ED William Anderson, AD Jeannine Oppewall, SONG "Over You" by Bobby Hart & Austin Roberts†.

LP Robert Duvall* (Mac Sledge), Tess Harper (Rosa Lee), Betty Buckley (Dixie), Wilford Brimley (Harry), Ellen Barkin (Sue Anne), Allan Hubbard (Sonny), Lenny Von Dohlen (Robert).

Ex-alcoholic country-and-western singer Robert Duvall attempts a comeback after taking a job with widow Tess Harper, whom he marries. Lurking in the background is Duvall's ex-wife Betty Buckley, herself a country-and-western singer. Finally Duvall realizes that show business is not for him and that true happiness can be found with Harper and her young son Allan Hubbard.

3002. Tennessee Nights (1989, Nelson, US/Swiss, 95m, c). P Bernard Lang & Peter-Christian Fueter, D Nicolas Gessner, W Gessner & Laird Koenig (based on *Minnie* by Hans Werner Kettenbach), PH Pio Corradi, M Gabriel Yared, ED Marie-Therese Boiche.

LP Julian Sands (Wolfgang Leighton), Stacey Dash (Minnie), Ed Lauter, Ned Beatty, Denise Crosby, Brian McNamara, Rod Steiger.

The chaotic story sees uptight British lawyer Julian Sands, who specializes in music contracts, visiting Nashville and taking a side trip into the world of Kafka.

3003. Tequila Sunrise (1988, Warner, 116m, c). P Thom Mount, D Robert Towne, W Towne, PH Conrad L. Hall†, M Dave Grusin, ED Claire Simpson, PD Richard Sylbert.

LP Mel Gibson (Dale McKussic), Kurt Russell (Lt. Nick Frescia), Michelle Pfeiffer (Jo Ann Vallenari), Raul Julia (Escalante), J.T. Walsh (Maguire), Arliss Howard (Gregg Lindroff), Ann Magnuson (Shaleen).

High school friends Mel Gibson, a retired cocaine dealer, and Kurt Russell, a L.A. narcotics cop, both fall for Michelle Pfeiffer, proprietor of a trendy restaurant. That's how it seems, but maybe Russell is just using the lovely lady to implicate his old buddy in a major drug deal.

3004. Terminal Choice (1985, Magder/Almi, Canada, 95m, c). P Gary Magder, D Sheldon Larry, W Neal Bell (based on a story by Peter Lawrence), PH Zale Magder, M Brian Bennett, ED Murray Magder, PD David Jaquest.

LP Joe Spano (Dr. Frank Holt), Diane Venora (Anna Lang), David McCallum (Dr. Dodson), Robert Joy (Dr. Harvey Rimmer), Don Francks (Chauncey Rand), Nicholas Campbell (Henderson), Ellen Barkin (Mary O'Connor).

A modern computer-managed hospital has patients dying at an alarming rate. Is it human or computer error? Accident or a sinister plot?

3005. Terminal Entry (1988, TBA/International, 95m, c). P Sharyon Reis Cobe, D John Kincade, W David Mickey Evans & Mark Sobel (based on a story by Sobel), PH James L. Carter, M Gene Hobson, ED Dean Goodhill, AD Alexandra Kicenik.

LP Edward Albert (Capt. Danny Jackson), Kabir Bedi (Terrorist Commander), Heidi Helmer (Chris), Mazhar Khan (Abdul), Yaphet Kotto (Styles), Patrick Laborteaux (Bob), Yvette Nipar (Tina), Kavi Raz (Mahaddi), Paul Smith (Stewart).

Teenage computer hackers break into the Terminal Entry program and mistake it for an interactive terrorist game. Actually the program is an information source for terrorists planning to assassinate the president.

Terminal Exposure see **Double Exposure**

3006. The Terminator (1984, Orion, 108m, c). P Gale Anne Hurd, D James

Cameron, W Cameron, Hurd & William Wisher, Jr., PH Adam Greenberg, M Brad Fiedel, ED Mark Goldblatt, AD George Costello.

LP Arnold Schwarzenegger (Terminator), Michael Biehn (Kyle Reese), Linda Hamilton (Sarah Connor), Paul Winfield (Traxler), Lance Henriksen (Vukovich), Rick Rossovich (Matt), Bess Motta (Ginger).

In this sf thriller Arnold Schwarzenegger is a death-dealing android sent back from the 21st century to assassinate Linda Hamilton. But he must contend with Michael Biehn, also from the future, hot on his trail.

3007. Termini Station (1989, Astral Bellevue Pathe, Canada, 108m, c). P&D Allan King, W Colleen Murphy, PH Brian Hebb, M Mychall Dama, ED Gordon McClellan, PD Lillian Sarafinchan.

LP Colleen Dewhurst (Molly Dushane), Megan Follows (Micheline), Gordon Clapp (Harvey Dushane), Norma Dell'Agnese (Val), Debra McGrath, Leon Pownall.

Boozing widow Colleen Dewhurst lives with her businessman son Gordon Clapp and his wife. Her daughter Megan Follows is a hooker in a small Ontario mining town. Everyone's problems stem from a longtime affair Dewhurst had with a businessman who is the true father of her daughter.

3008. Terms of Endearment* (1983, Paramount, 130m, c). P James L. Brooks, Penney Finkelman & Martin Jurow, D Brooks*, W Brooks* (based on the novel by Larry McMurtry), PH Andrzej Bartkowiak, M Michael Gore†, ED Richard Marks†, PD Polly Platt, AD/SD Platt, Harold Michelson, Tom Pedigo & Anthony Mondell†, SOUND Donald O. Mitchell, Rick Kline, Kevin O'Connell & Jim Alexander†.

LP Debra Winger† (Emma Horton), Shirley MacLaine* (Aurora Greenway), Jack Nicholson* (Garrett Breedlove), Danny DeVito (Vernon Dahlart), Jeff Daniels (Flap Horton), John Lithgow† (Sam Burns), Betty King (Rosie), Lisa Hart Carroll (Patsy Clark), Huckleberry Fox (Toddy), Megan Morris (Melanie), Troy Bishop (Tommy).

In a five-handkerchief weeper, eccentric Shirley MacLaine fends off suitors and interferes with her daughter Debra Winger's life and marriage. Winger develops an incurable cancer and takes about a reel to die, giving all the performers the opportunity to show off their dramatic talents.

Terror Eyes   see   Night School

The Terror Factor   see   Scared to Death

Terror in the Forest   see   The Forest

3009.   Terror Squad (1988, Matterhorn/Manson, 92m, c). P&D Peter Maris, W Chuck Rose (based on a story by Mark Verheiden), PH Peter Jensen, M Chuck Cirino, ED Jack Tucker.

LP Chuck Connors (Chief Rawlings), Brodie Greer (Capt. Steiner), Bill Calvert (Johnny), Kerry Brennan (Jennifer), Kavi Raz (Yassir), Joseph Nasser (Gamel), Budge Threlkeld (Mr. Nero), Dennis Moynahan (Norman).

When Libyan terrorists attack a nuclear power plant in Kokomo, Indiana, sheriff Chuck Connors has his hands full.

3010.   Terror Train (1980, 20th Century-Fox, Canada, 97m, c, aka *Train of Terror*). P Harold Greenberg, D Roger Spottiswoode, W T.Y. Drake, PH John Alcott, Rene Verzier, Peter Benison & Al Smith, M John Mills-Cockell, ED Anne Henderson, PD Glenn Bydwell.

LP Ben Johnson (Carne), Jamie Lee Curtis (Alana), Hart Bochner (Doc), David Copperfield (The Magician), Derek MacKinnon (Kenny Hampson), Sandee Currie (Mitchy), Timothy Webber (Mo), Anthony Sherwood (Jackson).

Revelers at a wild party aboard a train are killed one-by-one by a mysterious psychotic.

3011.   The Terror Within (1989, Concorde, 86m, c). P Roger Corman, D Thierry Notz, W Thomas M. Cleaver, PH Ronn Schmidt, M Rick Conrad, ED Brent Schoenfeld, PD Kathleen B. Cooper.

LP George Kennedy (Hal), Andrew Stevens (David), Starr Andreeff (Sue), Terri Treas (Linda), John LaFayette (Andre), Tommy Hinchley (Neil), Yvonne Saa (Karen), Roren Sumner (Gargoyle).

Almost the entire human race has been killed by the plague. A group of scientists in the underground Mojave Lab for Disease Control are running out of food and must constantly fight off marauding mutants topside. They find a pregnant girl whose child, a real little monster, bursts from her chest and terrorizes everyone.

3012.   Terrorvision (1986, Empire Pictures, 82m, c). P Albert Band, D&W Ted Nicolaou, PH Romano Albani, M Richard Band, ED Tom Meshelski, PD Giovanni Natalucci.

LP Diane Franklin (Suzy), Gerrit Graham (Stanley), Mary Woronov (Raquel), Chad Allen (Sherman), Jonathan Gries (O.D.), Jennifer Richards (Medusa), Alejandro Rey (Spiro), Bert Remsen (Gramps).

In this wacky sf/horror flick, a high-tech TV satellite turns into a real-life terror.

3013.   The Terry Fox Story (1983, 20th Century-Fox, Canada, 98m, c). P Robert Cooper, D Ralph L. Thomas, W Edward Hume (based on a story by John & Rose Kastner), PH Richard Ciupka, M Bill Conti, ED Ron Wisman, AD Gavin Mitchell.

LP Robert Duvall (Bill Vigars), Eric Fryer (Terry Fox), Michael Zelniker (Alward), Chris Makepeace (Darrell Fox), Rosalind Chao (Rika), Elva Mai Hoover (Betty Fox), Frank Adamson (Rolly Fox), Marie McCann (Judith Fox).

Unfortunately the filming of this true story of a young Canadian who loses his leg to cancer, and runs across the country to raise money for research before he dies, is not engrossing drama.

3014.   Tess† (1980, Columbia, France/GB, 170m, c). P Claude Berri, D Roman Polanski†, W Polanski, Gerard Brach & John Brownjohn (based on the novel *Tess of the d'Urbervilles* by Thomas Hardy), PH Geoffrey Unsworth & Ghislain Cloquet*, M Philippe Sarde†, ED Alastair McIntyre & Tom Priestley, PD Pierre Guffroy*, SD Jack Stephens*, COS Anthony Powell*.

LP Nastassja Kinski (Tess Durbeyfield), Leigh Lawson (Alec d'Urberville), Peter Firth (Angel Clare), John Collin

(John Durbeyfield), David Markham (Rev. Mr. Clare), Rosemary Martin (Mrs. Durbeyfield), Richard Pearson (Vicar of Marlott), Carolyn Pickles (Marian).

Peasant girl Nastassja Kinski attempts to prove her noble heritage but is betrayed by Leigh Lawson, a cocky young nobleman, who seduces her and sends her home pregnant. The baby dies and Kinski takes work on a dairy farm where she attracts the attention of Peter Firth. He marries her, but leaves her on their wedding night, unable to accept her past. She returns to Lawson, but Firth soon changes his mind and comes for her. Kinski lashes out at Lawson and fatally stabs him. She and Firth spend a final idyllic evening together before she is arrested and hanged for her crime.

A Test of Love see Annie's Coming Out

3015. *Testament* (1983, Paramount, 90m, c). P Jonathan Bernstein & Lynne Littman, D Littman, W John Sacret Young (based on the story *The Last Testament* by Carol Amen), PH Steven Poster, M James Horner, ED Suzanne Pettit, PD David Nichols.

LP Jane Alexander† (Carol Wetherly), William Devane (Tom Wetherly), Ross Harris (Brad Wetherly), Roxana Zal (Mary Liz Wetherly), Lukas Haas (Scottie Wetherly), Philip Anglim (Hollis), Lilia Skala (Fania), Leon Ames (Henry Abhart), Lurene Tuttle (Rosemary Abhart), Rebecca DeMornay (Cathy Pitkin), Kevin Costner (Phil Pitkin).

The film opens on a typical American family living in Hamlin, California. A nuclear bomb is dropped, the government issues reassuring statements, but then people begin to die. Jane Alexander's family, now minus father William Devane, who one assumes is dead because he never reappears after the bomb is dropped, relies on memories to get them through the horror.

3016. *Testimony* (1988, GB, 157m, c/b&w). P,D,ED&PD Tony Palmer, W David Rudkin & Palmer (based on Memoirs of Dimitri Shostakovich as edited by Solomon Volkov), PH Nic Knowland.

LP Ben Kingsley (Dimitri Shostako-

vich), Terence Rigby (Josef Stalin), Ronald Pickup (Tukhachevsky), John Shrapnel (Andrei Zhdanov), Sherry Baines (Nina Shostakovich), Robert Stephens (Meyerhold), Murray Melvin (Film Editor), Robert Urquhart (Journalist).

Although Ben Kingsley is admirable as composer Dimitri Shostakovich, this overly long biopic is a banal production. As the film concentrates on the political problems of an artist in the Soviet Union, the pretentious film makes little use of the master's music.

3017. *Tex* (1982, Buena Vista, 103m, c). P Tim Zinnemann, D Tim Hunter, W Hunter & Charlie Haas (based on the novel by S.E. Hinton), PH Ric Waite, M Pino Donaggio, ED Howard Smith, PD Jack T. Collis.

LP Matt Dillon (Tex McCormick), Jim Metzler (Mason McCormick), Meg Tilly (Jamie Collins), Bill McKinney (Pop McCormick), Frances Lee McCain (Mrs. Johnson), Ben Johnson (Cole Collins), Emilio Estevez (Johnny Collins), Zeljko Ivanek (Hitchhiker).

Disney treats audiences to a realistic look at adolescent growing pains in this story of young motherless brothers Matt Dillon and Jim Metzler, living by themselves in the Southwest when their father takes off. They must learn to take responsibility for their lives and settle their differences.

3018. *The Texas Chainsaw Massacre Part 2* (1986, Cannon, 95m, c). P Menahem Golan & Yoram Globus, D Tobe Hooper, W L.M. Kit Carson, PH Richard Kooris, M Hooper & Jerry Lambert, ED Alain Jakybowicz, PD Cary White, SE Tom Savini.

LP Dennis Hopper (Lt. "Lefty" Enright), Caroline Williams (Vanita "Stretch" Brock), Bill Johnson (Leatherface), Jim Siedow (Cook/Drayton Sawyer), Bill Moseley (Chop-Top), Lou Perry (L.G. McPeters).

"Leatherface" returns in this sequel to the 1974 shocker, with his powerful and deadly hand tool. The blood splatters in all directions as the screaming starts up again.

Texas Chainsaw Massacre 3 see Leatherface: Texas Chainsaw 3

3019. ***Texas Lightning*** (1981, Film Ventures, 93m, c). P Jim Sotos, D&W Gary Graver.

LP Cameron Mitchell, Channing Mitchell, Maureen McCormick, Peter Jason, Danone Camden, J.L. Clark.

Father and son truck drivers spend their free time in a honky-tonk cowboy bar.

3020. ***That Championship Season*** (1982, Cannon, 110m, c). P Menahem Golan & Yoram Globus, D&W Jason Miller (based on his play), PH John Bailey, M Bill Conti, ED Richard Halsey, PD Ward Preston.

LP Bruce Dern (George Sitkowski), Stacy Keach (James Daley), Robert Mitchum (Coach Delaney), Martin Sheen (Tom Daley), Paul Sorvino (Phil Romano), Arthur Franz (Macken), Michael Bernosky (Jacks), James M. Langan (Cooney).

This Pulitzer Prize–winning play makes a boring movie. Basketball coach Robert Mitchum and four of his five former players from a championship team 20 years earlier get together for a reunion. At first they are happy to be together, but a few drinks begin to reveal the envy, bitterness and anger they really feel for each other. But it's all talk, talk, talk. Slam dunk this one.

3021. ***That Summer of White Roses*** (1989, Amy Intl./Jadran, GB/Yugo., 103m, c). P Simon MacCorkindale & Mike Mihalic, D Rajko Grlic, W Grlic, MacCorkindale & Borislav Pekic (based on Pekic's book *Defense and the Last Days*), PH Tomislav Pinter, M Brane Zivkovic, Junior Campbell & Mike O'Donnell, ED Damir F. German.

LP Tom Conti (Andrija Gavrilovic), Susan George (Ana), Rod Steiger (Martin), Nitzan Sharron (Danny), Alun Armstrong (Zemba), John Gill (Doctor), John Sharp (Mayor).

Simpleminded Yugoslavian lifeguard Tom Conti can't seem to do anything right when he tries to do right. In the last year of the war he hides Susan George and her son, refugees from the Germans. He plans to marry her to protect her because she has no papers. In the meantime he rescues the one and only person ever in danger of drowning in his peaceful lake.

It turns out to be the new German commandant of the area. The Germans treat Conti as a hero; the rest of the town folk consider him a collaborator.

3022. ***That Was Then...This Is Now*** (1985, Paramount, 102m, c). P Gary R. Lindberg & John M. Ondov, D Christopher Cain, W Emilio Estevez (based on the novel by S.E. Hinton), PH Juan Ruiz Anchia, M Keith Olsen & Bill Cuomo, ED Ken Johnson, AD Chester Kaczenski.

LP Emilio Estevez (Mark Jennings), Craig Sheffer (Byron Douglas), Kim Delaney (Cathy Carlson), Jill Schoelen (Angela Shepard), Barbara Babcock (Mrs. Douglas), Frank Howard (M&M Carlson), Frank McCarthy (Mr. Carlson), Larry B. Scott (Terry Jones), Morgan Freeman (Charlie Woods).

Emilio Estevez and Craig Sheffer are raised as brothers by the latter's widowed mother Barbara Babcock. They react differently to the challenges of growing up. Sheffer becomes responsible, determined to make something of himself. Estevez deals in drugs and steals cars.

3023. ***That's Dancing*** (1985, MGM, 105m, c/b&w). P David Niven, Jr. & Jack Haley, Jr., D&W Jack Haley, Jr., ADDITIONAL PH Andrew Laszlo & Paul Lohmann, ED Bud Friedgen & Michael J. Sheridan, M Henry Mancini.

LP Mikhail Baryshnikov, Ray Bolger, Sammy Davis, Jr., Gene Kelly, Liza Minnelli.

This dance compilation film features scenes from many movies starring dancing greats such as Fred Astaire, Mikhail Baryshnikov, Ray Bolger, James Cagney, Cyd Charisse, Dan Dailey, Sammy Davis, Jr., Isadora Duncan, Dame Margot Fonteyn, Bob Fosse, Carol Haney, Michael Jackson, Ruby Keeler, Gene Kelly, Paula Kelly, Michael Kidd, Shirley MacLaine, Ann Miller, The Nicholas Brothers, Rudolf Nureyev, Donald O'Connor, Anna Pavlova, Eleanor Powell, Jane Powell, Debbie Reynolds, Chita Rivera, Bill "Bojangles" Robinson, Ginger Rogers, Shirley Temple, John Travolta & Vera-Ellen.

That's Life *see* ***Blake Edward's That's Life***

3024. *That's My Baby* (1985, Gemini, Canada, 98m, c). P Edie Yolles, D&W Jon Bradshaw & Yolles, PH W.W. Reeve, M Eric N. Robertson, ED Stephen Withrow.

LP Timothy Webber (Louis), Sonja Smits (Suzanne), Joann McIntyre (Sugar), Lenore Zann (Sally), Derek McGrath (Bob Morgan).

Career-woman Sonja Smits rejects all of Timothy Weber's urgings for paternity until he agrees to become a house-husband and free her from all domestic chores.

3025. *There Goes the Bride* (1980, Vanguard, GB, 88m, c). P Ray Cooney & Martin Schute, D Terence Marcel, W Cooney, Marcel & John Chapman (based on the play by Cooney), PH James Devis, M Harry Robinson, ED Alan Jones, PD Peter Mullins.

LP Tom Smothers (Timothy Westerby), Twiggy (Polly), Martin Balsam (Mr. Babcock), Sylvia Syms (Ursula Westerby), Michael Whitney (Bill Shorter), Geoffrey Sumner (Gerald Drimond), Graham Stark (Rossi), Hermione Baddeley (Daphne Drimond), Jim Backus (Mr. Perkins), Toria Fuller (Judy Westerby).

Since this film is one of the least funny comedies ever thrust onto unsuspecting audiences, one must conclude that either Dickie Smothers had all the talent or the film's writers are incredibly untalented hacks. Tommy Smothers is the father of bride-to-be Toria Fuller. The proceedings are interrupted by Twiggy, the ghost of a 20s model, who only Tommy can see.

3026. *They All Laughed* (1981, 20th Century–Fox/United Artists, 115m, c). P George Morfogen & Blaine Novak, D&W Peter Bogdanovich, PH Robby Muller, M Douglas Dilge, ED Scott Vickrey, AD Kert Lundell.

LP Audrey Hepburn (Angela Niotes), Ben Gazzara (John Russo), John Ritter (Charles Rutledge), Colleen Camp (Christy Miller), Patti Hansen (Deborah "Sam" Wilson), Dorothy Stratten (Dolores Martin), George Morfogen (Leon Leondopolous), Blaine Novak (Arthur Brodsky).

Three agency detectives, Ben Gazarra, John Ritter and Blaine Novak, fall in and out of love with the three women, Audrey Hepburn, Patti Hansen and Dorothy Stratten, they have been hired to trail. The film is good enough to be remembered for more than being Stratten's last picture—she was murdered by her husband after its completion (possibly because of her affair with director Peter Bogdanovich while this movie was in production).

3027. *They Call Me Bruce* (1980, Film Ventures, 88m, c, aka *A Fistful of Chopsticks*). P&D Elliott Hong, W Hong, David Randolph, Johnny Yune & Tim Clawson, PH Robert Roth, M Tommy Vig.

LP Johnny Yune (Bruce), Ralph Mauro (Freddy), Pam Huntington (Anita), Margaux Hemingway (Karmen), Tony Brande (Boss of Bosses), Bill Capizzi (Lil Pete), Martin Azarow (Big Al).

Korean comic Johnny Yune is mistaken for Bruce Lee, giving him the opportunity to emulate his martial arts hero. There are some funny bits in this story of an Oriental working as an Italian chef when he gets involved with the mob.

3028. *They Live* (1988, Universal, 93m, c). P Larry Franco, D John Carpenter, W Frank Armitage [Carpenter] (based on the short story "Eight O'Clock in the Morning" by Ray Nelson), PH Gary B. Kibbe, M Carpenter & Alan Howarth, ED Frank E. Jimenez, AD William J. Durrell, Jr.

LP Roddy Piper (John Nada), Keith David (Frank), Meg Foster (Holly), George "Buck" Flower (Drifter), Peter Jason (Gilbert), Raymond St. Jacques (Street Preacher), Jason Robards, III (Family Man), John Lawrence (Bearded Man).

When construction worker Roddy Piper comes into possession of a special pair of sunglasses, they reveal ordinary looking people to be aliens.

3029. *They Still Call Me Bruce* (1987, Shapiro, 91m, c). P,C&W Johnny Yune & James Orr, PH R. Michael Delahoussaye, M Morton Stevens, ED Roy Watts, AD Jeff McManus.

LP Johnny Yune (Bruce Won), Robert Guillaume (V.A. Officer), Pat Paulsen (Psychiatrist), David Mendenhall (Orphan), Carl Bensen (Mr. B.), Joey Travolta, Bethany Wright, Don Gibb.

Funnier and faster than the original, this martial arts comedy stars Korean comedian Johnny Yune as a bungling karate expert who takes on a bunch of baddies with a magic sock.

3030. *They're Playing with Fire* (1984, New World, 96m, c). P Howard Avedis & Marlene Schmidt, D Avedis, W Avedis & Schmidt, PH Gary Graver, M John Cacavas, ED Jack Tucker, ED Rosemary Brandenburg.

LP Sybil Danning (Dianne Stevens), Eric Brown (Jay Richards), Andrew Prine (Michael Stevens), Paul Clemens (Martin "Bird" Johnson), K.T. Stevens (Lillian Stevens), Gene Bicknell (George Johnson).

Professor Sybil Danning seduces her student Eric Brown and then enlists him in a plot to kill her husband Andrew Prine, but things don't quite follow her lesson plan.

3031. *Thief* (1981, United Artists, 122m, c, aka *Violent Streets*). P Jerry Bruckheimer & Ronnie Caan, D&W Michael Mann (based on the book *The Home Invaders* by Frank Hohimer), PH Donald Thorin, M Tangerine Dream, ED Dov Hoenig, PD Mel Bourne.

LP James Caan (Frank), Tuesday Weld (Jessie), Willie Nelson (Okla), James Belushi (Barry), Robert Prosky (Leo), Tom Signorelli (Attaglia), Dennis Farina (Carl), Nick Nickeas (Nick), Bill Brown (Mitch).

James Caan, a professional thief, enjoys working alone, but is forced to slave for a crime syndicate to bring in more money for his family.

3032. *Thief of Hearts* (1984, Paramount, 100m, c). P Don Simpson & Jerry Bruckheimer, D&W Douglas Day Stewart, PH Andrew Laszlo, M Harold Faltermeyer, ED Tom Rolf, AD Edward Richardson.

LP Steven Bauer (Scott Muller), Barbara Williams (Mickey Davis), John Getz (Ray Davis), David Caruso (Buddy Calamara), Christine Ebersole (Janie Pointer), George Wendt (Marty Morrison), Alan North (Sweeney).

San Francisco burglar Steven Bauer breaks into the house of Barbara Williams and her husband John Getz. Besides money, he takes Williams' private journals in which she describes her fantasies. Bauer becomes obsessed with fulfilling her fantasies. He arranges for them to meet and knowing what she's looking for, it's no time before they are having the affair she always dreamed of — but dreams can become nightmares.

3033. *The Thing* (1982, Universal, 108m, c). P David Foster & Lawrence Turman, D John Carpenter, W Bill Lancaster (based on the story "Who Goes There?" by John W. Campbell, Jr.), PH Dean Cundey, M Ennio Morricone, ED Todd Ramsay, PD John J. Lloyd.

LP Kurt Russell (MacReady), A. Wilford Brimley (Blair), T.K. Carter (Nauls), David Clennon (Palmer), Keith David (Childs), Richard Dysart (Dr. Copper), Charles Hallahan (Norris), Peter Maloney (Bennings).

This remake of the 1951 science fiction classic is disappointing. The filmmakers seem to have learned nothing in the intervening 30 years. While more faithful to the source work by John W. Campbell, it's not nearly as entertaining as the earlier film. Scientists at an isolated outpost in the Antarctic (is there any other kind on the southern continent?), discover the presence of an alien which can transform itself into an exact replica of any living thing, including any of the scientists.

3034. *Things and Other Stuff* (1989, Lynchpin & Tosh, Australia, 88m, c). P Michael Lynch, D&W Tony Wellington, PH Kim Batterham, M Dale Barlow, ED Marcus D'Arcy, PD Judith Harvey.

LP Kelly Dingwall (David), Rebecca Rigg (Michelle), John Polson (Billy), Barry Leane, Jan Ringrose, Kate Reid, Sylvia Coleman.

Director Tom Wellington attempts an Australian *Breakfast Club*-type film of meaningful teen interplay. Kelly Dingwall and a reluctant Rebecca Rigg, with John Polson tagging along, break into a mansion to get some money. Emotional and class barriers are torn down almost violently as complex relationships among the three are explored.

3035. *Things Are Tough All Over* (1982, Columbia, 90m, c). P Howard Brown, D Thomas K. Avildsen, W "Cheech" Marin & Thomas Chong, PH Bobby Byrne, M Gaye Delorme, ED Dennis Dolan, PD Richard Tom Sawyer.

LP Richard "Cheech" Marin (Himself/Mr. Slyman), Tommy Chong (Himself/Prince Habib), Michael Aragon (Cheech's Double), Toni Attell (Cocktail Waitress), Mike Bacarella (Cop), Billy Beck (Pop).

The comedy of Cheech and Chong is an acquired taste perhaps not worth acquiring. Playing both themselves and Arab princes, C&C are tricked into transporting money to Las Vegas to be laundered.

3036. *Things Change* (1988, Columbia, 105m, c). P Michael Hausman, D David Mamet, W Mamet & Shel Silverstein, PH Juan Ruiz Anchia, M Alaric Jans, ED Trudy Ship, PD Michael Merritt.

LP Don Ameche (Gino), Joe Mantegna (Jerry), Robert Prosky (Joseph Vincent), J.J. Johnston (Frankie), Ricky Jay (Mr. Silver), Mike Nussbaum (Mr. Green), Jack Wallace (Repair Shop Owner), Dan Conway (Butler).

Bearing a remarkable resemblance to a mobster facing a long jail term, Italian shoeshine man Don Ameche agrees to take the rap and go to prison. His none-too-reliable, mob-soldier guard, Joe Mantegna, decides to give Ameche one last hurrah at Lake Tahoe. Both performances sparkle.

3037. *Thinkin' Big* (1988, AFC/Arista, 94m, c). P Jim C. Harris, D S.F. Brownrigg, W Robert Joseph Sterling & Loretta Yeargin, PH Brian H. Hooper, M John Boy Cooke, ED Hooper.

LP Bruce Anderson (Pud), Nancy Buechler (Morgan), Darla Ralston (Liz), Kenny Sargent (The Chief), Randy Jandt (Wong), Derek Hunter (Barry), Regina Mikel (Dee-Dee), Claudia Church (Wendy), April Burrage (Georgia).

The one-joke plot of this sophomoric teen comedy is that Randy Jandt is believed to have a three-foot-long member. This makes him very popular with the buxomy bikini-clad girls on the Texas shore.

3038. *The 13th Floor* (1989, Premiere, Australia, 94m, c). P David Hannay & Charles Hannah, D Chris Roache, W Roache, PH Stephen Prime, M Mick Coleman, ED Peter McBain, PD Darrell Lass.

LP Lisa Hensley (Heather Thompson), Tim McKenzie (John Burke), Miranda Otto (Rebecca), Jeff Truman (Bert), Vic Rooney (Brenner), Michael Caton (Dr. Fletcher), Tony Blackett (Thompson), Paul Hunt (Nick).

An 8-year-old witnesses her politician father ordering the torture of a man on the 13th floor of a building under construction. The victim is accidentally electrocuted. Years later, the girl, grown to be Lisa Hensley, is estranged from her father. With druggie friend Miranda Otto, she camps out on the 13th floor of the building, still unoccupied because it is reported to be haunted. Indeed it is, by the ghost of the electrocuted lad—but he's a friendly spirit.

3039. *This Is Elvis* (1981, Warner, 101m, c/b&w). P,D&W Malcolm Leo & Andrew Solt, PH Gil Hubbs, M Walter Scharf, ED Bud Friedgen & Glenn Farr.

LP David Scott (Elvis at 18), Paul Boensch, III (Elvis at 10), Johnny Harra (Elvis at 42), Lawrence Koller (Vernon Presley), Rhonda Lyn (Priscilla Presley), Debbie Edge (Gladys Presley), Larry Raspberry (Dewey Phillips), Liz Robinson (Minnie Mae Presley), Dana MacKay (Elvis at 35).

This harmless pseudodocumentary of the king of rock 'n' roll combines film clips and dramatic reconstructions of episodes in Elvis' life. It's not very interesting or revealing. Viewers are exposed to the myth, not the man.

3040. *This Is Spinal Tap* (1984, Embassy, 82m, c, aka *Spinal Tap*). P Karen Murphy, D Rob Reiner, W Christopher Guest, Michael McKean, Harry Shearer & Reiner, PH Peter Smokler, M Guest, McKean, Shearer & Reiner, ED Kent Beyda, Kim Secrist & Robert Leighton, PD Bryan Jones.

LP Rob Reiner (Marty DiBergi), Michael McKean (David St. Hubbins), Christopher Guest (Nigel Tufnel), Harry Shearer (Derek Smalls), R.J. Parnell (Mick Shrimpton), David Kaff (Vic

Savage), Tony Hendra (Ian Faith), Bruno Kirby (Tommy Pischedda).

In this hilarious, good-natured spoof, Rob Reiner is a documentary filmmaker covering the American tour of aging British rock group "Spinal Tap." It has risen from obscurity to become England's loudest group. The film has achieved cult status.

3041.   *Those Glory, Glory Days* (1986, Cinecom, 91m, c). P Chris Griffin, D Philip Saville, W Julie Welch, PH Phil Meheux, ED Max Lemon, AD Maurice Cain.

LP Julia McKenzie (Mrs. Herrick), Elizabeth Spriggs (Coalhole), Julia Goodman (Julia, journalist), Rachael Meidman (Young Danny), Zoe Nathenson (Danny), Liz Campion (Jailbird), Sara Sugarman (Toni).

Thirteen-year-old Rachael Meidman, mad about soccer, drives her parents and teachers crazy. She grows up to become sports reporter Zoe Nathenson.

3042.   *Those Lips, Those Eyes* (1980, United Artists, 107m, c). P Steven-Charles Jaffe & Michael Pressman, D Pressman, W David Shaber, PH Bobby Byrne, M Michael Small, ED Millie Moore, PD Walter Scott Herndon.

LP Frank Langella (Harry Crystal), Glynnis O'Connor (Ramona), Thomas Hulce (Artie Shoemaker), Kevin McCarthy (Mickey Bellinger), Jerry Stiller (Mr. Shoemaker), Herbert Berghof (Dr. Julius Fuldauer).

Pre-med student Tom Hulce takes a summer job with an outdoor Ohio theater. He is befriended by never-has-been and never-will-be professional actor Frank Langella. The latter helps Hulce with his job and his romance with chorus girl Glynnis O'Connor.

3043.   *Thou Shall Not Kill...Except* (1987, Filmworld, 94m, c). P Scott Spiegel, D Josh Becker, W Becker & Spiegel (based on a story by Becker, Sheldon Lettich & Bruce Campbell), M Joseph Lo Duca, SE Gary Jones.

LP Brian Schulz (Sgt. Jack Stryker), John Manfredi (Miller), Robert Rickman (Jackson), Tim Quill (Tyler), Sam Raimi (Cult Leader), Cheryl Hanson (Sally), Perry Mallette (Otis), Rick Hudson (Kennel Owner).

Unless you were in Detroit in September, 1987, you likely missed this feature, shown theatrically only in the Motor City where it was filmed. Brian Schulz, in the guise of Stryker (a macho name very popular with helmers of horror, action/adventure and science fiction movies) is a Vietnam vet. After his fiancée Cheryl Hanson is kidnapped by a Charlie Manson–like cult headed by Sam Raimi, he calls on his ex-army buddies to help him kick a little ass.

3044.   *Thrashin'* (1986, Fries, 90m, c). P Alan Sacks, D David Winters, W Paul Brown & Sacks, PH Chuck Colwell, M Barry Goldberg, ED Nicholas Smith & Lorenzo De Stefano, PD Katheryn Hardwick.

LP Josh Brolin (Cory Webster), Robert Rusler (Tommy Hook), Pamela Gidley (Chrissy), Brooke McCarter (Tyler), Brett Marx (Bozo), Josh Richman (Radley), David Wagner (Little Stevie), Sherilyn Fenn (Velvet).

Josh Brolin, a skateboard riding fool, is newly arrived in a California neighborhood inhabited by unfriendly leather and chain clad skateboarders.

3045.   *Three Amigos* (1986, Orion, 105m, c). P Lorne Michaels & George Folsey, Jr., D John Landis, W Steve Martin, Michaels & Randy Newman, PH Ronald W. Browne, M Elmer Bernstein, ED Malcolm Campbell, PD Richard Sawyer.

LP Chevy Chase (Dusty Bottoms), Steve Martin (Lucky Day), Martin Short (Ned Nederlander), Patrice Martinez (Carmen), Alfonso Arau (El Guapo), Tony Plana (Jefe), Joe Mantegna (Harry Flugelman).

Saturday Night Live alums Chevy Chase, Steve Martin and Martin Short do not cover themselves with glory in this tom-foolery about three movie cowboys faced with taking on real bandits in a Mexican town. The Magnificent Three they are not.

3046.   *3:15 The Moment of Truth* (1986, Dakota Ent. Corp., 92m, c). P Dennis Brody & Robert Kenner, D Larry Gross, W Sam Bernard & Michael Jacobs, PH Misha Suslov, M Gary Chang, ED Steven Kemper.

LP Adam Baldwin (Jeff Hanna), Deborah Foreman (Sherry Haviland), Rene Auberjonois (Horner), Ed Lauter (Moran).

Filmed in 1984, this is a typical low-budget teen gang film with little to recommend it.

3047. *Three for the Road* (1987, New Century/Vista, 88m, c). P Herb Jaffe & Mort Engelberg, D B.W.L. Norton, W Richard Martini, Tim Metcalfe & Miguel Tejada-Flores (based on a story by Martini), PH Steve Posey, M Barry Goldberg, ED Christopher Greenbury, PD Linda Allen.

LP Charlie Sheen (Paul Tracy), Kerri Green (Robin Kitteridge), Alan Ruck (Tommy "T.S."), Sally Kellerman (Blanche), Blair Tefkin (Missy), Raymond J. Barry (Sen. Kitteridge), Alexa Hamilton (Virginia), Bert Remsen (Stu), James Avery (Clarence).

Young congressional aide Charlie Sheen is chosen by Senator Raymond J. Barry to accompany the latter's teenage daughter Kerri Green to a school for troubled youngsters. Sheen talks his friend Alan Ruck into going along for the ride. The guys discover that Green's father is the problem as time after time she tries to escape from her escorts. Finally Sheen and Ruck deliver Green to her mother Sally Kellerman, rather than the reformatory-like institution her father had picked out to rid himself of her.

3048. *Three Fugitives* (1989, Buena Vista, 96m, c, aka *Fugitives*). P Lauren Shuler-Donner, D&W Francis Veber, PH Haskell Wexler, M David McHugh, ED Bruce Green, PD Rick Carter.

LP Nick Nolte (Lucas), Martin Short (Perry), Sarah Rowland Doroff (Meg), James Earl Jones (Dugan), Alan Ruck (Tener), Kenneth McMillan (Horvath).

Just out of prison, Nick Nolte innocently enters a bank to open an account where he is taken hostage by novice bank robber Martin Short. The police figure Nolte is involved; so he must go on the run with Short and the latter's little daughter Sarah Rowland Doroff. This is director Francis Veber's remake of his French film *Les Fugitifs*.

3049. *Three Kinds of Heat* (1987, Cannon, 87m, c, aka *Fireworks*). P Mi-

chael J. Kagan, D&W Leslie Stevens, PH Terry Cole, M Michael Bishop & Scott Page, ED Bob Dearberg, PD Duncan Cameron.

LP Robert Ginty (Elliot Cromwell), Victoria Barrett (Sgt. Terry O'Shea), Shakti (Maj. Shan), Sylvester McCoy (Harry Pimm), Barry Foster (George Norris), Jeannie Brown (Angelica).

The film begins with a New York shoot-out between rival warring Oriental underworld factions. Interpol assigns three of its crack investigators Robert Ginty, Victoria Barrett and Shakti to track down dangerous Chinese crime boss Sylvester McCoy. There's plenty more gunfire in the final confrontation.

3050. *Three Men and a Baby* (1987, Buena Vista, 99m, c). P Ted Field, Robert W. Cort & Edward Teets, D Leonard Nimoy, W James Orr & Jim Cruickshank (based on the French film *Trois Hommes et un Couffin* by Coline Serreau), PH Adam Greenberg, M Marvin Hamlisch, ED Michael A. Stevenson, PD Peter Larkin.

LP Tom Selleck (Peter Mitchell), Steve Guttenberg (Michael Kellam), Ted Danson (Jack Holden), Nancy Travis (Sylvia), Margaret Colin (Rebecca), Lisa & Michelle Blair (Mary), Celeste Holm (Mrs. Holden), Philip Bosco (Det. Melkowitz), Derek de Lint (Jan Clopatz).

Apparently lacking confidence in their stars or having a poor opinion of American audiences, the makers of this film were not content to merely make an English-language film of the French comedy *Three Men and a Cradle*. They added a hokey subplot about a misdirected drug shipment. The real story has Nancy Travis dropping off the baby fathered by Ted Danson at the luxurious apartment he shares with two equally swinging bachelor playboys Tom Selleck and Steve Guttenberg. Although initially they are very poor at caring for an infant, they come to adore the baby.

3051. *Three O'Clock High* (1987, Universal, 97m, c). P David E. Vogel, D Phil Joanou, W Richard Christian Matheson & Thomas Szollosi, PH Barry Sonnenfeld, M Tangerine Dream, ED Joe Anne Fogle, PD Bill Matthews & Tom Bugenhaven.

LP Casey Siemaszko (Jerry Mitchell), Anne Ryan (Franny Perrins), Stacey Glick (Brei Mitchell), Jonathan Wise (Vincent Costello), Richard Tyson (Buddy Revell), Jeffrey Tambor (Mr. Rice), Liza Morrow (Karen Clarke).

It's not Casey Siemaszko's day. His car has a flat on the way to school and he's sent to the dean's office for being late. Worse yet he's incurred the wrath of mean, nasty new student Richard Tyson, with whom he has a 3 o'clock appointment for a fight.

3052.   *Threshold* (1983, 20th Century–Fox, Canada, 97m, c). P Jon Slan & Michael Burns, D Richard Pearce, W James Salter, PH Michel Brault, M Micky Erbe & Maribeth Solomon, ED Susan Martin, PD Anne Pritchard.

LP Donald Sutherland (Dr. Thomas Vrain), Jeff Goldblum (Dr. Aldo Gehring), Allan Nicholls (Dr. Basil Rents), Sharon Acker (Tilla Vrain), Jana Stinson (Sally Vrain), Jessica Steen (Tracy Vrain), Mavor Moore (Usher), Mare Winningham (Carol Severance).

Donald Sutherland gives a fine performance as a surgeon who plants an artificial heart in Mare Winningham, her only chance of survival.

3053.   *Thrilled to Death* (1989, Platinum, 92m, c). P&D Chuck Vincent, W Craig Horrall, PH Larry Revene, M Joey Mennonna, ED James Davalos & Marc Ubell [Vincent].

LP Blake Bahner (Cliff Jackson), Rebecca Lynn (Elaine Jackson), Richard Maris (Darryl Christie), Christine Moore (Nan Christie), Harvey Siegel (Val), Scott Baker (Bill), Karen Nielsen (Trudy).

Innocent young couple Blake Bahner and Rebecca Lynn become mixed up with sinister twosome Richard Maris and Christine Moore when Bahner researches a novel at a club for swingers. They find themselves involved with drugs, sex and murder.

3054.   *Thrillkill* (1988, Brightstar, Canada, 87m, c). P Anthony Kramreither, D Kramreither & Anthony D'Andrea, W D'Andrea, PH John Clement, M Tim McCauley, ED Nick Rotundo, AD Andrew Deskin.

LP Robin Ward (Frank), Gina Massey (Bobbie Kendell), Laura Robinson (Adrian), Diana Reis (Carly), Colleen Embree (Parrish), Kurt Reis (Schofield), Eugene Clark (Grissom), Frank Moore (Caspar), Joy Boushel (Maggie).

Filmed in 1984 the movie was held up until 1988 before going directly to video. Gina Massey is featured as a young woman who finds herself caught up in a multimillion dollar theft by computer when her sister Diana Reis, a software whiz mysteriously vanishes.

3055.   *Throw Momma from the Train* (1987, Orion, 88m, c). P Larry Brezner, D Danny DeVito, W Stu Silver, PH Barry Sonnenfeld, M David Newman, ED Michael Jablow, PD Ida Random.

LP Danny DeVito (Owen), Billy Crystal (Larry), Kim Greist (Beth), Anne Ramsey† (Momma), Kate Mulgrew (Margaret), Branford Marsalis (Lester), Rob Reiner (Joel).

Getting the idea from a filming of *Strangers on a Train,* Danny De Vito believes he has made a bargain with his creative writing teacher Billy Crystal to trade murders. DeVito will kill Crystal's ex-wife Kate Mulgrew, while Crystal is to reciprocate by eliminating DeVito's nasty, overbearing mother Anne Ramsey. Crystal believes Mulgrew stole his best-selling novel and is the cause of his present severe case of writer's block. DeVito is treated like a piece of garbage by his momma. The results are funnier than in the Hitchcock movie.

3056.   *Thunder Alley* (1985, Cannon, 92m, c). P William R. Ewing, D&W J.S. Cardone, PH Karen Grossman, M Robert Folk, ED Daniel Wetherbee, PD Joseph T. Garrity, AD Pat Tagliaferro.

LP Roger Wilson (Richie), Jill Schoelen (Beth), Scott McGinnis (Donnie), Cynthia Eilbacher (Lorraine), Clancy Brown (Weasel), Leif Garrett (Skip), Phil Brock (Butch), Brian Cole (Wolf).

Keyboardist Scott McGinnis starts a rock 'n' roll band. Lead singer Leif Garrett and guitarist Roger Wilson don't get along, but the band seems on its way to success until McGinnis gets hooked on drugs.

3057.   *Thunder Run* (1986, Lynn-Davis, Australia, 91m, c). P Carol Lynn, D Gary Hudson, W Charles Davis & Carol

Heyer (based on a story by Clifford Wenger, Sr. & Lynn), PH Harvey Genkins, M Matthew McCauley & Jay Levy, ED Burton Lee Harry, AD Heyer.

LP Forrest Tucker (Charlie Morrison), John Ireland (George Adams), John Sheperd (Chris), Jill Whitlow (Kim), Wally Ward (Paul), Cheryl M. Lynn (Jilly), Marilyn O'Connor (Maggie Morrison), Graham Ludlow (Mike).

John Ireland persuades old army buddy Forrest Tucker to act as bait to catch terrorists. It's a grade Z bomb.

3058. *Thunder Warrior* (1983, Trans-World, Italy, 91m, c). P Fabrizio De Angelis, D Larry Ludman [Fabrizio De Angelis], W David Parker, Jr. & Ludman, M Francesco De Masi, ED Eugenio Alabiso, AD & COS Massimo Lentini (based on a story by Parker), PH Sergio Salvati.

LP Mark Gregory (Thunder), Bo Svenson (Sheriff Roger), Raymund Harmstorf (Rusty), Karen Reel (Sheena), Paolo Malco (Sherman), Valerie Ross (Sheila).

Young American Indian Mark Gregory explodes with all the violence of a one-man war party against injustice to his people and himself.

3059. *Thunder Warrior II* (1987, TransWorld, Italy, 93m, c). P Larry Ludman [Fabrizio De Angelis], D David Parker, Jr. & Ludman, PH Sergio Salvati, M Walter Ritz, ED Albert Moryalty.

LP Mark Gregory (Thunder), Bo Svenson (Sheriff Roger), Raymund Harmstorf (Rusty), Karen Reel (Sheena), William Rice, Vic Roych, Clayton Tevis, Bill Rossly.

Indian Mark Gregory has been pardoned by the governor of Arizona for his exploits in the original film. He teams up with sheriff Bo Svenson to combat drug traffickers who are making life hell for the Indians.

Thursday the 12th see Pandemonium

3060. *Ticket to Heaven* (1981, United Artists, Canada, 107m, c). P Vivienne Leebosh, D Ralph L. Thomas, W Thomas & Anne Cameron (based on the book *Moonwebs* by Josh Freed), PH Richard Leiterman, M Micky Erbe & Maribeth Solomon, ED Ron Wisman, PD Susan Longmire.

LP Nick Mancuso (David), Saul Rubinek (Larry), Meg Foster (Ingrid), Kim Cattrall (Ruthie), R.H. Thompson (Linc Strunk), Jennifer Dale (Lisa), Guy Bond (Eric), Dixie Seatle (Sarah), Paul Soles (Morley).

After breaking up with his girlfriend, young Canadian Nick Mancuso visits San Francisco where he is seduced into joining a religious cult by the group's Meg Foster and Kim Cattrall. Thoroughly brainwashed, Mancuso rejects his family and his past. His best friend Saul Rubinek sets out to deprogram him.

3061. *Tiger Shark* (1989, Chappell, 99m, c). P Lana Lee Jones, D Emmet Alston, W Mike Stone & Ivan Rogers, PH Robert Ebinger, M Quito Colayco, ED Uncredited, AD Lito Nicdao.

LP Mike Stone (Tava, Tiger Shark), John Quade (Dave, Cowboy), Pamela Bryant (Karen), Vic Silayan (Col. Barro), Roy Alvarez (Tony), Roland Dantes (Ponsok), Jimmy Fabrigas (Vladimir), Lana Lee Jones (Jan Carter).

Mike Stone, who runs a Hawaiian martial arts academy, is helped by his old war buddy John Quade to rescue his kidnapped girlfriend Pamela Bryant.

3062. *Tiger Warsaw* (1988, Continental/Sony, 93m, c). P&D Amin Q. Chaudhri, W Roy London, PH Robert Draper, M Ernest Troost, ED Brian Smedley-Aston, PD Tom Targownik.

LP Patrick Swayze (Chuck "Tiger" Warsaw), Piper Laurie (Frances Warsaw), Lee Richardson (Mitchell Warsaw), Mary McDonnell (Paula Warsaw), Barbara Williams (Karen), Bobby DiCicco (Tony), Jenny Chrisinger (Val).

As she plans her wedding, Mary McDonnell's black sheep brother Patrick Swayze shows up for the first time in 15 years. His mother Piper Laurie is happy to see him, but his father Lee Richardson doesn't want him around. Swayze rekindles a romance with former girlfriend Barbara Williams and chums around with his old buddy Bobby DiCicco.

3063. *A Tiger's Tale* (1988, Atlantic, 97m, c). P&D Peter Douglas, W Douglas (based on the book *Love and Other Natural Disasters* by Allen Hannay 3d), PH Tony Pierce-Roberts, M Lee Holdridge, PD Shay Austin.

LP Ann-Margret (Rose), C. Thomas Howell (Bubber), Charles Durning

(Charlie), Kelly Preston (Shirley), Ann Wedgeworth (Claudine), Angel Tompkins (La Vonne), William Zabka (Randy), Tim Thomerson (Lonny).

When Texas teen C. Thomas Howell has an affair with his ex-girlfriend Kelly Preston's divorced mother Ann-Margret, a pregnancy results because Preston punches a hole in her mom's diaphram. What a nasty kid!

3064. *Tightrope* (1984, Warner, 114m, c). P Clint Eastwood & Fritz Manes, D&W Richard Tuggle, PH Bruce Surtees, M Lennie Niehaus, ED Joel Cox, PD Edward Carfagno.

LP Clint Eastwood (Wes Block), Genevieve Bujold (Beryl Thibodeaux), Dan Hedaya (Detective Molinari), Alison Eastwood (Amanda Block), Jennifer Beck (Penny Block), Marco St. John (Leander Wolfe), Rebecca Perle (Becky Jacklin), Regina Richardson (Sarita), Randi Brooks (Jamie Cory).

New Orleans vice cop Clint Eastwood, separated from his wife and raising two daughters (one played by his own daughter Alison), searches for a serial killer whose victims are the very same prostitutes whom Eastwood now and then takes comfort and kink with.

3065. *Tim* (1981, Pisces/Satori, Australia, 90m, c). P,D&W Michael Pate (based on a novel by Colleen McCullough), PH Paul Onorato, M Eric Jupp, ED David Stiven, AD John Carroll.

LP Piper Laurie (Mary Horton), Mel Gibson (Tim Melville), Alwyn Kurts (Ron Melville), Pat Evison (Emily Melville), Peter Gwynne (Tom Ainsley), Deborah Kennedy (Dawn Melville), David Foster (Mick Harrington).

Piper Laurie is an older woman who falls in love with slightly retarded but gorgeous hunk Mel Gibson. She teaches him to read rather than how to respond to her lust for him.

3066. *Time After Time* (1985, BBC-TV Arts & Entertainment, GB, 103m, c). P Terry Coles, D Bill Hays, W Andrew Davis (based on the novel by Molly Keane), PH John McGlashan, M Jim Parker, ED Dave King, PD Don Taylor.

LP John Gielgud (Jasper Swift), Googie Withers (Leda Klein), Helen Cherry (April Grange-Gorman), Ursula Howells (May Swift), Brenda Bruce (June Swift), Mark Lambert (Christy Lucy), Trevor Howard (Brigadier Crowshawe), Freddie Jones (Ulick Uniake), Mavis Walker (Lady Alys Crowshawe).

In this witty comedy, John Gielgud lives on an estate with his three elderly and eccentric sisters. Their lives are significantly altered by the arrival of their manipulative cousin Googie Withers.

3067. *Time Bandits* (1981, Avco Embassy, 110m, c). P&D Terry Gilliam, W Michael Palin & Gilliam, PH Peter Biziou, M Mike Moran, ED Julian Doyle, PD Millie Burns.

LP John Cleese (Robin Hood), Sean Connery (King Agamemnon), Shelley Duvall (Pansy), Katherine Helmond (Mrs. Ogre), Ian Holm (Napoleon), Michael Palin (Vincent), Ralph Richardson (Supreme Being), Peter Vaughan (Ogre), David Warner (Evil Genius), David Rappaport (Randall), Kenny Baker (Fidget), Jack Purvis (Wally), Mike Edmunds (Og), Malcolm Dixon (Strutter), Tiny Ross (Vermin), Craig Warnock (Kevin).

Six dwarves and young Warnock make their way through the universe with a map that reveals gaps in time. They travel through history encountering such famous fictional and real characters as Robin Hood, King Agamemnon and Napoleon. Coming from the pen of Monty Python members it has the sharp, clever slapstick edge associated with that troupe.

3068. *Time Burst: The Final Alliance* (1989, Action Intl., 93m, c). P&D Peter Yuval, W Yuval & Michael Bogert, PH Paul Maibaum, M Todd Hayen, ED Todd Felker.

LP Scott David King (Urbane), Michiko (Jane English), Gerald Okamura (Master), Jay Richardson (Mueller), Craig Ng (Takeda/Akira), Chet Hood, Jack Vogel, Richard Rogers.

After surviving a plane crash, Scott David King develops amnesia. He becomes involved with a group of Japanese samauri of an earlier time seeking some ancient tablets.

3069. *A Time of Destiny* (1988, Columbia, 118m, c). P Anna Thomas, D Gregory Nava, W Nava & Thomas, PH

James Glennon, M Ennio Morricone, ED Betsy Blankett, PD Henry Bumstead.

LP William Hurt (Martin Larraneta), Timothy Hutton (Jack McKenna), Melissa Leo (Josie Larraneta), Francisco Rabal (Jorge Larraneta), Concha Hidalgo (Sebastiana Larraneta), Stockard Channing (Margaret Larraneta).

In this old-fashioned soap opera, Basque-American William Hurt vows revenge when his father is killed trying to prevent Timothy Hutton from eloping with Hurt's sister Melissa Leo. During World War II, Hurt is attached to Hutton's unit and tries to kill him. Neither of the two very fine actors, Hurt and Hutton, are in top form in this one.

3070. *Time of the Beast* (1989, Liberty Films, 89m, c). P Russell Markowitz, D John R. Bowey, W Lynn Rose Higgins, M Rene Veldsman, SE Robert Burman.

LP Brion James, Carolyn Ann Clark, Milton Raphael Murrill, Neil McCarthy, Brian O'Shaughnessy.

The beast of this film comes into existence as the result of a foul-up in a genetic laboratory. It's tame and routine—the movie, that is, not the beast.

Time Raiders see Warrior of the Apocalypse

3071. *Time Trackers* (1989, Concorde, 87m, c). P Roger Corman, D&W Howard R. Cohen, PH Ronn Schmidt, M Parmer Fuller, ED Brent Schoenfeld, AD Peter Flynn.

LP Ned Beatty (Harry), Wil Shriner (Charles), Kathleen Beller (R.J.), Bridget Hoffman (Madeline), Alex Hyde-White (Edgar), Lee Bergere (Zandor).

A group of young scientists travel backwards in time from the year 2033 to prevent evil scientist Lee Bergere from changing history. No one seems to note or care that their presence in the past will have a like effect.

3072. *Time Walker* (1982, New World, 83m, c). P Dimitri Villard & Jason Williams, D Tom Kennedy, W Karen Levitt & Tom Friedman, PH Robbie Greenberg, M Richard Band, ED Joseph Yanuzzi, AD R.A. Burns & Joe Garrity.

LP Ben Murphy (Doug McCadden), Nina Axelrod (Susy Fuller), Kevin Brophy (Peter), James Karen (Wendell Rossmore), Robert Random (Parker), Austin Stoker (Dr. Ken Melrose), Shari Belafonte-Harper (Linda).

When jewels from the sarcophagus of an Egyptian mummy brought to a California university by archaeologist Ben Murphy are stolen, the mummy comes alive. Its touch is fatal to humans.

3073. *Timerider, The Adventures of Lyle Swann* (1983, Jensen-Farley, 93m, c). P Harry Gittes, D William Dear, W Dear & Michael Nesmith, PH Larry Pizer, M Nesmith, ED Suzanne Pettit, Kim Secrist & R.J. Kizer, AD Linda Pearl.

LP Fred Ward (Lyle Swann), Belinda Bauer (Clair Cygne), Peter Coyote (Porter Reese), Ed Lauter (Padre), Richard Masur (Claude Dorsett), Tracey Walter (Carl Dorsett), L.Q. Jones (Ben Potter), Chris Mulkey (Daniels).

Fred Ward, a modern motorcycle rider, passes through a time warp and finds himself and his bike on dusty plains with outlaw horsemen of the old West.

3074. *Times Square* (1980, Butterfly Valley/AFD, 111m, c). P Robert Stigwood & Jacob Brackman, D Alan Moyle, W Brackman (based on a story by Moyle & Leanne Unger), PH James A. Contner, ED Tom Priestley, PD Stuart Wurtzel.

LP Tim Curry (Johnny Laguardia), Trini Alvarado (Pamela Pearl), Robin Johnson (Nicky Marotta), Peter Coffield (David Pearl), Herbert Berghof (Dr. Huber), David Margulies (Dr. Zymabsky), Anna Maria Horsford (Rosie Washington), Michael Margotta (JoJo).

Wealthy Trini Alvarado runs away from her uncaring politician father with Robin Johnson to Times Square. There she becomes a stripper and he, a punk rock star. DJ Tim Curry turns them both into media celebrities.

3075. *Tin Man* (1983, Goldfarb, 95m, c). P&D John G. Thomas, W Bishop Holiday, PH Virgil Harper, M Holiday.

LP Timothy Bottoms, Deana Jurgens, John Phillip Law, Troy Donahue.

Born deaf and dumb, auto mechanic Timothy Bottoms invents a computer that becomes his ears and tongue.

3076. *Tin Men* (1987, Buena Vista, 110m, c). P Mark Johnson, D&W Barry Levinson, PH Peter Sova, M Fine Young Cannibals, ED Stu Linder, PD Peter Jamison.

LP Richard Dreyfuss (Bill "BB" Babowsky), Danny DeVito (Ernest Tilley), Barbara Hershey (Nora Tilley), John Mahoney (Moe), Jackie Gayle (Sam), Stanley Brock (Gil), Seymour Cassel (Cheese), Bruno Kirby (Mouse), J.T. Walsh (Wing), Richard Portnow (Carly), Matt Craven (Looney), Alan Blumenfeld (Stanley), Brad Sullivan (Masters).

In as fine a film as was made in 1987, audiences laughed at the antics of aluminum siding con-artist salesmen Richard Dreyfuss and Danny DeVito, but not at them. The film is very touching as well as amusing. The trouble begins when DeVito and Dreyfuss, "tin men" for different companies, run their new Cadillacs into each other in Baltimore of the early 60s. They spend much of the rest of the movie seeking ways to get even with each other. Dreyfuss even seduces De-Vito's wife Barbara Hershey, only to find Danny glad to be rid of her. Dreyfuss falls in love with Hershey. Both men lose their licenses to sell aluminum siding because of the various crooked scams they used.

3077. *Tin Star Void* (1988, Double Helix, 95m, c). P Jean Bodon, Paul Falcone, Tom Gniazdowski & Leopold Wurm, D Gniazdowski, PH Adam Goldfine, M David Perlman, ED Michael Lang.

LP Daniel Chapman (Wade Holt), Ruth Collins (Annie), Loren Blackwell (Hawk), Karen Rizzo (Star), Phillip Nutman (Tough), John Pierce (Kid).

In this comedy crime western, Daniel Chapman is sent to a seedy prison, but returns to take revenge on the punk cowboys who framed him. The latter all drive around in 50s roadsters, rather than riding ponies.

Titan Find   see   Creature

3078. *Title Shot* (1982, Cinepax, Canada, 96m, c). P Bob Iveson, D Les Rose, W John Saxton (based on a story by Richard Gabourie), PH Henry Fiks, M Paul

James Zaza, ED Ronald Sanders, AD Karen Bromley.

LP Tony Curtis (Frank Renzetti), Richard Gabourie (Blake), Susan Hogan (Sylvia), Allan Royal (Dunlop), Robert Delbert (Rufus Taylor), Natsuko Ohama (Terry), Jack Duffy (Mr. Green), Sean McCann (Lt. Grace).

Mafia chief Tony Curtis plots to kill the heavyweight boxing champion during a match. Richard Gabourie is a tough cop out to stop him.

3079. *To All a Goodnight* (1980, IRC-IWC, 84m, c). P Sandy Gobe, D David Hess, W Alex Rebar, PH B. Godsey, M Rich Tufo, PD Joe Garrity.

LP Buck West (Weird Ralph), Sam Shamshak (Polansky), Katherine Herington (Mrs. Jensen), Jennifer Runyon, Forrest Swanson, Linda Gentile, William Lauer, J. Bridges.

Five young couples expect to have a good time during Christmas vacation at The Calvin Finishing School for Girls, but a mad Santa Claus slaughters them one by one.

3080. *To Be or Not to Be* (1983, 20th Century-Fox, 108m, c). P Mel Brooks, D Alan Johnson, W Thomas Meehan & Ronny Graham (based on the film by Ernst Lubitsch, written by Edwin Justus Mayer), PH Gerald Hirschfeld, M John Morris, ED Alan Balsam, PD Terence Marsh.

LP Mel Brooks (Frederick Bronski), Anne Bancroft (Anna Bronski), Tim Matheson (Lt. Andre Sobinski), Charles Durning† (Col. Erhardt), Jose Ferrer (Prof. Siletski), Christopher Lloyd (Capt. Shultz), James Haake (Sasha), George Gaynes (Ravitch), George Wyner (Ratkowski).

Older film fans have fond memories of the 1942 version of this film. This may be due to an appreciation of the talents of Jack Benny, the tragic conclusion of the film for Carole Lombard, killed in a plane crash before her final scenes were shot, and the comedy of the "Lubitsch touch." The material at the time seemed fresh and daring. Forty years later with Mel Brooks and Anne Bancroft it seems trite and dated.

3081. *To Die For* (1989, Skouras, 90m, c). P Barin Kumar, D Devan

Sarafian, W Leslie King, PH David Boyd, M Cliff Eidelman, ED Dennis Dolan, PD Maxine Shepard, AD Greg Oehler, SE John Carl Buechler.

LP Brendan Hughes (Vlad Tepish), Sydney Walsh (Kate Wooten), Amanda Wyss (Celia Kett), Scott Jacoby (Martin Planting), Micah Grant (Mike Dunn), Duane Jones (Simon Little), Steve Bond (Tom), Remy O'Neill (Jane).

The filmmakers attempt unsuccessfully to demonstrate that the pleasures and eroticism of a bite from a handsome vampire, such as Brendan Hughes, may be worth the consequences to a woman like Sydney Walsh, afraid she may never experience the grand passion of uncontrollable love.

To Elvis with Love see ***Touched by Love***

3082. ***To Kill a Priest*** (1988, Columbia, US/France, 117m, c). P Jean-Pierre Alessandri, D Agnieszka Holland, W Holland & Jean-Yves Pitoun, PH Adam Holender, M Georges Delerue, ED Herve de Luze, AD Emile Ghigo.

LP Christopher Lambert (Father Alek), Ed Harris (Stefan), Joanne Whalley (Anna), Joss Ackland (The Colonel), David Suchet (The Bishop), Tim Roth (Feliks), Peter Postlethwaite (Joseph).

Polish filmmaker Agnieszka Holland presents the story of priest Christopher Lambert. He is a charismatic spokesman for the Solidarity Labor movement. He is pursued by police chief Ed Harris who believes himself to be under orders from high in the government to silence the troublesome priest. The story is a bit passé now, considering all that has happened in Poland, but is still a suspenseful chase film.

3083. ***To Kill a Stranger*** (1985, Angel-Radio Video-Star World, 88m, c). P Raul Vale, D Juan Lopez-Moctezuma, W Emerich Oross, Rafael Bunuel, Michael Elliot, Lopez-Moctezuma & Morrie Ruvinsky, PH Alex Phillips, M Mort Garson, ED Carlos Savage.

LP Angelica Maria (Cristina Carver), Dean Stockwell (John Carver), Donald Pleasence (Col. Kostik), Aldo Ray (Inspector Benedict), Sergio Aragones (Maj.

Keller), Ken Grant (Tom), Jill Franklyn (Susan).

In an unidentified South American country, Angelica Maria kills unknown attacker Donald Pleasence who tries to rape her after she helps him following an accident. She and hubby discover that the deceased was a war hero and the militaristic government is not sympathetic to her actions.

3084. ***To Live and Die in L.A.*** (1985, MGM/United Artists, 116m, c). P Irving H. Levin, D William Friedkin, W Friedkin & Gerald Petievich (based on Petievich's novel), PH Robby Muller, M Wang Chung, ED Scott Smith & Bud Smith, PD Lilly Kilvert.

LP William L. Petersen (Richard Chance), Willem Dafoe (Eric Masters), John Pankow (John Vukovich), Debra Feuer (Bianca Torres), John Turturro (Carl Cody), Darlanne Fluegel (Ruth Lanier), Dean Stockwell (Bob Grimes), Steve W. James (Jeff Rice), Robert Downey (Thomas Bateman).

Filmed in the style of a music video, director William Friedkin attempts to make a sort of West Coast *French Connection*. Secret Service agent William L. Petersen is out to nab counterfeiter Willem Dafoe. The characters are vulgar and the story is trite. A hair-raising car chase is the best thing in an otherwise unappealing film.

3085. ***Toby McTeague*** (1986, Spectra-film, Canada, 95m, c). P Nicolas Clermont, D Jean-Claude Lord, W Jeff Maguire, Djordje Milicevic & Jamie Brown, PH Rene Verzier, M Claude Demers, ED Yves Langlois.

LP Winston Rekert (Tom McTeague), Yannick Bisson (Toby McTeague), Timothy Webber (Edison Crowe), Stephanie Morgenstern (Sara), Andrew Bednarski (Sam McTeague), Liliane Clune (Jenny Lessard), George Clutesi (Chief George Wild Dog).

In this children's story, Canadian teenager Yannick Bisson must take over the reins of his father Winston Rekert's dog team for the big race.

3086. ***Tom Horn*** (1980, Warner, 98m, c). P Fred Weintraub, D William Wiard, W Thomas McGuane & Bud Shrake (based on *Life of Tom Horn*,

Government Scout and Interpreter by Tom Horn), PH John Alonzo, M Ernest Gold, ED George Grenville, AD Ron Hobbs.

LP Steve McQueen (Tom Horn), Linda Evans (Glendolene Kimmel), Richard Farnsworth (John Coble), Billy Green Bush (Joe Belle), Slim Pickens (Sam Creedmore), Peter Canon (Assistant Prosecutor), Elisha Cook (Stable Hand).

It's based on the true story of Old West gunman Tom Horn. By the age of 40 he had already been a railroad worker, stagecoach driver, U.S. Cavalry scout, silver miner, Rough Rider with Teddy Roosevelt at Sam Juan Hill and a Pinkerton detective. The movie picks up with Steve McQueen as Horn invited by Wyoming ranchers to put an end to rustling on their lands.

3087. The Tomb (1986, TransWorld, 84m, c). P Fred Olen Ray & Ronnie Hadar, D Ray, W Kenneth J. Hall, PH Paul Elliott, M Drew Neumann, ED Miriam L. Preissel, AD Maxine Shepard.

LP Cameron Mitchell (Prof. Phillips), John Carradine (Mr. Androheb), Sybil Danning (Jade), Susan Stokey (Helen), Richard Alan Hench (David Manners), Michelle Bauer (Nefratis), David Pearson (John Banning).

Long dead Egyptian princess Michelle Bauer wreaks havoc in the modern world. Don't look for sparkling dialogue.

3088. Tomboy (1985, Crown, 91m, c). P Marilyn J. Tenser & Michael D. Castle, D Herb Freed, W Ben Zelig (based on an idea by Mark Tenser), PH Daniel Yarussi, ED Richard E. Westover, AD Randy Ser.

LP Betsy Russell (Tommy Boyd), Jerry Dinome (Randy Starr), Kristi Somers (Seville Ritz), Richard Erdman (Chester), Philip Sterling (Earl Delarue), Eric Douglas (Ernie Leeds, Jr.), Paul Gunning (Frankie).

Baby-faced, neatly built Betsy Russell has a hard-edged sexiness which seems appropriate for the S&M scenes. In this film she's a female mechanic determined to win the love of Jerry Dinome, a pretty boy superstar race driver. Just in case he's confused by her name and tomboy behavior, she frequently takes off her shirt to reassure him.

3089. Too Much (1987, Cannon, 89m, c). P Menahem Golan & Yoram Globus, D Eric Rochat, W Rochat & Joan Laine, PH Daisaku Kimura, M George S. Clinton, ED Alain Jakubowicz, AD Tsuneo Kantake, SE Osamu Kung.

LP Bridgette Andersen (Suzy/Narrator), Masato Fukazama (Too Much), Hiroyuki Watanabe ("Uncle" Tetsuro), Char Fontana (Prof. Finkel), Uganda (Bernie).

Not even the most easily-pleased dull child will be able to stomach this comedy about adorable little Bridgette Andersen, her robot friend Masato Fukazama and their experiences in Japan.

3090. Too Outrageous (1987, Spectrafilm, Canada, 105m, c). P Roy Krost, D&W Dick Benner, PH Fred Guthe, M Russ Little, ED George Appleby, AD Andris Hausmanis.

LP Craig Russell (Robin Turner), Hollis McLaren (Liza Connors), David McIlwraith (Bob), Ron White (Luke), Lynn Cormack (Betty Treisman), Michael J. Reynolds (Lee Sturges), Timothy Jenkins (Rothchild).

Female inpersonator Craig Russell becomes a smash in the Big Apple. His story isn't interesting, but he sure can make you believe he's Barbra Streisand, Mae West, etc.

3091. Too Scared to Scream (1985, Movie Store, 104m, c). P Mike Connors, D Tony Lo Bianco, W Neal Barbera & Glenn Leopold, PH Larry Pizer, M George Garvarentz, ED Ed Beyer & Michael Economou, PD Lilly Kilvert.

LP Mike Connors (Lt. Dinardo), Anne Archer (Kate), Leon Isaac Kennedy (Frank), Ian McShane (Hardwick), Ruth Ford (Irma), John Heard (Lab Technician), Carrie Nye (Graziella), Maureen O'Sullivan (Mother).

New York police detective Mike Connors teams up with female undercover cop Anne Archer to solve a series of bizarre murders of females in a Manhattan apartment building. The prime suspect is Shakespeare-quoting doorman Ian McShane who lives with his invalid mother Maureen O'Sullivan in a luxurious brownstone.

3092. *Tootsie†* (1982, Columbia, 116m, c). P Sydney Pollack & Dick Richards, D Pollack†, W Larry Gelbart, Murray Schisgal & Don McGuire† (uncredited, Elaine May, based on a story by Don McGuire & Gelbert), PH Owen Roizman†, M Dave Grusin, ED Fredric Steinkamp & William Steinkamp†, PD Peter Larkin, SD Tom Tonery, SONG "It Might Be You" by Dave Grusin, Alan & Marilyn Bergman, SOUND Arthur Plantadosi, Les Fresholtz, Dick Alexander & Les Lazarowitz†.

LP Dustin Hoffman† (Michael Dorsey/Dorothy Michaels), Jessica Lange* (Julie), Teri Garr† (Sandy), Dabney Coleman (Ron), Charles Durning (Les), Bill Murray (Jeff), Sydney Pollack (George Fields), George Gaynes (John Van Horn), Geena Davis (April), Doris Belack (Rita), Ellen Foley (Jacqui).

Unable to find work, actor Dustin Hoffman dresses up as a woman and wins a pivotal role on a soap opera. He falls for Jessica Lange, who sees "her" as a confidant. How to win the girl of his dreams and remain employed is his problem. Oh, that and the fact that Lange's father Charles Durning has the hots for "her."

3093. *Top Gun* (1986, Paramount, 109m, c). P Don Simpson & Jerry Bruckheimer, D Tony Scott, W Jim Cash & Jack Epps, Jr., PH Jeffrey Kimball, M Harold Faltermeyer, ED Billy Weber & Chris Lebenzon†, SOUND EFFECTS EDITING Cecelia Hall & George Walters, II†, PD John F. De Cuir, Jr., M/L "Take My Breath Away" by Giorgio Moroder & Tom Whitlock*, SOUND Donald O. Mitchell, Kevin O'Connell, Rick Kline & William B. Kaplan†.

LP Tom Cruise (Maverick), Kelly McGillis (Charlie), Val Kilmer (Ice), Anthony Edwards (Goose), Tom Skerritt (Viper), Michael Ironside (Jester), John Stockwell (Cougar), Barry Tubb (Wolfman), Rick Rossovich (Slider), Tim Robbins (Merlin), Clarence Gilyard, Jr. (Sundown), Whip Hubley (Hollywood), Meg Ryan (Carole).

The film is a long winded tribute to naval fighter pilots. The story isn't much and beautiful Kelly McGillis is wasted, but the scenes in the sky almost make it worth the price of admission.

3094. *Top Secret!* (1984, Paramount, 90m, c). P Jon Davison & Hunt Lowry, D Jim Abrahams, David Zucker & Jerry Zucker, W Abrahams, D. & J. Zucker & Martyn Burke, Ph Christopher Challis, M Maurice Jarre, ED Bernard Gribble, PD Peter Lamont.

LP Omar Sharif (Cedric), Jeremy Kemp (Gen. Streck), Warren Clarke (Col. Von Horst), Tristram Jellinek (Maj. Crumpler), Val Kilmer (Nick Rivers), Billy J. Mitchell (Martin), Major Wiley (Porter), Gertan Klauber (Mayor).

The creators of the disaster spoofs *Airplane* and *Airplane II* try their hands at a satire featuring Val Kilmer as an Elvis-like entertainer. They find time for surf, spy and cold war intrigue in their zany script.

3095. *Torch Song Trilogy* (1988, New Line, 120m, c). P Howard Gottfried, D Paul Bogart, W Harvey Fierstein (based on his play), PH Mikael Salomon, M Peter Matz, ED Nicholas C. Smith, PD Richard Hoover.

LP Anne Bancroft (Ma), Matthew Broderick (Alan), Harvey Fierstein (Arnold Beckoff), Brian Kerwin (Ed), Karen Young (Laurel), Eddie Castrodad (David), Ken Page (Murray), Charles Pierce (Bertha Venation), Axel Vera (Marina Del Rey).

Gay female impersonator Harvey Fierstein falls in love with bisexual teacher Brian Kerwin but loses him to Karen Young. Fierstein takes up with Matthew Broderick, a young model, in what seems to be a permanent relationship, but Broderick is beaten to death by a gang of gay bashers, just as the couple are about to adopt troubled teen Eddie Castrodad. Fierstein takes his role as "father" to Castrodad very seriously and renews his relationship with Kerwin, who has broken with his wife Young.

3096. *Torchlight* (1984, Film Ventures, 91m, c). P Joel Douglas & Michael Schroeder, D Tom Wright, W Pamela Sue Martin & Eliza Moorman, PH Alex Phillips, M Michael Cannon, AD Craig Stearns.

LP Pamela Sue Martin (Lillian Gregory), Steve Railsback (Jake Gregory), Ian McShane (Sidney), Al Corley (Al), Rita Taggart (Rita), Arnie Moore (Richard).

Artist Pamela Sue Martin marries Steve Railsback, the rich owner of an L.A. construction firm. Wealthy art dealer Ian McShane introduces them to free-basing cocaine and their life begins to crumble.

3097.   Torment (1986, New World, 90m, c). P,D&W Samson Aslanian & John Hopkins, PH Stephen Carpenter, M Christopher Young, ED John Penney, Earl Ghaffari, Bret Shelton, AD Chris Hopkins.

LP Taylor Gilbert (Jennifer), William Witt (Father), Eve Brenner (Mrs. Courtland), Warren Lincoln (Michael), Najean Cherry (Helen), Stan Weston (Bogartis), Doug Leach (Officer Tilman), Lisa Ramirez (Dianne).

Middle-aged William Witt becomes a psychopathic killer when he's rejected by a young woman. He preys on single San Francisco women. Taylor Gilbert appears to be his next intended victim.

3098.   Touch and Go (1980, Mutiny/Great Union, Australia, 92m, c). P John Pellatt, D Peter Maxwell, W Peter Yeldham (based on a story by Maxwell & Yeldham), PH John McLean, ED Sara Bennett & Paul Maxwell.

LP Wendy Hughes (Eva Gilmour), Chantal Contouri (Fiona Latham), Carmen Duncan (Millicent Hoffman), Jeanie Drynan (Gina Tesoriero), Liddy Clark (Helen Preston), Christine Amor (Sue Fullerton), Jon English (Frank Butterfield).

Three beautiful women turn to grand larceny to keep the local kindergarten in operation.

3099.   Touch and Go (1987, Tri-Star, 101m, c). P Stephen Friedman, D Robert Mandel, W Alan Ormsby, Bob Sand & Harry Colomby, PH Richard H. Kline, M Sylvester Levay, ED Walt Mulconery, PD Charles Rosen.

LP Michael Keaton (Bobby Barbato), Maria Conchita Alonso (Denise DeLeon), Ajay Naidu (Louis DeLeon), John Reilly (Jerry Pepper), Maria Tucci (Dee Dee), Richard Venture (Gower), Max Wright (Lester), Michael Zelniker (McDonald).

Self-centered and emotionally isolated hockey player Michael Keaton becomes involved with Maria Conchita Alonso and her 11-year-old prospective juvenile delinquent son Ajay Naidu in this "feel-good" movie.

3100.   Touched (1983, Lorimar, 93m, c). P Dick Petersmann & Barclay Lottimer, D John Flynn, W Lyle Kessler, PH Fred Murphy, M Shirley Walker, ED Harry Keramidas, PD Patrizia von Brandenstein.

LP Robert Hays (Daniel), Kathleen Beller (Jennifer), Ned Beatty (Herbie), Gilbert Lewis (Ernie), Lyle Kessler (Timothy), Farnham Scott (Thomas), Meg Myles (Jennifer's Mother), Mady Kaplan (Arlene).

In a well-meaning but dramatically emotionless story, Robert Hays and Kathleen Beller leave a mental institution and struggle against all odds to set up a normal household.

3101.   Touched by Love (1980, Columbia, 95m, c, aka *To Elvis, with Love*). P Michael Viner, D Gus Trikonis, W Hesper Anderson (based on the story "To Elvis, with Love" by Lena Canada), PH Richard H. Kline, M John Barry, ED Fred Chulack, AD Claudio Guzman.

LP Deborah Raffin (Lena Canada), Diane Lane (Karen), Michael Learned (Dr. Bell), John Amos (Tony), Christina Raines (Amy), Mary Wickes (Margaret), Clu Gulager (Don Fielder), Twyla Volkins (Monica).

The film is based on the true story of a girl suffering from cerebral palsy, here played by Diane Lane, who learns the power of love from a dedicated teacher played by Deborah Raffin. The two write a letter to Elvis Presley. He responds and they begin a correspondence that brings great joy to the girl.

3102.   Tough Enough (1983, 20th Century–Fox, 107m, c). P William S. Gilmore, D Richard O. Fleischer, W John Leone, PH James A. Contner, M Michael Lloyd & Steve Wax, ED Dann Cahn, PD Bill Kenney.

LP Dennis Quaid (Art Long), Carlene Watkins (Caroline Long), Stan Shaw (P.T. Coolidge), Pam Grier (Myra), Warren Oates (James Neese), Bruce McGill (Tony Fallon), Wilford Brimley (Bill Long), Fran Ryan (Gert Long).

Hoping to raise money to finance his

country-western singing career, Dennis Quaid enters the boxing ring and finds himself developing into an up-and-coming contender.

3103. *Tough Guys* (1986, Buena Vista, 102m, c). P Joe Wizan, D Jeff Kanew, W James Orr & Jim Cruickshank, PH King Baggot, M James Newton Howard, ED Kaja Fehr, PD Todd Hallowell.

LP Burt Lancaster (Harry Doyle), Kirk Douglas (Archie Long), Charles Durning (Deke Yablonski), Alexis Smith (Belle), Dana Carvey (Richie Evans), Darlanne Fluegel (Skye Foster), Eli Wallach (Leon B. Little).

Seventy-two year old Burt Lancaster and 69-year-old Kirk Douglas don't embarrass themselves portraying two flamboyant train robbers released from prison after serving a thirty year stretch. Unable to adjust to the modern world, they return to what they know best. Douglas does look a wee bit out of place with swinging young Darlanne Fluegel as his main squeeze. Lancaster has the better sense to take up with Alexis Smith, someone more nearly his age.

3104. *Tough Guys Don't Dance* (1987, Cannon, 108m, c). P Menahem Golan & Yoram Globus, D&W Norman Mailer (based on his novel), PH John Bailey, M Angelo Badalamenti, ED Debra McDermott, PD Armin Ganz.

LP Ryan O'Neal (Tim Madden), Isabella Rossellini (Madeline), Debra Sandlund (Patty Lareine), Wings Hauser (Regency), John Bedford Lloyd (Wardley Meeks, III), Clarence Williams, III (Bolo), Lawrence Tierney (Dougy Madden), Penn Jillette (Big Stoop), Frances Fisher (Jessica Pond).

Loser Ryan O'Neal may have committed murder but he can't remember. Look for a sparkling performance from Lawrence Tierney as O'Neal's no-nonsense father in this tribute to film noir.

3105. *Tougher Than Leather* (1988, New Line, 92m, c). P Vincent Giordano, D Rick Rubin, W Ric Menello & Rubin (based on a story by Bill Adler, Lyor Cohen & Menello), PH Feliks Parnell, ED Steven Brown.

LP Joseph Simmons (Run), Darryl McDaniels (DMC), Jason Mizell (Jam Master Jay), Richard Edson (Bernie), Jenny Lumet (Pam), Rick Rubin (Vic), Lois Ayer (Charlotte), George Godfrey (Nathan), Russell Simmons (Russell).

If you didn't get enough of rap music stories with *Wild Style, Beat Street, Breakin', The Disorderlies* and *Krush Groove,* this subpar action picture features Run DMC doing their thing.

Tower of Evil see Beyond the Fog

3106. *The Toxic Avenger* (1985, Troma, 81m, c). P Lloyd Kaufman & Michael Herz, D Herz & Samuel Weil, W Joe Ritter (additional material by Kaufman, Gay Terry & Stuart Strutin), PH James London & Kaufman, ED Richard Haines & Alan J. Polyniak, AD Barry Shapiro & Alexandra Mazur, SE Jennifer Aspinall & Tom Lauten.

LP Andree Maranda (Sara), Mitchell Cohen (The Toxic Avenger), Jennifer Baptist (Wanda), Cindy Manion (Julie), Robert Prichard (Slug), Gary Schneider (Bozo), Pat Ryan, Jr. (Mayor Belgoody), Mark Torgl (Melvin), Dick Martinsen (Officer O'Clancy), Chris Liano (Walter Harris).

Despite some sick humor, this film, about a nerdish pool attendant thrown into a tub of toxic waste, only to emerge with special powers which he uses as a crimefighter, has some very funny moments.

3107. *The Toxic Avenger: Part II* (1989, Troma, 95m, c). P&D Lloyd Kaufman & Michael Herz, W Gay Partington Terry (based on an original story by Kaufman), PH James London, M Barrie Guard, ED Michael Schweitzer, AD Alex Grey, SE Pericles Lewnes.

LP Ron Fazio & John Altamura (The Toxic Avenger), Phoebe Legere (Claire), Rick Collins (Apocalypse Inc. Chairman), Rikiya Yasuoka (Big Mac), Tsutomu Sekine (Announcer), Shinoburyu (Shockikuyama), Lisa Gaye (Malfaire).

While the original had a few laughs, this sequel has jokes so bad five-year-olds will groan. Toxic makes it to Japan to seek out his father Big Mac, the head cheese in an underworld gang—you know, Big Mac with cheese. Terrible!

3108. *The Toxic Avenger Part III: The Last Temptation of Toxie* (1989, Troma, 89m, c). P&D Michael Herz & Lloyd Kaufman, W Gay Partington Terry & Kaufman (based on a story by Kaufman), PH James London, M Christopher DeMarco (based on music by Antonin Dvorak), ED Joseph McGirr.

LP Ron Fazio & John Altamura (The Toxic Avenger), Phoebe Legere (Claire), Rick Collins (Chairman/The Devil), Lisa Gaye (Malfaire), Jessica Dublin (Mrs. Junko).

The former nerd who became a deformed superhero after emerging from a vat of toxic waste is back in a stupid second sequel which unfortunately may not be the last. Not so long as there are young people with a limited imagination and a weird notion of what's funny. Among other things Toxie, played by both Ron Fazio and John Altamura, attempts to raise money needed for an operation to restore the sight of his "beautiful blind buxom bimbo" Phoebe Legere (that's how she's frequently referred to in the film).

3109. *The Toy* (1982, Columbia, 99m, c). P Phil Feldman, D Richard Donner, W Carol Sobieski (based on the film *Le Jouet* by Francis Veber), PH Laszlo Kovacs, M Patrick Williams, ED Richard Harris & Michael A. Stevenson, PD Charles Rosen.

LP Richard Pryor (Jack Brown), Jackie Gleason (U.S. Bates), Ned Beatty (Mr. Morehouse), Scott Schwartz (Eric Bates), Teresa Ganzel (Fancy Bates), Wilfrid Hyde-White (Barkley), Annazette Chase (Angela), Tony King (Clifford), Don Hood (O'Brien).

Janitor Richard Pryor finds himself the new "toy" of Scott Schwartz, the son of department store owner Jackie Gleason. Pryor gets to play a modern day slave in this not very funny movie.

3110. *Toy Soldiers* (1984, New World, 91m, c). P E. Darrell Hallenbeck, D David A. Fisher, W Fisher & Walter Fox, PH Francisco Bojorquez, M Leland Bond, ED Geoffrey Rowland.

LP Jason Miller (Sarge), Cleavon Little (Buck), Rodolfo De Anda (Col. Lopez), Terri Garber (Amy), Tracy Scoggins (Monique), Willard Pugh (Ace), Jim Greenleaf (Tom), Mary Beth Evans (Buffy), Tim Robbins (Boe).

A group of kids from Beverly Hills are on a relaxing cruise off Central America when they are taken captive and held for ransom. They escape and join-up with a seasoned mercenary who turns them into a vigilante force.

3111. *Track 29* (1988, Island, GB, 90m, c). P Rick McCallum, D Nicolas Roeg, W Dennis Potter, PH Alex Thomson, M Stanley Myers, ED Tony Lawson, PD David Brockhurst.

LP Theresa Russell (Linda Henry), Gary Oldman (Martin), Sandra Bernhard (Nurse Stein), Christopher Lloyd (Dr. Henry Henry), Colleen Camp (Arlanda), Seymour Cassel (Dr. Bernard Fairmont), Leon Rippy (Trucker).

Texas housewife Theresa Russell's husband Christopher Lloyd is more interested in model trains and nurse Sandra Bernhard than in her. Russell encounters mysterious Englishman Gary Oldman: Is he the son she abandoned years ago? It's a bewildering story.

3112. *Trading Hearts* (1988, Cineworld, 88m, c). P Herb Jaffe & Mort Engelberg, D Neil Leifer, W Frank Deford, PH Karen Grossman, M Stanley Myers, ED Rick Shaine, PD George Goodridge.

LP Raul Julia (Vinnie), Beverly D'Angelo (Donna), Jenny Lewis (Yvonne), Parris Buckner (Robert), Robert Gwaltney (Ducky), Ruben Rabasa (Pepe), Mark Harris (Ralph).

Set in 1957 Miami, Raul Julia, a washed-up pitcher with the Boston Red Sox, is released during spring training. Cute tomboy Jenny Lewis believes that Julia would make a neat new father, but her mother, lounge singer Beverly D'Angelo, isn't buying him.

3113. *Trading Places* (1983, Paramount, 106m, c). P Aaron Russo, D John Landis, W Timothy Harris & Herschel Weingrod, PH Robert Paynter, M Elmer Bernstein†, ED Malcolm Campbell, PD Gene Rudolf.

LP Dan Aykroyd (Louis Winthorpe, III), Eddie Murphy (Billy Ray Valentine), Ralph Bellamy (Randolph Duke), Don Ameche (Mortimer Duke), Denholm Elliott (Coleman), Jamie Lee Curtis (Ophelia), Kristin Holby (Penelope Witherspoon), Paul Gleason (Clarence Beeks).

Eddie Murphy establishes himself as a major star in this movie in which all participants deserve praise for their comedy work. Rich fat cat brothers Ralph Bellamy and Don Ameche make a bet about what will happen if Dan Aykroyd, who has had all the advantages that money and class can bring him, is forced to change places with poor black beggar Murphy. Ultimately, Aykroyd and Murphy turn the tables on Bellamy and Ameche, with the help of butler Denholm Elliott and prostitute Jamie Lee Curtis.

3114. *Trail of the Pink Panther* (1982, MGM/United Artists, 97m, c). P Blake Edwards & Tony Adams, D Edwards, W Frank Waldman, Tom Waldman, B. Edwards & Geoffrey Edwards, Friz Freleng (based on a story by B. Edwards and characters created by David H. DePatie & Frelang, PH Dick Bush, M Henry Mancini, ED Alan Jones, PD Peter Mullins.

LP Peter Sellers (Inspector Clouseau), David Niven (Sir Charles Litton), Herbert Lom (Dreyfus), Richard Mulligan (Clouseau Sr.), Joanna Lumley (Marie Jouvet), Capucine (Lady Litton), Robert Loggia (Bruno), Harvey Korman (Prof. Balls), Burt Kwouk (Cato), Graham Stark (Hercule), Peter Arne (Col. Bufoni).

As this movie clearly demonstrates, there is no respect for the dead in Hollywood. Using outtakes of earlier Pink Panther movies and peppering the scenes with characters who appeared in them, director Blake Edwards gets one last sick laugh from the late Peter Sellers. Clouseau is reported missing after falling from a ship at sea. TV reporter Joanna Lumley interviews all who knew him including a ghastly looking David Niven, then suffering from Lou Gehrig's disease which would soon take his life.

Train of Terror see *Terror Train*

Trancers see *Future Cop*

3115. *The Transformers – The Movie* (1986, DeLaurentiis, animated, 86m, c). P Joe Bacal & Tom Griffin, D Nelson Shin, W Ron Friedman, M Vince DiCola.

VOICES Eric Idle (Wreck Gar), Judd Nelson (Hot Rod/Rodimus Prime), Leonard Nimoy (Galvatron), Robert Stack (Ultra Magnus), Lionel Stander (Kup), Orson Welles (Unicron), Scatman Crothers (Jazz), Clive Revill (Kickback).

The popular TV characters, who convert to cars and dinosaurs to fight evil, face their biggest challenge in combatting the sinister forces of Orson Welles.

3116. *Transylvania 6-5000* (1985, New World, 93m, c). P Mace Neufeld & Thomas H. Brodek, D&W Rudy DeLuca, PH Tom Pinter, M Lee Holdridge & Alfie Kabiljo, ED Harry Keller, PD Zeljko Senecic.

LP Jeff Goldblum (Jack Harrison), Joseph Bologna (Dr. Malavaqua), Ed Begley, Jr. (Gil Turner), Carol Kane (Lupi), Jeffrey Jones (Lepescu), John Byner (Radu), Geena Davis (Odette), Donald Gibb (Wolfman).

In a film that can only be described as dumb, dumb and dumb, klutzy reporters Jeff Goldblum and Ed Begley, Jr., go to modern day Transylvania where they encounter an array of comedic monsters. The wolfman has all the best lines.

3117. *Trapper County War* (1989, Noble Ent. Group/Alpine, 95m, c). P Michael W. Leighton, D Worth Keeter, W Russel V. Manzatt, PH Irl Dixon, M Shuki Levy, ED Miriam L. Preisel, PD R. Clifford Searcy.

LP Robert Estes (Ryan Cassidy), Betsy Russell (Lacey Luddigger), Bo Hopkins (Sheriff Sam Frost), Don Swayze (Walt Luddiger), Noah Black (Bobby Keal), Sarah Hunley (Mom Luddigger), R.G. Armstrong (Pop Luddigger).

This city folks vs. rednecks story is better than most of its kind. Robert Estes and Noah Black are young New Jersey musicians who run into trouble in a small North Carolina community when they strike up a friendship with bored waitress Betsy Russell, who'd like to become a singer. The violent climax looks like the start of another civil war.

3118. *The Traveller* (1989, BLP/Lighthouse, Canada, 96m, c). P Bruno Lazaro Pacheco & Raymond Massey, D Pacheco, W Pacheco & Jean Pierre Lefebvre (based on an original story and

French screenplay by Guy P. Buckholtzer), PH Thomas H. Turnbull, M Daniel Ross, ED Pacheco & Patricia Lambkin.

LP R. Lewis Morrison (Robert Braun), Ginette St. Denis (Ginette), Denise Brillon, Phillip Stewart, James Stevens, Arlen Jones.

Wooden performances and direction doom this story of businessman R. Lewis Morrison who is in Vancouver to buy Pacific Northwest Indian masks. He has sort of a mid-life crisis because he's torn between his lucrative business exploiting the Indians and the fact that he was raised by the Indians and married one of their maidens.

3119.   *Travelling North* (1988, View Pictures, Australia, 97m, c). P Ben Gannon, D Carl Schultz, W David Williamson (based on his play), PH Julian Penney, M Alan John, Beethoven, Mozart & Vivaldi, ED Henry Dangar, PD Owen Paterson.

LP Leo McKern (Frank), Julia Blake (Frances), Graham Kennedy (Freddie), Henri Szeps (Saul), Michele Fawdon (Helen), Diane Craig (Sophie), Andrea Moor (Joan), Drew Forsythe (Martin), John Gregg (Jim), Rob Steele (Syd).

Crusty seventyish Melbourne civil engineer Leo McKern retires. He convinces much younger widow Julie Blake to join him in starting a new life in subtropical northern Australia.

3120.   *Traxx* (1988, DEG, 84m, c). P Gary De Vore & Richard McWhorter, D Jerome Gary, W Gary De Vore, PH Giuseppe Maccari, M Jay Gruska, ED Michael Kahane, PD Jack Poplin.

LP Shadoe Stevens (Traxx), Priscilla Barnes (Mayor Alexandria Cray), Willard E. Pugh (Deeter), John Hancock (Chief Emmett Decker), Hugh Gillin (Comm. R.B. Davis), Hershal Sparber, Jonathan Lutz & Lucius Houghton (Guziks), Darrow Igus (Wendall).

Ex-cop turned mercenary Shadoe Stevens starts a cookie business in a Texas town. Hoping for reward money from sexy mayor Priscilla Barnes, he teams with black sidekick Willard E. Pugh to take on the local Mafia and clean up a crime-ridden neighborhood.

3121.   *Treasure of the Yankee Zephyr* (1984, Film Ventures, 90m, c, AKA *Race for the Yankee Zephyr*). P Anthony I. Ginnane, John Barnett & David Hemmings, D Hemmings, W Everett de Roche, PH Vincent Morton, M Brian May, ED John Laing, PD Bernard Hides.

LP Ken Wahl (Barney), Lesley Ann Warren (Sally), Donald Pleasence (Gibbie), George Peppard (Theo Brown), Bruno Lawrence & Robert Bruce (Barkers), Grant Tilly (Coin Collector), Harry Rutherford-Jones (Harry).

Wahl, Warren and Pleasence set off across New Zealand to find a plane that went down 40 years earlier carrying a cache of gold bars worth $50 million.

3122.   *Tree of Hands* (1989, Greenpoint Film, GB, 90m, c). P Ann Scott, D Giles Foster, W Gordon Williams (based on the novel by Ruth Rendell), PH Kenneth MacMillan, M Richard Hartley, ED David Martin, PD Adrian Smith.

LP Helen Shaver (Benet Archdale), Lauren Bacall (Marsha Archdale), Malcolm Stoddard (Dr. Ian Raeburn), Peter Firth (Terence), Paul McGann (Barry), Kate Hardie (Carol).

Set in contemporary London, bestselling author Helen Shaver lives with her young son. Her mother Lauren Bacall, with a history of mental illness, arrives from the United States, intent on mending fences between her daughter and herself, and building a relationship with her grandson. When the boy dies unexpectedly, Bacall brings home a youngster she's found in the streets, beaten and abandoned by his parents. The two women decide to keep the child for a while. Shaver, posing as a journalist, gets to know his bickering parents, who are into kinky sex. There seems to be more plot here than director Giles Foster can handle.

3123.   *Trenchcoat* (1983, Buena Vista, 91m, c). P Jerry Leider, D Michael Tuchner, W Jeffrey Price & Peter Seaman, PH Tonino Delli Colli, M Charles Fox, ED Frank J. Urioste, PD Rodger Maus.

LP Margot Kidder (Mickey Raymond), Robert Hays (Terry Leonard), David Suchet (Inspector Stagnos), Gila Von Weitershausen (Eva Werner), Daniel Faraldo (Nino Tenucci), Ronald Lacey (Princess Aida), John Justin (Marquis DePina).

In this detective spoof, aspiring mystery writer Margot Kidder heads to Malta to write a story and finds herself drawn into a real-life conspiracy.

3124. *Trespasses* (1987, Shapiro, 100m, c). P Loren Bivens & Richard Rosetta, D Adam Roarke & Bivens, W Bivens & Lou Diamond Phillips & Jo Carol Pierce, PH Monte Dhooge & Phil Curry, M Wayne Bell & Chuck Pennell, ED Sherri Galloway, AD Becky Block & Lisa Knight.

LP Robert Kuhn (Franklin Ramsey), Van Brooks (Richard), Mary Pillot (Sharon Rae), Adam Roarke & Lou Diamond Phillips (Drifters), Ben Johnson (August Klein), Deborah Neumann (Catherine), Thom Meyer (Johnny Ramsey).

Shot in 1983, this is the inane story of the relationship of cattleman Robert Kuhn and married rape victim Mary Pillot.

3125. *Tribute* (1980, 20th Century–Fox, Canada, 123m, c). P Joel B. Michaels & Garth B. Drabinsky, D Bob Clark, W Bernard Slade (based on his stage play), PH Reginald H. Morris, M Kenn Wannberg, Barry Manilow, Jack Feldman, Bruce Sussman, Jack Lemmon & Alan Jay Lerner, ED Richard Halsey, PD Trevor Williams.

LP Jack Lemmon† (Scottie Templeton), Robby Benson (Jud Templeton), Lee Remick (Maggie Stratton), Kim Cattrall (Sally Haines), Colleen Dewhurst (Gladys Petrelli), John Marley (Lou Daniels), Gale Garnett (Hilary).

Dying Broadway press agent Jack Lemmon is determined to achieve a reconciliation with his son Robby Benson. With the help of his ex-wife Lee Remick, he succeeds. Benson arranges for a testimonial dinner for his father before he dies.

3126. *Trick or Treat* (1986, DeLaurentiis, 97m, c). P Michael S. Murphey & Joel Soisson, D Charles Martin Smith, W Murphey, Soisson & Rhet Topham (based on a story by Topham), PH Robert Elswit, M Christopher Young & Fastway, ED Jane Schwartz Jaffe, PD Curt Schnell.

LP Marc Price (Eddie Weinbauer), Tony Fields (Sammi Curr), Lisa Orgolini (Leslie Graham), Doug Savant (Tim Hainey), Elaine Joyce (Angie Weinbauer), Glen Morgan (Roger Mockus), Gene Simmons (Nuke), Ozzy Osbourne (Rev. Aaron Gilstrom).

High school nerd and school scapegoat Marc Price conjures up the disfigured ghost of his late rock idol Tony Fields to help him take revenge on his numerous tormentors. The film is a comical homage to heavy-metal horror.

3127. *Trick or Treats* (1982, Lone Star, 91m, c). P,D,W,PH&ED Gary Graver, SD Michael Railsback.

LP Jackelyn Giroux (Linda), Peter Jason (Malcolm), Chris Graver (Christopher), David Carradine (Richard), Carrie Snodgress (Joan), Jillian Kesner (Andrea), Dan Pastorini & Tim Rossovich (Men in White Shorts).

The film is another of the many *Halloween* rip-offs, no better or worse than the average. It's a strange tribute to a moneymaker that has its own poorly produced clones.

3128. *The Trip to Bountiful* (1985, Island, 105m, c). P Sterling VanWagenen & Horton Foote, D Peter Masterson, W Foote† (based on his play), PH Fred Murphy, M J.A.C. Redford, ED Jay Freund, PD Neil Spisak.

LP Geraldine Page* (Mrs. Watts), John Heard (Ludie Watts), Carlin Glynn (Jessie Mae Watts), Richard Bradford (Sheriff), Rebecca De Mornay (Thelma), Kevin Cooney (Roy), Norman Bennett & Harvey Lewis (Bus Ticket Men), Kirk Sisco (Ticket Agent, Houston Train Station), Dave Tanner (Billy Davis).

Geraldine Page is perfection as an old woman in 1947 living in cramped quarters in a Houston Texas apartment with her wimpy son John Heard and his shrewish wife Carlin Glynn. Page's heart is not strong and the only dream she has left in life is to return to the small town of Bountiful where she was born and grew up. She hides her pension check from Glynn and escapes to the bus station when her daughter-in-law is away. The town is a ruin and her ex-home is an abandoned shack, but the sheriff of the region allows her one last look at the place which means so much to her. She sees it as it was and doesn't mind so much when her son and his wife come for her to take her back to Houston.

3129. *Triumph of the Spirit* (1989, Nova Intl., 120m, c). P Arnold Kopelson & Shimon Arama, D Robert M. Young, W Andrzej Krakowski & Laurence Heath (based on a story by Arama & Zion Haen), PH Curtis Clark, M Cliff Eidelman, ED Arthur Coburn, PD Jerzy Maslowska.

LP Willem Dafoe (Salamo Arouch), Edward James Olmos (Gypsy), Robert Loggia (Poppa), Wendy Gazelle (Allegra), Kelly Wolf (Elena), Costas Mandylor (Avram), Kario Salem (Jacko), Edward Zentara (Janush), Hartmut Becker (Maj. Rauscher).

Filmed almost entirely inside the Auschwitz/Birkenau Nazi death camps, the film presents the true story of a Greek boxing champion (Willem Dafoe) who saved his life by entertaining Nazi officers by defeating opponents in a ring at Auschwitz. The vanquished were sent to the gas chamber and the contestants were aware that was to be the fate of the losers. The film fails to be great drama because it is so obvious and sentimental. Then too, the director doesn't explore the moral anguish that the boxer must have felt.

3130. *Triumphs of a Man Called Horse* (1984, Redwing/Jensen Farley, US/Mex., 86m, c). P Derek Gibson, D John Hough, W Ken Blackwell & Carlos Aured (based on a story by Jack DeWitt and a character created by Dorothy M. Johnson), PH John Alcott & John Cabrera, M George Garvarentz, ED Roy Watts, PD Alan Roderick-Jones.

LP Richard Harris (Man Called Horse), Michael Beck (Koda), Ana De Sade (Redwing), Vaughn Armstrong (Capt. Cummings), Anne Seymour (Elk Woman), Buck Taylor (Sgt. Bridges), Simon Andreu (Gance), Lautaro Murua (Perkins).

In this dumb rip-off of the "Man Called Horse" series, Richard Harris appears very briefly as the white man who has led a Sioux tribe for 30 years. It is his half-breed son Michael Beck who must save his people from prospectors and once more bring peace to his land.

3131. *Troll* (1986, Marvin Films, 86m, c). P Albert Band, D John Buechler, W Ed Naha, PH Romano Albani, M Richard Band, ED Lee Percy.

LP June Lockhart (Eunice St. Clair), Jenny Beck (Wendy Potter), Anne Lockhart (Young Eunice St. Clair), Shelley Hack (Mrs. Potter), Michael Moriarty (Mr. Potter), Sonny Bono (Peter Dickenson).

In this fantasy, a malevolent troll haunts an apartment building. It plans to turn all humans into trolls.

3132. *Troma's War* (1988, Troma, 99m, c). P Lloyd Kaufman & Michael Herz, D Herz & Samuel Weil, W Mitchell Dana & Kaufman (based on a story by Kaufman), PH Jane London, PD Alexis Grey.

LP Carolyn Beauchamp (Lydia), Sean Bowen (Taylor), Michael Ryder (Parker), Patrick Weathers (Kirkland), Jessica Dublin (Dottie), Steven Crossley (Marshall), Lorayn Lane DeLuca (Maria), Charles Kay Hune (Hardwick).

A group of survivors of an air crash find themselves fighting terrorists with plans of infecting the people of the U.S. with an AIDS virus. Timely, but dumb.

3133. *Tron* (1982, Buena Vista, 96m, c). P Donald Kushner, D&W Steven Lisberger (based on a story by Lisberger & Bonnie MacBird), PH Bruce Logan, M Wendy Carlos, ED Jeff Gourson, PD Dean Edward Mitzner, COS Elois Jenssen & Rosanna Norton†, SOUND Michael Minkler, Bob Minkler, Lee Minkler & Jim La Rue.

LP Jeff Bridges (Kevin Flynn/Clu), Bruce Boxleitner (Alan Bradley/Tron), David Warner (Ed Dillinger/Sark), Cindy Morgan (Lora/Yori), Barnard Hughes (Dr. Walter Gibbs/Dumont), Dan Shor (Ram), Peter Jurasik (Crom).

Video game designer Jeff Bridges is scientifically transformed into a component of a computer and must battle his own creations in the "Tron" dimension in order to survive. It's the old western good guys wear white, bad guys wear black shtick with a science fiction twist.

3134. *Troop Beverly Hills* (1989, Columbia, 100m, c). P Ava Ostern Fries, D

Jeff Kanew, W Pamela Norris & Margaret Grieco Oberman, PH Donald E. Thorin, M Randy Edelman, ED Mark Melnick, PD Robert F. Boyle, AD Jack G. Taylor, Jr.

LP Shelley Long (Phyllis Nefler), Craig T. Nelson (Freddy Nefler), Betty Thomas (Velda Plendor), Mary Gross (Annie Herman), Stephanie Beacham (Vicki Sprantz), Audra Lindley (Frances Temple), Carla Gugino (Chica Barnfell).

How can you not like spoiled princess Shelley Long? Well, it's possible if she doesn't soon add some other facets to her act. Still tossing her hair, wearing smart clothes and being the know-it-all that we came to love on TV's "Cheers" and in a few movies, Long is den mother to a group of Beverly Hills girls scouts. Somehow the fancy locale is supposed to make a difference. OK Shelley, we'll let you get away with it one more time — but for goodness' sake grow up!

3135. *Tropical Snow* (1989, PSM Ent., 88m, c). P J.D. Leif, D&W Ciro Duran, PH Eduardo Serra, M Alan DerMarderosian, ED Duncan Burns, Oscar Alzate.

LP Nick Corri (Gustavo [Tavo]), Madeleine Stowe (Marina), David Carradine (Oskar), Argermiro Catiblanco, Alfonso Ortiz, Merena Dimont, Libia Tenorio, Roger Melo, Celmira Yepes, William Mesa, Sonia Ceballos, Antonio Corral.

In view of Colombia's attempted crackdown on druglords, this movie filmed in Bogotá and Barranquilla in 1986 is at least timely. Colombian couple Nick Corri and Madeleine Stowe want to leave their country for New York to find a better life. They are offered free passage by David Carradine if they will do him a little favor — smuggle a lot of cocaine into the States.

3136. *Trouble in Mind* (1985, Raincity/Alive, 111m, c). P Carolyn Pfeiffer & David Blocker, D&W Alan Rudolph, PH Toyomichi Kurita, M Mark Isham, ED Sally Coryn Allen & Tom Walls, PD Steven Legler.

LP Kris Kristofferson (Hawk), Keith Carradine (Coop), Lori Singer (Georgia), Genevieve Bujold (Wanda), Joe Morton (Solo), Divine (Hilly Blue), George Kirby (Lt. Gunther), John Considine (Nate Nathanson), Dirk Blocker (Rambo), Albert Hall (Leo).

Former detective Kris Kristofferson returns home after serving a prison term for killing a mobster. He moves into an apartment over a seedy diner run by his former lover Genevieve Bujold. Small-time hood Keith Carradine and girlfriend Lori Singer move their camper next door to the diner. Kristofferson falls for Singer. When Crime boss Divine (in his only nondrag role) orders a hit on Carradine, Kristofferson intervenes for Singer's sake.

3137. *The Trouble with Dick* (1987, Frolix, 93m, c). P Gary Walkow & Leslie Robins, D&W Walkow, PH Daryl Studebaker, M Roger Bourland, ED G.A. Walkowishky, PD Eric Jones.

LP Tom Villard (Dick Kendred), Susan Dey (Diane), Elaine Giftos (Sheila Dibble), Elizabeth Gorcey (Haley Dibble), David Clennon (Lars), Jack Carter (Samsa), Marianne Muellerleile (Betty).

Tom Villard, a struggling writer of "literary science fiction," is suffering from writer's block. While he would like to renew a romance with Susan Dey, she's not interested so he seeks his muse with his divorced landlady Elaine Giftos and her hot-to-trot daughter Elizabeth Gorcey, but this only earns him a nervous breakdown.

3138. *The Trouble with Spies* (1987, DEG-HBO, 91m, c). P,D&W Burt Kennedy (based on the novel *Apple Pie in the Sky* by Marc Lovell), PH Alex Phillips, M Ken Thorne, ED Warner E. Leighton, PD Jose Maria Tapiador.

LP Donald Sutherland (Appleton Porter), Ned Beatty (Harry Lewis), Ruth Gordon (Mrs. Arkwright), Lucy Gutteridge (Mona Smith), Michael Hordern (Jason Lock), Robert Morley (Angus Watkins), Gregory Sierra (Capt. Sanchez).

Made for HBO in 1984 but never shown on cable, Donald Sutherland appears as a bumbling British agent sent to the Mediterranean isle of Ibiza to find Soviet spies who have developed a truth serum. Sutherland is no Peter Sellers in this poor attempt to imitate an Inspector Clouseau/Pink Panther film.

3139. *True Believer* (1989, Columbia, 104m, c). P Walter F. Parkes & Lawrence

Lasker, D Joseph Ruben, W Wesley Strick, PH John W. Lindley, M Brad Fiedel, ED George Bowers, PD Lawrence Miller.

LP James Woods (Eddie Dodd), Robert Downey, Jr. (Roger Baron), Margaret Colin (Kitty Greer), Yuji Okumoto (Shu Kai Kim), Kurtwood Smith (Robert Reynard), Tom Bower (Cecil Skell), Miguel Fernandes (Art Esparza).

Woods, a 60s-style liberal, idealistic lawyer, is still taking cases for the underdog in the 80s. He's hired by a Japanese woman to defend her son in prison for murder. As part of a prison gang he has become implicated in another murder. Lawyers like Woods are adept at espousing conspiracy theories against their clients. They often defend clients that the general public already believe guilty from reading and listening to news stories about the cases. We need such attorneys, even if we don't always relish their working methods.

3140.   *True Blood* (1989, Fries Ent., 97m, c). P Peter Maris, D&W Frank Kerr, PH Mark H.L. Morris, M Scott Roewe, ED Mac Haight.

LP Jeff Fahey (Ray Trueblood), Chad Lowe (Donny Trueblood), Sherilyn Fenn (Jennifer), James Tolkan (Lt. Joe Hanley), Billy Drago (Spider Masters), Ken Foree (Charlie).

The film is a predictable crime drama about street gangs and rumbles. It's violent enough but for no noticeable purpose.

3141.   *True Confessions* (1981, United Artists, 108m, c). P Irwin Winkler & Robert Chartoff, D Ulu Grosbard, W John Gregory Dunne & Joan Didion (based on the novel by Dunne), PH Owen Roizman, M Georges Delerue, ED Lynzee Klingman, PD Stephen S. Grimes.

LP Robert De Niro (Des Spellacy), Robert Duvall (Tom Spellacy), Charles Durning (Jack Amsterdam), Ed Flanders (Dan T. Champion), Burgess Meredith (Seamus Fargo), Rose Gregorio (Brenda Samuels), Cyril Cusack (Cardinal Danaher), Kenneth McMillan (Frank Crotty), Dan Hedeya (Howard Terkel).

In 1948 L.A. homicide detective Robert Duvall clashes with his brother Robert De Niro, a bright young monsignor with quite a future in the Catholic Church.

The bone of contention is former pimp and hood Charles Durning, striving desperately for respectability, trying to buy his way to heaven with his contributions to the church. Duvall wants to burn Durning for the murder of a "Black Dahlia"-like whore, while De Niro is forced to award Durning the title "Catholic Layman of the Year." Duvall wins out and the scandal ruins De Niro's career, condemning him to a life as the pastor of a tiny run-down church in the desert. DeNiro and Duvall, two of the best "star" characters actors in the business, are both superb.

3142.   *True Love* (1989, United Artists, 104m, c). P Richard Guay & Shelley Houis, D Nancy Savoca, W Savoca & Guay, PH Lisa Rinzler, M Various Composers, ED John Tintori, PD Lester W. Cohen.

LP Annabella Sciorra (Donna), Ron Eldard (Michael), Aida Turturro (Grace), Roger Rignack (Dom), Star Jasper (J.C.), Michael J. Wolfe (Brian), Kelly Cinnante (Yvonne), Rick Shapiro (Kevin).

Hollywood brought audiences *Moonstruck,* the story of a romance in New York's Little Italy. Now director Nancy Savoca invites us to a large, rambunctious Italian-American wedding – and anyone who has attended one knows how much fun they can be. This one doesn't disappoint and neither does this touching, amusing and memorable film.

3143.   *True Stories* (1986, Warner, 111m, c). P Gary Kurfirst, D David Byrne, W Stephen Tobolowsky, Beth Henley & Byrne, PH Ed Lachman, M Talking Heads, ED Caroline Biggerstaff, PD Barbara Ling.

LP John Goodman (Louis Fyne), Annie McEnroe (Kay Culver), Jo Harvey Allen (The Lying Woman), Spalding Gray (Earl Culver), Alix Elias (The Cute Woman), Roebuck "Pops" Staples (Mr. Tucker), Humberto "Tito" Larriva (Ramon), John Ingle (The Preacher), Swoosie Kurtz (The Lazy Woman), David Byrne (Narrator).

This is a long-rock video with head Talking Head David Byrne presenting audiences who care with the eccentric lives of the weird folks who reside in the fictional town of Virgil, Texas. For Talking

Head fans, ignore the movie; listen to the soundtrack LP.

3144. *Trust Me* (1989, Cinecom, 104m, c). P George Edwards, D Bobby Houston, W Houston & Gary Rigdon, PH Thomas Jewett, M Pray for Rain, ED Barry Zetlin.

LP Adam Ant (James Callendar), David Packer (Sam Brown), Talia Balsam (Catherine Walker), William DeAcutis (Billy Brawthwaite), Joyce Van Patten (Nettie Brown), Barbara Bain (Mary Casal), Brooke Da Vida (Denise Tipton), Simon McQueen (Holly Windsor), Alma Beltran (Imelda), Marilyn Tokuda (Chic Girl).

Adam Ant stars as an art gallery owner who doesn't know much about art, but does know that a dead painter's work brings in more money than a live one. He tries to drive artist David Packer over the brink so he'll leave this vale of tears, which will quickly be followed by a mark-up of his cute little cherubs in flight.

3145. *Tuck Everlasting* (1981, Vestron, animated, 100m, c). P Howard Kling, W Stratton Rawson, Fred A. Keller, F.K. Keller, Jim Bisco, M Malcolm Dalglish, Grey Larson, AD Michael Bucur, D Frederick King Keller (based on the novel by Natalie Babbitt).

VOICES Margaret Chamberlain, Paul Flessa, Fred A. Keller, James McGuire, Sonia Raimi, Bruce D'Auria.

Dreamy young Margaret Chamberlain befriends a family with an incredible secret in this entertaining fable.

3146. *Tucker: The Man and His Dream* (1988, Paramount, 111m, c). P Fred Roos & Fred Fuchs, D Francis Ford Coppola, W Arnold Schulman & David Seidler, PH Vittorio Storaro, M Joe Jackson, ED Priscilla Nedd, PD Dean Tavoularis†, AD Alex Tavoularis, SD Armin Ganz†, COS Milena Canonero.

LP Jeff Bridges (Preston Tucker), Joan Allen (Vera Tucker), Martin Landau† (Abe Karatz), Frederic Forrest (Eddie Dean), Mako (Jimmy Sakuyama), Lloyd Bridges (Senator Homer Ferguson), Elias Koteas (Alex Tremulis), Christian Slater (Junior), Nina Siemaszko (Marilyn Lee Tucker), Dean Stockwell (Howard Hughes).

In the late 1940s, Preston Tucker, part visionary, part conman, has a dream of building the best car possible, with aerodynamic design, seat belts, rear engine, fuel injection, disc brakes, pop-out windows, etc., features which only in recent years found their ways into cars. In the late 1940s, he attempts to make that dream a reality, with the Tucker automobile, "The Car of Tomorrow — Today!" Unfortunately, he tries to sell the cars even before he had a working model. This minor drawback, combined with the opposition of the major automobile makers of the time and the politicians they have in their pockets, is enough to grease the skids for the exuberant world-beater-to-be, and destroy his dream.

3147. *Tuff Turf* (1985, New World, 112m, c). P Donald P. Borchers, D Fritz Kiersch, W Jette Rinck (based on a story by Greg Collins O'Neill & Murray Michaels), PH Willy Kurant, M Jonathan Elias, ED Marc Grossman, AD Craig Stearns.

LP James Spader (Morgan Hiller), Kim Richards (Frankie Croyden), Paul Mones (Nick Hauser), Matt Clark (Stuart Hiller), Claudette Nevins (Page Hiller), Robert Downey, Jr. (Jimmy Parker), Olivia Barash (Ronnie).

The new kid in a lowerclass section of L.A., tough but brainy James Spader engages local gang leader Paul Mones in a bitter turf dispute.

3148. *Tulips* (1981, Avco Embassy, Canada, 92m, c). P Don Carmody, D Stan Ferris (Mark Warren, Rex Bromfield, Al Waxman), W Fred Sappho (Bromfield, Waxman, Henry Olek & Gabe Kaplan), PH Francois Protat, M Eddie Karam, ED Alan Collins & Yurij Lohovy, AD Ted Watkins.

LP Gabe Kaplan (Leland Irving), Bernadette Peters (Rutanya Wallace), Al Waxman (Bert Irving), Henry Gibson (Maurice "Boom Boom" Avocado), David Boxer (Dr. Carl Walburn), Jazzmine Lauzane (Metermaid).

Believing that he has nothing to live for but unable to commit suicide, Gabe Kaplan takes out a contract on his life, then meets Bernadette Peters, who makes him want to live — but how do they cancel his "hit"?

Tunnels see Criminal Act

3149.   *Turk 182!* (1985, 20th Century–Fox, 98m, c). P Ted Field & Rene Dupont, D Bob Clark, W James Gregory Kingston, Denis Hamill & John Hamill (based on a story by Kingston), PH Reginald H. Morris, M Paul Zaza, ED Stan Cole, PD Harry Pottle.

LP Timothy Hutton (Jimmy Lynch), Robert Urich (Terry Lynch), Kim Cattrall (Danny Boudreau), Robert Culp (Mayor Tyler), Darren McGavin (Detective Kowalski), Steven Keats (Jockamo), Paul Sorvino (Himself), Peter Boyle (Detective Ryan), James S. Tolkan (Hanley).

When New York fireman Robert Urich is disabled rescuing a little girl from a burning building, he is denied his pension because he was off duty and drunk at the time. His angry brother Timothy Hutton takes on City Hall to win back his brother's rights.

3150.   *Turkey Shoot* (1983, Hemdale, Australia, 92m, c, aka *Escape 2000*). P Anthony I. Ginnane & William Fayman, D Brian Trenchard-Smith, W Jon George & Neill Hicks (based on a story by George Schenck, Robert Williams & David Lawrence), PH John McLean, M Brian May, ED Alan Lake, PD Bernard Hides.

LP Steve Railsback (Paul Anders), Olivia Hussey (Chris Walters), Michael Craig (Charles Thatcher), Carmen Duncan (Jennifer), Noel Ferrier (Mallory), Lynda Stoner (Rita Daniels), Roger Ward (Ritter), Michael Petrovich (Tito).

In this sadistic, futuristic bloodbath, individuality is considered a crime and those who fail to conform are hunted down like animals in a jungle.

3151.   *Turner and Hooch* (1989, Touchstone, 98m, c). P Raymond Wagner, D Roger Spottiswoode, W Dennis Shryack, Michael Blodgett, Daniel Petrie, Jr., Jim Cash & Jack Epps, Jr. (based on a story by Shryack, Blodgett and Petrie), PH Adam Greenberg, M Charles Gross, ED Paul Seydor, Mark Conte, Kenneth Morrisey & Lois Freeman-Fox, PD John De Cuir, Jr.

LP Tom Hanks (Scott Turner), Mare Winningham (Emily Carson), Beasley (Hooch), Craig T. Nelson (Chief Hyde), Reginald VelJohnson (David Sutton), Scott Paulin (Zack Gregory), J.C. Quinn (Walter Boyett), John McIntire (Amos Reed).

Tom Hanks has worked with many funny partners including John Candy, Dan Aykroyd, Shelley Long and Jackie Gleason, but none were any more appealing than his canine partner Beasley. Fussy police detective Hanks is investigating the murder of the master of the massive, ugly creature with huge floppy jowls and a constantly drooling mouth.

3152.   *Turtle Diary* (1985, Goldwyn, GB, 97m, c). P Richard Johnson, D John Irvin, W Harold Pinter (based on a novel by Russell Hoban), PH Peter Hannan, M Geoffrey Burgon, ED Peter Tanner, PD Leo Austin.

LP Glenda Jackson (Neaera Duncan), Ben Kingsley (William Snow), Richard Johnson (Mr. Johnson), Michael Gambon (George Fairbairn), Rosemary Leach (Mrs. Inchcliff), Eleanor Bron (Miss Neap), Jeroen Krabbe (Sandor).

In this witty, eccentric comedy, writer-artist Glenda Jackson and bookstore clerk Ben Kingsley, both self-admitted "characters," take it upon themselves to release turtles from captivity in the London Zoo.

3153.   *Twice Dead* (1988, Concorde, 85m, c). P Guy J. Louthan & Robert McDonnell, D Bert Dragin, W Bert Dragin & Robert McDonnell, PH Zoran Hochstatter, M David Bergeaud, ED Patrick Rand, PD Stephan Rice.

LP Tom Breznahan (Scott), Jill Whitlow (Robin/Myrna), Jonathan Chapin (Crip/Tyler), Christopher Burgard (Silk), Sam Melville (Harry), Brooke Bundy (Sylvia), Todd Bridges (Petie), Shawn Player (Stony).

When an All-American family moves into a home that a street gang has been using for a clubhouse, the punks aren't happy and terrorize the family. A ghost in the home helps the family foil the gang.

3154.   *Twice in a Lifetime* (1985, Yorkin, 117m, c). P&D Bud Yorkin, W Colin Welland, PH Nick McLean, M Pat Metheny, ED Robert C. Jones & Catherine L. Peacock, PD William J. Creber.

LP Gene Hackman (Harry MacKenzie), Ann-Margret (Audrey Minelli), Ellen Burstyn (Kate MacKenzie), Amy Madigan† (Sunny Sobel), Ally Sheedy

(Helen MacKenzie), Brian Dennehy (Nick), Stephen Lang (Keith Sobel), Darrell Larson (Jerry MacKenzie), Chris Parker (Tim).

Gene Hackman turns fifty and decides to make a clean break with his family and start a new life with busty barmaid Ann-Margret. His self-sacrificing wife Ellen Burstyn puts aside her despair at being deserted to plan her daughter's wedding. It's just another midlife-crisis comedy drama with no new insights into the problem.

3155. *Twice Upon a Time* (1983, Warner, animated, 75m, c). P Bill Couturie, D John Korty & Charles Swenson, W Korty, Swenson, Suella Kennedy & Couturie (based on a story by Korty, Couturie & Kennedy), M Dawn Atkinson & Ken Melville, ED Jennifer Gallagher, AD Harley Jessup.

VOICES Lorenzo Music (Ralph), Judith Kahan Kampmann (Fairy Godmother), Marshall Elfron (Synonamess Botch), James Cranna (Rod Rescueman/Scuzzbopper), Julie Payne (Flora Fauna), Hamilton Camp (Greensleeves), Paul Frees (Narrator/Chief of Stage/Judge/Bailiff).

Using a pseudo-cutout style called "Lumage," this animated feature pits a silly bunch of would-be heroes against the evil bosses of Murkworks who wish to doom the world to perpetual darkness. Young kids aren't going to get it, older kids and adults probably won't care.

3156. *Twilight Zone – The Movie* (1983, Warner, 102m, c). P Steven Spielberg & John Landis, D&W Landis (Segment 1 & Prologue); D Spielberg, W George Clayton Johnson, Richard Matheson & Josh Rogan (Segment 2); D Joe Dante, W Matheson (based on a story by Jerome Bixby) (Segment 3); D George Miller, W Matheson (based on his story) (Segment 4) (All based on stories which appeared on Rod Serling's TV series "Twilight Zone"), PH Stevan Larner, Allen Daviau & John Hora, M Jerry Goldsmith, ED Malcolm Campbell, Michael Kahn, Tina Hirsch & Howard Smith, PD James D. Bissell.

LP Segment 1 and Prolog: Dan Aykroyd (Passenger), Albert Brooks (Driver), Vic Morrow (Bill), Doug McGrath (Larry), Charles Hallahan

(Ray); Segment 2: Scatman Crothers (Bloom), Bill Quinn (Conroy), Martin Garner (Weinstein), Selma Diamond (Mrs. Weinstein), Helen Shaw (Mrs. Dempsey), Murray Matheson (Agee); Segment 3: Kathleen Quinlan (Helen), Jeremy Licht (Anthony), Kevin McCarthy (Uncle Walt), Patricia Barry (Mother), William Schallert (Father); Segment 4: John Lithgow (Valentine), Abbe Lane (Senior Stewardess), Donna Dixon (Junior Stewardess), Larry Cedar (Creature).

In the only segment not based on an original episode of TV's "Twilight Zone," Vic Morrow portrays a big-mouthed bigot who is transported in time to Nazi-occupied France where he is a persecuted Jew, to the South as a black being tracked by the KKK, and then to Vietnam where he is a "gook" hunted by American soldiers. Tragically, Morrow and two Vietnamese children were killed in an accident during the making of this segment. In the second segment, based on "Kick the Can," Scatman Crothers arrives at a retirement home, where he gets the old folks to play a game of kick-the-can; they are transformed into youthful incarnations of themselves, but only briefly. In the third segment, based on the episode "It's a Good Life," Jeremy Licht is a little boy who has everyone in the house where he lives terrified of him because he is able to turn them into cartoon characters on TV. In the final segment, based on "Nightmare at 20,000 Feet," John Lithgow appears as a plane passenger deathly afraid of flying. His phobia causes him to see a menacing creature standing on the wing of the plane in flight. Of course no one else sees the creature – save the audience, that is.

3157. *Twinkle, Twinkle, "Killer" Kane* (1980, Warner, 105m, c, aka *The Ninth Configuration*). P,D&W William Peter Blatty (based on his novel), PH Gerry Fisher, M Barry DeVorzon, ED T. Battle Davis, Peter Lee Thompson & Roberto Silvi, PD Bill Malley & J. Dennis Washington.

LP Stacy Keach (Col. Kane), Scott Wilson (Capt. Cutshaw), Jason Miller (Lt. Reno), Ed Flanders (Col. Fell), Neville Brand (Groper), George DiCenzo

(Capt. Fairbanks), Moses Gunn (Maj. Nammack), Robert Loggia (Lt. Bennish), Joe Spinell (Spinell), Alejandro Rey (Lt. Gomez).

Stacy Keach, the new psychiatrist at a military mental institution, may be crazier than his patients.

3158.   *Twins* (1988, Universal, 112m, c). P&D Ivan Reitman, W William Davies, William Osborne, Timothy Harris & Herschel Weingrod, PH Andrzej Bartkowiak, M Georges Delerue & Randy Edelman, ED Sheldon Kahn & Donn Cambern, PD James D. Bissell.

LP Arnold Schwarzenegger (Julius Benedict), Danny DeVito (Vincent Benedict), Kelly Preston (Marnie Mason), Chloe Webb (Linda Mason), Bonnie Bartlett (Mary Ann Benedict), Marshall Bell (Webster), Trey Wilson (Beetroot McKinley), David Caruso (Al Greco), Hugh O'Brien (Granger), Nehemiah Persoff (Mitchell Traven).

Danny DeVito is a very droll little man. Arnold Schwarzenegger has a way to go before he can be considered intentionally funny. In this outlandish comedy, DeVito carries his musclebound partner, with the two playing twins, their difference the result of a genetic experiment. They are separated after birth, Arnie raised by a scientist, not only to be a perfect physical specimen, but a perfect man. DeVito is—well, DeVito, kicked out of his orphanage for corrupting a nun, grown to being a womanizing, thieving conman. Things get going when the two are reunited.

The Twisted Legend of Dr. Hunter S. Thompson see ***Where the Buffalo Roam***

3159.   *Twisted Nightmare* (1988, United Filmmakers, 94m, c). P Sandy Horowitz, D Paul Hunt, W Hunt, PH Hunt & Gary Graver, ED Allen Persselin, SE Cleve Hall.

LP Rhonda Gray (Laura), Cleve Hall, Brad Bartrum, Robert Padillo, Heather Sullivan, Scott King, Juliet Martin.

Seven young couples are murdered one-by-one at a secluded backwoods camp by an unseen killer. If it sounds like dozens of other slasher films—that's because it is.

3160.   *Twister* (1989, Vestron, 94m, c). P Wieland Schulz-Keil, D&W Michael Almereyda (based on the novel *Oh* by Mary Robison), PH Renato Berta, M Hans Zimmer, ED Roberto Silvi, PD David Wasco.

LP Harry Dean Stanton (Eugene Cleveland), Suzy Amis (Maureen Cleveland), Crispin Glover (Howdy Cleveland), Dylan McDermott (Chris), Jenny Wright (Stephanie), Charlaine Woodard (Lola), Lois Chiles (Virginia), William S. Burroughs (Man in Bar).

Retired soda pop tycoon Harry Dean Stanton presides over a fruitcake Kansas family consisting of his do-nothing daughter, Suzy Amis, his would-be-but-probably-never-will-be artist son, Crispin Glover, the latter's fiancé, Jenny Wright, an uppity black maid, Charlaine Woodard, and his own fiancée, Lois Chiles. Arriving just ahead of an impending twister is Amis' estranged husband Dylan McDermott, who for some weird reason would like to once more be part of this oddball group.

3161.   *Two for the Money* (1985, Bonner Films, 75m, c). P Mary Holland, D Lee Bonner, W Bonner & Leif Elsmo, PH David Insley, M John Palumbo, ED Bonner & Randy Aitken, PD Vincent Peranio.

LP Ronald Hunter (Walter), Sean Murphy (Betsy), Steve Beauchamp (Skipper), Peter Walker (Oliver), Hans Kramm (Bartender), Joseph Cimino, Art Donovan, Marcello Rollando & George Stover (Gangsters).

In this routine crime thriller Ronald Hunter is in trouble with the mob. It's pay up or be shut up, for good.

3162.   *Two Moon Junction* (1988, Lorimar, 104m, c). P Donald P. Borchers, D Zalman King, W King (based on a story by King & MacGregor Douglas), PH Mark Plummer, M Jonathan Elias, ED Marc Grossman, PD Michelle Minch.

LP Sherilyn Fenn (April Delongpre), Richard Tyson (Perry), Louise Fletcher (Belle), Kristy McNichol (Patti-Jean), Martin Hewitt (Chad Douglas Fairchild), Burl Ives (Sheriff Earl Hawkins), Juanita Moore (Delilah), Don Galloway (Senator Delongpre), Millie Perkins (Mrs. Delongpre), Herve Villechaize (Smiley).

In this softcore porn movie, wealthy engaged Southern girl Sherilyn Fenn gets an itch, which she scratches, to take off with Richard Tyson, a Conan-like hunk working with a carnival. Her grandma Louise Fletcher and sheriff Burl Ives conspire to ruin her fun. No one in this movie ever restrains themselves when it comes to sex. Clothes come off often in great sensual frenzies.

3163. *Two of a Kind* (1983, 20th Century–Fox, 87m, c). P Roger M. Rothstein & Joe Wizan, D&W John Herzfeld, PH Fred Koenekamp, M Patrick Williams, ED Jack Hofstra, PD Albert Brenner.

LP John Travolta (Zack), Olivia Newton-John (Debbie), Charles Durning (Charlie), Beatrice Straight (Ruth), Scatman Crothers (Earl), Castulo Guerra (Gonzales), Oliver Reed (Beazley), Richard Bright (Stuart).

Four angels propose to an angry God that the earth be spared from a second flood if two arbitrarily chosen human beings can be seen to perform a great sacrifice for each other. The makers of this film must have hoped that John Travolta and Olivia Newton-John would recapture some of the magic of *Grease*. They didn't and we could understand God's opening up the skies and letting the rain begin to fall, if the world depends on these two.

3164. *2010* (1984, MGM/United Artists, 114m, c). P,D&W Peter Hyams (based on the novel *2010: Odyssey Two* by Arthur C. Clarke), M David Shire, Richard Strauss & Gyorgi Ligeti, ED James Mitchell & Mia Goldman, PD Albert Brenner†, SD Rick Simpson†, COS Patricia Norris†, SOUND Michael J. Kohut, Aaron Rochin, Carlos de Larios & Gene S. Cantamessa†, VE Richard Edlund, Neil Krepela, George Jensen & Mark Stetson†, MK Michael Westmore†.

LP Roy Scheider (Heywood Floyd), John Lithgow (Walter Curnow), Helen Mirren (Tanya Kirbuk), Bob Balaban (R. Chandra), Keir Dullea (Dave Bowman), Douglas Rain (Voice of HAL 9000), Madolyn Smith (Caroline Floyd), Dana Elcar (Dimitri Moisevitch), Taliesin Jaffe (Christopher Floyd).

With Earth on the brink of war, the U.S. and the U.S.S.R. reluctantly join forces to reclaim the spaceship *Discovery* before its decaying orbit around Jupiter

causes it to crash on the planet. Scientists seek the meaning of the black monolith. It's a tame sequel to 2001, offering little in the way of story or spectacular special effects.

3165. *The Two Worlds of Angelita* (1983, First Run Features, 73m, c). P&D Jane Morrison, W Jose Manuel Torres Santiago, Rose Rosenblatt & Jane Morrison (based on the novel *Angelita* by Wendy Kesselman), PH Affonso Beato, M Dom Salvador, ED Suzanne Fenn, PD Randy Barcelo.

LP Marien Perez Riera (Angelita), Rosalba Rolon (Fela), Angel Domenech Soto (Chuito), Delia Esther Quinones (Dona Angela), Roberto Rivera Negron (Don Curro), Pedro Juan Texidor (Manolo), Idalia Perez Garay (Fortuna).

The problems of Puerto Rican families who have moved into the barrios of New York City are seen through the eyes of nine-year-old Marien Perez Riera.

3166. *Two Wrongs Make a Right* (1989, Paradigm, 83m, c). P Ivan Rogers, D Robert Brown, W Rogers, PH David Yosha, M Tony Byrne, ED Sheri J. Galloway, AD Yosha.

LP Ivan Rogers (Fletcher Quinn), Eva Wu (Jayna), Rick Komenich (Lake), R. Michael Pyle (Lt. Zander), Michael G. Rizk (Sgt. Vellosi), Ron Blackstone (Jack Balantine).

The film is a low-key blaxploitation film, starring Ivan Rogers as a nightclub owner whose club is shot up by gangsters when he refuses to sell. They also beat up his Asian-American girlfriend Eva Wu, making him extremely irritated and turning this mild-mannered man into a vigilante.

3167. *Uforia* (1985, Universal, 100m, c). P Gordon Wolf & Susan Spinks, D&W John Binder, PH David Myers, M Richard Baskin, ED Dennis M. Hill, PD Bill Malley.

LP Cindy Williams (Arlene), Harry Dean Stanton (Brother Bud), Fred Ward (Sheldon), Beverly Hope Atkinson (Naomi), Harry Carey, Jr. (George Martin), Diane Diefendorf (Delores), Robert Gray (Emile).

Filmed in 1981, this quirky little film is the story of born-again Christian Cindy

Williams who believes that salvation will come to earth in the form of a flying saucer. Crooked evangelist Harry Dean Stanton pumps all he can out of this notion.

3168. *UHF* (1989, Orion, 96m, c). P Gene Kirkwood & John Hyde, D Jay Levey, W Al Yankovic & Levey, PH David Lewis, M John Du Prez, ED Dennis O'Connor, PD Ward Preston.

LP Weird Al Yankovic (George Newman), Victoria Jackson (Teri), Kevin McCarthy (R.J. Fletcher), Michael Richards (Stanley Spadowski), David Bowie (Bob), Stanley Brock (Uncle Harvey), Anthony Geary (Philo), Trinidad Silva (Raul Hernandez), Gedde Watanabe (Kuni), Billy Barty (Noodles), Sue Ane Langdon (Aunt Esther).

That particular breed of musical madness fan—those who adore Weird Al Yankovic's music parodies—may find this movie a scream. Their hero inherits a dinky little TV station and makes it a success by appealing to the wackos in TV land. Even though Yankovic's dream sequences, in which he parodies some Steven Spielberg movies, are fun, the film just won't make it with most audiences.

3169. *The Ultimate Solution of Grace Quigley* (1984, MGM/UA/Cannon, 102m, c, aka *Grace Quigley*). P Menahem Golan & Yoram Globus, D Anthony Harvey, W A. Martin Zweiback, PH Larry Pizer, M John Addison, ED Robert Raetano, PD Gary Weist.

LP Katharine Hepburn (Grace Quigley), Nick Nolte (Seymour Flint), Elizabeth Wilson (Emily Watkins), Chip Zien (Dr. Herman), Kit Le Fever (Muriel), William Duell (Mr. Jenkins), Walter Abel (Homer).

Dotty old Katharine Hepburn convinces hit man Nick Nolte to kill off her elderly friends who don't want to live anymore. It's a tender little comedy, filled with love. But if you're one of the victims to be, don't change your mind.

The Umbrella Woman* see *The Good Wife

3170. *The Unbearable Lightness of Being* (1988, Orion, 171m, c). P Saul Zaentz, D Philip Kaufman, W Jean-Claude Carriere & Kaufman† (based on the novel by Milan Kundera), PH Sven Nykvist†, M Mark Adler, Keith Richards & Leos Janacek, ED Walter Murch, PD Pierre Guffroy.

LP Daniel Day-Lewis (Tomas), Juliette Binoche (Tereza), Lena Olin (Sabina), Derek de Lint (Franz), Erland Josephson (The Ambassador), Pavel Landovsky (Pavel), Donald Moffat (Chief Surgeon), Daniel Olbrychski (Interior Ministry Official), Stellan Skarsgard (The Engineer), Tomek Bork (Jiri), Bruce Myers (Czech Editor).

Director Philip Kaufman provides a fascinating production of Czech writer Milan Kundera's story of Daniel Day-Lewis, a free-spirited brain surgeon, who has romantic interludes with shy waitress Juliette Binoche and assertive Lena Olin. The complex saga of sex, love, and fidelity takes place in Prague in 1968, shortly after Soviet tanks invade the country to prevent deviation from communist unity. The mixture of sex and politics is extremely well-handled in this provocative but sometimes confusing film. It's a delight, as are the three leading performers.

3171. *The Unbelievable Truth* (1989, Action Features, 98m, c). P Bruce Weiss & Hal Hartley, D&W Hartley, PH Michael Spiller, M Jim Coleman, ED Hartley, PD Cara Gerona.

LP Adrienne Shelly (Audry Hugo), Robert Burke (Josh Hutton), Christopher Cooke (Victor Hugo), Julia McNeal (Pearl), Gary Sauer (Emmett), Mark Bailey (Mike), Katherine Mayfield (Liz).

Adrienne Shelly, a contrary 17-year-old sexpot, dumps her long-time boyfriend, passes on college, makes it big as a model in Manhattan, shacks up with a photographer and puts the make on Robert Burke, an ex-con who works as a mechanic in the small-town garage owned by her father. It's a full life.

3172. *Uncle Buck* (1989, Universal, 100m, c). P John Hughes & Tom Jacobson, D&W Hughes, PH Ralf D. Bode, M Ira Newborn, ED Lou Lombardo, Tony Lombardo & Peck Prior, PD John W. Corso.

LP John Candy (Buck Russell), Amy Madigan (Chanice Kobolowski), Jean Louisa Kelly (Tia Russell), Gaby Hoffman (Maizy Russell), Macaulay Culkin (Miles Russell), Elaine Bromka (Cindy Russell),

Garrett M. Brown (Bob Russell), Laurie Metcalf (Marcie), Jay Underwood (Bug).

John Candy is quite good portraying men who are strangely appealing despite numerous faults or defects. In this comedy he's a ne'er-do-well, uncouth, unwelcome member of the family, pressed into service to stay with three kids when their parents rush from suburban Chicago to be at the side of Elaine Bromka's father, who has suffered a heart attack, From this point on the film is a typical TV situation comedy, dealing rather poorly with the generation gap. The kids are mortified by Candy's coarse behavior and furious with his crude meddling in their affairs. We hope the very funny Mr. Candy will find better vehicles than those he was stuck with in 1989.

3173. *Uncle Scam* (1981, New World Pictures of Philadelphia, 105m, c). P&D Tom Pileggi & Michael Levanios, Jr., W Pileggi, Levanios, Jr., Tom Pilong & Joe Ryan, PH John Burke, M Michael Levanios, III, ED Levanios, Jr.

LP Tom McCarthy (Tom Ryan), Maxine Greene (Ginger), John Russell (Art), James E. Myers (Steve Vitali), Sharon Victoria (Linda), David Cassling (Herbie), Matt Myers (Governor Jones), Pat Cooper (Agency Chief).

Federal agents attempt to solicit bribes à la the Abscam scandal. They do but the cameras catch the feds in some extramarital activities. It was meant to be funny — we think.

3174. *Uncommon Valor* (1983, Paramount, 105m, c). P John Milius & Buzz Feitshans, D Ted Kotcheff, W Joe Gayton, PH Stephen H. Burum & Ric Waite, M James Horner, ED Mark Melnick, PD James L. Schoppe.

LP Gene Hackman (Col. Rhodes), Robert Stack (MacGregor), Fred Ward (Wilkes), Reb Brown (Blaster), Randall "Tex" Cobb (Sailor), Patrick Swayze (Scott), Harold Sylvester (Johnson), Tim Thomerson (Charts), Alice Lau [Lau Nga Lai] (Lai Fun), Kwan Hi Lim (Jiang).

Retired Colonel Gene Hackman goes to Vietnam to locate his son declared missing in action. There's about an even mix of suspense and clichés.

3175. *Under Cover* (1987, Cannon, 94m, c). P Menahem Golan & Yoram

Globus, D John Stockwell, W Stockwell & Scott Fields, PH Alexander Gruszynski, M Todd Rundgren, ED Sharyn L. Ross, PD Becky Block.

LP David Neidorf (Sheffield), Jennifer Jason Leigh (La Rue), Barry Corbin (Sgt. Irwin Lee), David Harris (Lucas), Kathleen Wilhoite (Corrine), Brad Leland (Drug Dealer).

Baltimore cop David Neidorf goes undercover in a South Carolina high school in order to organize a mass bust on kids using drugs.

3176. *Under Fire* (1983, Orion, 127m, c). P Jonathan Taplin, D Roger Spottiswoode, W Ron Shelton & Clayton Frohman (based on a story by Frohman), PH John Alcott, M Jerry Goldsmith†, ED John Bloom, AD Augustin Ytuarte & Toby Rafelson.

LP Nick Nolte (Russell Price), Ed Harris (Oates), Gene Hackman (Alex Grazier), Joanna Cassidy (Claire), Alma Martinez (Isela), Holly Palance (Journalist), Ella Laboriel (Nightclub Singer), Hamilton Camp (Regis Seydor), Jean-Louis Trintignant (Jazy), Richard Masur (Hub Kittle).

Journalists in Nicaragua become involved in the revolutionary cause when they encounter double-dealing in the political regime. This raises serious ethical concerns for them.

3177. *Under the Boardwalk* (1988, New World, 104m, c, aka *Wipeout*). P Steven H. Chanin & Gregory S. Blackwell, D Fritz Kiersch, W Robert King (based on a story by Matthew Irmas & King), PH Don Burgess, M David Kitay, ED Daniel Gross, PD Maxine Shepard.

LP Keith Coogan (Andy), Danielle Von Zerneck (Allie), Richard Joseph Paul (Nick Rainwood), Roxana Zal (Gitch).

Two teenagers from different backgrounds find romance and love amidst the world of surfing.

3178. *Under the Cherry Moon* (1986, Warner, 98m, c). P Robert Cavallo, Joseph Ruffalo & Steven Fargnoli, D Prince, W Becky Johnston, PH Michael Ballhaus, M Prince, ED Eva Gardos, PD Richard Sylbert.

LP Prince (Christopher Tracy), Jerome Benton (Tricky), Kristin Scott Thomas (Mary Sharon), Steven Berkoff

(Mr. Sharon), Emmanuelle Sallet (Katy), Alexandra Stewart (Mrs. Sharon), Francesca Annis (Mrs. Wellington).

In this vanity piece, Prince portrays an American gigolo/entertainer in the south of France who women find irresistible.

3179.   Under the Gun (1989, Marquis Picture, 89m, c). P Warren Stein, D James Sbardellati, W Almer John Davis, James Devney & Sbardellati (based on Devney's story), PH Gary Thieltges, M Edna Sterling, ED George Copanas, PD James Shumaker.

LP Sam Jones (Mike Braxton), Vanessa Williams (Samantha Richards), John Russell (Stone), Michael Halsey (Frank), Nick Cassavetes (Tony), Steven Williams (Gallagher), Bill McKinney (Miller).

Dethroned Miss America Vanessa Williams makes her film debut as the lawyer of plutonium thief John Russell. His henchmen have killed St. Louis cop Sam Jones' brother Nick Cassavetes. Jones wants revenge and Williams has the information which can put Russell away for good.

3180.   Under the Rainbow (1981, Warner, 98m, c). P Fred Bauer, D Steve Rash, W Pat McCormick, Harry Hurwitz, Martin Smith, Pat Bradley & Bauer (based on a story by Bradley & Bauer), PH Frank Stanley, M Joe Renzetti, ED David Blewitt, PD Peter Wooley.

LP Chevy Chase (Bruce Thorpe), Carrie Fisher (Annie Clark), Billy Barty (Otto Kriegling), Eve Arden (Duchess), Joseph Maher (Duke), Robert Donner (Assassin), Mako (Nakamura), Cork Hubbert (Rollo Sweet), Pat McCormick (Tiny), Adam Arkin (Henry Hudson), Richard Stahl (Lester).

Set in 1938, this is purported to be the story of the hundreds of midgets brought to Hollywood to appear in *The Wizard of Oz*. The film concentrates on their destructive, drunken carousing at the hotel where they are staying. It's all done in extremely bad taste.

3181.   Under the Volcano (1984, Universal, 112m, c). P Moritz Borman & Wieland Schulz-Keil, D John Huston, W Guy Gallo (based on the novel by Malcolm Lowry), PH Gabriel Figueroa, M Alex North†, ED Roberto Silvi, PD Gunther Gerzso.

LP Albert Finney† (Geoffrey Firmin), Jacqueline Bisset (Yvonne Firmin), Anthony Andrews (Hugh Firmin), Ignacio Lopez Tarso (Dr. Vigil), Katy Jurado (Senora Gregoria), James Villiers (Brit), Dawson Bray (Quincey), Carlos Riquelme (Bustamante), Jim McCarthy (Gringo).

Set in 1938, the film is a superb production of Malcolm Lowry's masterpiece about the last day in the life of alcoholic ex-consul Albert Finney in Mexico. Finney's alcoholism, aggravated by his wife Jacqueline Bisset's infidelity with his half-brother Anthony Andrews, is the device used to liken his descent into a personal hell with the self-destruction taking place in the world at the time.

3182.   The   Underachievers (1988, PMS/Lightning, 90m, c). P&D Jackie Kong, W Kong, Tony Rosato & Gary Thompson (based on a story by Rosato), PH Chuck Colwell, M Don Preston, ED Tom Meshelski, PD Jay Burkhardt.

LP Edward Albert (Danny Warren), Barbara Carrera (Katherine), Michael Pataki (Murphy), Susan Tyrrell (Mrs. Grant), Mark Blankfield (Kline), Garrett Morris (Dummont), Vic Tayback (Coach), Jesse Aragon (Carlos).

This tepid comedy is set in a night school, where various society rejects gather.

3183.   Underground Aces (1981, Filmways, 95m, c). P Jay Weston, D Robert Butler, W Jim Carabatsos, Lenore Wright & Andrew Peter Marin, PH Tom Del Ruth, M Pete Rugolo, ED Argyle Nelson.

LP Dirk Benedict (Huff), Melanie Griffith (Lucy), Robert Hegyes (Tico), Jerry Orbach (Penlitter), Frank Gorshin (Kruger), Rick Podell (Joe), Randi Brooks (Ollie), T.K. Carter (DeeJay), Joshua Daniel (Wally).

A group of parking attendants at a large hotel amuse themselves with sex, carousing and wrecking the vehicles of the guests.

3184.   Underground   Terror (1989, SVS Film, 90m, c). P Steven Mackler, D James McCalmont, W Robert Zimmerman & Brian O'Hara (based on O'Hara's story), PH Anghel Deca, M Taj, ED Keith Reamer, PD Mikhail Fishgoyt.

LP Doc Dougherty (John Willis), Lennie Loftin (Boris), B.J. Geordan (Kim Knowles), Ric Siler (Weasel), Joe Bachana, James Davies, Alan L. Rickman.

A ruthless gang lives in the subway, preying on unsuspecting travelers.

3185. *Underground U.S.A.* (1980, New Cinema, 85m, c). P Eric Mitchell & Erdner Rauschalle, D&W Mitchell, PH Tom DiCillo, M Various Artists, ED J.P. Roland-Levy.

LP Patti Astor (Vickie), Eric Mitchell (Hustler), Rene Ricard (Kenneth), Tom Wright (Frank), Jackie Curtis (Roommate), Cookie Mueller, Taylor Mead, Duncan Smith, Steve Mass.

Hustler Eric Mitchell takes up with Patti Astor, a film star whose career is almost all behind her. The film gives audiences a peek at the underground art scene.

3186. *The Understudy: Graveyard Shift II* (1989, Cinema Ventures, 88m, c). P Stephen R. Flaks & Arnold H. Bruce, D&W Gerard Ciccoritti, PH Barry Stone, M Philip Stern, ED Neil Grieve, PD Ciccoritti.

LP Wendy Gazelle (Camilla/Patti), Mark Soper (Matthew), Silvio Oliviero (Baissez), Ilse Von Glatz (Ash), Tim Kelleher (Duke/Larry).

Real vampire Silvio Oliviero takes the place of an actor who is to appear as a vampire in a movie.

3187. *Underworld* (1985, Limehouse Pictures, GB, 100m, c). P Kevin Attew, Don Hawkins & Graham Ford, D George Pavlou, W Clive Barker & James Caplin, PH Sydney Macartney, M Freur, ED Chris Ridsdale.

LP Denholm Elliott (Dr. Savary), Steven Berkoff (Hugo Motherskille), Larry Lamb (Roy Bain), Miranda Richardson (Oriel), Art Malik (Fluke), Nicola Cowper (Nicole), Ingrid Pitt (Pepperdine), Irina Brook (Bianca).

Mad scientist Denholm Elliott develops a serum which allows a user to experience his or her fantasies in real life. The catch is that there's an aftereffect which horribly disfigures the users, forcing them to hide underground.

3188. *Uneasy Silence* (1989, Full Circle, 90m, c). P Wanda Rohm & Robert Rothman, D John Strysik, W Rothman & Strysik, PH Michael Goi, M Elliott Delman, ED Strysik, PD Thomas B. Mitchell.

LP Robert Rothman (Sam), Kathleen Sykora (Sarah), Michael Bacarella (Astro), Carolyn Kodes (Terry Quinn), Charles Gerace (T.J.).

Robert Rothman and Kathleen Sykora are not very believable as Chicago vagrants trying to eke out an existence, in this downbeat movie.

3189. *Unfaithfully Yours* (1984, 20th Century–Fox, 96m, c). P Marvin Worth & Joe Wizan, D Howard Zieff, W Valerie Curtin, Barry Levinson & Robert Klane (based on the screenplay by Preston Sturges), PH David M. Walsh, M Bill Conti, Tchaikovsky violin concerto, ED Sheldon Kahn, PD Albert Brenner.

LP Dudley Moore (Claude Eastman), Nastassja Kinski (Daniella Eastman), Armand Assante (Maxmillian Stein), Albert Brooks (Norman Robbins), Cassie Yates (Carla Robbins), Richard Libertini (Giuseppe), Richard B. Shull (Jess Keller), Jan Triska (Jerzy Czyrek).

This a modernized version of Preston Sturges' 1948 film, which starred Rex Harrison as an orchestral conductor who believes his wife is being unfaithful. While he's conducting he imagines three different ways of dealing with the situation. In the remake, conductor Dudley Moore wrongly believes wife Nastassja Kinski is having an affair with guest violinist Armand Assante. The little actor imagines a perfect scheme to have his revenge, but it goes awry when he tries to put his plan into practice.

3190. *Unfinished Business* (1985, Unfinished Business Pty., Australia, 78m, c). P Rebel Penfold-Russell, D&W Bob Ellis, PH Andrew Lesnie, ED Amanda Robson, PD Jane Johnston.

LP John Clayton (Geoff), Michele Fawdon (Maureen), Norman Kaye (George), Bob Ellis (Geoff's Flatmate), Andrew Lesnie (Telegraph Boy).

After leaving his wife and three children in the U.S., John Clayton returns to Australia, where he encounters old flame Michele Fawdon. She's now married but unfulfilled because she has no children. She suggests that Clayton impregnate her. He's delighted, but the process isn't all the fun he was hoping for.

3191. *Unfinished Business* (1987, American Film Institute, 65m, c). P Dale Ann Stieber, Chrisann Verges & Suzanne Kent, D&W Viveca Lindfors, PH Sean McLin, M Patricia Lee Stotter, Don Rebic & Matt Sullivan, ED Dale Ann Stieber & Sharyn G. Blumenthal, PD Johanna Leovey.

LP Viveca Lindfors (Helena), Peter Donat (Ferenzy), Gina Hecht (Vickie), James Morrison (Jonathan), Anna Devere Smith (Anna), Haley Taylor-Block (Kristina), Herriett Guiar (Cynthia).

Actress Viveca Lindfors is preparing to appear in a production of "Brecht on Brecht." Her former lover Peter Donat, who left her 15 years earlier, resurfaces in her life, dragging along his mistress. He'd like to get back with Lindfors, and by the end of the film this seems as certain as that the film is dull.

Unforgettable see Chances Are

3192. *The Unholy* (1988, Vestron, 100m, c). P Mathew Hayden, D Camilo Vila, W Philip Yordan & Fernando Fonseca, PH Henry Vargas, M Roger Bellon, ED Mark Melnick, PD Fonseca.

LP Ben Cross (Father Michael), Ned Beatty (Lt. Stern), Jill Carroll (Millie), William Russ (Luke), Hal Holbrook (Archbishop Mosely), Trevor Howard (Father Silva), Peter Frechette (Claude), Claudia Robinson (Teresa Montez), Nicole Fortier (Demon).

In this confusing horror nonsense, Ben Cross is a priest who has mysteriously survived a fall. He's assigned to a parish in New Orleans where he unravels the mystery of the death of two priests who previously prayed before the altar of the church. He must resist beautiful naked redheaded demon Nicole Fortier, who attempts to seduce him.

3193. *The Uninvited* (1988, Heritage, 89m, c). P,D&W Greydon Clark, PH Nicholas Von Sternberg, M Dan Slider, ED Travis Clark, PD Peter Paul Raubertas.

LP George Kennedy (Mike Harvey), Alex Cord (Walter Graham), Clu Gulager (Albert), Toni Hudson (Rachel), Eric Larson (Martin), Clare Carey (Bobbie), Rob Estes (Corey), Shari Shattuck (Suzanne).

The "uninvited" in this film is a cat that shows up now and then, spits out a puppet head which gnaws people to death, and disappears. All of this takes place on dishonest Alex Cord's yacht, skippered by Toni Hudson. Along for the ride are guests Clare Carey and Shari Shattuck, and three guys that they invited along for a trip to Bimini.

3194. *Union City* (1980, Kinesis, 87m, c). P Graham Belin, D&W Mark Reichert (based on the short story "The Corpse Next Door" by Cornell Woolrich), PH Edward Lachman, M Chris Stein, ED Eric Albertson, Lana Tokel & J. Michaels, AD George Stavrinos.

LP Dennis Lipscomb (Harlan), Deborah Harry (Lillian), Irina Maleeva (Contessa), Everett McGill (Larry Longacre), Sam McMurray (Young Vagrant), Terina Lewis (Evelyn), Pat Benatar (Jeanette).

In this gloomy film, Deborah Harry, the lead singer with the defunct New Wave band Blondie, is a mousy-looking brunette married to neurotic Dennis Lipscomb. His obsession is to trap vagrant Sam McMurray, who steals a drink of milk out of a bottle delivered to Lipscomb's door each day. Things escalate into madness and murder.

3195. *The Unnamable* (1988, Yankee Classic, 87m, c). P Dean Ramser & Jean-Paul Ouellette, D&W Ouellette (based on a story by H.P. Lovecraft), PH Tom Fraser, M David Bergeaud, ED Wendy J. Plump, PD Gene Abel.

LP Charles King (Howard Damon), Mark Kinsey Stephenson (Randolph Carter), Alexandra Durrell (Tanya), Laura Albert (Wendy), Katrin Alexandre (Alyda Winthrop), Eben Ham (Bruce), Blane Wheatley (John Babcock), Mark Parra (Joel Manton).

This direct-to-video horror film takes place in a small college town where two young couples spend the night in an ancient mansion. The 17th century owner, a warlock, was horribly murdered by a creature that he kept chained in the attic. Well, it's still there.

3196. *Unni* (1989, Malabar, 113m, c). P Kitty Morgan & Bill Rothman, D G.

Aravindan, W Rothman & Morgan, PH Sunny Joseph, M Aravindan, ED Beena Venugopal, AD Aravindan.

LP Tara Johannessen (Tara), Gijie Abraham (Unni), Sethu (Sethu), Elizabeth Anthony (Mary), Vivian Colodro (Maggie), Bill Swotes (Bill).

This meandering film follows the adventures of American student Tara Johannessen in Kerala, a section of southern India.

3197. *An Unremarkable Life* (1989, SVS/Continental, 92m, c). P&D Amin Q. Chaudhri, W Marcia Dinneen, PH Alan Hall, M Avery Sharpe, ED Sandi Gerling, PD Norman B. Dodge, Jr.

LP Patricia Neal (Frances McEllany), Shelley Winters (Evelyn), Mako (Max Chin), Rochelle Oliver, Charles Dutton, Lily Knight, Jenny Chrisinger.

Patricia Neal and Shelley Winters portray two aging sisters who share a household and live with their memories. When Neal takes up with Mako, a happy Asian auto mechanic, Winters, who doesn't care for foreigners, makes her opinions known. It's a rather drab movie about drab, unremarkable lives, but the leads Neal and Winters give solid performances.

3198. *The Unseen* (1981, World Northal, 89m, c). P Anthony Unger & Don P. Behrns, D Peter Foleg, W Michael L. Grace, PH Roberto Quezada, Irv Goodnoff & James Carter, M Michael J. Lewis, ED Jonathan Braun, AD Dena Roth, SE Harry Woolman.

LP Barbara Bach (Jennifer), Sidney Lassick (Ernest Keller), Stephen Furst (Junior), Lelia Goldoni (Virginia Keller), Karen Lamm (Karen), Doug Barr (Tony), Lois Young (Vicki).

When three female reporters are forced to take lodging in a private home because all the hotels are completely booked during a festival they are covering, they find that their host is not what he seems. In addition there is living in the cellar a monster who gets out to torment them.

3199. *An Unsuitable Job for a Woman* (1985, Castle Hill, GB, 90m, c). P Michael Relph & Peter McKay, D Christopher Petit, W Elizabeth McKay, Brian Scobie & Petit (based on the novel by

P.D. James), PH Martin Schafer, M Chaz Jankel, Philip Bagenal & Peter Van-Hooke, ED Mick Audsley.

LP Billie Whitelaw (Elizabeth Leaming), Paul Freeman (James Calender), Pippa Guard (Cordelia Gray), Dominic Guard (Andrew Lunn), Elizabeth Spriggs (Miss Markland), David Horovitch (Sgt. Maskell), Dawn Archibald (Isobel).

Twenty-three year old novice detective Pippa Guard is hired to investigate the apparent suicide of a wealthy young man. She becomes obsessed with him, living in his cottage, wearing his clothes and speaking to him using tape recordings.

3200. *Until September* (1984, MGM/ United Artists, 95m, c). P Michael Gruskoff, D Richard Marquand, W Janice Lee Graham, PH Philippe Welt, M John Barry, ED Sean Barton, PD Hilton McConnico.

LP Karen Allen (Mo Alexander), Thierry Lhermitte (Xavier De La Perouse), Christopher Cazenove (Philip), Hutton Cobb (Andrew), Michael Mellinger (Col. Viola), Nitza Saul (Sylvia), Rochelle Robertson (Carol).

Stranded in Paris, American Karen Allen meets and falls in love with married banker Thierry Lhermitte. She accepts his suggestion that they be lovers until summer is over. It's a little hard to believe that she'd buy the arrangement, particularly since his attitude and behavior doesn't mark him as Mr. Wonderful.

3201. *The Untouchables* (1987, Paramount, 119m, c). P Art Linson, D Brian DePalma, W David Mamet, PH Stephen H. Burum, M Ennio Morricone†, ED Jerry Greenberg & Bill Pankow, AD William A. Elliott, Patrizia Von Brandenstein†, SD Hal Gausman†, COS Marilyn Vance-Straker†.

LP Kevin Costner (Eliot Ness), Sean Connery* (James Malone), Charles Martin Smith (Oscar Wallace), Andy Garcia (George Stone), Robert De Niro (Al Capone), Richard Bradford (Mike), Jack Kehoe (Walter Payne), Brad Sullivan (George), Billy Drago (Frank Nitti), Patricia Clarkson (Catherine Ness).

Kevin Costner is the naive, incorruptible T-man, brought into Chicago to find some means of putting away notorious Al

Capone. With the help of Sean Connery as a tough Irish cop, marksman Andy Garcia and tax expert Charles Martin Smith, the Untouchables are able to send Scarface to prison for tax evasion. The film has plenty of bloodshed and killings for those seeking that kind of action, but it is the relationship between Connery as grizzled mentor and the unemotional Costner that makes the film special.

3202. *Up the Academy* (1980, Warner, 88m, c, aka *Mad Magazine's Up the Academy; The Brave Young Men of Weinberg*). P Marvin Worth & Danton Rissner, D Robert Downey, W Tom Patchett & Jay Tarses, PH Harry Stradling, Jr., M Jody Taylor Worth, ED Bud Molin, PD Peter Wooley.

LP Ron Leibman (Major), Wendell Brown (Ike), Tom Citera (Hash), J. Hutchinson (Oliver), Ralph Macchio (Chooch), Harry Teinowitz (Ververgaert), Tom Poston (Sisson), Ian Wolfe (Commandant Caseway), Stacey Nelkin (Candy), Barbara Bach (Bliss).

In this tasteless teenage sexual comedy, Ron Leibman runs the Sheldon R. Weinberg Military Academy with an iron fist. But four new students lay waste timeless traditions and enrage their talentless teachers. The film was sponsored by *Mad* magazine, but even they have disowned it.

3203. *Up the Creek* (1984, Orion, 95m, c). P Michael L. Metzer & Fred Baum, D Robert Butler, W Jim Kouf (based on a story by Kouf, Jeff Sherman & Douglas Grossman), PH James Glennon, M William Goldstein, ED Bill Butler, PD William M. Hiney.

LP Tim Matheson (Bob McGraw), Jennifer Runyon (Heather Merriweather), Stephen Furst (Gonzer), Dan Monahan (Max), Sandy Helberg (Irwin), Jeff East (Rex), Blaine Novak (Braverman), James B. Sikking (Tozer).

The boys from Lepetomane University (named after a performer in turn-of-the-century French theaters whose specialty was passing gas in rhythm at various pitches), are off to a raft-race. It's a vulgar, scatological, violent but funny film.

3204. *Up Your Alley* (1989, Unknown Film Co., 88m, c). P Murray Langston, D Bob Logan, W Langston & Logan, PH

Mark Melville, M Paul Ventimiglia, ED Tom Siiter.

LP Linda Blair (Vickie Adderly), Murray Langston (David), Bob Zany (Sonny), Ruth Buzzi (Marilyn), Johnny Dark (Nick), Jack Hanrahan (Joe), Glen Vincent (Lance), Melissa Shear (Pauline).

Unknown comic Murray Langston is responsible for this stinker, presenting the story of street people, who, as if they didn't have enough to contend with, are being knocked off by some madman.

3205. *Uphill All the Way* (1986, New World, 86m, c). P Burr Smidt & David L. Ford, D&W Frank Q. Dobbs, PH Roland Smith, M Dennis M. Pratt, ED Chuck Weiss, PD Hal Matheny.

LP Roy Clark (Ben), Mel Tillis (Booger Skaggs), Burl Ives (Sheriff), Glen Campbell (Capt. Hazleton), Trish Van Devere (Widow Quinn), Richard Paul (Dillman), Burt Reynolds (Poker Player), Elaine Joyce (Jesse), Jacque Lynn Colton (Lucinda).

Country singers Roy Clark and Mel Tillis portray inept robbers in the old West in a film filled with cameo appearances and pitifully short on laughs.

The Upstate Murders see Savage Weekends

3206. *Urban Cowboy* (1980, Paramount, 135m, c). P Robert Evans & Irving Azoff, D James Bridges, W Bridges & Aaron Latham (based on a story by Latham), PH Ray Villalobos, M Ralph Burns, ED Dave Rawlins, PD Stephen Grimes.

LP John Travolta (Bud), Debra Winger (Sissy), Scott Glenn (Wes), Madolyn Smith (Pam), Barry Corbin (Uncle Bob), Brooke Alderson (Aunt Corene), Cooper Huckabee (Marshall), James Gammon (Steve Strange).

Texas oil-field worker John Travolta seeks love and adventure in Gilley's country and western bar, which features a mechanical bull to ride. He falls for Debra Winger, but their romance goes sour once they are married. Dumb blond hussy Madolyn Smith separates Travolta from Winger. She takes up with rat Scott Glenn. Travolta and Winger get together again, but it really doesn't matter for those who have had enough of the bull in this film, mechanical or otherwise.

3207. *Used Cars* (1980, Columbia, 113m, c). P Bob Gale, D Robert Zemeckis, W Zemeckis & Gale, PH Donald M. Morgan, M Patrick Williams, ED Michael Kahn, PD Peter M. Jamison.

LP Kurt Russell (Rudy Russo), Jack Warden (Roy L. Fuchs/Luke Fuchs), Gerrit Graham (Jeff), Frank McRae (Jim), Deborah Harmon (Barbara Fuchs), Joseph P. Flaherty (Sam Slaton), David L. Lander (Freddie Paris), Michael McKean (Eddie Winslow).

Jack Warden portrays two brothers with competing used car lots. Kurt Russell is the head salesman, for the less successful lot. He and his partner Gerrit Graham will try any scam to sell a car.

3208. *Utilities* (1983, New World, Canada, 91m, c, aka *Getting Even*). P Robert Cooper, D Harvey Hart, W David Greenwalt & M. James Kouf, Jr., PH Richard Leiterman, M John Erbe & Mickey Solomon, ED John Kelly, PD Bill Boeton.

LP Robert Hays (Bob), Brooke Adams (Marion), John Marley (Roy), James Blendick (Kenneth), Ben Gordon (Eddie), Jane Mallet (Dr. Rogers), Toby Tarnow (Gilda), Helen Burns (Ruby), Lee Broker (Jack).

Crusading social worker Robert Hays teams up with beautiful lady cop Brooke Adams to take on a local utilities company.

3209. *Utu* (1984, Glitteron, New Zealand, 104m, c). P Geoff Murphy & Don Blakeney, D Murphy, W Murphy & Keith Aberdein, PH Graeme Cowley, M John Charles, ED Michael Horton & Ian John, PD Ron Highfield.

LP Anzac Wallace (Te Wheke), Bruno Lawrence (Williamson), Kelly Johnson (Lt. Scott), Wi Kuki Kaa (Wiremu), Tim Elliot (Col. Elliot), Ilona Rodgers (Emily), Tania Bristowe (Kura), Martyn Sanderson (Vicar).

In a New Zealand "western," in 1870 the Maoris seek retribution after the colonials have squeezed them off their land.

3210. *The Vacant Lot* (1989, Picture Plant, Canada, 100m, c). P Terry Greenlaw, D&W William D. MacGillivray, PH Lionel Simmons, ED Angela Baker & MacGillivray, AD Angela Murphy.

LP Trudi Petersen (Trudi), Grant Fullerton (David), Barbara Nicholson, Rick Mercer, Caitlyn Colquhoun, Cheryl Reid, Tara Wilde.

"The Vacant Lot" is the name of a female punk rock band, featuring Trudi Petersen as the rhythm guitarist. She takes up with Grant Fullerton, an older ex-guitar great of the 60s. He joins the band when Petersen breaks her arm in a car accident. They go on a mini road trip — but nothing very interesting happens.

3211. *Valentino Returns* (1989, Skouras, 88m, c). P Peter Hoffman & David Wisnievitz, D Hoffman, W Leonard Gardner (based on his story "Christ Has Returned to Earth and Preaches Here Nightly"), PH Jerzy Zielinski, ED Denine Rowan, AD Woody Romine.

LP Barry Tubb (Wayne Gibbs), Frederic Forrest (Sonny Gibbs), Veronica Cartwright (Patricia Gibbs), Jenny Wright (Sylvia), David Packer (Count Messner), Seth Isler (Harry Ames), Miguel Ferrer (The Biker), Kit McDonough (Ruth Fuller).

In this bit of Americana, small-town teen Barry Tubb's rites of passage in the 50s are not smooth. We follow one important night in his life when everything goes wrong.

3212. *Valet Girls* (1987, Lexyn/Empire, 82m, c). P Dennis Murphy, D Rafal Zielinski, W Clark Carlton, PH Nicholas Von Sternberg, M Robert Parr, ED Akiko B. Metz, AD Dins Danielsen.

LP Meri D. Marshall (Lucy), April Stewart (Rosalind), Mary Kohnert (Carnation), Christopher Weeks (Dirk Zebra), Patricia Scott Michel (Tina Zebra), John Sharp (Lindsay Brawnsworth), Michael Karm (Alvin Sunday).

Three shapely, enterprising girls put themselves through school running a parking service. Their uniforms on the job include high heels, hot pants and not much else.

3213. *Valley Girl* (1983, Atlantic, 95m, c). P Wayne Crawford & Andrew Lane, D Martha Coolidge, W Crawford & Lane, PH Frederick Elmes, M Scott Wilk & Marc Levinthal, ED Eva Gardos, PD Mary Delia Javier.

LP Nicolas Cage (Randy), Deborah Foreman (Julie Richman), Elizabeth Daily (Loryn), Michael Bowen (Tommy), Cameron Dye (Fred), Heidi Holicker (Stacey), Michelle Meyrink (Suzie), Tina Theberge (Samantha), Lee Purcell (Beth Brent), Colleen Camp (Sarah Richman), Frederic Forrest (Steve Richman).

This is the Romeo and Juliet tale of Valley Girl (i.e., L.A. valley as in the Frank & Moon Zappa hit song) Deborah Foreman and Hollywood punker Nicolas Cage. Her friends try to get her back with an old flame, while his pals crash Valley parties to cause trouble. Director Martha Coolidge deserves praise for giving audiences a cute film about clashing cultures, even though few viewers can identify with either of them.

3214. Valmont (1989, Orion, 134m, c). P Paul Rassam & Michael Hausman, D Milos Forman, W Jean-Claude Carrière (based on the novel *Les Liaisons Dangereuses* by Choderlos de Laclos), PH Miroslav Ondricek, M Christopher Palmer, ED Alan Heim & Nena Danevic, PD Pierre Guffroy, COS Theodor Pistek†.

LP Colin Firth (Valmont), Annette Bening (Mme. de Merteuil), Meg Tilly (Mme. de Tourvel), Fairuza Balk (Cecile), Sian Phillips (Mme. de Volanges), Fabia Drake (Mme. de Rosemonde), Jeffrey Jones (Gercourt), Henry Thomas (Danceny), T.P. McKenna (Baron).

This adaptation of the familiar story of sex and love used as weapons to gain power over others is at a disadvantage in following Stephen Frear's very popular version, *Dangerous Liaisons,* by only a year. Yet it is a lovely production with a beautiful performance by Annette Bening which easily rivals that of Glenn Close in the 1988 film. Colin Firth as the title character and Meg Tilly as his virtuous conquest are less compelling than John Malkovich and Michelle Pfeiffer. Young Fairuza Balk as 15-year-old Cecile is different in every way than Uma Thurman, but no less impressive.

3215. The Vals (1985, Sundowner, 100m, c). P&D James Polakof, W Polakof & Deborah Amelon (based on a story by Polakof), PH G.W. "Dink" Read, M Daphne Edwards, ED Millie Paul.

LP Jill Carroll (Samantha), Elena Stratheros (Trish), Michelle Laurita (Beth), Gina Calabrase (Annie), Chuck Connors (Trish's Father), Tiffany Bolling (Samantha's Mother), Sue Ane Langdon (TV Star), Sonny Bono (Spaced-out Guest), John Carradine (Mr. Stanton).

Scheduled for a 1983 release to take advantage of the popularity of California's "Valley Girls," popularized by Frank and Moon Zappa in 1982, instead this loser sat on the shelf for a couple of years until it was decided that it might make back some of its cost from videocassettes. The Vals of the title are four teen girls trying to save an orphanage by conning the needed funds from drug dealers.

3216. Vamp (1986, New World, 93m, c). P Donald P. Borchers, D&W Richard Wenk (based on a story by Borchers & Wenk), PH Elliot Davis, M Jonathan Elias, ED Marc Grossman, PD Alan Roderick-Jones.

LP Chris Makepeace (Keith), Sandy Baron (Vic), Robert Rusler (A.J.), Dedee Pfeiffer (Amaretto), Gedde Watanabe (Duncan), Grace Jones (Katrina), Billy Drago (Snow), Brad Logan (Vlad), Lisa Lyon (Cimmaron).

In order to be taken into a college fraternity, Chris Makepeace and Robert Rusler must arrange for a stripper to appear at the frat's big party. Together with weirdo Gedde Watanabe, the boys make their way to the After Dark Club where they engage Grace Jones for the job, unaware that she is a bloodsucking vampire.

3217. Vamping (1984, Atlantic, 107m, c). P Howard Kling & Stratton Rawson, D Frederick King Keller, W Michael Healy & Robert Seidman (based on a story by Keller), PH Skip Roessel, M Ken Kaufman, ED Darren Kloomok, PD Kling, Karen Morse & Rawson.

LP Patrick Duffy (Harry Baranski), Catherine Hyland (Diane Anderson), Rod Arrants (Raymond O'Brien), Fred A. Keller (Fat Man), David Booze (Benjamin), Jed Cooper (Lennie), Steve Gilborn (Jimmy).

Down-on-his-luck saxophonist Patrick Duffy moonlights as a burglar to raise money. He falls for one of his victims.

3218. Vampire at Midnight (1988, Skouras, 93m, c). P Jason Williams & Tom Friedman, D Gregory McClatchy,

W Dulhany Ross Clements (based on a story by Williams & Friedman), PH Daniel Yarussi, M Robert Etoll, ED Kaye Davis.

LP Jason Williams (Det. Roger Stutter), Gustav Vintas (Victor Radkoff), Lesley Milne (Jenny Carlon), Jeanie Moore (Amalia), Esther Alise (Lucia), Ted Hamaguchi (Capt. Takato), Robert Random (Childress).

Police detective Jason Williams is on the trail of a fiendishly clever serial killer who may be a vampire.

3219. *Vampire's Kiss* (1989, Hemdale, 105m, c). P Barbara Zitwer & Barry Shils, D Robert Bierman, W Joseph Minion, PH Stefan Czapsky, M Colin Towns, ED Angus Newton, PD Christopher Nowak.

LP Nicolas Cage (Peter Loew), Maria Conchita Alonso (Alva Restrepo), Jennifer Beals (Rachel), Elizabeth Ashley (Dr. Glaser), Kasi Lemmons (Jackie), Bob Lujan (Emilio), Jessica Lundy (Sharon).

Literary agent Nicolas Cage is fearful of romantic commitments. When he does find the perfect woman, Jennifer Beals, she's a vampire. Once again Cage demonstrates his limitations as an actor.

3220. *Variety* (1984, Horizon, 100m, c). P Renee Schafransky & Bette Gordon, W Kathy Acker (based on a story by Gordon), PH Tom Di Cillo & John Foster, M John Lurie, ED Ila Von Hasperg.

LP Sandy McLeod (Christine), Will Patton (Mark), Richard Davidson (Louie), Luis Guzman (Jose), Nan Goldin (Nan), Lee Tucker (Projectionist), Peter Rizzo (Driver).

Despite an initial aversion to porno films, Sandy McLeod, a ticket-taker at the Variety, one of the oldest theaters in New York, and now a triple-X rated movie theater, becomes fascinated with the patrons. She follows one around after working hours. The message about women, pornography and power that the independent filmmakers are trying to make is garbled.

3221. *Vasectomy: A Delicate Matter* (1986, Vandom International, 90m, c). P Robert Burge & Lou Wills, D Burge, W Robert Hilliard & Burge, PH Gary Thieltges, M Fred Karlin, ED Beth Conwell.

LP Paul Sorvino (Gino), Cassandra Edwards (Anna), Abe Vigoda (Detective Edwards), Ina Balin (Regine), Lorne Greene (Theo Marshall), June Wilkinson, William Marshall.

This comedy about a man whose wife wishes him to have the title operation is about as funny as a knee in the groin.

3222. *Vendetta* (1986, Concorde, 88m, c). P Jeff Begun, Ken Solomon & Ken Dalton, D Bruce Logan, ED Glenn Morgan, W Emil Farkas, Simon Maskell, Laura Cavestani & John Adams, PH Robert New, M David Newman, AD Chris Clarens.

LP Sandy Martin (Kay), Kin Shriner (Steve Nelson), Greg Bradford (Joe-Bob), Holly Butler (Movie Star), Karen Chase (Laurie), Lisa Clarson (Bobo), Roberta Collins (Miss Dice), Pilar Delano (Inmate), Eugene Rogert Glazer (David Greene).

Stuntwoman Karen Chase deliberately commits crimes which will get her sent to the same prison where her younger sister was killed by a prison gang, so she may take vengeance.

Vengeance: The Demon see Pumpkinhead

3223. *Venom* (1982, Paramount, GB, 93m, c). P Martin Bregman, D Piers Haggard, W Robert Carrington (based on the novel by Alan Scholefield), PH Gilbert Taylor & Denys Coop, M Michael Kamen, ED Michael Bradsell, SE Alan Whibley & Richard Dean.

LP Klaus Kinski (Jacmel), Oliver Reed (Dave), Nicol Williamson (Cmdr. William Bulloch), Sarah Miles (Dr. Marion Stowe), Sterling Hayden (Howard Anderson), Corelia Sharpe (Ruth Hopkins), Mike Gwilym (Det. Constable Dan Spencer), Lance Holcomb (Philip Hopkins).

A big game hunter and his asthmatic grandson are held for ransom in a house where a black mamba, one of the most deadly of snakes, is loose.

3224. *Venus Peter* (1989, Atlantic, GB, 92m, c). P Christopher Young, D Ian Sellar, W Sellar & Christopher Rush, PH Gabriel Beristain, M Jonathan Dove, ED David Spiers, PD Andy Harris.

LP George R. Strachan (Peter), Ray McAnally (Grandfather), David Hayman (Kinnear), Sinead Cusack (Miss Balsilbie), Caroline Paterson (Peter's Mother),

Peter Caffrey (Peter's Father), Alex Mc-Avoy (Beadle), Emma Dingwall (Jenny).

Set in the windswept Orkney Islands north of Scotland, the film is the story of young George R. Strachan who lives with his mother and grandfather. His father is missing. The boy likes to imagine he's a ship's captain. Things in this family film slowly reach a moving climax after the father, who had grown tired of living on the island, returns.

3225.   *The Verdict*† (1982, 20th Century–Fox, 129m, c). P Richard D. Zanuck & David Brown, D Sidney Lumet†, W David Mamet† (based on the novel by Barry Reed), PH Andrzej Bartkowiak, M Johnny Mandel, ED Peter Frank, PD Edward Pisoni.

LP Paul Newman† (Frank Galvin), Charlotte Rampling (Laura Fischer), Jack Warden (Mickey Morrissey), James Mason† (Ed Concannon), Milo O'Shea (Judge Hoyle), Lindsay Crouse (Kaitlin Costello Price), Edward Binns (Bishop Brophy), Julie Bovasso (Maureen Rooney), Roxanne Hart (Sally Doneghy), James Handy (Kevin Doneghy).

Aging, alcoholic attorney Paul Newman is unexpectedly given a case of medical malpractice and successfully sues a hospital. It's an interesting examination of legal and medical ethics, with Newman giving another of his first rate performances, as does James Mason.

3226.   *Verne Miller* (1988, Three Aces/Alive, 95m, c). P Ann Broke Ashley, D&W Ron Hewitt, PH Misha Suslov, M Tom Chase & Steve Rucker, ED John O'Connor, PD Victoria Paul.

LP Scott Glenn (Verne Miller), Barbara Stock (Vi Miles), Thomas G. Waites (Al Capone), Lucinda Jenney (Bobby), Sonny Carl Davis (Frank "Baldy" Nash), Diane Salinger (Mortician's wife), Ed O'Ross (Ralph Capone), Vyto Rugins (Fitzsimmons), Andrew Robinson (Pretty Boy Floyd), Joseph Carberry (Hymie Ross).

Former lawman Scott Glenn has two talents, killing and bedding any woman he wants. He develops his skills in both areas, then moves to Chicago to offer half of his services to Al Capone. He's given several assignments to "hit" opponents of the South Side mob chief, but ultimately finds a contract has been put out on him when he becomes too ambitious. Don't wonder why you missed this film. It's so poorly done, it went directly to video.

3227.   *Vibes* (1988, Columbia, 99m, c). P Deborah Blum & Tony Ganz, D Ken Kwapis, W Lowell Ganz (based on a story by Blum, Lowell Ganz & Babaloo Mandel), PH John Bailey, M James Horner, ED Carol Littleton, PD Richard Sawyer.

LP Cyndi Lauper (Sylvia Pickel), Jeff Goldblum (Nick Deezy), Julian Sands (Dr. Harrison Steele), Googy Gress (Ingo Swedlin), Peter Falk (Harry Buscafusco), Michael Lerner (Burt Wilder), Ramon Bieri (Eli Diamond), Elizabeth Pena (Consuela).

In her feature film debut, psychic Cyndi Lauper joins psychometric (one who can tell an object's history merely by touching it) Jeff Goldblum and conman Peter Falk to seek a lost city of gold in Ecuador.

3228.   *Vice Squad* (1982, Avco Embassy/Hemdale, 97m, c). P Brian Frankish, D Gary A. Sherman, W Sandy Howard, Kenneth Peters & Robert Vincent O'Neil, PH John Alcott, M Keith Rubinstein, ED Roy Watts, PD Lee G. Fischer.

LP Season Hubley (Princess), Gary Swanson (Tom Walsh), Joseph DiGiroloma (Kowalski), Wings Hauser (Ramrod), Pepe Serna (Pete Mendez), Beverly Todd (Louise Williams), Maurice Emmanuel (Edwards).

It's the sleazy story of L.A.'s underbelly, featuring a whore helping the police capture a vicious wire-hanger–wielding pimp.

3229.   *Vice Versa* (1988, Columbia, 98m, c). P Dick Clement & Ian La Frenais, D Brian Gilbert, W Clement & La Frenais, PH King Baggot, M David Shire, ED David Garfield, PD Jim Schoppe.

LP Judge Reinhold (Marshall Seymour), Fred Savage (Charlie Seymour), Corinne Bohrer (Sam), Swoosie Kurtz (Tina), David Proval (Turk), Jane Kaczmarek (Robyn), Gloria Gifford (Marcie), William Prince (Avery).

The device of a preadolescent boy or a teen exchanging bodies with an adult has been overworked recently and this entry is the least effective. Overworked businessman Judge Reinhold and his neglected son Fred Savage develop a greater respect for each other after spending some time in the other's world and body.

3230. *Vicious* (1988, SVS, Australia, 88m, c). P David Hannay & Charles Hannah, D Karl Zwicky, W Paul J. Hogan & Zwicky (based on an original idea by Hogan), PH John Stokes, M Robert Scott & John Sleith, ED Roy Mason.

LP Tambly Lord (Damon Kennedy), Craig Pearce (Terry), Tiffiny Dowe (Sondra Price), John Godden (Felix), Kelly Dingwall (Benny), Leather (Claire), Joanna Lockwood (Diane Kennedy), Frank McNamara (Gerry).

In a terrible exploitation film, Tambly Lord is a rich youngster who becomes a ruthless killer after falling in with a trio of juvenile delinquents.

3231. *Victor/Victoria* (1982, MGM/United Artists, GB, 133m, c). P Blake Edwards & Tony Adams, D Edwards, W Edwards† (based on the film *Viktor und Viktoria* by Rheinhold Schuenzel & Hans Hoemburg), PH Dick Bush, M Henry Mancini, ED Ralph E. Winters, PD Rodger Maus, AD Maus, Tim Hutchinson & William Craig Smith†, SD Harry Cordwell†, COS Patricia Norris†, M/L Mancini & Leslie Bricusse*.

LP Julie Andrews† (Victor/Victoria), James Garner (King), Robert Preston† (Toddy), Lesley Ann Warren† (Norma), Alex Karras (Squash), John Rhys-Davies (Cassell), Graham Stark (Waiter), Peter Arne (Labisse), SherloqueTanney(Bovin).

This delightful sex-farce did not become the box-office success it deserved to be. Set in Paris during the Depression, British singer Julie Andrews and aging homosexual performer Robert Preston both have hit rock bottom. Things start to turn around when Preston convinces Andrews to pose as a female impersonator singer-dancer. She becomes the toast of the town. Entering the picture is James Garner, a Chicago gangster, travelling with his cheap blonde mistress Lesley Ann Warren and his bodyguard Alex Karras. He is attracted to Andrews, suspecting she really is a woman. When he discovers that he is right, he must go along with the masquerade because of her career. Now everyone believes that he's gay, something he's discovered is true of Karras. It all

works out in the end. Preston and Warren are excellent in their roles, as is Graham Stark as a waiter who has seen it all.

3232. *Victory* (1981, Paramount, 117m, c, aka *Escape to Victory*). P Freddie Fields, D John Huston, W Evan Jones & Yabo Yablonsky (based on a story by Yablonsky, Djordje Milicevic & Jeff Maguire, PH Gerry Fisher, M Bill Conti, ED Roberto Silvi, PD J. Dennis Washington.

LP Sylvester Stallone (Robert Hatch), Michael Caine (John Colby), Pele (Luís Fernández), Bobby Moore (Terry Brady), Osvaldo Ardiles (Carlos Rey), Paul Van Himst (Michel Fileu), Kazimierz Deyna (Paul Wolchek), Hallvar Thorensen (Gunnar Hilsson), Max von Sydow (Maj. Karl Von Steiner).

Various international soccer stars including Pele appear in this routine prisoner-of-war film with a sports connection. Both the Germans and the prisoners have their own reasons for wanting a soccer match between a team of "all-star" prisoners and the German National Team. The Germans see it as a public relations opportunity and the prisoners plan to use it as a chance to escape.

3233. *The Video Dead* (1987, Interstate 5-Highlight, 90m, c). P,D&W Robert Scott, PH Greg Becker, M Stuart Rabinowitsk, Kevin McMahon & Leonard Marcel, ED Bob Sarles, PD Katalin Rogers, SE Dale Hall, Jr.

LP Roxanna Augeson (Zoe Blair), Rocky Duvall (Jeff Blair), Michael St. Michaels (Henry Jordan), Al Millan (Taxi Driver), Sam David McClelland (Joshua Daniels), Jennifer Miro (The Woman), Libby Russler (Maria).

An old TV set gets only one channel, which plays the same horror film over and over. The set also releases zombies and evil monsters to do their damnedest on a quiet tree-lined street.

Video Madness see Joysticks

3234. *Videodrome* (1983, Unviersal, Canada, 88m, c). P Claude Heroux, D&W David Cronenberg, PH Mark Irwin, M Howard Shore, ED Ronald Sanders, PD Carol Spier.

LP James Woods (Max Renn), Sonja Smits (Bianca O'Blivion), Deborah Harry (Nicki Brand), Peter Dvorsky (Harlan),

Les Carlson (Barry Convex), Jack Creley (Prof. Brian O'Blivion), Lynne Gorman (Masha).

Ambitious cable TV programmer James Woods schedules programs with soft-porn and S&M content whose signals he has pirated from satellite disks. When he tries to find out where the programs come from, he discovers he has bitten off more than he can chew.

3235. *A View to a Kill* (1985, MGM/ United Artists, GB, 131m, c). P Albert R. Broccoli & Michael G. Wilson, D John Glen, W Richard Maibaum & Wilson (based on characters created by Ian Fleming), PH Alan Hume, M John Barry, ED Peter Davies, PD Peter Lamont.

LP Roger Moore (James Bond), Christopher Walken (Max Zorin), Tanya Roberts (Stacey Sutton), Grace Jones (May Day), Patrick Macnee (Tibbett), Patrick Bauchau (Scarpine), David Yip (Chuck Lee), Fiona Fullerton (Pola Ivanova), Manning Redwood (Bob Conley).

In what we trust will be Roger Moore's last venture as 007, he is teamed with lovely Tanya Roberts, a woman who moves so fluidly but acts so woodenly. Their adversary is mean-spirited Christopher Walken, who seems to be playing the role in his sleep. The latter's "right-hand man" is Grace Jones, who chews up the scenery to a fair-thee-well. But as Bond cannot be resisted by any woman, she gives her life in the end to save our hero when Walken has found it prudent to sacrifice her so he may escape.

3236. *Vigil* (1984, Enterprise, New Zealand, 90m, c). P John Maynard, D Vincent Ward, W Ward & Graeme Tetley, PH Alun Bollinger, M Jack Body, ED Simon Reece, PD Kai Hawkins.

LP Penelope Stewart (Elizabeth), Frank Whitten (Ethan), Bill Kerr (Birdie), Fiona Kay (Toss), Gordon Shields, Arthur Sutton, Snow Turner.

The film is seen through the eyes of 11-year-old Fiona Kay, who must learn to deal with the death of her father as well as the new man in her mother's life and hers.

3237. *Vigilante* (1983, Film Ventures, 90m, c, aka *Street Gang*). P Andrew Garroni & William Lustig, D Lustig, W Richard Vetere, PH James Lemmo, M

Jay Chattaway, ED Lorenzo Marinelli, PD Mischa Petrow.

LP Robert Forster (Eddie), Fred Williamson (Nick), Richard Bright (Burke), Rutanya Alda (Vickie), Don Blakely (Prago), Joseph Carberry (Ramon), Willie Colon (Rico), Joe Spinell (Eisenberg), Carol Lynley (D.A. Fletcher), Woody Strode (Rake).

Factory worker Robert Forster resists joining the vigilante group put together by Fred Williamson and others until a Puerto Rican gang victimizes his family, killing his son. When the leader of the gang goes free because of a corrupt judicial system, Forster joins Williamson's group and the bloodletting begins.

3238. *Vincent — The Life and Death of Vincent Van Gogh* (1988, Australia, 103m, c). P Tony Llewellyn-Jones, D,W,PH&ED Paul Cox (based on the letters of Vincent Van Gogh), M Norman Kaye, PD Neil Angwin.

VOICE John Hurt.

John Hurt reads the letters of Vincent Van Gogh to his brother Theo, providing the only text of this tribute to the passionate painter by Australian director Paul Cox, who visualizes the world of trees, sunflowers, sky and fields as he imagines Van Gogh saw them.

Vindicator see Desert Warrior

Violent Streets see Thief

3239. *Violent Zone* (1989, Arista Films, 90m, c). P&D John Garwood, W John Bushelman & Daved Pritchard, PH Roger Estrada, M Mark Josephson & Malcolm Cecil, ED Steve Bushelman.

LP John Jay Douglas (Steve Ryker), Christopher Weeks (Charles Townsend), Chard Hayward (Norman McKloskey), Cynthia Killion (Linda Blomberg), Daved Pritchard (Rick O'Brien), Michael Myracle (Doris).

In this direct-to-video movie, John Jay Douglas is recruited for a special mission 43 years after he fought the Japanese on Kao Teng Island. He will return to the island with a team he trains to rescue Christopher Weeks' son who has been held captive by the communists since 1974.

3240. *Violets Are Blue* (1986, Columbia, 90m, c). P Marykay Powell, D Jack Fisk, W Naomi Foner, PH Ralf Bode, M Patrick Williams, ED Edward Warschilka, PD Peter Jamison, M/L "One Day" by Williams & Will Jennings (sung by Laura Brannigan).

LP Sissy Spacek (Gussie Sawyer), Kevin Kline (Henry Squires), Bonnie Bedelia (Ruth Squires), John Kellogg (Ralph Sawyer), Jim Standiford (Addy Squires), Augusta Dabney (Ethel Sawyer), Kate McGregor-Stewart (Sara Mae), Adrian Sparks (George), Annalee Jefferies (Sally).

During high school, dreamers Sissy Spacek and Kevin Kline were lovers. He stayed home, taking over the family newspaper, and marrying local girl Bonnie Bedelia. She became a world-traveling photojournalist. When she returns home for R&R, the spark is still there as they team up for a news exposé.

3241. *The Violins Came with the Americans* (1987, Sun and Moon Prods., 94m, c). P David Greene, D Kevin Conway, W M. Quiros, Mila Burnette, PH Benjamin Davis, M Fred Weinberg, ED John Tintori.

LP Mila Burnette (Annie Adams), Joaquim de Almeida (David Garcia), Jose Ferrer (Don Fulhencio), Maria Norman, Kevin Conway, Norma Candal.

Disenchanted with her marriage, Mila Burnette leaves Manhattan for the South Bronx. There she falls in love with Puerto Rican lawyer Joaquim de Almeida and helps him organize the tenants of a tenement to force their absent landlord to make improvements.

3242. *Viper* (1988, Fries Distribution, 94m, c). P&D Peter Maris, W Frank Kerr, PH Gerald Wolfe, M Scott Roewe, ED Jack Tucker.

LP Linda Purl (Laura McCalla), James Tolkan (Col. Tanzer), Jeff Kober (Richard Gelb), Ken Force (Harley Trueblood), Chris Robinson (Jim McCalla), David M. Sterling (Powell), Charles Hoyes (Broadnax).

CIA agents kill members of the administration of a university, blaming it on Middle Eastern terrorists. The government then has justification for taking military action against an Arab nation. It takes the widow of an assassinated operative to unravel the circumstances surrounding her husband's death and expose the plot.

3243. *The Virgin Queen of St. Francis High* (1987, Crown International, Canada, 94m, c). D&W Francesco Lucente, PH Joseph Bitoni & Kevin Alexander, M Danny Lowe, Brad Steckel & Brian Island, ED Lucente.

LP Joseph R. Straface (Mike), Stacy Christensen (Diane), J.T. Wotton (Charles), Anna-Lisa Iapaolo (Judy), Lee Barringer (Randy), Bev Wotton (Diane's Mother).

Nicknamed "Snow White" because she's saving herself for marriage, Stacy Christensen, the prettiest, most virginal girl at St. Francis High, is the dream girl of nerdish Joseph R. Straface. Obnoxious Lee Barringer taunts Straface into accepting a bet that he can bet Christensen to go with him to the local lover's lane. He does but they don't have sex. Instead they become friends.

3244. *Vision Quest* (1985, Warner, 107m, c). P Jon Peters & Peter Guber, D Harold Becker, W Darryl Ponicsan (based on the novel by Terry Davis), PH Owen Roizman, M Tangerine Dream, ED Maury Winetrobe, PD Bill Malley.

LP Matthew Modine (Louden Swain), Linda Fiorentino (Carla), Michael Schoeffling (Kuch), Ronny Cox (Louden's Dad), Harold Sylvester (Tanneran), Charles Hallahan (Coach), J.C. Quinn (Elmo), Daphne Zuniga (Margie Epstein), R.H. Thompson (Kevin).

Wanting to compete against the city's best wrestler, high school athlete Matthew Modine goes on a starvation diet to get himself down from 190 to 168 pounds so he can be matched with the champ.

3245. *Visiting Hours* (1982, 20th Century-Fox, Canada, 105m, c, aka *The Fright; Get Well Soon*). P Claude Heroux, D Jean Claude Lord, W Brian Taggert, PH Rene Verzier, M Jonathan Goldsmith, ED Lord & Lise Thouin.

LP Michael Ironside (Colt Hawker), Lee Grant (Deborah Ballin), Linda Purl (Sheila Munroe), William Shatner (Gary Baylor), Lenore Zann (Lisa), Harvey Atkin (Vinnie Bradshaw), Helen Hughes (Louise Shepherd), Michael J. Reynolds (Porter Halstrom).

In another of the many slasher movies, a killer stalks the corridors of a major medical center.

3246. *Volunteers* (1985, Tri-Star, 106m, c). P Richard Shepherd & Walter F. Parkes, D Nicholas Meyer, W Ken Levine & David Isaacs (based on a story by Keith Critchlow), PH Ric Waite & Jack Green, M James Horner, ED Ronald Roose & Steven Polivka, PD James L. Schoppe.

LP Tom Hanks (Lawrence Bourne, III), John Candy (Tom Tuttle from Tacoma), Rita Wilson (Beth Wexler), Tim Thomerson (John Reynolds), Gedde Watanabe (At Toon), George Plimpton (Lawrence Bourne, Jr.), Ernest Harada (Chung Mee).

Faced with elimination by gangsters when his father won't bail him out from his gambling debts, filthy-rich Ivy League graduate Tom Hanks trades his convertible for a friend's seat on a plane to Bangkok where he is to work in the Peace Corps (Hanks is forced to throw in his fiancée as well). If you think that Thailand and the experience of helping others will change him, making him more humble, think again.

3247. *Vortex* (1982, B Movies, 90m, c). D&W Scott B., Beth B., PH Steven Fierberg, M Adele Bertei, Richard Edson, Lydia Lunch, Scott B. & Beth B., ED Scott B. & Beth B.

LP James Russo (Anthony Demmer), Lydia Lunch (Angel Powers), Bill Rice (Frederick Fields), Ann Magnuson (Pamela Fleming), Brent Collins (Peter), Bill Corsair (John Allen), Tom Webber (Ron Gavers).

Detective Lydia Lunch becomes involved in corporate wars and the manipulation of politicians by companies seeking defense contracts.

3248. *Voyage of the Rock Aliens* (1988, Inter Planetary Curb, 95m, c). P Micheline H. Keller & Brian Russell, D James Fargo & Bob Giraldi, W S. James Guidotti, Edward Gold & Charles Hairston, PH Gil Taylor & Dante Spinotti, M Jack White, ED Billy Williams & Malcolm Campbell, PD Ninkey Dalton.

LP Pia Zadora (Dee Dee), Tom Nolan (Abed), Craig Sheffer (Frankie), Alison LaPiaca (Diane), Michael Berryman (Chainsaw), Ruth Gordon (Sheriff), Jermaine Jackson (Rain).

This stupid spoof combines the worst elements of science fiction, musicals and beach party movies. Alien Tom Nolan and his rock band search the universe for signs of intelligent life—which is recognized as any world which plays rock music.

3249. *Wacko* (1983, Jensen Farley, 84m, c). P&D Greydon Clark, W Dana Olsen, Michael Spound, M. James Kouf, Jr. & David Greenwalt, PH Nicholas von Sternberg, M Arthur Kempel, ED Earl Watson & Curtis Burch.

LP Joe Don Baker (Harbinger), Stella Stevens (Marg Graves), George Kennedy (Dr. Graves), Julia Duffy (Mary Graves), Scott McGinnis (Norman), Andrew Clay (Tony), Elizabeth Daily (Bambi), Michele Tobin (Rosie).

Greydon Clark, struggling to maintain his reputation as among the worst directors presently working, gives audiences an *Airplane*-like parody of slasher movies; they want to give it back.

3250. *Wagner* (1983, London Trust Cultural, GB/Hung./Austria, 300m, c). P Alan Wright, D Tony Palmer, W Charlie Wood, PH Vittorio Storaro, M Richard Wagner, ED Graham Bunn, PD Kenneth Carey.

LP Richard Burton (Richard Wagner), Vanessa Redgrave (Cosima Wagner), Gemma Craven (Minna), Laszlo Galffi (King Ludwig II of Bavaria), John Gielgud (Pfistermeister), Ralph Richardson (Pfordten), Laurence Olivier (Pfeufer), Ekkerhard Schall (Franz Liszt), Ronald Pickup (Friedrich Nietzsche), Miguel Herz-Kestranek (Hans von Bulow).

Originally filmed to run nine hours, this epic movie biography of the great German composer attempts to touch on every important event in his life. This being the case, nothing is presented in a satisfactory manner. The photography is excellent and the supporting cast impressive, but as a whole, it disappoints.

3251. *Wait Until Spring, Bandini* (1989, Orion Classics, Bel./Fr./Ital./US, 100m, c). P Erwin Provoost, Tom Luddy & Fred Roos, D Dominique Deruddere, W Deruddere (based on a novel by John Fante), PH Jean-Francois Robin, M Angelo Badalamenti, ED Ludo Troch, PD Robert Ziembicki.

LP Joe Mantegna (Svevo Bandini), Ornella Muti (Maria Bandini), Faye Dunaway (Mrs. Effi Hildegarde), Michael Bacall (Arturo Bandini), Burt Young (Rocco Saccone), Tanya Lopert (Sister Celia).

The film features a family of Italian immigrants in Colorado in 1925. Bricklayer Joe Mantegna wastes his money in pool halls before becoming a handyman in more ways than one for wealthy widow Faye Dunaway. He moves in with her, leaving his wife Ornella Muti and family to fend for themselves. His 12-year-old son Michael Bacall is finally able to bring his parents back together.

3252. *Waiting for the Moon* (1987, Skouras, 88m, c). P Sandra Schulberg, D Jill Godmilow, W Mark Magill (based on a story by Godmilow & Magill), PH Andre Neau, M Michael Sahl, ED Georges Klotz, PD Patrice Mercier.

LP Linda Hunt (Alice B. Toklas), Linda Bassett (Gertrude Stein), Bernadette Lafont (Fernande Olivier), Bruce McGill (Ernest Hemingway), Jacques Boudet (Guillaume Apollinaire), Andrew McCarthy (Henry Hopper).

This witty biography explores the 39-year relationship of Alice B. Toklas and American writer Gertrude Stein.

3253. *Waitress* (1982, Troma, 88m, c, aka *Soup to Nuts*). P Lloyd Kaufman & Michael Herz, D Samuel Weil & Herz, W Michael Stone & Charles Kaufman, PH L. Kaufman, ED Dan Lowenthal, AD Barry Shapiro.

LP Carol Drake (Andrea), Jim Harris (Jerry), Carol Bevar (Jennifer), Renata Majer (Lindsey), David Hunt (Bill), Anthony Sarrero (Moe), Ed Fenton (Mr. Bellerman), Augie Grompone (Piebalt), Bonnie Horan (Mrs. Bellerman).

There isn't much of a plot to the story of three women working as waitresses in a New York restaurant, hoping for something better in their lives.

3254. *Walk Like a Man* (1987, MGM/United Artists, 86m, c). P Leonard Kroll, D Melvin Frank, W Robert Klane, PH Victor J. Kemper, M Lee Holdridge, ED Bill Butler & Steve Butler, PD Bill Malley.

LP Howie Mandel (Bobo Shand), Christopher Lloyd (Reggie Henry), Cloris Leachman (Margaret Shand), Colleen Camp (Rhonda Shand), Amy Steel (Penny).

Weird stand-up comedian Howie Mandel portrays a young man separated from his family as an infant and raised in the wilderness by a pack of wolves. When this innocent rejoins his family, he finds that two-legged wolves are far more dangerous.

3255. *A Walk on the Moon* (1987, Benenson-Midwest, 95m, c). P Diane Silver, D Raphael Silver, W William B. Mai, PH Adam Greenberg, M Paul Chihara, ED Peter Frank, PD Holger Gross.

LP Kevin Anderson (Everett Jones), Terry Kinney (Lew Ellis), Laila Robins (Marty Ellis), Patrice Martinez (India), Pedro Armendariz, Jr. (Doctor), Roberto Sosa (Candy).

At the time of the Vietnam war, after the death of Bobby Kennedy and Martin Luther King, new Peace Corpsman Kevin Anderson, assigned to a village in Colombia, still has his idealism. Not so for the married couple Terry Kinney and Laila Robins, whose two year stint and marriage are both about finished. Before long, Anderson has a nervous breakdown, the village is almost destroyed by a torrential downpour and Kinney and Robins renew their love.

3256. *Walker* (1987, Universal, 95m, c). P Lorenzo O'Brien & Angel Flores Marini, D Alex Cox, W Rudy Wurlitzer, PH David Bridges, M Joe Strummer, ED Carlos Puente Ortega & Cox, PD Bruno Rubeo.

LP Ed Harris (William Walker), Richard Masur (Ephraim Squier), Rene Auberjonois (Maj. Siegried Henningson), Keith Szarabajka (Timothy Crocker), John Diehl (Stebbins), Peter Boyle (Commodore Cornelius Vanderbilt), Marlee Matlin (Ellen Martin), Alfonso Arau (Raousset), Pedro Armendariz, Jr. (Munoz).

In what is meant to be a farcical parable of the current U.S. policy in Latin America, Ed Harris portrays the 19th century American soldier-of-fortune who declares himself president of Nicaragua. Marlee Matlin, as Harris' militant deaf girlfriend, dies early in the movie, but the film dies even earlier.

3257. Walking the Edge (1985, Empire, 93m, c). P Sergei Goncharoff, D Norbert Meisel, W Curt Allen, PH Ernie Poulos, M Jay Chattaway, ED Warren Chadwick, AD Dena Roth.

LP Robert Forster (Jason Walk), Nancy Kwan (Christine), Joe Spinell (Brusstar), A. Martinez (Tony), Aarika Wells (Julia), Wayne Woodson (McKee), James McIntire (Jimmy), Russ Courtney (Leon).

Unhappy cabdriver Robert Forster innocently becomes involved with guntoting Nancy Kwan's plans to blow away Joe Spinell, the man who killed her husband and son.

3258. Wall Street (1987, 20th Century-Fox, 124m, c). P Edward R. Pressman & A. Kitman Ho, D Oliver Stone, W Stone & Stanley Weiser, PH Robert Richardson, M Stewart Copeland, ED Claire Simpson, PD Stephen Hendrickson.

LP Charlie Sheen (Bud Fox), Michael Douglas* (Gordon Gekko), Martin Sheen (Carl Fox), Terence Stamp (Sir Larry Wildman), Sean Young (Kate Gekko), Daryl Hannah (Darien Taylor), Sylvia Miles (Realtor), James Spader (Roger Barnes), Hal Holbrook (Lou Mannheim), Saul Rubinek (Harold Salt).

Michael Douglas and Charlie Sheen star in an effective morality tale about movers and shakers in a world of stocks and bonds. Douglas manipulates companies and people, but produces nothing except money. Douglas argues that greed is good and young Sheen buys the whole spiel, despite warnings from his hardworking father Martin Sheen and decent stockbroker Hal Holbrook. In the end Charlie goes to jail for his insider dealings, taking Douglas with him, but the "crime doesn't pay" ending seems out of place in a day and age where on the contrary it seems quite lucrative.

3259. Walter and June (1986, Film Forum, GB, 110m, c, aka *Loving Walter*). P Richard Creasey, D Stephen Frears, W David Cook (based on his book *Winter Doves*), PH Chris Menges, M George Fenton, ED Mick Audsley, AD Michael Minas.

LP Ian McKellen (Walter), Sarah Miles (June), Barbara Jefford, Arthur Whybrow.

Ian McKellan is excellent as an unloved mentally retarded man. His bleak existence is briefly interrupted when mentally ill Sarah Miles seduces him.

3260. Waltz Across Texas (1982, Atlantic, 99m, c). P Martin Jurow & Scott Rosenfelt, D Ernest Day, W Bill Svanoe (based on a story by Terry Jastrow & Anne Archer), PH Robert Elswit, M Steve Dorff, ED Jay Lash Cassidy, PD Michael Erler.

LP Anne Archer (Gail Weston), Terry Jastrow (John Taylor), Noah Beery, Jr. (Joe Locker), Mary Kay Place (Kit Peabody), Josh Taylor (Luke Jarvis), Richard Farnsworth (Frank Walker), Ben Piazza (Bill Wrather).

Husband and wife team Anne Archer and Terry Jastrow try to resurrect the romantic comedies of the 30s with this story of two people whose mutual dislike for each other turns to love when they join a quest to discover oil in West Texas. Unfortunately the resurrection doesn't take.

3261. Wanted: Dead or Alive (1987, New World, 104m, c). P Robert C. Peters, D Gary Sherman, W Michael Patrick Goodman, Brian Taggert & Sherman, PH Alex Nepomniaschy, M Joseph Renzetti, ED Ross Albert, PD Paul Eads.

LP Rutger Hauer (Nick Randall), Gene Simmons (Malak Al Rahim), Robert Guillaume (Philmore Walker), Mel Harris (Terry), William Russ (Danny Quintz), Susan McDonald (Louise Quintz), Jerry Hardin (John Lipton).

Former CIA career agent Rutger Hauer is a sort of modern-day bounty hunter, collecting society's scum for very good prices. But the tables are turned when an FBI-CIA conspiracy uses him as bait, with the quarry an international terrorist.

3262. War (1988, Troma, 99m, c). P Lloyd Kaufman & Michael Herz, D Herz & Samuel Weil, W Mitchell Dana, Eric Hattler, Thomas Martinek & Kaufman (based on a story by Kaufman), PH James London, M Christopher De Marco, SE William Jennings & Pericles Lewnes.

LP Carolyn Beauchamp (Lydia), Sean Bowen (Taylor), Michael Ryder (Parker), Patrick Weathers (Kirkland), Jessica

Dublin (Dottie), Steven Crossley (Marshall), Charles Kay Hune (Hardwick), Lorayn Lane DeLuca (Maria).

A planeload of New Jersey residents crashland on a remote tropical island overrun with terrorists plotting attacks on the U.S. The survivors band together to frustrate the terrorists' plans.

3263. War and Love (1985, Cannon, 112m, c). P Jack P. Eisner, D Moshe Mizrahi, W Abby Mann (based on the book *The Survivor* by Eisner), PH Adam Greenberg, M Gustav Mahler, ED Peter Zinner.

LP Sebastian Keneas (Jacek), Kyra Sedgwick (Halina), David Spielberg (Aron), Cheryl Gianini (Zlatka), Eda Reiss-Merin (Masha), Brita Youngblood (Hela), Reuel Schiller (Lutek), Eric Faber (Yankele).

The film is based on the experiences of producer Jack P. Eisner, who as a young man survived the horrors of the Warsaw ghetto and Nazi concentration camps.

3264. War Birds (1989, Vidmark, 88m, c). P Kurt Eggert & Joanne Watkins, D Ulli Lommel, W Clifford B. Wellman & Lommel, PH Deland Nuse, M Jerry Lambert, ED Joe Negron, PD Angela Allaire.

LP Jim Eldert (Billy Hawkins), Timothy Hicks (Jim Harris), Bill Brinsfield (Lt. Col. Ronson), Cully Holland (Vince Costello), David Schroeder (Van Dam), Joanne Watkins (Carolyn), Rick Anthony Monroe (Salim).

Bill Brinsfield recruits some "Top Gun" school graduates to fly into El Alahaim, a U.S. ally to aid the pro-American sheik fight some nasty rebels.

3265. War of the Roses (1989, 20th Century-Fox, 116m, c). P James L. Brooks & Arnon Milchan, D Danny DeVito, W Michael Leeson (based on the novel by Warren Adler), PH Stephen H. Burum, M David Newman, ED Lynzee Klingman, PD Ida Random.

LP Michael Douglas (Oliver Rose), Kathleen Turner (Barbara Rose), Danny DeVito (Gavin D'Amato), Marianne Sagebrecht (Susan), Sean Astin (Josh at 17), Heather Fairfield (Carolyn at 17), G.D. Spradlin (Harry Thurmont), Peter Donat (Larrabee).

This witty black comedy is the story of the dissolution of the marriage of Michael Douglas and Kathleen Turner. After all the years of scrimping and saving have paid off and they have both made it big, Turner wants out. All that she demands from the divorce is their luxuriously and tastefully furnished home. Douglas wants it also. Both are advised by their lawyers not to vacate their shared home. As a result the home becomes an emotional and physical battlefield with no holds barred. Douglas and Turner have never been better, separately or as a team, and Danny DeVito is proving he's a damn good director as well as a very funny man. It's to his credit and writer Michael Leeson's that the film doesn't wimp out in the end, although not everyone is going to be happy with the outcome.

3266. War Party (1989, Hemdale, 96m, c). P John Daly, Derek Gibson & Bernard Williams, D Franc Roddam, W Spencer Eastman, PH Brian Tufano, M Chaz Jankel, ED Sean Barton, PD Michael Bingham.

LP Billy Wirth (Sonny Crowkiller), Kevin Dillon (Skitty Harris), Tim Sampson (Warren Cutfoot), Jimmie Ray Weeks (Jay Stivic), Kevyn Major Howard (Calvin Morrisey), Jerry Hardin (Sheriff), Tantoo Cardinal (Sonny's Mother), Bill McKinney (Mayor).

This fictional account of a group of modern young Indians, who say "enough is enough" and violently rise up against the government in Montana, snuck into theaters for the briefest of stays and left without much attention. The filmmakers maintain the fiction that they are showing concern for the treatment of the redman but really they only want to exploit conditions in order to show a bloodbath as in the good old days of racist westerns.

3267. Wargames (1983, MGM/United Artists, 113m, c). P Harold Schneider, D John Badham, W Lawrence Lasker & Walter F. Parkes†, PH William A. Fraker†, M Arthur B. Rubinstein, ED Tom Rolf, PD Angelo P. Graham, SOUND Michael J. Kohut, Carlos de Larios, Aaron Rochin & Willie D. Burton†.

LP Matthew Broderick (David), Dabney Coleman (McKittrick), John Wood (Falken), Ally Sheedy (Jennifer), Barry Corbin (Gen. Beringer), Juanin Clay (Pat Healy), Kent Williams (Cabot), Dennis Lipscomb (Watson).

Teenage computer whiz Matthew Broderick taps into a top-secret Pentagon computer and sets in motion "Global Thermonuclear War" which he thinks is a video game, but it's the real thing.

3268. Warlock (1989, New World, GB, 102m, c). P&D Steve Miner, W David Twohy, PH David Eggby, ED David Finfer, PD Roy Forge Smith.

LP Richard E. Grant (Giles Redferne), Julian Sands (The Warlock), Lori Singer (Kassandra), Kevin O'Brien (Chas), Richard Kuse (Mennonite), Juli Burkhart (Daughter-in-law), Chip Johnson (Farmer), David Carpenter (Pastor), Anna Levine (Pastor's Wife).

While being prepared for execution in the Massachusetts Bay Colony of 1691, warlock Julian Sands and witch hunter Richard E. Grant are transported to 1988 L.A. From then on the film resembles *Time After Time* (1980), in which Jack the Ripper escaped to the 20th century, only to be pursued by H.G. Wells.

3269. Warlords (1989, American-Independent, 85m, c). P Harel Goldstein & Fred Olen Ray, D Fred Olen Ray, W Scott Ressler, PH Laslo Regos, M William Belote, ED William Shaffer, AD Corey Kaplan.

LP David Carradine (Dow), Dawn Wildsmith (Danny), Sid Haig (Warlord), Ross Hagen (Beaumont), Fox Harris (Col. Cox), Robert Quarry (Dr. Mathers), Brinke Stevens (Dow's wife), Victoria Sellers (Desert Girl).

In a tongue-in-cheek "Mad Max"-type film, David Carradine is the clone of a famous warrior. After a nuclear war and an uprising by mutants, he seeks his wife, being held by powerful warlord Sid Haig.

Warlords of the 21st Century see Battletruck

3270. Warning Sign (1985, 20th Century–Fox, 100m, c). P Jim Bloom, D Hal Barwood, W Barwood & Matthew Robbins, PH Dean Cundey, M Craig Safan, ED Robert Lawrence, PD Henry Bumstead.

LP Sam Waterston (Cal Morse), Kathleen Quinlan (Joanie Morse), Yaphet Kotto (Maj. Connolly), Jeffrey De Munn (Dan Fairchild), Richard Dysart (Dr. Nielsen), G.W. Bailey (Tom Schmidt), Jerry Hardin (Vic Flint), Rick Rossovich (Bob).

When an experiment in gene-splicing headed by fanatical scientist Richard Dysart goes awry in a secret germ warfare lab in Utah, workers are turned into homicidal zombies.

3271. The Warrior and the Sorceress (1984, New World, 81m, c). P Frank Isaac & John Broderick, D&W Broderick (based on a story by Broderick & William Stout), PH Leonard Solis, M Louis Saunders, ED Silvia Ripoll, SE Chris Biggs.

LP David Carradine (Kain), Luke Askew (Zeg), Maria Socas (Naja), Anthony DeLongis (Kief), Harry Townes (Bludge), William Marin (Bal Caz), Arthur Clark (Burgo), Daniel March (Blather).

In this sword and sorcery flop, wandering warrior David Carradine sells his services to both sides in a dispute over a well.

3272. Warrior Queen (1987, Seymour Borde, 69m, c). P Harry Alan Towers, D Chuck Vincent, W Rick Marx (based on a story by Peter Welbeck [Towers]), PH Lorenzo Battaglia, M Ian Shaw & Kai Joffe, ED Vincent, Joel Bender & Tony Delcampo, PD Lucio Parisi.

LP Sybil Danning (Berenice), Donald Pleasence (Claudius), Richard Hill (Marcus), Josephine Jacqueline Jones (Chloe), Tally Chanel (Vespa), Stasia Micula [Samantha Fox] (Philomena/Augusta), Suzanna Smith (Veneria).

This softcore sword and sorcery film has no plot that is readily apparent. It's set in Pompeii, a Roman brothel and a gladiator ring. Somehow or other these are supposed to be related, but it's not clear how.

3273. Warriors of the Apocalypse (1987, Film Concept, 95m, c, aka *Time Raiders; Searchers of the Voodoo Mountain*). P&D Bobby A. Suarez, W Ken Metcalfe (based on a story by Suarez), PH Juanito Pereira, M Ole Hoyer, PD Ruben Arthur Nicado.

LP Michael James (Trapper), Deborah Moore (Sheba), Franco Guerrero

(Anouk), Ken Metcalfe (Goruk), Robert Marius, Charlotte Cain, David Light, Mike Cohen.

About 150 years in the future, Michael James and his nomadic followers come across 100-year-old Franco Guerrero. They travel with him in search of Voodoo Mountain, ruled by Ken Metcalfe and his queen, Deborah Moore. The mountain hides a nuclear power plant, operated by slave labor. The battle lines are drawn.

3274. *The Wash* (1988, Skouras/Exclusive, 93m, c). P Calvin Skaggs, D Michael Toshiyuki Uno, W Philip Kan Gotanda (based on his play), PH Walt Lloyd, M John Morris, ED Jay Freund, PD David Wasco.

LP Mako (Nobu), Nobu McCarthy (Masi), Patti Yasutake (Marsha), Marian Yue (Judy), Sab Shimono (Sadao), Shizuko Hoshi (Kiyoko), Danny Kamekona (Blackie), Takayo Fischer (Chiyo), Ken Narasaki (Brad).

San Francisco is the setting for this admirable off-beat romantic comedy. Sour old codger Mako never sweetens up as the movie progresses. His 60-year-old wife Nobu McCarthy, who has left him, makes a weekly visit to bring him clean laundry. She finally comes out of her shell, finding happiness with a pleasant widower. Mako can't understand why she should want a divorce and upset their arrangement.

3275. *The Watcher in the Woods* (1980, Disney/Buena Vista, GB, 100m, c). P Ron Miller, D John Hough & Vincent McEveety (uncredited), W Brian Clemens, Harry Spalding & Rosemary Anne Sisson (based on the novel by Florence Engel Randall), PH Alan Hume, M Stanley Myers, ED Geoffrey Foot, PD Elliot Scott.

LP Bette Davis (Mrs. Aylwood), Carroll Baker (Helen Curtis), David McCallum (Paul Curtis), Lynn-Holly Johnson (Jan Curtis), Kyle Richards (Ellie Curtis), Ian Bannen (John Keller), Richard Pasco (Tom Colley).

In this Gothic horror story, the Curtis family rents a woodland mansion. Their teenage daughter is haunted by visions. Bette Davis, the owner of the mansion, lives in a small guest house on the grounds and seeks her daughter who was lost 30 years ago as a child and is trapped in another dimension.

3276. *Watchers* (1988, Universal, Canada, 92m, c). P Damian Lee & David Mitchell, D Jon Hess, W Bill Freed & Lee (based on the novel by Dean R. Koontz), PH Richard Leiterman, M Joel Goldsmith, Rick Fields, ED Bill Freda & Carolle Alain, PD Richard Wilcox Kent.

LP Corey Haim (Travis), Barbara Williams (Nora), Michael Ironside (Lem), Lala Sloatman (Tracey), Duncan Fraser (Sheriff Gaines), Blue Mankuma (Cliff), Colleen Winton (Deputy Porter), Norman Browning (Hockney).

We're not sure who's watching whom in this ridiculous sf/horror film about a hairy orange monster named Oxcom who hates a very bright, loveable little dog. Both are part of a government secret project that has gone awry. It doesn't really matter, because the film hasn't had many watchers.

3277. *Water* (1986, Atlantic, GB, 91m, c). P Ian La Frenais, D Dick Clement, W Clement, La Frenais & Bill Persky (based on a story by Persky), PH Douglas Slocombe, M Mike Moran, ED John Victor Smith, PD Norman Garwood.

LP Michael Caine (Baxter), Valerie Perrine (Pamela), Brenda Vaccaro (Bianca), Billy Connolly (Delgado), Leonard Rossiter (Sir Malcolm), Dennis Dugan (Rob), Fulton MacKay (Eric), Chris Tummings (Garfield).

This satire about the discovery of a delicious mineral water source in a British colony doesn't do much more than give Michael Caine another paycheck in one of his busier years.

3278. *Wavelength* (1983, New World, 88m, c). P James Rosenfield, D&W Mike Gray, PH Paul Goldsmith, M Tangerine Dream, ED Mark Goldblatt & Robert Leighton, AD Linda Pearl.

LP Robert Carradine (Bobby Sinclaire), Cherie Currie (Iris Longacre), Keenan Wynn (Dan), Cal Bowman (Gen. Milton Ward), James Hess (Col. James MacGruder), Terry Burns (Capt. Hinsdale), Eric Morris (Dr. Vernon Cottrell).

In this thriller military advisors and scientists perform an autopsy on an alien creature while three others are stored in frozen containers. It turns out that Cherie

Currie can communicate telepathically with the creatures.

3279. *The Way It Is* (1986, Spring Films, Inc., 80m, b&w). P Daniel Sales & Eric Mitchell, D&W Mitchell, PH Bobby Bukowski, M Vincent Gallo, ED Bob Gould & Sue Graef.

LP Kai Eric (Orpheus), Boris Major (Eurydice), Vincent Gallo (Vic), Jessica Stutchbury (Vera), Mark Boone, Jr. (Hank), Steve Buscemi (Willy), Rockets Redglare (Frank), Daniel Rosen (Dave).

East Village artists bore audiences with their production of Cocteau's "Orpheus."

3280. *Waxwork* (1988, Vestron, 97m, c/b&w). P Staffan Ahrenberg, D&W Anthony Hickox, PH Gerry Lively, M Roger Bellon, ED Christopher Cibelli, PD Gianni Quaranta, SE Bob Keen.

LP Zach Galligan (Mark), Deborah Foreman (Sarah), Michelle Johnson (China), David Warner (Mr. Lincoln), Dana Ashbrook (Tony), Patrick Macnee (Sir Wilfred), Charles McCaughan (Det. Roberts), J. Kenneth Campbell (Marquis De Sade), Miles O'Keeffe (Count Dracula), John Rhys-Davies (Anton Weber).

In a horror story loosely based on Paul Leni's 1924 classic *Waxworks,* David Warner is the proprietor of a wax museum featuring movie monsters and real-looking horrors. He is able to revive them and turn them loose on an unsuspecting mankind. It's up to a bunch of dimwitted teens to thwart his plans.

3281. *We of the Never Never* (1983, Triumph, Australia, 132m, c). P Greg Tepper & John B. Murray, D Igor Auzins, W Peter Schreck (based on the book by Jane Taylor Gunn), PH Gary Hansen, M Peter Best, ED Clifford Hayes, PD Josephine Ford.

LP Angela Punch-McGregor (Jeannie), Arthur Dignam (Aeneas Gunn), Tony Barry (Mac), Tommy Lewis (Jackeroo), Lewis Fitz-Gerald (Jack), Martin Vaughan (Dan), John Jarratt (Dandy), Tex Morton (Landlord).

It's the story of the first white woman ever to travel to the aborigine wilderness known as the "Never Never."

3282. *We Think the World of You* (1988, Cinecom, GB, 94m, c). P Tommaso Jandelli & Paul Cowan, D Colin Gregg, W Hugh Stoddart (based on the novel by J.R. Ackerley), PH Mike Garfath, M Julian Jacobson, ED Peter Delfgou, PD Jamie Leonard.

LP Alan Bates (Frank Meadows), Gary Oldman (Johnny), Frances Barber (Megan), Liz Smith (Millie), Max Wall (Tom), Kerry Wise (Rita).

Set in the mid-50s, this off-beat comedy about love and obsession centers on a friendship between Alan Bates and Gary Oldman, the latter's wife Frances Barber and a beautiful dog, Evie.

3283. *Weeds* (1987, Kingsgate, 115m, c). P Bill Badalato, D John Hancock, W Dorothy Tristan & Hancock, PH Jan Weincke, M Angelo Badalamenti, ED Dennis O'Connor, PD Joseph T. Garrity.

LP Nick Nolte (Lee Umstetter), Lane Smith (Claude), William Forsythe (Burt the Booster), John Toles-Bey (Navarro), Joe Mantegna (Carmine), Ernie Hudson (Bagdad), Mark Rolston (Dave), J.J. Johnson (Lazarus).

Prisoner Nick Nolte develops a love for theater while in the joint. After winning a pardon, he forms a group of traveling actors who perform in prisons.

3284. *Weekend at Bernie's* (1989, 20th Century-Fox, 97m, c). P Victor Drai, D Ted Kotcheff, W Robert Klane, PH Francois Protat, M Andy Summers, ED Joan E. Chapman, PD Peter Jamison.

LP Andrew McCarthy (Larry Wilson), Jonathan Silverman (Richard Parker), Catherine Mary Stewart (Gwen Saunders), Terry Kiser (Bernie Lomax), Don Calfa (Paulie), Catherine Parks (Tina), Eloise Broady (Tawny), Gregory Salata (Marty), Louis Giambalvo (Vito), Ted Kotcheff (Jack Parker).

Insurance go-getters Andrew McCarthy and Jonathan Silverman show up for a weekend at the island home of their slimy boss Terry Kiser, only to find he's been bumped off by the mob. No one else visiting that weekend seems to notice that Kiser is deceased for reasons not adequately explained to the audience. McCarthy and Silverman feel they must get Kiser's body off the island, before it's discovered he's expired.

3285. *Weekend Pass* (1984, Crown, 92m, c). P Marilyn J. Tenser & Michael

D. Castle, D&W Lawrence Bassoff (based on a story by Tenser), PH Bryan England, M John Baer, ED Harry B. Miller, III.

LP D.W. Brown (Paul Fricker), Peter Ellenstein (Lester Gidley), Patrick Hauser (Webster Adams), Chip McAllister (Bunker Hill), Pamela G. Kay (Tina Wells), Hilary Shapiro (Cindy Hazard), Graem McGavin (Tawny Ryatt).

Four wiseguy rookie sailors just having finished boot camp are off on a fun-filled amorous weekend pass.

3286. *Weekend Warriors* (1986, The Movie Store, 85m, c). P Hannah Hempstead, D Bert Convy, W Bruce Belland & Roy M. Rogosin (based on a story by Belland), PH Charles Minsky, M Perry Botkin, ED Raja Gosnell, PD Chester Kaczenski.

LP Chris Lemmon (Vince Tucker), Vic Tayback (Sgt. Burge), Lloyd Bridges (Col. Archer), Graham Jarvis (Congressman Balljoy), Daniel Greene (Phil McCracken), Marty Cohen (Decola), Brian Bradley (Cory Seacomb).

In an effort to avoid the draft, a group of young men join the National Guard. Lots of guys did that before the Korean War and found themselves cannon fodder when hostilities broke out. Nothing like that happens here; it's a sloppy comedy.

3287. *Weird Science* (1985, Universal, 94m, c). P Joel Silver, D&W John Hughes, PH Matthew F. Leonetti, M Ira Newborn, ED Mark Warner, Christopher Lebenzon & Scott Wallace, PD John W. Corso.

LP Anthony Michael Hall (Gary), Kelly LeBrock (Lisa), Ilan Mitchell-Smith (Wyatt), Bill Paxton (Chet), Suzanne Snyder (Deb), Judie Aronson (Hilly), Robert Downey (Ian), Robert Rusler (Max), Vernon Wells (Lord General).

Anthony Michael Hall and Ilan Mitchell-Smith are like car-chasing dogs; once they catch one, they don't know what to do with it. Brilliant nerds, the boys use their computer expertise to create the perfect women, Kelly LeBrock. She's a bit much for our heroes. Before the film is out the boys are happy to settle for some teenage girls who are more their speed.

3288. *Welcome Home* (1989, Columbia, 87m, c). P Martin Ransohoff, D Franklin J. Schaffner, W Maggie Kleinman, PH Fred J. Koenekamp, ED Bob Swink, PD Dan Yarhi & Dennis Davenport.

LP Kris Kristofferson (Jake Robbins), JoBeth Williams (Sarah), Brian Keith (Jake's Father), Sam Waterston (Woody), Trey Wilson (Col. Barnes), J.J. [John Marshall Jones, Jr.] (Dwayne), Thomas Wilson Brown (Tyler), Kieu Chinh [Nguyen] (Leang).

Kris Kristofferson portrays an American officer who returns to his Vermont home after 17 years in Cambodia. He is married to Kieu Chinh who has borne him two children. The military wishes he had stayed put, and at least initially so does JoBeth Williams, the wife he left so long ago. She's now living with her new husband Sam Waterston, Kristofferson's son and Kris' widower father Brian Keith.

3289. *Welcome to Canada* (1989, National Film Board, Canada, 88m, c). D John N. Smith, W Sam Grana & Smith, PH David de Volpi & Roger Martin, ED Smith, Grana & Martial Ethier.

LP Noreen Power, Brendan Foley, Madonna Hawkins, Kasivisanathan Kathrigasoo, Kumasraselvy Kathrigasoo, Pathanjali Prasad.

Using nonprofessional actors, the film explores what might have happened to the 1987 Tamil refugees from Sri Lanka who were dropped off the coast of Newfoundland where they were detained by Immigration officers. In this fictional account the Newfies are able to make personal contact with the refugees.

3290. *Welcome to 18* (1986, American Distribution Group, 91m, c). P David C. Thomas, D Terry Carr, W Judith Sherman Wolin & Carr, PH Stephen L. Posey, M Tony Berg, ED Lois Freeman-Fox, PD Steven Legler.

LP Courtney Thorne-Smith (Lindsey), Mariska Hargitay (Joey), Jo Ann Willette (Robin), Cristen Kaufman (Talia), E. Erich Anderson (Roscoe), Jeff MacGregor (Cliff), John Putch (Corey).

Three teenage girls learn something about the hard cruel world in the summer between graduation from high school and beginning college.

3291. *We're No Angels* (1989, Paramount, 108m, c). P Art Linson, D Neil Jordan, W David Mamet (loosely based on the 1955 movie *We're No Angels,* screenplay by Ranald MacDougall, adapted from the play *My Three Angels* by Sam and Bella Spewak and the play *La Cuisine de Anges* by Albert Husson), PH Philippe Rousselot, M George Fenton, ED Mick Audsley & Joke Van Wijk, PD Wolf Kroeger.

LP Robert DeNiro (Ned), Sean Penn (Jim), Demi Moore (Molly), Hoyt Axton (Father Levesque), Bruno Kirby (Deputy), Ray McAnally (Warden), James Russo (Bobby), Wallace Shawn (Translator), John C. Reilly (Young Monk), Jay Brazeau (Sheriff), Ken Buhay (Bishop Nogulich).

The time is 1935. The place is a state somewhere near the Canadian border. Robert DeNiro and Sean Penn are small-time, dimwitted hoods sentenced to hard labor. Forced to take part in a prison breakout, they take refuge in a small border town where the local monastery is celebrated for a shrine of "the Weeping Madonna." They are mistaken for visiting ecclesiastical monks and they gleefully go along with the deception. The two are redeemed in spite of themselves. Based loosely on the 1955 film, starring Humphrey Bogart, Aldo Ray and Peter Ustinov, this version isn't as funny. Maybe it misses Aldo Ray's accommodating poisonous snake "Adolphe."

3292. *Wetherby* (1985, MGM/United Artist Classics, GB, 102m, c). P Simon Relph, D&W David Hare, PH Stuart Harris, M Nick Bicat, ED Chris Wimble, PD Hayden Griffin.

LP Vanessa Redgrave (Jean Travers), Ian Holm (Stanley Pilborough), Judi Dench (Marcia Pilborough), Marjorie Yates (Verity Braithwaite), Tom Wilkinson (Roger Braithwaite), Tim McInnerny (John Morgan), Suzanna Hamilton (Karen Creasy), Stuart Wilson (Mike Langdon).

Wetherby is a small town in Yorkshire. There a stranger kills himself in school teacher Vanessa Redgrave's home in surely one of the most surprising and shocking suicides to be filmed. Police investigations reveal some secrets in Redgrave's past.

3293. *The Whales of August* (1987, Alice-Circle-Nelson, 90m, c/b&w). P Carolyn Pfeiffer & Mike Kaplan, D Lindsay Anderson, W David Berry (based on his play), PH Mike Fash, M Alan Price, ED Nicolas Gaster, MD Derek Wadsworth, PD Jocelyn Herbert.

LP Bette Davis (Libby Strong), Lillian Gish (Sarah Webber), Vincent Price (Mr. Nikolai Maranov), Ann Sothern† (Tisha Doughty), Harry Carey, Jr. (Joshua Brackett), Frank Grimes (Mr. Beckwith), Frank Pitkin (Old Randall), Mike Bush (Young Randall).

In her last film role Bette Davis appears as an elderly blind woman, tenderly cared for by her sister Lillian Gish. Art may be imitating life as Davis is quarrelsome, embittered and always willing to pass judgment on the failings of others, while Gish is saintly patient. It's always a pleasure to see these giants of the silver screen — and come to think of it, now that Bette is gone, isn't it time the Academy of Arts and Sciences presented Gish with a special Oscar for lifetime achievement before it's too late?

3294. *What Comes Around* (1986, A.W.O. Associates, 86m, c). P Ted Evanson, D Jerry Reed, W Peter Herrecks (based on a story by Gary Smith & Dave Franklin), PH James Pergola, M Al Delory, ED William Carruth, PD Don K. Ivey.

LP Jerry Reed (Joe Hawkins), Barry Corbin (Leon), Bo Hopkins (Tom Hawkins), Arte Johnson (Malone), Ernest Dixon (Big Jay), Hugh Jarrett (Ralph), Buck Ford (Chester).

Bo Hopkins kidnaps his older brother, country-western singer Jerry Reed, who is hooked on booze and drugs, in an attempt to save him from his self-destruction.

3295. *What You Take for Granted* (1984, Iris Feminist Collective, 75m, c). P,D&W Michelle Citron, PH Frances Reid, M Karen Pritikin, ED Citron.

LP Belinda Cloud (Dianna the Doctor), Donna Blue Lachman (Anna the Truck Driver), Mosetta Harris (Cable Splicer), Fran Hart (Philosophy Professor), Helen Larimore (Sculptor).

In this tedious pseudodocumentary, interviews are held with women doing jobs not ordinarily associated with women. These are intercut with fictional scenes of such women relating to each other.

3296. *Whatever It Takes* (1986, Aquarius Films, 93m, c). P,D&ED Bob Demchuk, W Chris Weatherhead & Demchuk, PH John Drake, M Garry Sherman.

LP Tom Mason (Jeff Perchick), Martin Balsam (Hap Pershicksky), Chris Weatherhead (Lee Bickford), James Rebhorn (Michael Manion), Maura Shea (Eren Haberfield), Bill Bogert (Timothy Shaughnessy), Rosetta LeNoire (Millie), Joey Ginza (Curley), Fred Morsell (Mr. Bunyon), Edward Binns (Mr. Kingsley).

Tom Mason is a cartoonist trying anything to make it to syndication and all the perks which go with it.

3297. *What's Up, Hideous Sun Demon* (1989, Greystone, 71m, b&w/c). P Greg Brown, Jeff Montgomery, Hadi Salem, D Craig Mitchell, W Mitchell, PH John Lambert & Steve Dubin, M Fred Myrow, ED Glenn Morgan.

LP Robert Clarke (Gil/Pitnik), Patricia Manning (Polly), Nan Petersen (Trudy/Bunny), Patrick Whyte (Major), Del Courtney, Fred La Porta, Bill Hampton.

This is a revamped version of Robert Clarke's 1959 monster film with voice dubbings of Jay Leno, Susan Tyrrell, Barbara Goodson and Bernard Behrens. The laughs will guarantee the film plenty of midnight showings. For those who don't recall the 1959 pic, Clarke is a research scientist exposed to radioactive poisoning. It turns him into a humanoid reptilian monster with a bad temper.

Wheels of Fire see *Desert Warrior*

3298. *When Harry Met Sally...* (1989, Columbia, 95m, c). P Rob Reiner & Andrew Scheinman, D Reiner, W Nora Ephron†, PH Barry Sonnenfeld, M Marc Shaiman, ED Robert Leighton, PD Jane Musky.

LP Billy Crystal (Harry Burns), Meg Ryan (Sally Albright), Carrie Fisher (Marie), Bruno Kirby (Jess), Steven Ford (Joe), Lisa Jane Persky (Alice), Michelle Nicastro (Amanda).

Director Rob Reiner and writer Nora Ephron owe a great deal to Woody Allen movies, starring Allen and Diane Keaton, such as *Annie Hall* and *Manhattan*. This romantic comedy presents Billy Crystal and Meg Ryan as friends enjoying a platonic relationship, but it doesn't stay that way. It's a cute summer movie—if one can be satisfied with that and not look for any messages or new insights into relationships between men and women.

3299. *When Nature Calls* (1985, Troma, 85m, c). P Frank Vitale & Charles Kaufman, D Kaufman, W Kaufman & Straw Weisman, PH Mike Spera, M Arthur Custer, ED Michael Jacobi, PD Susan Kaufman.

LP David Orange (Greg), Barbara Marineau (Barb), Nicky Beim (Little Billy), Tina Marie Staiano (Bambi), David Strathairn (Weejun), Silas Davis (O'Malley), Mike Brancato (Milos), Patricia Clement (Cleaning Lady).

This screwball comedy features a typical American family, grown tired of city living, that takes to the great outdoors. It's merely an excuse for a scattergun series of gags, including one about a telethon to raise money to cure the Jerry Lewis disease.

3300. *When the Whales Came* (1989, 20th Century–Fox, GB, 99m, c). P Simon Channing Williams, D Clive Rees, W Michael Morpurgo (based on his novel *Why the Whales Came*), PH Robert Paytner, M Christopher Gunning, ED Andrew Boulton, PD Bruce Grimes.

LP Paul Scofield (The Birdman), David Threlfall (Jack Jenkins), Helen Mirren (Clemmie Jenkins), David Suchet (Will), Helen Pearce (Grace Jenkins), Max Rennie (Daniel Pender), Jeremy Kemp (Mr. Wellbeloved).

Mysterious Paul Scofield seems to be the only one to know why in 1844 the island of Samson in the Scilly Isles was abandoned by its inhabitants. A whale washed up on the beach, which the locals killed. After this their wells dried up and they left their homes believing the island to be cursed. Now in 1914, a neighboring isle may experience the same fate. When a whale beaches itself Scofield convinces the people to carry the whale back to the seas and drive off a herd of narwhals heading for shore.

3301. *When the Wind Blows* (1988, Kings Road, GB, animated, 81m, c). P

John Coates, D Jimmy T. Murakami, W Raymond Briggs (based on his novel), ED John Cary, MD Ray Williams, AD/ANIM Richard Fawdry, M Roger Waters.

VOICES Dame Peggy Ashcroft (Hilda Bloogs), Sir John Mills (James Bloggs), Robin Houston (Announcer), James Russell, David Dundas, Matt Irving.

This brutal animated black comedy shows an elderly British couple who foolishly follow the advice of the government on surviving a nuclear attack. A very effective and thought-provoking film.

3302. *When Time Ran Out* (1980, Warner, 121m, c). P Irwin Allen, D James Goldstone, W Carl Foreman & Stirling Silliphant (based on the novel *The Day the World Ended* by Gordon Thomas & Max Morgan Witts), PH Fred J. Koenekamp, M Lalo Schifrin, ED Edward Biery & Freeman A. Davies, PD Philip M. Jefferies, COS Paul Zastupnevich†.

LP Paul Newman (Hank Anderson), Jacqueline Bisset (Kay Kirby), William Holden (Shelby Gilmore), Edward Albert (Brian), Red Buttons (Francis Fendly), Barbara Carrera (Iolani), Valentina Cortesa (Rose Valdez), Veronica Hamel (Nikki), Alex Karras (Tiny Baker), Burgess Meredith (Rene Valdez), Ernest Borgnine (Tom Conti), James Franciscus (Bob Spangler).

In this disaster spectacular, an assortment of familiar names and faces are staying at a splendid resort on a beautiful tropical Polynesian island. A long-dormant volcano unexpectedly explodes, turning the paradise into a hell cut off from the outside world.

3303. *Where Are the Children* (1986, Columbia, 92m, c). P Zev Braun, D Bruce Malmuth, W Jack Sholder (based on the novel by Mary Higgins Clark), PH Larry Pizer, M Sylvester Levay, ED Roy Watts, PD Robb Wilson King.

LP Jill Clayburgh (Nancy Eldridge), Max Gail (Clay Eldridge), Harley Cross (Michael Eldridge), Elisabeth Harnois (Missy Eldridge), Elizabeth Wilson (Dorothy Prentiss), Barnard Hughes (Jonathan Knowles), Frederic Forrest (Courtney Parrish).

Having survived the trauma of being cleared of murdering her kids, Jill Clayburgh is hit with more heartbreak when her mate from a previous marriage kidnaps her children from her present marriage.

3304. *Where Is Parsifal?* (1984, Terence Young, GB, 84m, c). P Daniel Carrillo, D Henri Helman, W Berta Dominguez D, PH Norman Langley, M Hubert Rostaing & Ivan Jullien, ED Russell Lloyd & Peter Hollywood, PD Malcolm Stone.

LP Tony Curtis (Parsifal Katzenellenbogen), Cassandra Domenica "Dominguez D. Berta" (Elba), Erik Estrada (Henry Board, II), Peter Lawford (Montague Chippendale), Ron Moody (Beersbohm), Donald Pleasence (Mackintosh), Orson Welles (Klingsor).

Tony Curtis, a wild hypochondriac, has invented a laser skywriter which he hopes will provide him with the money he needs to pay for his unusual life style and the crazies who live with him.

3305. *Where the Boys Are '84* (1984, Tri-Star, 97m, c). P Allan Carr, D Hy Averback, W Stu Krieger & Jeff Burkhart (based on the novel *Where the Boys Are* by Glendon Swarthout), PH James A. Contner, M Sylvester Levay, ED Melvin Shapiro & Bobbie Shapiro, PD Michael Baugh.

LP Lisa Hartman (Jennie), Wendy Schaal (Sandra), Lorna Luft (Carol), Lynn-Holly Johnson (Laurie), Russell Todd (Scott), Christopher McDonald (Tony), Howard McGillian (Chip), Daniel McDonald (Camden), Alana Stewart (Maggie), Louise Sorel (Barbara).

How times have changed. In the 1960 movie, the girls flocked to Florida to be where the boys were, but they were seeking a wedding band before going to bed. Doing it in the other order brought tragedy to one girl. In 1984, sexual abstinence is not even a consideration for the females pouring into the sunny south for Spring Break. They know exactly the effect their openness and bikini-clad bodies have on the male population.

3306. *Where the Buffalo Roam* (1980, Universal, 96m, c). P&D Art Linson, W John Kaye (based on the writings of Hunter S. Thompson), PH Tak Fujimoto, M Neil Young, ED Christopher Greenbury, PD Richard Sawyer.

LP Peter Boyle (Lazlo), Bill Murray (Hunter S. Thompson), Bruno Kirby (Marty Lewis), Rene Auberjonois (Harris), R.G. Armstrong (Judge Simpson), Danny Goldman (Porter), Rafael Campos (Rojas).

Bill Murray portrays psychotic journalist Hunter S. Thompson, who attempts to cover everything from the Superbowl to Nixon's reelection campaign. It's a strangely quirky film. Murray really gets into his role as the Gonzo journalist but the script is a stinker.

3307. *Where the River Runs Black* (1986, MGM, 100m, c). P Joe Roth & Harry Ufland, D Christopher Cain, W Peter Silverman & Neal Jimenez (based on the book *Lazaro* by David Kendall), PH Juan Ruiz Anchia, M James Horner, ED Richard Chew, PD Marcos Flaksman.

LP Charles Durning (Father O'Reilly), Alessandro Rabelo (Lazaro), Ajay Naidu (Segundo), Divana Brandao (Eagle Woman), Peter Horton (Father Mahoney), Castulo Guerra (Orlando Santos), Conchata Ferrell (Mother Marta), Dana Delany (Sister Ana).

Born of a mysterious Indian woman, Alessandro Rabelo is a child of nature, living along the Rio Negro in an Amazon rain forest. When his mother is killed, he is taken to an orphanage by Charles Durning, a priest determined to save his soul. It's a difficult adjustment for the youngster.

3308. *Where the Spirit Lives* (1989, CBC, Canada, 97m, c). P Heather Goldin, Eric Jordan & Mary Young Leckie, D Bruce Pittman, W Keith Ross Leckie, PH Rene Ohashi, M Buffy Sainte Marie, ED Michael Todd.

LP Michelle St. John (Komi/Amelia), Clayton Julian (Pita/Abraham), Heather Hess (Rachel), Ann-Marie MacDonald (Kathleen), Ron White (Taggert), Chapelle Jaffe (Miss Appleby), David Hemblen (Rev. Buckley), Patricia Collins (Mrs. Barrington).

The film tells a fictitious story about the former Canadian Federal government's actual practice of kidnapping Indian children from their reserves and keeping them virtual prisoners in religious schools. There, all vestiges of their Indian heritage are beaten out of them.

3309. *A Whisper to a Scream* (1989, Distant Horizon, Canada, 96m, c). P&W Gerard Ciccoritti & Robert Bergman, D Bergman, PH Paul Witte, M Barry Fasman & Dana Walden, ED Richard Bond, PD Ciccoritti.

LP Nadia Capone (Gabrielle), Silvio Oliviero (Frank), Yaphet Kotto (Det. Taillard), Lawrence Bayne (Ohwyn Peters), Michael Lebovic (Tullio), Denise Ryan (Mia), Soo Garay (Mimi).

In this Canadian horror film, an obsessed soundman kills strippers.

3310. *The Whistle Blower* (1987, Hemdale, GB, 104m, c). P Geoffrey Reeve, D Simon Langton, W Julian Bond (based on the novel by John Hale), PH Fred Tammes, M John Scott, ED Robert Morgan, PD Morley Smith.

LP Michael Caine (Frank Jones), James Fox (Lord), Nigel Havers (Robert Jones), Felicity Dean (Cynthia Goodburn), John Gielgud (Sir Adrian Chapple), Gordon Jackson (Bruce), Barry Foster (Charles Greig), Kenneth Colley (Bill Pickett), Dinah Stabb (Rose).

Michael Caine searches for the answers to why his only son is killed, in a thriller which abounds with spies and counterspies.

3311. *White Elephant* (1984, Worldoc, GB, 99m, c). P&D Werner Grusch, W Grusch & Ashley Pharoah (based on an idea by Grusch), PH Tom D. Hurwitz, M Various Artists, ED Thomas Schwalm.

LP Peter Firth (Peter Davidson), Peter Sarpong (Bishop of Kumasi), Nana Seowg (High Priestess), Ejissu Jasantua (Fetish Priest), Frederick Lawluwi (Reverend in Angola).

White businessman Peter Firth arrives in Ghana with plans of modernizing the country through high tech. He is met with resistance, finally succumbing to the charm of simpler ways of life.

3312. *White Ghost* (1988, Gibralter, 93m, c). P Jay Davidson & William Fay, D B.J. Davis, W Gary Thompson, PH Hans Kuhle, M Parmer Fuller, ED Ettie Feldman.

LP William Katt (Steve Shepard), Rosalind Chao (Thi Hau), Martin Hewitt (Waco), Wayne Crawford (Capt.

Walker), Reb Brown (Major Cross), Raymond Ma (Camp Commander), Karl Johnson (Brownie), Graham Clark (Doc).

Fifteen years after all other American troops pulled out of Southeast Asia, William Katt, wearing spooky white kabuki makeup, is still fighting on in a Vietnam/Cambodia border war. Katt signals for some help and Reb Brown sends in a band of mercenaries to find him.

3313.   *White Mischief* (1988, Columbia, GB, 107m, c). P Simon Perry, D Michael Radford, W Radford & Jonathan Gems (based on the book by James Fox), PH Roger Deakins, M George Fenton, ED Tom Priestley, PD Roger Hall.

LP Sarah Miles (Alice de Janze), Joss Ackland (Sir John "Jock" Delves Broughton), John Hurt (Gilbert Colvile), Greta Scacchi (Diana Caldwell), Charles Dance (Josslyn Hay, Earl of Erroll), Susan Fleetwood (Gwladys, Lady Delamere), Alan Dobie (Harragin), Jacqueline Pearce (Lady Idina Gordon).

Based on fact, this film is the story of decadence in the British upper class in Kenya around 1940 and the suspected murder of notorious playboy Charles Dance by a jealous husband. It's tedious stuff.

3314.   *White Nights* (1985, Columbia, 136m, c). P Taylor Hackford & William S. Gilmore, D Hackford, W James Goldman, Eric Hughes & Nancy Dowd (based on a story by Goldman), PH David Watkin, M Michel Colombier, ED Fredric Steinkamp & William Steinkamp, PD Philip Harrison, SONG "Say You, Say Me" by Lionel Richie*, SONG "Separate Lives" by Stephen Bishop†.

LP Mikhail Baryshnikov (Nikolai "Kolya" Rodchenko), Gregory Hines (Raymond Greenwood), Jerzy Skolimowski (Col. Chaiko), Helen Mirren (Galina Ivanova), Geraldine Page (Anne Wyatt), Isabella Rossellini (Darya Greenwood), John Glover (Wynn Scott).

Former Soviet ballet star Mikhail Baryshnikov, a defector to the West, survives a plane crash in Russia. He is captured and is put in the care of Gregory Hines, an American tap dancer. The latter is supposed to convince Baryshnikov

to once again dance with the Kirov Ballet Company. Before long the two become friends and together plot an escape from the U.S.S.R.

3315.   *White of the Eye* (1988, Cannon, 111m, c). P Cassian Elwes & Brad Wyman, D Donald Cammell, W China Cammell & Donald Cammell (based on the novel *Mrs. White* by Margaret Tracy), PH Larry McConkey, M Nick Mason & Rick Fenn, ED Terry Rawlings, PD Philip Thomas.

LP David Keith (Paul White), Cathy Moriarty (Joan White), Art Evans (Detective Charles Mendoza), Alan Rosenberg (Mike Desantos), Michael Greene (Phil Ross), Danielle Smith (Danielle White), Alberta Watson (Ann Mason).

Philandering married audio expert David Keith is cop Art Evans' number one suspect in a series of local housewife murders. Keith's wife Cathy Moriarty and daughter Danielle Smith are menaced by the killer.

3316.   *White Phantom* (1987, Spectrum, 89m, c). P Roy McAree & K.L. Lim, D Dusty Nelson, W David Hamilton & Chris Gallagher (based on a story by Nelson), PH Alan Brennecke, M Robert J. Resetar, Kevin Klingler & Bob Mamet, ED Carole A. Kenneally.

LP Jay Roberts, Jr. (Willi), Page Leong (Mai Lin), Jimmy Lee (Hanzo), Bo Svenson (Col. Slater), H.F. Chiang (Bookstore Owner), Kathy McClure (Daughter).

This straight to video package takes audiences into the world of the ninja fighters. It represents a modernday battle between good and evil. Such films are above—or below—criticism.

3317.   *White Water Summer* (1987, Columbia, 90m, c). P Mark Tarlov, D Jeff Bleckner, W Manya Starr & Ernest Kinoy, PH John Alcott, M Michael Boddicker, ED David Ray.

LP Kevin Bacon (Vic), Sean Astin (Alan Block/Narrator), Jonathan Ward (Mitch), K.C. Martel (George), Matt Adler (Chris), Caroline McWilliams (Virginia Block), Charles Siebert (Jerry Block), Joseph Passarelli (Storekeeper).

Gung-ho Kevin Bacon leads a group of teens on a three week camping trip. He's particularly tough on city-kid Sean Astin, who doesn't want to be there and isn't too crazy about strenuous activities. When Bacon is injured, this least-likely kid takes charge. Sounds like John Wayne and John Agar in *Sands of Iwo Jima*.

3318. Whiteforce (1989, Eastern, Australian/Philippines, 85m, c). P Lope V. Juban & Marilyn G. Ong, D Eddie Romero, W Henry Tefay, PH Jose Batac, M Ryan Cayabyab, ED Gervacio Santos.

LP Sam Jones (Johnny Quinn), Kimberley Pistone (Nicki), Timothy Hughes (Alex Korda), Raoul Aragonn (Briggs), Jimmy Fabregas (Wizard), Vic Diaz, Rubin Rustia, Ken Metcalfe, Mike Monty.

Accused of murdering his partner Ken Metcalfe, Sam Jones, with some help from Kimberly Pistone, Metcalfe's daughter, dodges bullets as he tries to prove that the real villain is druglord Timothy Hughes.

3319. Who? (1982, Lorimar, GB/Ger., 93m, c, aka *A Man Without a Face; Prisoner of the Skull; The Man in the Skull Mask*). P Barry Levinson, D Jack Gold, W John Gould [Jack Gold] (based on the novel by Algis Budrys), PH Petrus Schloemp, M John Cameron, ED Norman Wanstall.

LP Elliott Gould (Sean Rogers), Trevor Howard (Col. Azarin), Joe Bova (Dr. Lucas Martino), Ed Grover (Finchley), James Noble (Gen. Deptford), John Lehne (Haller), Kay Tornborg (Edith), Lyndon Brook (Dr. Barrister).

Shot in 1975 this production underwent many title changes before reaching U.S. theaters. American scientist Joe Bova is nearly killed in an accident along the Soviet border. Russian doctors perform life-saving surgery that makes him half-man, half-machine. But who is he going to work for?

Who Dares Win see The Final Option

3320. Who Framed Roger Rabbit? (1988, Buena Vista, part-animated, 103m, c). P Robert Watts & Frank Marshall, D Robert Zemeckis, W Jeffrey Price & Peter S. Seaman (based on the book *Who Censored Roger Rabbit?* by Gary K. Wolf), PH Dean Cundey†, M Alan Silvestri, ED Arthur Schmidt*, PD Elliot Scott & Roger Cain, AD Stephen Scott†, SD Peter Howitt†, SOUND Robert Knudson, John Boyd, Don Digiroamo & Tony Dawe†, SOUND EFFECTS Charles L. Campbell*, VE Ken Ralston, Richard Williams, Edward Jones & George Gibbs*, ANIM Richard Williams.

LP Bob Hoskins (Eddie Valiant), Christopher Lloyd (Judge Doom), Joanna Cassidy (Dolores), Stubby Kaye (Marvin Acme), Charles Fleischer (Roger Rabbit/Greasy/Psycho/Benny the Cab), Lou Hirsch (Baby Herman), Kathleen Turner (Jessica Rabbit), Amy Irving (Jessica Rabbit's Singing Voice), Alan Tilvern (R.K. Maroon), Richard le Parmentier (Lt. Santino).

In an amazing blending of live-action and animation, Robert Zemeckis brings forth a 40s comical film noir. Set in 1947 Hollywood, cartoon characters, second class citizens, are relegated to a Toon Town ghetto. Private eye Bob Hoskins reluctantly agrees to help slapstick Toon Roger Rabbit, the major suspect when a despised producer is murdered. Kathleen Turner, the speaking voice of Roger's glamorous wife Jessica, just about walks away with the honors in this truly remarkable movie breakthrough. It must be seen to be believed.

3321. Who Has Seen the Wind (1980, Cinema World, Canada, 100m, c). P Pierre Lamy, D Allan King, W Patricia Watson (based on the novel by W.O. Mitchell), PH Richard Leiterman, M Eldon Rathburn, ED Arla Saare, AD Anne Pritchard.

LP Brian Painchaud (Brian), Douglas Junor (The Young Ben), Gordon Pinsent (Gerald O'Connal), Chapelle Jaffe (Maggie), Jose Ferrer (The Ben), Charmion King (Mrs. Abercrombie), David Gardner (Rev. Powelly).

Brian Painchaud stars in this production of a classic Canadian children's novel. He's sort of a Tom Sawyer growing up with his father and assorted pets in Depression-era Saskatchewan.

3322. Wholly Moses (1980, Columbia, 109m, c). P Freddie Fields, D Gary Weis, W Guy Thomas, PH Frank Stanley, M Patrick Williams, ED Sidney Levin, PD Dale Hennesy.

LP Dudley Moore (Harvey/Herschel), Laraine Newman (Zoe/Zerelda), James Coco (Hyssop), Paul Sand (Angel of the Lord), Jack Gilford (Tailor), Dom DeLuise (Shadrach), John Houseman (Archangel), Madeline Kahn (Sorceress), Richard Pryor (Pharaoh), John Ritter (Devil).

This comedy is so sophomoric, you'd swear it was written and directed by Mel Brooks. But no, it's a bunch of other chaps slinging the crap. Dudley Moore portrays Herschel, who mistakenly believes that he, rather than Moses, is the man chosen by God to lead the Israelites out of Egypt.

3323. The Whoopee Boys (1986, Paramount, 88m, c). P Adam Fields & Peter MacGregor-Scott, D John Byrum, W Steve Zacharias, Jeff Buhai & David Obst, PH Ralf Bode, M Jack Nitzsche, ED Eric Jenkins, PD Charles Rosen.

LP Michael O'Keefe (Jake), Paul Rodriguez (Barney), Denholm Elliott (Col. Phelps), Carole Shelley (Henrietta Phelps), Andy Bumatai (Roy Raja), Eddie Deezen (Eddie), Marsha Warfield (Officer White), Elizabeth Arlen (Shelley).

Michael O'Keefe's problem is that he's in love with a Palm Beach heiress who must marry a wealthy, refined gentleman in order to earn her own inheritance. Being neither rich nor refined, he has his work cut out for him.

3324. Whoops Apocalypse (1987, MGM, GB, 89m, c). P Brian Eastman, D Tom Bussmann, W Andrew Marshall & David Renwick, PH Ron Robson, M Patrick Gowers, ED Peter Boyle, PD Tony Noble.

LP Loretta Swit (President Barbara Adams), Peter Cook (Sir Mortimer Chris), Michael Richards (Lacrobat), Rik Mayall (Specialist Catering Commander), Ian Richardson (Rear Adm. Bendish), Alexei Sayle (Himself), Herbert Lom (Gen. Mosquera), Joanne Pearce (Princess Wendy).

Based on a successful British TV series, this comedy consists of news coverage of the events leading up to World War III. It's filled with wit, expletives included,

zinging one-liners, manic energy and nontopical garbage.

3325. Who's Harry Crumb? (1989, Tri-Star, 87m, c). P Arnon Milchan, D Paul Flaherty, W Robert Conte & Peter Martin Wortmann, PH Stephen M. Katz, M Michel Colombier, ED Danford B. Greene, PD Trevor Williams.

LP John Candy (Harry Crumb), Jeffrey Jones (Eliot Draisen), Annie Potts (Helen Downing), Tim Thomerson (Vince), Barry Corbin (P.J. Downing), Shawnee Smith (Nikki Downing), Wesley Mann (Tim).

Teddy bear John Candy plays a bumbling, know-it-all private eye so dumb that he takes an incriminating photograph of his own client rather than of the woman's husband. He's called to L.A. by his family's detective firm to investigate the kidnapping of a beautiful heiress. He's given lines so stupid that one almost flinches. Still as expected he somehow manages to get the detecting job done—but hasn't got a clue how to get some laughs out of the script.

3326. Who's That Girl? (1987, Warner, 94m, c). P Rosilyn Heller & Bernard Williams, D James Foley, W Andrew Smith & Ken Finkleman (based on a story by Andrew Smith), PH Jan DeBont, M Stephen Bray & Patrick Leonard, ED Pembroke Herring, PD Ida Random.

LP Madonna (Nikki Finn), Griffin Dunne (Loudon Trutt), Haviland Morris (Wendy Worthington), John McMartin (Simon Worthington), Robert Swan (Detective Bellson), Drew Pillsbury (Detective Doyle), Coati Mundi (Raoul), Dennis Burkley (Benny).

In this screwy comedy, straitlaced lawyer Griffin Dunne and zany parolee Madonna seek out the nasty guy who framed her.

3327. Whose Life Is It Anyway? (1981, MGM/United Artists, 119m, c). P Lawrence P. Bachmann, D John Badham, W Brian Clark & Reginald Rose (based on the play by Clark), PH Mario Tosi, M Arthur B. Rubinstein, ED Frank Morriss, PD Gene Callahan.

LP Richard Dreyfuss (Ken Harrion), John Cassavetes (Dr. Michael Emerson), Christine Lahti (Dr. Clare Scott), Bob

Balaban (Carter Hill), Kenneth McMillan (Judge Wyler), Kaki Hunter (Mary Jo).

Totally paralyzed after a car accident, talented, successful, married sculptor Richard Dreyfuss uses the only part of his body not injured, his brain, to decide he wishes to die. He hires a lawyer to fight for his right to terminate his life. It's a thought-provoking film.

3328. *Why Not Stay for Breakfast* (1985, Artgrove, GB, 95m, c). P Martin Schute & Alan Cluer, D Terence Martel, W Martel & Ray Cooney (based on the play by Gene Stone & Cooney), PH James Devis, M Harry Robinson, ED Alan Jones.

LP George Chakaris (George Clark), Gemma Craven (Louise Hamilton), Yvonne Wilder (Helen), Ray Charleson (Davey), David Baxt (Boy), Carinthia West (Girl), Vic Gallucci (Neighbor), Baby Dale (Baby).

Produced in 1979, the film was not released until 1985. Divorced New York postal clerk George Chakaris assumes the role of protector of English girl Gemma Craven and her baby, Baby Dale.

3329. *Why Would I Lie?* (1980, MGM/United Artists, 105m, c). P Pancho Kohner, D Larry Peerce, W Peter Stone (based on the novel *The Fabricator* by Hollis Hodges), PH Gerald Hirschfeld, M Charles Fox, ED John C. Howard.

LP Treat Williams (Cletus), Lisa Eichhorn (Kay), Gabriel Swann (Jeorge), Susan Heldfond (Amy), Anne Byrne (Faith), Valerie Curtin (Mrs. Bok), Jocelyn Brando (Mrs. Crumpe), Nicolas Coster (Walter).

Thoroughly unlikeable social worker Treat Williams is a confirmed and colorful liar. He romances feminist Lisa Eichhorn while espousing his half-baked philosophical ideas.

3330. *The Wicked Lady* (1983, MGM/United Artists, GB, 99m, c). P Menahem Golan & Yoram Globus, D Michael Winner, W Winner & Leslie Arliss (based on the novel *The Life and Death of the Wicked Lady Skelton* by Magdalen King-Hall), PH Jack Cardiff, M Tony Banks, ED Arnold Crust, AD John Blezard, COS John Bloomfield.

LP Faye Dunaway (Lady Barbara Skelton), Alan Bates (Capt. Jerry Jackson), John Gielgud (Hogarth), Denholm Elliott (Sir Ralph Skelton), Prunella Scales (Lady Kingsclere), Oliver Tobias (Kit Locksby), Glynis Barber (Caroline), Joan Hickson (Aunt Agatha Trimble).

This remake of the 1946 film starring Margaret Lockwood and James Mason features Faye Dunaway in constant danger of falling out of the bodice of her dress. Her breasts and those of the other "ladies" in the film are in a constant jiggle. But all of the mammary glands and nude lovemaking don't make audiences forget that there is almost no plot to this story of a bored aristocratic lady who becomes a highway robber. Dunaway chews up the sets to a fare-thee-well, looking more than a little deranged most of the time.

3331. *Wicked Stepmother* (1989, MGM/United Artists, 92m, c). P Robert Littman, D&W Larry Cohen, PH Bryan England, M Robert Folk, ED David Kern.

LP Bette Davis (Miranda), Barbara Carrera (Priscilla), Colleen Camp (Jenny), David Rasche (Steve), Lionel Stander (Sam), Tom Bosley (Lt. MacIntosh), Shawn Donahue (Mike), Richard Moll (Nat), Evelyn Keyes (Witch Mistress).

Colleen Camp and David Rasche return from vacation to find that dad Lionel Stander has taken a new wife, Bette Davis. Seems Davis is a witch being tracked by detective Tom Bosley. About halfway through the film Bette disappears without explanation. Barbara Carrera shows up claiming to be Davis' daughter. It's sad to see Davis reduced to appearing in such crap. (The film was made before Davis' appearance in *The Whale of August*). Come to think of it, it's a shame to see Bosley, Stander and Evelyn Keyes in the same boat.

3332. *The Wild Duck* (1983, Orion, Australia, 96m, c). P Phillip Emanuel & Basil Appleby, D Henri Safran, W Safran, Peter Smalley & John Lind (based on the play by Henrik Ibsen), PH Peter James, M Simon Walker, ED Don Saunders, PD Darrell Lass.

LP Liv Ullmann (Gina), Jeremy Irons (Harold), Lucinda Jones (Henrietta), John Meillon (Maj. Ackland), Arthur Dignam (Gregory), Michael Pate

(George), Colin Croft (Mollison), Rhys McConnochie (Dr. Roland).

Henrik Ibsen's play is not dull but this needless update is. It's the story of young Pollyannaish Lucinda Jones, whose birth is kept a secret, straining the relationship between mother Liv Ullmann and her egotistical husband Jeremy Irons.

3333.   *Wild Geese II* (1986, Universal, 125m, c). P Euan Lloyd, D Peter Hunt, W Reginald Rose (based on the book *The Square Circle* by Daniel Carney), PH Michael Reed, M Roy Budd, ED Keith Palmer, PD Syd Cain.

LP Scott Glenn (John Haddad), Barbara Carrera (Kathy Lukas), Edward Fox (Alex Faulkner), Laurence Olivier (Rudolf Hess), Robert Webber (Robert McCann), Robert Freitag (Heinrich Stroebling), Kenneth Haigh (Col. Reed-Henry), Stratford Johns (Mustapha El Ali).

This film has nothing to do with *Wild Geese* (1978). Its strange plot deals with an attempt to kidnap imprisoned Nazi Rudolf Hess, played by Laurence Olivier. At the end of his film career, the latter seemed willing to do anything for a paycheck.

3334.   *Wild Horses* (1984, Satori, New Zealand, 90m, c). P John Barnett, D Derek Morton, W Kevin O'Sullivan [Kevin J. Wilson], PH Doug Milsome, M Dave Fraser, ED Simon Reece, PD Jose Bleakley.

LP Keith Aberdein (Dan "Mitch" Mitchell), John Bach (Jack Sullivan), Kevin J. Wilson (Harry Sullivan), Kathy Rawlings (Mary Mitchell), Helena Wilson (Anne Mitchell), Robyn Gibbes (Sara), Tom Poata (Sam Richardson).

In this New Zealand "western," horse wranglers in a national park are at odds with deerhunters. The scenery is beautiful, the story is routine.

3335.   *The Wild Life* (1984, Universal, 96m, c). P Art Linson, Cameron Crowe & Don Phillips, D Linson, W Crowe, PH James Glennon, M Edward Van Halen & Donn Landee, ED Michael Jablow, PD William Sandell.

LP Christopher Penn (Tom Drake), Ilan Mitchell-Smith (Jim Conrad), Eric Stoltz (Bill Conrad), Jenny Wright (Eileen), Lea Thompson (Anita), Brin

Berliner (Tony), Rick Moranis (Harry), Hart Bochner (David Curtiss).

Many of the same people who brought us *Fast Times at Ridgemont High* are responsible for this disappointing followup. Christopher Penn is the leader of a bunch of teens trying to grow up too fast. Life seems to revolve around getting laid, with little else being of any importance.

3336.   *The Wild Pair* (1987, TransWorld Ent., 88m, c, aka *Devil's Odds*). P Paul Mason & Randall Torno, D Beau Bridges, W Joseph Gunn (based on a story by Gunn & John Crowther), PH Peter Stein, M John Debney, ED Christopher Holmes & Scott Conrad, PD Stephen Berger.

LP Beau Bridges (Joe Jennings), Bubba Smith (Benny Avalon), Lloyd Bridges (Col. Hester), Gary Lockwood (Capt. Kramer), Raymond St. Jacques (Ivory), Danny De La Paz (Tucker), Lela Rochon (Debby), Ellen Geer (Fern Willis).

Beau Bridges and Bubba Smith challenge a private army led by Lloyd Bridges. This action-adventure film is for those who like exciting buddy-films but aren't concerned with plots.

The Wild Side   see   Suburbia

3337.   *Wild Style* (1983, First Run Features, 85m, c). P,D&W Charlie Ahearn, PH Clive Davidson & John Foster, M Chris Stein, ED Steve Brown.

LP Lee George Quinones (Raymond), Frederick Brathwaite (Phade), Sandra Pink Fabara (Rose), Patti Astor (Virginia), Andrew Zephyr Witten (Zroc), Carlos Morales (Raymond's Brother).

In this semidocumentary, featuring rap singing and break dancing, a promoter helps graffiti artist Lee George Quinones escape the ghetto and find a place in the art world.

3338.   *Wild Thing* (1987, Atlantic, US/Canada, 92m, c). P David Calloway & Nicolas Clermont, D Max Reid, W John Sayles (based on a story by Sayles & Larry Stamper), PH Rene Verzier, M George S. Clinton, ED Battle Davis & Steven Rosenblum, PD John Meighen & Jocelyn Joli.

LP Rob Knepper (Wild Thing), Kathleen Quinlan (Jane), Robert Davi (Chopper), Maury Chaykin (Det. Trask), Betty Buckley (Leah), Guillaume Lemay-Thivierge (Wild Thing 10 Years Old), Clark Johnson (Winston), Sean Hewitt (Father Quinn).

Orphaned at age three, Rob Knepper has learned to survive on his own into adulthood. He becomes a legend as "Wild Thing," protector of Montreal's ghetto people from villains.

3339. *Wildcats* (1986, Warner, 107m, c). P Anthea Sylbert, D Michael Ritchie, W Ezra Sacks, PH Donald E. Thorin, M Hawk Wolinski & James Newton Howard, ED Richard A. Harris, PD Boris Leven.

LP Goldie Hawn (Molly), Swoosie Kurtz (Verna), Robyn Lively (Alice), Brandy Gold (Marian), James Keach (Frank), Jan Hooks (Stephanie), Bruce McGill (Darwell), Nipsy Russell (Edwards), Mykel T. Williamson (Bird).

The Wildcats, a high school football team, get no respect and no wins until Goldie Hawn is made coach. It's as predictable as the smell of sweaty gym clothes.

3340. *Wildfire* (1988, Zupnik Cinema Group, 98m, c). P Jerry Tokofsky & Hunt Lowry, D Zalman King, W Matthew Bright & King (based on a story by Bright), PH Bill Butler, M Maurice Jarre, ED Caroline Biggerstaff, PD Geoffrey Kirkland.

LP Steven Bauer (Frank), Linda Fiorentino (Kay), Will Patton (Mike), Marshall Bell (Lewis), Sandra Seacat, Richard Bradford, Alisha Byrd-Pena, Jonah Ellers-Isaacs, Michelle Mayberry.

Steven Bauer and Linda Fiorentino meet in an orphanage. They break out and hit the road. Broke, Bauer robs a bank, is caught and sent to prison, while Fiorentino is adopted by a middleclass family. She marries yuppie Will Patton and is happy until Bauer shows up again, wishing to renew their relationship. The result is violence.

3341. *Wildrose* (1985, Troma, 95m, c). P Sandra Schulberg, D John Hanson, W Hanson & Eugene Corr (based on a story by Schulberg & Hanson), PH Peter Stein, M Bernard Krause, Gary S. Remal & Cris Williamson, ED Arthur Coburn.

LP Lisa Eichhorn (June Lorich), Tom Bower (Rick Ogaard), Jim Cada (Pavich), Cinda Jackson (Karen), Dan Nemanick (Ricotti), Lydia Olsen (Katri Sippola), Bill Schoppert (Timo Maki), James Stowell (Doobie).

Feisty Lisa Eichhorn, a female heavy-machine operator in the Mesabi Range of Minnesota, is at odds with her coworkers, experiencing sexist attitudes when reassigned to an otherwise all male crew. Recently divorced from a drunken wife-beater, she has an unexpected love affair with Tom Bower, the only one of her crew not to harrass her.

3342. *Willie and Phil* (1980, 20th Century–Fox, 116m, c). P Paul Mazursky & Tony Ray, D&W Mazursky, PH Sven Nykvist, M Claude Bolling & Georges Delerue, ED Donn Cambern, PD Pato Guzman.

LP Michael Ontkean (Willie Kaufman), Margot Kidder (Jeanette Sutherland), Ray Sharkey (Phil D'Amico), Jan Miner (Mrs. Kaufman), Tom Brennan (Mr. Kaufman), Julie Bovasso (Mrs. D'Amico), Louis Guss (Mr. D'Amico), Kathleen Maguire (Mrs. Sutherland), Kaki Hunter (Patti Sutherland).

In this attempt to film an American *Jules et Jim,* friends Michael Ontkean and Ray Sharkey share Margot Kidder in a veritable ménage-à-trois throughout the 70s.

3343. *Willow* (1988, MGM/United Artists, 125m, c). P Nigel Wooll, D Ron Howard, W Bob Dolman (based on a story by George Lucas), PH Adrian Biddle, M James Horner, ED Daniel Hanley & Michael Hill, PD Allan Cameron, SOUND EFFECTS ED Ben Burtt & Richard Hymns†, VE Dennis Muren, Michael McAlister, Phil Tippett & Chris Evans†.

LP Val Kilmer (Madmartigan), Joanne Whalley (Sorsha), Warwick Davis (Willow), Jean Marsh (Queen Bavmorda), Patricia Hayes (Fin Raziel), Billy Barty (High Aldwin), Pat Roach (Gen. Kael), Gavan O'Herlihy (Airk Thaughbaer), David Steinberg (Meegosh), Phil Fondacaro (Vohnkar).

In this sword and sorcery tale, evil queen Jean Marsh is determined to destroy the baby which prophecy claims will destroy her. The baby falls into the hands of amicable dwarf Warwick Davis, who with the reluctant help of mercenary Val Kilmer, sorceress Patricia Hayes and Marsh's own daughter Joanne Whalley, is able to defeat the evil one.

3344. Wills and Burke (1985, Greater Union, Australia, 101m, c). P Bob Weis & Margot McDonald, D Weis, W Philip Dalkin, PH Gaetano Nino Martinetti, M Red Symonds & Paul Grabowsky, ED Edward McQueen Mason, PD Tracy Watt.

LP Garry McDonald (Robert O'Hara Burke), Kim Gyngell (William John Wills), Jonathan Hardy (John Macadam), Peter Collingwood (Sir William Stawell), Mark Little (John King), Roy Baldwin (Charley Gray).

Familiar to every Aussie schoolboy, the epic and tedious comedy tells the story of Burke and Wills, intrepid explorers, who set out to cross the Australian continent and return. They die on the way home. It is a weak piece, with little hope of attracting an audience away from Down Under.

Willy Milly see Something Special

3345. Wilt (1989, Rank, GB, 91m, c). P Brian Eastman, D Michael Tuchner, W Andrew Marshall & David Renwick (based on the novel by Tom Sharpe), PH Norman Langley, M Anne Dudley, ED Chris Blunden, PD Leo Austin.

LP Griff Rhys Jones (Wilt), Mel Smith (Flint), Alison Steadman (Eva), Diana Quick (Sally), Jeremy Clyde (Hugh), Roger Allam (Dave), David Ryall (Rev. Froude), Roger Lloyd-Pack (Dr. Pittman).

Disillusioned college lecturer Griff Rhys Jones spends much of his time walking his dog and daydreaming about murdering his domineering wife Alison Steadman. When she disappears after a night in which Rhys Jones gets dead drunk, police inspector Mel Smith is put on the case. The banter between the two British TV comedians is moderately amusing, but not enough to make this movie a commercial success.

3346. Wimps (1987, Vestron, 84m, c). P&D Chuck Vincent, W Vincent & Craig Horrall, PH Larry Revene, M Ian Shaw & Kai Joffe, ED Marc Ubell [Vincent] & James Davalos, AD D. Gary Phelps.

LP Louis Bonanno (Francis), Deborah Blaisdell (Roxanne), Jim Abele (Charles Conrad), Jane Hamilton [Veronica Hart] (Tracy), Eddie Prevot, Derrick R. Roberts, Philip Campanero, Michael Heintzman.

In this updating of *Cyrano de Bergerac,* nerd Louis Bonanno helps star college quarterback Jim Abele woo fetching librarian Deborah Blaisdell. See *Roxanne* instead.

3347. The Wind (1987, Omega, 93m, c). P&D Nico Mastorakis, W Mastorakis & Fred C. Perry (based on a story by Mastorakis), PH Andreas Bellis, M Stanley Myers & Hans Zimmer, ED Mastorakis & Bruce Cannon, PD Lester Gallagher.

LP Meg Foster (Sian Anderson), Wings Hauser (Phil), David McCallum (John), Robert Morley (Elias Appleby), Steve Railsback (Kesner), Michael Yannatos (Policeman), Summer Thomas (Sian's Friend).

Mystery writer Meg Foster rents a house on a Greek Island from eccentric Robert Morley, despite the latter's warnings of the dangerous winds in the region and the presence of creepy caretaker Wings Hauser. When she begins to write about the characters of the island in a new mystery story, life begins to imitate art.

3348. Windows (1980, United Artists, 96m, c). P Michael Lobell, D Gordon Willis, W Barry Siegel, PH Willis, M Ennio Morricone, ED Barry Malkin, PD Melvin Bourne.

LP Talia Shire (Emily Hollander), Joseph Cortese (Bob Luffrono), Elizabeth Ashley (Andrea Glassen), Kay Medford (Ida Marx), Michael Gorrin (Sam Marx), Russell Horton (Steven Hollander), Michael Lipton (Dr. Marin).

Cinematographer Gordon Willis *(Manhattan)* makes his directorial debut with pretty pictures but an ugly psychological thriller about the unhealthy relationship between mousey Talia Shire and crazed lesbian Elizabeth Ashley.

3349. Windrider (1987, MGM/United Artists, Australia, 92m, c). P Paul Barron, D Vincent Monton, W Everett De Roche & Bonnie Harris, PH Joe Pickering, M Kevin Peak, ED John Scott, AD Steve Jodrell.

LP Tom Burlinson (P.C. Simpson), Nicole Kidman (Jade), Charles Tingwell (Simpson, Sr.), Jill Perryman (Miss Dodge), Simon Chilvers, Kim Bullad, Matt Parkinson, Penny Brown.

Windsurfer Tom Burlinson and rock star Nicole Kidman become romantically involved in a little bit of nothing.

3350. *Windwalker* (1981, Pacific International, 108m, c). P Arthur R. Dubs & Thomas E. Ballard, D Keith Merrill, W Ray Goldrup (based on the novel by Blaine M. Yorgason), PH Reed Smoot, M Merrill Jensen, ED Stephen L. Johnson, Janice Hampton & Peter L. McCrea, PD Thomas Pratt.

LP Trevor Howard (Windwalker), Nick Ramus (Smiling Wolf/Twin Brother/Narrator), James Remar (Windwalker as a young man), Serene Hedin (Tashina), Dusty Iron Wing McCrea (Dancing Moon), Silvana Gallardo (Little Feather), Billy Drago (Crow Scout).

This is an interesting presentation of the life of American Indians of the late 18th century before the white man arrived. Except for Trevor Howard and James Remar the cast consists of Indian actors speaking in the dialects of the Crow and Cheyenne with English subtitles.

3351. *Windy City* (1984, Warner, 102m, c). P Alan Greisman, D&W Armyan Bernstein, PH Reynaldo Villalobos, M Jack Nitzsche, ED Clifford Jones & Christoher Rouse, PD Bill Kenney.

LP John Shea (Danny Morgan), Kate Capshaw (Emily Reubens), Josh Mostel (Sol), Jim Borrelli (Mickey), Jeffrey DeMunn (Bobby), Eric Pierpoint (Pete), Lewis J. Stadlen (Marty), James Sutorius (Eddie).

It's an uneven but ambitious attempt to make something meaningful of the last hurrah of some South Side Chicago adults who have known and cared for each other since childhood. Their lives and dreams haven't turned out quite as they planned.

Winged Serpent see Q: Quetzalcoatl

3352. *Winners Take All* (1987, Apollo/Embassy, 105m, c). P Christopher W. Knight & Tom Tatum, D Fritz

Kiersch, W Ed Turner (based on a story by Tatum & Knight), PH Fred V. Murphy, II, M Doug Timm, ED Lorenzo De Stefano, PD Steve P. Sardanis.

LP Don Michael Paul (Rick Melon), Kathleen York (Judy McCormick), Robert Krantz ("Bad" Billy Robinson), Deborah Richter (Cindy Wickes), Peter DeLuise (Wally Briskin), Courtney Gains (Goose Trammel).

Top motorcycle racer Robert Krantz rides for a corporate sponsored team. He returns to his hometown for a race and once again finds himself in competition with Don Michael Paul, both on the track and with Krantz's old girlfriend Deborah Richter.

3353. *Winter Flight* (1984, Enigma/Goldcrest, GB, 103m, c). P Susan Richards & Robin Douet, D Roy Battersby, W Alan Janes, PH Chris Menges, M Richard Harvey, ED Lesley Walker.

LP Reece Dinsdale (Mal Stanton), Nicola Cowper (Angie), Gary Olsen (Dave), Sean Benn (Hooker), Beverly Hewitt (Lara), Shelagh Stephenson (Kel), Michael Percival (Doctor), Anthony Trent (Sgt. Bowyer).

In a routine story, Reece Dinsdale's job is to keep seagulls off a Royal Air Force runway. He becomes romantically involved with Nicola Cowper, an unmarried mother-to-be.

3354. *Winter of Our Dreams* (1982, Vega Enterprises/Satori, Australia, 89m, c). P Richard Mason, D&W John Duigan, PH Tom Cowan, M Sharon Calcraft, ED Henry Dangar, PD Lee Whitmore.

LP Judy Davis (Lou), Bryan Brown (Rob), Cathy Downes (Fretel), Baz Luhrmann (Pete), Peter Mochrie (Tim), Mervyn Drak (Mick), Margie McCrae (Lisa), Mercie Deane-Johns (Angela).

Sidney prostitute Judy Davis tries desperately to escape her life of drugs and degradation.

3355. *Winter People* (1989, Columbia, 110m, c). P Robert H. Solo, D Ted Kotcheff, W Carol Sobieski (based on the novel by John Ehle), PH Francois Protat, M John Scott, ED Thom Noble, PD Ron Foreman.

LP Kurt Russell (Wayland Jackson), Kelly McGillis (Collie Wright), Lloyd

Bridges (William Wright), Jeffrey Meek (Cole Campbell), Mitchell Ryan (Drury Campbell), Amelia Burnette (Paula Jackson), Eileen Ryan (Annie Wright), Lanny Flaherty (Gudger Wright).

Clockmaker widower Kurt Russell sets off with his young daughter, Amelia Burnette, and her pet pig, in search of a better life. His car breaks down near the cabin of unwed mother Kelly McGillis. She allows Russell and his daughter to live in a tiny shack near hers, scandalizing her family and the neighbors once again. Russell wants to be part of McGillis' life but first everyone has to deal with a Hatfield and McCoy–like feud.

Wipeout see Under the Boardwalk

3356. Wired (1989, Taurus, 108m, c). P Edward S. Feldman & Charles R. Meeker, D Larry Peerce, W Earl Mac Rauch (based on the book by Bob Woodward), PH Tony Imi, M Basil Poledouris, ED Eric Sears, PD Brian Eatwell.

LP Michael Chiklis (John Belushi), Ray Sharkey (Angel Velasquez), J.T. Walsh (Bob Woodward), Patti D'Arbanville (Cathy Smith), Lucinda Jenney (Judy Belushi), Alex Rocco (Arnie Fromson), Gary Groomes (Dan Aykroyd), Jere Burns (Lou).

Don't blame Michael Chiklis for the failure of this movie about the life of comedian John Belushi. Although he seems a little young for the role he gives it all he's got. Unfortunately, the director and screenwriter provide him very little to work with. The film opens with Belushi already dead, but not quite down. He escapes from his body bag in the morgue and is picked up by cabbie Ray Sharkey who turns out to be the funny man's guardian angel. The rest of the movie jumps around in time and place with no apparent goal in mind, except not to offend any of Belushi's pals or acquaintances who might sue if they were shown in the wrong light or perhaps even mentioned.

3357. Wired to Kill (1986, American Distribution Group, 96m, c). P Jim Buchfuehrer, D&W Franky Schaeffer, PH Tom Fraser, M Russell Ferrante & The Yellow Jackets, ED Daniel Agulian & Schaeffer.

LP Emily Longstreth (Rebecca), Devin Hoelscher (Steve), Merritt Butrick (Reegus), Frank Collison (Sly), Garth Gardner (Loady), Kim Milford (Rooster), Michael Wollet (Zero).

In the year 1998, a deadly virus has wiped out most of the population of the United States. Mutant gangs victimize the survivors. But when they kill Devin Hoelscher's girlfriend, he invents deadly booby traps to take revenge.

3358. Wisdom (1986, 20th Century–Fox, 108m, c). P Bernard Williams, D&W Emilio Estevez, PH Adam Greenberg, M Danny Elfman, ED Michael Kahn, PD Dennis Gassner.

LP Demi Moore (Karen Simmons), Emilio Estevez (John Wisdom), Tom Skerritt (Lloyd Wisdom), Veronica Cartwright (Samantha Wisdom), William Allen Young (Williamson), Richard Minchenberg (Cooper).

Emilio Estevez becomes the youngest person ever to write, direct and star in a movie, but he can't claim the result is much to brag about. He is a modern day Robin Hood, with pretty Demi Moore as his Maid Marian, but such shenanigans are not allowed today. He dies in a hail of bullets which he deliberately calls down on himself. Not so wise!

3359. Wise Blood (1980, New Line, 108m, c). P Michael Fitzgerald & Kathy Fitzgerald, D John Huston, W Benedict Fitzgerald (based on the novel by Flannery O'Connor), PH Gerald Fisher, M Alex North, ED Roberto Silvi.

LP Brad Dourif (Hazel Motes), Ned Beatty (Hoover Shoates), Harry Dean Stanton (Asa Hawks), Daniel Shor (Enoch Emery), Amy Wright (Sabbath Lilly), Mary Nell Santacroce (Landlady), John Huston (Grandfather).

The film traces the strange career of religious fanatic Brad Dourif. He attempts to found a church without salvation in retaliation for his past sufferings at the hands of his hellfire-and-brimstone preaching grandfather.

3360. Wise Guys (1986, MGM/United Artists, 92m, c). P Aaron Russo, D Brian DePalma, W George Gallo, PH Fred Schuler, M Ira Newborn, ED Jerry Greenberg, PD Edward Pisoni.

LP Danny DeVito (Harry Valentini),

Joe Piscopo (Moe Dickstein), Harvey Keitel (Bobby DiLea), Ray Sharkey (Marco), Dan Hedaya (Anthony Castelo), Capt. Lou Albano (Frank "The Fixer"), Julie Bovasso (Lil Dickstein), Patti LuPone (Wanda Valentini), Antonia Rey (Aunt Sadie), Mimi Cecchini (Grandma Valentini).

You have to enjoy Danny DeVito to enjoy this movie. He and Joe Piscopo are two lamebrain minor gangsters working for Ray Sharkey. When they make the wrong wager at the racetrack for their boss, their futures don't look very bright. To add to the fun, these best friends are told to "hit" each other. How they get around that is somewhat amusing.

3361. *Wish You Were Here* (1987, Atlantic, GB, 92m, c). P Sarah Radclyffe, D&W David Leland, PH Ian Wilson, M Stanley Myers, ED George Akers, PD Caroline Amies.

LP Emily Lloyd (Lynda), Tom Bell (Eric), Clare Clifford (Mrs. Parfitt), Barbara Durkin (Valerie), Geoffrey Hutchings (Hubert), Charlotte Barker (Gillian), Chloe Leland (Margaret), Trudy Cavanagh (Tap Dancing Lady), Jesse Birdsall (Dave).

Emily Lloyd makes a triumphant debut as a spunky but troubled British teen, living at a seaside resort during the 50s. Still grieving over the death of her mother, Lloyd rebels against her father. She has ill-fated sexual encounters, including one with sleazy but oddly magnetic Tom Bell, a friend of her father. Her favorite expression is "Up your bum."

The Witch see Superstition

3362. *Witchboard* (1987, Cinema Group, 98m, c). P Gerold Geoffray, D&W Kevin S. Tenney, PH Roy H. Wagner, M Dennis Michael Tenney, ED Daniel Duncan & Stephen J. Waller, AD Sarah Burdick.

LP Todd Allen (Jim Morar), Tawny Kitaen (Linda Brewster), Steven Nichols (Brandon Sinclair), Kathleen Wilhoite (Zarabeth), Burke Byrnes (Lt. Dewhurst), Rose Marie (Mrs. Moses), James W. Quinn (Lloyd).

The witchboard can turn an innocent player into a righteous person or a possessed murderer.

3363. *The Witches of Eastwick* (1987, Warner, 118m, c). P Neil Canton, Peter Guber & Jon Peters, D George Miller, W Michael Cristofer (based on a novel by John Updike), PH Vilmos Zsigmond, M John Williams†, ED Richard Francis-Bruce & Hubert C. De La Bouillerie, PD Polly Platt, SOUND Wayne Artman, Tom Beckett, Tom Dahl & Art Rochester†.

LP Jack Nicholson (Daryl Van Horne), Cher (Alexandra Medford), Susan Sarandon (Jane Spofford), Michelle Pfeiffer (Sukie Ridgemont), Veronica Cartwright (Felicia Alden), Richard Jenkins (Clyde Alden), Keith Jochim (Walter Neff), Carel Struycken (Fidel).

The first half of this film is intriguing. Three recently divorced women, sculptor Cher, high school music teacher Susan Sarandon and newspaper writer Michelle Pfeiffer, find their quiet and boring lives in the small New England town of Eastwick drastically changed by the arrival of that "horny little devil" Jack Nicholson. He takes all three as lovers and apparently knows how to satisfy women. The second half is a typical exploitation sex and horror film, gross and disgusting.

3364. *Witchtrap* (1989, Cinema Plus/GCO, 90m, c). P Kevin S. Tenney & Dan Duncan, D&W Tenney, PH Thomas Jewett, M Dennis Michael Tenney, ED William O. Sullivan.

LP James W. Quinn (Tony Vicente), Kathleen Bailey (Whitney), Judy Tatum (Agnes), Rob Zapple (Felix), Jack W. Thompson (Frank Murphy), Clyde Talley, 2d (Levi Jackson), Linnea Quigley (Ginger), Keith S. Tenney (Devin Lauter).

Kevin S. Tenney calls in a team of paranormal experts to exorcise the haunted house he's inherited from his uncle.

3365. *Withnail and I* (1987, Cineplex Odeon, GB, 108m, c). P Paul M. Heller, D&W Bruce Robinson (based on his novel), PH Peter Hannan, M David Dundas, ED Alan Strachan, PD Michael Pickwoad.

LP Richard E. Grant (Withnail), Paul McGann (Marwood [I]), Richard Griffiths (Monty), Ralph Brown (Danny), Michael Elphick (Jake), Daragh O'Mallery (Irishman), Michael Wardle (Isaac Parkin), Una Brandon-Jones (Mrs. Parkin).

In this hilarious black comedy-drama, Richard E. Grant and Paul McGann are two struggling actors of the late 60s. They share drugs, alcohol and their failures in a seedy London flat. Looking for some recuperative cure, the two decide to spend a weekend in the country and find this just as taxing and terrifying as their city life.

3366. *Without a Clue* (1988, Orion, 106m, c). P Marc Stirdivant, D Thom Eberhardt, W Gary Murphy & Larry Strawther, PH Alan Hume, M Henry Mancini, ED Peter Tanner, PD Brian Ackland-Snow.

LP Michael Caine ("Sherlock Holmes"/Reginald Kincaid), Ben Kingsley (Dr. Watson), Jeffrey Jones (Inspector Lestrade), Lysette Anthony (Fake Leslie), Matthew Sim (Real Leslie), Paul Freeman (Dr. Moriarty), Nigel Davenport (Lord Smithwick), Pat Keen (Mrs. Hudson), Peter Cook (Greenhough).

Suppose Sherlock Holmes was merely an invention of Dr. Watson, who was the true brilliant sleuth. Suppose further that the time has come for Watson to produce Holmes. Then suppose that Watson hires a drunken, none-too-bright actor to portray Holmes. And suppose further that the pair actually has to track down the nefarious Dr. Moriarty with the phony sleuth starting to believe his press clippings and his supposed brilliance in deduction. With all these suppositions, one must come to the conclusion that this film is less interesting than the least exciting tale written by Arthur Conan Doyle.

3367. *Without a Trace* (1983, 20th Century-Fox, 121m, c). P&D Stanley R. Jaffe, W Beth Gutcheon (based on her novel *Still Missing*), PH John Bailey, M Jack Nitzsche, ED Cynthia Scheider, PD Paul Sylbert.

LP Kate Nelligan (Susan Selky), Judd Hirsch (Al Menetti), David Dukes (Graham Selky), Stockard Channing (Jocelyn Norris), Jacqueline Brookes (Margaret Mayo), Keith McDermott (Phillippe), Kathleen Widdoes (Ms. Hauser), Daniel Bryan Corkill (Alex Selky).

When Kate Nelligan's son disappears, she and New York detective Judd Hirsch search all over the city until they find the child.

3368. *Without Warning* (1980, Filmways, 89m, c, aka *It Came... Without Warning*). P&D Greydon Clark, W Lyn Freeman, Daniel Grodnik, Ben Nett & Steve Mathis, PH Dean Cundey, M Dan Wyman, ED Curtis Burch, PD Jack DeWolf.

LP Jack Palance (Taylor), Martin Landau (Fred Dobbs), Tarah Nutter (Sandy), Christopher S. Nelson (Greg), Cameron Mitchell (Hunter), Neville Brand (Leo), Sue Ane Langdon (Aggy), Larry Storch (Scoutmaster), Ralph Meeker (Dave).

A small town is taken over by space invaders who resemble giant leeches, Prospective viewers have now been warned.

3369. *Witness*† (1985, Paramount, 112m, c). P Edward S. Feldman, D Peter Weir†, W Earl W. Wallace & William Kelley (based on a story by Kelley, Earl W. Wallace & Pamela Wallace*), PH John Seale†, M Maurice Jarre†, ED Thom Noble*, PD Stan Jolley, AD Stan Jolley†, SD John Anderson†.

LP Harrison Ford† (John Book), Kelly McGillis (Rachel), Josef Sommer (Schaeffer), Lukas Haas (Samuel), Jan Rubes (Eli Lapp), Alexander Godunov (Daniel Hochleitner), Patti LuPone (Elaine), Danny Glover (McFee), Brent Jennings (Carter).

Amish lad Lukas Haas witnesses a murder committed by crooked cop Danny Glover. Harrison Ford is a tough police detective who takes it on himself to flee with the boy and the lad's beautiful widowed mother Kelly McGillis to the Pennsylvania Dutch country to hide from the murderers. Ford and McGillis have time to fall in love before the bad guys show up and there is one hell of a shoot-out.

Wits End   see   The G.I. Executioners

3370. *The Wizard* (1989, Universal, 97m, c). P David Chisholm & Ken Topolsky, D Todd Holland, W Chisholm, PH Robert Yeoman, M J. Peter Robinson, ED Tom Finan, PD Michael Mayer.

LP Fred Savage (Corey), Luke Edwards (Jimmy), Jenny Lewis (Haley), Christian Slater (Nick), Beau Bridges (Sam).

Warning to all adults. Do not accompany your children to this kiddie knockoff of *Rain Man*. Just drop them off at the theater and pick them up about an hour-and-a-half later. Television's "Wonder Years" star, 13-year-old Fred Savage leads his troubled, uncommunicative younger half-brother Luke Edwards on a cross-country journey. They end up in the world's video game championship, where Edwards shows his stuff. The entire film is one giant advertisement for Nintendo and Universal Studio Tours.

3371. The Wizard of Loneliness (1988, Skouras, 110m, c). P Thom Tyson & Philip Porcella, D Jenny Bowen, W Nancy Larson & Bowen (based on the novel by John Nichols), PH Richard Bowen, M Michel Colombier, ED Lisa Day, PD Jeffrey Beecroft.

LP Lukas Haas (Wendall Olet), Lea Thompson (Sybil), Lance Guest (John T.), John Randolph (Doc), Dylan Baker (Duffy), Anne Pitoniak (Cornelia), Jeremiah Warner (Tom), Steve Hendrickson (Fred).

Set in Vermont during World War II, Lukas Haas is a spoiled kid from Los Angeles. He is sent to live with his grandparents after his mother dies and his father is shipped overseas. He is greatly affected by his disabled Uncle Lance Guest and Aunt Lea Thompson, who gives birth to an illegitimate child.

3372. Wizards of the Lost Kingdom (1985, Concorde, US/Arg., 75m, c). P Frank Isaac & Alex Sessa, D Hector Olivera, W Tom Edwards, PH Leonard Solis, M James Horner & Chris Young, ED Silvia Roberts, PD Mary Bertram.

LP Bo Svenson (Kor), Vidal Peterson (Simon), Thom Christopher (Shurka), Barbara Stock (Udea), Maria Socas (Acrasia), Dolores Michaels (Aura), Edward Morrow (Wulfrick/Old Simon/Gulfax), August Larreta (King Tylor).

Great warrior Bo Svenson helps boy magician Vidal Peterson battle monsters, mermaids and other mystical beings in order to restore justice to the magical kingdom.

3373. Wolfen (1981, Warner, 115m, c). P Rupert Hitzig, D Michael Wadleigh, W David Eyre & Wadleigh (based on the novel by Whitley Strieber), PH Gerry Fisher, M James Horner, ED Chris Leb-

enzon, Dennis Dolan, Martin Bram & Marshall M. Borden, PD Paul Sylbert, MK Carl Fullerton.

LP Albert Finney (Dewey Wilson), Diane Venora (Rebecca Neff), Edward James Olmos (Eddie Holt), Gregory Hines (Whittington), Tom Noonan (Ferguson), Dick O'Neill (Warren), Dehl Berti (Old Indian).

Mutilation murders in New York City are discovered to be the work of savage beasts. They have descended from Indian hunters who went underground, despairing of the future of the human race.

3374. Wolfman (1980, Omni, 101m, c). P Earl Owensby, D&W Worth Keeter, PH Darrell Cathcart, M Arthur Smith & David Floyd, ED Richard Aldridge, AD David Cadell, SE Al Yehoe, MK Sandy Barber & Keeter.

LP Earl Owensby (Colin Glasgow), Ed L. Grady (Rev. Leonard), Julian Morton (Edwin Glasgow), Kristine Reynolds (Lynn Randolph), Richard Dedmon (Uncle Clement), Maggie Lauterer (Aunt Elizabeth), Sid Rancer (Dr. Tate).

Earl Owensby slowly comes to the realization that he has inherited the family curse and will become a wolfman.

3375. The Wolves of Willoughby Chase (1988, Atlantic, GB, 98m, c). P Mark Forstater, D Stuart Orme, W William M. Akers (based on the novel by Joan Aiken), PH Paul Beeson, M Colin Towns, ED Martin Walsh, PD Christopher Hobbs.

LP Stephanie Beacham (Slighcarp), Mel Smith (Grimshaw), Geraldine James (Mrs. Brisket), Emily Hudson (Bonnie), Aleks Darowska (Sylvia), Lynton Dearden (Simon), Richard O'Brien (James), Jane Horrocks (Pattern).

When her parents go abroad, Emily Hudson and her timid cousin Aleks Darowska are left in the care of sinister governess Stephanie Beacham. The latter has plans to claim Willoughby Chase manor for herself. She commands a pack of wolves. It takes all of the wit and courage of the two girls to foil the evil governess in this fantasy-adventure film set in Victorian England.

3376. The Woman in Red (1984, Orion, 87m, c). P Victor Drai, D&W

Gene Wilder (based on the screenplay *Pardon Mon Affair* by Jean-Loup Dabadie & Yves Robert), PH Fred Schuler, M John Morris, ED Christopher Greenbury, PD David L. Snyder.

LP Gene Wilder (Theodore Pierce), Charles Grodin (Buddy), Joseph Bologna (Joe), Judith Ivey (Didi), Michael Huddleston (Michael), Kelly LeBrock (Charlotte), Gilda Radner (Ms. Milner), Kyle T. Heffner (Richard), Michael Zorek (Shelly).

Kelly LeBrock is a knock-out. Charles Grodin and Joseph Bologna are outstanding character actors who can always be counted on to please. Stevie Wonder's "I Just Called to Say I Love You" is one of his best songs. Everything else about this film is disappointingly dumb and sexist. The premise is that married Gene Wilder spies LeBrock dancing over an air vent in a parking garage. As the wind swirls up her sexy red dress, showing her very fine legs and panties, Wilder is a goner. Unfortunately, as is the case with Dudley Moore in *10,* he gets a chance to meet and bed his mysterious lady — but it's not as good as he imagines. Still the ending of the film suggests that Wilder has learned nothing from his experiences.

3377. The Woman Inside (1981, 20th Century-Fox, 94m, c). P Sidney H. Levine, D&W Joseph Van Winkle, PH Ron Johnson, M Eddy Lawrence Manson, ED John Duffy.

LP Gloria Manon (Holly/Hollis), Dane Clark (Dr. Rassner), Joan Blondell (Aunt Coll), Michael Champion (Nolan), Marlene Tracy (Dr. Parris), Michael Mancini (Marco), Luce Morgan (Maggie), Terri Haven (Agnes).

Joan Blondell makes her final film appearance in this story of wounded veteran Gloria Manon, who wants a sex change operation so "he" can become a woman.

3378. A Woman Obsessed (1989, Platinum, 105m, c). P&D Larry Vincent, W Craig Horrall, PH Larry Revene, M Joey Mennonna, ED James Davalos, AD Hilary Wright.

LP Ruth Raymond (Arlene Bellings), Linda Blair (Evie Barnes), Gregory Patrick (Ted Barnes), Troy Donahue (Jack Barnes), Carolyn Van Bellinghen

(Wanda Barnes), Frank Stewart (Bobby Trumbal).

Yuppie lawyer Gregory Patrick discovers that what appears to be a nude portrait of him, for which he never posed, is actually the work of Ruth Raymond, who claims to be Patrick's mother. Her model was Patrick's father. Momma Raymond is not too stable and she's talented in mixing poison as well as paints.

3379. The Women's Club (1987, Lightning Pictures, 89m, c). P Fred Weintraub, D&W Sandra Weintraub, PH Kent Wakeford, M David Wheatley & Paul F. Antonelli, ED Martin Cohen, AD Tim Duffey.

LP Michael Pare (Patrick), Maud Adams (Angie), Eddie Velez (Carlos).

In this comedy, what seems a perfect job for young stud Michael Pare, servicing Adams' friends, becomes a nightmare.

3380. Wonderland (1989, Vestron, GB, 103m, c). P Steve Morrison, D Philip Saville, W Frank Clarke, PH Dick Pope, M Hans Zimmer, ED Richard Bedford, PD David Brockhurst.

LP Emile Charles (Eddie), Tony Forsyth (Michael), Robert Stephens (Vincent), Clare Higgins (Eve), Bruce Payne (Echo), Robbie Coltrane (Annabelle), Carsten Norgaard (Dolphin Man).

Emile Charles and Tony Forsyth are two gay Liverpool teenagers who dream of finding someplace where they can be happy. The film doesn't seem to suggest that they will ever find it. Charles identifies with the performing dolphins at Wonderland, even sneaking in to swim with them.

3381. Working Girl† (1988, 20th Century-Fox, 113m, c). P Douglas Wick, D Mike Nichols†, W Kevin Wade, PH Michael Ballhaus, M Carly Simon, ED Sam O'Steen, PD Patrizia Von Brandenstein, AD Doug Kraner, SD George De Titta, M/L "Let the River Run" by Simon & Phil Collins*.

LP Melanie Griffith† (Tess McGill), Harrison Ford (Jack Trainer), Sigourney Weaver† (Katherine Parker), Joan Cusack† (Cyn), Alec Baldwin (Mick Dugan), Philip Bosco (Oren Trask), Nora Dunn (Ginny), Oliver Platt (Lutz), James

Lally (Turkel), Kevin Spacey (Bob Spreck), Robert Easton (Armbrister), Olympia Dukakis (Personnel Director).

Melanie Griffith is a delight as a sweet, scrappy and sexy secretary who makes the most of the opportunity presented to her when her boss Sigourney Weaver has a skiing accident. Griffith not only shows she's a Wall Street whiz, she also snags Weaver's gentleman friend Harrison Ford in the bargain. When she tells off the obnoxious Weaver, audiences cheer, although some may object to the reference to Weaver's "bony ass." An excellent performance is given by Joan Cusack as Griffith's gum-chewing, bouffant-hairdo, clunky jewelry and gobs of eyeshadow girlfriend. She will never be anything more than a member of the steno pool, but she's there to cheer her friend on.

3382. *Working Girls* (1986, Miramax, 90m, c). P Lizzie Borden & Andi Gladstone, D Borden, W Borden & Sandra Kay (based on a story by Borden), PH Judy Irola, M David van Tieghem & Roma Baran, ED Borden, PD Kurt Ossenfort.

LP Louise Smith (Molly), Ellen McElduff (Lucy), Amanda Goodwin (Dawn), Marusia Zach (Gina), Janne Peters (April), Helen Nicholas (Mary).

The film follows a group of prostitutes through a day (or night) in their work at a high class brothel. The notorious documentary-like film is an interesting examination of sexual politics in action.

3383. *The World According to Garp* (1982, Warner, 136m, c). P George Roy Hill & Robert L. Crawford, D Hill, W Steve Tesich (based on the novel by John Irving), PH Miroslav Ondricek, ED Ronald Roose & Stephen A. Rotter, PD Henry Bumstead.

LP Robin Williams (T.S. Garp), Marybeth Hurt (Helen Holm), Glenn Close† (Jenny Fields), John Lithgow† (Roberta Muldoon), Hume Cronyn (Mr. Fields), Jessica Tandy (Mrs. Fields), Swoosie Kurtz (Hooker), James McCall (Young Garp), Peter Michael Goetz (John Wolfe).

Based on John Irving's novel, which many believed could not be filmed, the result is an episodic adaptation which perhaps shouldn't have been filmed. It is the comical and tragic life of Robin Williams, a man deliberately conceived by

his nurse mother Glenn Close, using a dying, insane soldier as an unaware source of sperm. The performances of Close and John Lithgow as a transsexual former professional football player are very good.

3384. *A World Apart* (1988, Atlantic, GB, 113m, c). P Sarah Radclyffe, D Chris Menges, W Shawn Slovo, PH Peter Biziou, M Hans Zimmer, ED Nicolas Gaster, PD Brian Morris.

LP Barbara Hershey (Diana Roth), Jodhi May (Molly Roth), Jeroen Krabbe (Gus Roth), Carolyn Clayton-Cragg (Miriam Roth), Merav Gruer (Jude Roth), Yvonne Bryceland (Bertha), Albee Lesotho (Solomon), Linda Mvusi (Elsie), Rosalie Crutchley (Mrs. Harris).

In 1963, a crackdown on antiapartheid protests causes dissident Jeroen Krabbe to flee South Africa, leaving behind his wife Barbara Hershey and two daughters, Carolyn Clayton-Cragg and Jodhi May. The latter's resentment towards her mother grows in direct proportion to the continuing fight Hershey makes against apartheid, leaving little time for her daughters.

3385. *World Gone Wild* (1988, Lorimar, 94m, c). P Robert L. Rosen, D Lee H. Kazin, W Jorge Zamacona, PH Don Burgess, M Laurence Juber, ED Gary A. Griffen, PD Donald L. Harris.

LP Bruce Dern (Ethan), Michael Pare (George Landon), Catherine Mary Stewart (Angie), Adam Ant (Derek Abernathy), Anthony James (Ten Watt), Rick Podell (Exline), Julius Carry, III (Nitro), Alan Autry (Hank).

In a postapocalyptic world, survivors, jealously guarding their precious supply of water, are attacked by white-clad thugs led by androgynous Adam Ant, who quotes from Charles Manson as inspiration for the carnage of his cult.

3386. *The World Is Full of Married Men* (1980, New Line, GB, 106m, c). P Malcolm Fancey & Oscar S. Lerman, D Robert Young, W Jackie Collins & Terry Howard (based on her novel), PH Ray Parslow, M Frank Musker & Dominic Bugatti, ED David Campling.

LP Anthony Franciosa (David Cooper), Carroll Baker (Linda Cooper), Gareth Hunt (Jay Grossman), Georgina Hale (Lori Grossman), Anthony Steel

(Conrad Lee), Sherrie Cronn (Claudia Parker), Paul Nicholas (Gem Gemini), Jean Gilpin (Miss Field), John Nolan (Joe).

In this tedious production of Jackie Collins' trashy novel, the wife of advertising executive Anthony Franciosa decides to pay him back in kind for his frequent infidelities.

3387. The Worm Eaters (1981, New American, 94m, c). P Ted V. Mikels, D&W Herb Robins (based on a story by Nancy Kapner), PH Willis Hawkins, M Theodore Stern, ED Soly Bina, PD Jack DeWolf.

LP Herb Robins (Hermann Umgar), Lindsay Armstrong Black, Joseph Sacket, Robert Garrison, Muriel Cooper, Mike Garrison, Barry Hostetler.

An eccentric, club-footed hermit attempts to settle the score with a nearby small California community by setting loose a horde of worms to destroy their food supply.

3388. Worth Winning (1989, 20th Century-Fox, 102m, c). P Gil Friesen & Dale Pollock, D Will Mackenzie, W Josann McGibbon & Sara Parriott (based on the novel by Dan Lewandowski), PH Adam Greenberg, M Patrick Williams, ED Sidney Wolinsky, PD Lilly Kilvert.

LP Mark Harmon (Taylor Worth), Madeleine Stowe (Veronica Briskow), Lesley Ann Warren (Eleanor Larimore), Maria Holvoe (Erin Cooper), Mark Blum (Ned Braudy), Andrea Martin (Claire Braudy), Tony Longo (Terry Childs), Alan Blumenfeld (Howard Larimore).

The sexual innuendoes in this lost-in-space comedy are not so much tasteless as they are childish. TV weatherman Mark Harmon is very, very popular with the ladies — at least the ladies of great pulchritude and little brains, the only type to appear in the film. Harmon's friends bet him he can't get three women to agree to marry him and the lout accepts the bet, wins, but finds true love. Who cares?

3389. The Wraith (1986, New Century, 92m, c). P John Kemeny, D&W Mike Marvin, PH Reed Smoot, M Michael Hoenig & J. Peter Robinson, ED Scott Conrad & Gary Rocklin.

LP Charlie Sheen (The Wraith/Jake), Nick Cassavetes (Packard), Sherilyn Fenn (Keri), Randy Quaid (Loomis), Matthew Barry (Billy), David Sherrill (Skank), Jamie Bozian (Gutterboy), Clint Howard (Rughead).

Charlie Sheen is a hero sent from the skies to challenge the evil forces in a rural community.

3390. The Wrong Guys (1988, New World, 86m, c). P Chuck Gordon & Ronald E. Frazier, D Danny Bilson, W Bilson & Paul de Meo, PH Frank Byers, M Joseph Conlan, ED Frank J. Jimenez, PD George Costello.

LP Louie Anderson (Louie), Richard Lewis (Richard), Richard Belzer (Belz), Franklyn Ajaye (Franklyn), Tim Thomerson (Tim), Brion James (Glen Grunski), Biff Manard (Mark Grunski), John Goodman (Duke Earl).

Louie Anderson is the leader of a group of stand-up comedians appearing as members of a former Boy Scout troop on a camping trip. They encounter escaped convict John Goodman who mistakes them for the CIA. Dumb! Dumb! Dumb!

3391. Wrong Is Right (1982, Columbia, 117m, c, aka *The Man with the Deadly Lens*). P,D&W Richard Brooks (based on the novel *The Better Angels* by Charles McCarry), PH Fred J. Koenekamp, M Artie Kane, ED George Grenville, PD Edward Carfagno.

LP Sean Connery (Patrick Hale), George Grizzard (President Lockwood), Robert Conrad (Gen. Wombat), Katharine Ross (Sally Blake), G.D. Spradlin (Philindros), John Saxon (Homer Hubbard), Henry Silva (Rafeeq), Leslie Nielsen (Mallory), Robert Webber (Harvey), Rosalind Cash (Mrs. Ford), Hardy Kruger (Helmut Unger), Dean Stockwell (Hacker), Ron Moody (King Awad).

International TV commentator Sean Connery discovers that the world is being manipulated by the CIA. So what else is news?

3392. Xanadu (1980, Universal, 93m, c). P Lawrence Gordon, D Robert Greenwald, W Richard Christian Danus, Marc Reid Rubel & Michael Kane, PH Victor J. Kemper, M Barry DeVorzon, ED Dennis Virkler, PD John W. Corso.

LP Olivia Newton-John (Kira), Gene Kelly (Danny McGuire), Michael Beck (Sonny Malone), James Sloyan (Simpson), Dimitra Arliss (Helen), Katie Hanley (Sandra), Fred McCarren (Richie), Ren Woods (Jo).

This attempt to prove that 40s musicals could succeed in the 80s fell flat on its face. The muse Terpsichore (Olivia Newton-John) comes to earth to inspire artist Michael Beck who wants to open a rock 'n' roll hall. Poor Gene Kelly finds himself at the twilight of his career in possibly the worst of all musicals, after having appeared in many of the best. The story seems inspired by the not very good 1947 film *Down to Earth*.

3393. *Xtro* (1983, New Line, GB, 80m, c). P Mark Forstater, D Harry Bromley Davenport, W Iain Cassie, Robert Smith & Jo Ann Kaplan (based on a screenplay by Michel Parry & Davenport), PH John Metcalfe & John Simmons, M Davenport & Shelton Leigh Palmer, ED Nick Gaster & Kaplan, AD Andrew Mollo & Peter Body, SE Tom Harris.

LP Philip Sayer (Sam Phillips), Bernice Stegers (Rachel Phillips), Danny Brainin (Joe Daniels), Simon Nash (Tony Phillips), Maryam D'Abo (Analise), David Cardy (Michael), Anna Wing (Miss Goodman).

In a vile film filled with grotesque special effects, mostly involving a series of repulsive bladder problems, father Philip Sayer is abducted by aliens. He returns to his family three years later in the form of a crablike monster. He infects his son, kills any number of people and turns the family's au pair into an alien breeding machine.

The XYZ Murders see Crimewave

3394. *The Year My Voice Broke* (1988, Avenue, Australia, 103m, c). P Terry Hayes, Doug Mitchell & George Miller, D&W John Duigan, PH Geoff Burton, M Christine Woodruff, ED Neil Thumpston, PD Roger Ford.

LP Noah Taylor (Danny), Loene Carmen (Freya), Ben Mendelsohn (Trevor), Graeme Blundell (Nils Olson), Lynette Curran (Anne Olson), Malcolm Robertson (Bruce Embling), Judi Farr (Sheila Embling).

This coming of age film is set in New South Wales in 1962. Long-time pals Noah Taylor and Loene Carmen begin to experience their first feelings of sexual desire, he for her, she for an older, wilder lad. Carmen scandalizes the town when she becomes pregnant, miscarries and must leave her home, never to be seen again by her friend Taylor.

3395. *The Year of Living Dangerously* (1983, MGM, Australia, 115m, c). P James McElroy, D Peter Weir, W David Williamson, Weir & C.J. Koch (based on the novel by Koch), PH Russell Boyd, M Maurice Jarre, ED Bill Anderson, AD Herbert Pinter.

LP Mel Gibson (Guy Hamilton), Sigourney Weaver (Jill Bryant), Linda Hunt* (Billy Kwan), Michael Murphy (Pete Curtis), Bembol Roco (Kumar), Domingo Landicho (Hortono), Hermono De Guzman (Immigration Officer), Noel Ferrier (Wally O'Sullivan), Paul Sonkkila (Kevin Condon), Ali Nur (Ali).

Young Australian journalist Mel Gibson has his first international assignment in Indonesia in 1965 when the Sukarno regime was toppling. The film belongs to diminutive Linda Hunt, playing a man who plays cupid for Gibson and British diplomatic attaché Sigourney Weaver.

3396. *Year of the Dragon* (1985, MGM/United Artists, 136m, c). P Dino De Laurentiis, D Michael Cimino, W Cimino & Oliver Stone (based on the novel by Robert Daley), PH Alex Thomson, M David Mansfield, ED Francoise Bonnot, PD Wolf Kroeger.

LP Mickey Rourke (Stanley White), John Lone (Joey Tai), Ariane (Tracy Tzu), Leonard Termo (Angelo Rizzo), Raymond Barry (Louis Bukowski), Caroline Kava (Connie White), Eddie Jones (William McKenna), Joey Chin (Ronnie Chang), Victor Wong (Harry Yung).

In a violent, racist, sexist film, Mickey Rourke portrays a police officer trying to break up Chinese youth gangs in New York's Chinatown.

3397. *Yellow Hair and the Fortress of Gold* (1984, Crown, US/Spain, 102m, c). P John Ghaffari & Diego G. Sempre, D Matt Cimber, W Cimber & John Kershaw (based on characters and story by

Cimber), PH John Cabrera, M Franco Piersanti, ED Claudio Cutry.

LP Laurene Landon (Yellow Hair), Ken Roberson (Pecos Kid), John Ghaffari (Shayowteewah), Luis Lorenzo (Col. Torres), Claudia Gravi (Grey Cloud), Aldo Sambrel (Flores), Eduardo Fajardo (Man-Who-Knows).

Seeking a fortress of gold, princess Laurene Landon looks for help from a strange man who lives in an elk's horn.

3398. *Yellowbeard* (1983, Orion, 101m, c). P Carter De Haven, D Mel Damski, W Graham Chapman, Peter Cook & Bernard McKenna, PH Gerry Fisher, M John Morris, ED William Reynolds, PD Joseph R. Jennings.

LP Graham Chapman (Yellowbeard), Peter Boyle (Moon), Richard "Cheech" Marin (El Segundo), Tommy Chong (El Nebuloso), Peter Cook (Lord Lambourn), Marty Feldman (Gilbert), Martin Hewitt (Dan), Michael Hordern (Dr. Gilpin), Eric Idle (Cmdr. Clement), Madeline Kahn (Betty), James Mason (Capt. Hughes), John Cleese (Blind Pew), Kenneth Mars (Crisp/Verdugo), Spike Milligan (Flunkie), Susannah York (Lady Churchill), Beryl Reid (Lady Lambourn).

This directionless farce follows the adventures of a 17th century pirate captain, Graham Chapman. It is the useless tasteless stuff expected from Monty Python but without the wit. Marty Feldman makes his final screen appearance, having died during production.

3399. *Yentl* (1983, MGM/United Artists, GB, 134m, c). P Barbra Streisand & Rusty Lemorande, D Streisand, W Streisand & Jack Rosenthal (based on the short story "Yentl the Yeshiva Boy" by Isaac Bashevis Singer), PH David Watkin, M Michel Legrand, Alan & Marilyn Bergman†, ED Terry Rawlings, PD Roy Walker, AD Walker & Leslie Tomkins†, SD Tessa Davies, M/L "Papa Can You Hear Me?" and "The Way He Makes Me Feel" by Legrand, Alan & Marilyn Berman†.

LP Barbra Streisand (Yentl), Mandy Patinkin (Avigdor), Amy Irving† (Hadass), Nehemiah Persoff (Papa), Steven Hill (Reb Alter Vishkower), Allan Corduner (Shimmele), Ruth Goring (Esther Rachel), David DeKeyser (Rabbi Zalman).

Many years ago in Poland, a young woman, played by Barbra Streisand, has a thirst for knowledge which is denied to one of her sex. Not to be denied she cuts her hair, puts on men's clothes and attends a yeshiva as a male. She falls in love with fellow student Mandy Patinkin, but through a series of misunderstandings, finds herself married to Amy Irving. It's a heavy-handed personal statement by Streisand which most of the industry ignored, as did audiences.

3400. *Yes, Giorgio* (1982, MGM/United Artists, 110m, c). P Peter Fetterman, D Franklin J. Schaffner, W Norman Steinberg (based on the novel by Anne Piper), PH Fred J. Koenekamp, M John Williams, ED Michael F. Anderson, PD William J. Creber, SONG "If We Were in Love" by John Williams, Alan & Marilyn Bergman*.

LP Luciano Pavarotti (Giorgio Fini), Kathryn Harrold (Pamela Taylor), Eddie Albert (Henry Pollack), Paola Borboni (Sister Teresa), James Hong (Kwan), Beulah Quo (Mei Ling), Norman Steinberg (Dr. Barmen).

Luciano Pavarotti is a magnificent tenor. He is not an accomplished actor, but even if he was, he'd be defeated by this ridiculous story in which he is asked to be a caricature of himself. His character's overbearing ego and male chauvinistic attitudes barely gets in the way of his romance with beautiful throat specialist Kathryn Harrold. She is called in when he unexpectedly loses his voice while on a U.S. tour.

You Better Watch Out see ***Christmas Evil***

3401. *You Can't Hurry Love* (1988, Lightning Pictures, 92m, c). P Jonathan D. Krane, D&W Richard Martini, PH Peter Lyons Collister & John Schwartzman, M Bob Esty, ED Richard Candib.

LP David Packer (Eddie Hayes), Scott McGinnis (Skip), Bridget Fonda (Peggy), David Leisure (Newcomb), Luana Anders (Macie Hayes), Judy Balduzzi (Glenda), Frank Bonner (Chuck Hayes), Anthony Geary (Tony), Charles Grodin (Mr. Glerman), Sally Kellerman (Kelly Bones), Kristy McNichol (Rhonda).

In a very dim comedy, David Packer is

a hick from Akron who finds life in Los Angeles to be rather unsettling. He employs a dating service, which gives the filmmakers a reason to show a number of underdressed and undressed pretty young women. Charles Grodin, Sally Kellerman and Kristy McNichol make throwaway cameo appearances.

3402. *You Talkin' to Me?* (1987, MGM/United Artists, 97m, c). P Michael Polaire, D&W Charles Winkler, PH Paul Ryan, M Joel McNeely, ED David Handman.

LP Jim Youngs (Bronson Green), James Noble (Peter Archer), Mykel T. Williamson (Thatcher Marks), Faith Ford (Dana Archer), Bess Motta (Judith Margolis), Rex Ryon (Kevin), Brian Thompson (James), Alan King (Himself).

Jim Youngs is a Robert DeNiro fan, inspired by watching *Taxi Driver* over and over. He goes to Southern California where he confronts a white supremacy group and rescues his friend, black male model Mykel T. Williamson.

3403. *Young Doctors in Love* (1982, 20th Century-Fox, 95m, c). P Jerry Bruckheimer, D Garry Marshall, W Michael Elias & Rich Eustis, PH Don Peterman, M Maurice Jarre, ED Dov Hoenig, PD Polly Platt.

LP Michael McKean (Dr. Simon August), Sean Young (Dr. Stephanie Brody), Harry Dean Stanton (Dr. Oliver Ludwig), Patrick Macnee (Dr. Jacobs), Hector Elizondo (Angelo/Angela), Dabney Coleman (Dr. Joseph Prang), Pamela Reed (Norine Sprockett), Taylor Negron (Dr. Phil Burns), Saul Rubinek (Dr. Floyd Kurtzman), Patrick Collins (Dr. Walter Rist).

This comedy about a team of new interns at a big city hospital is an *Airplane*-like spoof both of medical films and TV soap operas (to insure this point is made, several soap opera stars make cameo appearances). The jokes are hit and miss, some cruel, some obscene, some gross, some scatological, some sexist, some even funny.

3404. *Young Einstein* (1989, Warner, Australia, 90m, c). P Yahoo Serious, Warwick Ross & David Roach, D Serious, W Serious & Roach, PH Jeff Darling, M William Motzing, Martin Armiger & Tommy Tycho, ED Roach, Neil Thumpston, Peter Whitmore & Amanda Robson.

LP Yahoo Serious (Albert Einstein), Odile Le Clezio (Marie Curie), John Howard (Preston Preston), Pee Wee Wilson (Mr. Einstein), Su Cruickshank (Mrs. Einstein), Lulu Pinkus (The Blonde).

One has to be in a zany mood to appreciate this weird import from down under. It's merely a series of uneven sketches featuring Yahoo Serious as a none-too-serious Albert Einstein. Those who enjoy Monty Python might find this fun.

3405. *Young Guns* (1988, 20th Century-Fox, 97m, c). P Joe Roth & Christopher Cain, D Cain, W John Fusco, PH Dean Semler, M Anthony Marinelli & Brian Banks, ED Jack Hofstra, PD Jane Musky.

LP Emilio Estevez (William H. Bonney, aka "Billy the Kid"), Kiefer Sutherland (Josiah "Doc" Scurlock), Lou Diamond Phillips (Chevez Y Chavez), Charlie Sheen (Dick Brewer), Dermot Mulroney ("Dirty Steve" Stephens), Casey Siemaszko (Charley Bowdre), Terence Stamp (John Henry Tunstall), Jack Palance (Lawrence G. Murphy), Terrance O'Quinn (Alex McSween), Sharon Thomas (Susan McSween), Brian Keith (Buckshot Roberts), Patrick Wayne (Pat Garrett), Cody Palance (Baker).

Westerns appear to be a dead genre and this attempt to bring it back to life raised only the slightest pulse in the cadaver. It's the story of the Lincoln County War. Kindly British rancher Terence Stamp gathers together a group of scruffy young men to act as hired guns for his battle with evil beef baron Jack Palance. When Stamp is killed the war is on, with Emilio Estevez finding that he really enjoys killing people.

Young Lady Chatterley II see Private Property

3406. *Young Nurses in Love* (1989, Platinum Pictures, 76m, c). P&D Chuck Vincent, W Vincent & Craig Horrall, PH Larry Revene, M Bill Heller, ED "Marc Ubell" (Vincent) & James Davalos.

LP Jeanne Marie (Nurse Ellis), Alan

Fisler (Dr. Reilly), Jane Hamilton (Francesca), Jamie Gillis (Dr. Spencer), Harv Siegel (Dr. Young), James Davies, Barbara Robb, Jennifer Delora, Beth Broderick, Annie Sprinkle.

This answer to *Young Doctors in Love* (1982) is a cheap sex comedy about Soviet spy Jeanne Marie who infiltrates a hospital posing as an American nurse. Her assignment is to steal the sperm deposits of geniuses such as Einstein and Edison being stored at the hospital.

3407.   *Young Sherlock Holmes* (1985, Paramount, 109m, c). P Mark Johnson, D Barry Levinson, W Chris Columbus (based on the characters created by Sir Arthur Conan Doyle), PH Stephen Goldblatt, M Bruce Broughton, ED Stu Linder, PD Norman Reynolds, VE Dennis Muren, Kit West, John Ellis & David Allen†.

LP Nicholas Rowe (Sherlock Holmes), Alan Cox (John H. Watson), Sophie Ward (Elizabeth), Anthony Higgins (Rathe), Susan Fleetwood (Mrs. Dribb), Freddie Jones (Cragwitch), Nigel Stock (Waxflatter), Roger Ashton-Griffiths (Lestrade), Earl Rhodes (Dudley).

The notion of making a picture about a precocious lad who will grow up to be the world's most famous fictional detective seems like a capital idea. Unfortunately Chris Columbus is no Conan Doyle and the story shows more the influence of co-executive producer Steven Spielberg than an author who lived and wrote during the Victorian era. It will probably appeal more to those who have never read any of the Holmes stories than to Baker Street Irregulars.

3408.   *Young Warriors* (1983, Cannon, 105m, c). P Victoria Paige Meyerink, D Lawrence D. Foldes, W Foldes & Russell W. Colgin, PH Mac Ahlberg, M Rob Walsh, ED Ted Nicolaou, PD Karl Pogany.

LP Ernest Borgnine (Lt. Bob Carrigan), Richard Roundtree (Sgt. John Austin), Lynda Day George (Beverly Carrigan), James Van Patten (Kevin Carrigan), Anne Lockhart (Lucy), Tom Reilly (Scott), Ed De Stefane (Stan), Mike Norris (Fred).

In this *Death Wish* clone, cop Ernest Borgnine cooperates with authorities when his daughter is raped and killed by a gang of young punks. But his son James Van Patten organizes a bunch of his fraternity brothers into a vigilante group who roam the streets looking for the killers. They take on any criminals they encounter during their patrols.

3409.   *Youngblood* (1986, MGM/United Artists, 110m, c). P Peter Bart & Patrick Wells, D&W Peter Markle (based on a story by Markle & John Whitman), PH Mark Irwin, M William Orbit/Torchsong & Chris Boardman, ED Stephen E. Rivkin & Jack Hofstra, AD Alicia Keywan & Alta Louise Doyle.

LP Rob Lowe (Dean Youngblood), Cynthia Gibb (Jessie Chadwick), Patrick Swayze (Derek Sutton), Ed Lauter (Murray Chadwick), Jim Youngs (Kelly Youngblood), Eric Nesterenko (Blane Youngblood), George Finn (Racki), Fionnula Flanagan (Miss Gill), Ken James (Frazier).

Meant to be the *Rocky* of hockey, this puck doesn't make it across the blue line. Rob Lowe, no Wayne Gretzsky, lacks the killer instinct needed to become a real star. Everyone in the film acts as if they fell on the ice when they weren't wearing their helmets.

3410.   *Zadar! Cow from Hell* (1989, Stone Peach Production, 87m, c). P&D Robert C. Hughes, W Merle Kessler (based on the story by Duck's Breath Mystery Theater), PH James Mathers, M Greg Brown, ED Michael Ruscio, AD Ginni Barr.

LP Bill Allard (Mr. Nifty), Dan Coffey (Rex), Merle Kessler (Sleepless Walker), Leon Martell (Dan Tension), Jim Turner (Max), Deborah Gwinn (Amy Walker), Eric Topham (Ralph, Jr.), Ned Holbrook (Chip).

This film within a film is the story of a movie crew returning to the director's home in Iowa to make a horror film about an enormous cow. It is meant to be a comedy, but it's a long time between clever ideas, let alone laughs.

3411.   *Zapped!* (1982, Embassy, 96m, c). P Jeffrey D. Apple, D Robert J. Rosenthal, W Rosenthal & Bruce Rubin, PH Daniel Pearl, M Charles Fox, ED Bob Bring & Robert Ferretti, SE Robert Blalack, Dick Albain & Ron Nary.

LP Scott Baio (Barney), Willie Aames (Peyton), Robert Mandan (Walter Johnson), Felice Schachter (Bernadette), Scatman Crothers (Dexter Jones), Roger Bowen (Mr. Springboro), Marya Small (Mrs. Springboro), Sue Ane Langdon (Rose), Heather Thomas (Jane).

In another teenage exploitation film, a chemistry experiment explosion gifts Scott Baio with telekinetic powers. He uses these in the best tradition of such movies to get girls stripped to the buff. Stupid stuff!

3412. *A Zed and Two Noughts* (1985, Skouras, GB/Netherlands, 115m, c). P Peter Sainsbury & Kees Kasander, D&W Peter Greenaway, PH Sacha Vierny, M Michael Nyman, ED John Wilson, PD Ben van Os.

LP Andrea Ferreol (Alba Bewick), Brian Deacon (Oswald Deuce), Eric Deacon (Oliver Deuce), Frances Barber (Venus De Milo), Joss Ackland (Van Hoyten), Jim Davidson (Joshua Plate), Agnes Brulet (Beta Bewick).

Dutch zoologist twin brothers, Brian & Eric Deacon, become obsessed with the decay of animals after their wives are both killed in an automobile accident in which the driver Andrea Ferreol loses a leg. The brothers plan to set free all the animals in the zoo. They also have a ménage à trois with Ferreol. As a result she gives birth to twin sons. She has her remaining leg amputated and takes up with another double amputee, whom she names as the legal father of her sons before she dies. The brothers commit joint suicide. It's certainly an unusual film.

3413. *Zelig* (1983, Warner, 80m, c/b&w). P Robert Greenhut, D&W Woody Allen, PH Gordon Willis†, M Dick Hyman, ED Susan E. Morse, PD Mel Bourne, COS Santo Loquasto†.

LP Woody Allen (Leonard Zelig), Mia Farrow (Dr. Eudora Fletcher), John Buckwalter (Dr. Sindell), Marvin Chatinover (Glandular Diagnosis Doctor), Paul Nevens (Dr. Birsky), Sol Lomita (Martin Geist), Mary Louise Wilson (Sister Ruth), Sharon Ferrol (Miss Baker).

Director-writer Woody Allen produces a parody documentary about a chameleon-like nonentity. Played by Allen, the little man manages to show up at every major event of the 20th century. The remarkable recreations of old newsreels in which Allen's character is introduced is a cinematic breakthrough. Gordon Willis deserves special praise.

3414. *Zelly and Me* (1988, Columbia, 87m, c). P Sue Jett & Tony Mark, D Tina Rathborne, W Rathborne, PH Mikael Salomon, M Pino Donaggio & Jeremiah Clarke, ED Cindy Kaplan Rooney, PD David Morong.

LP Alexandra Johnes (Phoebe), Isabella Rossellini (Joan "Zelly"), Glynis Johns (CoCo), Kaiulani Lee (Nora), David Lynch (Willie), Joe Morton (Earl), Courtney Vickery (Dora), Lindsay Dickon (Kitty).

The film is the story of the struggle between orphaned eight-year-old Alexandra Johnes and her saintly but rather strange grandmother Glynis Johns. Only equally strange nanny Isabella Rossellini can referee their differences.

3415. *The Zero Boys* (1987, Omega, 89m, c). P&D Nico Mastorakis, W Mastorakis & Fred C. Perry (based on a story by Mastorakis), PH Steve Shaw, M Stanley Myers & Hans Zimmer, ED George Rosenberg.

LP Daniel Hirsch (Steve), Kelli Maroney (Jamie), Nicole Rio (Sue), Tom Shell (Larry), Jared Moses (Rip), Crystal Carson (Trish), Joe Phelan (Killer), Gary Jochimsen (Killer No. 2), John Michaels (Casey), Elise Turner (Victim), T.K. Webb (Killer No. 3).

When three survival-game champions and their girlfriends are invited to a party in the backwoods, they find themselves in a murderous plot which will really test their survival skills.

3416. *Zilch* (1989, Park Avenue Prods./Vardex, New Zealand, 95m, c). P Amanda Hocquard & Richard Riddiford, D Riddiford, W Riddiford & Jonathan Dowling, PH Murray Milne, M Chris Knox, ED Chris Todd.

LP Michael Mizrahi (Sam), Lucy Sheehan (Anna).

Telephone toll operator Michael Mizrahi listens in and tapes phone conversations. This is how he learns of a blackmail plot against a government minister by operators of a construction company (they want the pol's support for their efforts to get the contract for building a harbor crossing). Also, the politician seems fond of standing naked in a shower while Lucy Sheehan, an occasional lover of Mizrahi, pelts him with tomatoes.

3417. *Zina* (1985, Hemdale, GB, 92m, c/b&w). P&D Ken McMullen, W McMullen & Terry James, PH Bryan Loftus, M David Cunningham, Barrie Guard & Simon Heyworth, ED Robert Hargreaves, PD Paul Cheetham.

LP Domiziana Giordano, Ian McKellen, Philip Madoc, Ron Anderson, Micha Bergese, Gabrielle Dellal, Paul Geoffrey, William Hootkins, Leonie Mellinger, Maureen O'Brien.

Domiziana Giordano portrays the daughter of Leon Trotsky. The film examines her problems and obsessions while in psychoanalysis in pre–World War II Berlin.

3418. *Zombie High* (1987, Cinema Group, 91m, c).P Marc Toberoff & Aziz Ghazai, D Ron Link, W Tim Doyle, Elizabeth Passerelli & Ghazai, PH David Lux & Brian Coyne, M Daniel May, ED Shawn Hardin & James Whitney, PD Matthew Kozinets.

LP Virginia Madsen (Andrea Miller), Richard Cox (Prof. Philo), Kay Kuter (Dean Eisner), James Wilder (Barry), Sherilyn Fenn (Suzi), Paul Feig (Emerson), T. Scott Coffey (Felner), Paul Williams (Ignatius).

Virginia Madsen is one of the first coeds to enroll at a previously all male prep school. The girls find all the boys to be nerdish bores, only interested in studying. Madsen discovers the reason: the instructors have lobotomized the boys to make a serum that gives everlasting life.

3419. *Zombie Island Massacre* (1984, Troma, 95m, c). P David Broadnax, D&ED John N. Carter, W William Stoddard & Logan O'Neill (based on a story by Broadnax), M Harry Manfredini, SE Dennis Eger.

LP David Broadnax, Rita Jenrette, Tom Cantrell, Diane Clayre Holub, Ian MacMillan, George Peters, Dennis Stephenson.

Rita Jenrette, the former wife of a real-life Abscam congressman, appears nude in three early scenes. This seems to have nothing to do with the plot about bad

things happening on a zombie-infested island.

3420. *Zombie   Nightmare* (1987, Gold-Gems, 83m, c). P Pierre Grise, D John Bravman, W David Wellington, PH Robert Racine, M Jon-Miki Thor, ED David Franko, AD David Blanchard.

LP Adam West (Capt. Churchman), Jon-Miki Thor (Tony Washington), Tia Carrere (Amy), Manuska Rigaud (Molly), Frank Dietz (Frank), Linda Singer (Maggie), Francesca Bonacorsa (Tony's Wife).

Rock singer Jon-Miki Thor portrays a man killed by some irresponsible teenagers. He is brought back to life as a zombie by his widow and a Haitian woman who wants to use him to take revenge on those who raped her years before. Thor beats everyone he can catch with a baseball bat.

3421. *Zone Troopers* (1986, Empire, 88m, c). P Paul DeMeo, D Danny Bilson, W Bilson & DeMeo, PH Mac Ahlberg, M Richard Band, ED Ted Nicolaou, SE John Buechler.

LP Tim Thomerson (Sarge), Timothy Van Patten (Joey), Art LaFleur (Mittens), Biff Manard (Dolan), William Paulson (Alien).

What a dumb idea! During World War II a troop of American soldiers lost behind German lines encounter space aliens.

3422. *The Zoo Gang* (1985, New World, 96m, c). P Pen Densham, John Watson & Richard Barton Lewis, D&W Densham & Watson (based on a story by Stuart Birnbaum, David Dashev, Densham & Watson), PH Robert New, M Patrick Gleeson, ED James Symons, PD Steve Legler.

LP Ben Vereen (Leatherface), Jack Earle Haley (Little Joe), Tiffany Helm (Kate), Jason Gedrick (Hardin), Eric Gurry (Danny), Marc Price (Val), Gina Battist (Bobbi), Darwyn Swalve (Goose).

A group of youngsters want to start their own nightclub for teens, but other adolescents spoil their plans. Isn't that always the way?

3423. *Zoot Suit* (1982, Universal, 103m, c). P Peter Burrell, Kenneth Brecher & William P. Wingate, D&W Luis Valdez (based on his play), PH

David Myers, M Daniel Valdez & Shorty Rogers, ED Jacqueline Cambas, PD Tom H. John.

LP Daniel Valdez (Henry Reyna), Edward James Olmos (El Pachuco), Charles Aidman (George), Tyne Daly (Alice), John Anderson (Judge), Abel Franco (Enrique), Mike Gomez (Joey), Alma Rose Martinez (Lupe).

This film is based on the true story of a group of Chicanos who in 1942 were convicted of murder on some trumped-up charges. Attempts to free them were to no avail.

3424. *Zorro, the Gay Blade* (1981, 20th Century-Fox, 93m, c). P George Hamilton & C.O. Erickson, D Peter Medak, W Hal Dresner (based on a story by Dresner, Greg Alt, Don Moriarty & Bob Randall), PH John A. Alonzo, M Ian Fraser, ED Hillary Jane Kranze, PD Herman A. Blumenthal.

LP George Hamilton (Don Diego Vega/Bunny Wigglesworth), Lauren Hutton (Charlotte), Brenda Vaccaro (Florinda), Ron Leibman (Esteban), Donovan Scott (Paco), James Booth (Velasquez), Helen Burns (Consuela), Clive Revill (Garcia), Carolyn Seymour (Dolores), Eduardo Noriega (Don Francisco).

Having parodied *Dracula* with *Love at First Bite,* George Hamilton is back to take on another legendary movie, *Zorro.* He apparently thought it would be a scream if the dashing masked California hero of the oppressed had a twin brother with a limp wrist. He was wrong.

3425. *Zulu Dawn* (1980, Warner, GB, 117m, c). P Nate Kohn, D Douglas Hickox, W Cy Endfield & Anthony Storey (based on a story by Endfield), PH Ousama Rawi, M Elmer Bernstein, ED Malcolm Cooke, PD John Rosewarne.

LP Burt Lancaster (Col. Durnford), Peter O'Toole (Lord Chelmsford), Simon Ward (William Vereker), John Mills (Sir Bartle Frere), Nigel Davenport (Col. Hamilton-Brown), Michael Jayston (Col. Crealock), Ronald Lacey (Norris Newman), Denholm Elliott (Lt. Col. Pulleine), Freddie Jones (Bishop Colenso), Anna Calder-Marshall (Fanny Colenso).

This film is a prequel to *Zulu* (1964), the exciting action film about an 1879 British stand against the Zulu at Rorke's Drift. This film deals with the battle which preceeded the one at Rorke's Drift. In it, 1300 British soldiers are massacred at Ulundi by Zulu warriors led by King Cetshwayo.

Index

Numbers refer to the entry number, not page number.